lonely planet

Micronesia

Kate Galbraith
Glenda Bendure
Ned Friary

LONELY PLANET PUBLICATIONS
Melbourne • Oakland • London • Paris

Micronesia
4th edition – September 2000
First published – April 1988

Published by
Lonely Planet Publications Pty Ltd A.C.N. 005 607 983
192 Burwood Rd, Hawthorn, Victoria 3122, Australia

Lonely Planet Offices
Australia PO Box 617, Hawthorn, Victoria 3122
USA 150 Linden St, Oakland, CA 94607
UK 10a Spring Place, London NW5 3BH
France 1 rue du Dahomey, 75011 Paris

Photographs
Many of the images in this guide are available for licensing from
Lonely Planet Images.
email: lpi@lonelyplanet.com.au

Front cover photograph
Diving in Palau, Micronesia (Michael Aw, LPI)

ISBN 1 86450 104 9

Diving in Blue Corner, Palau

Orange-finned anemonefish, Palau

ASTRID WITTE & CASEY MAHANEY

Sea turtle and diver

MICHAEL AW

Pink soft coral, Chuuk

MICHAEL AW

Pink anemonefish, Chuuk

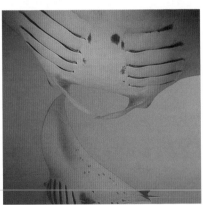

MICHAEL AW

Manta rays, Palau

ASTRID WITTE & CASEY MAHANEY

Whipcoral reef scene, Palau

ASTRID WITTE & CASEY MAHANEY

Schooling blue-stripe snappers, Palau

Contents – Text

2 Contents – Text

NAURU

FEDERATED STATES OF MICRONESIA

PALAU

US TERRITORIES 351

GLOSSARY 355

INDEX 361

MAP LEGEND back page

METRIC CONVERSION inside back cover

Contents – Maps

The Authors

Kate Galbraith

Kate is a US-based freelance writer who graduated from Harvard with a degree in English literature and has since worked mostly in Eastern Europe. Covering the nations of Micronesia for this book was a big change from her last Lonely Planet assignment (Bosnia) and her next (Latvia). Hourly applications of sun screen stopped Kate from frying in the tropical sun, and she's also proud to have survived vulturous Kiribati immigration authorities. Kate now lives in London.

Glenda Bendure & Ned Friary

Glenda grew up in California's Mojave Desert and first travelled overseas as a high school AFS exchange student to India. A few years later a Chuukese exchange student living with Glenda's family introduced her to Micronesia. Ned grew up near Boston and studied Social Thought & Political Economy at the University of Massachusetts in Amherst. After meeting in Santa Cruz, California, where Glenda was finishing up her university studies, they took to the road and spent years travelling throughout Asia and the Pacific, including long-term stints in Japan where Ned taught English and Glenda edited a magazine. They eventually came back to the USA, settling down on Cape Cod in Massachusetts. Ned and Glenda are the authors of several Lonely Planet guides, including *Hawaii, Oahu, Bermuda, Eastern Caribbean* and *Denmark*, and they also write the Norway and Denmark chapters of Lonely Planet's *Scandinavian & Baltic Europe*.

From Kate

Infinite thanks go to Ben of the Marshall Islands Visitors Authority, my ever-patient virtual helper. On Palau, my gratitude goes to the Tmetuchl family for the best hospitality, food, company and guide service I could ever imagine; you are in my thoughts. On Nauru, great thanks to Ellamaine of Air Nauru for her gracious impromptu guide service and to Helen Bogdan in Melbourne. Thanks to the tourist office on Tarawa for their generous assistance, and the same to Simeon at Chuuk Visitors Bureau, Tony of Guam Visitors Bureau and the tourist bureaus across Micronesia. On Saipan, thanks to Simon for the illuminating back-alley tour – and the surfing lesson. And to the innumerable others who gave me advice, information and guidance, my greatest thanks.

This Book

Glenda and Ned wrote the first three editions of *Micronesia*. This fourth edition was updated by Kate, who also wrote the three new chapters covering Kiribati, Nauru and the US Territories.

From the Publisher

The editing of *Micronesia* was coordinated by Bruce Evans, who was assisted by Kate Daly and Hilary Eriksen. Helping with the proofing were Errol Hunt, Martin Heng, Kristin Odijk and Rebecca Turner.

Corinne Waddell coordinated the mapping and design, assisted by Jenny Jones and Tim Uden. Jane Hart checked the maps and the layout.

Illustrations were co-ordinated by Matt King and drawn by Kate Nolan and Martin Harris. Valerie Tellini of Lonely Planet Images sourced the great shots, Maria Vallianos designed the book's cover, and Leonie Mugavin helped with fact checking and travel information.

Acknowledgments

Thanks

Many thanks to the travellers who used the last edition and wrote to us with helpful hints, useful advice and interesting anecdotes. Your names follow:

Dr Hartwig Bailer, Henry Barbauta, Bob Bergevin, Paul Binford, Loretta Brooks, Rod & Maryanne Calver, Jerry Ann Campbell, Rusty Cartmill, Dave Casey, Matt Chabot, Chao Chang, Christopher Chong, H Chong, Judith Coker, Garry Cope, Doug Crowe, Caroline Crowell, Laurie Darian, Lars Dessen, Julie Douglas, Terry Edge, Mary Evans, Deborah Fisher, George Gorski-Popiel, Jennifer Gray, Bill Groble, David Groom, Charles Hood, Steve Johnson, Tom Kintner, Mike Komlos, Matthew Konsa, Diana Lamb, Garrick C Law, Glenn H Manglona, David Maude, J Keith Mercer, Tim Morton, Christopher Neill, Larry & Merran Oakley, Paul Padberg, Eric Phan-Kim, Peter Phillips, Julie & Ben Pugh, Joachim Reinhart, Stephanie Riddle, Gary Robson, Jamie Salamon, Andrea Streit Schreiner, Adrian Stuerm, Rod Szasz, Karen Toy, Paul D Varady, Janicke Volkmar, Morlie L Wang, Marshall Weisler, Darren Williams.

Foreword

ABOUT LONELY PLANET GUIDEBOOKS

The story begins with a classic travel adventure: Tony and Maureen Wheeler's 1972 journey across Europe and Asia to Australia. Useful information about the overland trail did not exist at that time, so Tony and Maureen published the first Lonely Planet guidebook to meet a growing need.

From a kitchen table, then from a tiny office in Melbourne (Australia), Lonely Planet has become the largest independent travel publisher in the world, an international company with offices in Melbourne, Oakland (USA), London (UK) and Paris (France).

Today Lonely Planet guidebooks cover the globe. There is an ever-growing list of books and there's information in a variety of forms and media. Some things haven't changed. The main aim is still to help make it possible for adventurous travellers to get out there – to explore and better understand the world.

At Lonely Planet we believe travellers can make a positive contribution to the countries they visit – if they respect their host communities and spend their money wisely. Since 1986 a percentage of the income from each book has been donated to aid projects and human rights campaigns.

Updates Lonely Planet thoroughly updates each guidebook as often as possible. This usually means there are around two years between editions, although for more unusual or more stable destinations the gap can be longer. Check the imprint page (following the colour title page at the beginning of the book) for publication dates.

Between editions up-to-date information is available in two free newsletters – the paper *Planet Talk* and email *Comet* (to subscribe, contact any Lonely Planet office) – and on our Web site at www.lonelyplanet.com. The *Upgrades* section of the Web site covers a number of important and volatile destinations and is regularly updated by Lonely Planet authors. *Scoop* covers news and current affairs relevant to travellers. And, lastly, the *Thorn Tree* bulletin board and *Postcards* section of the site carry unverified, but fascinating, reports from travellers.

Correspondence The process of creating new editions begins with the letters, postcards and emails received from travellers. This correspondence often includes suggestions, criticisms and comments about the current editions. Interesting excerpts are immediately passed on via newsletters and the Web site, and everything goes to our authors to be verified when they're researching on the road. We're keen to get more feedback from organisations or individuals who represent communities visited by travellers.

Lonely Planet gathers information for everyone who's curious about the planet – and especially for those who explore it first-hand. Through guidebooks, phrasebooks, activity guides, maps, literature, newsletters, image library, TV series and Web site we act as an information exchange for a worldwide community of travellers.

Research Authors aim to gather sufficient practical information to enable travellers to make informed choices and to make the mechanics of a journey run smoothly. They also research historical and cultural background to help enrich the travel experience and allow travellers to understand and respond appropriately to cultural and environmental issues.

Authors don't stay in every hotel because that would mean spending a couple of months in each medium-sized city and, no, they don't eat at every restaurant because that would mean stretching belts beyond capacity. They do visit hotels and restaurants to check standards and prices, but feedback based on readers' direct experiences can be very helpful.

Many of our authors work undercover, others aren't so secretive. None of them accept freebies in exchange for positive write-ups. And none of our guidebooks contain any advertising.

Production Authors submit their raw manuscripts and maps to offices in Australia, USA, UK or France. Editors and cartographers – all experienced travellers themselves – then begin the process of assembling the pieces. When the book finally hits the shops, some things are already out of date, we start getting feedback from readers and the process begins again ...

WARNING & REQUEST

Things change – prices go up, schedules change, good places go bad and bad places go bankrupt – nothing stays the same. So, if you find things better or worse, recently opened or long since closed, please tell us and help make the next edition even more accurate and useful. We genuinely value all the feedback we receive. Julie Young coordinates a well travelled team that reads and acknowledges every letter, postcard and email and ensures that every morsel of information finds its way to the appropriate authors, editors and cartographers for verification.

Everyone who writes to us will find their name in the next edition of the appropriate guidebook. They will also receive the latest issue of *Planet Talk*, our quarterly printed newsletter, or *Comet*, our monthly email newsletter. Subscriptions to both newsletters are free. The very best contributions will be rewarded with a free guidebook.

Excerpts from your correspondence may appear in new editions of Lonely Planet guidebooks, the Lonely Planet Web site, *Planet Talk* or *Comet*, so please let us know if you *don't* want your letter published or your name acknowledged.

Send all correspondence to the Lonely Planet office closest to you:

Australia: PO Box 617, Hawthorn, Victoria 3122
USA: 150 Linden St, Oakland, CA 94607
UK: 10A Spring Place, London NW5 3BH
France: 1 rue du Dahomey, 75011 Paris

Or email us at: talk2us@lonelyplanet.com.au

For news, views and updates see our Web site: www.lonelyplanet.com

HOW TO USE A LONELY PLANET GUIDEBOOK

The best way to use a Lonely Planet guidebook is any way you choose. At Lonely Planet we believe the most memorable travel experiences are often those that are unexpected, and the finest discoveries are those you make yourself. Guidebooks are not intended to be used as if they provide a detailed set of infallible instructions!

Contents All Lonely Planet guidebooks follow roughly the same format. The Facts about the Destination chapters or sections give background information ranging from history to weather. Facts for the Visitor gives practical information on issues like visas and health. Getting There & Away gives a brief starting point for researching travel to and from the destination. Getting Around gives an overview of the transport options when you arrive.

The peculiar demands of each destination determine how subsequent chapters are broken up, but some things remain constant. We always start with background, then proceed to sights, places to stay, places to eat, entertainment, getting there and away, and getting around information – in that order.

Heading Hierarchy Lonely Planet headings are used in a strict hierarchical structure that can be visualised as a set of Russian dolls. Each heading (and its following text) is encompassed by any preceding heading that is higher on the hierarchical ladder.

Entry Points We do not assume guidebooks will be read from beginning to end, but that people will dip into them. The traditional entry points are the list of contents and the index. In addition, however, some books have a complete list of maps and an index map illustrating map coverage.

There may also be a colour map that shows highlights. These highlights are dealt with in greater detail in the Facts for the Visitor chapter, along with planning questions and suggested itineraries. Each chapter covering a geographical region usually begins with a locator map and another list of highlights. Once you find something of interest in a list of highlights, turn to the index.

Maps Maps play a crucial role in Lonely Planet guidebooks and include a huge amount of information. A legend is printed on the back page. We seek to have complete consistency between maps and text, and to have every important place in the text captured on a map. Map key numbers usually start in the top left corner.

Although inclusion in a guidebook usually implies a recommendation we cannot list every good place. Exclusion does not necessarily imply criticism. In fact there are a number of reasons why we might exclude a place – sometimes it is simply inappropriate to encourage an influx of travellers.

Introduction

The North Pacific, home to most of Micronesia, may not conjure up the exotic images of the South Pacific, but all the idyllic island cliches fit perfectly: warm aqua waters lapping at pristine beaches, swaying coconut palms, lush tropical jungles, tumbling waterfalls and rustic thatched huts.

Micronesia's more than 2000 islands lie scattered between Hawai'i and the Philippines. In contrast to the vast seas they span, their total land area is so small that many world maps don't even bother dotting them in.

Four colonial powers have used these tiny specks of land as stepping stones between continents, first as provision stops on trade routes and later as military bastions. Following WWII, the USA took over the administration of much of Micronesia, and those island groups have only recently emerged as 'island nations', though their futures all remain firmly bound up with the USA. Other islands – those of Kiribati and Nauru – were administered by the British and Australians respectively, but they too emerged from the colonial umbrella in the 1960s and 1970s.

Not only are Micronesia's island groups spread out over a great distance but each also has its own culture and character. Inhabited areas vary from idyllic villages with no cars or electricity to the high-rise resort developments of Guam and Saipan.

Steeped in a rich yet largely unknown history, the ruins of the great stone cities of Pohnpei's Nan Madol and Kosrae's Lelu are on an archaeological par with the stone statues of Easter Island and the Mayan ruins

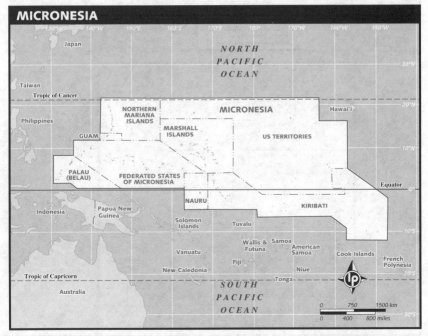

MICRONESIA

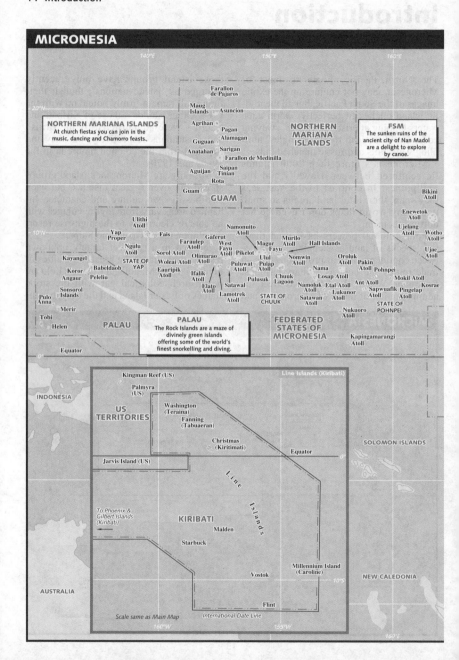

MICRONESIA

NORTHERN MARIANA ISLANDS
At church fiestas you can join in the music, dancing and Chamorro feasts.

FSM
The sunken ruins of the ancient city of Nan Madol are a delight to explore by canoe.

PALAU
The Rock Islands are a maze of divinely green islands offering some of the world's finest snorkelling and diving.

NORTHERN MARIANA ISLANDS

Farallon de Pajaros
Maug Islands
Asuncion
Agrihan
Pagan
Guguan
Alamagan
Anatahan
Sarigan
Farallon de Medinilla
Aguijan
Saipan
Tinian
Rota
Guam
GUAM

Bikini Atoll
Enewetok Atoll
Ujelang Atoll
Wotho Atoll
Ujae Atoll

STATE OF YAP
Ulithi Atoll
Yap Proper
Fais
Namonuito Atoll
Ngulu Atoll
Gaferut
Magur
Murilo Atoll
Hall Islands
Faraulep Atoll
West Fayu
Fayu
Kayangel
Sorol Atoll
Olimarao Atoll
Pikelot
Ulul
Nomwin Atoll
Oroluk Atoll
Pakin Atoll
Koror
Babeldaob
Woleai Atoll
Pulap Atoll
Pohnpei
Angaur
Peleliu
Eauripik Atoll
Puluwat Atoll
Nama
Mokil Atoll
Sonsorol Islands
Ifalik Atoll
Pulusuk
Chuuk Lagoon
Losap Atoll
Ant Atoll
Sapwuafik Atoll
Pingelap Atoll
Kosrae
Pulo Anna
Elato Atoll
Satawal
Namoluk Atoll
Etal Atoll
Lukunor Atoll
Merir
Lamotrek Atoll
STATE OF CHUUK
Satawan Atoll
STATE OF POHNPEI
Tobi
PALAU
Nukuoro Atoll
Helen
FEDERATED STATES OF MICRONESIA
Kapingamarangi Atoll
Equator

Kingman Reef (US)
Line Islands (Kiribati)
Palmyra (US)
US TERRITORIES
Washington (Teraina)
Fanning (Tabuaeran)
Christmas (Kiritimati)
Equator
INDONESIA
Jarvis Island (US)
Line Islands
SOLOMON ISLANDS
To Phoenix & Gilbert Islands (Kiribati)
KIRIBATI
Malden
Starbuck
Millennium Island (Caroline)
Vostok
NEW CALEDONIA
AUSTRALIA
Flint
Scale same as Main Map
International Date Line

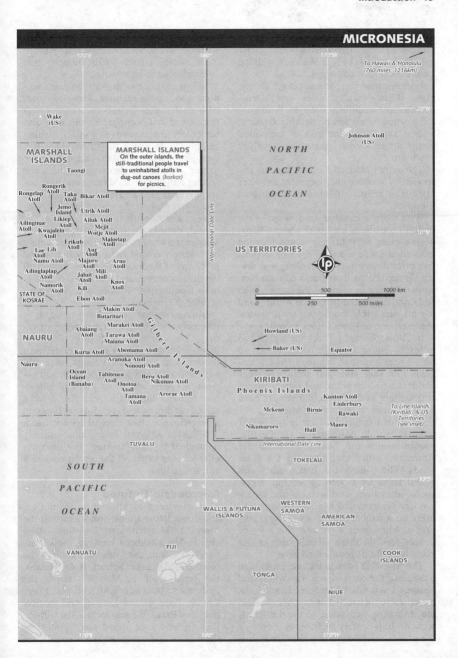

MICRONESIA

To Hawaii & Honolulu
(760 miles, 1216km)

Wake
(US)

Johnson Atoll
(US)

**MARSHALL
ISLANDS**

Taongi

MARSHALL ISLANDS
On the outer islands, the still-traditional people travel to uninhabited atolls in dug-out canoes (korkor) for picnics.

N O R T H

P A C I F I C

O C E A N

Rongerik
Atoll

Rongelap
Atoll

Taka
Atoll

Bikar Atoll

Jemo
Island

Likiep
Atoll

Utrik Atoll

Ailinginae
Atoll

Kwajalein
Atoll

Ailuk Atoll

Mejit

Wotje Atoll

Erikub
Atoll

Maloelap
Atoll

Lae Lib
Atoll

Aur
Atoll

Namu Atoll

Majuro
Atoll

Arno
Atoll

Ailinglaplap
Atoll

Jaluit
Atoll

Mili
Atoll

Namorik
Atoll

Kili

Knox
Atoll

**STATE OF
KOSRAE**

Ebon Atoll

International Date Line

US TERRITORIES

0   500   1000 km
0   250   500 miles

Makin Atoll

Butaritari

Marakei Atoll

Abaiang
Atoll

Tarawa Atoll

Maiana Atoll

NAURU

Kuria Atoll

Abemama Atoll

G i l b e r t   I s l a n d s

Howland (US)

Baker (US)

Equator

Nauru

Ocean
Island
(Banaba)

Tabiteuea
Atoll

Aranuka Atoll

Nonouti Atoll

Onotoa
Atoll

Beru Atoll

Nikunau Atoll

KIRIBATI
Phoenix Islands

Kanton Atoll

Tamana
Atoll

Arorae Atoll

Mckean

Birnie

Enderbury

Rawaki

To Line Islands
(Kiribati) & US
Territories
(see inset)

Nikumaroro

Hull

Manra

TUVALU

International Date Line

TOKELAU

S O U T H

P A C I F I C

O C E A N

WESTERN
SAMOA

**WALLIS & FUTUNA
ISLANDS**

AMERICAN
SAMOA

VANUATU

FIJI

COOK
ISLANDS

TONGA

NIUE

of Central America. You can still get a glimpse of these abandoned worlds by navigating the canals of Nan Madol or walking Lelu's coral rock pathways.

Unfrequented Yap has giant stone money, grass skirts, 'men's houses' and Micronesia's most traditional lifestyle. With only a few small hotels and no developed tourist sights, Yap offers the sort of unspoiled earthy attractions that independent travellers yearn for.

The outer islands of Kiribati, too, are unspoiled by Western encroachment and offer visitors a chance to observe traditional lifestyles.

With more ocean than land, some of the region's top sights are under water. Micronesia's clear 80°F (27°C) waters teeming with coral gardens and zillions of tropical fish offer unsurpassed snorkelling and diving. Around Palau, three ocean currents converge to bring in some of the most varied and dazzling marine life in the world – and it's all accessible from your own private beach on one of Palau's Rock Islands.

In Chuuk (formerly Truk), the lagoon bed holds an entire Japanese fleet, frozen in time where it sank in February 1944. Complete with sake cups and skeletons, jeeps and tanks tied on board and fighter planes still waiting in the holds, the wrecks have been declared an underwater museum.

Some of the bloodiest battles of WWII were fought in Micronesia. On Peleliu, Saipan, Tinian and Tarawa, Japanese and Americans killed each other by the thousands. These days the battle scars and WWII ruins have been turned into sightseeing attractions, and both US and Japanese war veterans and relatives of war dead make up a sizable (though dwindling) portion of Micronesia's visitors. Not a lot of people live on these islands, the saying goes, but a lot of people died here.

The Marshall Islands include more than a thousand flat coral islands with white sand beaches and turquoise lagoons. To some it's a tropical paradise but many Marshallese are struggling with some of the nastier effects of 20th-century technology. Some of the islands served as testing sites for atomic

bombs and as a consequence many Marshallese have suffered radioactivity poisoning. Some islands still remain too contaminated to be resettled.

Micronesia is caught between past traditions and present realities. Many islanders who still make their homes of coconut fronds and sail outrigger canoes now also have electric generators and VCRs; visiting neighbours to watch the latest video is a popular pastime. Some islanders have moved away from subsistence farming and fishing only to find hard times and high unemployment in district centres such as Weno and Majuro. As elsewhere, it's a society in a state of flux.

Still, outside the larger towns, many of Micronesia's more remote islands remain refreshingly distant from the pollution and problems of the modern world – though all the district centres are now linked by air, as both Continental Airlines and Air Nauru service the region.

Micronesia can be explored in depth or taken in small chunks; there is plenty of variety. You can take small prop planes or two-week ship journeys to some of the most remote and unspoiled islands on earth, where you can stay in thatched huts and become a beachcomber; or you can island-hop through the district centres, drive a rented car around and spend sunset hours on a beach lounge chair, tropical drink in hand.

Much of Micronesia remains virtually untouched by mass tourism. For the traveller looking to get off the beaten track, it's still a rare find.

Micronesia Defined

The boundaries of Micronesia are not cut and dried. In this guidebook we include the Mariana, Marshall and Caroline island chains. The islands covered are: the US territory of Guam, the Commonwealth of the Northern Marianas (Saipan, Rota, Tinian), the Republic of the Marshall Islands, the Federated States of Micronesia (Yap, Chuuk, Pohnpei and Kosrae) and the Republic of Palau. We also include the Gilbert, Phoenix and Line island chains; most of their islands belong to the Republic of

Kiribati but some are unincorporated US territories. The Republic of Nauru, belonging to no island chain, is also included.

These islands (with the exception of Guam, Kiribati, Nauru and the US territories) were grouped together after WWII as the Trust Territory of the Pacific Islands – officially a United Nations territory, but for all practical purposes a US colony, which has only recently been dissolved. Because these islands have in many ways been thought of as a single unit since the end of the war, we occasionally refer to them as American Micronesia, though the Micronesian region as a whole extends well beyond its borders.

Facts about the Region

HISTORY
Early Settlers
The first Micronesians canoed across the Pacific from the Philippines and Indonesia to settle on the high western islands of the Marianas, Yap and Palau somewhere between 2000 and 4000 BC. Much later voyagers from Melanesia settled the eastern islands of the Marshall island group and then worked their way westwards to Kosrae, Pohnpei and Chuuk. In time they continued still farther west, settling the outer atolls of Yap and Palau as well as Nauru and Kiribati's Gilbert Islands.

Though they occupy an enormous expanse of ocean, the islands settled by these Melanesian descendants still share related cultures and languages, but Micronesians have no legends of a life outside Micronesia. The earliest artefacts discovered so far in Micronesia were found on the Bikini Atoll.

Micronesia's inhabited island groups had thriving cultures and well-established societies. As the islands had no metals, the most impressive archaeological remains of these societies are in stone – the great stone cities of Nan Madol on Pohnpei and Lelu on Kosrae.

The Chamorro people of the Marianas quarried large stones to use as foundation pillars, called *latte*, for their buildings.

The Yapese quarried immense circles out of the limestone found on Palau to use as money, carrying the stones back to Yap on barges behind their canoes. They were superb ocean navigators and built an empire that stretched across hundreds of kilometres of ocean.

In Palau, on the northernmost point of the main island of Babeldaob, there are two rows of large basalt monoliths. Their original use remains a mystery but their size and layout suggest they may have been part of a structure that held thousands of people. There are also elaborately terraced hillsides nearby that date back to AD 100 though no-one knows who built them or why.

COURTESY OF THE GUAM VISITORS BUREAU

Ancient *latte* stones were common in the Mariana Islands and are thought to have been used as building pillars.

Most of what is known about ancient Micronesian societies comes from village remains or archaeological digs. Before European contact the islanders had no written languages and passed down all information through oral histories, many of which were lost when the Europeans arrived.

European Contact

In the late 15th century Portuguese explorers, in a quest for spices, established a trade route around Africa and across the Indian Ocean to the Spice Islands, or the Moluccas, which are part of present-day Indonesia. The Spanish, who were denied use of this Portuguese trade route by a decree from the pope, were forced to sail west to get to the East.

The search for an alternate route to the Spice Islands led to a flurry of exploration, beginning with Christopher Columbus, who discovered parts of the Americas while floundering around the Atlantic looking for a route to the Pacific.

The first Europeans to set foot in Micronesia were with the Spanish expedition of Portuguese explorer Ferdinand Magellan in 1521. It had taken 30 years to find a way around the Americas. Magellan became the first navigator to lead his ships around the tip of South America into the Pacific and the expedition was the first to circumnavigate the globe.

It is an indication of the vastness of the Pacific and the smallness of its islands that Magellan managed to sail across the entire ocean from South America to the Mariana Islands, close to the Asian mainland, without encountering any of the thousands of islands along the way.

By the time they arrived in the Marianas, Magellan and his scurvy-ridden crew were eating rats and boiled leather to ward off complete starvation. Although the islanders provided the crew with food, drink and shelter, they also helped themselves to whatever they could carry off the ships.

This first contact between Micronesians and Europeans was to establish a recurring pattern: To the Micronesians all property was shared, but when they helped themselves to the ship's provisions and one of its skiffs Magellan's men retaliated swiftly and brutally, killing seven islanders and burning 40 of their houses to the ground.

The Spanish Period

Numerous explorers soon followed in Magellan's path. Micronesia's tiny islands, devoid of cloves or gold, held little interest for the explorers other than as a quick stopover to replenish water and food supplies. Certainly no-one ever set out to 'discover' Micronesia and it took more than 300 years for all the islands to get added to European charts.

In 1565 Spanish trade ships started making annual trips between Mexico and the Philippines. These 'Manila Galleons' loaded up with silk, spices and tea from Chinese traders in Manila and took them across to Acapulco, where they took aboard newly mined silver for transport back to the Philippines.

The 'new' transpacific shipping corridors, established by the Spanish traders to take advantage of favourable trade winds, actually followed routes the ocean-going Micronesians had been sailing for centuries. Because the ships attempted to stick to these precise routes very few Micronesian islands outside these corridors were discovered during the 16th and 17th centuries; Nauru, Kiribati and many islands of the Marshall group were off the existing beaten track.

In one notable exception, after a mutiny in 1565, the Spanish ship *San Lucas* dropped a few degrees from the usual route to avoid other Spanish ships. It became the first European vessel to come upon Chuuk Lagoon and some of the Marshallese atolls.

Spanish missionaries arrived in the Marianas in 1668, accompanied by the military and government authorities sent to establish colonial rule. Outside the Marianas, however, there were no significant European influences in Micronesia until the late 18th century when British, American and European traders began plying the waters for commercial purposes.

Whalers, Traders & Missionaries

Beginning in 1817 Russian and French explorers began carefully exploring and mapping Micronesia's islands. They also wrote and sketched some colourful accounts of the island people and their lifestyles.

The first British whalers began to arrive in the early 19th century, and American whale ships out of New England arrived a couple of decades later in much greater numbers. During the whaling boom, which reached its peak in the 1840s, there were as many as 500 ships hunting whales in the Pacific.

Whaling was tough, back-breaking work. The whale ships were virtual factories which could stay at sea for years on end, boiling down blubber into oil and storing it in tanks on board. When the whalers stopped off in Micronesia to replenish supplies desertion was common.

Traders also infiltrated Micronesia, setting up posts to deal in copra and beche-de-mer (sea cucumbers). Also during this time US and British companies combed the Pacific for phosphate. Peleliu in Palau was mined, as were Howland and Baker islands (now US territories) and later Nauru and Banaba (Ocean Island, in present-day Kiribati).

Whalers and traders were hardly the cream of civilised society. The sailors picked fights, taunted the islanders, slept with local women and provoked massacres, although quite often it was the islanders who would do away with the crews. Kosrae had so much trouble with the 'degenerate whites' who jumped ship that the chief initiated a policy of putting deserters on the next ship that pulled out of port. The whalers also introduced foreign diseases such as syphilis, smallpox, measles and influenza that ravaged the islands' populations.

Protestant missionaries started going to eastern Micronesia in 1870, after two decades of successful work in Hawai'i. Like their Catholic counterparts in the western part of the region, they brought more than religion. They introduced Western clothing for the scantily clad islanders, as well as Western laws and values. They put the native languages into a written form, primarily so the Bible could be translated, and they set up schools.

But their work was also destructive. Native lore and customs were lost during this time, resulting in a sort of cultural amnesia brought on by the missionaries' zealous efforts at religious conversion.

In addition to these changes, the 19th century saw the introduction of alcohol, firearms, new animals, new tools and new ideas.

German Period

Disregarding Spanish claims in the region, the Germans arrived in Micronesia in the 19th century to develop the copra trade. Initially German involvement was more of a commercial venture than an attempt at colonisation.

The first German company to set up operations in Micronesia was Godeffroy & Sons which, from its New Guinea headquarters, opened an office in Yap in 1869. Meanwhile, 2200 miles (3550km) to the east, Germany was negotiating with the chiefs of Jaluit Atoll in the Marshall Islands to make a treaty which in 1878 established a German protectorate over the Marshalls. Nauru was added to the protectorate 10 years later.

Spain grumbled about German activity in the Caroline Islands (now the Federated States of Micronesia) but did little else until 1885 when the dispute was taken to Pope Leo XIII for arbitration. The pope ruled that Spain owned the land and had administrative rights, but that Germany had a right to establish plantations and commerce.

In 1898 the USA, looking to get in on the action, abruptly declared war on a reluctant Spain. As an outcome of the Spanish-American War, the USA was given Spain's Pacific possessions of Guam, the Philippines and Wake Island.

Not particularly keen on selling her remaining Micronesian possessions to gunboat diplomats, Spain went into secret negotiations with Germany for the sale of the Carolines and the remaining Marianas.

In 1899 the Germans, now eager to become an established colonial power, agreed on a purchase price of 25 million pesetas.

The 15-year German administration in the Marianas thus began with a simple real estate transaction. Commercial development was mainly in copra production, though there were also phosphate-mining operations. German interests, led by the Jaluit Company, controlled the copra trade in the Marshalls and eastern Carolines, governing the islands through local chiefs. On Yap and Palau the copra market was dominated by Japanese traders.

To support the copra trade, Micronesians were encouraged to grow coconuts and were given seeds, tools and long-term contracts. To increase the labour supply, outer islanders were sometimes forcibly removed from their atolls. Communally held land, often seemingly idle, was redistributed to the new arrivals or leased by the government to private businesses. Germany's main legacy in Micronesia rests in the social disruptions caused by forced relocations and altered land-use policies.

The German presence, however, was limited to a small group of government officials, businessmen and missionaries, and its total population in Micronesia was well under 1000. Some businesses, such as the German South Seas Phosphate Company in Angaur and the Jaluit Company, made money, but overall German government subsidies to faltering businesses outweighed the total profits taken in Micronesia.

A classic case was phosphate-rich Nauru, the wealth of which the German administrators had been ignorant of until the British emerged claiming their rights. The Germans hastily negotiated for company shares and royalties; those shares were sold in London for £600,000 at the start of WWI.

With the onset of WWI German forces fled Micronesia, allowing the Japanese fleet to sail in without resistance.

Japanese Period

Japan controlled all of Micronesia except for Guam, Kiribati and Nauru between the two world wars. A triumvirate of Australia, Britain and New Zealand governed Nauru and busily expanded phosphate operations to keep pace with ballooning post-war demand. The Gilbert Islands (now in Kiribati), which had been incorporated into the British Gilbert & Ellice Islands Protectorate in 1892, became a fully fledged colony in 1916.

Throughout Germany's occupation, Japan increased its economic ties with Micronesia. Just before WWI more than 80% of its trade was with 'German Micronesia'. The Japanese imported turtle shell, mother-of-pearl, beche-de-mer and other products from the islands.

With the outbreak of hostilities in Europe, Japan moved to strengthen its ties to Micronesia and in October 1914 the Japanese navy seized possession of the German colonies under the pretext of alliance obligations with Britain. The Japanese then proceeded to occupy the islands, starting in the east with the Marshalls and moving westwards.

Japan wasted no time developing the infrastructure and administration necessary for the complete annexation of Micronesia. The League of Nations formally mandated control of Micronesia to Japan in 1920.

By this time Saipan, the nearest island to Japan, was already home to a growing number of Japanese colonists and entrepreneurs who had sugar-cane production under way. A Japanese conglomerate, the South Seas Development Company, bought them out in 1921 and came to dominate Micronesia's development and exploitation.

Micronesia was an extension of the Japanese empire's boundaries, and the Japanese left no doubt that they were there to stay. They intended to make Micronesia as Japanese as possible, building Buddhist temples and Shinto shrines, geisha houses and public baths.

The construction of roads, harbours, hospitals and water systems was followed by seaplane ramps, airfields and fortifications that violated the League of Nations mandate. The Japanese withdrew from the league in 1935 but remained firmly in control of Micronesia.

Administrative buildings were made of heavy concrete capable of withstanding not only typhoons but also direct aerial bombings. Many weathered both in WWII.

Although the mandate called for the economic and social development of Micronesia, the Japanese geared such development toward supporting and fortifying their own settlements, not toward the local population. By 1940 the Japanese population in the Marianas, Carolines and Marshalls was more than 70,000, far outnumbering the 50,000 Micronesians.

In the Marianas, railroads were built to carry sugar cane from the plantations to harbourside refineries. From there the sugar and alcohol were shipped to Japan. Throughout Micronesia, fisheries projects, copra, tapioca and trochus shell production and phosphate and bauxite mining began to thrive.

The Japanese, drawing from experience with their resource-scarce home islands, created an astonishing level of agricultural activity in Micronesia. With exports exceeding imports, they achieved an economic viability that would never be remotely approached under the Americans. In terms of production it was Micronesia's heyday.

It was not the most pleasant time for the Micronesians, whose place in this profitable system was clearly at the bottom. The two-tiered education system saw Japanese children attending excellent schools, while the three years of compulsory education for Micronesians was primarily geared to teaching them a servant's form of Japanese. This subordination prevailed in wage scales and social treatment.

The Micronesians saw only trickle-down benefits from the impressive Japanese-crafted economy and during wartime, when the trickle stopped, it was the local islanders who were the first to feel hard times and hunger.

The Japanese not only made the islands more productive than ever before, but also set Micronesia on a shifting course from a traditional subsistence lifestyle to a monetary economy. In boom towns like Garapan and Koror, the sudden development awed many locals who acquired a taste for the imported goods in store windows, such as rice, canned food and sweets.

WWII

Though Nauru had a brush with WWII on 6 December 1940, when the Germans sank four offshore ships, the war in the Pacific came into force with the Japanese air attack on Pearl Harbor on 7 December 1941 and against the US territory of Guam on the same day (8 December across the International Date Line).

Undefended, Guam surrendered two days later, just hours after Japanese forces came ashore. With Guam's capture, the Japanese possessed most of Micronesia. Unopposed, the Japanese seized many of the Gilbert Islands in December 1941 and gained Nauru in August 1942. In November 1943, the USA launched its first major counter-offensive in the bloody Battle of Tarawa.

On 1 February 1944, the USA started its drive across the Pacific with an attack on Kwajalein Atoll, a major Japanese air and naval base in the Marshall Islands. By 4 February it had captured Kwajalein and the undefended Majuro Atoll to the south, and from these two outposts the USA began air raids on Japanese bases in the western Carolines.

On 17 February the USA made a surprise attack on a fleet of Japanese warships and commercial vessels harboured in Chuuk Lagoon (then called Truk Lagoon). This supposedly impenetrable fortress was the Imperial Japanese Fleet's most important central Pacific base. The USA destroyed more than 200 planes on the ground and sank nearly 60 ships. The 200,000 tons of equipment sunk in the two days of fighting was a WWII record.

With the Chuuk base neutralised and no longer able to provide support to other Pacific bases, the USA continued moving westwards from Majuro, capturing Enewetok and other smaller atolls and islands in the Marshalls.

In June 1944, US forces moved westwards from the Marshalls with the largest armada ever assembled. The fight for the Marianas began with the US invasion of Saipan on 15 June. Tinian and Guam were invaded in July and all three islands were 'liberated' by the beginning of August. These battles, some of the war's most brutal and costly, marked a major turning point as they put the US air bases within striking distance of Japan.

With the Marianas secured, only Palau was left. In retrospect it should have been bypassed: Although US officers feared that air raids from Palau would threaten a planned US invasion of the Philippines, Japanese air power in the western Pacific had nearly collapsed and the Palau bases had little significance in the declining days of the war. Nevertheless, the USA attacked the Palauan island of Peleliu on 15 September and secured it after a month of battles even bloodier than those on the Marianas.

With planes taking off from Micronesian airstrips, the air bombing of Japan began in force in November 1944. In August 1945 two planes, leaving from Tinian, dropped atomic bombs on Japan's industrial ports of Hiroshima and Nagasaki. The devastation of those cities was followed days later by Japan's unconditional surrender.

The Micronesians had watched the Japanese construct fortified command posts, communications buildings, hospitals, airports and harbours. Caught in the crossfire, they watched as the USA turned it all into rubble. Whole towns such as Koror, Garapan and Sapou were levelled, some never to be rebuilt. For Micronesia, the Rising Sun had set.

In the months following the war thousands of Japanese were shipped home from Micronesia, most of them civilians or soldiers from uninvaded islands. The USA took few military prisoners since most Japanese soldiers fought to the death or committed suicide rather than surrender. Many Japanese civilians killed themselves as well, rather than risk the torture which they believed the Americans would inflict. Thousands of Americans and tens of thousands of Japanese died fighting in Micronesia.

Thousands of Micronesians died during the war too, though in all the volumes written about WWII they are scarcely mentioned. Their islands were the stage – with even uninhabited islands such as Canton, Palmyra, Christmas and Johnston becoming vital air stations – but the islanders were not the players, merely the victims.

The Americans Move In

The US government immediately began to treat Micronesia as its 'spoils of war'. From the Micronesians' perspective, the occupying forces were suddenly American instead of Japanese.

The US navy took command of the islands in 1945 and effectively sealed Micronesia off to visitors – with the exception of Nauru and Kiribati, where the Australians and British respectively reassumed control. Some areas remained closed until 1962.

The islands' remoteness and the relative paucity of Micronesians left the islands unseen and isolated to all beyond their shores. It was an isolation that the US military took measures to maintain (and still does on some islands: see the chapters on the Marshall Islands and the US territories).

The Nuclear Age

For the Marshallese the destruction did not cease with the end of the Pacific conflict; for them the most fearsome display of firepower was still to come.

Soon after the war, the USA took over sections of the Marshalls to test nuclear weapons and research the little-understood effects of radiation.

On 1 July 1946 the first nuclear bomb explosion, part of a perversely theatrical testing program dubbed 'Operation Crossroads', took place at Bikini Atoll, with dignitaries and military officials from around the world brought in to witness the event. Without any fanfare, nuclear testing was

Operation Crossroads

Operation Crossroads, a dual-bomb test which took place at Bikini Atoll, was the first peacetime explosion of atomic bombs. Nearly 100 decommissioned and captured warships were anchored in the lagoon as target subjects to test the effectiveness of the nuclear bomb in sinking an enemy fleet. The first bomb was detonated on 1 July 1946 directly above the lagoon while the second bomb was exploded underwater from the lagoon floor on 25 July. It all took place with the bizarre fanfare of a gala international event and rates as the biggest public relations coup of the early Cold War.

Scores of congressmen, foreign dignitaries and scientists were invited to witness the event, a blitz of media personnel were brought in and over 200 movie cameras were used to shoot 18 tons of film, equal to half the world's film supply at the time. It's little wonder that the mushroom cloud that resulted from the explosion has since been used as a backdrop in hundreds of programs and movies.

Back in the USA, radio programs were interrupted to broadcast the event. Reports were replete with such patronising sound bites as 'The islanders aren't exactly sure what the atom bomb means but at least they admit it'. Congressional observers compared it to a huge firecracker and complained they weren't allowed to get closer to the explosion.

Of those present at the testing, more than 1000 people, including the military newscaster, later filed disability claims for radiation-induced cancer.

expanded to a second Marshallese atoll, Enewetok, in 1948. There would be 66 nuclear tests which would leave some atolls uninhabitable and hundreds of islanders victims of radiation poisoning.

The most powerful bomb ever tested by the USA was detonated over Bikini's lagoon in 'Operation Bravo' on 1 March 1954. The 15-megaton hydrogen bomb had an equivalent tonnage of TNT greater than the total tonnage of explosives used during WWII and was 1000 times more powerful than the bomb dropped on Hiroshima.

Pulverised coral from Bikini's reef was scattered as radioactive fallout over an area of about 50,000 sq miles (130,000 sq km). It filtered down as ash upon the Marshallese on the atolls of Rongelap and Utrik, upon US weather station personnel on Rongerik Atoll and upon the unlucky crew of the Japanese fishing vessel *Lucky Dragon*. Hundreds of people and their offspring were affected. The USA evacuated the Rongelapese 48 hours later, but by that time many had already suffered severe radiation burns from 'Bikini snow'. Although the USA downplayed the extent of the contamination, it's now believed that nearly two dozen Marshallese atolls were affected.

Nuclear experiments ended in 1958 with an international test-ban treaty, just before US plans to blast nuclear warheads into space from Bikini Atoll. In 1959, however, the British commenced nuclear testing off Christmas Island in present-day Kiribati, and the USA, relocating Bikini, joined them for testing in 1961–62. The tests were conducted high in the atmosphere rather than on the ground and have had no obvious long-term effects on the island.

Trust Territory

In 1947 the UN established a trusteeship in Micronesia. Called the Trust Territory of the Pacific Islands, it had six districts: the Northern Marianas, Pohnpei (including Kosrae), Chuuk, Yap, the Marshalls and Palau. The USA was given exclusive rights to administer the islands.

The UN designated the area a 'strategic trust', allowing the USA to establish and maintain military bases in Micronesia and to prevent other nations from doing the same.

Nauru became a separate trust territory in 1947, administered principally by Australia, while Kiribati remained a British colony.

Under UN guidelines, the USA was obliged to foster the development of political and economic institutions with the goal of helping the Micronesians to achieve self-government and self-sufficiency. Instead, 20 years of neglect were followed by 20 years of promoting dependency on welfare.

Rather than developing an economic infrastructure and promoting industry, the USA pumped in money for government-operated services. Rather than encouraging farming and fishing, they passed out food commodities. They built airports, schools and aged-care centres and initiated other projects, creating an abundance of government jobs in an economy reliant on imported greenbacks.

With anticolonial sentiment high in the 1960s, the USA found itself coming under mounting criticism. Yielding to Micronesian aspirations, it allowed the islanders to assume a degree of self-government. In 1965 the USA agreed to the formation of the Congress of Micronesia as a forum for islanders to deliberate their future political status. The congress was a two-house legislature made up of elected representatives from all island groups.

Executive authority in the Trust Territory, however, remained under the control of the US High Commissioner. The CIA kept tabs on island legislators by bugging the offices of the Congress of Micronesia.

Peace Corps

The Peace Corps arrived in 1966, bringing a new breed of Americans. They were more concerned with the interests of the people of Micronesia than with the strategic interests of the USA. For the first time, Americans slept, ate and lived with the Micronesians, and a fair number stayed on to marry into Micronesian life. (Whether the Peace Corps volunteers introduced the islands to marijuana remains a matter of some debate.)

The US government saw the Peace Corps as a way of spreading American influence and for a while there was one volunteer for every 100 Micronesians. By putting a volunteer on every inhabited island, they brought English as a unifying language to the distant corners of Micronesia. What they hadn't calculated on was the volunteers' idealism and their critical outlook on US policies.

The Peace Corps still has volunteers in most Micronesian countries; many are teaching on the outer islands. The Australian Volunteer Service Abroad program also has young people placed in Kiribati and the Marshall Islands.

Emerging States

Nauru gained its independence in 1968, after lobbying successfully for control of its phosphate resources. Kiribati, taking its cue from independence movements in the Solomon Islands and Fiji, emerged from British colonial rule in 1979, shortly after the Ellice Islands split off to become the independent nation of Tuvalu.

For its part, the USA had initially expected that the seven Trust Territory districts under its jurisdiction (Kosrae had become a separate district in 1977) would become one Micronesian nation, but this was not to be.

In January 1978 the people of the Northern Marianas opted to become US citizens under US commonwealth status, becoming the Commonwealth of the Northern Mariana Islands (CNMI).

In July 1978 the remaining six districts voted in a referendum to form a federation. It failed to pass in the Marshalls and Palau, but Pohnpei, Kosrae, Chuuk and Yap became the Federated States of Micronesia (FSM). Its constitution took effect in May 1979.

The Marshalls became a separate political entity, the Republic of the Marshall Islands. Its constitution also became effective in May 1979.

The Palauans, opting to become the Republic of Palau, voted for a constitution that went into effect in January 1981.

In 1982 these new nations signed separate Compacts of Free Association with the USA, all striking their own economic deals. In theory the compacts allow the new nations to manage their internal affairs, although their relationships with other nations are subject to US restrictions. In return for an aid package totalling about three billion US dollars, the compacts allow the USA to maintain sweeping military rights throughout Micronesia.

As part of the terms for the dissolution of the Trust Territory, each compact had to be approved by four separate groups in turn: by the people of each new nation in a general referendum, by the legislatures of those nations, by the US Congress and by the UN Security Council.

The compacts of the FSM and the Marshalls were approved in plebiscites in 1983 and then ratified by their respective congresses. Finally the US Congress approved the two compacts, which took effect in November 1986.

However, over the next few years unresolved issues in Palau (see Independence & the Compact of Free Association in the chapter on Palau) stalled its political process and the dissolution of the Trust Territory.

In December 1990 the UN Security Council voted (with only Cuba dissenting) to terminate the trusteeship for the CNMI, the FSM and the Marshalls, allowing Palau to be dealt with separately.

In 1993, following a vote to amend their constitution, Palauans ratified their compact with the USA by a simple majority. In October 1994, Palau became an independent nation and later that year became the 185th member of the UN.

With Palau's independence, the last of the 11 UN-mandated trusteeships of former colonial possessions was finally abolished.

GEOGRAPHY

Counting Micronesia's islands is no easy task – there are more than 2300. Some are just small flat specks that disappear and reappear with the tides – some are still growing, through coral build-up or volcanic flows – but most are uninhabited. As the vast majority of these islands cover less than one square mile (2.6 sq km) each, they are aptly named Micronesia – Greek for 'small islands'.

Micronesia's islands are scattered over millions of square kilometres of the western Pacific between Hawai'i and the Philippines. They divide geographically into four archipelagoes – the Marshall, Caroline,

Coral Atolls

Charles Darwin was the first to recognise that atolls are made from coral growth which has built up around the edges of a submerged volcanic mountain peak.

In a process taking hundreds of thousands of years, coral first builds up around the shores of a high island producing a fringing reef. Then, as the island begins to slowly sink under its own weight, the coral grows upwards at about the same rate to stay close to the water's surface. This forms a barrier reef which is separated from the shore by a lagoon. By the time the island has completely submerged, the coral growth has become a base for an atoll, marking the place where the island's coastline used to be.

The classic atoll shape is roughly oval, with islands of coral rubble and sand built up on the higher points of the reef. There are usually breaks in the reef rim large enough for boats to enter the sheltered lagoon.

The coral is made up of millions of tiny rock-like limestone skeletons. These are created by tentacled coral polyps which draw calcium from the water and then excrete it to form hardened shells to protect their soft bodies. Only the outer layer of coral is alive. As polyps reproduce and die, the new polyps attach themselves in successive layers to the empty skeletons already in place.

Mariana and Gilbert islands. Kiribati, although a Micronesian nation, also incorporates the Line and Phoenix islands – which are counted part of Polynesia.

All are in the tropics, except two of the Marianas which poke up just north of the Tropic of Cancer. The southernmost island in Micronesia is Arorae, one of the Gilbert Islands, which is 2.39° south.

The islands have a total land mass of about 1240 sq miles (3225 sq km). In comparison, Hawai'i totals 6450 sq miles (16,770 sq km) and the island of Tahiti is 402 sq miles (1045 sq km). From north to south, Micronesia spans 1595 miles (2572km), from the Northern Mariana

Islands to Arorae in Kiribati. East to west, Micronesia spans 45 degrees of longitude. From Tobi, a small Palauan island in the west, to Arorae is a 3135-mile (5056km) stretch.

GEOLOGY

Micronesia's islands are classified as either 'high' or 'low'. The main islands in western Micronesia are high types and are actually the exposed, deeply eroded peaks of a volcanic mountain ridge that runs from Japan through the Northern Marianas, Guam and Palau on down to New Guinea. The Northern Marianas have six to eight active volcanoes – Micronesia's only active volcanoes. Palau's unique Rock Islands, shaped like green mushrooms, were formed by dissolved limestone.

While basically of volcanic formation, some of the western Micronesian islands are partly or wholly capped with a layer of limestone. Pohnpei, Kosrae and Chuuk, in the eastern Carolines, are also high volcanic islands, while Yap is a raised part of the Asian continental shelf.

High islands, which make up the vast majority of Micronesia's land area, usually have good soil, abundant water and lush vegetation. Guam is the largest island, followed by Babeldaob in Palau.

Micronesia's highest point is 3166 feet above sea level, on Agrihan Island in the Northern Marianas. A submarine canyon, known as the Mariana Trench, runs for 1835 miles (2960km) parallel to and just west of the Mariana Islands and has the world's greatest known ocean depth – formed because the Pacific plate is diving down nearly vertically beneath the Philippine plate into the earth's mantle. The canyon is more than seven miles (11km) deep, so, if measured from the bottom of the canyon, the Mariana Islands are the highest mountains in the world.

All of the Marshall Islands (more than 1100) are low coral islands or atolls, as are most of Kiribati's islands and the hundreds of small islands of the central Carolines between Yap Proper and Chuuk, and the outer islands of Pohnpei and Palau.

Typhoons

A typhoon is a tropical storm in the western Pacific with winds of over 75 miles per hour. (The same storm in the Atlantic would be called a hurricane; in the eastern Pacific they are called cyclones.)

While typhoons can occur any time, they are most frequent in Micronesia between August and December. Guam and the Northern Marianas, directly in the main storm track, are particularly susceptible.

For travellers staying in modern hotels, getting caught in a typhoon mostly means enduring heavy winds and rains, damp rooms and the loss of a day or two outdoors. Most of the serious damage affects thatched huts and tin-roofed shanties which easily get blown apart or wrecked by downed trees. Typhoons that sweep across low coral islands have been known to destroy every home and wipe out most of the trees and vegetation.

Supertyphoons, such as the one that pounded Guam in 1997, are those with winds in excess of 150 miles per hour. At the other end of the scale are 'banana typhoons', those with winds that do little more than knock down banana trees.

Some of these low coral islands are like the archetypal cartoon island – just a patch of white sand with a single coconut tree – while others are grouped together on the rims of atolls. Micronesia contains about one-quarter of the world's atolls. Kwajalein Atoll is the world's largest atoll measured by lagoon area, and Christmas Island is the world's largest measured by land area.

Low islands have little topsoil and the sand has a high salt content, so vegetation is limited. Though the islands have no springs or rivers, many sit atop freshwater pockets that can be tapped by wells.

CLIMATE

Micronesia has a tropical oceanic climate that is consistently warm and humid, with some of the world's most uniform year-round temperatures. Temperatures range

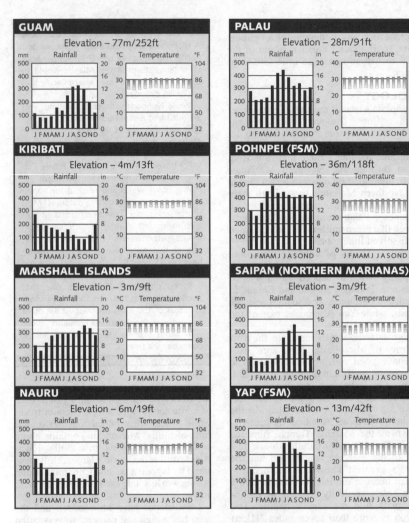

GUAM — Elevation – 77m/252ft

KIRIBATI — Elevation – 4m/13ft

MARSHALL ISLANDS — Elevation – 3m/9ft

NAURU — Elevation – 6m/19ft

PALAU — Elevation – 28m/91ft

POHNPEI (FSM) — Elevation – 36m/118ft

SAIPAN (NORTHERN MARIANAS) — Elevation – 3m/9ft

YAP (FSM) — Elevation – 13m/42ft

from 70° to 90°F (21° to 32°C), with the average daily temperature about 81°F (27°C). Humidity levels average well over 70%.

Generally the more comfortable months are December through March, when there is less rainfall, somewhat lower humidity, slightly cooler weather and refreshing north-easterly trade winds. However, Micro-

nesians report that in the last several years the climate has become less predictable.

The average annual rainfall is about 85 inches to 150 inches (216cm to 380cm), but this varies from place to place. Some of the northern Marshalls and the Phoenix Islands get less than 20 inches a year, while Pohnpei's rainforest interior gets over 400 inches annually. Average rainfall decreases in the Carolines as one goes from east to west.

ECOLOGY & ENVIRONMENT

The threat of global warming (see the boxed text 'Global Warming') is very real for Micronesia. Particularly vulnerable are the low coral atolls that could be easily flooded by severe storms or submerged by rising sea levels. During the late 1990s, locals throughout Micronesia claimed that weather patterns had become totally unpredictable – whether as a result of global warming or the passing El Niño/La Niña phenomenon of 1997/1998. Most nations in Micronesia experienced severe drought during those years, and as a result many were declared disaster areas in spring 1998.

Rising sea levels have contributed to growing erosion along the islands' coasts, where the vast majority of Micronesians live. Many burial grounds near the coast are reportedly crumbling into the ocean. Some countries, such as Kiribati and the Marshalls, are enduring unexpected, unpredictable storm surges, and some have responded to the threat by building sea walls, but even Majuro's eight-foot sea wall cannot prevent occasional flooding of the airport. The sea walls, moreover, can be counter-productive because they alter currents, and in any case they cannot prevent salt water from seeping into taro patches.

Rising water temperature and salinity, combined with some pollution, has resulted in coral bleaching. Around Palau, for example, corals are changing their colours to yellow, purple or pale white.

FLORA & FAUNA
Flora

The coconut palm tree is Micronesia's most important plant. Copra, the dried meat of the nut from which coconut oil is made, is the region's principal export and the main source of revenue for outer islanders. The nut also provides food and drinking liquid, while sap from different parts of the tree is used to make *tuba* (wine) or a beer-like substance called *kaokioki* in Kiribati. Rope is made from the green coconut husks, while fuel and charcoal are made from mature husks. The wood is used for lumber and carving, the fronds for thatch and baskets.

Breadfruit trees provide timber and their large, green globular fruits are a major food source. Timber also comes from tropical mahogany and other trees including the betel nut tree (areca palm), although the latter is more treasured for its nuts (see the boxed text 'Betel Nut' in the FSM chapter). The fruit of the pandanus is eaten and the leaves are used for making mats, baskets and fans.

Other traditional food plants include taro, yams, tapioca and bananas. The lush, heart-shaped leaves of the taro plant, which is cultivated in mud flats, are big enough to use as umbrellas.

Mangrove swamps are common along the shores of many of the high islands. Mangrove trees are easily recognised by their looping roots that arch above the water before reaching down into the mud. The trees help to expand the shoreline as their roots extend away from shore and sediments build up around them, creating new soil.

Colourful tropical plants and flowers are abundant in Micronesia, especially on the high islands. Common varieties include hibiscus, bougainvillea, beach morning glories, plumeria, lilies, lantana and crotons. The Marianas are especially noted for their flame trees (royal poinciana) which have scarlet blossoms.

Plants such as coleus, caladium and philodendron grow in wild abandon in Micronesia, reaching huge proportions.

Two of the more peculiar plants found in Micronesia are the low-growing insectivorous pitcher plant and the 'sensitive plant', a small green ground cover with thin compound leaves that close up when touched.

Fauna

The closer an island group is to the Asian landmasses, the more numerous its birds and animals. High islands have a greater variety of fauna and support larger populations than coral atolls. Thus the isolated Marshall

Global Warming

Since the Industrial Revolution in the 18th century, the concentration of greenhouse gases in the Earth's atmosphere has risen dramatically – particularly carbon dioxide from burning fossil fuels. These gases increase the Earth's natural greenhouse effect, reducing the loss of heat to space and raising the Earth's temperature. The predicted increase in average temperature may seem small – about 6°F (4°C) in the next 100 years – but this rate of increase is vastly faster than any change in the last 10,000 years.

One of the most obvious effects of global warming will be a rise in sea level from thermal expansion of the oceans and the melting of polar icecaps – a 1½ feet to three feet (0.5m to 1m) increase in the next 100 years is a conservative estimate. Other important effects are an increase in the severity of storms in some regions, an increase in the frequency of droughts in other areas, and coral bleaching (see Effects).

Although it is difficult to accurately calculate the causes and effects of global warming, there is no longer any doubt that it is occurring. It's accepted that global temperatures are increasing and polar ice breaking up, but claims of increasing storm severity and the exact cause of coral bleaching are hotly debated. There are even claims that the earth's warming is not a result of the industrial countries high carbon dioxide emissions but a natural event.

There are people who express doubt about the whole issue of global warming –and they're not *all* groups with vested interests, such as oil companies. Some doubters claim the risks are being exaggerated by extreme 'green' movements. However, these dire predictions are sourced from the United Nations Environment Program, the Intergovernmental Panel on Climate Change, and the South Pacific Regional Environment Program – hardly the lunatic left!

Effects

Rising sea levels will cause devastating sea flooding and coastal erosion in many Pacific countries, most disastrously on low-lying coral atolls. However, even on 'high' islands most agriculture, population centres and infrastructure are in low-lying coastal areas. As well as the loss of land, higher seas will increase the effects of storms and cyclones, and the rising seawater table will poison crops and reduce the available fresh ground water.

Recently it has been found that even small increases in sea temperatures can kill off coral reefs (coral cannot survive in water warmer than 83°F). Called 'coral bleaching', the first symptom of the process is the expulsion of the colourful symbiotic algae that lives within coral. Colourless, dead coral is left behind. As well as meaning the loss of precious fisheries, the absence of coral reefs will decrease islands' protection against storms already worsened by the rising sea level.

Freshwater contamination, land erosion, increased storms, lost fisheries and lost agricultural land will make some marginal, resource-poor atolls uninhabitable, forcing the relocation of large numbers of refugees.

Countries with both high and low islands will be able to relocate people and infrastructure inland, although at enormous financial cost, and can relocate atoll dwellers to the higher islands. People in countries composed only of atolls and low-lying islands, such as Kiribati and the Marshall Islands, will have no choice but to emigrate entirely to other countries – risking the extinction of their unique cultures. These countries may not survive the next century.

Ironically, the developed Pacific rim countries that will probably bear the brunt of relocation costs (the USA, Canada, Australia and New Zealand) are among the world's worst producers of greenhouse gasses per capita.

Errol Hunt

Brown Tree Snake

The brown tree snake, which is native to the Solomon Islands and was accidentally introduced to Guam with military cargo in the late 1940s, has wiped out virtually all of Guam's forest birds. In the 1960s it was noted that the number of Guam's birds was declining and by the late 1970s many species survived only in a small forested area in the north. At first pesticides and avian disease were suspected and it wasn't until the 1980s that the snake was identified as the culprit. For most birds it was too late. Nine of the island's endemic species, including the Guam flycatcher and the Guam broadbill, are now extinct, and others survive only in precariously low numbers.

Meanwhile there are millions of brown tree snakes living without predators on Guam, roaming the forest trees at night and polishing off birds and eggs, or at least what's left of them. With so few birds left to eat, the snakes are resorting to chicken eggs, rodents and lizards.

Adult snakes can reach up to eight feet in length and though they'll take a threatening stance when cornered they pose little danger to humans (other than infants), as their toxin is mild and is injected through chewing rather than a strike.

In addition to the devastation of the native ecology, the snakes commonly climb around power lines, causing frequent power outages on Guam. So far little has been done to address the problem, though other Pacific islands are very worried that the snake may slink onto their islands via cargo from Guam; it's already been sighted on Saipan, Wake and Oahu.

Islands, as well as the Line, Phoenix and Gilbert islands, have few creatures other than sea birds and shore birds, while Palau has Micronesia's greatest variety of fauna.

The only land mammals native to Micronesia are bats. Fruit bats with wingspans of up to three feet are found on all island groups except the Marshalls. They are common at dusk in Palau's Rock Islands and on Chuuk, Pohnpei and Yap. Rota has a large bat population – between 1000 and 2000 – but bats are rare on Tinian and Saipan. On Guam, brown tree snakes prey upon young fruit bats. The bats have also been hunted and are now on the endangered species list. Legislation passed in the early 1990s prohibits the import of bats, now a protected species, to Guam and other Mariana islands, but they are hunted and eaten on some of Micronesia's other islands.

Introduced animals include dogs, cats, mice, rats, pigs, cattle, horses and goats. Feral cats wreaked severe havoc on the birds in the Phoenix Islands until they were largely eradicated in the 1960s. Angaur in Palau has monkeys. The seldom-seen sambar deer are found on Pohnpei, Rota, Guam and Saipan.

Guam has carabao (water buffalo), which were probably brought in by Jesuit missionaries in the 17th century. Carabao are most often seen in southern Guam, where they work on small farms. They are large, clumsy animals and not always good-tempered with strangers.

Palau is the only island to have estuarine crocodiles (and a few New Guinea crocodiles) that frequent both saltwater and freshwater areas, favouring muddy mangrove swamps. They are primarily nocturnal, but sometimes bask in the sun during the day. Adult crocodiles average about nine feet in length and can be dangerous. After a spearfisherman was eaten in the late 1960s, Australian hunters were brought in to pick off Palau's largest crocodiles. The one that killed the fisherman was captured and part of the man's arm and flashlight were found in its stomach.

On several islands you might come across monitor lizards sunning themselves on the roads or hanging out in caves or muddy swamps. They can reach up to six feet in length but are more commonly half that size.

Other than venomous but non-aggressive sea snakes and worm-sized blind snakes, Micronesia's only snakes are on Guam and Palau. Palau has the Pacific Island boa in its forests, the Palau tree snake in its small trees and shrubs, and the dog-faced water snake in its mangrove swamps. None poses a threat to people. Guam's infamous brown tree snake has spelled extinction for most of that island's forest birds, but is not a danger to adults (see the boxed text 'Brown Tree Snake' in this chapter).

Micronesia's numerous native skinks include a green variety that can grow up to one foot in length, and others with bright iridescent blue tails. The endearing gecko, a small common house lizard that scampers along walls and ceilings by means of suction-cup-like feet, has a loud call. It prefers to live indoors with people, paying its way by eating mosquitoes and other pesky insects.

Micronesia has a variety of crabs, including coconut crabs and mangrove crabs which both make good eating. Coconut crabs are sometimes caught by islanders and kept in cages while they grow to a meatier size, which can be up to three feet long. They are strong enough to tear open a metal rubbish bin and pry apart the bars of a steel barbecue grill. And, yes, they can also rip through coconut husks and shells.

Micronesia has about 7000 varieties of insects. Mosquitoes, beach gnats and cockroaches are the most common annoyances. Butterflies are particularly noticeable on Guam, largely because the birds and skinks that once preyed on the caterpillars have been decimated by the brown tree snake.

Marine Life Micronesia has an abundance of marine life, including a wide range of hard and soft corals, anemones, sponges and many varieties of shellfish, the best known being the giant tridacna clam (see the boxed text 'Giant Clams' in the Palau chapter).

Sea turtles, including hawksbills, green turtles and leatherbacks, which are all endangered species, lay eggs on uninhabited sandy beaches. Turtles and their eggs have been an important native food source for centuries and are still eaten, especially by outer islanders.

Micronesian waters hold porpoises, sperm whales and beaked whales. Palau has less than 200 of the endangered dugong, or sea cow, which is an herbivorous, seal-like mammal about nine feet in length and weighing up to 900 pounds.

Sea cucumbers, particularly common in the Marianas, dot the bottom of shallow waters near shore. Their entrails squish underfoot if you happen to step on one, but they're harmless. One variety is the beche-de-mer sought by traders in the 19th century. When boiled, dried and smoked they are considered delicacies in China and South-East Asia.

Sportsfishing fans like Christmas Island for its bonefish.

Birds More than 200 species of birds have been recorded in Micronesia and about 85 species breed in the area.

The cardinal honeyeater, a small bright-red-and-black bird, is endangered in Guam but easily seen elsewhere. It's found in gardens and forests, poking its curved bill into the centres of hibiscus and other flowers. The Northern Marianas have a beautifully plumed golden honeyeater.

The white or grey Pacific reef heron is common on reefs and in shallow water, where it uses its long beak to hunt for fish and small crabs. Cattle egrets are sometimes seen in open grassy areas and are particularly common in western Micronesia during the winter months of November to February.

Kingfishers in Micronesia seldom fish. These pretty blue-and-white birds, with cinnamon-coloured touches, are found on Pohnpei, Palau and in the Marianas. They feed mainly on insects and lizards.

Micronesian starlings are common and widespread. Starlings like to eat papayas and some islanders like to eat starlings.

Red ginger, common on Kosrae

Traditional dance, Satawal Atoll, Yap

The Rock Islands of Palau

The Sleeping Lady, Kosrae

Sunset over russet waters, Lamotrek Atoll, Yap

Bird Island, Saipan, a nesting site for brown noddies and other sea birds

MH

White-tailed tropicbirds are often seen in Micronesia.

The best place to see the endangered Micronesian megapode is on Palau's Rock Islands, where some of these ground-living birds have built nests on the picnic beaches. The megapode does not incubate its eggs but lays them in the ground, warming them with dirt and decaying matter. Endemic to Micronesia, this species is now extinct on Guam and Rota, but there is a small group near Saipan's Suicide Cliff.

The Guam rail, a flightless bird indigenous to Guam but wiped out there by the brown tree snake, was introduced on Rota in 1990 and 1991 after a successful captive breeding program saved the bird from extinction. Unfortunately, most of the rails released on Rota have died or disappeared. In 1998 rails were reintroduced to Guam in an area where snakes have been controlled through trapping. Some rails have already nested and are raising young; a barrier prevents snake access to the release areas.

Nauru's frigate bird is slowly encountering a similar fate to that of the Guam rail, as human habitation and environmental degradation edge it out of its habitat.

Some of the more commonly seen shore birds in Micronesia, especially during spring and autumn migrations, include the lesser golden plover, wandering tattler, whimbrel and ruddy turnstone. Common sea birds include the brown noddy, black noddy and white tern.

Christmas Island is a bird-watcher's paradise, with 18 sea bird and one shore bird species. The nearby Phoenix Islands, many of which are wildlife refuges, are also havens for migratory birds.

White-tailed tropicbirds, distinguishable by two long, white tail feathers, are often seen riding the air currents around the cliffs where they build their nests.

Serious bird-watchers should get hold of the 12-page *Checklist of the Birds of Micronesia* by Peter Pyle & John Engbring. It's available for US$2 from the Hawaii Audubon Society (☎ 808-528 1432), 850 Richards St, Suite 505, Honolulu, HI 96813. For a suggested bird-watching guide, see Books in the Regional Facts for the Visitor chapter.

National Parks & Reserves

With so little land area, it's not surprising that Micronesia has few public parks. On these islands the land, as well as the reef and waters surrounding it, are traditionally part of an extended family or clan's property. Consequently more traditional islands, such as those of the FSM, Marshalls or Kiribati, lack vast tracts of public land for parks. On Guam and Saipan, where colonial powers eroded cultural traditions, there is more public space, but even there parks are limited.

Guam has several hundred acres of land, called the War in the Pacific National Historical Park, which have been set aside to preserve WWII battle sites. In addition, there's a conservation preserve in southwestern Guam with hiking trails up to a couple of mountain ridges and down to a secluded bay that once held a Chamorro village. In 1993 Ritidian Point, at the northern tip of Guam, became a new national wildlife refuge.

On Saipan, the Marpi Commonwealth Forest in the north is an upland forest large enough for an hour or so of hiking. There is also the American Memorial Park in Garapan.

Palau has set aside a group of its uninhabited Rock Islands, known as 70 Islands, as a marine preserve, prohibiting public access to prevent disturbance of nesting turtles and sea birds.

Jarvis, Baker and Howland islands – unincorporated US territories located in the Phoenix Islands – were designated national wildlife refuges in 1974. The wildlife refuge status of Johnston Island, also a US territory, is temporarily subordinated to the US military's use of the island as a weapons destruction site.

GOVERNMENT & POLITICS

Guam is an incorporated US territory. The Commonwealth of the Northern Marianas is a commonwealth of the USA. The Republic of the Marshall Islands, the Federated States of Micronesia and the Republic of Palau, all formerly under the USA's sphere of influence, are independent nations. The Republic of Nauru and the Republic of Kiribati are members of the British Commonwealth.

The internal governments of FSM, the Northern Marianas and Palau are based on the US system of executive, legislative and judicial branches; the Marshallese government incorporates elements of the British parliamentary system. In all three nations, traditional village councils and high-ranking chiefs retain some powers through advisory boards.

District Centres

The term 'district centre' refers to the main centre within a cluster of islands. This is generally the place where services are based, including the international airport, main medical centre, government offices and tourist facilities.

The main district centres in Micronesia are: Majuro (Marshall Islands), Koror (Palau), Saipan (Northern Marianas), Tarawa and Christmas Island (Kiribati) and, in the Federated States of Micronesia, Pohnpei Island (Pohnpei), Weno Island (Chuuk), Yap Proper (Yap) and Kosrae. Guam acts as a district centre for the entire Micronesian region and has the most developed commercial, medical and educational facilities.

A few of the more widely-scattered island groups, such as the Marshalls, further designate domestic district centres (sometimes called sub-districts) within their own political unit.

ECONOMY

The economy of American Micronesia depends heavily upon US appropriations. This makes it possible for island governments to employ roughly 60% of the total workforce. On most islands their payrolls form the backbone of the entire economy.

The Marshalls, the FSM and Palau have entered 15-year Compacts of Free Association with the USA. In all three cases (though less so in Palau), the money was spent much too freely in the early years of the compact, and the governments are now struggling to economise before the money expires. In the 1998 financial year, grants of US$72 million went to the Federated States of Micronesia, US$37 million to the Marshall Islands and US$19 million to Palau.

Palau's compact expires in 2009, while those of the Marshalls and the FSM expire in 2001. The latter two will try to negotiate another deal with the USA. The FSM is worried about the future of its funding, but the Marshalls have a bargaining chip – Kwajalein, a US missile-testing site which the USA plans to retain.

In the short term, Micronesia's economy is unsustainable. Exports are limited to copra, handicrafts and a few marine products. The total value of all exports doesn't generate enough income to pay even Micronesia's fuel bills.

Apart from their subsistence Micronesians produce very little. The few private-sector jobs deal largely in imported goods. Virtually none of the products in the department stores, markets, bars, office suppliers or car dealers are produced in Micronesia.

US expenditures in Micronesia have created dependency rather than self-sufficiency. Micronesia's main asset, aside from its land coveted by the US military, is its sea. Micronesia's waters are rich in tuna – the Pacific holds 90% of the world's tuna (skipjack, yellowfin, bigeye and albacore). Unfortunately, prospective local operations are hindered by lack of expertise and equipment and so cannot develop large-scale fishing operations. Consequently, each nation leases its waters to foreign fishing boats, including US, Japanese, Chinese and Russian vessels.

At the end of the trusteeship, the USA undertook extensive capital improvement projects in Micronesia, including new airports, docks, water and sewerage systems, paved roads and hospitals. However, with their multi-million dollar annual maintenance and operation costs, many of these capital improvements represent yet another economic liability. It is telling that despite all the funding, most district centres still lack potable water.

Nauru and Kiribati, never under the US umbrella, are both somewhat different. Kiribati survives largely on Australian aid grants and revenue from foreign fishing licences. Phosphate-rich Nauru was one of the world's wealthiest nations per capita in the mid-20th century. Now the money has been squandered through poor investments, the phosphate is about to run out and Nauru has no colonial power to fall back upon.

The per capita Gross Domestic Product (GDP) varies greatly between Micronesian nations. Guam has the highest per capita GDP (actually, Gross Island Product!) at US\$19,200, while the scale bottoms out with Kiribati at US\$535.

POPULATION & PEOPLE

The region's population is about 521,000. Micronesia has high birth rates and one of the world's highest proportions of people under age 18.

The people of the eastern and central islands are thought to be predominately of Melanesian descent, while those of the western islands are believed to be of South-East Asian descent. Micronesian societies evolved in relative isolation and maintained fairly undiluted indigenous cultures. The Chamorro people of the Mariana Islands have the only notable admixture of Western blood, a result of 17th-century Spanish conquest in those islands and a policy of cultural absorption.

Many migrants from compact countries have settled in Guam, the Northern Mari-

anas and Hawai'i, bypassing usual US immigration laws.

EDUCATION

Free public education is provided in Micronesia through to high school, but on most islands it's mandatory to attend school only to the 8th grade or to age 14.

There are colleges in all major district centres. Micronesia's only on-site university is the University of Guam, which has a high enrolment of students from other Micronesian islands. The University of the South Pacific's main campus is on Fiji but there are university centres on Tarawa, Majuro and Nauru.

ARTS
Dance

Traditional dancing is important on many Micronesian islands, especially those less affected by Westernisation such as Yap, the outer Caroline islands and Kiribati. Micronesian dancers wear colourful traditional costumes and commonly accompany their movements with chanting in unison. Dancing is done in groups, with the women and men customarily dancing separately. Dances can be performed marching, sitting or standing. One form, known as stick dancing, involves beating bamboo poles together to create a rhythm.

Most dancing in the outer islands takes place only on special occasions or for village events, but in a few district centres, notably Pohnpei, Koror, Tarawa and Christmas Island, visitors can arrange to watch a show of traditional dancing.

Traditional Architecture

While Western ways now mix with traditional architectural styles, many islands still have traditional community buildings constructed in the centuries-old manner with planks of native mahogany or coconut palms and roofs of thatched nipa palm, bound by hand-twisted coconut sennit. On Pohnpei, these traditional buildings are called *nahs* and are used as ceremonial houses. On Palau, they're called *bai* and serve as men's meeting houses, while Yap has *pebai*, which are community meeting houses, and *faluw*, or men's houses (see Traditional Community Houses under Society & Conduct in the FSM chapter). Kiribati's ubiquitous structures are called *maneaba* and serve as community meeting houses.

Canoes

While speedboats are more common, traditional outrigger canoes are still found throughout Micronesia. The canoes have a single outrigger and are generally made from a breadfruit tree trunk that's hollowed out and crafted using simple hand tools. Model versions are handcrafted on a few islands including the Marshalls, Kiribati and Pohnpei.

Stone Money

There were many forms of indigenous money in Micronesia, including those made of beads, turtle shell and rare clams. The most notable was Yapese stone money, called *rai*, which was made of a single stone that could reach 12 feet in diameter and weigh as much as five tons. It was carved into a disc shape and carried by means of a hole bored through the centre, which gave it the appearance of a giant wheel. Although the stones are no longer 'minted', Yap still has many impressive stone money 'banks', as village paths lined with rai are called.

Tattooing

Before the arrival of missionaries, tattooing was a common practice on many Micronesian islands. It was considered a rite of passage to adulthood, with the extent and design of tattoos often signifying the wearer's place within the social hierarchy. Chiefs were often the only people permitted to have facial tattoos.

Tattoos were generally simple repetitive patterns that either extended horizontally or formed a triangular design. Women were tattooed less extensively than men. On the Marshalls, for example, only a woman's shoulders, arms and thighs could be tattooed. If she was royalty her hands were also tattooed. Traditional tattooing is a dying art, though some youngsters are still tattooed on Kiribati's outer islands.

Handicrafts

Some items traditionally used in daily life are still made by islanders, sometimes for practical use, other times for sale as souvenirs. Some handicrafts have dual functions, as for example the finely woven hibiscus-fibre skirts known as *lava-lava* that are worn by Yapese women and which also make lovely wall hangings.

In some cases the souvenir market has kept the traditional art alive. Examples are Marshallese stick charts, which were once used to teach traditional navigation methods, and carved Palauan storyboards, which are smaller versions of legends that once decorated traditional buildings.

Other common handicrafts are baskets woven of pandanus or coconut fibres (some of the finest are found in the Marshall Islands) and detailed woodcarvings such as the dolphins, manta rays and sharks created by the Kapingamarangi people in Pohnpei. Miniature shark-tooth swords from Kiribati make brilliant gifts.

Nauru's handicraft industry, supplanted by phosphate, is sadly near extinction.

SOCIETY & CONDUCT
Traditional Society

Traditional Micronesian societies can be divided into two groups: those on the high islands and those on the low islands.

On the high islands people developed a land-based subsistence livelihood and tended to be homebodies. The food sources were reliable and supported relatively large populations. Because life wasn't a constant struggle for survival, the high islanders were able to develop stable and elaborate societies, some of which became highly stratified with caste hierarchies, chiefs, royalty and the like.

Low atoll islanders, such as those in the Marshalls or Kiribati, had to eke out their living from the sea rather than the land. They became expert navigators, sailors and

COURTESY OF THE GUAM VISITORS BUREAU

Warriors and commoners in an ancient Chamorro village in the Mariana Islands

fishers. They travelled great distances and though their next-door neighbours were sometimes hundreds of kilometres away, visits were not infrequent.

Canoe journeys between islands brought trade, warfare and new ideas. Neighbouring islands share cultural elements and islanders can often understand each other's languages, whereas islands at opposite ends of Micronesia are culturally quite different and their languages mutually unintelligible. On the low islands, people travelled farther and thus today maintain a shared culture across a greater distance.

Micronesian societies are made up of clan groupings descended matrilineally (except Yap, which has a patrilineal system) from a common ancestor. The head clan on each island can trace its lineage back to the original settlers and clan members usually retain certain privileges.

Extended families are the norm and it's not uncommon for grandparents, cousins, children and adopted clan members to live under the same roof. If one family member gets a good job, other relatives may well move in and live off the income.

Traditional Canoes & Navigation

Some of the greatest navigators in the Pacific have come from the resource-scarce low islands of Micronesia. With their sandy soil offering limited food supplies, the low islanders took to the oceans. In general, the smaller the island, the more ocean-going the islanders.

Without compasses or maps, Micronesians used a combination of natural aids to navigate around the Pacific.

The long Marshallese atolls, which are fairly close together in a north-south orientation, interrupt the large swells that move across the Pacific from east to west. Marshallese navigation depended largely on learning to feel and interpret the patterns of the currents and waves that were deflected around their islands.

The Carolinians' main navigational focus was the sky. Because most travel was in an east-west line, they could keep on course by watching the sun and by identifying individual stars that would rise or set over particular islands. They memorised ancient chants detailing star patterns and other navigational directions.

The Micronesians also observed other natural phenomena. For instance, to see if land was nearby they would watch for birds returning home to their island nests in the evening. A single stationary cloud off in the distance was often moist ocean air hovering over a high island. Although coral atolls are too flat to be seen from far away, their shallow aqua-coloured lagoons reflect a pale green light onto the underside of clouds.

In protected areas islanders used simple dugout canoes made from a single tree trunk. On the open ocean they used huge canoes, up to 100 feet long, constructed of planks tied together with cord made from coconut husk fibres. These ocean-going vessels were often larger and faster than the ships of the early European explorers and could hold more than 100 passengers.

Avoiding Offence

Outside Guam, Saipan or the beaches of resort hotels, skimpy swimsuits are apt to get you more attention than you'll want and may cause offence.

In most parts of the FSM short skirts and even shorts are deemed inappropriate for women. In Yap, Kosrae, Chuuk and some of the outer islands it's considered offensive for women to expose their thighs. In those places, although it's OK to wear a swimsuit in the water, women are expected to put on a skirt when they get out.

Though skimpy clothing is not appropriate anywhere in Micronesia, things are a bit more relaxed on the more developed parts of Palau and in Guam and the Northern Marianas, where longer shorts don't pose a problem for women. Always watch what the locals are wearing.

For the most part it's acceptable for men to wear shorts throughout Micronesia, even on islands like Pohnpei and Weno where most local men sweat it out in long pants.

RELIGION

Micronesia has been almost completely Christianised. Spanish Catholics got to the Marianas and the western islands first and New England Protestants converted the Marshalls and the eastern islands. They met somewhere in the middle, with Chuuk, Nauru, Kiribati and Pohnpei having fairly equal numbers of Catholic and Protestant followers. Church singing is popular throughout Micronesia, and going to church on Sunday is an unsurpassed way to experience local culture.

LANGUAGE

Micronesian languages are in the Austronesian language group. The major native languages are: Marshallese in the Marshall Islands; Palauan in Palau; Chamorro in Guam and the Northern Marianas; Yapese, Ulithian and Woleaian in Yap; Pohnpeian and Kapingamarangi-Nukuoro in Pohnpei; Chuukese and Mortlockese in Chuuk; Kosraean in Kosrae; Gilbertese in Kiribati; and Nauruan in Nauru. In addition there are numerous languages on the outer islands, some spoken by fewer than 100 people. These island languages developed separately and for the most part are not mutually intelligible.

English is spoken throughout Micronesia and serves as the medium of communication among the far-flung states, though within an island group the local language will predominate.

Regional Facts for the Visitor

HIGHLIGHTS

The highlights of Micronesia are far too many to name, and indeed all visitors will emerge with long lists of their own. Nonetheless, the following deserve a special thumbs up.

Micronesia is famous for its expressive, rhythmic **dancing**. Often accompanied by singing or chanting, the dances stand out for their variety of creative forms.

For **underwater wrecks** Chuuk Lagoon and Bikini Atoll are tops, and for gigantic **manta rays** Yap is unsurpassed. Palau offers wonderful variety and **stunning scenery**, as does less crowded Pohnpei.

A full day's kayak or boat trip through the gloriously lush, mushroom-shaped **Rock Islands of Palau** is paradise defined. Bring your snorkel and dive gear along!

For **traditional culture** no island group holds so strongly to its old ways as Yap, also known for its giant **stone money**. Visiting the outer islands away from any district centre also offers a refreshing immersion in **traditional culture**.

Try the **local food** – the tuna in Pohnpei, the sashimi and mangrove crabs in Palau, the lobster and giant prawns in Kiribati. These delicacies plucked from the sea are everyday menu items. Even a simple local meal may include fried bananas or breadfruit, tapioca, taro balls coated with sugar and coconut milk, and drinking coconuts or coconut home-brew.

Micronesia abounds with **WWII relics** – old cannons, shipwrecks and shells. Among the most moving but least visited sites is the runway on Tinian, from which the planes carrying atomic bombs for Hiroshima and Nagasaki took off.

Micronesia holds the ruins of two impressive **archaeological sites**: the stone cities of Nan Madol on Pohnpei and Lelu on Kosrae, which were once the centres of mighty island kingdoms.

As you would expect, Micronesia has endless **fabulous beaches**. Among our favourites was Ritidian Point – an unexpectedly gorgeous stretch of white sands on northern Guam, pleasantly deserted during weekdays and filled with picnicking families during weekends.

There are six annual **fiestas** on the Northern Mariana Islands and 19 on Guam. These colourful events feature heaped platefuls of local food, an abundance of crafts and local dance performances, and extraordinary hospitality.

Yap, Pohnpei and now Kosrae all offer accommodation in beautiful **traditional-style bungalows** with thatched roofs that provide intimate getaways. Some of the normal amenities (such as in-room phones and televisions) are absent, but you're guaranteed never to miss them!

SUGGESTED ITINERARIES

Any itinerary in Micronesia depends largely on your point of entry and the type of airline ticket you are willing to purchase. Since Micronesia offers a broad range of activities, it's important also to identify what kind of experience you're after. A week is the bare minimum for spending time in Micronesia – anything less could set flying time equal to vacation time!

If you have just one week, the best choice is to visit Palau and Yap. Besides offering spectacular scenery (the Rock Islands, Palau) and a comfortable opportunity to view traditional culture (Yap), both are also top-notch diving and snorkelling destinations.

From Australia, consider flying Air Nauru, which offers good prices (if you book well in advance) and dependable service. Tarawa and its outer islands would make a nice stopover en route to Fiji, or as an endpoint in themselves. Air Nauru also flies from Australia via Nauru to Pohnpei, another pleasant and peaceful vacation spot, and on to Guam.

From Hawai'i, sportsfishing fans and divers can most easily access Kiribati's

Christmas Island, which is serviced once a week by an Aloha Airlines charter flight.

Given three or four weeks in Micronesia, you'll want to purchase a Circle Micronesia or Visit Micronesia pass, or an island-hopper ticket, that will permit open stopovers on multiple islands. Palau and Yap are outstanding choices for any potential itinerary. See Air Passes later in the Getting There & Away chapter for details about Continental's flight policies.

PLANNING
When to Go

By and large, you should schedule your trip to Micronesia when it's most convenient for you. This being the tropics, the temperature is not a major variable, though it's a tad more comfortable in the drier and less humid months of December to March (see Climate in the Facts about the Region chapter). Those are also generally the busiest months.

If you're visiting Guam, Saipan or Palau, it's wise to avoid traditional Japanese holiday seasons when most mid-range and top-end hotels get quite booked up. The Japanese peak seasons include: Christmas through to the first week of January, Golden Week (the last week of April and the first week of May) and Obon (August).

The rest of Micronesia still lies well off the package tourist track and doesn't tend to see seasonal flocks of visitors.

What Kind of Trip

Micronesia can be visited alone or as part of a broader Pacific islands swing. Some travellers use Micronesia as a break during travel between Asia and the western USA or Australia.

Most travellers come by plane, but it's also possible to 'island-hop' by private yacht, which is a pleasant way to visit some of Micronesia's outer islands and more remote areas.

Maps

Local tourist offices often have simple island maps that they distribute free to visitors. The quality varies from hand-drawn approximations to a fold-out public highway map on Guam. On most islands, the Lands & Survey division of the government sells more accurate poster-size maps for US$10 and above.

The US Geological Service (USGS) has topographical maps, last updated in the early 1980s, for many Micronesian islands. They can be ordered from the US Geological Service, Box 25286, Denver Federal Center, Denver, CO 80225.

A very good source for maps is Omni Resources (☎ 1-800-742 2677, 336-227 8300, fax 227 3748), 1004 South Mebane St, PO Box 2096, Burlington, NC 27216-2096. It has maps of Palau, FSM, Kiribati, Guam and the Northern Marianas. The Web site is at www.omnimap.com.

Pacific Magazine (fax 808-852 6325), Box 37551, Honolulu, Hawai'i 96837, publishes a nice map which delineates the various Pacific island nations. It costs US$7; add US$2 for overseas airmail.

What to Bring

Travelling light, a good policy anywhere, is easier in the tropics as sleeping bags, heavy jackets and bulky clothing are unnecessary.

Dress is definitely casual. For men, dressing up means wearing a Hawai'ian-print shirt; women should bring a loose, lightweight cotton dress that covers the knees if they are visiting islands other than Guam, Saipan and Palau.

Ideal clothes are made of breathable cotton, are loose fitting and can be hand washed in a sink and hung up to dry without wrinkling.

One long-sleeved shirt, lightweight cotton jacket or windbreaker might be useful against indoor air-con and outside insects. There are mosquitoes in Micronesia so if you use insect repellent, bring some.

An umbrella or rain jacket to protect against occasional tropical downpours is advisable, though if you get caught out in the rain banana leaves also make a handy shelter.

Footwear in Micronesia is predominately rubber thongs (flip-flops), which are sold everywhere, or other casual sandals. Sneakers are useful for hiking and for walking along rough coral reefs.

A torch is useful for occasional power blackouts and is essential for exploring caves. A Swiss Army knife is worth its weight in gold. If you plan to do a lot of snorkelling or scuba diving, particularly in more remote islands, it's a good idea to bring your own gear.

You might want to consider a passport pouch or money belt to wear around your neck or waist.

Sealable plastic sandwich bags are indispensable for keeping valuables such as camera, film, passport and airline tickets dry.

If you plan to use a laptop computer or other electrical device, bring a converter and adaptor; remember that Kiribati and Nauru use a different voltage from the rest of Micronesia. See Electricity later in this chapter.

Medical supplies and toiletries are available in most places, though outside Guam and Saipan the selection will be limited. Kmart in Guam is a good place to stock up on essentials.

A one-cup immersion heater, usually available for a few dollars from hardware or department stores, and a durable lightweight cup are handy for making coffee, tea or instant soup. Otherwise bring some iodine tablets to treat water.

Lastly and most importantly, bring your patience. People may not be there when you need them, dive operations and hotels may not answer their telephones. Just call back later – it's island time.

Considerations for Responsible Diving

The popularity of diving is placing immense pressure on many sites. Please consider the following tips when diving and help preserve the ecology and the beauty of the reefs:

- Do not use anchors on the reef, and take care not to ground boats on coral. Encourage dive operators and regulatory bodies to establish permanent moorings at popular dive sites.
- Avoid touching living marine organisms with your body or dragging equipment across the reef. Polyps can be damaged by even the gentlest contact. Never stand on corals, even if they look solid and robust. If you must hold on to the reef, only touch exposed rock or dead coral.
- Be conscious of your fins. Even without contact the surge from heavy fin strokes near the reef can damage delicate organisms. When treading water in shallow reef areas, take care not to kick up clouds of sand. Settling sand can easily smother the delicate organisms of the reef.
- Practise and maintain proper buoyancy control. Major damage can be done by divers descending too fast and colliding with the reef. Make sure you are correctly weighted and that your weight belt is positioned so that you stay horizontal. If you have not dived for a while, have a practice dive in a pool before taking to the reef. Be aware that buoyancy can change over the period of an extended trip: initially you may breathe harder and need more weight; a few days later you may breathe more easily and need less weight.
- Take great care in underwater caves. Spend as little time within them as possible as your air bubbles may be caught within the roof and so leave previously submerged organisms high and dry. Taking turns to inspect the interior of a small cave will lessen the chances of damaging contact.
- Resist the temptation to collect or buy corals or shells. The same goes for marine archaeological sites (mainly shipwrecks).
- Ensure that you take home all your rubbish and any litter you may find as well. Plastics in particular are a serious threat to marine life. Turtles can mistake plastic for jellyfish and eat it.
- Resist the temptation to feed fish. You may disturb their normal eating habits, encourage aggressive behaviour or feed them food that is detrimental to their health.
- Minimise your disturbance of marine animals. In particular, do not ride on the backs of turtles as this causes them great anxiety.

RESPONSIBLE TOURISM

Island eco-systems are fragile, and it's important when visiting Micronesia to leave nature as pristine as you found it. This applies to activities on land (hiking) and on sea (diving); divers should not touch or otherwise disturb the fragile coral.

In interacting with the local people, respect is paramount. It's always wise to ask permission before taking photographs, and it's essential in Yap where people rightly take issue with having cameras arbitrarily pointed at them.

Campers should always ask permission before setting down a tent, as almost all land in Micronesia is privately owned.

TOURIST OFFICES

All the island groups give out brochures, maps and other standard tourist information. You can also write in advance and have the information mailed to you, but give yourself extra time as the responses can be slow.

Consult the individual chapters about local tourist offices.

Tourist Offices Abroad

Only Guam, Kiribati and Palau have tourist offices abroad (see those countries' chapters for details).

VISAS & DOCUMENTS
Passport

US citizens need a passport and visa to enter Nauru and Kiribati but not elsewhere in Micronesia, though it makes things much simpler to carry one. Without a passport, some other proof of US citizenship, such as an official birth or naturalisation certificate combined with a driving licence or similar photo ID, is required.

All other nationalities must carry a valid passport throughout Micronesia.

Visas & Travel Permits

US citizens must obtain a visa or visitors permit to visit most of Micronesia's islands, but these are obtainable upon arrival. Most non-US visitors also need visas or visitors permits to all Micronesian countries. See the individual country sections that follow for details. Visitors to Guam (other than US citizens, Canadians and those travelling on a visa waiver) must obtain a US visa in advance. Further details are in the destination subheadings that follow.

Immigration officials in Micronesia commonly ask how long you're planning to stay and then stamp that exact number of days into your passport. It's a good idea to go for the maximum or at least give yourself a buffer, so you won't have to bother about getting (or paying for) an extension if you decide to stay a bit longer.

Most island groups require visitors to have return or onward tickets. Nauru and Kiribati are particularly strict on this, but other countries only occasionally require you to show your onward ticket.

It's wise to obtain visas for onward travel before arriving in Micronesia, as there are only a few embassies in the region, and most offer only limited services.

Guam All non-US citizens need a US visa to visit Guam, except Canadians and those eligible for Guam's visa waiver program.

Under Guam's visa waiver program, citizens of the following countries may enter Guam for up to 15 days for business or pleasure without obtaining a US visa: Australia, Brunei, Hong Kong, Indonesia, Japan, Malaysia, Myanmar (Burma), Nauru, New Zealand, Papua New Guinea, Singapore, Solomon Islands, South Korea, Taiwan, the UK, Vanuatu and Samoa.

Under the visa waiver program it's not possible to extend your stay.

Northern Mariana Islands US citizens need no visa and can stay as long as they like. Non-US citizens don't need a visa for tourist stays of up to 30 days. Tourists can get an extension of up to 60 days by applying to the immigration office and paying a non-refundable fee of US$100.

Marshall Islands Visas are not required for tourist visits of up to 30 days. Upon arrival visitors will be issued an entry permit valid for 30 days. The permit can be extended twice, for a maximum stay of 90 days, for US$10 per extension.

Kiribati Citizens of the following countries can enter visa-free for a maximum stay of 28 days: Canada, Cyprus, Denmark, Fiji, Iceland, India, Jamaica, Kenya, Malaysia, Malta, New Zealand, Norway, Samoa, Singapore, Solomon Islands, Spain, Sweden, Switzerland, Tonga, Tuvalu, United Kingdom (not Northern Ireland), Uruguay, Vanuatu and Zimbabwe. This also applies to holders of passports of the following Commonwealth countries: Bermuda, Britain, Virgin Islands, Cayman Islands, Cook Islands, Falkland Islands and Gibraltar.

Citizens with passports issued by the following authorities can stay for the stated amount of time without a visa: American Samoa, Guam, Trust Territories of the Pacific Islands and Ecuador (20 days), South Korea (30 days) and the Philippines (21 days).

Citizens of all other countries should apply for a visa at a Kiribati diplomatic mission abroad prior to arrival. Single-entry visas cost A$40, multiple-entry visas cost A$70. To get a visa you must complete an application and send your passport, one passport photo and the payment. Three-day processing is available but allow time for courier mail. Upon arrival, you may request a visitors permit allowing you to stay a maximum of four months in a 12-month period.

Although the official word is that you must obtain a visa before arriving, in reality Kiribati will issue visas upon arrival. If you're travelling through the region and would like to enter Kiribati but have no visa, call the immigration office in Tarawa in advance of your arrival. It should be willing to grant you a visa on the border; if asked, emphasise that you're on the road and haven't had time to send off your passport to obtain a visa. Ask the immigration officer to fax you a letter approving your arrival, and show this document to immigration authorities at the airport.

Upon arrival in Kiribati, all visitors (except those whose visa-free stay is limited, as detailed above) will be given a one-month visitors permit. Tourists can extend these three times.

Travellers from Hawai'i to Christmas Island can get visas right before departure, as Kiribati's Honorary Consul in Hawai'i shows up at the Honolulu Airport a few hours before the weekly flight. It's best to notify him in advance of your plans. Be ready with the cash or certified cheque.

A cautionary note: If you notify the Kiribati immigration authorities that you are doing anthropological work or any other type of 'research', you will be charged at least an A$250 cultural fee plus an A$120 immigration fee, payable shortly after arrival. The theory is that you're 'taking something out' of their country.

Nauru Visas for up to 30 days can be granted to visitors upon arrival in Nauru. Tourists should bring an official letter from one of Nauru's hotels to show a pre-arranged booking. If you show up without a booking, they'll undoubtedly let you in so long as the hotels have vacancies (which they usually do). Visitors on business must show a letter from a local sponsor upon arrival and will be issued a business visa, valid for a maximum of three months.

Both tourists and business visitors arriving without a visa must give their passports to the immigration authorities; the passports can be picked up from the immigration office the next working day. Transit passengers will not need to give up their passports; they will be allowed to stay on Nauru until the departure date of the next plane to their destination. Nationals of New Zealand do not need a visa for Nauru.

To carry over A$1000 in cash out of Nauru you must obtain authorisation from the Bank of Nauru. This pesky regulation is because the Bank of Nauru is very low on cash and the country can't afford to have cash leaking out. Thus, anyone bringing more than A$1000 into the country would be advised to document it thoroughly, to minimise hassle on the way out.

Federated States of Micronesia Visas are not required for tourist visits of up to 30 days. Each of the four FSM states (Kosrae, Pohnpei, Chuuk, Yap) has its own immigration process so you automatically get a new entry permit, good for up to 30 days, each time you fly into a new district centre. Entry permits can be extended through the immigration offices without fee for a total stay of up to 90 days, or up to 365 days for US citizens. One-year permits can also be issued for free; you'll need police and medical clearance from your previous place of residence, plus a copy of your passport.

Palau All tourists may stay in Palau for 30 days without a visa. After that, two extensions of 30 days each may be granted by the immigration office. Apply for your extensions at least seven days before the expiration of your current visa (though they can probably process it in one day). The cost is US$100 for each extension.

Travel Insurance

Whatever your destination, make sure you take out a comprehensive travel insurance policy that covers medical expenses, luggage theft or loss, and cancellation or delays in your travel arrangements. Ticket loss should also be covered. For students, international student travel policies handled by STA travel and other student travel organisations are usually quite good value.

Buy insurance as early as possible; some agencies require time to process the application and may require you to get a medical checkup. Check the small print as some policies specifically exclude 'dangerous activities' – even scuba diving! Check whether the policy covers an emergency flight home.

Paying for your ticket with a credit card often provides limited travel insurance, and you may be able to reclaim the payment if the operator doesn't deliver.

Driving Licence

Bring your home driving licence and if it's in a language other than English it's a good idea to also bring an International Driving Permit. Foreign driving licences are gener-ally valid for two weeks or one month after your arrival in a given country. You can obtain a local driving licence in most countries by simply bringing your home licence and taking a test or paying a small fee.

International Health Card

If you're coming from an area infected with cholera or yellow fever, such as South America or Africa, you must carry an International Health Certificate showing that you've been vaccinated to present to immigration authorities.

Other Documents

Divers of course must bring their certification cards.

Copies

Make two photocopies of all important documents, including your passport, airplane tickets and travellers cheque numbers. Leave one copy at home and keep another in a separate part of your luggage.

It's also a good idea to store details of your vital travel documents in Lonely Planet's free online Travel Vault in case you lose the photocopies or can't be bothered with them. Your password-protected Travel Vault is accessible online anywhere in the world – create it at www.ekno.lonelyplanet.com.

EMBASSIES & CONSULATES
Micronesian Embassies & Consulates Abroad

The following are Micronesian embassies and consulates abroad:

Australia
Kiribati Consul General (☎ 02-9371 7808, fax 9371 0248), 35 Dover Road, Rose Bay, NSW 2029
Nauru Consul General (☎ 03-9653 5709, fax 9654 4738), Nauru House, 80 Collins St, Level 50, Melbourne, Victoria 3000
Nauru Consulate (☎ 02-9922 7722, fax 9923 1133), Box 1303, 47 Falcon St, Crows Nest, Sydney, NSW 2065
Fiji
FSM Embassy (☎ 304 180, fax 304 081), Box 15493, Suva
Marshall Islands Embassy (☎ 387 899, fax 387 115), 41 Borron Rd, Box 2038, Suva

Nauru Embassy (☎ 313 566, fax 313 249), 7th floor, Ratu Sukuna House, MacArthur St, Suva

Japan

FSM Embassy (☎ 03-3585 5456, fax 3585 5348), 2nd floor, Reinanzaka Building, 1-14-2, Akasaka 1-chome, Minato-ku, Tokyo 107

Marshall Islands Embassy (☎ 03-5379 1701, fax 5379 1810), Meiji Park Heights, 1st floor, 9-9 Minamimoto-Machi, Shinjuku-ku, Tokyo 160

Palau Embassy (☎ 03-3354 5500, fax 3354 5200), 2nd floor, 201 Pare Cristal, 1-2 Katamachi, Shinjuku-ku, Tokyo 160-001

New Zealand

Kiribati Consul (☎ 09-419 0404, fax 419 1414), 3 Gladstone Rd, Northcote, Auckland, PO Box 40205

UK

Kiribati Consulate (☎/fax 187-3840 375), The Great House Llanddewi, Rhydderch Monmouthshire NP7 UY

Nauru Representative (☎ 020-7235 6911, fax 7235 7423), Nauru Government Office, 3 Chesham St, London SWIX8ND

USA

FSM Embassy (☎ 202-223 4383, fax 223 4391), 1725 N Street NW, Washington DC 20036

FSM Consulate (☎ 808-836 4775, fax 836 6896), 3049 Ualena St, Suite 408, Honolulu, Hawai'i 96819

Kiribati Consul (☎ 808-521 7703, fax 521 8304), 850 Richard St, Suite 503, Honolulu, Hawai'i 96813

Marshall Islands Embassy (☎ 202-234 5414, fax 232 3236), 2433 Massachusetts Ave NW, Washington DC 20008

Marshall Islands Consulate (☎ 808-545 7767, fax 545 7211), 1888 Lusitana St, Suite 301, Honolulu, Hawai'i 96813

Palau Embassy (☎ 202-452 6814, fax 452 6281), 2000 L St NW, Suite 407, Washington DC 20036

Embassies & Consulates in Micronesia

The following foreign embassies are located in Micronesia.

Australia

FSM: Australian Embassy (☎ 320 5448), Box 5, Kolonia, Pohnpei

Kiribati: Australian High Commissioner (☎ 21 184, fax 21 440), Box 77, Bairiki, Tarawa

China

FSM: Chinese Embassy (☎ 320 5575), Box 1530, Kolonia, Pohnpei

Kiribati: Chinese Embassy (☎ 21 486, fax 21 116), Box 30, Bairiki, Tarawa

Nauru: Chinese Embassy (☎ 555 4399, fax 555 4594), NPC Settlement

Federated States of Micronesia

Guam: FSM Embassy (☎ 646 9154, fax 649 6320), PO Box 10630, Suite 613, Tamuning, Guam 96931

Japan

Guam: Japanese Consulate (☎ 646 5220), ITC Building, Marine Drive, Tamuning

Northern Mariana Islands: Japanese Consulate (☎ 234 7201), Horiguchi Building, Garapan, Saipan

Palau: Japanese Consulate (☎ 488 6455), Palau Pacific Resort

Korea

Guam: Korean Consulate (☎ 472 3097), 305 GCIC Building, Hagåtña

Kiribati: Korean Consulate (☎ 26 536, fax 26 367), Box 470, Betio, Tarawa

---

Your Own Embassy

It's important to realise what your own embassy – the embassy of the country of which you are a citizen – can and can't do to help you if you get into trouble.

Generally speaking, it won't be much help in emergencies if the trouble you're in is remotely your own fault. Remember that you are bound by the laws of the country you are in. Your embassy will not be sympathetic if you end up in jail after committing a crime locally, even if such actions are legal in your own country.

In genuine emergencies you might get some assistance, but only if other channels have been exhausted. For example, if you need to get home urgently, a free ticket home is exceedingly unlikely – the embassy would expect you to have insurance. If you have all your money and documents stolen, it might assist with getting a new passport, but a loan for onward travel is out of the question.

Some embassies used to keep letters for travellers or have a small reading room with home newspapers, but these days the mail holding service has usually been stopped and even newspapers tend to be out of date.

Nauru
 Guam: Nauru Consulate (☎ 649 8300), Pacific Star Hotel, Tumon
 Northern Mariana Islands: Nauru Representative (☎ 234 6841), Nauru Building, Susupe, Saipan
New Zealand
 Kiribati: NZ High Commissioner (☎ 21 400, fax 21 402), Box 53, Bairiki, Tarawa
Philippines
 Guam: Philippines Consulate (☎ 646 4620), ITC Building, Marine Drive, Tamuning
 Northern Mariana Islands: Philippines Consulate (☎ 234 1848), Beach Road, San Jose, Saipan
 Palau: Philippines Embassy (☎ 488 5482)
USA
 Marshall Islands: US Embassy (☎ 247 4011), Airport Rd, Majuro
 Palau: US Embassy (☎ 488 2920), Topside
 FSM: US Embassy (☎ 320 2187), Box 1286, Kolonia, Pohnpei

CUSTOMS

Sometimes Micronesian customs officers carry out baggage checks, though these tend to be brief and cursory.

As elsewhere, Micronesian nations prohibit the entry of drugs, weapons, large quantities of alcohol or cigarettes, and fruits and plants that might contain insects or diseases harmful to local crops. Handicraft items purchased on other islands should be declared but will be waved through.

MONEY
Currency

The US dollar is used throughout Micronesia except in Nauru and Kiribati, where the Australian dollar is the currency. There are commercial banks on all major islands in Micronesia; check individual chapters for the listings. On the outer islands you should always bring enough cash to last the duration of your stay – though you won't need much.

Exchange Rates

country	unit		US$
Australia	A$1	=	$0.61
Canada	C$1	=	$0.68
euro	€1	=	$0.95
France	10FF	=	$1.45
Germany	DM1	=	$0.49
Japan	¥100	=	$0.97
New Zealand	NZ$1	=	$0.49
UK	UK£1	=	$1.59

Exchanging Money

Travellers Cheques Except on the remote outer islands which have no banks, travellers cheques in US dollars are universally accepted. You'll rarely have to wait in a bank queue to change them since most hotels, restaurants and larger stores will accept them as cash. The one exception is cash-strapped Nauru, where the bank severely limits the amount of travellers cheques you can cash. It's wise to bring sufficient Australian dollars (in cash) into Nauru to cover your stay. It's always economical to bring travellers cheques in the currency of the country you're travelling to – ie, have cheques in US dollars except in Kiribati and Nauru.

ATMs ATM machines are a dime a dozen on Guam and Saipan and almost as prevalent in Palau. Islands with one ATM are Rota, Tinian, Chuuk, Pohnpei and Majuro. Some islands with none are Tarawa, Christmas Island, Yap, Nauru, Kosrae, Ebeye and Kwajalein. Do not rely solely on ATMs, particularly on islands where there is only one, as the machines frequently run out of cash or otherwise malfunction.

Credit Cards Major credit cards are well integrated in Guam, Saipan and Palau. They are also used by some hotels and a few restaurants on Pohnpei and Kosrae; at most major car rentals and some dive shops throughout the islands; and by travel agents and Continental Airlines and Air Nauru agents everywhere. However, many places are still adjusting to credit cards, and you may be charged a hefty 2.5% to 5% commission for plastic payment.

Costs

Because the islands are so spread out and many of their goods are imported, Micronesia can be an expensive place to travel.

For most people the biggest cost will be airfare. Depending on your itinerary and point of origin, your airfare could easily reach a few thousand dollars. It's certainly an area worth researching well before you go.

Although prices vary between islands, accommodation is generally expensive; see the Accommodation section later in this chapter for details.

Food prices vary a bit between islands but if you stick to local foods, including fresh fish, it's quite reasonable. On most islands you could get by eating on US$15 a day, though it would be easy to spend double that amount without any big splurges.

Public transport is limited and most visitors opt to rent a car for at least part of their stay. Expect to pay about US$50 a day including petrol. Add an extra US$10 to US$15 for collision insurance.

For scuba divers, a full day of diving will add another US$70 to US$120 to your budget.

Tipping & Bargaining

Tipping of 10% to 15% is expected in restaurants on Guam, Saipan and (increasingly) Palau. Elsewhere in Micronesia, tipping is uncommon except in upper-end restaurants with predominantly European clientele.

Bargaining is not customary as stores sell most items for fixed prices. In some cases, bargaining may even be perceived as insulting. Some hotels may drop a few dollars off the price if you press your case, but that is the exception rather than the norm.

Taxes & Refunds

There are no value-added taxes in Micronesia. Of more significance to travellers are hotel room taxes: 5% on Kosrae, 6% on Pohnpei, a flat US$2 or US$3 plus 8% per night in the Marshalls and 10% on all the other islands except tax-free Nauru. Some hotels include tax in the price quoted and others don't; always ask.

Refund policies vary from shop to shop, and from organisation to organisation.

POST & COMMUNICATIONS
Postal Rates

Except for Nauru and Kiribati, Micronesia is under the umbrella of the US Postal Service, which handles Micronesia's international mail (US postage rates apply). Nauru and Kiribati have their own mail services.

Airmail rates from American Micronesia are US$0.33 for a one-ounce letter and US$0.20 for a postcard to the USA or within Micronesia; US$0.55 for a one-ounce letter and US$0.45 for a postcard to Canada; and US$0.60 for a half-ounce letter and US$0.55 for a postcard to any other foreign country except Mexico.

Guam and the Northern Marianas use US stamps, but the Marshalls, FSM, Palau, Nauru and Kiribati print their own stamps, which can only be used from those particular island groups.

Except for Nauru and Kiribati, Micronesia is in US Postal Zone 8 (the same as Hawai'i) for calculating parcel rates to US destinations.

Sending Mail

Service is reasonably efficient between major islands of Micronesia and the outside world. International mail to Micronesia goes through either Honolulu or Guam and generally takes a week to 10 days to arrive, depending on the district centre. Priority mail may get items to their destination in about half that time – but remember, the mail can't go before the plane leaves!

Mail delivery to and from the outer islands depends on the frequency of field trip ships and/or commuter flights and can be very slow. If you're writing to someone on an outer island, you need to include their island's name, in addition to the district centre's address and zip code.

Except on Guam, most places in Micronesia receive mail at post office boxes. When providing contact information, Lonely Planet has not included these box numbers because they are unnecessary: Micronesia is such a small place that if you address mail to the business, island, country and zip code it will get there. For example, write to Kosrae Village Resort, Kosrae, Federated States of Micronesia 96944 and there can be no mistake.

In accordance with US postal regulations, each area in Micronesia (except Nauru and Kiribati) has a zip code and its own two-letter 'state' abbreviation – MH for the Marshall Islands, PW for Palau, GU for Guam, FM for the Federated States of Micronesia and MP for the Northern Marianas. However, since these abbreviations are not well known outside the region, it's advisable to write out the country name instead of the abbreviation. When sending mail from outside the USA, also add 'via USA' below the address.

Receiving Mail

You can have mail sent to you care of General Delivery (or poste restante) at any district centre post office and it will be held for 30 days. While Guam has numerous post offices, general delivery is only available at the general post office (GPO) so all mail should be addressed: General Delivery GMF, Barrigada, Guam 96921.

The following are the zip codes for the main postal areas in Micronesia, excluding Guam (which has multiple postal codes) and Nauru and Kiribati (which have no postal codes).

Chuuk, FSM	96942
Ebeye, Marshall Islands	96970
Koror, Palau	96940
Kosrae, FSM	96944
Majuro, Marshall Islands	96960
Pohnpei, FSM	96941
Rota, Northern Mariana Islands	96951
Saipan, Northern Mariana Islands	96950
Tinian, Northern Mariana Islands	96952
Yap, FSM	96943

Telephone

All district centres have phone systems. Outer islands can be reached by radio; each island generally has a certain time period within which it communicates daily. None of the countries in Micronesia have telephone area codes.

Guam and Saipan have pay phones readily available in public places. Many hotels throughout Micronesia have in-room phones, though some, particularly the upper-end ones, charge US$0.25 or more for local calls. Otherwise, just ask to use the phone in a shop or hotel front desk, and people are generally accommodating.

Almost all district centres have a 24-hour telecommunications office where you can make both local and long-distance calls and pay in cash; the FSM offices accept Visa and MasterCard payment. On average international calls cost US$3 to US$5 per minute, usually with a three-minute minimum.

The FSM has debit card phones, as do Tarawa (Kiribati) and Guam; the cards can be purchased at the telecommunications office. As there are very few cardphones beyond the telecommunications office, the card system is most useful in avoiding the three-minute minimum charge.

Cellular phone users travelling through Micronesia will find it almost impossible to stay connected, particularly if they're island-hopping. Contact Guam Cellular & Paging (☎ 649 7243), which may be able to arrange a connection for Guam and Saipan and may give the latest tips for the rest of Micronesia.

To call direct to Micronesia from overseas, dial the overseas access code for the country you're in, followed by the Micronesian country code for the island you're calling and the seven-digit local number.

Micronesian country codes are:

Northern Mariana Islands	☎ 670
Guam	☎ 671
Palau	☎ 680
FSM	☎ 691
Marshall Islands	☎ 692
(To call Kwajalein Island, dial ☎ 808-471 1836 and then give the five-digit extension.)	
Nauru	☎ 674
Kiribati	☎ 686

Fax, Telex & Telegraph

Fax, telex and telegraph services are available in the district centres through the telecommunications offices. More information is given in individual country chapters.

Email & Internet Access

Much of Micronesia is now connected to the Internet, and a surprising number of businesses have Web pages and email.

Visitors can find public computers with Internet access in all district centres except

Nauru, Rota, Tinian, Ebeye and Christmas Island. There are plenty of Internet terminals on Guam and Saipan. On Majuro and Palau terminals are available during working hours at the businesses listed. Each telecommunications centre in the FSM states has one or two computers where Internet access costs US$4 per hour, and the Tarawa telecommunications centre charges A$30 per hour.

Each island country has a local server, and people planning to settle on one of the islands may want to set up a local account. Prices vary, but in general it's not prohibitively expensive. On Tarawa, which is on the high side, setting up a tskl.net.ki account entails paying a set-up fee of A$40, an A$32 monthly access fee, an A$8 per-hour fee and an A$100 security deposit.

INTERNET RESOURCES

The World Wide Web is a rich resource for travellers. You can research your trip, hunt down bargain air fares, book hotels, check on weather conditions or chat with locals and other travellers about the best places to visit (or avoid!).

There's no better place to start your Web explorations than the Lonely Planet Web site (www.lonelyplanet.com). Here you'll find succinct summaries on travelling to most places on earth, postcards from other travellers and the Thorn Tree bulletin board, where you can ask questions before you go or dispense advice when you get back. You can also find travel news and updates to many of our most popular guidebooks, and the subWWWay section links you to the most useful travel resources elsewhere on the Web.

The Web site of the US Department of Insular Affairs (www.doi.gov/oia/), which has jurisdiction over the compact territories and the unincorporated US territories, gives helpful background information on the islands and has an outstanding page of links.

The CocoNET wireless Web site (www.uq.edu.au/jrn/coco/) is a good source of news on the South Pacific and has well-organised links to magazines and newspapers in the region.

Tourist office Web sites include: Guam (www.visitguam.org); Northern Mariana Islands (www.visit-marianas.com); Palau (www.visit-palau.com); Chuuk (www.fsmgov.org/info/chuuk/); Yap (www.fsmgov.org/info/yap/); Pohnpei (www.fsmgov.org/info/pohnpei); and Kosrae (www.fsmgov.org/info/kosrae). If you're looking to find a package tour to Micronesia, it's a good idea to check the tourist office Web pages, which keep fresh links on groups doing package tours to their countries.

For information on the Marshall Islands, the best site is www.rmiembassyus.org; for Nauru try www.airnauru.com.au; and for Kiribati try www.tskl.net.ki/kiribati/.

One of Micronesia's funkier sites is the Bikini Atoll home page (www.bikiniatoll.com), which mixes thorough information about the atoll with insights into such matters as the evolution of the bikini bathing suit.

Because Web addresses change constantly, and for space reasons, we do not list all of them in this book. We do, however, list email addresses, from which Web site addresses can often be derived. Web site addresses can also be located by a simple search on the Internet.

BOOKS

Most books are published in different editions by different publishers in different countries. As a result, a book might be a hardcover rarity in one country while it's readily available in paperback in another. Fortunately, bookshops and libraries search by title or author, so your local bookshop or library is best placed to advise you on the availability of the following recommendations.

Lonely Planet

The Lonely Planet Pisces series covers the top dive sites around the world – and Micronesia not least among them! LP's Pisces series by Tim Rock includes *Diving & Snorkeling Palau*, *Diving & Snorkeling Chuuk Lagoon, Pohnpei & Kosrae* and *Diving & Snorkeling Guam & Yap*; all describe the dive sites on those respective islands and are illustrated with stunning underwater photography.

If you're visiting Micronesia as part of a regional excursion, watch for the inaugural edition of *South Pacific*, which unites all glorious Pacific sites within one comprehensive book.

Travel & Guidebooks

A Field Guide to the Birds of Hawai'i & the Tropical Pacific by HD Pratt, PL Bruner & DG Berrett (1987) is the best general bird guide to the area.

Yachties should check *Landfalls of Paradise: Cruising Guide to the Pacific Islands* by Earl Hinz (1999). It has information on ports of entry, suggested anchorages and data on oceanographic phenomena for islands throughout Micronesia, Melanesia and Polynesia.

Hikers might want to get *Making Tracks in the Mariana Islands* and *The Best Tracks on Guam: A Guide to the Hiking Trails*, available in bookshops on Guam and Saipan. These pamphlets by David Lotz, a Guam parks administrator, detail hiking trails on Saipan, Tinian, Rota and Guam, with maps and write-ups on time, difficulty and distance.

Atlas of Micronesia, by Bruce Karolle (1994), is the broadest overview of Micronesia's geography, though the book has serious editing flaws.

This Living Reef by environmentalist Douglas Faulkner (1974), is a beautiful book, heavy on colour photographs of coral, fish and underwater life in Palau.

Micronesian Reef Fishes, by Robert F Myers (1991), is a comprehensive book with 975 quality colour photos. This superb book identifies more than 1250 of the most common reef fishes found in Micronesian waters, as well as 150 pelagic fish.

History & Politics

Destiny's Landfall: A History of Guam, by Robert F Rogers (1995), comprehensively and articulately traces Guam's history from Magellan's landing to the present day, with good attention to Chamorro cultural heritage.

The First Taint of Civilization, by Francis X Hezel (1994), is an excellent anecdotal history of the Caroline and Marshall Islands during the pre-colonial era from 1521 to 1885.

History of Micronesia, edited by Rodrigue Levesque, is a hefty, comprehensive 10-volume history of the region, told through colourful source documents.

Nan'yo: The Rise & Fall of the Japanese in Micronesia, 1885–1945, by Mark R Peattie, is one of the best books about the Japanese colonial empire in Micronesia.

A Handful of Emeralds: On Patrol With the Hanna in the Postwar Pacific, by Joseph Meredith (1997), describes patrolling through Micronesia in the early 1950s. The author, a ship's captain, discusses the Pacific war and strategies.

For some insights into Micronesian society, pick up *The Edge of Paradise*, by PF Kluge (1993), a perceptive account of the effects of cultural imperialism on Micronesians written by a former Peace Corps volunteer.

Operation Crossroads: The Atomic Tests at Bikini Atoll by Jonathan M Weisgall (1994), the lawyer for the Bikini islanders, explores the inner workings of the agencies responsible for the atomic bomb tests over Bikini and the various US cover-ups.

Atoll Politics: The Republic of Kiribati, edited by Howard Van Trease, is a collection of essays by leading I-Kiribati politicians and scholars who address a variety of issues relevant to Kiribati, including politics, economic and social development and the environment.

Culture

There are a good number of scholarly anthropological works about Micronesian culture, many written by individuals who have lived on remote islands and studied a single group of people in depth. The following books about Micronesian culture are geared more to the general reader.

An Introduction to the Peoples and Cultures of Micronesia, by G Alkire (1972), is a bible of sorts on Micronesian cultural anthropology, resulting from Alkire's 3½ years of field work in Micronesia.

Prehistoric Architecture in Micronesia by William N Morgan (1988) is a study of the unique traditional architecture found on Kosrae, Pohnpei, Yap, Palau and the Marianas, including the stone cities of Lelu and Nan Madol.

We, the Navigators: The Ancient Art of Landfinding in the Pacific, by David Lewis (1994), comprehensively traces navigational routes and methods of early Micronesian and Polynesian sailors.

Language

The PALI Language Texts, published by the University of Hawai'i in Honolulu, provide the most comprehensive Micronesian language series.

The University of Guam also has a series on the more prominent Micronesian languages, but it is aimed at helping English-speaking teachers instruct young non-English-speaking children. Each book starts with a bit of history and culture, incorporates a long word list and ends with native language songs.

General

The classic *A Reporter in Micronesia*, by EJ Kahn, is a very readable log of Kahn's travels around the islands. His journeys were mostly by field ship, as Micronesia then had no jet traffic, no tourist hotels and very few visitors.

The Happy Isles of Oceania: Paddling the Pacific, by Paul Theroux, is a lively narration of the renowned travel-writer's trip to the South Pacific. Though the trip concentrates on French Polynesia, New Guinea and New Zealand and includes almost nothing of Micronesia, it's still a worthwhile read to get the flavour of the South Pacific.

Micronesian Customs & Beliefs and *Never and Always: Micronesian Stories of the Origins of Islands, Landmarks, and Customs*, compiled by Gene Ashby (1989), are collections of legends and stories written by the students at the College of Micronesia.

And No Birds Sing: A True Ecological Thriller Set in a Tropical Paradise, by Mark Jaffe, touches on the brown tree snake and Guam's other ecological troubles.

FILMS

Two award-winning documentary films on Bikini Atoll in the Marshall Islands are real eye-openers. *Radio Bikini*, produced by the Corporation for Public Broadcasting in 1988, is a compilation of historic footage on the events surrounding the exile of the Bikinians and the actual bomb tests. *Bikini: Forbidden Paradise*, produced by the ABC television network in 1993, gives a contemporary account of conditions on Bikini, including some interesting underwater footage of the decommissioned warships sunk in the lagoon during the testing. *The Atomic Café* (1982), directed by Jayne Loader, also graphically covers the nuclear bomb fever of the 1940s and 1950s.

Those interested in Yapese culture can order Eric Metzgar's *Lamotrek: Heritage of an Island* and *Spirits of the Voyage*, available from Triton Films (✉ tritonfilms@vcnet.com, 5177 Mesquite St, Camarillo, CA 93102-6724).

WWII buffs should seek out *Famous Marine Battles: Tarawa* and *Death Tide at Tarawa*, both of which show gripping original footage from the 1943 Battle of Tarawa; order the latter from A&E Home Video (AAE-10017), Box HV1, 235 E 45th St, New York, NY 10017.

NEWSPAPERS & MAGAZINES

Micronesia's only daily newspaper is Guam's *Pacific Daily News*, which is flown to capital towns around Micronesia. PDN, as the paper is commonly called, is a member of the Gannett group of newspapers and provides a good mix of regional and international news.

The Marshalls has a weekly newspaper, the *Marshall Islands Journal*. Palau has a biweekly newspaper, *Tia Belau*. In the Northern Marianas the *Marianas Variety* is published six days a week and the *Saipan Tribune* five days a week.

A good news magazine for Micronesian events is *Pacific Magazine* (PO Box 37551, Honolulu, HI 96837), published six times a year. It covers all the Pacific but gives a fair weight to Micronesia, with an emphasis on politics, business and new developments.

Subscriptions cost US$15 a year surface mail; add US$12 for airmail to the USA or US$24 to other countries.

Another excellent Pacific region magazine with less coverage of Micronesia is *Pacific Islands Monthly* (GPO Box 1167, Suva, Fiji), which costs US$45 a year to overseas destinations.

The University of Guam's *Isla: A Journal of Micronesia Studies* (Graduate School & Research, UOG Station, 303 University Drive, Mangilao, Guam 96923) is a semiannual scholarly journal devoted exclusively to Micronesia. An annual subscription costs US$20.

Another excellent scholarly journal about the South Pacific region is the semiannual *The Contemporary Pacific: A Journal of Island Affairs* (University of Hawai'i Press, Journals Department, 2840 Kolowalu St, Honolulu, HI 96822-1888, USA). Subscriptions are US$35 from Hawai'i and other countries, US$23 for most Pacific Islands.

The Journal of Pacific Studies (University of the South Pacific, PO Box 1168, Suva, Fiji) is a semiannual publication that occasionally runs features on Micronesia.

The *Washington Pacific Report* (☎ 703-519 7757, PO Box 26142, Alexandria VA 22313-642), a newsletter published twice a month, gives brief but useful news updates on the Pacific and occasionally on Micronesia. Subscriptions are US$169 a year (US$189 outside the USA).

RADIO & TV

All the district centres have radio stations with local broadcasting and all, with the exceptions of Kosrae, Nauru, Tarawa and Christmas Island, have cable TV. Tarawa, Christmas Island and Kosrae have no TV whatsoever; Nauru has two channels (one is a sports channel, the other mostly plays CNN). Cable TV on the other islands always includes live CNN news but beyond that the coverage varies.

VIDEO SYSTEMS

If you want to record or buy video tapes to play back home, you won't get a picture unless the 'image registration' system is the same. Three systems are used in the world, and each one is completely incompatible with the others. The three formats are NTSC, used in North America and Japan; PAL, used in Australia, New Zealand and most of Europe; and SECAM, used in metropolitan France.

All of the Micronesian countries in this book, with the exception of Nauru, use the NTSC system. Nauru uses the PAL system.

PHOTOGRAPHY & VIDEO

The high temperatures and high humidity in the tropics can accelerate the deterioration of film. The sooner you have exposed film developed, the better the results. Print film and some slide films can be professionally processed on Pohnpei, Palau, Saipan and Guam.

Don't leave your camera in direct sunshine longer than necessary. A locked car can heat up like an oven very quickly.

Another problem that often arises is moisture condensing on film and lenses that have been taken from air-con rooms into the warm, moist outside air. Keep your camera in an area of the room less affected by the air-con, such as a closet or the bathroom, or try keeping it wrapped inside a camera case or carry-bag for an hour or so after leaving a place with air-con.

Sand and water are intense reflectors and in bright light they'll often leave foreground subjects shadowy. You can compensate by adjusting your f-stop or attaching a polarising filter, or both, but the most effective technique is to take photos in the gentler light of early morning and late afternoon.

Print film is available on the main islands, though slide film is reliably available only in Guam and Saipan. Film can be more expensive in Micronesia than elsewhere and expiry dates should be checked carefully.

Photographing People

In general, Micronesians enjoy being photographed but it's always courteous to ask. On Yap, photographing a person without asking is a major affront: The Yapese do not wish to be treated as anthropological subjects. If you ask, though, they'll gladly oblige.

On most islands, it's tough to get a natural shot since everyone insists on posing.

TIME

The International Date Line runs between Hawai'i and the Marshalls and takes an eastward swoop around Kiribati; see the Kiribati chapter for the curious explanation behind the date line bulge. Going from the USA to Micronesia you lose a day, while on the return you gain a day.

Micronesia spans many different time zones. Guam is 10 hours ahead of Greenwich Mean Time.

When it's noon in Guam, the Northern Marianas, Yap and Chuuk it is: 11 am in Palau; 1 pm in Pohnpei and Kosrae, 2 pm in Majuro, Nauru and Tarawa, and 4 pm on Christmas Island. It is also noon in Port Moresby, Sydney and Melbourne; 11 am in Tokyo; 10 am in Manila and Hong Kong; 2 am in London; 4 pm the day before in Honolulu; 6 pm the day before in San Francisco; and 9 pm the day before in New York.

Note that these times do not take summer (daylight savings) time into account, which advances Australia by one hour November to March, and the United States by one hour April to October. It's wise to double-check flight times if you have an international flight during the transition time.

Because Micronesia is so close to the equator it does not use daylight savings time.

ELECTRICITY

Electricity in Guam, the Northern Marianas, FSM, Palau and the Marshalls is 110/120V AC, 60Hz, and a US-type flat two-pronged plug is used. In Nauru and Kiribati, electricity is supplied at 240V AC, 50Hz, and an Australian-type three-pin plug is used (though on Christmas Island, some of the plugs are two-prong US-style).

WEIGHTS & MEASURES

American Micronesia, like the USA, uses the imperial system of measurement. Kiribati and Nauru usually go by the metric system, though miles sometimes sneak into local discourse. Using imperial measurements, distances are in inches, feet, yards and miles; weights are in ounces, pounds and tons. There is a conversion table at the back of this book.

LAUNDRY

There are self-service coin laundries in most main district centres. Rates vary, but US$1 to wash a load of clothes and US$1 to dry will generally cover it. Your hotel can do your laundry for an additional fee.

TOILETS

As you would expect, toilet facilities vary widely through Micronesia. All district centre hotels listed in Lonely Planet have Western-style toilets. On the outer islands, a few guesthouses may have Western-style toilets but otherwise prepare to squat. Unfortunately, particularly in Kiribati, there is a lack of available toilets, outhouse-style or otherwise. This means that locals tend to use the beach as a toilet. Needless to say, refrain from swimming.

HEALTH

Travel health depends on your preparations prior to departure, your daily health care while travelling and how you handle any medical problem that does develop. While the potential dangers can seem quite frightening, in reality few travellers experience anything more than an upset stomach.

Micronesia is not an unhealthy place to visit. Still, sunburn, fungal infections, diarrhoea and other gut infections all warrant precautions.

If you're new to the heat and humidity you may find yourself easily fatigued and more susceptible to minor ailments. Acclimatise yourself by slowing down your pace – take a cue from the Micronesians.

Many of the district centres throughout Micronesia have small hospitals that have been built in recent times with American aid. Some are modern with good services; others are distinctly unmodern, and with limited services. The best medical treatment is generally found on Guam and Saipan, though costs there are high, on a par with mainland USA.

Most outer islands have no health services so if you're going somewhere remote it's a good idea to take along a first-aid kit with some basic medical supplies.

Travel Health Guides

Lonely Planet's *Healthy Travel: Australia, New Zealand & the Pacific* is a handy pocket size and packed with useful information including pre-trip planning, emergency first aid, immunisation and disease information and what to do if you get sick on the road. *Travel with Children* from Lonely Planet also includes advice on travel health for younger children.

There are also a number of excellent travel health sites on the Internet. From the Lonely Planet home page there are links at www.lonelyplanet.com/weblinks/ to the World Health Organization and the US Centers for Disease Control & Prevention.

Other Preparations

Make sure you're healthy before you start travelling. If you intend to be in Micronesia a long time make sure your teeth are OK; dental care outside of Guam and Saipan varies a lot. If you wear glasses take a spare pair and your prescription.

If you require a particular medication take an adequate supply, as it will probably not be available locally. Take part of the packaging showing the generic name rather than the brand, which will make getting replacements easier. It's a good idea to have a legible prescription or letter from your doctor to show that you legally use the medication to avoid any problems.

Immunisations

The only immunisations required to enter Micronesia are for cholera and yellow fever, but that's only if you're coming from an infected area. It is recommended (though not required) that the following vaccinations, which are usually administered in childhood, are up to date; record all vaccinations on an International Health Certificate, which your physician should provide.

Medical Kit Check List

Following is a list of items you should consider including in your medical kit – consult your pharmacist for brands available in your country.

- ☐ **Aspirin or paracetamol (acetaminophen in the USA)** – for pain or fever
- ☐ **Antihistamine** – for allergies, eg, hay fever; to ease the itch from insect bites or stings; and to prevent motion sickness
- ☐ **Cold and flu tablets, throat lozenges and nasal decongestant**
- ☐ **Multivitamins** – consider for long trips, when dietary vitamin intake may be inadequate
- ☐ **Antibiotics** – consider including these if you're travelling well off the beaten track; see your doctor, as they must be prescribed, and carry the prescription with you
- ☐ **Loperamide or diphenoxylate** –'blockers' for diarrhoea
- ☐ **Prochlorperazine or metaclopramide** – for nausea and vomiting
- ☐ **Rehydration mixture** – to prevent dehydration, which may occur, for example, during bouts of diarrhoea; particularly important when travelling with children
- ☐ **Insect repellent, sunscreen, lip balm and eye drops**
- ☐ **Calamine lotion, sting relief spray or aloe vera** – to ease irritation from sunburn and insect bites or stings
- ☐ **Antifungal cream or powder** – for fungal skin infections and thrush
- ☐ **Antiseptic (such as povidone-iodine)** – for cuts and grazes
- ☐ **Bandages, Band-Aids (plasters) and other wound dressings**
- ☐ **Water purification tablets or iodine**
- ☐ **Scissors, tweezers and a thermometer** – note that mercury thermometers are prohibited by airlines
- ☐ **Syringes and needles** – in case you need injections in a country with medical hygiene problems; ask your doctor for a note explaining why you have them

Diphtheria & Tetanus Vaccinations for these two diseases are usually combined and are recommended for everyone. After an initial course of three injections (usually given in childhood), boosters are necessary every 10 years.

Polio Everyone should keep up to date with this vaccination, normally given in childhood. A booster every 10 years maintains immunity.

Typhoid This is an important vaccination to have where hygiene is a problem and especially recommended for travel to Chuuk, Nauru and the Marshalls. The vaccine is available either as an injection or in oral capsules.

Hepatitis A The hepatitis A vaccine (eg Avaxim, Havrix 1440 or VAQTA), recommended for travellers to Micronesia, provides long-term immunity (possibly more than 10 years) after an initial injection and a booster at six to 12 months.

Alternatively, an injection of gamma globulin can provide short-term protection against hepatitis A – two to six months, depending on the dose given. It is not a vaccine but a ready-made antibody collected from blood donations. It is reasonably effective and, unlike the vaccine, it is protective immediately, but because it is a blood product there are current concerns about its long-term safety.

Hepatitis A vaccine is also available in a combined form, Twinrix, with hepatitis B vaccine. Three injections over a six-month period are required, the first two providing substantial protection against hepatitis A.

Hepatitis B Travellers who should consider vaccination against hepatitis B include those on a long trip, as well as those visiting countries where there are high levels of hepatitis B infection, where blood transfusions may not be adequately screened or where sexual contact or needle sharing is a possibility. Vaccination involves three injections, with a booster at 12 months. More rapid courses are available if necessary.

Basic Rules

Care in what you eat and drink is the most important health rule; stomach upsets, though relatively minor, are the most common travel health problem. Don't become paranoid, as trying the local food is part of the experience of travel after all.

Food Food in Micronesia is usually sanitarily prepared and requires no unusual precautions, but avoid pre-cooked foods that are sold in the marketplace on smaller islands, and ice cream that may be made with untreated water. As a general rule, places that look clean and well run are preferable to those that look run down.

Make sure your diet is well balanced and you get enough protein. Rice and fish are very plentiful in Micronesia, so this shouldn't be much of a problem. Fruit, also plentiful, is a good source of vitamins, though paradoxically fresh fruit is rarely available in shops. If you're going to spend significant time on outer islands or on field-trip ships you might want to pack a bottle of vitamins.

Poisonous Fish Ciguatera fish poisoning (resulting from eating reef-dwelling fish that have ingested plankton-produced toxins) is a problem throughout the Pacific and is most common in areas, such as the Marshalls, where coral reefs are well developed.

More than 300 species of fish can become toxic. Sometimes the same species can be safe in some areas and poisonous in others, so get local advice before eating your catch. Cooking the fish doesn't destroy the toxin.

Reef fish served in restaurants pose little risk as restaurateurs know which species to avoid. Tuna, the most common fish served in Micronesia, is an unaffected deep-water fish.

The symptoms, if you do eat the wrong fish, can include nausea, stomach cramps, diarrhoea, paralysis, tingling and numbness of the face, fingers and toes, and a reversal of temperature feelings so that hot things feel cold and vice versa. Extreme cases can result in unconsciousness and even death. Vomit until your stomach is empty and get immediate medical help.

Water Tap water is generally not safe to drink, the only exceptions being Guam and, to a lesser extent, Rota. There are a lot of parasites in Micronesia, including giardia and amoeba, and unclean water is a great place to find them.

Often the problem comes not so much from impure water as from poor water distribution. On many islands ageing sewer and water pipes are laid alongside each other, and when the water is turned off for more than a few hours for rationing purposes cross-seepage can occur.

When in doubt stick with readily available canned beverages or bottled water. Tea or coffee should also be OK, since the water should have been boiled.

To avoid dehydration, make a conscious effort to drink ample liquids to replace the body fluids you quickly lose in the heat and humidity. Always carry a water bottle on long trips. Drinking coconuts, readily available in many places, are an excellent rehydration drink, full of vitamins and minerals.

Water Purification The simplest way to purify water is to boil it thoroughly.

Consider purchasing a water filter for a long trip. There are two main kinds of filters. Total filters take out all parasites, bacteria and viruses and make water safe to drink. They are often expensive, but they can be more cost-effective than buying bottled water. Simple filters (which can even be a nylon mesh bag) remove dirt and larger foreign bodies from the water so that chemical solutions work much more effectively; if water is dirty, chemical solutions may not work at all. It's very important when buying a filter to read the specifications so that you know exactly what it removes from the water and what it doesn't.

Simple filtering will not remove all dangerous organisms, so if you cannot boil water it should be treated chemically. Chlorine tablets will kill many pathogens, but not some parasites like giardia and amoebic

Everyday Health

Normal body temperature is 37°C (98.6°F); more than 2°C (4°F) higher indicates a high fever. The normal adult pulse rate is 60 to 100 per minute (children 80 to 100, babies 100 to 140). As a general rule the pulse increases about 20 beats per minute for each 1°C (2°F) rise in fever.

Respiration (breathing) rate is also an indicator of illness. Count the number of breaths per minute: between 12 and 20 is normal for adults and older children (up to 30 for younger children, 40 for babies). People with a high fever or serious respiratory illness breathe more quickly than normal. More than 40 shallow breaths a minute may indicate pneumonia.

cysts. Iodine is more effective in purifying water and is available in tablet form. Follow the directions carefully and remember that too much iodine can be harmful.

Medical Treatment

Hospital care varies widely in Micronesia. All district centres have hospitals, but outside of Guam and Saipan the facilities tend to be rather run down and have only a limited supply of prescription drugs. Insist on an air-conditioned room.

Some island hospitals (in Guam, Kiribati and Palau) have dive decompression chambers; Lonely Planet has mentioned these in the Information section within individual chapters.

Carry your health insurance policy with you at all times so that there will be no delay in treatment in any emergency.

Anyone needing unusual or long-term treatment will have to fly to Guam or a hospital outside of Micronesia.

Environmental Hazards

Heat Exhaustion Dehydration and salt deficiency can cause heat exhaustion. Take time to acclimatise to high temperatures, drink sufficient liquids and do not do anything too physically demanding.

Salt deficiency is characterised by fatigue, lethargy, headaches, giddiness and muscle cramps; salt tablets may help, but adding extra salt to your food is better.

Heatstroke This serious, occasionally fatal, condition can occur if the body's heat-regulating mechanism breaks down and the body temperature rises to dangerous levels. Long, continuous periods of exposure to high temperatures and insufficient fluids can leave you vulnerable to heatstroke.

The symptoms are feeling unwell, not sweating very much (or at all) and a high body temperature (39° to 41°C, or 102° to 106°F). Where sweating has ceased, the skin becomes flushed and red. Severe, throbbing headaches and lack of coordination will also occur, and the sufferer may become confused or aggressive. Eventually the victim can become delirious or convulse. Hospitalisation is essential, but in the interim get victims out of the sun, remove their clothing, cover them with a wet sheet or towel and then fan continually. Give fluids if they are conscious.

Motion Sickness Eating lightly before and during a trip will reduce the chances of motion sickness. Fresh air usually helps; reading and cigarette smoke don't. Commercial motion sickness preparations, which can cause drowsiness, have to be taken before the trip commences. Ginger (available in capsule form) and peppermint (including mint-flavoured sweets) are natural preventatives.

Prickly Heat Prickly heat is an itchy rash caused by excessive perspiration trapped under the skin. It usually strikes people who have just arrived in a hot climate. Keeping cool, bathing often, drying the skin and using a mild talcum or prickly heat powder, or taking refuge in air-conditioning, may help.

Sunburn Since Micronesia is so near to the equator, you can get sunburned surprisingly quickly, even on a cloudy day. Use sunscreen, a hat and barrier cream for your nose and lips. Calamine lotion or a commercial after-sun preparation are good for mild sunburn. Protect your eyes with good quality sunglasses.

Fair-skinned people can get first and second degree burns in the hot Micronesian sun, which is most severe between 10 am and 2 pm but powerful all day.

Sunscreen with a SPF (sun protection factor) of 15 and above is recommended. If you're going into the water, choose a brand that's water-resistant. You may want to wear a T-shirt (or even light cotton pants) while snorkelling, especially if you plan to be out in the water for a long time.

Fungal Infections The same climate that produces lush tropical forests also promotes a prolific growth of skin fungi and bacteria. Hot weather fungal infections are most likely to occur on the scalp, between the toes or fingers (athlete's foot) or in the groin.

To prevent fungal infections, keeping your skin cool and allowing air to circulate is essential. Choose cotton clothing rather than artificial fibres and sandals instead of shoes.

If you do get an infection, wash the infected area daily with a disinfectant or medicated soap and water, and rinse and dry well. Apply an antifungal powder like the widely available tolnaftate. Try to expose the infected area to air or sunlight as much as possible and wash all towels and underwear in hot water and change them often.

Infectious Diseases

Diarrhoea Simple things like a change of water, food or climate can cause a mild bout of diarrhoea, but a few rushed toilet trips with no other symptoms is not indicative of a major problem.

Dehydration is the main danger with any diarrhoea, particularly in children or the elderly as it can occur quite quickly. Under all circumstances *fluid replacement* (at least equal to the volume being lost in vomit or bowel movements) is the most important thing to remember. Weak black tea with a little sugar, soda water, or soft drinks allowed to go flat and diluted 50% with clean water are all good. With severe diarrhoea a rehydrating solution is preferable to replace lost minerals and salts. Commercially available oral rehydration salts (ORS) are very useful; add them to boiled or bottled water. In an emergency you can make up a solution of six teaspoons of sugar and a half teaspoon of salt to a litre of boiled or bottled water. Urine is the best guide to the adequacy of replacement – if you are producing small amounts of concentrated urine, you need to drink more. Keep drinking small amounts often. Stick to a bland diet as you recover.

Gut-paralysing drugs such as loperamide or diphenoxylate can bring relief from the symptoms, although they do not actually cure the problem. Only use these drugs if you do not have access to toilets, eg if you *must* travel. Note that these drugs are not recommended for children under 12 years.

In certain situations antibiotics may be required – diarrhoea with blood or mucus (dysentery), any diarrhoea with fever, profuse watery diarrhoea, persistent diarrhoea not improving after 48 hours and severe diarrhoea: These suggest a more serious cause of diarrhoea and in these situations gut-paralysing drugs should be avoided.

In these situations, a stool test may be necessary to diagnose what bug is causing your diarrhoea, so you should seek medical help urgently. Where this is not possible the recommended drugs for bacterial diarrhoea (the most likely cause of severe diarrhoea in travellers) are norfloxacin 400mg twice daily for three days or ciprofloxacin 500mg twice daily for five days. These are not recommended for children or pregnant women. The drug of choice for children would be co-trimoxazole with dosage dependent on weight. A five day course is given. Ampicillin or amoxycillin may be given in pregnancy, but medical care is necessary.

Two other causes of persistent diarrhoea in travellers, particularly those travelling off the beaten track, are giardiasis and amoebic dysentery.

Giardiasis Giardia is caused by a common parasite, *Giardia lamblia*. Symptoms include stomach cramps, nausea, a bloated stomach, watery, foul-smelling diarrhoea and frequent gas. Giardiasis can appear several weeks after you have been exposed to the parasite. The symptoms may disappear for a few days and then return; this can go on for several weeks.

Amoebic dysentery Amoebic dysentery, caused by the protozoan *Entamoeba histolytica*, is characterised by a gradual onset of low-grade diarrhoea, often with blood and mucus. Cramping abdominal pain and vomiting are less likely than in other types of diarrhoea, and fever may not be present. It will persist until treated and can recur and cause other health problems.

You should seek medical advice if you think you have giardiasis or amoebic dysentery, but where this is not possible, tinidazole or metronidazole are the recommended drugs. Treatment is a 2g single dose of

Micronesians' Health Problems

Much of Micronesian society – and particularly the district centres – has been traumatised by its exposure to Western culture and diet.

Although Micronesians eagerly took to a new diet heavy in processed sugars, genetically they have been unable to assimilate it. For example, the sugar-laced cereals and soft drinks and the extensive variety of packaged junk food that cram supermarket shelves have left 35% of the Marshall Islands population prone to diabetes. At Majuro's hospital, 75% of inpatients are diabetic. Nauru, with its heavy emphasis on Western products, has similarly high rates of diabetes. Other health problems of epidemic proportions include high blood pressure, alcoholism and radiation-related thyroid tumours.

Malnutrition is also severe. There have been cases of blindness from vitamin A deficiency, even though vitamin A-rich pandanus, papaya and pumpkins are locally grown. Rather than eating the produce, some families cart it off to the market and sell it to get money to buy more tantalising junk food.

tinidazole or 250mg of metronidazole three times daily for five to 10 days.

HIV/AIDS Infection with the human immunodeficiency virus (HIV) may lead to acquired immune deficiency syndrome (AIDS), which is a fatal disease. Any exposure to blood, blood products or body fluids presents a risk. The disease is often transmitted through sexual contact or dirty needles – vaccinations, acupuncture, tattooing and body piercing can be potentially as dangerous as intravenous drug use. HIV/AIDS can also be spread through infected blood transfusions; some developing countries cannot afford to screen blood used for transfusions.

If you do need an injection, ask to see the syringe unwrapped in front of you, or take a needle and syringe pack with you.

Fear of HIV infection should never preclude treatment for serious medical conditions.

Some countries such as the Marshall Islands require HIV testing for visitors staying more than 30 days and applicants for residency; for the Federated States of Micronesia it's 90 days.

Typhoid Typhoid fever is a dangerous gut infection caused by contaminated water and food. Medical help must be sought.

In its early stages sufferers may feel they have a bad cold or flu on the way, as early symptoms are a headache, body aches and a fever which rises a little each day until it is around 40°C (104°F) or more. The victim's pulse is often slow relative to the degree of fever present – unlike a normal fever where the pulse increases. There may also be vomiting, abdominal pain, diarrhoea or constipation.

In the second week the high fever and slow pulse continue and a few pink spots may appear on the body; trembling, delirium, weakness, weight loss and dehydration may occur. Complications such as pneumonia, perforated bowel or meningitis may occur.

The fever should be treated by keeping victims cool and giving them fluids, as dehydration should also be watched for.

Ciprofloxacin 750 mg twice a day for 10 days is good for adults.

Chloramphenicol is recommended in many countries. The adult dosage is two 250mg capsules, four times a day. Children aged between eight and 12 years should have half the adult dose, and younger children one-third the adult dose.

Sexually Transmitted Diseases HIV/AIDS and hepatitis B can be transmitted through sexual contact – see the relevant sections earlier for more details. Other STDs include gonorrhoea, herpes and syphilis; sores, blisters or rashes around the genitals and discharges or pain when urinating are common symptoms. In some STDs, such as wart virus or chlamydia, symptoms may be less marked or not observed at all, especially in women. Chlamydia infection can cause infertility in men and women before any symptoms have been noticed. Syphilis symptoms eventually disappear completely but the disease continues and can cause severe problems in later years. While abstinence from sexual contact is the only 100% effective prevention, using condoms is also effective. Gonorrhoea and syphilis are treated with antibiotics. Different kinds of sexually transmitted diseases require specific antibiotics.

Insect-Borne Diseases

Dengue Fever This viral disease, which is not uncommon in Micronesia, particularly in Kiribati, is transmitted by mosquitoes and is fast becoming one of the top public health problems in the tropical world. Unlike the malaria mosquito the *Aedes aegypti* mosquito, which transmits the dengue virus, is most active during the day, and is found mainly in urban areas, in and around human dwellings.

Signs and symptoms of dengue fever include a sudden onset of high fever, headache, joint and muscle pains (hence its old name, 'breakbone fever') and nausea and vomiting. A rash of small red spots sometimes appears three to four days after the onset of fever. In the early phase of illness, dengue may be mistaken for other infectious diseases, including malaria and influenza. Minor bleeding such as nose bleeds may occur in the course of the illness, but this does not necessarily mean that you have progressed to the potentially fatal dengue haemorrhagic fever (DHF). This is a severe illness, characterised by heavy bleeding, which is thought to be a result of second infection due to a different strain (there are four major strains) and usually affects residents of the country rather than travellers. Recovery even from simple dengue fever may be prolonged, with tiredness lasting for several weeks.

You should seek medical attention as soon as possible if you think you may be infected. A blood test can exclude malaria and indicate the possibility of dengue fever. There is no specific treatment for dengue. Aspirin should be avoided, as it increases the risk of haemorrhaging. There is no vaccine against dengue fever. The best prevention is to avoid mosquito bites at all times by covering up, using insect repellents containing the compound DEET and using mosquito nets.

Cone Shells

Cone shells should be left alone unless you're sure they're empty. There is no safe way of picking up a live cone shell, as the animal inside has a long stinging tail that can dart out and reach any place on its shell to deliver a puncture wound. Stings can result in numbness at the wound site, breathing difficulties and sight and speech impairment. A few species, such as the textile cone, have a venom so toxic that the sting could prove fatal. If you should get stung by such a shell, seek immediate medical attention.

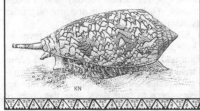

KN

Cuts, Bites & Stings

Cuts & Scratches Wash well and treat any cut with an antiseptic such as povidone-iodine. Where possible avoid bandages and Band-Aids, which can keep wounds wet. Coral cuts are notoriously slow to heal and if they are not adequately cleaned, small pieces of coral can become embedded in the wound.

Insect Bites & Stings Other than mosquitoes and sand gnats, there are very few biting insects in Micronesia. Calamine lotion will give relief for those that do.

Jellyfish Take a peek into the water before you plunge in, to make sure it's not jellyfish territory. These gelatinous creatures with stinging tentacles are fairly common around Guam, for example, where even the dangerous sea wasps and Portuguese man-of-war have occasionally been sighted.

The sting of a jellyfish varies from mild to severe, depending on the variety. A man-of-war sting is very painful, similar to a bad bee sting except that you're likely to get stung more than once from clusters of long tentacles. Even touching a man-of-war a few hours after it's washed up on shore can result in a burning sting.

You can at least partly neutralise the venom of a sting by dousing the skin with vinegar, or even urine. Calamine lotion, antihistamines and analgesics may reduce the reaction and relieve the pain. For serious stings, which are usually followed by swelling, bleeding, stomach spasms, difficulty in breathing or chest pains, seek immediate medical attention.

Women's Health

Gynaecological Problems Antibiotic use, synthetic underwear, sweating and contraceptive pills can lead to fungal vaginal infections, especially when travelling in hot climates. Fungal infections are characterised by a rash, itch and discharge and can be treated with a vinegar or lemon-juice douche, or with yogurt. Nystatin, miconazole or clotrimazole pessaries or vaginal cream are the usual treatment. Maintaining good personal hygiene and wearing loose-fitting clothes and cotton underwear may help prevent these infections.

Sexually transmitted diseases are a major cause of vaginal problems. Symptoms include a smelly discharge, painful intercourse and sometimes a burning sensation when urinating. Medical attention should be sought and male sexual partners must also be treated. For more details see the section on Sexually Transmitted Diseases earlier. Besides abstinence, the best thing is to practise safer sex using condoms.

WOMEN TRAVELLERS

Although most places in Micronesia shouldn't be a hassle, women travelling alone may occasionally get some unwanted attention. Chuuk, where unemployment and boredom have produced a culture of harassment, deservedly has the worst reputation. See the Chuuk section of the FSM chapter for a more specific warning.

Most other parts of Micronesia are relatively safe, but nonetheless women should use standard precautions and avoid walking alone in out-of-the-way places after dark.

GAY & LESBIAN TRAVELLERS

Most parts of Micronesia do not deal regularly with gay and lesbian issues, though most Micronesians assert that they would be accepting. Displays of affection are generally uncommon, be they gay or straight. Guam is the only place with specifically gay venues, though Saipan may soon follow.

DISABLED TRAVELLERS

Special facilities for the disabled are virtually nonexistent in Micronesia. Outside Guam, wheelchair-accessible accommodations are often difficult to find. Kosrae Village Resort, with a good emphasis on disabled travellers, is recommended.

SENIOR TRAVELLERS

With a warm climate, relaxed pace of life, and a culture of respect for elders, Micronesia could be a good place for elderly travellers. However, as the availability of services varies dramatically throughout Micronesia, seniors might do well to choose more developed places like Guam, Palau and the Northern Mariana Islands.

TRAVEL WITH CHILDREN

Awash with children itself, Micronesia will welcome visiting children with warmth and curiosity. Swimming, snorkelling, beach-combing, kayaking (for older children) and cultural events are all possible activities. Many mid-range and upper-end hotels allow children to share the room at a reduced rate.

Apply sunscreen generously to your child, and bring a baby carrier or nappies (diapers) if you need them, as they can be expensive.

Travel With Children by Maureen Wheeler, Lonely Planet's cofounder, has helpful tips for travelling with children anywhere in the world.

DANGERS & ANNOYANCES
Crime

There is very low incidence of crime in Micronesia – on the contrary, people are ready to give you gifts and assistance! The one exception is Chuuk, where cars have been stoned and people injured by violent young local men. See the Chuuk section for further details.

Marine Dangers

Most underwater experiences in Micronesia are safe, and while you shouldn't miss out for fear of monsters lurking in the depths, it's important to be aware of potential dangers.

There are a few venomous varieties of fish in Micronesian waters, including scorpion fish and stonefish which inhabit shallow waters and can inject venom through their dorsal spines.

Sharks

The probability of shark attacks on humans has been greatly exaggerated. Still, there are plenty of sharks in Micronesian waters and it doesn't hurt to have a healthy respect for them.

The few attacks that do occur in Micronesia are usually during spear fishing. When the shark tries to chomp down on a bloody, just-speared fish, the spearer sometimes gets in the way. Still, even these incidents are rare. And just for the record, the Yap Institute of Natural Science notes that people eat sharks 600,000 times more often than sharks eat people!

Sharks are attracted to shiny things and by anything bright red or yellow, which might influence your choice of swimsuit colour. Those popular Day-Glo orange life jackets are called 'yummy orange' in shark circles!

Strong Currents & Riptides

Be careful of water funnelling off the reefs into channels when the tide's going out as it can have a very strong pull.

You can quickly use up all your energy and lose ground if you try to fight a strong current. It's easier to swim across a current than against it. If you do find yourself being carried out through a reef passage, once outside the reef you should be able to move down along the reef and cross back over it to a calmer area.

Property

In Micronesia, most things are shared and individual property in the Western sense is a rather foreign concept. If you don't want visitors, particularly when you're out, be careful to leave your doors locked. The more remote the place you're staying, the more likely it is that you'll have the village kids just walking in.

Don't tempt anyone. If you have anything that looks appealing, lock it up in your bags. Two-way zippers on soft luggage and backpacks allow for use of a small lock, which might be enough to deter the overly curious.

The simplest way to feel at ease is to bring nothing you wouldn't mind parting with. Keep your passport and air tickets on you and if you have a camera you might want to bring a day pack to carry it around with you.

Privacy

The concept of privacy is also a different affair in Micronesia compared to most Western societies. You can often tell which house in a village has a VCR by the crowds standing outside looking in the windows; it's an acceptable way to watch a movie. Likewise, using a laptop in public will attract boldly curious children. If you stay with a local family and are given your own room it won't be uncommon for groups of the extended family to come by and join you for impromptu visits. You should see this not as an intrusion, but as an indication that you're being honoured and accepted as part of the family.

Payday Weekends

Throughout most of Micronesia every second Friday is payday. From payday until Sunday many Micronesian males go on a drinking binge and, for the most part, they don't make happy-go-lucky drunks, as many islanders have a low tolerance for alcohol. Domestic violence, suicide and the desire to settle up pent-up accounts all tend to come to a head on this weekend. A few places have responded by enacting prohibition, though most of Micronesia just sits it all out. The problem tends to be worse in district centres.

BUSINESS HOURS

Business hours vary throughout the islands, but 8 am to 4.30 pm Monday to Friday is fairly common. Banking hours also vary, though 10 am to 3 pm Monday to Thursday and 10 am to 5 pm on Fridays is average.

The last weeks of the year are very difficult for doing business. Not only do Christmas and New Year holidays and parties interfere, but many government employees scoot off then for their annual leave. On payday Fridays government workers leave work early (if they show up at all) to line up at the bank. This goes for the day after a holiday as well, as people have a habit of extending their holiday.

PUBLIC HOLIDAYS & SPECIAL EVENTS

Christian holidays, primarily Christmas and Easter, are celebrated throughout Micronesia with dancing, singing and festivities. New Year's Day, complete with firecrackers, is also observed. Most islands have an independence and/or a constitution day.

Fiestas are the basic annual festivities celebrated in Guam and the Northern Mariana Islands. Sporting events are also popular throughout the islands. The Micronesian games, locally known as the 'Micro Games', take place every four years and will be in Pohnpei in 2002; they include everything from running events to classic Micronesian-style events, such as outrigger canoe races.

ACTIVITIES
Diving & Snorkelling
What Micronesia lacks in land it makes up for in water. Some of the region's most spectacular scenery is under water and the traveller who never looks below the surface is missing out on some incredible sights.

Micronesia has an abundance of fish in every imaginable – and sometimes unimaginable – colour and shape. There are hundreds of types of hard and soft corals, anemones, and colourful sponges and many varieties of shellfish, including giant tridacna clams. There are also lots of reef sharks and manta rays.

Micronesia's water temperature is about 80°F (27°C). Wet suits are not required for warmth, although some divers wear them as protection against coral cuts.

Divers world-wide are drawn to the underwater wreck museums at Chuuk and Bikini and to Palau's terrific drop-offs. These are the finest diving spots in Micronesia and among the very best locales in the world.

There are many other superb, though less famous, diving opportunities in Micronesia, including unspoiled reefs, forests of towering sea fans, coral gardens, underwater caves and the scattered wrecks of whaleboats and WWII ships and planes.

There are dive shops in all district centres except Nauru. Specific information on dive shops, as well as diving and snorkelling locales, is given under Activities in each island section.

It's recommended that you bring your own buoyancy compensator and other personalised equipment with you, not only to save on the added rental charge, but to avoid the uneven quality that can be encountered when renting these particular items. A dive computer can be very useful, as can some advance training in decompression diving, especially if you plan to dive Chuuk's wrecks. Know your limits and make them clear to the dive master, as a few shops tend to pay less attention to depth and a diver's level of experience than they should.

If you've never been scuba diving before, here's your chance to learn. Some dive shops offer non-divers an introductory dive down to about 30 feet, which costs anywhere from US$60 to US$100. An intensive three- or four-day certification course is sometimes an option.

On the other hand you could just pack a mask and snorkel – and flippers if you have room – and enjoy it all for free. If you prefer to travel light, snorkelling gear can be rented at many places for about US$10 a day.

For information on diving holiday packages, refer to the Tours section in the Getting There & Away chapter.

Other Water Sports
While diving is clearly the region's major attraction, numerous other water sports can be enjoyed. Kayak rentals are widely available. Windsurfing is quite popular in Saipan and although conditions aren't as good it's also possible to windsurf in Guam. Guam is the only island where board surfing enjoys any popularity. Both Saipan and Guam have beach huts offering recreational water activities such as outrigger canoe rides, banana boats, jetskis etc, although these can be pricey as they are geared to Japanese package tourists.

Hiking
It takes but two minutes to walk from one side to the other of some of the smaller islands, so hiking is obviously limited to a stroll down the road. Most of the larger high islands have at least a couple of tracks to

scenic points or waterfalls that can make for a bit of exercise. Outside Guam and the Northern Marianas, most trails cross private land so hikers will often have to consult with the local municipal office to get permission to cross or to arrange a guide. Kosrae and Pohnpei each have a variety of interesting hikes.

An interesting option is to join one of the expat-led Hash House Harrier groups that lead guided 'harrier' walk/runs on most of the larger islands. The runs generally take place on Saturdays – on Tarawa it's Wednesday – and are as much social events as exercise, ending with beer and American company.

Golf
The islands of Guam and Saipan both have numerous 18-hole golf courses, while Rota and Nauru each have one nine-hole course.

Fishing
Deep-sea fishing is available on a charter basis in many places, but is most popular on Guam, the Marshalls and Yap. Christmas Island, where bonefish abound, is a popular sportsfishing venue.

ACCOMMODATION
Camping
Throughout Micronesia most of the land, including the beaches, is privately owned and uninvited campers are about as welcome as they would be if they walked into your backyard at home and started pitching a tent. If you want to camp, get permission from the landowners first. In any case, camping is very uncommon in many places.

While there are no established camping grounds in Micronesia, there are some possibilities for roughing it. The best are on the Rock Islands and Peleliu in Palau, on Tinian in the Northern Marianas, at Bechiyal village in Yap, along the beaches of Kosrae and on the uninhabited islands off Pohnpei. Details on camping are given in each island section.

If you decide it's worth your while to carry camping gear, don't bother about a sleeping bag but *do* bring along some sort of gnat- and mosquito-proof covering.

Hotels
All the main islands have Western-style hotels. Overall, Micronesian hotels tend to be a bit pricey for what you get and, with the exception of Rota's cheery new youth hostel, there aren't many real cheapies.

Hotel rates usually start between US$35 and US$50. What you get for the lowest rate varies quite a bit from island to island. A few are rock-bottom places where the mattresses sag, the walls are dirty and the bathroom is down the hall. Others are clean and comfortable, with private bathrooms, air-con and a friendly atmosphere.

Hotels with Micronesian influences are far too few in number, though the Pathways Hotel in Yap, the Village Hotel in Pohnpei and the Kosrae Village Resort in Kosrae are excellent exceptions. Each has traditionally designed thatched cottages that balance native aesthetics with modern conveniences.

Outside the district centres you can experience Micronesian hospitality in some nice island-style accommodation for US$15 to US$25 a night. These include the men's house in the traditional village of Bechiyal on Yap, family guest houses in Palau, homestays on North Tarawa and beach huts on Pohnpei's lagoon islands.

Most main islands have a few mid-range hotels with standard comforts at rates between US$60 and US$90.

Guam, Saipan, Rota, Majuro and Palau have luxurious beachside resort hotels, though rates are upwards of US$125. Most are geared toward package tourists but also welcome individuals or families. A new resort hotel is being built on Yap.

Many upper-end hotels offer discounts to locals, government employees, Peace Corps volunteers, the military and businesspeople.

Outer Islands
Few of the outer islands have hotels or guesthouses for visitors. It's best to arrange accommodation in advance through the island's mayor or chief magistrate. Although you could try doing it by mail, it's less confusing to radio ahead from the district centre. Local airlines can also be helpful in arranging a place to stay on islands they service.

Soaking up a waterfall, Pohnpei

Canoeing in Pohnpei

Fish Eye Marine Park jetty, Guam

Manta Ray Bay Hotel, Yap

SIMON ROWE

Fetching coconuts, Yap

MICHAEL AW

Paradisal beachside pavilion, Yap

MICHAEL AW

The moody outline of Sokehs Rock, Pohnpei

MICHAEL AW

Palau Pacific Resort, Palau

MICHAEL AW

Thatched hut, Yap

If you do just fly out to one of the islands or get off a boat somewhere, the local school principal might allow you to stay in the schoolhouse, especially if school's not in session. You could also approach the local mayor or chief.

Usually people are warm and friendly and will help you out. However, because islanders feel obligated to provide for visitors, foreigners can sometimes impose without realising it. Be careful not to take advantage of Micronesian hospitality. While islanders readily welcome each other into their homes, it's a long-established system founded on reciprocity and kinship obligations and the casual visitor should not expect the same rights.

If you stay with a family you should offer them something, but unless money is requested, giving coffee, rice, tobacco or other gifts is probably a more appropriate way to pay for your stay.

FOOD
Considering the geographic spread, it's surprising how similar the food is throughout Micronesia.

Western foods like hamburgers, sandwiches, fried chicken and steak are found on most menus. Almost equally as common is Japanese food, such as fresh sashimi, teriyaki and ramen. Breakfasts are typically Western style, with toast, eggs, bacon (or Spam!) and French toast. There's a great deal of variety in Guam and Saipan and to a lesser extent Palau. On those islands it's easy to find Mexican food and Korean, Chinese, Thai and other Asian cuisines. Chinese food has the monopoly on Nauru. On Saipan and Guam, US fast-food chains are also ubiquitous.

Fish is plentiful, fresh and delicious throughout the islands. Grilled tuna is often one of the best and cheapest meals available.

On most of the islands restaurants are quite simple local eateries – don't expect to find quaint cafes, pastry shops or coffee bars.

Local Food
Fish, shellfish, coconuts, breadfruit, taro, tapioca and bananas are Micronesian staples.

Traditional local dishes are not often served in restaurants however, although mangrove crab and fried breadfruit find their way onto a few menus.

Breadfruit is prepared much like potatoes – either boiled, fried, mashed, roasted or baked. Preserved (fermented) breadfruit, which was traditionally a provision food for long canoe journeys, is definitely an acquired taste. Taro root is eaten baked or boiled, rather than smashed up into a Hawai'ian-style *poi* (paste).

Micronesians developed a taste for rice during the Japanese era and it remains the single largest imported food. Canned fish and high-salt, high-fat canned meats are other popular imported foods, as are chocolate chip cookies and candy bars. In grocery stores banana cake mix may be easier to find than bananas.

Some of Micronesia's more exotic dishes include crocodile (Palau), fruit bat, mangrove crab and coconut crab. In Kiribati they favour *te babai*, swamp taro cooked for special occasions.

If you've imagined a wild abundance of exotic tropical fruits in Micronesia you'll be disappointed. You can sometimes buy bananas, papayas and coconuts in local markets, but despite year-round sun, many fruits in Micronesia are seasonal. Moreover, families generally grow just enough for their own use and feed the surplus to their pigs, so those sweet papayas you were hoping to see on the breakfast menu might go to the family porker instead. Other fruits are grown for export.

Fresh vegetables, especially crisp salad types, are imported and scarce, so what you do find often looks ready for composting.

Self-Catering
There are grocery stores, where you can buy packaged and canned Western foods, on all the main islands. Although the selection varies widely, on the larger islands it's generally quite extensive. Many islands also have simple farmer's markets where you can pick up fresh fruits and limited local produce. When buying groceries, check the expiry dates.

DRINKS
Nonalcoholic Drinks
Tap water may be safe in Guam and Rota, but it's risky elsewhere in Micronesia and it's a good idea to boil it when you're unsure – or avoid it altogether.

Bottled water is usually available in grocery stores throughout the islands. Soft drinks, coffee and tea are easy to get almost everywhere.

Coconuts are plentiful and refreshing to drink, but devilishly hard to open. If you buy a coconut from a fruit stall the vendor will open it for you. Otherwise, if you've got a coconut that's already husked, look for the three dots that resemble a face with two eyes and a mouth. If you have a pocketknife, it's easy to poke a hole in the 'mouth'.

Alcoholic Drinks
There are bars serving alcohol almost everywhere in Micronesia. Chuuk is dry only on paper, and Kosrae ostensibly requires visitors to get a drinking permit. Budweiser is generally the king of beers, though Victoria Bitter reigns throughout Nauru and Kiribati. For locally brewed beer, try Red Rooster in Palau.

Among island drinks, *tuba*, which is laboriously made from coconut sap, is quite common; sour toddy is Kiribati's beer-like coconut equivalent. *Sakau* (or kava), a non-alcoholic intoxicant made from the root of a pepper plant, is drunk on Pohnpei – see the boxed text 'Sakau' in the FSM chapter.

SHOPPING
There's some fine woodwork and weaving to be found on many of the islands.

Yap has some of the most interesting traditional crafts, including hibiscus fibre skirts and other functional items still used

---

Things Not to Buy

Sea turtle shells make beautiful jewellery – too beautiful, in fact, for the welfare of the turtles. Although the islanders have taken turtles for subsistence purposes for centuries, a combination of drift-netting and worldwide demand for the ornamental shells has thrown sea turtles onto the endangered species list. Tortoise shell jewellery, as well as the whole shells, are prohibited entry into the USA, Canada, Australia and most other countries.

The importation of black coral is likewise banned in more than 100 countries. The purchase of other corals, which are often dynamited from their fragile reef ecosystem and sold in chunks or made into jewellery, should also give pause to the environmentally conscious.

---

by the Yapese. The Marshall Islands have stick charts and high-quality baskets; Palau has intricately carved wooden storyboards; Kiribati has shark-tooth swords and outrigger canoes; and Chuuk has carved love sticks and masks. The Northern Marianas and Guam are devoid of any real native handicrafts. Kosrae's handicrafts are good all-around, and Nauru, while devoid of traditional handicrafts, offers some novel phosphate paperweights.

Some of the best woodcarvings in Micronesia are those of marine animals made by the Kapingamarangi islanders on Pohnpei. Gourmet pepper and island-made coconut soaps and oils are other Pohnpeian specialities. All islands except Guam and the Northern Mariana Islands sell their own colourful postage stamps which make lightweight souvenirs.

Getting There & Away

AIR
Airports & Airlines

The main air gateways into Micronesia are Honolulu and Guam, but there are also direct flights from Asia to Saipan, in the Northern Marianas, and Palau and from Australia to Nauru and Guam.

Continental Airlines is Micronesia's main carrier. As it is the only airline with direct flights between Honolulu and Guam, Continental is the best option for US travellers.

Air Nauru, a reliable airline which uses a 737 and mostly Australian pilots, is the only airline with access to Nauru and Tarawa (Kiribati). Air Nauru has one weekly flight to Nauru from Australia; from there you can connect to Tarawa and Fiji in one direction, and Pohnpei, Guam and Manila in the other.

For service from Asian destinations there are a number of carriers, including Japan Airlines, All Nippon Airways, Asiana Airlines, Continental Airlines and Northwest Airlines. Almost all terminate in Guam or Saipan, so if you plan to explore other islands you'll need to transfer to Continental (for American Micronesia) or Air Nauru (for Nauru and Tarawa).

For Continental, high season – and higher prices – is the period from mid-December to mid-January and from June to mid-September.

Air Passes

Continental Airlines offers two money-saving passes, called Circle Micronesia and Visit Micronesia. Both passes are infinitely preferable to Continental's exorbitant one-way and return fares among the islands.

Circle Micronesia fares are best for travellers wanting to go the 'island-hopper' route (see later), but they are only available to travellers flying from the USA. Visit Micronesia fares allow travellers to fly from Asia or from Cairns (Australia), Continental's only Australian destination.

Both tickets allow for open stopovers. However, given Continental's reduced flight schedule, seating availability for such heavily discounted fares can be limited, particularly as you near Guam or Honolulu. Make reservations early. If you're put on a waiting list, check in as early as possible and don't despair – most flights have lots of no-shows.

Children receive discounted fares on these Micronesia air passes of up to 67%.

Outside of Honolulu and Micronesia, travel agents are usually rather baffled when faced with the complicated fare structure of a Circle Micronesia or Visit Micronesia air pass. Make sure you can clearly communicate your desired itinerary so that the agent gets everything right. On the other hand, the confusion means that everything

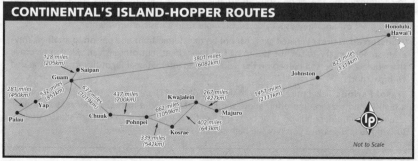

CONTINENTAL'S ISLAND-HOPPER ROUTES

Honolulu, Hawai'i

128 miles (205km)

Saipan

3801 miles (6082km)

Johnston

821 miles (1314km)

281 miles (450km)

532 miles (851km)

Guam

637 miles (1019km)

437 miles (700km)

Kwajalein

267 miles (427km)

1457 miles (2331km)

Yap

Majuro

Palau

Chuuk

662 miles (1059km)

Pohnpei

402 miles (643km)

Kosrae

339 miles (542km)

Not to Scale

Air Travel Glossary

Cancellation Penalties If you have to cancel or change a discounted ticket, there are often heavy penalties involved; insurance can sometimes be taken out against these penalties. Some airlines impose penalties on regular tickets as well, particularly against 'no-show' passengers.

Courier Fares Businesses often need to send urgent documents or freight securely and quickly. Courier companies hire people to accompany the package through customs and, in return, offer a discount ticket which is sometimes a phenomenal bargain. However, you may have to surrender all your baggage allowance and take only carry-on luggage.

Full Fares Airlines traditionally offer 1st class (coded F), business class (coded J) and economy class (coded Y) tickets. These days there are so many promotional and discounted fares available that few passengers pay full economy fare.

Lost Tickets If you lose your airline ticket an airline will usually treat it like a travellers cheque and, after inquiries, issue you with another one. Legally, however, an airline is entitled to treat it like cash and if you lose it then it's gone forever. Take good care of your tickets.

Onward Tickets An entry requirement for many countries is that you have a ticket out of the country. If you're unsure of your next move, the easiest solution is to buy the cheapest onward ticket to a neighbouring country or a ticket from a reliable airline which can later be refunded if you do not use it.

Open-Jaw Tickets These are return tickets where you fly out to one place but return from another. If available, this can save you backtracking to your arrival point.

Overbooking Since every flight has some passengers who fail to show up, airlines often book more passengers than they have seats. Usually excess passengers make up for the no-shows, but occasionally somebody gets 'bumped' onto the next available flight. Guess who it is most likely to be? The passengers who check in late.

Promotional Fares These are officially discounted fares, available from travel agencies or direct from the airline.

Reconfirmation If you don't reconfirm your flight at least 72 hours prior to departure, the airline may delete your name from the passenger list. Ring to find out if your airline requires reconfirmation.

Restrictions Discounted tickets often have various restrictions on them – such as needing to be paid for in advance and incurring a penalty to be altered. Others are restrictions on the minimum and maximum period you must be away.

Round-the-World Tickets RTW tickets give you a limited period (usually a year) in which to circumnavigate the globe. You can go anywhere the carrying airlines go, as long as you don't backtrack. The number of stopovers or total number of separate flights is decided before you set off and they usually cost a bit more than a basic return flight.

Transferred Tickets Airline tickets cannot be transferred from one person to another. Travellers sometimes try to sell the return half of their ticket, but officials can ask you to prove that you are the person named on the ticket. On an international flight tickets are compared with passports.

Travel Periods Ticket prices vary with the time of year. There is a low (off-peak) season and a high (peak) season, and often a low-shoulder season and a high-shoulder season as well. Usually the fare depends on your outward flight – if you depart in the high season and return in the low season, you pay the high-season fare.

is ultimately a little bit flexible. Nobody really knows the rules: even when you have your ticket the Continental agents are not necessarily going to understand it. One agent will tell you one thing, another agent another. So if you need to make a change, call up your best negotiating skills.

It will be easier to understand the explanations below if you refer to the 'Continental's Island-hopper Routes' map in this chapter.

Circle Micronesia Circle Micronesia air fares are return tickets that originate in Honolulu, Los Angeles or San Francisco and allow travel on an open ticket via Continental's island-hopper route through Micronesia. One leg is always a nonstop flight between Honolulu and Guam; the other is the island-hopper portion, which means that between Guam and Honolulu the plane stops on Chuuk, Pohnpei, Kosrae, Kwajalein, Majuro and (for refuelling) Johnston Island, a US military territory. You can get off at any of these stops except Johnston Island.

The base fare of a Circle Micronesia itinerary depends on your turn-around point, which can be Guam, Saipan, Yap or Koror (Palau). If it's Guam, the base fare from Honolulu is US$920; from San Francisco or Los Angeles it's US$1230. For Saipan the fares are US$975/1280 from Honolulu/San Francisco or Los Angeles, for Yap it's US$1150/1500, and for Palau US$1250/1650. Add US$300 if you're coming from the USA's east coast.

On all routes intermediate stops can include Honolulu, Majuro, Kwajalein, Kosrae, Pohnpei, Chuuk and Guam. Yap can be added as a stopover if you're turning around at Palau; Guam can also be an intermediate stop for anyone terminating in Palau, Yap or Saipan.

Four 'free' stopovers are included in the base fare. Additional intermediate stops are US$50 each. If you build these extra stopovers into your original ticket you'll avoid a US$50 ticket-reissuing fee. You must work your stopovers into your ticket before you disembark at the desired stop.

If your turn-around point is Palau or Yap, one of your stopovers cannot be Saipan. The reverse also applies: If you choose Saipan as an turn-around point, you will have to buy a separate ticket to Palau and/or Yap. This is because Saipan is in a different direction from Guam than Palau and Yap (look at the map). If you wish to visit Palau/Yap and Saipan, it's best to opt for Yap or Palau as your turn-around point and take one of the frequent and cheap commuter planes from Guam to Saipan. (Continental's flight from Guam to Saipan is much more expensive.)

The Circle Micronesia tickets are valid year round and have a minimum stay of 10 days and maximum stay of six months. Ticketing must be done seven days before departure. There is a full refund for cancellations made more than seven days before departure. If you cancel less than a week before departure, there's a 25% cancellation fee.

Visit Micronesia Continental also offers a Visit Micronesia pass, which starts and ends in Guam or Saipan and allows travel to Guam or Saipan, Palau, Chuuk and Yap for a set fee. Pohnpei and Kosrae can be added for an additional charge.

The pass must be purchased outside Micronesia in conjunction with an international ticket to Guam or Saipan on Continental or Northwest. Citizens of Guam and Saipan are ineligible. The pass is valid for 30 days, and travel must begin within 60 days of arrival on Guam or Saipan.

The price differs depending on the country you start out from and your island stopovers.

A Visit Micronesia pass for those flying from North or South America for Guam, Saipan, Palau and Yap is US$400; for Guam, Saipan, Chuuk, Yap and Palau it's US$500; and for Palau, Saipan, Chuuk, Yap, Guam, Pohnpei and Kosrae it's US$600.

Your total allowed stopovers will equal one less than the total number of islands on your ticket. Your turn-around point (Guam or Saipan) counts as a stopover if you stay there more than 24 hours. Thus for the Guam, Saipan, Palau and Yap fare you can stop only on three of the four islands; for Guam, Saipan, Chuuk, Yap and Palau you will be allowed to stay on only four of those islands; and so on.

For those originating from Cairns, Australia, there is no four-island pass; the five-island pass (choosing four islands from Guam, Saipan, Chuuk, Yap and Palau) is US$625, and it's US$775 for the six-island pass.

These fares do not include taxes.

Micronesian-Based Airlines

The phone numbers for the main airlines servicing Micronesia are:

Continental Airlines
  Australia: (in Sydney ☎ 02-9244 2242; in Melbourne ☎ 03-9920 3858)
  Canada: (☎ 1-800-231 0856)
  Guam: (☎ 647 6453)
  Hong Kong: (☎ 2525 7759)
  Indonesia: (☎ 0361-287 774)
  Japan: (☎ 03-3508 6411)
  Korea: (☎ 02-773 0100)
  Philippines: (☎ 02-818 8701)
  USA: (☎ 1-800-525 0280)

Air Nauru
  Australia: (in Sydney ☎ 02-8267 0727, fax 8627 0705; in Melbourne ☎ 03-9653 5602, fax 9650 4925; in Brisbane ☎ 07-3229 6455, fax 3229 6344)
  Fiji (☎ 313 731, fax 308 687; Nadi Airport ☎ 722 795, fax 721 010)
  New Zealand: (☎ 64-9-636 6444, fax 636 6777)
  Philippines: (☎ 02-879 5787, fax 879 5785)
  USA: (☎ 310-670 7302, fax 338 0708)

USA

Island-Hopping Continental is the only airline that island-hops between Honolulu and Guam. The route is: Honolulu, Johnston, Majuro, Kwajalein, Kosrae, Pohnpei, Chuuk and Guam.

The island-hopper flights go twice a week. They cross the International Date Line after Johnston Island and before arriving at Majuro. Majuro is the first destination where civilians are allowed to disembark.

Continental Flight Times

Honolulu-Johnston	two hours
Johnston-Majuro	three hours
Majuro-Kwajalein	50 minutes
Kwajalein-Kosrae	one hour
Kosrae-Pohnpei	one hour
Pohnpei-Chuuk	one hour
Chuuk-Guam	1½ hours
Guam-Yap	1½ hours
Yap-Koror	50 minutes
Guam-Koror	two hours
Guam-Saipan	35 minutes
Guam-Honolulu (direct)	7½ hours

The plane refuels on Johnston but unless you have permission from the US military you will not be permitted to get off the plane.

Kwajalein, the stop after Majuro, is another off-limits military base, but visitors can disembark there and take the ferry to nearby Ebeye Island.

Continental offers only unrestricted fares in economy class for flights between the islands. There are no advance purchase fares and no maximum stay for return tickets.

The one-way, unrestricted island-hopper fare allowing any or all stopovers between Honolulu and Guam is US$700. Airport taxes between Honolulu and Guam total US$28; there may also be an additional 'hidden charge' when you plug in your actual dates.

The same ticket coming from Los Angeles or San Francisco (via Northwest) starts at US$900.

It costs US$70 to add Saipan to the island-hopper tickets.

If you're planning to go to all of the islands you'll definitely save money by buying the island-hopper as opposed to point-to-point tickets, as the fares will be the same or nearly the same for inter-island segments.

Aloha Airlines has begun a weekly air service from Honolulu to the Marshall Islands and hopes to begin one to the Federated States of Micronesia. Fares from Honolulu to Majuro/Kwajalein are US$800/900 return.

Continental flies nonstop daily between Honolulu and Guam. Return excursion tickets to Guam are around US$825 from Honolulu and US$1100 from the US west coast. The tickets are valid for up to one year and return dates can be kept open.

Although tickets originating on the West Coast should allow a stopover in Honolulu, these excursion tickets don't allow for any island-hopping through Micronesia. If you want to island-hop one way and return on a direct flight, you need to piece together two one-way tickets.

You can continue from Guam to Yap and Koror (Palau) via Continental; tickets cost US$365 one way, US$730 return. This should allow a stopover in Yap. From Guam to Yap the fare is US$250 one way.

To beat these sky-high prices, have Yap and Palau added on to your original ticket to Micronesia.

Asia

Continental makes the five-hour flight between Bali (Indonesia) and Guam three days a week. The one-way fare is $463. An excursion ticket allowing a stay of up to 90 days costs US$712.

From Hong Kong, Continental flies to Guam via Saipan twice a week. The one-way fare to Guam is US$567; the 45-day excursion fare is US$890/707 in the high/low season.

Northwest Airlines flies daily from Hong Kong to Guam via Tokyo for US$574 one way or US$666 for a 45-day excursion (tax not included).

From the Philippines, Continental has a daily flight from Manila to Guam. A separate flight that stops in Palau on the way to Guam goes out of Manila twice a week. Once a week this flight also stops on Yap. The one-way fare from Manila to Guam is US$400 (including tax). A 14-day advance purchase excursion ticket, valid for two to 45 days, costs US$545/445 in high/low season. Seven-day advance purchase tickets cost a little more.

For flights between Manila and Palau, Continental charges US$350 one way or US$585 for a 45-day excursion.

Air Nauru has two flights a week from Manila to Guam for US$450 for a 45-day excursion. The flight continues on to Pohnpei, Nauru and Tarawa; the excursion fares, respectively, are US$590, US$734, US$867. The flight continues on from Tarawa to Fiji.

There are numerous daily flights from Japan to Saipan and Guam: from Tokyo on Japan Airlines and Northwest; from Osaka on Japan Airlines and All Nippon Airways; and from Nagoya on Japan Air Lines. Continental flies direct from those cities only to Guam. There's also a regular but less frequent service from other ports in Japan, including Sapporo, Sendai and Fukuoka.

Continental has two flights a week from Nigata, Japan, direct to Guam.

All Nippon Airways has daily flights from Osaka to Guam with 21-day advance purchase fares for US$397 not including taxes; 21 day maximum stay. The one-way fare is US$562.

Return fares from Japan begin at US$348 (Northwest from Tokyo) with a 14-day advance purchase fare and a 14-day maximum stay. From Tokyo to Saipan on Northwest tickets are US$437 return or US$543 one way.

Prices tend to fluctuate quite a bit, so it's worthwhile if you don't like a fare quote to call again the next day.

Reservations on flights from Japan are almost impossible to make around the time of Japan's New Year's vacation (Christmas through the first week of January), the Golden Week period (the last week of April and the first week of May) and during Obon (August), as almost all the seats are pre-booked for holiday package tours.

Asiana Airlines in Korea flies from Seoul to Guam with a one-way fare of US$414 and a one-month excursion ticket from US$604/685 for weekday/weekend travel. Fares from Seoul to Saipan are the same.

From Taiwan, Continental has a direct flight between Taipei and Guam which goes four days a week. The one-way fare is US$262, while a 45-day excursion ticket costs US$507.

Far Eastern Air Transport has two flights a week from Taipei to Palau for US$350 one way or US$690 return.

The Pacific

Air Nauru has two flights a week from Fiji to Tarawa (Kiribati); the flight continues on to Nauru, where you can connect to Air Nauru's other Micronesian destinations (Pohnpei or Guam).

Australia

Continental Airlines flies twice a week non-stop between Cairns and Guam for US$858 excursion; the fare is for a 14-day advance purchase and a maximum stay of one month, and is subject to a US$75 change penalty. The unrestricted one-way fare is US$878, but prices drop from September to December and January to May.

Air Nauru also has one direct flight per week between Nauru and Brisbane, with a one-way fare of A$783 and a 35-day excursion fare of A$817. The flight goes to Melbourne after Brisbane; fares between Melbourne and Nauru are A$880 one way, A$875 excursion. On the other end you can continue on via Air Nauru to Pohnpei, Guam and Manila or to Tarawa and Fiji in the other direction.

Standard fares aside, Air Nauru usually has excellent special fares that allow travel between Australia and Nauru for as low as A$600 return; you can continue elsewhere in Micronesia for not much more – but keep in mind that Air Nauru has only one plane and depending on timing you might have a few days' layover in Nauru. Air Nauru's Web site (www.airnauru.com.au) keeps lists of the current specials. If you're travelling on a special fare, confirm your seat well in advance as the low-fare seats tend to sell out.

It's vital to reconfirm your Air Nauru flight from Australia a few days in advance, otherwise they might fill your weight allotment with cargo.

SEA

Although you might think it would be handy to get around Micronesia by ship, in reality the islands are so spread out that travel by ship is only common among the island groupings within one country. To Christmas Island from Tarawa, for example, would take two weeks by ship – and that's within one country!

One of the few cruise lines with services to Micronesia is US-based Zegrahm Expeditions (☎ 1-800-628 8747, ✉ zoe@zeco .com), 1414 Dexter Ave N #327, Seattle, WA 98109, which has cruises to some of Micronesia's more remote and beautiful outer islands. Fares start at US$5390/6990 for the seven/10 day cruises.

If you travel by private yacht, your first stop in any country (or, as in the case of the FSM, any state) must be the district centre for immigration formalities. It is best to notify the harbour or immigration authorities in advance of your arrival. Wherever possible this book has included information about harbour facilities and lagoon passages for visiting yachts under the Getting There & Away sections of each chapter.

ORGANISED TOURS

There are an increasing number of US-based diving and speciality tours to Micronesia. Many of the dive holiday packages are substantially cheaper than if you pieced together the dives and hotels by yourself, especially if you want to stay in more upscale establishments.

It's a good idea to check the tourist office Web site of the country you want to visit, as there are often links to foreign dive tour companies. Those interested in cultural tours might ask at US universities, which very occasionally run guided trips to Micronesia.

The following prices do not include air fare, except where noted, and are based on double occupancy.

Cultural Tours

Oceanic Society Expeditions (☎ 1-800-326 7491, 415-441 1106, fax 474 3395), Fort Mason Center, Building E, San Francisco, CA 94123, is a nonprofit company with an ecotravel focus. It leads three 10-day snorkelling tours of Palau each year. A marine naturalist accompanies the tours and the trips emphasise Palauan culture. The cost is US$2790, including air fare from Honolulu, accommodation and picnic lunches. Web site: www.oceanic-society.org.

Valor Tours (☎ 1-800-842 4504, 415-332 7850, fax 332 6971, ✆ bobatsqv@aol.com), 10 Liberty Ship Way, Suite 160, Sausalito, CA 94965, USA, plans guided tours for history buffs and WWII veterans wanting to visit island and battle sites. Destinations include Majuro, Mili, Wotje and Maloelap in the Marshall Islands as well as Guam, Tinian, Palau and Tarawa. The trips are generally in November and can be multi-island. A tour of seven to ten days costs US$2000 to US$2500.

Dive Tours

Trip-N-Tour (☎ 1-800-348 0842, 760-724 0788, fax 724 9897, ✆ info@trip-n-tour.com), 2182 Foothill Drive, Vista, CA 92084, USA, has a variety of four- and seven-day dive packages to Chuuk, Yap, Palau, Pohnpei, Rota, Saipan, Kosrae and Guam. It also arranges live-aboard packages in Palau and Chuuk that start at US$1795.

World of Adventure Vacations (☎ 1-800-900 7657, 310-322 8100, fax 310 322 5111, ✆ info@worldofdiving.com) offers customised scuba, snorkel, fishing and kayaking trips to American Micronesia. Among the least expensive packages is a five-night special to Palau that includes three days of diving and air fare from the US West Coast for US$1499 (plus tax). Non-divers can subtract US$300; prices also drop during the summer. Multi-island itineraries can be arranged.

Tropical Adventures (☎ 1-800-247 3483, 206-441 3483, fax 206-441 5431, ✆ dive@divetropical.com), PO Box 4337 Seattle, WA 98104, USA, arranges a wide variety of customised dive vacations in Chuuk, Palau, Pohnpei, Kosrae, Guam and Yap. A four-day, five-night package at the Kosrae Village Resort, with a two-tank dive each day, is US$560; it's US$665 at Blue Lagoon Resort in Chuuk, and US$816 at the Outrigger Palasia in Palau.

The PADI Travel Network (☎ 1-800-729 7234, 949-858 7234, fax 858 9311, ✆ ptn1@padi.com), 30151 Tomas St, Rancho Santa Magarita, CA 92688-2125, USA, also offers customised dive trips to Palau, Chuuk and Yap. Two days and three nights in Palau, staying in the Carolines, costs US$447. Dive trips to Chuuk on the *Truk Aggressor* cost from US$2295 per person for a week. A Visit Yap package of three nights and two days of diving costs from US$391.

Live-Aboard Dive Boats

The SS *Thorfinn* and the *Truk Aggressor II*, based in Chuuk Lagoon, and the *Ocean Hunter*, *Sun Dancer II* and *Palau Aggressor*, based in Palau, are live-aboard dive boats with set rates that include diving, accommodation and meals. They can be booked directly or through certain travel agents; details are in the respective chapters.

DEPARTURE TAX

Airport departure taxes are US$5 on Pohnpei, US$20 in Palau, A$10 on Tarawa and Christmas Island, US$10 on Kosrae and Chuuk and US$15 on Majuro.

WARNING

The information in this chapter is particularly vulnerable to change: prices for international travel are volatile, routes are introduced and cancelled, schedules change, special deals come and go, and rules and visa requirements are amended. Prices quoted here were obtained at a time when Micronesia's tourist industry was being buffeted by the effects of an economic crisis in Asia which significantly reduced the amount of money tourists were willing or able to spend. As the Asian economies revive prices of travel will certainly increase.

Airlines and governments seem to take a perverse pleasure in making price structures and regulations as complicated as possible. Check directly with the airline or a travel agent to make sure you understand how a fare works. In addition, the travel industry is highly competitive and there are many lurks and perks.

The upshot of this is that you should get opinions, quotes and advice from as many airlines and travel agents as possible before you part with your hard-earned cash. The details given in this chapter should be regarded as mere pointers and are not a substitute for your own careful, up-to-date research.

Getting Around

AIR

Continental's air passes, which extend to flights coming in to Micronesia from countries such as the USA or Australia, are an affordable way to move around some of Micronesia's many islands. For details see Air Passes in the Getting There and Away chapter.

Within Micronesia, Continental Airlines links the nine major district centres of Majuro and Kwajalein/Ebeye (Marshall Islands); Kosrae, Pohnpei, Chuuk and Yap (FSM); Saipan (Northern Marianas); Guam and Palau.

While this book was being researched, Continental had scaled back its flights in response to low tourism numbers; this will change as the Asian economy revives. Hawai'i-based Aloha Airlines has also recently begun a Micronesia service.

Other international routes within Micronesia are flown by Air Nauru, which links Guam, Pohnpei, Nauru and Tarawa (Kiribati), and Air Marshall Islands, which links the Marshall Islands with Tarawa.

Some island groups have domestic airlines connecting the district centres with their outer islands. The government-supported Air Marshall Islands (AMI) and Air Kiribati are by far the most extensive, respectively linking almost every inhabited Marshall and Gilbert atoll. Caroline Islands Air links Pohnpei twice weekly with the outer islands of Pingelap and Mokil. On Yap, Pacific Missionary Aviation (PMA) flies between Yap Proper and the outer islands of Ulithi, Fais and Woleai. The fares for these small planes generally fall between US$60 and US$100 one way (though some of AMI's longer flights cost more).

None of the small airlines has very many planes, and there's always a risk that you may get stuck on an outer island if the aircraft breaks down. Flexibility is an asset.

Slightly larger and more reliable are the two commuter airlines based in the Northern Marianas, Freedom Air (code-shared

Airports

Guam's modern, newly-expanded airport is the hub of Micronesia, and Nauru has a pleasant, air-conditioned terminal. Most other airports, however, are partly or entirely open-air and have few services besides snack bars, handicraft stalls, restrooms and a telephone. When you deplane at these stops, the most striking thing is not the airport but the arrival ceremony. Particularly in the FSM and on Tarawa, locals gather en masse to greet the flight. Some are welcoming relatives; others merely want to watch the jet arrive and see who gets off. It can be quite overwhelming to step off the plane into an excited gaggle of locals, so if you get flustered by crowds be sure to have somebody from your hotel meet your plane (a good idea anyway, as most hotels offer airport pick-up and drop-off). Otherwise, enjoy this quintessentially Micronesian experience.

with Continental) and Pacific Island Aviation (PIA; code-shared with Northwest). They fly numerous times a day between Guam, Rota, Saipan and Tinian, charging from US$20 to US$74 a flight. PIA gives discounts to children ages two to 11. When planning your travel between Guam and the Northern Marianas, stay on top of fiesta dates, as many of the small planes will be fully booked around fiesta time.

More detailed information on these flights is provided in the respective island sections.

Island Airlines

The following airlines have services within Micronesia:

Air Kiribati
 Tarawa: (☎ 21 550)
Air Marshall Islands (AMI)
 Majuro: (☎ 625 3733)
 Ebeye: (☎ 329 3036)
 Tarawa: (☎ 21 557)

Air Nauru
Guam: (☎ 649 4253)
Nauru: (☎ 444 3141, fax 444 3705; airport
☎ 444 3218, fax 444 3170)
Pohnpei: (☎ 320 5963, fax 320 5932)
Tarawa: (☎ 26 715, fax 26 000)
Caroline Islands Air
Pohnpei: (☎ 320 8406)
Continental Airlines
Chuuk: (☎ 330 2424)
Guam: (☎ 647 6453)
Kosrae: (☎ 370 3024)
Majuro: (☎ 625 3209)
Palau: (☎ 488 2448)
Pohnpei: (☎ 320 2424)
Saipan: (☎ 234 6491)
Yap: (☎ 350 2127)
Freedom Air
Guam: (☎ 647 2294)
Rota: (☎ 532 3801)
Saipan: (☎ 234 8328)
Tinian: (☎ 433 3288)
Pacific Island Aviation
Guam: (☎ 647 3600)
Rota: (☎ 532 0397)
Saipan: (☎ 288 0770)
Tinian: (☎ 433 3600)
Pacific Missionary Aviation (PMA)
Yap: (☎ 350 2360)

BUS

In Kiribati; South Tarawa has an excellent minibus system, with inexpensive minibuses whizzing constantly up and down the island's only road. A fledgling public bus system operates on Guam and there's one minibus on Christmas Island, but the next closest thing to a public bus system in Micronesia is the not-too-useful school buses on Yap.

TAXI

In the Marshalls, Majuro has a good, inexpensive system of shared taxis that cruise up and down the main road. As long as the taxi is not full it will stop if you wave it down. Rates, charged per person according to destination, dip as low as 50 cents. In the FSM, Pohnpei also has a good shared taxi system, as does Weno Island (Chuuk), though many of its cabs are unlicensed.

Yap, Koror (Palau), Saipan and Guam have private taxis. Rates are quite reasonable in Yap and a bit more expensive in

Palau, while those in Saipan and Guam are comparable to fares in the USA or Australia. Tarawa also has a few private taxis, and Nauru has two taxis owned by the Menen Hotel.

CAR

Most of the major islands have fairly extensive road systems. Usually the main drag around town and the road out to the airport are paved but beyond that it varies, and unpaved roads are as common as not.

In some places you can just cruise along, while in others roads are little more than pitted, washed-out obstacle courses where it's easy to scrape the bottom of the car. To challenge you even further, car agencies often rent low-riding compact cars.

Rental cars are available on the major islands, though they may book out completely during busy times.

The minimum rates range from US$35 to US$45 per day (almost no companies have hourly rates), and there's never a mileage charge. Major car rental chains operate in Guam and the Northern Marianas and occasionally in some of the other district centres; you can book cars in advance from their overseas offices, which is a good idea anyway as otherwise the cheaper cars may be rented out when you arrive. Unless you have a pre-paid deal, there are no cancellation penalties. Many car companies will offer to pick you up at your hotel.

Upon renting a car, check it over carefully and note on the contract any major scratches, dents or other damage before you drive away, to avoid hassles when you return the car. Also check the tyres – it's common to get a car with dangerously bald tyres (and there may be contract clauses that hold you responsible for tyre damage!).

The major car rental firms all offer collision insurance for US$10 to US$15 but only some of the local companies do. Not getting insurance is a mixed bag – you save a few bucks, but if you, say, hit a big stone camouflaged by the roadside grass (as happened to one couple) it will be a huge, very expensive hassle.

Although motor scooters are one of the main modes of transportation on some islands, particularly Nauru and Kiribati, there are no companies anywhere in Micronesia that rent them out. If you ask around, though, you may be able to find a local willing to rent.

Road Rules

In Nauru and Kiribati driving is on the left-hand side of the road; everywhere else driving is on the right, as it is in the USA. Other US traffic laws generally apply, including stopping for school buses (for traffic in both directions) when the bus lights are flashing.

Driving licences are discussed in Driving Licences under Visas & Documents in the Facts for the Visitor chapter.

BICYCLE

Cycling is not a practical way to get around in Micronesia and bike rentals are hard to come by, though hotels and guest houses are increasingly renting them out for guests. Cycling can be dangerous as there are no bike lanes and drivers on some islands drive fast. Sunburn is also a hazard, as sweat removes sunscreen faster than it can be applied.

HITCHING

Hitching is never entirely safe in any country in the world, and we don't recommend it. Travellers who decide to hitch should understand that they are taking a small but potentially serious risk. People who do choose to hitch will be safer if they travel in pairs and let someone know where they are planning to go.

All the usual hitchhiking safety precautions apply, especially for women, but with the exception of Guam and Saipan, getting lifts in Micronesia is fairly easy.

BOAT

See Sea in the Getting There & Away chapter for information on private yachts.

Field-trip Ships

Field-trip ships link several of Micronesia's district centres with the outer islands, car-rying both supplies and passengers and loading copra for the return journeys. Very few travellers take them, but they're an interesting way to meet local people and to travel to the remote corners of Micronesia where the most traditional lifestyles prevail. They're also one of the cheapest ways of travelling in Micronesia.

Ships leave from Majuro in the Marshalls, from the FSM islands of Weno (Chuuk), Pohnpei and Yap Proper and from Tarawa (Kiribati).

Some of the routes have the ships out for weeks, while the shorter routes, such as Pohnpei to Pingelap or Tarawa to Butaritari, take only a few days. You can get lists of departure dates in advance, but they shouldn't be taken too seriously as the ships often run behind schedule. Occasionally the ships will skip a sailing altogether or even go into dry dock for months at a time. Ships sail a bit more frequently around election time when politicians head out to woo the outer islands.

Be prepared for a rugged travel experience – these are working ships, not cruise ships, and the boats get grubby after a few days of crowded human habitation.

The field-trip ships have both deck class and a handful of simple cabins. Priority for the cabins is generally given to government officials, village elders and those with medical needs. Even if you manage to book a cabin, you may get bumped if someone with more authority decides they need it at the last moment.

Deck class passengers should board the boat early and mark out a spot on deck as soon as they get on the ship. Guard your spot until the boundaries are established with your new neighbours, as extended families travelling together will have no qualms about moving unattended gear out of the way.

It's nice to get acquainted with your fellow passengers as Micronesians are generally quite hospitable and can be incredibly helpful if they learn you're travelling to their island.

The meals served on board usually consist of monotonous dishes of rice, canned fish and canned meat so you'll probably want to bring at least some of your own food, as well as sufficient water.

For more details, see the respective island sections.

Commuter and Private Boats

Chuuk is unique for its extensive weekday system of commuter boats that bring people to Weno from the other islands in Chuuk Lagoon in the morning and return them to their home islands in the late afternoon.

Chuuk also has fishing boats that double as passenger carriers, running sporadically between Weno and some of the islands outside Chuuk Lagoon. However, see the Chuuk section for safety concerns.

Palau has government boats that take passengers from Koror to Peleliu and An-

gaur twice weekly and to Kayangel and various points on the island of Babeldaob less frequently.

In Kiribati boats run almost daily between the Betio dock in South Tarawa and Abaiang, the nearest 'outer' Gilbert Island.

In the Northern Marianas, a boat sponsored by the Dynasty Casino runs daily between Saipan and Tinian.

Throughout Micronesia, numerous private speedboats commute back and forth between islands within the same lagoon. Depending on how rough the seas are, traffic sometimes crosses open ocean to neighbouring islands as well. Hitching a ride on one of these boats is not too difficult if you offer a few dollars to help pay for petrol. Just go down to the docks and ask around.

Guam

Guam, an unincorporated US territory, is the metropolis of Micronesia. With 210 sq miles (549 sq km) and 163,500 people, Guam is Micronesia's largest and most populous island. It is a haven for shoppers: The Japanese come by the planeload to scoop up the duty-free items available at innumerable malls, while locals from nearby islands haunt the enormous new Kmart, which stocks US goods at the cheapest prices around.

The Tumon Bay and Tamuning areas are flashily overcommercialised, awash with duty-free malls, fast-food chains and high-rise hotels. But beyond the bustle Guam becomes a rural kaleidoscope of sleepy villages, stunning waterfalls and pristine beaches. Part of Guam also belongs to the US military, which maintains naval and air force bases that are closed to casual visitation.

Guam's indigenous population, the Chamorro, are working to reassert their cultural heritage. There is a movement afoot to return Guam's villages to their pre-Spanish names. The capital city, Hagåtña, was the first to change, and the remaining villages should soon follow suit. Self-determination is also an inveterate dream, as Guam looks enviously towards the mutual agreement arrangement negotiated between the US and the Northern Mariana Islands, but Guam's political status is unlikely to change in the near future.

HIGHLIGHTS

- Ritidian Point – a deserted and gorgeous sandy beach
- Hagåtña's Chamorro Village – great local food, especially during the Wednesday evening mini-fiesta
- Fiestas – lively events brimming with local food and dances, hosted annually by each of Guam's 19 villages
- Two Lovers Point – a pleasantly landscaped point where two lovers, now represented in a spindly statue, plunged to a precipitous death

Facts about Guam

HISTORY
Early Settlers

The ancient Chamorro inhabited the Mariana Islands at least as early as 1500 BC. Believed to have migrated from Indonesia, they shared language and cultural similarities with South-East Asians. The Chamorro were the only Micronesians to cultivate rice prior to Western contact.

Their society was stratified and organised in matrilineal clans. Most farming, construction and canoe building was done by men while the cooking, reef fishing, pottery and basket making was done by women.

The social system had three main classes. The *matua* and *achoat*, or the nobles and the lesser nobility, owned the land while the *manachang*, or lower class, worked it. Only members of nobility could be warriors, sailors, artists and fishermen. The manachang had to bow down in the company of nobles and were not allowed to eat certain foods, including such basics as saltwater fish.

GUAM

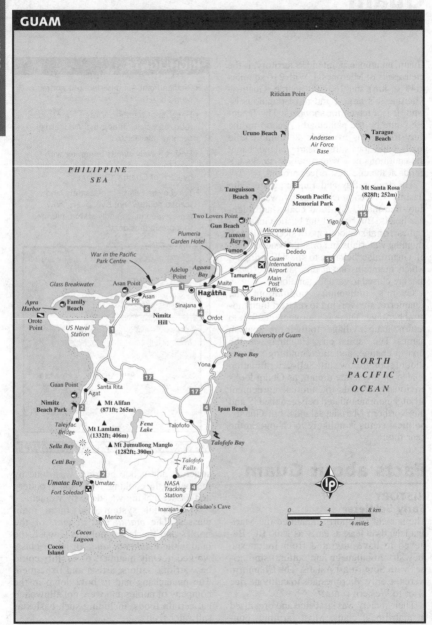

Ritidian Point

Uruno Beach

Andersen
Air Force
Base

Taragué
Beach

*PHILIPPINE
SEA*

Tanguisson
Beach

South Pacific
Memorial Park

Mt Santa Rosa
(828ft; 252m)

Two Lovers Point

Gun Beach

Yigo

15

*Plumeria
Garden Hotel*

*Tumon
Bay*

Micronesia Mall

Tumon

Dededo

1

War in the Pacific
Park Centre

Adelup
Point

*Agaña
Bay*

Tamuning

Guam
International
Airport

15

Glass Breakwater

Asan Point

Hagåtña

Maite

8

Main
Post
Office

*Apra
Harbor*

Family
Beach

Piti

Asan

6

Sinajana

Barrigada

Orote
Point

US Naval
Station

1

Nimitz
Hill

4

Ordot

University of Guam

Pago Bay

*NORTH
PACIFIC
OCEAN*

Yona

Gaan Point

Santa Rita

17

Agat

Nimitz
Beach Park

2

▲ Mt Alifan
(871ft; 265m)

17

Ipan Beach

*Taleyfac
Bridge*

▲ Mt Lamlam
(1332ft; 406m)

*Fena
Lake*

Talofofo

Sella Bay

▲ Mt Jumullong Manglo
(1282ft; 390m)

Talofofo Bay

Cetti Bay

*Talofofo
Falls*

Umatac Bay

2

Umatac

Fort Soledad

NASA
Tracking
Station

4

Merizo

Inarajan

Gadao's Cave

*Cocos
Lagoon*

4

0   4   8 km

0   2   4 miles

Cocos
Island

The island was divided into districts, each made up of one or more villages, mainly scattered along the coasts. The highest ranking district noble, the *chamorri*, was in charge of local affairs but there was no island-wide leader. As a consequence of this political structure the districts often fought, the villagers armed with slings and spears.

Spanish Period

The first Western contact in the Pacific islands was on 6 March 1521 when the *Trinidad*, captained by Ferdinand Magellan, sailed into Guam's Umatac Bay. As Magellan's ships dropped anchor, they were greeted by a flotilla of outrigger canoes.

The Spaniards noted that the triangular lateen sail used on the Chamorro canoes was superior in efficiency to the conventional European sails of the day. Consequently, Magellan named the chain of islands Islas de las Velas Latinas, 'Islands of Lateen Sails'. He retained the local name Guahan, meaning 'We Have', for the island of Guam.

Magellan and his crew had a fiery exchange with the Chamorros (see History in the Facts about the Region chapter), a scenario which was repeated often in the years that followed.

Miguel Lopez de Legazpi arrived in Guam in 1565 and officially claimed the Marianas for Spain before going on to establish the lucrative trade route between the Philippines and Mexico.

For the next 250 years Spanish galleons stopped at Guam to take on provisions during annual sailings between Manila and Acapulco. In addition to galleon layovers, there were occasional visits by Spanish, English and Dutch explorers. Yet almost 150 years passed between Magellan's landing and any real attempt at European settlement.

In 1668 the Jesuit priest Diego Luis de Sanvitores arrived with a small Spanish garrison and established a Catholic mission in the village of Hagåtña (which became Agaña under the Spanish). The Chamorro were initially receptive to the missionaries, but as the Jesuits gained influence they became more outspoken in opposing traditions such as ancestor worship and the

sexual initiation of young women. The priests insisted the islanders wear clothing, and blurred traditional caste lines by accepting converts from all classes.

It didn't take long for the Chamorro to realise that their very culture was under attack; this sparked rebellions and warfare that lasted for nearly two decades. Sanvitores was killed in 1672 after he baptised a chief's infant daughter against the chief's wishes. Spain sent soldiers to reinforce the missions and the battles escalated.

By 1690 the fighting was over, in large part because there were few Chamorro men left to fight. Between the bloodshed and the epidemics of smallpox and influenza, the Chamorro population had dropped from an estimated 100,000 to around 5000. The vast majority of those who survived were women and children.

Spanish soldiers and Filipino men, brought in to help repopulate the islands, intermarried with Chamorro women. Following local custom at that time, the men moved into their wives' houses on marriage, giving the women the chance to raise their children with some Chamorro influence. If not for this practice, the children would have grown up speaking Spanish and much of Chamorro culture would have been lost.

In addition to religion and disease, the Spanish introduced a written language, set up schools and taught construction and farming skills.

US Period

Although whale ships visited the Mariana Islands as early as 1798, it wasn't until 1822 that they stopped at Guam. Some of the whalers were British, but most were American; during the peak whaling years of the 1840s, hundreds of ships passed through Guam's waters.

In April 1898 the USA declared war on Spain. Two months later US captain Henry Glass sailed into Guam's Apra Harbor with guns firing. He was greeted warmly by the Spanish authorities who, having no idea that their two nations were at war, apologised for not having enough ammunition to return the salute. The next day the Spanish governor officially surrendered.

With the signing of the Treaty of Paris in late 1898, Spain ceded Guam (as well as Puerto Rico and the Philippines) to the USA, which for the next 40 years maintained largely unfortified naval control over the island. In February 1941, US president Franklin D Roosevelt set Guam off limits to all visitors except those authorised by the secretary of the navy. This travel restriction, dubbed the 'Coconut Curtain', remained until August 1962.

Japanese Occupation

Japanese bombers attacked Guam from Saipan on 8 December 1941, the same day as the Pearl Harbor attack across the International Date Line. Guam was an easy and undefended target. On 10 December, within hours of 5000 Japanese forces coming ashore, Guam's naval governor surrendered.

In anticipation of such an event, many Americans had been sent home just two months earlier. Those who remained were taken prisoner and sent to labour camps in Japan.

The Japanese administration in Guam immediately began the task of teaching the Chamorro the Japanese language. They renamed the island Omiyajima, 'Great Shrine Island'. Guam became part of an empire that the Japanese said would last for a thousand years. They held it for just 31 months.

In the beginning the Chamorro were largely left alone. Food supplies were rationed, but islanders could still live where they liked and workers were paid low wages for their labour.

Towards the end of Japanese control the military rule became quite harsh. Guamanians were placed in work camps to build fortifications and forced into farming to provide food for Japanese troops.

On 12 July 1944 the Japanese military command ordered all Guamanians into concentration camps on the eastern side of the island. The people didn't know where they were going or why, but, alarmed by a number of recent atrocities, many feared the worst. Particularly for some of the elderly

and the sick it did indeed become a death march. However, the move also saved many lives by concentrating the Guamanians away from areas, such as Hagåtña and the southwest coast, where the US pre-invasion bombing and subsequent combat was most intense.

Still, in the final days of conflict there were several incidents of massacres. The Japanese, hoping to kill as many Americans as possible before dying themselves, also took the lives of Chamorro who they thought might compromise that aim. In one infamous incident, 40 Chamorro men were taken at night from their camp to carry provisions as the Japanese retreated to the north. On arriving in Tarague the Japanese, fearing the men would go back to their camp and give away their positions to the advancing US forces, tied them to trees and beheaded them.

Americans Return

Pre-assault bombings by the USA began on 17 July 1944. Four days later, 55,000 US troops hit Guam's beaches at Agat and Asan. The USA secured Guam on 10 August after fierce fighting that resulted in 17,500 Japanese and 7000 US casualties.

Hagåtña was a city in ruins and many smaller villages were also destroyed. In the weeks that followed the population of the island swelled tenfold, as 200,000 US servicemen moved in to prepare for the invasion of Japan.

Large tracts of land, comprising roughly one-third of Guam, were confiscated by the US military. When the war ended the military kept the land and settled in, turning the bases into permanent facilities. These bases played a role in the Korean War and again in the Vietnam War, when Guam's Andersen Air Force Base was a take-off point for the B-52s that staged bombing raids over Indochina.

Although a 1986 class action lawsuit for dispossessed landowners won a multimillion dollar settlement from the US government, it is only in more recent times, with the closing and consolidating of US military bases worldwide, that Chamorro have hopes of any sizable tracts of land being returned. That issue has, for example, haunted the newly opened Ritidian Point on the northern end of Guam, where the former military land reverted to the US government rather than the original landowners.

GEOGRAPHY

The southernmost island in the Marianas chain, Guam is about 30 miles (48km) long and 9 miles (15km) wide. It narrows to about 4 miles (6.5km) in the centre, giving it a shape resembling a bow tie.

The northern part of Guam is largely a raised limestone plateau, sections of which have steep vertical cliffs. The south is a mix of high volcanic hills and valleys that contain numerous rivers and waterfalls.

Reef formations surround much of the island. The beaches on the west side tend to be calmer, while those on the east coast have heavier seas. The southern tip of the island has a number of protected bays.

Earthquakes are rare but not unknown. On 8 August 1993 Guam was rocked by the most powerful earthquake to hit Micronesia in a century. The quake, which measured 8.2 on the Richter scale, originated deep in the Mariana trench.

CLIMATE

Guam's climate is uniformly warm and humid throughout the year. Daily temperatures average a low of 72°F (22°C) and a high of 85°F (30°C).

Guam's annual rainfall averages 98 inches (2480mm). The most pleasant weather is during the dry season from January to the end of April when the dominant trade winds, which blow year round from the east or north-east, are strongest. The humidity is also slightly lower in the dry season and during that period the rainfall averages just 4.5 inches (114mm) monthly.

Guam lies in the path of typhoons and strong tropical storms, which are most frequent in the last half of the year but can occur in any month.

GOVERNMENT & POLITICS

Guam is an unincorporated territory of the USA. The Organic Act of Guam, passed in

Supertyphoon Paka

Centred in Micronesia's typhoon alley, Guam has seen plenty of typhoons in its day but nothing like Supertyphoon Paka, which struck on 16 December 1997. Wind gusts recorded at Andersen Air Force Base registered 235.7 miles per hour – the highest wind speed ever recorded – though the full fury of the storm passed 10 miles to the north of Guam. Miraculously no-one died, but 8000 homes and 2000 businesses were wrecked; non-concrete homes were particularly vulnerable. Guam was immediately declared a disaster area, and damages totalled near US$500 million. Not surprisingly, the 1997 Christmas season was full of neither joy nor light – not least because electricity was off for several weeks after the storm.

1950, installed a civilian government and granted all Guamanians US citizenship.

Guam's government structure resembles that of a US state. There's a 15-seat legislature, a governor and a lieutenant governor. But on a national level, Guam does not have a voice on par with the 50 states. The islanders cannot vote in national elections; in 1972 they were finally allowed to send one non-voting representative to the US Congress.

Many Guamanians feel that the Commonwealth of the Northern Mariana Islands brokered a much better deal with the USA than Guam, particularly in terms of self-government, and Guam is constantly trying to change its status from an unincorporated territory to a US commonwealth. But both the Clinton administration and Congress have, in effect, written off Guam's Commonwealth Bill, which was drafted in 1987 and would provide Guam with exemptions from some federal laws. It would also provide for a Chamorro-only vote for its political status.

ECONOMY

Despite the ending of the Cold War, Guam continues to have a heavily militarised economy. The US military maintains 6300 active-duty military personnel on Guam; 60% are with the navy, most of the remainder with the air force.

The biggest employer on the island is not the military, but rather local government. A bloated bureaucracy dubbed GovGuam, it employs over 14,000 people. If you include federal employees, Guam has the highest concentration of government employees of any US political entity.

Tourism, another pillar of the economy, was hard-hit by the Asian financial crisis of the 1990s, which caused many Japanese to stay home. Korean visits also plummeted following the fatal 1997 crash of a Korean jetliner just off Guam's runway.

POPULATION & PEOPLE

Guam's current population is 163,500. Although the Chamorro remain the largest ethnic group, they comprise less than 40% of the population and indigenous-rights groups are concerned that the Chamorro will end up losing control of their island to outsiders.

The next largest ethnic groups are Filipinos and other groups from Micronesia. Guam is also home to sizable numbers of Koreans, Chinese and Japanese as well as fewer numbers of other Pacific peoples.

There are about 23,000 US mainlanders, many of whom are active duty military personnel and their families.

Guam constantly contends with an influx of illegal immigrants – an estimated 700 in 1998 alone – many of whom are trying to enter from China by boat.

ARTS

Indigenous singing, dancing, chanting and cooking are showcased at Guam's many colourful fiestas. Guam has few indigenous handicrafts to speak of, aside from those sold in Hagåtña's Chamorro Village.

SOCIETY & CONDUCT

Present-day Chamorro culture is heavily influenced by the island's Spanish colonial past. The Spanish influence can be seen in the colourful *mestiza*, a full loose-fitting skirt and a frilled sleeveless blouse made of lightweight cotton and commonly patterned with tropical flowers. The mestiza is still worn by Chamorro women on special occasions and for festive events.

RELIGION

Over 90% of Guam's Chamorro population remains staunchly Roman Catholic, and Catholicism has a powerful sway on island culture – from Guam's unyielding anti-abortion laws to village fiestas that still centre around the church.

Chamorro Village Names

The Chamorro are pushing for a reassertion of their language. In 1998 the name of Guam's capital city, Agaña, was changed to Hagåtña, the pre-Spanish name. Legislation reverting the names of all Guam's villages to their original form was expected to pass in late 1999.

Spanish	Chamorro
Agaña	Hagåtña
Agaña Heights	Tutuhan
Tumon	Tomhom
Tamuning	Tamuneng
Dededo	Dededu
Yigo	Yigu
Mong Mong	Mong Mong
Toto	Toto
Maite	Maite'
Barrigada	Barigåda
Yona	Yo'ña
Sinajana	Sinåhånña
Chalan Pago	Chålan Pagu
Ordot	Otdot
Mangilao	Mangilao
Talofofo	Talo'fo'fo'
Merizo	Malesso'
Umatac	Humåtak
Inarajan	Inalåhan
Maina	Ma'Ina
Piti	Piti
Asan	Assan
Sumay	Sumai
Santa Rita	Sånta Rita
Agat	Hågat

LANGUAGE

Spanish never completely replaced the Chamorro language, even though an estimated 75% of modern Chamorro words are derived from Spanish. Although it has more guttural and repeated rhythmic sounds, Chamorro sounds a lot like Spanish.

The Chamorro language was first written by Spanish missionaries who, using their own language as a base, used 'y' for the Chamorro article 'the'. Western scholars later started writing it as 'i'.

Chamorro also has a unique sound that's something like 'dz', which is spelt 'y' in the Spanish style and 'j' in the English style. These two systems for spelling Chamorro words are still in use, so you can expect to see both.

In theory Chamorro and English are the official languages, and both are taught in schools and used in government documents. In practice, however, English is taking over as the language of choice.

Many common Chamorro phrases are the same as in Spanish: 'good morning' is *buenas dias* and 'goodbye' is *adios*.

The common Chamorro greeting is *hafa adai* (pronounced 'hoffa day'). Literally, it means 'what?' but it's sort of a 'hello', 'what's up?' and 'how are you?' all combined. 'Thank you' is *si yuus maasi*.

Facts for the Visitor

SUGGESTED ITINERARIES

Whether you have one day or one week, it's vital to get out of the Tumon Bay/Tamuning area. Guam's sights are individualised and scattered, so you can see a beach (Ritidian Point) one day, a waterfall (Talofofo Falls) the next day, then a cultural attraction (Inarajan) the next day, and so forth.

TOURIST OFFICES
Local Tourist Offices

The Guam Visitors Bureau is located in Tumon (see Information under Around Guam).

Tourist Offices Abroad

Overseas offices of the Guam Visitors Bureau include:

Hong Kong (☎ 540 6456, fax 559 0083) 7th floor West, Savoy Court, 101 Robinson Rd, Hong Kong
Japan (☎ 03-3212 3630, fax 3213 6087) Kokusai Building, 2nd floor, 3-1-1 Marunouchi, Chiyoda-ku, Tokyo 100
Korea (☎ 02-765 6161, fax 765 1134) Communications Korea, 3rd floor, Yeochundo Hoegwan, 1-1 Yeonji-dong, Chongro-ku, Seoul 110-470
Taiwan (☎ 02-2718 7661, fax 2718 7750) Compact Communications, 3rd floor, 150, Tun-Hwa North Road, Taipei 105
USA (☎ 1-800-873 4826, 510-865 5100, fax 865 5165) 1336-C Park Street, Alameda, California 94501

VISAS & DOCUMENTS

Being an unincorporated territory of the USA, visitors require a US visa to enter Guam. Visa requirements and other relevant information is given in the Regional Facts for the Visitor chapter.

MONEY

As is the case in much of Micronesia, the US dollar is the currency used in Guam. See under Money in the Regional Facts for the Visitor chapter for exchange rates and other relevant information.

The Bank of Guam and the Bank of Hawaii are the island's biggest banks, and together they have about 20 branches around Guam. Check the *Yellow Pages* for a list of locations.

Tipping

A tip of 10% to 15% is expected at most restaurants.

POST & COMMUNICATIONS
Post

Guam is under the US postal service and uses US stamps. Post restante mail for Guam must be picked up at the main post office on Route 16 in Barrigada. Mail should be addressed c/o General Delivery GMF, Barrigada, Guam 96921.

The post office has branches in Hagåtña and Tamuning.

Telephone

Guam's international telephone code is ☎ 671, and its largest long-distance carrier is IT&E. IT&E's main office is along Marine Dr in Tamuning and it also has offices in Dededo, Harmon, Agat and Sinajana. It is significantly cheaper to call the USA from Guam than from surrounding islands.

See Information under Around Guam for IT&E's opening hours and rates.

Email & Internet Access

Guam's public library has two overcrowded Internet terminals. The Coffee Beanery, in Tumon's Fountain Plaza, and Crystal Sand Multimedia Services, in Tamuning, also have Internet access. See Information under Around Guam for details.

INTERNET RESOURCES

The Guam Visitors Bureau (Web site www.visitguam.org) has some useful tourist information, as does the government Web site (ns.gov.gu).

BOOKS

Lonely Planet's *Diving & Snorkeling Guam & Yap* has descriptions and underwater photographs of Guam's best dive sites. *Destiny's Landfall – A History of Guam* (University of Hawai'i Press, Honolulu, 1995), by Robert F Rogers, comprehensively and articulately traces Guam's history from Magellan's landing to the present day, with good attention to Chamorro cultural heritage.

MEDIA

The main daily newspaper is the excellent *Pacific Daily News*, which costs US$0.75 on weekdays and US$1.25 on Sundays. It has hefty inside sections devoted to national, regional and international news. The *Guam Variety* is a recently launched daily focusing mainly on local news. *Latte Magazine* is a popular bimonthly local-interest magazine.

All hotels have cable TV, which includes CNN. Local news is broadcast at 6 and 10 pm on KUAM, Channel 8.

Guam has a number of radio stations, ranging from a Christian music station (92 FM) and easy listening (95.5 FM) to rock (98 FM and 105.1 FM).

LAUNDRY

Most of the budget hotels have a coin-operated laundry on the premises, while the larger resort hotels offer a laundry service.

PUBLIC HOLIDAYS & SPECIAL EVENTS

Guam's public holidays fall into two categories: US and Guam holidays. On the former, all government services are closed; on the latter, banks are typically closed while the post office and other federal government services remain open.

New Year's Day 1 January
Martin Luther King's Birthday 3rd Monday in January
President's Day 3rd Monday in February
Guam Discovery Day 1st Monday in March
Easter late March/early April
Memorial Day last Monday in May
US Independence Day 4 July
Liberation Day 21 July
Labor Day 1st Monday in September
Columbus Day 2nd Monday in October
All Souls Day 2 November
Veterans Day 11 November
Thanksgiving last Thursday in November
Immaculate Conception Day 8 December
Christmas Day 25 December

Guam Discovery Day marks Magellan's landing and is celebrated at Umatac, where festivities include a re-enactment of the landing, cultural dances, sports competitions, arts and crafts and the making of *tuba* (coconut wine).

Liberation Day celebrations bring feasts, fireworks and the largest parade of the year, which proceeds along Marine Dr.

For events dates, consult the Guam Visitors Bureau or the Guam phone book.

Guam's many fiestas take place year round:

January
Asan, Tumon, Chalan Pago, Mongmong
February
Maina, Yigo

Fiestas

Each of Guam's 19 villages hosts an annual fiesta honouring its patron saint. The Catholic-inspired fiestas are community affairs that begin with a Saturday evening mass in the local church and proceed with a procession around the village carrying a statue of the saint and then a buffet feast in the church hall. The festivities continue on Sunday, when groups of friends gather in private houses.

Fiestas are celebrated on the weekend closest to the saint's feast day so the dates vary slightly each year. The idea is to attract as many people as possible to the festivities, so everyone is welcome.

Guam's largest fiesta is held in Hagåtña on 8 December, a public holiday that honours Our Lady of the Immaculate Conception, the island's patron saint.

March
Inarajan
April
Barrigada, Merizo, Agafa Gumas
May
Malojloj, Santa Rita
June
Tamuning, Chalan Pago, Toto, Ordot
July
Agat
August
Piti, Barrigada
September
Canada-Barrigada, Hagåtña, Talofofo, Mangilao
October
Yona, Umatac, Sinajana
November
Agaña Heights
December
Dededo

ACTIVITIES
Diving & Snorkelling

Guam's waters are home to numerous war wrecks and a rich array of marine life – there are more than 800 species of fish and 300 species of coral.

There are a couple of dozen popular dive spots on the west coast, many in or south of Apra Harbor. One of the best known, for advanced divers, is Blue Hole at the end of Orote Peninsula. At about 60 feet (18m) a perpendicular shaft in the reef can be descended by divers in a free fall. At about 125 feet (38m) there's a window that allows divers to exit. The area is known for its large fish and superb visibility. At night there are flashlight fish in the deeper reaches.

One of the more unusual wreck dives is to the Tokai Maru, a Japanese freighter bombed during WWII in Apra Harbor. As it sank it landed beside the *Cormoran*, a German cruiser scuttled during WWI, which rests on its side on the ocean floor. At about 95 feet (29m) you can have one hand on each war. The uppermost part of the *Tokai Maru* is only 40 feet (12m) from the water's surface, so it can make a good beginner dive.

Some of the better snorkelling spots are Gun Beach in the Tumon Bay area (when the seas are calm), Ypao Beach next to the Hilton in Tumon, Outhouse Beach on the north side of Apra Harbor and the Piti Bomb Holes in Piti.

Dive Shops The five-star PADI Micronesian Divers Association (MDA; ☎ 472 6321, fax 477 6329, @ islands@mdaguam .com), at 855 Marine Drive, Piti, Guam 96925, is the region's largest dive operation and is geared to provide for English speakers. Located opposite the Piti Bomb Holes, MDA offers free guided shore dives at 9 am and 1 pm on Saturday and Sunday (two-tank gear can be rented for US$28). MDA offers a wide range of boat dives, most priced at US$40 for two tanks, plus gear rental.

The Coral Reef Marine Center (☎ 646 4895, fax 649 5209, @ chime@ite.net), behind the Tamuning post office, does not organise dives but sells, services and rents equipment at reasonable rates and fills tanks for US$3. A regulator or BC can be rented for US$5, tanks for US$4, mask and snorkel for US$3, fins for US$3 and weight belts for US$2.

Bob Odell at Real World Diving Co (☎ 646 8903, fax 646 4957), Box 2800, Hagåtña, Guam 96932, operating at the side of the PIA Resort in Tumon, offers some of the most exciting dives on the island and is a master at finding manta rays and dolphins. Two-tank boat dives cost US$95, but ask about the local rate which is US$15 cheaper. Real World offers half-day boat tours that include snorkelling and dolphin watching for US$65, gear included.

Guam Tropical Dive Station (☎ 477 2774, fax 477 2775, ✉ gtds@ite.net), on Marine Dr in Aniqua, offers two-tank dives for US$95, including lunch and hotel pick-up. You can hire regulator, BC, tanks and weights for US$15, a two-tank set for US$19 and a snorkel set for US$10.

Swimming

The calmest waters for swimming are usually along the west coast, with the greater Tumon Bay area having the busiest beaches. There are no fees at any of the island's 20 beach parks, many of which have showers, toilets and picnic tables. Before entering the water, check for jellyfish which occasionally float in, especially when the trade winds pick up.

There's a large public swimming pool on E O'Brien Dr in Hagåtña (☎ 472 8718), opposite the Agaña Shopping Center. It's open from 11 am to 8.30 pm Tuesday to Friday and from 11 am to 7.30 pm on weekends (admission US$0.50).

The resort hotels have swimming areas for their guests, many overseen by lifeguards.

Surfing

While Guam is not a prime surfing locale, surfing is possible. The best conditions are between December and June. Beginners generally prefer Talofofo Bay, while the more experienced surf the channel near Agaña Boat Basin. Surfboards can be rented at Primo Surf (☎ 472 2053), on Route 4 in Hagåtña, for US$30 to US$45.

Other Water Sports

Windsurfing is popular in Tumon Bay and in Cocos Lagoon off Merizo.

The Marianas Yacht Club (☎ 477 3533) at Apra Harbor sponsors several races throughout the year. These include the

Guam-Japan Goodwill Regatta in late February, the Rota and Return Race on Memorial Day weekend and the Round the Island Race in December. The club also has information about charter boats and sailing lessons.

The Marianas Paddle Sports Racing Association (☎ 649 6772) sponsors numerous races in six-person outrigger canoes in Tumon Bay and Apra Harbor. You can also catch an outrigger ride from Alupang Beach Club's branch (ABC; ☎ 649 9027) in the Pacific Star Hotel for US$16 an hour. ABC rents a range of other beach equipment, including kayaks (US$16 per hour) and snorkel gear (US$5 per hour).

Some of the larger Tumon Bay hotels, such as the Hyatt, have beach huts that offer outrigger canoe rides (through ABC) and windsurfing lessons and rent out catamarans and other water sports equipment, though prices tend to be high.

Fishing

Deep-sea fishing boats leave from Agaña Boat Basin and Apra Harbor on the search for marlin, wahoo, yellowfin tuna, sailfish, barracuda and mahimahi. A 1153-pound Pacific blue marlin, caught off Ritidian Point by a Guamanian in 1969, broke the world record at the time. For information on chartering a fishing boat, contact the Guam Visitors Bureau (☎ 646 5278).

Hiking

Guam has many hikes, ranging from short trails at Asan Park and up to the Piti guns to hardier hikes to Sella Bay and Mt Jumullong Manglo in southern Guam. Details are given under southern Guam later in this chapter.

The Department of Parks & Recreation sponsors guided forest walks most Saturdays, meeting at the Paseo Recreation Building in Paseo de Susana in Hagåtña and usually departing at 9 am (meet there earlier). Hikes are rated according to difficulty, and children aged under 12 are not allowed on the more strenuous routes. The cost is US$2 and hikers must provide their own transportation to the trailhead. Destinations include remote jungle war sites and secluded waterfalls; call ☎ 477 8280 or ☎ 477 8197 for the current schedule. David Lotz's glossy booklet *The Best Tracks on Guam – A Guide to the Hiking Trails*, available from the Bestseller bookshop, gives a thorough overview of the island's hiking opportunities.

Tennis

The Agaña Tennis Center (☎ 472 6270), next to the public pool in Hagåtña, has four courts open to the public on a first-come, first-served basis. There's no fee and the gates are never locked – the last player to leave each night must turn off the lights!

There are other public tennis courts scattered around the island, including two across Marine Dr from the ITC building, but most of those outside Hagåtña are not well maintained. Some larger hotels have tennis courts for their guests.

Golf

Guam has copious golf courses. The prices that follow include green fees and cart for weekday/weekend hire:

Alte Guam Golf Resort (☎ 632 1111) Dededo, 27 holes, US$130/170
Country Club of the Pacific (☎ 789 1361) Yona, 18 holes, US$100/130
Guam International Country Club (☎ 632 4445) Dededo, 18 holes, US$120/160
Guam Municipal Golf Course (☎ 632 1197) Dededo, 18 holes, US$110/150
Guam Takayama Golf Club (☎ 789 1612) Yona, 18 holes, US$80/97
Mangilao Golf Club (☎ 734 1111) Mangilao, 18 holes, US$120/170
Talofofo Golf Resort (☎ 789 5555) Talofofo, 18 holes, US$130/170
Tumon Golf Driving Range (☎ 649 8337) Upper Tumon, US$4 for a bucket of balls

Bowling

Guam has two bowling alleys: Central Lanes (☎ 646 9081) and Royal Lanes (☎ 646 8847), both in Tamuning. The cost to play a lane is US$3, though Central Lane drops to US$1.50 on weekday afternoons. Expect crowds on weekends.

Other Activities

The *Atlantis* submarine (☎ 477 4166, fax 477 4171) runs eight dives a day to Gab Gab Reef II in Apra Harbor. The 65-foot (19m) sub carries 48 passengers and has 26 viewport windows. Passengers spend about an hour on the sub, which goes to a depth of 50 to 90 feet (15 to 27.5m). The regular cost is US$96, including hotel pick-up; the local rate is US$50.

More moderately priced tours are offered on the *Nautilus Guam* (☎ 646 8331, fax 649 3253), a semi-submersible boat that has an underwater lower deck with port windows. It goes out from Apra Harbor for 45-minute cruises and charges US$25, if you avoid the inflated hotel pick-up rate, which pushes it up to US$55.

For something more local, the Adventure River Cruise (☎ 646 1710) run by Turtle Tours takes a catamaran riverboat up the Talofofo River to an ancient *latte* stone site where craft demonstrations are given. The outings begin at 9 am and 1 pm, last two hours and cost US$55, including pick-up at Tumon hotels. However, if you get to Talofofo Bay yourself, you might be able to join the tour at the US$20 local rate.

Discover Guam (☎ 649 8687, fax 649 3487) is a local company with various English-speaking tours of WWII sites, 'jungle adventures', a village cultural tour, and even a bar-hopping tour. Tours cost US$45 to US$85 per person.

ACCOMMODATION
Camping

Camping information is available from the Department of Parks & Recreation (☎ 477 8279) in Tiyan, behind the Revenue & Tax building in Barrigada. The office is open from 8 am to 5 pm weekdays. Camping permits are US$2 per head per night – it's best to go in the morning to allow for processing. Shelters are an additional US$10.

Camping is not that common on Guam. If you do camp alone or with just a couple of people it's advisable not to choose a roadside park as there's likely to be a few rowdy drinkers cruising the roads at night. Crime is also a factor.

Dano Park on isolated Cocos Island is one of more than 20 approved camping locations in the park system and is one of the more frequently recommended spots. Many of the parks have shelters. Digging and hammering in stakes is prohibited.

Hotels

The majority of Guam's 8700 hotel rooms are in the high-rises lining Tumon Bay, and their numbers keep on growing. These resorts are geared to Japanese package tourists and offer poor value for independent travellers. However, some of the international chain hotels, such as Hilton and Hyatt and the upcoming Outrigger, offer periodic promotions during which rates are substantially discounted.

Be aware that peak Japanese vacation periods extend from late December to early March and from June to September, and hotels will be crowded then. Generally, the farther you go from Tumon Bay, the easier it gets to find a room during those times.

Outside of Tumon Bay there are a number of small hotels. The majority are on or near Marine Dr in Tamuning, Hagåtña and Upper Tumon. A number of down-market hotels rent rooms by the hour to love-lorn travellers, and these are generally less well maintained. Avoid these spots if they make you feel uncomfortable. Many of the larger hotels charge for hotel transfers and local phone calls.

All rooms in Guam hotels have private bathrooms. An 11% room tax is added onto all rates. Almost all hotels, except for a few at the bottom end, accept Visa and Master-Card.

FOOD

Guam's multiethnic population and thousands of tourists support more than a hundred restaurants in the Hagåtña-Tumon area. The rainbow of cuisines includes Chamorro, Japanese, Chinese, Korean, Mexican, Indian, Italian, Vietnamese, Filipino and Thai. The restaurants at the luxury hotels generally excel in Japanese food. Most of the big hotels also feature a Sunday brunch – this is quite a popular feature so it's wise to make reservations.

Guam's tap water is treated and safe to drink.

SHOPPING

Guam isn't noted for its handicrafts and most of what passes for local souvenirs, including tacky coconut-husk carvings and shell items, are made in the Philippines. One reprieve is Chamorro Village in Hagåtña, where a law stipulates that wares be made locally. Handicraft stalls proliferate on Wednesday nights when Chamorro Village stays open until 9 pm.

Guam is the best place in Micronesia to buy supplies you may need on other islands. Islanders from around Micronesia make pilgrimages to Guam's new Kmart, a few miles (4km) south of the Micronesia Mall, which stocks everything from sun screen to beer to film at cheap prices.

Guam's main shopping centres are geared towards Japanese package tourists. The largest of these is the Micronesia Mall in Dededo, closely followed by the Premium Outlet Center in Tamuning and the Agaña Shopping Center in Hagåtña.

In Tumon Bay, the largest of many designer complexes is DFS, a duty-free shop that resembles an upmarket department store.

US citizens returning to the USA from Guam are allowed a higher than usual duty-free exemption on articles acquired abroad. They are permitted US$800 worth of duty-free items (US$400 is usual).

Getting There & Away

Guam is the main gateway to Micronesia. There are direct flights to Guam from Honolulu, Japan, Australia, Indonesia, the Philippines, South Korea and Taiwan. There is no departure tax to be paid when leaving Guam.

For complete information on getting to Guam refer to the Getting There & Away chapter earlier in this book.

AIR
Airports & Airlines
The busy Guam International Airport in Tamuning shines from its recent US$242 million expansion. The airport has a Thomas Cook foreign exchange booth, which, unlike most Micronesian banks, will exchange travellers cheques in foreign currency. It also has an information booth, pay phones, a hotel courtesy phone, car rental booths, a taxi stand and a duty-free shop. In addition there's a new food court and a branch of Shirley's Coffee Shop (open from 3 am daily).

Continental also has a deluxe President's Club Lounge, available to members only.

The following airlines have offices in Guam:

Air Nauru (☎ 642 4253) in Pacific Star Hotel, Tumon
All Nippon Airways (☎ 642 5555) Chalan Pasaheru, Tamuning
Asiana Airlines (☎ 646 9131) Marine Dr, Tamuning
Continental Airlines (☎ 647 6453) Route 14, Tamuning
Freedom Air (☎ 649 2294) in the local terminal
Japan Airlines (☎ 646 9195) in Guam Premium Outlets, Tamuning
Northwest Airlines (☎ 649 1665) Marine Dr, Tamuning
Pacific Island Aviation (☎ 647 3600) in the local terminal

SEA
Apra Harbor is the only port of entry for Guam. Visiting yachts should contact the Marianas Yacht Club (☎ 477 3533), at the Apra Harbor, on arrival.

Getting Around

It's virtually impossible to get around Guam without a car, especially if you want to tour the whole island. Hitchhiking is rarely practised and the public bus service isn't extensive or frequent enough to be practical for sightseeing.

TO/FROM THE AIRPORT
There are car rental booths and taxis at the airport, but the public bus does not serve the airport. Most of the hotels provide airport transport (see the Places to Stay section later in this chapter). The upmarket hotels generally charge US$15 return.

BUS
Guam Mass Transit Authority (☎ 475 7433) operates a limited public bus system that primarily serves central Guam. The most useful route for visitors runs from Hagåtña to Tamuning, Tumon Bay and the Micronesia Mall. Another line runs between Hagåtña and Agat, and another between Hagåtña and the University of Guam. Buses run approximately every hour from 5.30 am to 7.30 pm from Monday to Saturday, and on a limited schedule from 7.30 am to 6.30 pm on Sunday and public holidays. Rides cost US$1 (US$3 for a day pass) and US$0.35 for students, disabled passengers and seniors. The bus should make a special stop to pick you up if you call, but haste is unlikely.

Shuttle Bus
Every 10 to 15 minutes a shuttle bus runs between the malls and the major Tumon Bay hotels. Schedules are available at the malls or at the hotels. The buses operate roughly between 10 am and 9.30 pm and cost US$2 to US$5.

One shuttle operator is Turtle Tours (☎ 646 1710), which has buses between Kmart, the Tumon hotels and the DFS complex; another goes just between the malls. LamLam Tours (☎ 649 5314) runs buses from the Tumon hotels to Micronesia Mall and Guam Premium Outlets. Two other shuttle companies are Guam Sanco Transit (☎ 646 1548) and Micronesia Hospitality (☎ 649 2488).

CAR
Taxi
Taxi fares start at US$1.80 on flag fall. It's US$3 for the first mile (1.6km) and US$0.60 for each quarter mile (400m) thereafter. Perplexingly, the meters are also time-oriented: They will keep ticking as the built-in timer charges US$0.60 for every two minutes. Each piece of heavy luggage

is US$1. From Tumon Bay it costs about US$10 to catch a taxi to the airport or to Micronesia Mall and US$15 to US$20 to the Agaña Shopping Center. A 10% tip is customary.

Outside the airport, Kmart and the malls, you'll probably have to phone for a taxi. The larger companies include Hafa Adai Taxi Service (☎ 477 9629) and City Taxi (☎ 646 1155).

Rental
Budget (☎ 647 1446), Hertz (☎ 646 5875), National (649 0110), Toyota (☎ 642 3200), Avis (☎ 646 8156) and Nissan (☎ 632 7300) all have rental booths on the baggage claim level at the airport. Thrifty (☎ 646 6555), which is a mile (1.6km) from the airport, has a free airport shuttle. Prices tend to start at US$50 with unlimited mileage for a two-door manual subcompact, though in spring 1999 the slumping economy occasioned discounts of up to US$10.

Optional collision damage waivers (CDW) are available for an additional US$16 a day. Most companies will deliver cars to your hotel at no extra cost.

Dedicated budget travellers can try Cars Unlimited (☎ 646 7261), next to Winchell's Donuts on Route 1 in Tamuning. Older, run-down cars are rented for US$25 a day (US$140 a week) with unlimited mileage. It's always wise to agree in writing beforehand on all the bumps and scratches on the vehicle. Also be aware of the safety risks involved in driving an older, beaten-up car.

If you're on Guam for more than 30 days, you will need to get a local driving licence. This may be a good idea anyway, as flashing local identification may get you the cheaper local rates on everything from hotel rooms to sights to transportation. Bring your old licence, US$5 and half a brain (to pass the written test) to the Department of Revenue and Taxation, Motor Vehicle Division (☎ 475 5000), up Route 8 in Barrigada.

Driving is on the right-hand side of the road. The speed limit is 35 mph (56km/h) unless otherwise posted.

BICYCLE
Bicycles can be rented for US$13 a day at the Japanese-speaking Osaka Convenience Store (☎ 646 6080), about a quarter mile (400m) beyond the Visitors Bureau towards Tumon Bay along Route 4. It's the shop with the bicycles outside. Bicycle rental companies tend to come and go quickly; ask at your hotel or the tourist office about current operators.

Around Guam

Orientation
Most of Guam's main tourist and business facilities are centred in Tumon, Tamuning and Hagåtña, which cluster together on the western side of Guam.

The airport is in Tamuning, about a mile (1.6km) north-east of Route 1, which is also called Marine Drive.

A 50-mile (80km) road circles the lower half of the island, which is the most scenic and historic part of Guam.

Most of the driving around Guam is on excellent paved roads.

Maps A good map published by the Department of Public Works is available free of charge upon request at the Guam tourist office.

Information
Tourist Offices The Guam Visitors Bureau (☎ 646 5278, fax 646 8861, ✉ guaminfo@visitguam.org) is at 401 San Vitores Rd in Tumon, just north of the Hilton. It has helpful staff and a profusion of brochures and maps in English and Japanese, and is open from 8 am to 5 pm daily. Anyone planning to camp or to pursue eco-tourism in-depth should request a copy of *Guam's Natural, Cultural & Historical Guidebook*.

See Tourist Offices in the Facts for the Visitor section earlier for Guam tourist offices abroad.

Money ATMs are ubiquitous in Tumon, Tamuning and Hagåtña, and major credit cards are accepted at most of Guam's hotels, restaurants, and shops.

Post All poste restante mail for Guam (even mail marked Hagåtña) must be picked up at the less-than-central main post office on Route 16 in Barrigada. It is open from 9 am to 5 pm Monday to Friday and from 1 to 4 pm Saturday. Most mail is held for 30 days but express mail is held for only five days.

The branch post office in central Hagåtña is on Chalan Santo Papa, and the branch in Tamuning is behind the ITC Building.

Telephone You can make international calls through your hotel, generally for inflated rates, or head to the offices of IT&E (☎ 646 8886), Guam's largest long-distance carrier. The main office is along Marine Dr in Tamuning near Cinemas A&B and the Tamuning Plaza Hotel. IT&E has booths from which you can call for the following rates: USA, US$0.40 a minute; Australia, US$0.89 a minute; London, US$0.89 a minute. Using a phonecard, available at IT&E, the rates may drop a bit. The office is open from 8 am to 6 pm weekdays, from 8 am to 5 pm Saturday, from 8 am to noon Sunday and from 9 am to 1 pm on public holidays.

Email & Internet Access Guam's public library has two Internet terminals, but queues can be long and the time limit is 30 minutes. See under Libraries for opening hours.

The Coffee Beanery, in Fountain Plaza about half a mile (800m) north-east of the Visitors Bureau along Route 14, has three computers and charges US$8 per hour for Internet access.

Crystal Sand Multimedia Services (☎ 646 2227) in Tamuning has 12 terminals for US$8 per hour. Crystal Sand plans to open Cyber-Up cafe, with 14 additional Internet stations. If you're coming from Hagåtña, turn left off Marine Dr onto Route 30. At the first stop sign, turn right and Crystal Sand is past Payless on the left-hand side of the road.

Travel Agencies Among Guam's innumerable travel agencies, Travel Pacificana (☎ 472 8884), Guam's American Express Travel service representative, is recommended. The office is at 207 Martyr St in central Hagåtña and is open from 8 am to 5.30 pm weekdays and from 9 am to noon Saturday.

Bookshops Bestseller, on the second floor of the Micronesia Mall just north of Tumon (and with a branch in Agaña Shopping Center), is the largest of Micronesia's bookshops. It has a wide variety of magazines and sells the Sunday *New York Times* (US$6). Faith Bookstore, in Agaña Shopping Center, has a comprehensive section of travel and local books.

Libraries The Guam public library (☎ 472 6417), on the corner of Route 4 and W O'Brien Dr in central Hagåtña, is open from 9.30 am to 6 pm on Monday, Wednesday, and Friday, from 9.30 am to 8 pm on Tuesday and Thursday, from 10 am to 4 pm on Saturday and from noon to 4 pm on Sunday. It has two free and much-in-demand Internet terminals. There are other public libraries in Barrigada, Dededo, Agat, Merizo and Yona.

There's also a good general library at the University of Guam, as well as a more Pacific-oriented research library at the university's Micronesian Area Research Center.

Weather Information For the latest pre-recorded weather forecast, including wind, wave and tide updates, dial ☎ 711.

Medical Services The main civilian hospital is the Guam Memorial Hospital (☎ 647 2330) on Route 30 in Tamuning. The emergency room can be reached on ☎ 647 2489. The Naval Hospital (☎ 344 9232), along Route 7 just above Hagåtña, will take civilians in emergencies only. For routine medical issues, the Seventh-Day Adventist Clinic (☎ 636 0894) on Ypao Rd in Tamuning has a good service.

Divers with the bends (decompression sickness) are sent to SRF Guam Recompression Chamber (☎ 339 7143) at the naval base, which is staffed 24 hours. The Crisis Hotline is ☎ 477 4357.

GUAM

Emergency For police, fire or ambulance emergencies dial ☎ 911. The non-emergency police number is ☎ 472 8911.

Access to US Military Bases The land administered by the US air force and the US navy has many historical landmarks worth visiting and many hiking trails. Highlights of the navy's land include a fine naval museum, and the air force has the world's largest operational fire-fighting tanks.

Civilians are not allowed onto either military base without a pass. To obtain a day-pass to visit navy land, call the Navy Public Affairs Office (☎ 339 2115). It may clear you for a day visit; you'll need to present your driving licence and car rental agreement to pick up the pass. The US air force is a bit more parsimonious with passes. It's best to fax your request to public affairs (☎/fax 366 4202); headline it 36 ABW, Attn Community Affairs. Emphasise that you are interested in learning about air force history and that your visit is not tied to a commercial venture.

Hagåtña

The capital city of Hagåtña (pronounced Hag-**aht**-nya), formerly named Agaña, has been the main centre of Guam since the Spanish period. With its parks, bridges and historic sites it's a pleasant place to spend a few hours sightseeing. If you have a car, it's easiest to park in the area by Chamorro Village. From there you can visit most of the sights on foot.

Plaza de España Plaza de España, in the heart of Hagåtña, is a peaceful refuge of Spanish-era ruins, old stone walls and flowering trees.

The plaza was the centre of Spanish administration from 1669 and served as the hub of religious, cultural and government activities. US naval governors, who replaced the Spanish administrators in 1898, continued to use it as a seat of government, as did the Japanese during WWII.

Buildings once completely surrounded the central park area and included schools, priests' quarters, the governor's residence, a hospital, military compound, arsenal and town hall. Most were constructed of *ifil* wood and a concoction of lime mortar and coral called *manposteria*, and were roofed with clay tiles. Only a few of these buildings survived the US pre-invasion bombings in July 1944.

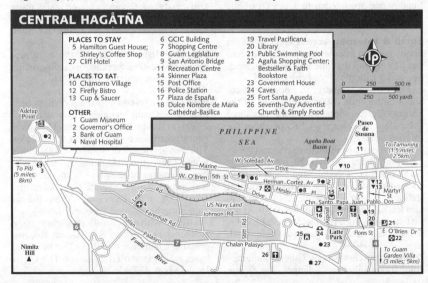

CENTRAL HAGÅTÑA

PLACES TO STAY
5 Hamilton Guest House;
    Shirley's Coffee Shop
27 Cliff Hotel

PLACES TO EAT
10 Chamorro Village
12 Firefly Bistro
13 Cup & Saucer

OTHER
1 Guam Museum
2 Governor's Office
3 Bank of Guam
4 Naval Hospital

6 GCIC Building
7 Shopping Centre
8 Guam Legislature
9 San Antonio Bridge
11 Recreation Centre
14 Skinner Plaza
15 Post Office
16 Police Station
17 Plaza de España
18 Dulce Nombre de Maria
    Cathedral-Basilica

19 Travel Pacificana
20 Library
21 Public Swimming Pool
22 Agaña Shopping Center;
    Bestseller & Faith
    Bookstore
23 Government House
24 Caves
25 Fort Santa Agueda
26 Seventh-Day Adventist
    Church & Simply Food

Among those that remain is the **Garden House**, which once served as a storage shed. A minute's walk north brings you to the **Chocolate House**, a small white circular building with a pointed tiled roof. It's so named because it was used by the wives of Spanish governors to serve afternoon refreshments, most commonly hot chocolate, to their guests.

Immediately west of the Chocolate House are the remains of **Casa Gobierno**, the Governor's Palace. The house itself is long gone but a raised, open-air terrace that once served as its foundation remains intact. Also notable are the three stone arches that are used as an entrance into the adjacent garden. The arches date from 1736 and were originally part of the arsenal.

There's a 10.5 foot (3m) roadside **statue** of Pope John Paul II, north of the plaza on the site where he held Mass on a visit to Guam in 1981. Uniquely, this pope revolves, making one complete turn every 24 hours. Near the statue is a **war memorial** honouring Guamanians killed during the Japanese invasion of 10 December 1941.

Dulce Nombre de Maria Cathedral-Basilica The newly renovated basilica in the Plaza de España was first built in 1669, although the current building dates to 1958. Chief Quipuha and other Chamorro chiefs and church leaders are buried beneath the basilica floor.

Above the main altar is a 12-inch **statue** of Santa Marian Camarin, carved in ironwood and with human hair and a face made of ivory. Local lore says that it was found in the waters off Merizo in the early 1800s by a fisherman who watched as the figurine was guided to shore by two gold crabs, each with a lighted candle between its claws.

The basilica is the main scene of activity during Hagåtña's two annual fiestas, which honour the Sweet Name of Mary, in early September, and the Feast of the Immaculate Conception, on 8 December.

Latte Park The **latte stones** in Latte Park, at the base of Kasamata Hill, are thought to

---

Latte Stones

Latte stones are the most visible remains of early Chamorro culture. The upright posts were quarried from limestone and the rounded top capstones were of either limestone or brain coral. The stones are of such antiquity that at the time of the first Western contact the islanders no longer knew what their purpose had been. Historians now believe the stones were used as foundation pillars for men's houses and for the homes of nobility. *Latte* stones vary from a few feet high to as tall as 20 feet.

NED FRIARY

---

be house pillars dating from about AD 500. They were moved to this site from an ancient Chamorro village in the south-central interior of Guam.

There are a number of Japanese-era **caves**, built by Chamorro forced labour, in the hill face at the park and farther west along O'Brien Dr. The caves in the park have been reinforced with cinder blocks and converted into fallout shelters.

Government House The governor's residence, called Government House (☎ 477 9850), is a Spanish-style structure built in 1952 on Kasamata Hill, one-third of a mile (500m) up Route 7 from O'Brien Dr. It has a panoramic view of Hagåtña and a **visitor gallery** with a small collection of Chamorro beads, baskets, model canoes, and the First Lady's collections.

If you're on foot, it takes about 10 minutes to reach Government House from Latte Stone Park. Visitors are requested to call before coming.

Fort Santa Agueda All that remains of Fort Santa Agueda is part of its stone foundation, built of coral and burnt limestone. The fort, which once had 10 cannons, was built in 1800 as a lookout, and this is the best reason to visit it now. A 10-minute walk from Government House, the view it affords of Hagåtña and the turquoise waters of the bay is unbeatable!

This is also the site of Guam's first Catholic mission, established in 1668, though nothing remains from that era. The fort is on the first road on the right, after heading uphill from Government House.

Skinner Plaza Guam's first civilian governor, Carlton Skinner, lends his name to this rather nondescript grassy strip. It contains a few memorials to Guam's war heroes, including a **statue** of General Douglas MacArthur.

San Antonio Bridge The San Antonio Bridge, also known as the 'Old Spanish Bridge' or *To lai Achu*, was built of cut stone in 1800 to cross an artificial branch of the Agaña River. The bridge survived WWII bombing raids but during the reconstruction of Hagåtña the canal it spanned was filled and the river diverted. The San Antonio Bridge now crosses just a shallow pool, though the park-like setting with its seasonal flame trees is attractive. A stone plaque on the bridge honours St Anthony of Padua.

Near the bridge is a statue of **Sirena the Mermaid**. According to legend, Sirena was a girl whose mother turned her into a mermaid because of her disobedience.

Paseo de Susana Paseo de Susana, north of central Hagåtña, sits upon an artificial peninsula that was created during the Hagåtña reconstruction. The military, needing to dispose of the rubble and debris of the levelled city, opted to bulldoze it here as coastal landfill.

KATE GALBRAITH

Sirena the Mermaid

Today it's a popular park and recreation centre, as well as the site of Hagåtña's public market. Known as **Chamorro Village**, the market has kiosks with food vendors, produce sellers and a few handicraft artists. The park's **baseball stadium** is used by Guam's league teams and as a winter training camp by the Yomiuri Giants, a top Japanese major league baseball team.

The **Agaña Boat Basin** is along the west side of the park. At the park's northern tip there's a tacky miniature replica of the **Statue of Liberty** and beyond that a breakwater where local surfers challenge the waves.

In the south-east section of the park, a **statue of Chief Quipuha** stands forever condemned to survey Hagåtña's congested traffic on Marine Dr. Quipuha was Hagåtña's highest ranking chief when the first mission was built on Guam, and he was the first Chamorro adult to be baptised. Under Jesuit persuasion, Quipuha donated the land for Guam's first Catholic church, the site of the present Dulce Nombre de Maria Cathedral-Basilica.

Tumon Bay (Tomhom)

Tumon Bay, the tourist centre of Guam, is Micronesia's most developed resort area. Its fringing white-sand beach is lined with

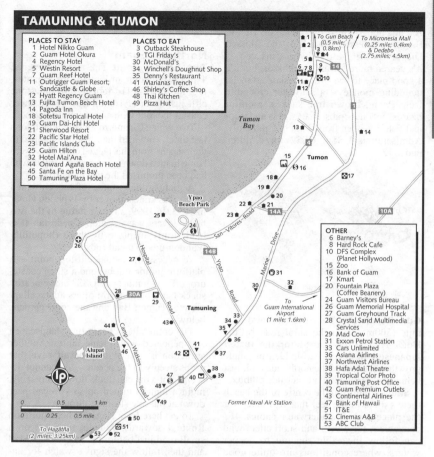

TAMUNING & TUMON

PLACES TO STAY
1 Hotel Nikko Guam
2 Guam Hotel Okura
4 Regency Hotel
5 Westin Resort
7 Guam Reef Hotel
11 Outrigger Guam Resort;
   Sandcastle & Globe
12 Hyatt Regency Guam
13 Fujita Tumon Beach Hotel
14 Pagoda Inn
18 Sotetsu Tropical Hotel
19 Guam Dai-Ichi Hotel
21 Sherwood Resort
22 Pacific Star Hotel
23 Pacific Islands Club
25 Guam Hilton
32 Hotel Mai'Ana
44 Onward Agaña Beach Hotel
45 Santa Fe on the Bay
50 Tamuning Plaza Hotel

PLACES TO EAT
3 Outback Steakhouse
9 TGI Friday's
30 McDonald's
34 Winchell's Doughnut Shop
35 Denny's Restaurant
41 Marianas Trench
46 Shirley's Coffee Shop
48 Thai Kitchen
49 Pizza Hut

OTHER
6 Barney's
8 Hard Rock Cafe
10 DFS Complex
   (Planet Hollywood)
15 Zoo
16 Bank of Guam
17 Kmart
20 Fountain Plaza
   (Coffee Beanery)
24 Guam Visitors Bureau
26 Guam Memorial Hospital
27 Guam Greyhound Track
28 Crystal Sand Multimedia
   Services
29 Mad Cow
31 Exxon Petrol Station
33 Cars Unlimited
36 Asiana Airlines
37 Northwest Airlines
38 Hafa Adai Theatre
39 Tropical Color Photo
40 Tamuning Post Office
42 Guam Premium Outlets
43 Continental Airlines
47 Bank of Hawaii
51 IT&E
52 Cinemas A&B
53 ABC Club

hotels, clubs and restaurants. Duty-free shops and upmarket eateries join Planet Hollywood, the glitzy Sandcastle and other tourist-targeted businesses along the road. Among other changes are the addition of the towering new Outrigger Hotel and the burial of telephone wires underground. Overall, Tumon is geared to Japanese package tourists, which translates to high prices for everything from hotels to dinner shows to diving.

Tumon Bay is quite shallow at low tide and it's possible to wade clear out to the reef. If you're not a strong swimmer be cautious, as it's possible to unwittingly get stuck on the reef by incoming tides.

Governor Joseph F Flores Beach Park
Governor Joseph F Flores Beach is a large beach park along the south-west side of Tumon Bay. It was once the location of an ancient Chamorro village and in the late 1800s was the site of a penal and leper colony.

The park has playground equipment, picnic facilities and a large beachfront with white sand and turquoise waters. It's a popular weekend spot for local families and sometimes hosts festivals and other celebrations.

Zoo Jimmy Cushing runs a small, funky zoo and aquarium (☎ 646 1477) on Tumon Bay, opposite the Church of the Blessed Diego. Tourists largely bypass the zoo as it's geared more towards local kids, but it's a good place to see 'Micronesian' animals, including monkeys, a saltwater crocodile from Palau, brown tree snakes, monitor lizards, coconut crabs, sharks, eels and tropical fish. It's open from 9 am to 5 pm daily. Admission is US$4, US$2 for children under 12.

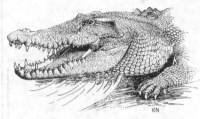

Saltwater crocodile

Gun Beach Gun Beach is one-third of a mile (500m) down the coral road by the Hotel Nikko. It's named for the **rusted Japanese gun** that is half-hidden in jungle growth at the foot of the north-side cliff, just behind the remains of a beachside **pillbox**.

Straight out from the centre of the beach there's a cut in the reef that was made for the placement of underwater cables. It's convenient for divers and snorkellers who can follow the cable run out to deeper waters, where conditions are quite good when the water's calm.

The sand at Gun Beach is fascinating, as it's largely comprised of tiny orange grains with little star-shaped points. Known as star sand, it's actually the calcium carbonate shells of a common protozoan found on Guam's reefs.

Gun Beach is pleasant enough, but past the gun and around the point to the north is an even nicer crescent of white sand. At low tide it's possible to wade around the point and at high tide you can swim or snorkel around it. There was once an old Chamorro village in this area and **latte stones** can be

found by following an overgrown trail that leads inland.

Northern Guam

Two Lovers Point The newly reopened Two Lovers Point, or Puntan Dos Amantes, is at the top of a 410-foot (125m) limestone cliff just north of Tumon Bay. It is a sheer coastal lookout with an intriguing legend.

Two young Chamorro lovers, 'united for a last time', entwined their hair and jumped to their deaths from this jagged cliff. They were being hunted down by a Spanish captain who had been promised the girl in marriage.

A giant gilded statue of the entwined lovers was knocked over by Typhoon Omar in 1993. In 1999, a recast **statue** of the two lanky lovers was set atop a pedestal. It is held firmly in place by three (hopefully typhoon-proof) metal rods.

To access the actual clifftop point – a platform jutting out beyond a steep coastal dropoff – you must pay US$3 at the nearby snack bar. The platform offers an excellent view of Tumon Bay and the coral gardens below.

The entire site is beautifully landscaped and peppered with picnic tables. Another attraction is a very deep **basalt cave** that drops steeply to the ocean – you cannot descend but you can look down into it. At night a light is turned on so you can peer down at the tide sloshing through.

To get here from Hagåtña, head north on Route 1 towards Dededo, turn left on a small road just before the Micronesia Mall and then follow the signs – watch for unmarked speed bumps. Two Lovers Point is open from 9 am to 8 pm daily and it's splendid at sunset. Besides the small snack bar, a vendor selling fresh coconut drinks is planned, as is a small art museum.

Ritidian Point At the northernmost tip of Guam, the Fish and Wildlife Service (FWS) administered Ritidian Point (☎ 355 5096), a national **wildlife refuge**, is the site of one of Guam's most pristine sandy beaches. On weekdays, the **beach** is gorgeously empty except for a few stray fishermen. On weekends it fills with families and picnickers. Swimming is possible but keep very close to shore to avoid the vicious currents further out. Besides the beach, the centre has a short path through the coconut-tree jungle, one of few signs that the land is a former coconut plantation. If you call ahead, the FWS might give you a quick tour of the nearby **limestone caves** (a guide is required).

Ritidian Point land is the subject of some controversy. The US navy took over the area in the 1950s, but in the early 1990s decided it didn't need it any more and the FWS eagerly claimed it. Some locals contest this, asserting that the land should revert to whoever owned it prior to the navy's takeover. However, a 1997 court case ruled that the Navy had claimed the land legally, and thus it was legally passed to FWS. With the court battle out of the way, the FWS is going ahead with plans to construct a visitor center on site by late 2000.

The refuge, which is reached by following Route 3 north and then branching left on 3A, is open from 8 am to 5 pm daily. No camping is allowed.

Other Northern Beaches Flanking Ritidian Point, on the island's northern tip, are two of Guam's best beaches: **Tarague Beach** and **Uruno Beach**. However, although these beaches are open to the public the only land access to them is through Andersen Air Force Base and without a visitor pass non-military personnel can't reach them.

South of Uruno Beach is **Tanguisson Beach**, which can be reached by taking the turn-off from Route 1 towards Two Lovers Point. Follow the main sealed road, which passes a sewage treatment plant before winding down to the shore. Tanguisson is a popular place for local picnickers but a huge power plant at the south end of the beach mars the view.

You can reach more appealing sandy beaches by continuing along the road, which runs parallel to the ocean. The final beach, which is about 2 miles (3km) north of Tanguisson and called **Shark's Hole**, has a turquoise hold with very good snorkel-

ling. There are two channels into the hole so beware of the currents.

South Pacific Memorial Park This park in Yigo is a memorial site for those who participated in WWII. The main monument is a 30-foot (9m) **abstract sculpture** of a pair of large white hands folded in prayer, which is surrounded by personalised memorial plaques in Japanese script. A small **chapel** called Queen of Peace is staffed by Buddhist monks.

Steps lead down the hill from the monument to four **caves** that served as the last Japanese Army command post. On 11 August 1944, US soldiers detonated 400-pound blocks of TNT at the opening of the caves. When the caves were reopened a few days later more than 60 bodies were removed, including that of Japanese commander Lieutenant General Hideoyoshi Obata, who had taken his own life. The caves are surrounded by a bamboo forest that creaks in the wind and is spooky enough to conjure up images of restless spirits.

The park, on Route 1 in Yigo, is open from 8 am to 5 pm daily.

University of Guam The University of Guam, which is in Mangilao on the east coast, is noted for its marine lab, a pioneer in the field of marine biology. The university's Micronesian Area Research Center (☎ 734 2921) has an excellent collection of books, maps and documents on the Pacific region, and the library staff are very helpful if you're interested in research.

Southern Guam

If you had only one full day on Guam, you couldn't do better than to rent a car and circle the southern part of the island, taking time to stroll through historic sites and catch the scenery along the way. Southern villages such as Umatac and Inarajan give a glimpse of a more rural Guam, the character of which remains unaffected by tourism.

If you start in Hagåtña and go down the west coast in the morning and up the east coast in the afternoon you'll keep the sun at your back for photography and views.

Ricardo J Bordallo Governor's Complex About a quarter mile (400m) south of Hagåtña on the western coastal road is Adelup Point, which was once heavily fortified by the Japanese. This is now the site of a Spanish-style complex that houses government administration offices.

Guam Museum This worthwhile museum (☎ 477 3325) stands atop a gorgeous ocean overlook on Adelup Point. It occupies an adobe-type building that was once the site of an open-air Spanish plaza. Objects from Guam's long history are displayed here, including an actual outrigger canoe, portraits of Chamorro chiefs, traditional fishing equipment and even stones representing different geological eras. The written explanations are concise and illuminating.

The museum is open 9 am to 4 pm weekdays and 10 am to 2 pm on Saturday. Admission is US$3 for adults, US$1 for students; children under 12 and seniors free.

Route 6 You might want to take the 5-mile (8km) Route 6 loop from Adelup Point through the Nimitz Hill area to Piti. You'll get some views of the west coast as well as glimpses into the island's interior.

About 1½ miles (2.5km) up Route 6 there are two **bunkers** in the hillside, visible on the right-hand side of the road, which once served as a Japanese command post. **Nimitz Hill**, incidentally, takes its name from US Admiral Chester Nimitz, the first commander of the Naval Forces Marianas to take up residence on the hill.

Past the school on Nimitz Hill, in the upper corner of War in the Pacific National Historical Park, is the **Asan Bay Overlook**. It was from here that Japanese soldiers watched in consternation as Americans seized the beaches to reclaim the island. Now the wind-blown overlook is home to a moving new WWII monument, a crescent-shaped stone wall inscribed with the names of US and Chamorro soldiers who perished or suffered during the war.

War in the Pacific National Historical Park This park has a visitor centre and WWII museum in Asan, almost a mile (1.6km) south-west of Adelup Point on Route 1. Period photos and military paraphernalia help present the history of Guam during the war years.

Movies are shown continuously in the centre's **theatre**; the most common is a 30-minute footage film of the US retaking of Guam. You can also request to see anything from the extensive library of tapes, which are in four languages, but you'll need to call ahead to schedule a viewing time. Subjects include Guam's brown tree snake, Chamorro history and culture, environmental issues and battles around the Pacific.

The centre is open from 9 am to 4.30 pm weekdays and from 10 am to 5 pm on weekends. Admission is free, as are brochures that map out the various battle sites around Guam.

A number of separate parcels of land that were WWII battlefield sites are part of the park's historical holdings.

The park's Asan Beach unit includes **Asan Point**, a big, grassy beach park a mile (1.6km) farther south, which has guns, torpedoes and monuments. Asan Beach was one of the major sites of the US invasion in July 1944. An octagonal marble monument flanked by coconut trees was erected on the beach in 1994 to mark the invasion's 50th anniversary. The area is now a favourite kite-flying and picnicking spot. On the south-west side of the park, a 15-minute loop trail takes in a cave and a couple of Japanese gun emplacements.

Piti Bomb Holes & Fish Eye Marine Park The Piti Bomb Holes, carved in the reef about 100 yards offshore from Piti, are ideal for beginner divers as they bottom out at around 30 feet (9m). Seen from Tepungan Beach, the holes look like dark blue circles in the aqua shades of the shallower water. It's just local lore that the holes are bomb craters – they're actually natural sinkholes.

Snorkellers might enjoy the hard yellow corals around the edges of the holes, but the water is deep enough in the centres to make it difficult to see the bottom. Closer to shore you'll see bright blue starfish, zebra damsels, pufferfish and other small tropicals. If you want to snorkel out to the holes rather than wade, the best time is high tide, as otherwise the nearshore waters can be quite shallow. Watch out for strong currents around the holes farthest out.

A new, environmentally controversial underwater observatory, called Fish Eye Marine Park, has been erected in the largest bombhole. The facility is well visited by Japanese tourists and is quite fascinating. Portholes 30 feet (9m) underwater afford close-up views of fish, corals and scuba divers swimming among the fish. This rotund structure is at the end of a long walkway jutting out from the beach. The observatory is open from 9 am to 5 pm weekdays and costs US$20 for adults, US$10 for children.

Piti Guns On a hill behind the Catholic church in Piti are three Japanese coastal defence guns, now part of the War in the Pacific National Historical Park holdings.

To get here, turn left off Route 1 onto JM Tumcap St in Piti and turn right into Assumption St, at the stop sign. You can park under the big monkeypod tree to the left of the church social hall (the building with the white cross on the front) and then take the concrete steps that lead up the hill. The path is fairly well defined, although slightly overgrown with hibiscus bushes. It's only five minutes up to the first gun, which is amazingly well preserved. The second gun is a couple of minutes farther along the same path while the third is at the end of a side path.

Apra Harbor Apra Harbor, Guam's huge deepwater harbour, was named San Luis de Apra by the Spanish who developed it in the 1700s as a port of call for their Manila galleons.

The US Naval Station holds all of the land surrounding Apra Harbor, including Orote Peninsula on the south side. In addition to home-ported US navy vessels, Apra Harbor has extensive commercial operations, a small boat harbour and space for cruise ships. A slew of **sunken ships** makes the harbour a popular diving spot.

The north side of the harbour is marked by a peninsula, called Cabras Island, which is extended by a long breakwater. About halfway out, along the harbour side of the peninsula, is a **recreational dock** used by glass-bottom boats and the *Nautilus* semi-submarine, as well as for other recreational activities. Just beyond the dock, look for a grove of ironwood trees on the left side of the road; they mark **Family Beach**, a sandy harbourside strand that's popular for weekend outings.

Dogleg Reef, fronting Family Beach, is a good place for snorkellers to see both soft and hard corals as well as anemone colonies with clownfish. The waters are protected and the top of the reef, which starts just a few feet (1m) underwater, is visible from shore.

When the seas are calm, **Luminao Reef**, which stretches along the north side of the peninsula, can also be snorkelled. It has good coral and small fish in waters five to 15 feet (1.5 to 4.5m) deep and it can be accessed in several places along the road by short paths.

To get to Family Beach, turn right onto Route 11 at the traffic lights, go straight past the Port Authority and oil tanks until the road ends. To get to Luminao Reef take the upper road to the right at the oil tanks.

Back on Route 1, an artificial (we hope!) Polaris missile guards the entrance to Polaris Point, part of the naval station.

To continue south around the island, turn left at the traffic lights just past the US Army Reserve Center. This is not well marked and if you miss the turn you will wind up at a guarded US Navy gate.

South of the harbour, Route 1 briefly becomes Route 2A and then turns to Route 2. The bright yellow flowers you may see growing tall along the roadside are *Cassia alata*, more commonly called golden candles, and the pink flowers among the trees are known as chain of love, as each tiny flower on the vine is shaped like a heart.

Gaan Point The park at Gaan Point, on Route 2 in Agat, was one of the main landing sites for the US invasion of southern Guam. On 21 July 1944, US marine and army combat divisions came ashore here to battle with the heavily fortified Japanese infantry.

From their coastal caves and pillboxes the Japanese cut down the Americans as they jumped from their landing crafts. In the first hours of the assault there were more than 1000 US casualties and it wasn't until the third day of fighting, after US tanks made it ashore and managed to knock the Japanese out from behind, that the beachhead was finally secured.

Known also as the War in the Pacific National Historical Park's Agat unit, Gaan Point has a large 20cm naval **coastal defence gun**, an **anti-aircraft cannon** and intact **bunkers** that can be explored.

There's a US WWII **amtrac** underwater about 400 yards out and 50 feet (15m) down, popular with divers.

Much of the reef off the Agat area can be snorkelled or dived. Agat is also the site of a new small-boat marina, Nimitz Beach Park and the Taleyfac Bridge.

Taleyfac Bridge In the late 1700s the Spanish built a bullock cart coastal road to link Hagåtña with Umatac and other southern villages. The road, known as the Camino del Real, was connected by several stone bridges.

The best-preserved Spanish bridge is in Agat at Taleyfac, just a little beyond Nimitz Beach Park, on the ocean side of the road. It's a few hundred feet (70m) back from Route 2 just before the Ocean Side Market store. The picturesque bridge, which is 36 feet (10.8m) long, has twin stone arches that span a narrow river.

Sella Bay Vista Point & Trail A couple of miles (about 4km) south of Agat, the road rises up the coastal hills to a roadside lookout offering a fine view of Sella Bay and the surrounding coast. If it's been raining recently, be sure to glance inland to the northeast for a view of a cascading waterfall.

From the lookout parking area a well-defined red clay trail leads down to Sella Bay, the site of an ancient Chamorro village. The walk is wonderfully scenic, but watch out for slippery mud and for the trail-side sword grasses which can cut. An **old Spanish bridge** that dates to the 1790s still crosses the Sella River close to the coast. There are also a few other overgrown remnants of earlier habitation, including an old **beehive oven** and some **latte stones**. Give yourself about 1½ hours to make the hike down and back.

Some people prefer to make a day of this walk, continuing south from Sella Bay along the shore to Cetti Bay and then up the Cetti River Valley. Before the valley dead-ends at Cetti Falls, there's a trail to the left that goes up to the main road.

Cetti Bay Vista Point The most panoramic roadside vista on the south-west coast is from the Cetti Bay Vista Point. It's just a two-minute walk up the steps to the lookout, which offers a commanding view of the palm-lined Cetti River Valley and picturesque Cetti Bay. You can also see Cocos Island and the Merizo Barrier Reef, which encloses Cocos Lagoon, and the whole south-west coastline.

Mts Lamlam & Jumullong Manglo Inland from the Cetti Bay Vista Point and topped with large wooden crosses is Mt Jumullong Manglo, or Humuyung Manglu, the final destination of cross-bearers during the island's annual Good Friday procession.

The starting point for a trail that goes up the 1282-foot (390m) Mt Jumullong Manglo is across the road from the Cetti Bay Vista Point. You begin by heading up an eroded hill then continue along the mostly well-defined trail. At the divide, go to the right to reach the crosses. There are excellent views of both the coast and the interior forests on the way and the hike should take about an hour. A more difficult and obscure trail continues left from the divide to the 1332-foot (406m) Mt Lamlam, Guam's highest point. Lamlam means 'lightning' and legend calls it the source of the winds.

Memorial Vista Memorias Para I Lalahita is a Vietnam War memorial about 1 mile (1.6km) north of Umatac. It is in a small roadside park graced with two *latte* stones and a hilltop view of Umatac Valley.

Umatac Umatac is an unspoilt, friendly village, steeped in history. Magellan's 1521 landing in Umatac Bay is celebrated in the village each March with four days of activities, including a re-enactment of the event. There's a tall concrete **monument to Magellan** in the village centre.

Umatac Bay was a port of call for Spanish galleons for more than 200 years, though little remains of the four forts that once protected the bay.

Opposite the Magellan monument are the ruins of the **Saint Dionicio Church**, which was originally built in the 1690s, reconstructed in 1862 and destroyed by an earthquake in 1902. All that remains today are rubble and a few stone pillars.

The rusting skeleton of a Japanese midget submarine used to be visible offshore at the river mouth but it's now buried under the sand bar. There's a **Japanese Zero** fighter plane in the bay about 150 yards from the beach and 50 feet (15m) under water that makes a good dive.

On your way out of town you'll see the decorative **Umatac Bridge** with its spiral staircase towers that are intended to symbolise Guam's Chamorro-Spanish heritage.

Fort Soledad Fort Nuestra Senora de la Soledad offers a lovely hilltop view of Umatac Bay and the coastline to the north. To get there take the ironwood-lined road on the right after crossing the Umatac Bridge.

The fort was built by the Spanish in the early 1800s to protect their treasure-laden Manila galleons from pirates roaming the western Pacific. Today the main remnant of the fort is a small hillside sentry post.

If you have a keen eye you can see the remains of **Fort Santo Angel**, which was built in 1742 on a rock jutting out on the northwest side of the bay.

Merizo (Malesso') Merizo, like neighbouring Inarajan, was founded in 1695 largely as a resettlement site for Chamorro who were forced to abandon their homes in

---

The Spanish Reduction

The villages of Merizo and neighbouring Inarajan were founded in 1695, largely as re-settlement sites for Chamorros who were forced to move from the Northern Marianas to southern Guam as part of a Spanish policy known as 'reduction'. Reduction was intended to more effectively convert and 'Hispanicize' the natives by centralising them on one island. To this day many inhabitants in Merizo and Inarajan can trace their lineage to the still un-inhabited islands of the Northern Marianas that their ancestors had to abandon.

---

the Northern Marianas and migrate to southern Guam to be converted to Christianity under the Spanish 'reduction' policy.

The courtyard of **San Dimas Church** in Merizo, Guam's southernmost village, holds a monument to the 46 Chamorro executed by the Japanese in July 1944, one week before the US invasion of Guam.

Next door are the ruins of **Merizo Conbento**, which was built by the Spanish in 1856, soon after the smallpox epidemic that killed almost two-thirds of the population. The *conbento* (convent) was constructed of ifil wood and manposteria (burnt limestone mixed with coral rocks) and was still in use as a parish house until it was heavily damaged by Typhoon Russ in December 1990. It is now being rebuilt.

Directly across the street is Kampanayun Malessu, the **Merizo Bell Tower**, built in 1910 under the direction of Father Cristobal De Canals. It was restored in 1981.

Cocos Island About 2½ miles (4km) offshore from Merizo is Cocos Island, a 1½-mile (2.4km) long atoll that sits within a huge barrier reef. The island has good beaches and the lagoon's calm waters are ideal for many water sports.

Cocos Island Resort (☎ 828 8691), on the eastern side of the island, is a day-trip destination catering mainly to the Japanese younger set, offering jet-skiing, parasailing, kayaking, banana boats, snorkelling, diving, dolphin adventure cruises, windsurfing

GUAM

lessons, rentals and a hodgepodge of tours and other activities.

Boats go to the resort from Merizo Pier between 9 am and 4 pm a dozen times a day. The US$40 price tag (US$12 for locals) includes the 10-minute boat ride, the day-use fee and lunch. Once on the island, water sports cost extra (US$25 to US$80). Visitors are not allowed to bring food or beverages to the resort; there's a snack bar with expensive burgers and plate lunches.

While most of Cocos is privately owned, the west side of the island, formerly the site of a US Coast Guard station, is part of the territorial park system. To get to the public side, called Dano, you either have to hike over from the resort dock or find someone with a private boat to take you there from Merizo. Dano Park has restrooms, picnic tables and barbecue pits. Camping is allowed with a permit from the Department of Parks & Recreation (☎ 477 8279).

Inarajan (Inalåhan) Inarajan is another sleepy village. It was founded in 1695 and has a smattering of Spanish-era influence.

Along the roadside, just before reaching the village, you'll see **Salugula Pool**, a natural saltwater pool with diving platforms and arched bridges that are now in disrepair as a consequence of the harsh storms that have whipped the south coast in recent years. Jagged grey lava rocks separate the calm pool from the crashing ocean surf beyond, and there's an interesting coastal view.

The body of Chamorro priest Jesus Baza Duenas is buried beneath the altar of Inarajan's **Saint Joseph's Church**. Duenas, his nephew and two other Chamorro were beheaded by the Japanese near the end of the war for failing to reveal the whereabouts of US navy radio man George Tweed, who had survived the Japanese occupation in hiding. The church was heavily damaged in the 1993 earthquake but has been renovated and is open to the public.

Along the waterfront is the **Chamorro Cultural Village**, a publicly funded complex of bamboo and thatch shelters where traditional Chamorro crafts are demonstrated between 9 am and 11.30 am each morning

A Meeting of Chiefs

According to legend, Tumon's Chief Malaguana, weary of hearing exaggerated rumours about the strength of Gadao, a rival chief in the southern part of Guam, set out in his canoe for Inarajan determined to kill Gadao.

When Malaguana reached Inarajan a stranger invited him to dinner. Unknown to him, that man was Gadao. When Gadao asked his guest to get a coconut for dinner, Malaguana shook a coconut tree and the coconuts fell like rain. Gadao then picked up one of the coconuts and crushed it open with one hand.

After a few more such contests, Malaguana became worried – if this common Inarajan man was so strong, what would his chief be like? So Malaguana asked the man to take him back to Tumon by canoe. Both chiefs got in the canoe but paddled in opposite directions. The canoe broke in half but Malaguana, in his urgency to leave, was paddling so fast that he didn't even notice until he was back in Tumon.

(US$8 admission). It's a simple concept that's delightfully presented. You can see cookies being baked in an old beehive oven, watch coconut fronds being woven into hats and baskets, see the making of coconut candy and even ride a carabao.

Just beyond the cultural village are the crumbling ruins of a concrete **Baptist church**, built in 1925. Next to it a **bronze sculpture** depicts a local legend about an encounter between two powerful Chamorro chiefs, Malaguana of Tumon and Gadao of Inarajan.

Gadao's Cave From the statue of Gadao in Inarajan you can see some caves in the cliffs across the bay, not far from the point. One of them is Gadao's Cave, which has ancient pictographs said to be the canoe story drawn onto the wall by Gadao himself.

To get to the caves, drive north out of town on Route 4. Just across the bridge take the first sealed road to the right and park at the far end of the beach, just before the road turns inland.

Walk along the beach and take the trail across a meadow and up a cliff to the caves. The walk takes about 15 minutes. Some of this land may be private property, so if you see anyone along the way ask their permission to continue.

Talofofo Falls Talofofo Falls, a popular swimming and picnic spot, is a two-tier cascade, with pools beneath each waterfall. There's a 30-foot drop (9m) on the top fall, though it's usually gentle enough to stand beneath. The deeper and larger pool is at the base of the second fall, where the water flows gently over a very wide rockface.

The falls were recently made over into a full-scale tourist attraction, and now the area includes a **gondola** to ferry visitors down the steep grade from the parking area to the falls. You can also opt for the ten-minute steep walk but the gondola is free. At the bottom is a wooden **swinging bridge** with a splendid view of the falls. A small **museum** has colourful murals and historical models along its narrow passages.

To get here, take the marked turn-off about 2½ miles (4km) north of Inarajan on Route 4. Take a right-turn about 1½ miles (2.4km) on, just before the NASA Tracking Station, and follow the signs to the falls. Car parking for the falls is about a mile (1.6km) farther.

The park is open from 9 am to 5.30 pm daily. Admission is US$13, US$5 for children under age 12. A 10-minute trail through the jungle leads to the **Yokoi Caves**, where a Japanese soldier subsisted for 28 years after WWII. Bring a flashlight to descend into the caves.

Talofofo Beaches Back on Route 4, **Talofofo Bay Beach Park** is about 2 miles (3.3km) farther. This is one of Guam's prime surfing spots. The island's longest and widest river, the Talofofo, runs out into the bay and the sand is chocolate brown.

A couple of miles (4km) down the road is **Ipan Beach Park**, another popular swimming place with calm shallow water and

ironwood shade trees. Just north of Ipan is Jeff's Pirates Cove, a casual beachside restaurant that has moderately priced burgers and sandwiches, drinks and occasional live music.

Pago Bay Vista Point An unmarked viewpoint just past the town of Yona looks over the Pago River as it empties into broad Pago Bay. There was once a Spanish village at the mouth of the river but its inhabitants were wiped out in the 1856 smallpox epidemic.

The area between Pago Bay on the east coast and Agaña Bay on the west is the narrowest part of the island.

According to legend a giant fish which wanted to divide Guam in half used to visit the island and nibble away at this neck of land. Guam was saved by the women of the island who cut off their long hair, wove a big net from their locks and scooped up the fish with the net.

Places to Stay – Budget
Guam Garden Villa (☎ 477 8166, c/o Mrs Herta Laguana, Box 10167, Sinajana, Guam 96926, or 193 Ramirez Dr, Ordot Village) is Guam's only B&B. It is in a pleasant family setting in Ordot, about 3 miles (5km) from Hagåtña. The house is spacious, with a porch and garden, and two guest rooms with a shared bathroom. The rate is US$40/50 for singles/doubles (tax and a hearty breakfast included). Mrs Laguana can provide airport transfers for US$10 each way. The public bus stops nearby, but it is inconvenient without a car. Call well in advance to reserve.

The *Tamuning Plaza Hotel* (☎ 649 8646, fax 649 865, @ tphotel@kuentos.guam.net, 960 S Marine Drive, Tamuning, Guam 96911), near the Ben Franklin department store in Tamuning, has large rooms, each with a refrigerator, cable TV, air-con, phone (free local calls) and comfortable beds. The helpful front desk will rent bicycles for US$10 a day and send emails from the hotel account. It's better maintained than other hotels in this price range and is a recommended option. There's a laundrette on site, free airport transfers and restaurants aplenty nearby. Regular rates are US$60/70 but they will fall if the economy is bad.

The **Hamilton Guest House** (☎ 477 6701, fax 477 6700, 470 West Soledad Ave, Hagåtña, Guam 96910) is a bit tired, but clean and convenient to central Hagåtña. Its 44 red-carpeted rooms each have a TV, refrigerator and phone (free local calls). The price is US$40 per person (tax included) or US$200 for a week plus a US$5 refundable key deposit (there are hourly rate customers as well). The staff are friendly, there's free coffee downstairs, and – best of all – a branch of Shirley's Coffee Shop is just off the lobby. Airport transfers are not available.

The **Harmon Loop Hotel** (☎ 632 3353, fax 632 3330, 1900 Harmon Loop Rd, Suite 107, Dededo, Guam 96912) has 61 rooms above a small shopping centre on Route 16, about 2 miles (3.2km) east of the airport. Rooms are plain but modern, with air-con, cable TV, a refrigerator and a double or queen-size bed. The location's not special but if you're just there to sleep it's good value at US$50/$55 for singles/doubles. There's free morning coffee, an Asian restaurant on site and a McDonald's across the street. Paradise? You decide. Airport pick-up, inexplicably, is available only between 2 and 6 am.

Kina Court Apartments (☎ 477 1261, fax 649 8401), on Toto-Canada Road off Route 8, has 30 plain but pleasant rooms each with a full kitchen, air-con and TV. There's also a laundrette, swimming pool and complimentary coffee in the lobby. Singles/doubles are US$45/55 (tax included). It's quite out of the way so a car is necessary.

The **Pagoda Inn** (☎ 646 1882, fax 646 9065, Box 9699, 801A N Marine Drive, Tumon, Guam 96910), opposite St John's School on a short driveway off Route 1 in Upper Tumon, has 41 rooms that are very small and lacklustre but otherwise OK. Each has a TV, refrigerator and phone. Singles or doubles cost US$45 (including tax), and it also has an hourly rate. There's free coffee in the lobby and the front desk can arrange a load of laundry for US$5. No airport trans-

fers are available. Major credit cards, except American Express, are accepted.

About a half mile (800m) up from the Plumeria on Route 8 is the cheapest hotel in Guam. The **Micronesian Hotel**'s rate of US$26 a night (tax included) barely exceeds the US$22 'short stay' fee. The ramshackle exterior masks tiny rooms and the shared hall bathroom is not terribly clean.

Places to Stay – Mid-Range

The gracefully aging **Plumeria Garden Hotel** (☎ 472 8831, fax 477 4914, @ plumeriagh @huentos.guam.net, Box 7863, Tamuning, Guam 96931), a favourite with repeat visitors, is on Route 8 in Maite, a quarter mile (400m) inland from Route 1. The 78 rooms are in the white two-storey complex that surrounds a courtyard and swimming pool. Each room has cable TV, a refrigerator and phone (local calls US$0.50), and there's free morning coffee. Singles/doubles cost US$55.50/61 (tax included), with a 20% discount for a week's stay.

With a cliffside location overlooking Hagåtña, the newly renovated **Cliff Hotel** (☎ 477 7675, 178 Francisco Javier Dr, Agaña Heights, Guam 96910) has a swimming pool, health club, tennis court and free airport transfers. Rooms with a TV, phone (local calls US$0.25) and small veranda go for US$77.70 (tax included). Studios with kitchenettes are US$122 (tax included).

The **Hotel Mai'Ana** (☎ 646 6961, fax 649 3230, @ maiana@ite.netis) is on the airport road a quarter mile (400m) west of the airport. Rates begin at US$88 for a studio and US$99 for a one-bedroom unit (tax included). All options have nice kitchens (ask to borrow kitchen equipment), air-con, refrigerators, TVs, and phones (local calls US$0.35). Other amenities include a pool, jacuzzi and sauna, a fitness centre, laundry facilities and a free airport shuttle service. Overall it's a very good value for those with a night's layover.

It's a 10-minute walk to the beach, but the **Regency Hotel** (☎ 649 8000, fax 646 8738, 1475 San Vitores Rd, Tumon, Guam 96911) is good value for the Tumon Bay area. The 126 rooms each have cable TV, phone (local calls US$0.50), refrigerator, bathtub and balcony. There's a 24-hour convenience store, a jacuzzi and free shuttle service to the beach and airport. The rate is US$85 for one person or two.

Places to Stay – Top End

The *Guam Hilton* (☎ 646 1835, fax 646 6038, @ gumhilt@ite.net) is at the quieter end of Tumon Bay, beside Ypao Beach. The hotel is a long-time favourite among international visitors and each room has cable TV, veranda and the other expected resort amenities (local calls cost US$0.75). Standard rooms begin at US$185/215, and the larger executive-floor rooms, complete with cosy ocean-view lounge and complimentary after-dinner cocktails, snacks and continental breakfast, go for US$260/290. There's a swimming pool and night-lit tennis courts.

The 455 room *Hyatt Regency Guam* (☎ 647 1234, fax 647 123; in the USA ☎ 1-800-233 1234) is among Tumon Bay's swankiest. It has a grand pillared lobby, beautifully landscaped grounds and a fun series of pools and interconnecting waterways. The rooms each have a large oceanfront balcony, heavy shade curtains, marble vanity, a soaking tub and separate shower, minibar, room safe and voice mail (local calls US$0.50). A nonsmoking floor and king-size beds are available. The staff are friendly, the hotel has excellent restaurants and there's often live beachfront music. Rates begin at US$210/225 plus tax. Airport transfers cost US$15 round-trip.

Built in 1996, the *Westin Resort* (☎ 647 1020, fax 647 0999, @ guamm@westin .com, 105 Gun Beach Road, Tumon, Guam, 96911) is a high-rise with an intriguing, angular interior design. Pleasant rooms each have cable TV, a phone, minibar, separate bathtub and shower areas and complimentary coffee and tea service. Rooms begin at US$235/255 and airport transfers are US$15 round-trip.

The *Sherwood Resort* (☎ 647 1188, fax 647 1166, @ sherwood@hafa.net.gu) may not have a beach for a yard, but in other respects this 260 room hotel in Tumon Bay is

an excellent choice. Like the grand lobby area below, the rooms are spacious and immaculate – each comes with a phone, TV, tub, refrigerator and fancy bathroom. For a luxury hotel, the rates are reasonable at US$150 for singles/doubles, or US$170 for an ocean view (request a high floor). Add US$35 for a third person. Airport transfers are US$15 return.

The 600-room *Outrigger Guam Resort* (☎ 649 9000, fax 647 9068; in the USA ☎ 1-800-422 7309, @ resvmgr @outriggerguam.com) takes its place among Guam's top resort hotels along Tumon Bay. All rooms have an ocean view and refrigerators, cable TV, port connections for computers, phones and coffee and tea-making facilities. Rates range from US$240 to US$700, though promotions may cut these rates.

Places to Eat – Budget

The *Chamorro Village (I Sengsong Chamorro)*, Hagåtña's public market, is the best place for a cheap and tasty local meal. Numerous tidy huts sell plate lunches of local favourites, such as spicy chicken *kelaguen* and barbecued spareribs with red rice, for US$3 to US$5. Vegetarians will also find a plethora of options.

Within Chamorro Village, *Jamaican Grill* (☎ 472 2000) is a popular stop – patrons either take away or opt for the ocean-view seating outside. The restaurant grills heaped platefuls of excellent fish, ribs, tropical fruits and vegetables at reasonable prices. Try the paseo vegetarian, a colourful, scrumptious plate of grilled tomato, eggplant and onion on a heaped bed of rice. The restaurant is open from 10 am to 10 pm daily.

Also in Chamorro Village, *Carmen's* serves excellent Mexican food for US$4 to US$10. For Chamorro food, try a fiesta plate (US$5) or a fish plate (US$4) from *Terry's*, at the centre of the village.

Chamorro Village is also the best place to find fresh fruits and vegetables (not to mention betel nut). Most stalls are open from about 9 am to 5.30 pm daily. On Wednesday nights, starting at 6 pm, Chamorro Village turns into a mini-fiesta as crowds flock to the fabulous array of food stalls and enjoy local entertainment.

Shirley's Coffee Shop, a Guam institution with a well-earned reputation for great food and mammoth servings, has opened its largest branch on Route 30 in Tamuning. You name it, Shirley's has it – the endless menu includes, in no particular order, omelettes, mushroom dishes, steak dishes, cashew dishes, crepes, moccachinos, sandwiches, burgers, pasta and chop suey. Almost all meal items fall well under US$10. The Shirley's in Tamuning is open from 6 am to midnight Sunday through Thursday and 24 hours Friday to Saturday. Shirley's has branches in Harmon, Mangilao, Hagåtña and at the airport.

Simply Food, adjacent to the Seventh-Day Adventist church on Route 7 in Hagåtña, is a small health-food store with a snack bar serving vegetarian food. The store is open from 9 am to 5 pm Monday to Thursday, from 9 am to 3 pm on Fridays. The lunch counter, open from 11 am to 2 pm weekdays, has smoothies, soups, salads and build-your-own sandwiches for under US$4 and a daily lunch special for US$6.

For a fresh-baked treat try the **Cup & Saucer** on Martyr St, next to the Firefly Bistro in Hagåtña. The fresh-baked cinnamon rolls (US$1.25 to US$1.50) are fantastic. It's a comfortable place to sit with a cup of coffee (US$1.50) and read the Sunday *New York Times* for US$6. The bakery-cafe is open weekdays from 6.30 am to 6 pm, and Saturdays from 6.30 am to noon.

The **Micronesia Mall**, a mile (1.6km) north of Tumon on Route 1, has a large second-floor food court with stalls serving every conceivable Pacific Rim food, including Hawai'ian, Korean, Chinese, Japanese, Chamorro and American, and also Italian food. Most stalls have combo-plate lunches for US$5. There's also a mini food court at **Kmart**.

Fast food enthusiasts will mistake Guam for heaven. **McDonald's**, **Wendy's**, **Burger King**, **Pizza Hut**, **Subway**, **Winchell's**, **Denny's** and a host of others are ubiquitous, particularly on Marine Dr in Tamuning.

Chamorro Food

Chamorro food is a rich mix of Spanish, Filipino and Pacific dishes.

Ahu is grated coconut boiled in sugar water.

Bonelos aga is banana dipped in a sweet flour batter and deep fried.

Cadon guihan is fish cooked in coconut milk with onions and sweet peppers.

Escabeche is fresh fish marinated in vinegar and soy sauce.

Golai hagoin sumi is taro leaves cooked in coconut milk.

Kelaguen is minced chicken, fish, shrimp or Spam mixed with lemon, onions, pepper and shredded coconut.

Lumpia is similar to an egg roll, but dipped in garlic sauce or vinegar.

Pancit is a mix of shrimp, vegetables and garlic over noodles.

Poto is a ricecake of tuba, sugar and ricemeal.

Other local delicacies include whole roast pig, tropical fruits, yams, coconut crabs, red rice made with *achiote* (annatto) seeds and anything barbecued. To turn ordinary dishes into a Chamorro meal ask for *finadene*, a hot sauce made from fiery red peppers, soy sauce, lemon juice and chopped onions.

The best Chamorro food is generally found at village fiestas and private feasts; also try the Chamorro Village in Hagåtña.

Places to Eat – Mid-Range

Among Guam's umpteen steakhouses, the standout is **Outback Steakhouse**, just north of Planet Hollywood along San Vitores Rd in Tumon Bay. If you don't fill up on the bloomin' onion appetiser – a small forest of marvellously crispy, spicy onion sticks – try the Outback special, which is 12 ounces (375gm) of seasoned and seared sirloin (US$19). Burgers go for US$8.50.

Firefly Bistro, on Martyr St in Hagåtña, is an upmarket new bistro that serves an array of gourmet meat, seafood and pasta dishes from an ever-changing menu. The pepper-crusted tuna (US$18) is a perennial favourite dinner choice. It's a good place to escape the tumult of Tumon Bay. Lunch is served from 11.30 am to 2 pm weekdays, and dinner is from 6 to 9 pm Tuesday to Saturday.

Fabulous Thai food is served at *Thai Kitchen*, in a small block of shops on Marine Dr in Tamuning. If you're driving from Hagåtña, it's just past Pizza Hut on the left-hand side of the road in a tired-looking office complex. Pink tablecloths, low lighting and soft music create a romantic setting that's also comfortable for lone travellers. Dishes range from *pad Thai* to garlic shrimp to papaya salad, and main course dishes are priced from US$7 to US$12. It's open from 11 am to 2.30 pm and 6 to 9 pm Monday to Saturday.

The *Hard Rock Cafe*, in the Plaza across the street from DFS (duty-free shopping) complex in Tumon Bay, is a trendy lunch spot, as is *TGI Friday's* another chain restaurant that's just up from DFS. Both have burgers and sandwiches priced at US$10 and above.

Places to Eat – Top End

La Mirenda (☎ 546 3463), a cafe-style restaurant at the Hyatt hotel, has a good buffet lunch that includes fresh fruit and tempting cakes and pies. The full buffet is from 11.30 am to 2 pm Monday to Saturday and costs US$15.50. La Mirenda also does a more elaborate Sunday champagne brunch for US$25 and a popular seafood buffet Wednesday and Friday evenings. Advance reservations for buffets are recommended. Dinner is from 6 to 9.30 pm. A 10% gratuity is automatically added to the bill.

La Premier (☎ 647 7714) in the Onward Agaña Beach Hotel on Agaña Bay, has an all-you-can-eat soup and salad bar for US$6.50 and a full lunch buffet for US$10 from 11.30 am to 1.30 pm Monday to Saturday. On Thursday night the restaurant features an Indian dinner buffet for US$17, and on Friday night a seafood buffet for US$16. Children under 12 get discounts.

If you're only going to have one splurge night out on Guam, you couldn't do better than *Roy's Restaurant* (☎ 646 3193) in the Guam Hilton, which serves superb Pacific Rim cuisine. The goat cheese in filo with roasted red capsicum and eggplant salad makes a nice starter at US$6. There are nightly specials, but meals begin with complimentary hot *naan* served from a clay oven; for dessert the melting hot chocolate souffle (US$7) is a rare treat. Entertainment in the lounge is available Thursday to Saturday nights.

Entertainment

For local flavour, head to the *Chamorro Village* in Hagåtña on Wednesday evenings. Starting at 6 pm, the village bursts into a colourful mini-fiesta with bands, dances, craft stalls, barbecues, and all kinds of Chamorro food specialities. If a village fiesta is going on while you're in Guam, it's worth the drive to visit; see Public Holidays & Special Events earlier in this chapter for the dates.

Planet Hollywood, in the DFS complex, is a popular dining spot with the younger crowd and with Japanese tourists, as is the cavernous *Hard Rock Cafe*, which transforms from an expat family scene during the day to a lively local scene at night.

Most of Guam's classic beach bars closed down when beachfront resorts gobbled up their property, but the proud flag-bearer is *Barney's*, which has just moved to the beach by Tumon's Guam Reef Hotel. Barney's has gained the sworn loyalty of the US military with Dollar-A-Bud Thursdays (from 6 pm to midnight) and other nightly drink specials.

On a mellower note, there's a great sunset view from the wrap-around windows at the *Salon del Mar* in the Guam Hotel Okura. During happy hour, from 5 to 7 pm each day, beer costs US$2 and tropical drinks US$3.50, and there's usually complimentary popcorn and hors d'oeuvres. Another romantic upmarket sunset spot is the open-air seaside restaurant-bar at *Santa Fe on the Bay*, a new adobe-style hotel in Tamuning just past Shirley's on Route 30. Margaritas are US$6.50, but the daily happy hour (4 to 7 pm) knocks US$1 off drinks.

For glitz, the *Sandcastle* entertainment complex on San Vitores Rd is unrivalled. Besides hosting pricey Las Vegas-style cabaret and dinner shows, it also houses the enormous, multi-theme-room *Globe*. Don't even *think* of entering Globe's ritzy Manhattan Room in shorts. You'll find a disco here too. The whopping US$30 cover charge includes two free drinks.

TJ's at the Hyatt is another 20-somethings dance spot, with the live music Friday nights.

For the gay scene, check the *Mad Cow* (☎ 649 4945), on Route 14 in Tamuning next to the Golden Motel. It's one of Micronesia's few gay clubs and it has two pool tables and a dance floor. There's a cover charge of US$5 on Saturdays but it's

US$10 on drag night (every other Friday). The club also has information about other events in Guam's gay community, including the annual October Miss Pacificana drag pageant.

Guam has three main movie theatres: the *Micronesian Mall Theatre* (☎ 632 3456), *Guam Mexaplex Cinema* (☎ 646 0360), in Guam Premium Outlets in Tamuning, and the multiscreen *Hafa Adai Theatre* (☎ 646 4834) near the ITC Building in Tamuning. Movies cost US$7, children US$3.50, matinees cost US$5. Cinemas A&B, along Marine Drive near the Tamuning Plaza Hotel, have US$1.50 showings of recently released movies. Call Hafa Adai Theatre for details.

Northern Mariana Islands

The main islands of the Commonwealth of the Northern Mariana Islands are Saipan, Rota and Tinian.

Saipan, the largest island, with 90% of the total population, gets most of the tourist trade. Chamorro culture lies buried beneath American fast food, ubiquitous casinos and sex shops. Rota, the quiet and friendly island, has only one paved road running between the airport and the main village, and life on Tinian continues placidly in spite of a brand-new multi-million dollar casino-hotel at one end of the island.

The Northern Marianas hosted some of the Pacific War's most devastating battles between US and Japanese forces. Now the islands are wooing the Japanese back by turning war ruins into sightseeing spots, erecting peace monuments and developing resort hotels.

Facts about the Northern Mariana Islands

HISTORY
Early Settlers

The Northern Marianas were settled around 1500 BC by Chamorros, who shared cultural ties with Guam's indigenous people. See the Guam history section for details on early Chamorro culture.

Spanish Period

When Ferdinand Magellan came upon the Marianas in 1521 he called them Islas de los Ladrones (Islands of Thieves). They were renamed Las Marianas in 1668 by the Spanish priest Luis Diego Sanvitores, in honour of the Spanish queen Maria Ana of Austria. Sanvitores and five other Jesuit priests established the first mission in the Marianas. From the onset the missionaries received a hostile welcome, and the next two decades

---

HIGHLIGHTS

- The Grotto – Saipan's exhilarating diving challenge
- Suicide Cliff – a sobering reflection on the tragedies of WWII
- North Field – Tinian's now-deserted runways from where the *Enola Gay* took off in 1945 with the atomic bomb that devastated Hiroshima
- Rota – the peaceful, friendly island where everyone waves to each other

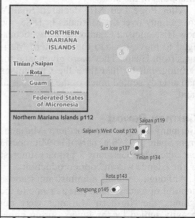

---

were marked by sporadic uprisings that cost the lives of a dozen priests and scores of Chamorros. By the late 1680s the Jesuits, with the help of Spanish troops, had clearly gained the upper hand and the uprisings ceased.

In the 1690s the Spanish, initiating a new policy termed 'reduction', swept down through the Marianas, rounded up the Chamorros and brought them to Guam in an effort to more effectively convert them to Christianity. On Rota several hundred Rotanese managed to hide in the hills and avoid capture, which is why some of the people of Rota today represent the purest Chamorro blood in the Marianas.

The other Northern Marianas were left uninhabited. Explorers who landed on the abandoned islands (including the British captain Samuel Wallis in 1768, soon after 'discovering' Tahiti) sometimes took advantage of the wild cattle and chickens found there, but most went instead to Guam to stock up on provisions.

Around 1820 the Spanish allowed islanders from the western Carolines to move to the larger Mariana islands. The Carolinians managed Spanish cattle herds and maintained a presence on the Marianas at a time when Spain was skittish over German intentions in the area.

After Pope Leo XIII declared Spain's sovereignty over the Marianas in 1885, the now Hispanicised Chamorros were encouraged to move back to the Northern Marianas from Guam. They were given land for farming, but by that time the Carolinians had already settled much of the best coastal land.

German Period

Germany bought the Northern Marianas from Spain in 1899 as part of its Micronesia package deal. Germany's primary interest in the islands was in copra production.

Although colonial administrators and a handful of teachers and priests came to the islands, the Northern Marianas were not heavily settled by foreigners during either the Spanish or German administrations.

Japanese Period

When the Japanese took the Northern Marianas from Germany at the beginning of WWI, there were fewer than 4000 Chamorros and Carolinians on the islands.

The Japanese had little interest in copra but had great expectations for sugar cane. They chopped down groves of coconut trees and cleared tropical forests and jungles to create level farmland. When *latte* stones from ancient villages got in the way, they were cast aside.

In the mid-1920s, after the success of Saipan's sugar industry, plantations were set

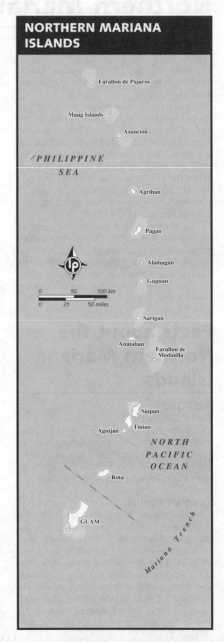

NORTHERN MARIANA ISLANDS

Farallon de Pajaros

Maug Islands

Asuncion

PHILIPPINE SEA

Agrihan

Pagan

Alamagan

Guguan

0   50   100 km
0   25   50 miles

Sarigan

Anatahan

Farallon de Medinilla

Saipan

Aguijan   Tinian

NORTH PACIFIC OCEAN

Rota

GUAM

Mariana Trench

up on Tinian and Rota. On all three islands sugar cane was loaded from the fields onto bullock carts and hauled to little narrow-gauge railroads where steam-powered trains carried the cane to mills for processing. Both sugar and alcohol made from the cane were major export items.

By the mid-1930s sugar operations in the Marianas were providing the Japanese with more than 60% of all revenues generated in Micronesia.

Many of the people who worked the cane fields came from Okinawa, where poor tenant farmers were recruited at low wages. The high influx of foreigners and the tendency of the colonisers to turn villages into miniature Japanese towns overwhelmed the native culture.

At the outbreak of WWII there were over 45,000 Japanese and immigrant workers in the Northern Marianas – more than 10 times the number of Micronesians.

WWII

One of WWII's largest military operations was Operation Forager, which captured the Mariana Islands for the USA. A US invasion force of 127,000 soldiers, 600 ships and 2000 planes attacked first Saipan and then Guam. American pre-invasion bombing attacks included the first-ever wartime use of napalm.

Operation Forager went into full swing on 15 June 1944, as two US Marine divisions landed on Saipan's south-west coast. The Japanese had 31,000 soldiers waiting. Resistance was fierce but by evening the USA had 20,000 men ashore.

That same night the Japanese First Mobile Fleet was detected in the Philippine Sea heading toward the Marianas. When squadrons of Zeros took off from those ships on 19 June, the US forces were ready. In the battle that became popularly known as the 'Marianas Turkey Shoot' both sides took part in a wild all-out air fight west of the Marianas. In two days the Japanese lost 402 planes and three aircraft carriers. The Americans lost only 50 planes, but on the return 80 more crashed into the sea when they ran out of fuel.

With the defeat of their fleet, Japanese forces in the Marianas lost any chance of rescue or reinforcement. On Saipan, the Americans advanced northward and into the island's mountainous interior.

Garapan, the Japanese administrative centre, fell on 3 July. When the battle for Saipan was declared over on 9 July, 3500 Americans, 30,000 Japanese defenders and 400 Saipanese were dead.

After the fall of Saipan the Japanese had no hope of holding onto Tinian. Still, the 9000 Japanese soldiers on the island chose to fight to the death rather than surrender.

The Americans made their first beach landing on Tinian's north-west shore on 24 July 1944, securing the island after nine days of heavy combat and the loss of 400 American and over 5000 Japanese lives. US troops immediately began extending the Japanese airbase on Tinian, and used it to stage air raids on Japan, including the atomic bomb drops on Hiroshima and Nagasaki.

US invasion forces bypassed Rota. The USA bombed the northern airstrips, but the Japanese held the island till the war's end and Rota emerged relatively unscathed.

Post-War Period

The fierce fighting reduced whole towns to rubble and in the years following the war there were no attempts to rebuild the sugar industry. The USA administered the islands by providing hand-outs rather than encouraging economic development.

In 1948 the CIA closed off half of Saipan to islanders and outsiders alike and used the northern part of the island for covert military manoeuvres. When the CIA moved out in 1962 the Northern Marianas were finally opened to visitors. The Trust Territory administration then moved its headquarters to Saipan, taking over the former CIA offices.

In 1961 Saipan and Rota petitioned the US government, asking to become integrated with Guam. The requests were made nearly every year until 1969, when Guam voters were allowed to vote in a referendum on the issue and rejected the idea. One

NORTHERN MARIANA ISLANDS

NORTHERN MARIANA ISLANDS

reason cited for the rejection was that many Guamanians still harboured ill feelings towards those Saipanese who had acted as interpreters during Guam's occupation by the Japanese.

In June 1975 the people of the Northern Marianas voted to become a US commonwealth, and in doing so became the first district to withdraw from the Trust Territory. Under the commonwealth agreement, which took effect in January 1978, the Northern Marianas retained the right to internal self-government, while the USA retained control over foreign affairs. In November 1986 the new commonwealth covenant became fully effective and the islanders became US citizens.

GEOGRAPHY

The Commonwealth of the Northern Mariana Islands is made up of 14 of the 15 islands in the Marianas archipelago. This archipelago curves 400 miles (645km) northward from Guam, the chain's southernmost island, dividing the Pacific Ocean and the Philippine Sea.

All the islands are high types of either volcanic or limestone formation. The total land area of the Northern Marianas is 184 sq miles (476 sq km); Saipan is 47 sq miles (121 sq km), Tinian is 39 sq miles (101 sq km) and Rota is 32 sq miles (83 sq km).

Mariana Trench

The Mariana Trench is an underwater canyon that extends 1835 miles (2953km) along the floor of the Pacific to the east of the Mariana Islands. At 38,635 feet (11,770m), the trench contains the world's greatest known ocean depth.

The Mariana Islands, which are the emerged tips of massive underwater mountains, can also make claim to another record. If measured from their bases deep in the Mariana Trench, the islands, which rise from the ocean floor more than 10,000 feet (3000m) higher than Mt Everest, would constitute the highest mountains in the world.

Northern (Outer) Islands

Except for Aguijan, which is just south of Tinian, the smaller Mariana islands run north of Saipan. All are rugged volcanic islands. The highest point in all of Micronesia is in the Marianas – 3166 feet (964m) on the remote island of Agrihan.

Pagan, which covers an area of 18½ sq miles (47.9 sq km), is the largest of these outer islands and one of the most beautiful. The Maug Islands and Sarigan island are protected nature preserves. Farallon de Medinilla is used on occasion as a bombing and gunnery target by both the US navy and air force.

Micronesia's only active volcanoes are located among these islands. Following weeks of seismic activity, Pagan's volcano erupted in May 1981, covering almost half of all the arable land with a coating of lava. All 54 residents were evacuated and ongoing seismic activity has prevented permanent resettlement. Interestingly, the volcanic ash that spewed out has proven useful as a cement additive and is now being mined and shipped to Saipan, Rota and Guam for use in new condo and resort developments.

In April 1990 all 21 residents of the island of Anatahan were evacuated to Saipan following an earthquake that measured 7.4 on the Richter scale and signs that a volcanic eruption was imminent.

The 1000-foot (300m) peak on Farallon de Pajaros and Asuncion's 3000-foot (914m) mountain sometimes send up smoke and steam as well.

CLIMATE

Saipan, which according to *The Guinness Book of Records* has the world's most equable temperature, averages 81°F (27°C) year-round. The rainy season is from July to October, when rainfall averages about 12 inches (300mm) a month, while from December to May monthly rainfall averages only about 4 inches (100mm).

Like Guam, the islands lie directly along the typhoon track, with typhoons most commonly occurring from August to December.

GOVERNMENT & POLITICS

As a US commonwealth, similar in status to Puerto Rico, the Northern Marianas have closer ties with the USA than other Micronesian island groups. The commonwealth has its own governor, lieutenant governor and a legislature with nine senators – three each from Saipan, Tinian and Rota – and 15 representatives – 13 from Saipan, one from Tinian and one from Rota. Each main island has its own mayor.

Although the people of the Northern Marianas are US citizens, they don't vote in US elections and are exempt from US income taxes. Representation in the US Congress is limited to non-voting observer status, although CNMI representatives can lobby and make presentations.

Pedro Tenorio is the current governor of CNMI and has the unenviable job of sparring with Washington about the garment industry (see boxed text 'Shady Labour Practices' in this section).

ECONOMY

Since the commonwealth covenant took effect, the USA has provided hundreds of millions of dollars for capital development, government operations and other programs in the Northern Marianas. The government is the largest single employer.

Still, the mainstay of the economy is tourism. The Asian economic crisis of the late 1990s hurt the CNMI badly, as visitor arrivals fell 20% between 1998 and 1999.

The CNMI minimum wage (US$3.05 an hour) is the lowest of any place under US jurisdiction. Unemployment and poverty among the Chamorro population are high, as 90% of private-sector jobs are held by low-paid Asian workers.

POPULATION & PEOPLE

With a 4.2% growth rate, the Northern Marianas is the fastest-growing area in Micronesia, with the population more than tripling from 1980 to 1995.

The population is 68,400, with approximately 90% on Saipan and 5% each on Tinian and Rota. Slightly more than half of the total population is resident foreigners, mostly

Shady Labour Practices

Under the commonwealth covenant, the CNMI government retains its own controls over immigration. Many US companies took advantage of Saipan's duty-free access to the USA and the estimated 40,000 low-paid Filipino and Chinese workers on Saipan and set up factories there in the 1980s. These infamous US$1.2 billion-per-year 'garment industry' factories turn out designer clothing tagged with 'Made in the USA' labels, and Saipan benefits from over US$2 million in annual taxes.

The industry has been an economic pillar of Saipan, but there are serious problems with the treatment of foreign workers, some of whom claim they have been beaten, locked into factories and forced to have abortions. Others claim that they must work up to 12 hours a day, seven days a week.

These complaints have gelled into a US$1 billion class-action lawsuit filed in the late 1990s by California and Saipan-based human-rights groups. The lawsuit named 18 high-profile US retailers as defendants, including big names like Tommy Hilfiger, J Crew and Gap.

On the political front, President Clinton has strongly criticised the CNMI's labour practices and immigration policies. There are strong indications that Congress will reassume control of these policies in the early 2000s, which would effectively end the garment industry. There is new legislation in Congress that would raise labour and immigration standards to federal levels. Other legislation would end Saipan's 'Made in the USA' labels and revoke Saipan's duty-free shipping status, which amounts to a US$200 million loss of federal tax revenue.

from the Philippines, China and Korea. Of the native population, roughly 75% is Chamorro; the remainder are Carolinian.

ARTS

Authenticity is hard to come by in the Northern Marianas, particularly on Saipan, where Chamorro culture has been subsumed by heavy commercialisation. Even on less-developed Tinian and Rota handicrafts are scarce, and those wanting cultural relics or performances must search for them.

SOCIETY & CONDUCT
The local Chamorro culture is a hybrid of native and Spanish colonial influences, with a powerful overlay of popular American trends. As on Guam, most cultural activities centre around the Catholic church.

RELIGION
Roman Catholicism predominates, especially among the Chamorro population and Filipino immigrants. There are also followers of the Baptist, Methodist, Mormon, Korean Presbyterian, Evangelical and Seventh-Day Adventist churches.

LANGUAGE
English is the official language. Chamorro and Carolinian are native tongues, and Japanese is spoken in some hotels and shops. *Hafa adai* is the traditional greeting, as it is in Guam, although the slang *howzit* is nearly as common.

Facts for the Visitor

SUGGESTED ITINERARIES
All three of the major CNMI islands can easily be visited within one week or 10 days. Peaceful and friendly Rota makes a fine getaway for a few days and is only a short trip via commuter flight from Guam. Saipan has good diving and historical points that could easily absorb a few days, if you can ignore the casinos and strip-joints. Tinian is an historical treasure-trove, but most of its accommodation options, except for the casino, aren't up to par.

TOURIST OFFICES
See under Information in the individual island sections later in this chapter for information on tourist offices.

VISAS & DOCUMENTS
See the Visas & Travel Permits section in the Regional Facts for the Visitor chapter for details of visa requirements and information on other documents.

MONEY
The Northern Marianas use US dollars (see Exchange Rates under Money in the Regional Facts for the Visitor chapter). Credit cards are widely used on Saipan, and are becoming more common on Rota and (more slowly) Tinian. Saipan has numerous ATMs, while Rota and Tinian have one each.

Prices quoted in this chapter, particularly hotel prices, will probably increase once the Asian economic crisis lifts.

POST & COMMUNICATIONS
Mail is handled by the US postal service and uses US stamps. Postal codes are: 96950 (Saipan), 96951 (Rota) and 96952 (Tinian). The Marianas' abbreviation is 'MP', but write 'via USA'. So you would address mail to: name, address, island, postal code, MP via USA.

The international telephone code is ☎ 670 and there are no area codes. Dial ☎ 411 for directory assistance. It costs US$0.25 a minute to call from one CNMI island to another. Internet access is possible on Saipan but not Rota or Tinian.

Per-minute rates for direct-dialled calls to Guam and the USA are US$0.40 for the first minute and US$0.15 for each additional minute. It costs US$0.89 per minute to Japan and Australia, US$1.22 to FSM or the Marshalls and US$1.78 to Palau.

Faxes can be sent from the IT&E office in San Jose for the price of a phone call plus US$2, and can be received (fax 234 8525) for US$0.50 a page.

INTERNET RESOURCES
See Internet Resources in the Facts for the Visitor chapter.

MEDIA
There are two newspapers published on Saipan: the *Marianas Variety* (US$0.50), published Monday to Saturday, and the

Saipan Tribune (US$0.25), published on weekdays. Guam's Pacific Daily News is flown in daily (US$0.85). You can pick up newspapers at most island grocery stores, petrol stations and hotels.

All islands have access to cable TV.

ELECTRICITY
See Electricity in the Regional Facts for the Visitor chapter.

WEIGHTS & MEASURES
Like the USA, the Northern Marianas use the imperial system.

HEALTH
Water on Rota is good to drink, but on Saipan and Tinian boil it first. Each of the main islands has a hospital, although Saipan's is the best.

BUSINESS HOURS
Most Saipan and Tinian businesses are open weekdays from 8 am to 5 pm. On Rota, hours are earlier: 7.30 to 11.30 am and 12.30 to 4.30 pm is usual. Banking hours are typically Monday to Thursday from 10 am to 3 pm and Friday from 10 am to 6 pm.

PUBLIC HOLIDAYS & SPECIAL EVENTS
Public holidays in the Northern Marianas include:

New Year's Day 1 January
Commonwealth Day 9 January
President's Day 3rd Monday in February
Covenant Day 24 March
Easter Sunday late March or early April
Good Friday Friday before Easter
Memorial Day last Monday in May
US Independence Day 4 July
Labor Day 1st Monday in September
Columbus Day 2nd Monday in October
Citizenship Day 4 November
Veterans Day 11 November
Thanksgiving last Thursday in November
Constitution Day 8 December
Christmas Day 25 December

Most villages have an annual fiesta honouring their patron saint, which is the big village bash of the year. Rota has two fiestas and

Tinian one, while Saipan has six. See the individual island sections for more details.

ACTIVITIES
All islands have good diving. A junkyard of WWII equipment lies just off Tinian, while Rota has some new 'wrecks' and Saipan has the challenging Grotto. Saipan and Rota have golf courses.

ACCOMMODATION & FOOD
Rota has the region's first youth hostel. Saipan has numerous resorts and Rota has one. Most food is Western style, though you can sometimes find Chamorro dishes. See the boxed text 'Chamorro Food' in the Guam chapter for an overview of Chamorro food.

Getting There & Away

AIR
Airports & Airlines
The modern airport on Saipan is the main airport in the Northern Marianas, and has car rental and airline offices. See the Saipan section later for details.

Departure Tax
None of the Northern Marianas have a departure tax.

Asia
There are daily flights to Saipan from Tokyo on Japan Airlines and Northwest Airlines; from Osaka to Saipan on Japan Airlines; and from Nagoya to Saipan on Japan Airlines. There's also regular but less frequent service from other ports in Japan. Continental Airlines serves Saipan via Guam from Japan.

Return fares from Tokyo start at around US$750 with Northwest, to around US$1131 on JAL. Keep in mind that peak holiday seasons, particularly 'Golden Week', which takes place in late April to early May, and the mid-summer O-bon festival, are when most Japanese travel.

Continental flies twice a week between Hong Kong and Saipan. Return fares are US$924/748 during the high/low season.

Continental flies three times a week between Saipan and Taipei for US$486 return in low season.

Within Micronesia

Pacific Island Aviation (PIA) flies twice daily between Saipan and Guam. One-way fares are US$77. Freedom Air also has two daily flights between Saipan and Guam for US$76/139 one way/return; discounts for children 11 and under. Freedom Air can arrange a special Guam-Rota-Saipan-Guam round-trip deal if you want to stop off in Rota.

Freedom Air and PIA also fly to Tinian and Rota; see details under Getting There & Away in those island sections.

If you have a Circle Micronesia ticket with Continental, you may be able to include the Guam-Saipan leg for an extra US$70 but it depends on your ticket.

All FSM and Palau connections to Saipan go through Guam, as do connections from Bali, Manila and Honolulu. For more details see the Getting There & Away chapter earlier in the book.

SEA

Yachties will be charged from US$62 for an entrance fee plus US$56 dockage on Saipan, though the fee may be waived altogether for pleasure boats. You can go straight to Rota (rather than going through Saipan), though its harbour facilities are worse than those of Saipan or Tinian; call Rota's seaport at ☎ 532 8489 in advance.

Getting Around

AIR

Freedom Air and PIA have flights every day between Saipan, Tinian and Rota. See the Tinian and Rota sections later in this chapter for details.

BUS

None of the Northern Marianas has public buses, but Saipan does have shuttle buses.

CAR & MOTORCYCLE

Only Saipan has taxis, but they're so expensive that it's more economical to rent a car. All three islands have major car-rental agencies; prices start around US$40 per day for unlimited mileage.

HITCHING

Hitching is dangerous on Saipan but is safer on Rota and Tinian.

Saipan

Saipan has the dubious distinction of being the fastest-growing island in Micronesia, with new golf courses and resorts continuously popping up. Tourists and foreign workers now outnumber the Saipanese, and much of the island's Micronesian character has been overshadowed by fast-food chains and poker houses.

Still, Saipan has gentle beaches on its west and south coasts, a rugged and rocky east coast, a hilly interior and dramatic cliffs on the north coast. The island is about 14 miles (22.5km) long and 5 miles (8km) wide.

The main sights are in the west coast town of Garapan and in the Marpi area at the northern end of the island. By car, most sights can be reached in just a few hours, though a more leisurely exploration would take a full day.

Orientation

Orientation is simple. The airport is at the southern end of the island. Most major hotels and services are on Beach Rd, which runs along the west coast, although some hotels and places of interest are along Middle Rd, an inland road parallel to Beach Rd.

Information

Tourist Offices The Marianas Visitors Authority (☎ 664 3200, fax 554 3237, @ mva@saipan.com) is on Beach Rd, south of Garapan. Its tiny sign can be easy to miss, so keep a lookout for the Nissan and Toyota car dealers on the inland side of the

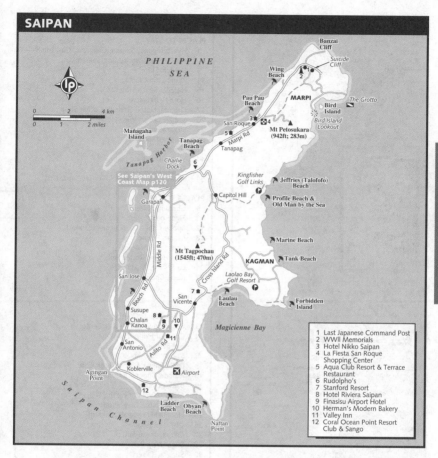

SAIPAN

PHILIPPINE SEA

Banzai Cliff

Suicide Cliff

Wing Beach

MARPI

The Grotto

Pau Pau Beach

Bird Island

Bird Island Lookout

San Roque

Mt Petosukara (942ft; 283m)

Mañagaha Island

Tanapag Beach

Marpi Rd

Tanapag

Tanapag Harbor

Charlie Dock

Kingfisher Golf Links

Jeffries (Talofofo) Beach

See Saipan's West Coast Map p120

Capitol Hill

Profile Beach & Old Man by the Sea

Garapan

Marine Beach

Mt Tagpochau (1545ft; 470m)

KAGMAN

Tank Beach

San Jose

Laolao Bay Golf Resort

Middle Rd

Cross Island Rd

Beach Rd

San Vicente

Laulau Beach

Forbidden Island

Susupe

Chalan Kanoa

Magicienne Bay

San Antonio

Aslito Rd

Koblerville

Airport

Agingan Point

Saipan Channel

Ladder Beach

Obyan Beach

Naftan Point

0 2 4 km
0 1 2 miles

1 Last Japanese Command Post
2 WWII Memorials
3 Hotel Nikko Saipan
4 La Fiesta San Roque Shopping Center
5 Aqua Club Resort & Terrace Restaurant
6 Rudolpho's
7 Stanford Resort
8 Hotel Riviera Saipan
9 Finasisu Airport Hotel
10 Herman's Modern Bakery
11 Valley Inn
12 Coral Ocean Point Resort Club & Sango

road. Most of the tourist brochures are in Korean or Japanese, but some are in English. The tourist office is open weekdays from 8 am to 5 pm.

Money Both the Bank of Guam and the Bank of Hawaii have branches in Garapan and Susupe. There are ATMs aplenty, at Wendy's and McDonald's, the supermarkets and the banks. Credit cards are widely accepted. The American Express representative is at the Marianas International Travel Agency (MITA) on Beach Rd on the south side of Garapan.

Post & Communications The main post office is in Chalan Kanoa and is open weekdays from 8.30 am to 4 pm and from 9 am to noon on Saturday. Pick up general delivery mail here rather than at branch offices.

Local and long-distance calls can be made from pay phones and most hotels.

International calls can be made via IT&E, a locally owned long-distance telephone company which has phone booths around the island and an office in San Jose. Calls can be placed at most booths 24 hours and at IT&E offices weekdays from 8 am to 6 pm (5 pm on weekends).

NORTHERN MARIANA ISLANDS

SAIPAN'S WEST COAST

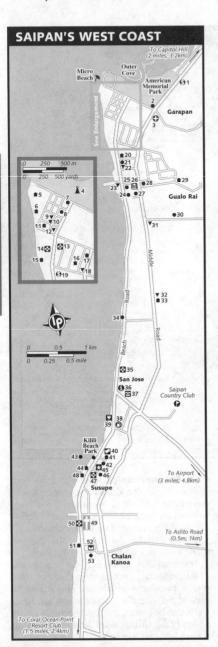

SAIPAN'S WEST COAST

PLACES TO STAY
5 Hyatt Regency Saipan; Gilligan's; Giovanni's; Kili Terrace; Windsurfing Saipan
6 Dai-Ichi Hotel
11 Remington Club
15 Hafadai Beach Hotel
16 Holiday In Saipan
17 Oriental Hotel; Shirley's Coffee Shop
20 Saipan Ocean View Hotel
29 Sugar King Hotel
33 Garden Motel
41 Sun Inn
44 Saipan Diamond Hotel
48 Saipan Grand Hotel
51 Pacific Gardenia Hotel; Sunset Bar & Grill

PLACES TO EAT
9 Chamorro House
10 Figueroa's
12 Bobby Cadillacs; Winchell's Donuts
18 Mom's Round II
22 Canton Restaurant
23 Thai House Restaurant
31 La Filipina
32 Kung Chun

OTHER
1 Bank of Hawaii
2 Public Tennis Courts
3 Commonwealth Health Center
4 Court of Honor Memorial
7 Fire Station
8 Saipan Scooters
13 DFS Galleria & Hard Rock Cafe
14 Hafadai Shopping Center
19 Bank of Guam
21 MITA Travel Office; Big Dipper
24 Abracadabra Dive Shop
25 Horiguchi (Federal) Building
26 CNMI Museum
27 Old Japanese Jail
28 Sugar King Park
30 Stingray Divers
34 Japanese Tank
35 Hakubotan
36 Marianas Visitors Authority
37 IT&E Office
38 24 Hour Petrol Station
39 Oleai Beach
40 Philippine Consulate
42 Island Farmer's Market
43 American Tanks (Offshore)
45 Police Station; Library
46 Nauru Building
47 Joeten Shopping Center
49 Mt Carmel Cathedral
50 Town House Shopping Center
52 Main Post Office
53 Saipan Farmers' Market

Bookshops Saipan's two bookstores both carry a limited selection of books on Micronesia. Bestseller, in the Joeten Shopping Center in Susupe, has magazines and a travel section (including Lonely Planet titles). Sablan Bookseller in the Sablan Building in Chalan Kanoa also has travel books.

Libraries The island's public library near the Joeten Shopping Center in Susupe is one of the most modern in Micronesia. It has good periodical and travel sections and Internet access. Opening hours are from 10 am to 6 pm weekdays and from 10 am to 4 pm on Saturday; the library is closed Wednesday and Sunday.

Emergency For police, fire and ambulance emergencies dial ☎ 911. Saipan's modern hospital, the Commonwealth Health Center (☎ 234 8950), is on Middle Rd in Garapan. For typhoon, storm, or medical evacuation emergencies call ☎ 322 9274.

Weather Information For 24-hour recorded weather information, including marine conditions, dial ☎ 234 5724.

Garapan
• pop 15,000

The Japanese developed Garapan, their administrative centre in the Marianas, into one of Micronesia's most bustling towns. Its streets were lined with neat rows of houses and its central area looked like a little Tokyo, with public baths, sake shops, Shinto shrines and Japanese schools and office buildings.

Garapan was completely levelled by US bombers during WWII and it wasn't until the 1960s that the Saipanese began to resettle the area.

These days Garapan has reawakened, thanks to Japanese tourists. The streets are lined with signs in Japanese announcing sushi shops, souvenir stores and karaoke clubs.

Micro Beach Micro Beach, Saipan's most attractive white-sand beach, is travel poster material. In fact, it's not that uncommon to find Japanese film crews shooting TV commercials on the shore. The broad beach has brilliant turquoise waters, a good view of Mañagaha Island and a fine angle for catching Saipan's lingering sunsets. It's also popular with windsurfers.

Water deep enough for swimming is a little way out but the wade is pleasant enough, except for a few squishy sea cucumbers, as the bottom is sandy.

There are public toilets and showers on the beach between the Dai-Ichi and Hyatt Hotels and at the north side of Micro Beach at American Memorial Park.

American Memorial Park The 133-acre (53-hectare) American Memorial Park, under the auspices of the US National Park Service, stretches north along the coast from the Hyatt hotel, encompassing the north end of Micro Beach and the Smiling Cove harbour area. To the east the park extends all the way to Middle Rd, and takes in a swamp forest that serves as an important bird habitat.

With the exception of public tennis courts on Middle Rd, all of the park's facilities are on the west side of Beach Rd. The park has beachside picnic grounds, restrooms and a popular ironwood-shaded jogging path that runs 1½ miles (2.4km) up the coast.

Along Beach Rd the park has erected two large memorials honouring Americans who died in the US invasions of Saipan and Tinian. One of these, the Court of Honor, is ringed by plaques inscribed with the names of the 2840 marines and 1824 infantrymen killed during the invasions, as well as the names of 505 navy personnel who died in the related battle of the Philippine Sea.

Sugar King Park Sugar King Park is a hodgepodge of historical and memorial sights on the east side of Middle Rd. A bright red railroad engine on a roadside grassy knoll makes the park easy to spot.

The steam-powered engine was once used to haul sugar cane from fields in the Marpi area to a factory in Chalan Kanoa where Mt Carmel Cathedral now stands. The route follows the present-day Middle Rd, although none of the train tracks remain.

The **bronze statue** in the centre of the park is of Haruji Matsue, head of the Nanyo Kohatsu Kaisha (South Seas Development Company), responsible for developing the sugar industry in the Marianas. The statue was erected in 1934 and survived the wartime bombings.

The rear section of the park is called the **Commonwealth Botanical Garden**. While it's not as extensive as the title might imply, there are some nice old trees and flowering bushes that make for pleasant strolling.

At the far end of the park, a red, river-less bridge leads to a **Japanese shrine** called the Katori Jinja. Originally built in 1911, it was destroyed in 1944 and rebuilt in concrete in 1985. Steps behind the shrine lead to a 15-minute loop trail that climbs around the back of the hill, stopping along the way at a **hexagonal prayer temple** dedicated to WWII Japanese soldiers.

CNMI Museum The ruins of the old Japanese hospital, on Middle Rd directly across from Sugar King Park, have been converted into a small air-conditioned historical museum. The museum has pottery, illustrations, and models from Saipan's history. The highlight is a few cases of trinkets recovered from the 17th-century wreckage of the Spanish galleon *Concepción*.

Old Japanese Jail A bit further south on Middle Rd, the old Japanese jail stands largely intact and makes for an interesting sight. You can walk down the corridor past the damp concrete cells, some of which still have barred steel doors attached. The main cell block row was for male civilian prisoners. Geishas who stole from their customers' pockets and women who didn't complete their employment contracts were held in a smaller building. There is a rumour that US aviator Amelia Earhart, who disappeared during her round-the-world flight in 1937, was shot down by the Japanese and held in this Saipan jail before being executed as a spy.

North of Garapan

North of Garapan are **Tanapag** and **San Roque**, once sleepy seaside villages that are being invaded by new resort developments. San Roque has a large shopping centre, La Fiesta San Roque, where you can stop and get a meal, and there are grocery stores in both Tanapag and San Roque.

The northern tip of the island, called **Marpi**, has most of Saipan's WWII tourist attractions and some of the island's prettiest scenery. It's easy to explore as the roads are well paved. Still, it's an undeveloped area, with much of the roadside lined with papaya trees and *tangan-tangan* bushes.

The defoliation of Saipan during WWII was so complete that the quick-growing tangan-tangan was aerially seeded to keep parts of the island from washing into the sea. Today this pervasive shrub is Saipan's most prevalent plant. While preventing major erosion, it has also choked out native flora and upset the natural pre-war ecosystem.

Pau Pau Beach Pau Pau Beach in San Roque has the splashy Hotel Nikko Saipan at its south end, but its north end remains

---

Sunken Treasure

In 1638 the Manila galleon *Nuestra Señora de la Concepción* went down in rough gales east of Agingan Point, scattering its rich treasure along the shallow reef that now borders the Coral Ocean Point Resort Club golf course.

In 1987, after searching through archives in Seville, Mexico City and Manila to research the location and cargo, an international crew of 30, including historians and archaeologists, began a two-year salvage operation. Some 10,000 dives later they had recovered scores of cannonballs and ballast stones, 1300 pieces of gold jewellery, many inlaid with precious gems, and 156 storage jars, some still filled with fragrant resins. Some of the pieces were recovered in as little as two feet of water.

Suicide Attack

The quiet village of Tanapag was the site of one of the most fanatical attacks of WWII. On the night of 6 July 1944, 4000 Japanese soldiers, many emboldened by sake, hurled themselves in a *banzai* attack upon US forces, which were lined up along Tanapag Beach. Some of the Japanese had guns, but most were armed with only clubs, bayonets, bamboo spears and grenades.

The Japanese, honour-bound to die one way or another in the face of defeat, were intent on taking as many Americans with them as possible. As wave after wave of Japanese soldiers rushed down in the surprise attack, the Americans were pushed out into the water, across Tanapag Harbor and all the way back onto the reef, firing continuously at the unrelenting enemy. By the next morning it was all over and 5000 men were dead.

pleasantly undeveloped. It has soft sand, a picnic shelter, fairly shallow waters, and good snorkelling and swimming during high tide.

Originally named Papau, meaning 'bitter root', the beach was inadvertently changed to its present name by Americans, and Pau Pau is now used by everyone except older Saipanese.

A paved road just north of the Hotel Nikko leads down to the beach.

Wing Beach Wing Beach was named after the US navy aircraft wing that lay half buried in the sand for decades before falling victim to an aluminium recycling program.

The south end of the beach has a shoreline coral shelf, but the north end is sandy and has good snorkelling.

Wing Beach is a mile (1.6km) north of Pau Pau Beach. Turn left off Marpi Rd just beyond the country club swimming pool. This unmarked road changes from packed coral to dirt after one-third of a mile (500m). You should be able to make it down in a car, though it might get a bit rough if there has been heavy rain. The beach sand is a pleasant mix of white shells and coral

bits; vines of white and purple morning-glory add a splash of colour.

Memorials A series of WWII memorial parks are neatly lined up along the road starting about 7½ miles (12km) north of Garapan. The first is the Korean Peace Memorial, the second park is dedicated to Okinawans and the Last Japanese Command Post is straight ahead.

Banzai Cliff Waves crash onto the jagged rocks below Banzai Cliff, one of the places where hundreds of Japanese civilians jumped to their deaths as the Americans were taking over the island in 1944.

Whole families lined up in order of age. Each child was pushed over the edge by the next oldest brother or sister, until the mother pushed the oldest child and the father pushed his wife before running backwards over the cliff himself. Although US soldiers dropped leaflets and shouted through loud-speakers that those who surrendered would not be harmed, the mass suicides were deemed preferable to the shame of capture and, it was presumed, torture.

Over the years the Japanese have put up a number of plaques and memorials to commemorate the spot, including a large **statue of Heiwa Kannon**, the Peaceful Goddess of Mercy.

The turn-off to Banzai Cliff is off Marpi Rd opposite the Okinawa Peace Memorial.

Last Japanese Command Post It was at the spot now known as the Last Command Post that troops of the Japanese Imperial Army readied themselves for their final desperate battle against American invasion forces.

Lieutenant General Yoshitsugo Saito, acknowledging defeat, asked his remaining soldiers to each take seven American lives for the emperor, triggering the banzai suicide attack at Tanapag Harbor. Saito then faced north-west towards Japan and committed hara-kiri, thrusting his sword into his stomach while his aide shot him in the head.

Guns, torpedoes and tanks have been placed on the lawn below the concrete bunker which served as the command post. The bunker, which was built into the rock face, is cleverly concealed. You can climb up inside and scramble around.

Suicide Cliff Half a mile (800m) beyond the Last Command Post, you'll come to a fork where you should bear right. At a second fork, which is a mile (1.6km) farther on, continue straight ahead to get to the Grotto and Bird Island, or bear right to get to Suicide Cliff.

From this turn-off, it's 2 miles (3.2km) up to Suicide Cliff. Follow the paved road all the way. Some of the signs read 'Laderan Banadero', the Chamorro name for this area.

There is also a paved roadside path leading from the Japanese command posts to the top of Suicide Cliff. In the early evenings, it becomes a popular (if challenging) spot for runners.

Suicide Cliff's 820-foot (249m) sheer rock face was another site for Japanese suicides, similar to those that took place on Banzai Cliff.

The cliff provides an excellent view of the northern tip of the island. Below the lookout you can see the remains of the North Field runway, an old Japanese fighter strip. White-tailed tropicbirds and fairy terns swoop and soar in the wind drafts along the cliffs.

The Grotto The Grotto, Saipan's unique diving spot, is a collapsed limestone cavern with a pool of cobalt-blue seawater filled by three underwater passageways. Sometimes the Grotto is calm and at other times powerful surges of water come whooshing in and out.

Once locals who wanted to swim in the Grotto had to shimmy down a rope, but there are now steep concrete stairs down to the water. Tiny stalactites drip from above and massive spider webs hanging overhead make interesting photographs if caught in the right light. The glowing blue light at the bottom of the rock wall comes from the tunnels that lead to the open sea. There's a viewpoint looking down into the Grotto at the top of the stairs to the left.

To get to the Grotto, turn left a quarter of a mile (400m) past the Suicide Cliff turn-off and follow the road to the end.

Bird Island Lookout Bird Island, a rocky limestone islet close to shore, is a wildlife sanctuary that provides a habitat for brown noddies and other seabirds.

The windy lookout affords a scenic view of **Bird Island**, the east side of which is battered by open ocean while the inland side is protected by a calm reef. The purple beach morning-glory that grows around the lookout cliff is known as *alalag-tasi* in Chamorro.

Bird Island Trail You can hike down to Bird Island but not from the lookout. Instead, head back the way you came and look for the start of the trail three-quarters of a mile (1.2km) on the right, shortly before the turn-off to the Grotto.

The beginning of the dirt footpath, which looks like an eroded driveway, leads down the hill through tall grass and a canopy of tangan-tangan.

At the bottom there's a coral sand beach. The water is clear and coral formations provide good snorkelling between Bird Island and the beach. Currents are rough beyond the reef.

Cross Island Road The Cross Island Rd heads north from Garapan, turns inland to Capitol Hill, circles around Mt Tagpochau, goes south through San Vicente and then heads back to the west coast, passing the Northern Marianas College on the left and ending up on Beach Rd in San Jose.

From various spots around Capitol Hill, and on the drive up from Garapan, there are excellent views of Tanapag Harbor, Mañagaha Island and the brilliant turquoise waters of the lagoon.

East of Garapan
Capitol Hill Capitol Hill is the site of most government offices for the Commonwealth of the Northern Marianas, including those of the governor and the legislature.

The complex of houses and office buildings that make up Capitol Hill was built in

1948 by the CIA as a base camp for secretly training Nationalist Chinese guerrillas to fight against Mao Zedong. The soldiers were trained in the Marpi area.

After the CIA moved out in 1962, Capitol Hill became the headquarters for the Trust Territory government. In the 1980s, as the Trust Territory was dismantled, the buildings were turned over to the emerging commonwealth government.

Mt Tagpochau You can drive right to the top of Mt Tagpochau which, at 1545 feet (463m), is Saipan's highest point. To get there take the crossroad opposite the convention centre on Capitol Hill, drive a short way up through the housing project and turn right up to the former Congress of Micronesia buildings, now marked as civil defence and energy agencies. Continue a few hundred yards beyond the buildings and take the dirt road heading down to the right. If it's been raining heavily you may need a 4WD vehicle from this point, but otherwise a sedan takes about 10 minutes to get to the top.

Each Easter, hundreds of Saipanese hike up Mt Tagpochau carrying a heavy wooden cross to plant at the top. There are excellent views of most of the island from the summit.

East Coast Beaches Much of Saipan's east coast is rugged shoreline battered by heavy seas, although there are some protected areas. Most of these beaches can be difficult to reach, as they are at the end of dirt roads that are subject to wash-outs after heavy rains.

Profile Beach is an isolated little beach with a limestone islet called Old Man by the Sea, which looks remarkably like the laughing head of an old man. To get there turn off Cross Island Rd at Esco's Bake House at the south end of Capitol Hill. Take a left at the fork and park about 100 feet (30m) down. The trailhead is on the right side of the road and it's about a 20-minute hike to the beach.

Alternatively, follow the road past Esco's Bake House to its end to reach **Jeffries (Talofofo) Beach**, which has a small pocket

beach and some nearby natural arches and blowholes.

Tank, Marine and Laulau are other east coast beaches that can all be reached by dirt roads. **Laulau Beach**, on the north side of Magicienne Bay, is one of the more popular and protected beaches on the east coast and is good for beach dives.

Another popular remote beach is **Forbidden Island**, which has a long stretch of beach, a grotto and a swimming hole. It's on an island-like peninsula south-east of the Laolao Bay Golf Resort and requires a 20-minute hike to reach.

South of Garapan

San Jose, Susupe, Chalan Kanoa and San Antonio were once distinct villages on Saipan's south-west coast until a decade of development turned Beach Rd into a nearly continuous strip of nightclubs, restaurants and shopping centres.

Susupe has the police station, courthouse and library. Chalan Kanoa has the main post office, the island's only remaining cinema and the picturesque Mt Carmel Cathedral. San Antonio is still the quieter end of the area, though it's being developed.

Southern Beaches Ladder and Obyan are two south coast beaches that get a few local picnickers, but are well off the tourist track. To reach them, go around the south-west tip of the airport runway. The road to Ladder Beach is on the right a quarter of a mile (400m) after passing the turn-off to Koblerville.

Ladder Beach is a rounded cove backed with 30-foot (9m) limestone cliffs. Most of the beach is covered with chunky coral pebbles, and the water is generally too rough for swimming. There are large caves in the cliffs that are used as picnic shelters, complete with picnic tables.

More appealing is **Obyan Beach**, a pretty white-sand beach with calm waters protected by Naftan Point. The expansive beach is good for shelling and snorkelling. At the head of the parking area is a large WWII concrete bunker, and about 75 yards east, just inland from a grove of coconut trees, are the remains of eight **latte stones** that have been carbon dated to around 1500 BC. The stones, which are easy to find, are in two parallel rows and are thought to have once supported a beachside structure.

The turn-off down to Obyan Beach is 1½ miles (2.4km) beyond Ladder Beach.

Mañagaha Island

Mañagaha, the island 1½ miles (2.4km) north-west of Micro Beach, is an old patch reef that geological forces lifted above sea level some 10,000 years ago. It's now covered with a fringing white-sand beach and has Saipan's best snorkelling. The clear waters surrounding the island have lots of colourful tropical fish and there's also abundant coral, although much of the near-shore coral shows signs of being trampled on – a consequence of the beach's heavy use.

This uninhabited island is small and only takes 20 minutes to walk around. The island has the rusting remains of a few war relics, including a pair of coastal cannons along the beach near the boat landing. On the other side of the island is a colourful statue and a small monument marking the burial site of the Yapese chief Aghurubw, who in 1815 led a group of settlers from the Satawal atoll in the Yap chain and established a Carolinian settlement on Saipan.

Once the domain of Saipanese picnickers, Mañagaha is now packed popular with tourists. Consequently the food and beach gear equipment are extremely pricey: US$15 will get you use of a beach mat or snorkel set, US$3 buys a soft drink and US$21 a barbecue lunch.

There are covered picnic tables and free changing rooms with toilets, showers and coin lockers for US$2 to US$3.

Getting There & Away All regularly scheduled boats to Mañagaha leave from the new Outer Cove marina. The crossing takes about 15 minutes.

The *Sounds of Saipan* leaves at 9, 10 and 11 am and 1 pm, and the last boat returns at 3.30 pm. The regular tourist price is US$35; Tasi Tours (☎ 234 7148) has current information.

The *Sounds of Coral* has a submerged lower deck with two rows of benches facing a series of windows. It is a better choice if you want to see a bit of the underwater world on the way to Mañagaha, as it takes a more scenic route, passing over a sunken Japanese Zero. It leaves four times a day and costs US$49 (US$35 for children). Reservations are made through Island Cruise Line (☎ 233 2556).

Saipan Marine Tours (☎ 322 9008) has a glass-bottom boat that also passes over the Japanese Zero and some coral heads on the way to Mañagaha. The cost is from US$25, children from US$20, including a free mask and snorkel but no lunch. Hit Tours (☎ 322 8778) has a slightly cheaper package for US$35 an adult, US$25 for children, without lunch.

Activities

Saipan rigorously observes a tiered pricing system, customised to tax everyone's wallet. For diving or other activities, there is typically one price quoted for locals and another for tourists. As in Guam, the trick to getting cheap 'local' rates is to visit the Marianas Bureau of Motor Vehicles (☎ 664 9066) in Susupe and obtain a Saipan driver's licence – though a Guam licence will qualify you as a local too. Just bring your current licence and a US$15 processing fee.

Diving & Snorkelling Saipan's most unusual and exciting dive is the Grotto, a natural cavern with waters 50 feet (15m) deep and tunnels to the open sea. Although it's a popular spot for locals to swim and for divers with a guide, the tricky currents can be quite dangerous for the uninitiated. Always get a thorough briefing before going out. You'll also need to be in good physical condition to do the dive, as it involves carrying tanks up and down a long, steep set of stairs.

Other popular dives include war wrecks in Tanapag Harbor, caves and garden eels at Obyan Beach, and a huge coral head offshore from the Saipan Grand Hotel.

Saipan's best snorkelling is at Mañagaha Island. Pau Pau, Laulau and Wing beaches have reasonably good snorkelling, as does Bird Island, though it requires a hike. You can also snorkel out around a couple of US Army tanks that rest in the shallow waters off Susupe's Kilili Beach, where US invasion forces first came ashore in June 1944. It's best to stick to the tank nearest the beach, as jet skiers commonly race around the tank farther offshore.

Dive Shops Most of Saipan's many dive operations are geared to the Japanese market. Among the English-language operations is Abracadabra (☎ 233 7234, fax 233 7235, ✆ ejcomfort@saipan.com) along Beach Rd south of Garapan. Ed and Jeannie give two-tank dives to shipwrecks for US$65; a full day at Tinian costs US$90. Gear costs US$45, but if you're diving consecutive days you don't have to re-rent the gear. Abracadabra plans to expand to include helicopter fly-ins and kayak eco-tours. It has a full-day kayak-dive for US$150. Snorkel sets can be rented for US$10.

Stingray Divers (☎ 233 6100, fax 234 3709, ✆ rick.northen@saipan.com) is at Gualo Rai (take the turn-off from Middle Rd toward the Honey Motel and take the first left). Another American-run operation, Stingray has beach dives from US$30 and boat dives for US$40 to US$45 per tank. Gear rents for US$20 to US$35 and introductory dives cost US$60. Staff will also motor over to Tinian upon request.

Other Water Sports Windsurfing is popular on Saipan, the only island in the Northern Marianas with a large lagoon, especially on Micro Beach.

Windsurfing Saipan (☎ 234 6965), inside the old WWII bunker on Micro Beach by the Hyatt, is run by a friendly English-speaking expat from Japan. Windsurfing equipment costs US$60 a day and US$40 a half day. Windsurfing lessons cost US$30 an hour, including equipment. The shop also rents snorkel sets for US$8 and one-person kayaks for US$15 an hour. Groups are taken to Mañagaha for US$20 a head.

There are more beach stands in front of the Dai-Ichi Hotel that rent various water sports equipment, including windsurfing gear, kayaks and catamarans. They can also make arrangements for water-skiing, para-sailing and trolling.

Hiking & Jogging Saipan has a number of options for good walking, including the jogging trail that begins at the north side of Micro Beach. The northern part of the island holds some overgrown forest trails. Joggers, roller-bladers and strollers can also enjoy the new Beach Pathway, a paved path running 2¾ miles (4.35km) along the coast north to Garapan from Kilili Beach Park.

Saipan has a Hash House Harriers group that meets fortnightly at the Bank of Guam across from DFS Galleria in Garapan at 3.30 on Saturday afternoons. They run a different route each time; a US$6 donation covers beer and snacks.

Golf Saipan has four 18-hole golf courses and one nine-hole course.

The nine-hole Saipan Country Club (☎ 234 8718) in Laulau Beach charges US$20/50 for locals/tourists.

The scenic Laolao Bay Golf Resort (☎ 256 8888), in the Kagman area, has an east course facing the sea and a mountainous west course. It charges US$170/150 for the east/west courses, though locals pay only US$30/25.

Coral Ocean Point Resort Club (☎ 234 7000) has an 18-hole golf course on the coast at Agingan Point, at the south side of the island. The cost for a round of golf, cart included, is US$130 for tourists.

The 18-hole golf course at the Marianas Country Club (☎ 322 2211) in Marpi charges US$50/$95 for locals/tourists.

Kingfisher Golf Links along the coast in Talofofo is an 18-hole course costing US$150 for tourists; locals pay US$35 on weekdays, US$50 weekends.

There is also Dandan Driving Range (☎ 288 7061), on the airport road about a mile (1.6km) north of the airport. A bucket of balls costs US$4.

Tennis The American Memorial Park maintains four public tennis courts at the north end of Middle Rd. The courts, lit for night play, are free.

Many 1st-class hotels have tennis courts that are free to their guests.

Bowling Saipan Bowling Center (☎ 233 7899), on Beach Rd south of Garapan, has 16 lanes and is open weekdays from 6 pm to midnight, and weekends from 5 pm to midnight. It costs US$13 per game.

Organised Tours

A number of tour companies with offices at the larger hotels offer land tours, sunset cruises, and trips to Rota and Tinian.

Most land tours of Saipan are geared to Japanese package tourists and they don't take you anywhere you can't easily explore on your own. Helicopter rides offer a more interesting alternative; try Macaw Helicopters (☎ 234 1304), which does flight-seeing tours of Saipan, operating out of Coral Ocean Point Resort Club in Koblerville. A 15-minute spin costs US$65 (children US$55) and a 30-minute ride costs US$99 (children US$81).

Freedom Air (☎ 234 8328) has Piper Cherokee six-seater planes that can be chartered for sightseeing at US$300 an hour.

A 48-passenger submarine goes out six times daily in the lagoon between Saipan and Mañagaha Island. Because the lagoon is fairly shallow, the sub descends only to about 45 feet (13m). Underwater sights include the ruins of a Japanese freighter and an American B-29. The tour runs just under two hours and costs US$82; call ☎ 322 7746 for info.

Special Events

Village fiestas are held in San Vicente in early April, in San Antonio in mid-June, at the Mt Carmel Cathedral in Chalan Kanoa in mid-July, in San Roque in mid-August, in Tanapag in early October and in Koblerville in late October.

The week-long Liberation Day Festival celebrates the American liberation of the islands and ends on 4 July, US Independence Day. Festivities include a beauty pageant,

nightly entertainment, games and food booths.

Sporting events are Saipan's forte. Saipan hosts a half marathon and a 10km fun run along Beach Rd in late January, the popular Tagaman triathlon (info ☎ 234 1001) in mid-May and a five-mile (8km) run (info ☎ 322 6201) up Mt Tagpochau on Thanksgiving. The Tagaman consists of a 2km swim, a 60km bike ride and a 15km run, and attracts international competitors.

The annual Micronesian Open Board-sailing Regatta and the Saipan Laguna Regatta are international windsurfing and catamaran competitions held at Micro Beach in mid-February; dial ☎ 234 6965 for info. There's also a Windsurfing Open (write to: CNMI Windsurfing Association, PPP 652 Box 10000), and a fishing tournament is held during the August marlin season.

Places to Stay

Most Saipan hotels, including the listings that follow, accept major credit cards. Add a 10% hotel tax to all room rates. Many resort hotels have periodic discounts; call to inquire.

Unless otherwise noted, the hotels below have air-con, cable TV, phones, mini-fridges and private bathroom.

During the Japanese holiday season, particularly Christmas through January and mid-July through August, it is more difficult to find accommodation, and advance reservations are recommended.

Places to Stay – Budget

Camping There are no developed camping grounds in Saipan, and the high local unemployment rate has spawned enough crime to deter campers. To build a bonfire on the beach you need permission from the Division of Coastal Resources Management (☎ 234 6623).

Uninhabited Mañagaha would be a good spot for overnighting, except for the hundreds of day tourists.

Hotels If you don't mind being inland, the *Valley Inn* (*☎ 234 7018, fax 234 7029*) is an excellent budget choice. The staff are

Chief's house or *bai*, Palau

Basket-weaving on Majuro

Majestic flame trees thrive in the Marianas

The lory, Pohnpei's state bird

The frigate bird, under threat of extinction

The notorious brown tree snake, Guam

Giant clam (tridacna cronea)

Gazebo on Pohnpei

cheery and helpful, and the pleasant rooms surround a central courtyard. The lowest-priced studio rooms are compact but cosy and have a separate kitchen. These studios go for US$45 (tax included) or US$550 per month, utilities included. There's free morning coffee, a coin-operated laundry and a barbecue grill. Lucky's Store is within walking distance. Free airport transfers are available but the location – a five-minute drive from the airport – is really only practical if you plan to rent a car.

The *Garden Motel* (☎ 234 3729) along Middle Rd is another small, family-run hotel with a comfortable atmosphere. Watch carefully for its sign, which is partially obscured by trees. Rooms with the usual amenities and a VCR go for US$39 (tax included). A cafe is on site and airport transfers are available.

The Korean-owned *Sun Palace Hotel* (☎ 234 3232, fax 235 6062), behind the baseball field in Susupe, has 36 large rooms at some of the best rates in Saipan. Singles/doubles start at US$30. Some of the rooms bear faint traces of cigarette smoke, and the air-con might not be really cold but it's cheap, safe and reliable.

The new *Stanford Resort* (☎ 235 8500, fax 235 3042), high on a hill beyond San Vicente, is a classic case of the late 1990s economic-crisis hotel malady. Pleasant, spacious and deserted rooms around a pool, once US$72, now go for US$29 (including tax). Rooms have a light and airy feel. Airport transfers are free; breakfast is just US$3. Up a pot-holed dirt road, this place should not be considered without a car.

The *Sugar King Hotel* (☎ 234 6164), in a quiet area above Sugar King Park, has 24 very cramped, run-down rooms in garishly coloured concrete duplex cottages. Rates are US$30 (including tax) for one or two people in a room with a platform-style double bed, refrigerator, air-con and TV but no phone. The swimming pool was being renovated at the time of research.

Places to Stay – Mid-Range

The locally owned *Pacific Gardenia Hotel* (☎ 234 3455, fax 234 3411) is on Beach Rd

at the north end of Chalan Kanoa. Despite being in a gambling area, there's a gorgeous white-sand beach at the back of the hotel. The 14 rooms, all on the 2nd floor along an atrium-like hallway, are large and well furnished and all but two have kitchens. The rate is US$54/60 for singles/doubles, including a continental breakfast and one free drink at the bar. The helpful staff can provide cribs, ironing boards and the like upon request. There's also a coin laundry and free airport transfers.

Finasisu Airport Hotel (☎ 235 6524, fax 235 8013, @ finasisuhotel@saipan.com), a short drive from the airport, is a large, architecturally bizarre-looking apartment complex with one wing converted for daily rentals. The units each have a full kitchen, living room and two bedrooms, one with two single beds and the other with a queen-size bed. Utensils are provided upon request. The rate is US$60. It's good value if you're looking for a lot of space and condo-like accommodation. There's a coin-operated laundry and a small coffee shop on site. Airport transfers are free, but you'll need a rental car.

The new *Hotel Riviera Saipan* (☎ 235 2111, fax 235 1614) is very near the Finasisu Airport Hotel. Promoted as 'Little Korea in Saipan', it caters almost exclusively to Korean and Japanese tourists. Large rooms with all amenities surround a pool; the open-air setup means you can hear birds chirping from your room. Free airport transfers are available. Rooms cost US$55.

The Japanese-owned *Remington Club* (☎ 234 5449, fax 234 5619) is an 18-room pension-style hotel in Garapan, just a minute's walk from Micro Beach. The rooms are simple but adequate. Considering that it's in the midst of Garapan's resort area, the hotel is a reasonable value at US$55/72 for singles/doubles. There are also a few twin rooms with kitchenettes and TV, and a two-bedroom suite for up to four people.

The 26-room *Holiday In Saipan* (☎ 234 3554, fax 235 5023), a couple of blocks inland from Beach Rd in Garapan, has decent rooms. Rates are US$50 for singles/doubles. There's a pool and airport transfers for US$10 each way.

Saipan Ocean View Hotel (☎ *234 8900, fax 234 9428*) is an 87-room hotel on Beach Rd in Garapan. Its modern rooms are tastefully arranged and are reasonably priced (US$55 for singles/doubles). There's a pool and free airport transfers.

The Chinese-owned **Oriental Hotel** (☎ *233 1420, fax 233 1424,* **@** *orientalhotel @saipan.com*), on Middle Rd opposite the Commonwealth Health Center, is a good choice for a mid-range hotel. Rooms have twin and double beds, minibar and bathtub. Singles/doubles cost US$54/60. It's a 10-minute walk to central Garapan and Micro Beach. Airport transfers are free.

Places to Stay – Top End

Because Saipan's larger hotels thrive on the package-tour trade, room rates are typically high, and there is a strong Japanese feel.

The seven-storey **Hyatt Regency Saipan** (☎ *234 1234, fax 234 7745*) is right on Micro Beach. All 325 rooms have balconies with sunset and ocean views. Rates start at US$275; prices in the newer south wing are from US$325, and rooms in the regency wing are higher still. Airport transfers are US$15 each way. The Hyatt, though the oldest of Saipan's resort hotels, has been refurbished and has the most international clientele and the best beach location. The grounds are pleasantly landscaped and the club has a pool, lit tennis courts, a fitness centre and excellent restaurants.

The **Aqua Resort Club** (☎ *322 1234, fax 322 1220*), on the beach in Tanapag, is among the top of the Japanese-oriented resorts. It has a casual yet classy ambience, with a pleasant open-air lobby that incorporates some Micronesian touches, a fabulous beachfront setting, large swimming pools, a good restaurant and friendly staff. All 91 rooms have verandas (most with ocean views), ceiling fans, room safes, refrigerators, minibar, and separate bathing and toilet areas as well as the usual amenities. Rates start at US$270. Airport transfers cost US$15 each way.

The **Hotel Nikko Saipan** (☎ *322 3311, fax 322 3144,* **@** *hnsrrv@itecnmi.com*), near Pau Pau beach in San Roque, is a plush hotel with 313 rooms from US$235.

Places to Eat

A tip of at least 10% is expected at most restaurants.

Places to Eat – Budget

The booths at Garapan's **Winchell's Donuts** on Beach Rd are a popular place to start the day. Doughnuts cost US$0.50 and you can get a decent cup of coffee for US$0.65, which is about half the price of most other places.

Bobby Cadillacs (☎ *234 3976*), a near neighbour to Winchell's, is all things to all people. Some swear by its US$4 pancakes, others by its pizzas and still others by its killer meat sandwiches. But all appreciate the US$2 Budweisers. Call ahead for takeaway.

Herman's Modern Bakery, on the airport road, is a local eatery with cheap breakfasts, sandwiches and lunch specials. Herman started his bakery in 1944 to bake bread for American GIs. By the time the GIs had moved out the Saipanese had developed a lasting taste for bread. Herman's continues to supply most of Saipan's cakes, bread and pastries. It opens at 6 am every day; come early for the freshest bread.

Shirley's Coffee Shop, in the Oriental Hotel, is a small branch of the beloved Guam restaurant. Here it's more a quick-stop than a restaurant, but you can still get a hearty meal and good coffee all day. Among the choices are omelettes, sandwiches, curry, seafood and steak, all at reasonable prices (US$6 and higher). Another branch is in Chalan Laulau.

Canton Restaurant on Beach Rd in Garapan has good, cheap weekday lunch specials. From 11 am to 2 pm you can select from numerous dishes, including standards like beef with vegetables or sweet and sour pork, served with rice and soup, for just US$5 to US$6. At dinner, from 5.30 to 10.30 pm, there's an extensive menu, with most items from US$9 to US$10. On weekend nights the place fills with Chinese families and groups.

Mom's Round II, a few blocks inland from the Hafadai Beach Hotel in Garapan, is a bar with dart boards and inexpensive Mexican food. You can get a taco, burrito or enchilada for US$5.50 and a cheeseburger with fries for US$6.50.

The cool spot for ice cream is *Big Dipper*, on Beach Rd beside the MITA office, where generous 'small' cones cost US$2. The ice cream itself is imported from the USA.

Saipan Farmers' Market, the 'Co-op of the Hardworking People', is a simple fruit and vegetable market opposite the post office in Chalan Kanoa. It sells local papaya, betel nut and taro, but much of the other produce is imported so prices are on the high side. The *Island Farmers' Market* in Susupe, also small, has some fruits and vegetables and casks of fresh fish. It also sells sushi lunch wraps and cold sandwiches.

Supermarkets in Saipan are modern and well stocked, at least by Micronesian standards. The *Hafadai Shopping Center* has the best selection of breads and cheese, the former supplied by the deli-bakery next door. It is open until 11 pm. *Joeten Supermarket*, in the eponymous shopping centre in Susupe, is also well stocked.

Places to Eat – Mid-Range

The friendly *Coffee Care*, half a mile (800m) up the Capitol Hill Rd, is run by a former Peace Corps worker and is a favourite expat watering hole. Besides lattes, cappuccinos and espressos galore, you can also get light meals such as sandwiches, soups, salads and desserts at reasonable prices. The US$10 Foccacia sandwich, one of the pricier sandwich options, is also popular. Veggie sandwiches are US$7. At dinner there are often specials, such as pasta or Thai food, for around US$10. It's open Monday to Saturday from 7 am to midnight, and Sunday from 8 am to midnight. There's an extensive bar.

Rudolpho's (☎ 322 3017), opposite the turn-off to Capitol Hill, has good, reasonably priced Mexican and Italian food. The

bar is a favourite expat hangout, and there's both indoor and outdoor seating. You can get a taco, burrito or enchilada with rice and beans for around US$7 to US$8, or lasagna with garlic bread for the same price. Seafood, chicken and steak meals cost from US$10 to US$17, and there are good pizzas and hearty sandwiches. It has great daily dinner specials like US$1 pizza or discount margaritas. Call for home delivery (US$1.50 delivery charge).

Thai House Restaurant on Beach Rd at the southern end of Garapan has good Thai food at moderate prices. It has weekday lunch specials for US$7 or you can order off the menu. Pad Thai, red or green curries and other dishes cost US$7 to US$8. The spring rolls make a great appetiser. If you're not used to hot food, order mild, as even moderate can be quite fiery and the Thai-hot is strictly for the initiated. Frosty 18-ounce (500g) mugs of Steinlager on tap cost US$3.50. It's open for lunch on weekdays from 11 am to 2 pm and for dinner daily from 5 to 10 pm. Domestic beer prices drop at the 4 to 6 pm happy hour.

Kung Chun (☎ 234 1249), a new Korean restaurant on Middle Rd, is popular for its cheap and tasty barbecue buffet; the dinner buffet is US$10, the lunch buffet US$8. The setting is spacious and comfortable, the service friendly. The restaurant is open daily from 7 am to 10 pm, noon to 3 pm and 6 to 10 pm.

Chamorro food is basically the same in Saipan as in Guam, except it's harder to find. One exception is *Chamorro House*, in the Micro Beach area, which serves quality local food, though prices are a bit high as it caters to the Japanese crowd. Its best deal is lunch, when Chamorro dishes such as *tinaktak katni* (beef strips in coconut milk) and *kelaguen mannok* (a tasty dish of grilled chicken and fresh shredded coconut in a light lemon sauce) go for US$7.50. Dinner prices are about double. At both meals these dishes are served with red rice, soup and salad. It's open daily from 6.30 am to 1.30 pm and from 5.30 to 9.30 pm.

For Filipino food, the clear choice is *La Filipina* along Middle Rd, which has tasty assorted seafood, pork, beef and vegetable offerings for very reasonable prices – generally US$7.50 to US$10. It's open daily from 9 am to 1 am.

The spacious, globe-shaped **Hard Rock Cafe** in the DFS Galleria building rocks to the usual tune of burgers, salads and sandwiches from around US$9. It's open daily from 9 am to 2 am.

The new **Figueroa's** (☎ 234 2739) in central Garapan has reliably good pizzas from US$9 to US$13, along with chicken, seafood, and meat dishes from US$9 to US$16. The restaurant has two free Internet terminals for patrons; it also has a van that does hotel pick-ups if you call. It's open daily from 11 am to 2 am. Happy hour is from 4 to 7 pm Monday to Saturday.

Places to Eat – Top End

The Aqua Resort Club's **Terrace Restaurant** (☎ 322 1234) has an Austrian chef and Saipan's best-value buffets. Friday nights feature fresh oysters, shrimp and other seafood; on Saturday there's Black Angus prime rib. The seafood buffet costs US$20 and the prime rib buffet a bit more. Both are accompanied by an extensive spread of hot dishes and appetisers, including sashimi, tempura and salads. There's an impressive dessert table and excellent service. Sunday features a sparkling wine brunch with prime rib, suckling pig and an array of other foods for US$19 (US$12 for children) from 10.30 am to 2 pm. On other days, from 11 am to 2 pm, there's a 'light and easy' luncheon buffet (US$12) that includes luncheon meats, soup, salads, desserts and iced tea.

The Hyatt's **Kili Terrace** has a reasonably good, though somewhat overpriced, lunch buffet from 11 am to 2 pm Monday to Saturday. You can sit out in the pleasant open-air terrace beside the pond and eat your fill of such dishes as mahimahi, sushi, soba, spareribs, breads, soup, salads and desserts for US$20. There's also an à la carte menu with a range of lunch and dinner dishes; spaghetti is US$13, steak US$20. Dinner also features tasty changing buffets which are a bit pricier.

The Hyatt's new and popular **Giovanni's**, just inside from Kili Terrace, has Italian pasta from US$12.50 to US$15.50 and a variety of gourmet pizzas priced around US$15. Giovanni's is open for dinner only from 6 to 10 pm.

Sango (☎ 234 7000) at the Coral Ocean Point Resort Club has an ocean view across the golf course and a good-value weekday bento box lunch that costs US$9 and includes three Japanese dishes, rice, miso soup and iced tea. Come early lest they run out. At other times there are various set meals for US$15 to US$25.

Entertainment

The open-air **Sunset Bar & Grill**, behind the Pacific Gardenia Hotel in Chalan Kanoa, is a fabulous sunset locale right on a white-sand beach. Happy hour is from 5 to 8 pm with US$2.50 beers and free popcorn, and live entertainment starts at 9 pm nightly except Monday. There's a beachside barbecue grill with chicken and steaks for US$15 to US$20; or make a tasty meal out of the bar's hors d'oeuvres.

The beachfront patio at **Oleai Beach**, a bar and grill in San Jose, is also a nice place to be at sunset. At happy hour, which on weekdays is all afternoon until 7 pm, drink prices drop US$0.50.

The **Remington Club** (see Places to Stay – Mid-Range) in Garapan is a local hangout popular for its pool table. There are live bands starting at 9.30 pm nightly except Tuesday, and the music is anything from cha cha to Jawaiian (an upbeat mix of reggae and contemporary Hawaiian music). Drinks are half-price from 5 to 7.30 pm.

Gilligan's in the Hyatt hosts dinner shows and then turns into a dance floor from 9 pm to 2 am (closed Monday). There's a US$5 cover charge.

There's a **cinema** in Chalan Kanoa on the west side of the post office and **cockfights** at the Saipan Game Club on Middle Rd in Garapan.

Shopping

Virtually none of the carvings, woven wall hangings or other handicrafts in Saipan are made on the island – even if they say 'Saipan'. Most are imported from the Philippines; prices are high and quality low.

Shopping in Saipan revolves around the duty-free market. The largest shopping malls are DFS Galleria in Garapan and Hakubotan in San Jose, both upmarket department stores. Another large shopping centre, La Fiesta San Roque, opposite the Hotel Nikko, has speciality clothing and gift shops as well as restaurants.

Getting There & Away

Air The Continental ticket office (☎ 234 6491), in the Oleai Center in San Jose, is open from 9 am to 5 pm Monday to Saturday. Reservations can be made by phone daily between 7 am and 6 pm. Other airlines centre their operations at the airport. The MITA office (☎ 234 7886, fax 234 6939), on Beach Rd near the Hafadai Shopping Center, handles business for Northwest, Continental, and Japan Airlines. Freedom Air (☎ 234 8328) and PIA (☎ 288 0770) are in the commuter airport.

Boat Saipan has an entrance fee of US$62 for boats with less than 1000 gross registered tonnage and a daily dockage fee of US$56 for boats under 100 feet long. Marina space can be tight, though, so call ahead to Saipan's seaport on ☎ 664 3550. The dockage fee is sometimes waived for pleasure boats.

Getting Around

To/From the Airport Saipan's modern airport, 8 miles (13km) south of Garapan, has car rental booths for Hertz, Tropical, Budget and Dollar, a small handicraft shop, a simple restaurant, restrooms, phones, a duty-free shop and an ATM. The separate local air terminal also has a snack bar. Islander Rent-A-Car (☎ 234 8233) is on the airport road and will come if you call.

Saipan has a good road system and traffic is light in most areas, but you can expect to see bumper-to-bumper traffic on busy Beach Rd. The traffic between San Jose and Chalan Kanoa, in particular, can slow to a crawl at any time of the day, especially rush hour.

Taxis and car rentals are available at the airport. Most hotels provide airport transport for their guests, though some charge a fee.

Bus There are three shuttle bus services. La Fiesta San Roque (☎ 322 0998) in San Roque has regular free shuttle buses to/from its shopping centre, with pick-up at major hotels approximately every 30 minutes. Similar hotel-to-shopping-centre shuttle services are the Gray Line Island Shuttle (☎ 234 7148), which has a half-day pass for US$5 and a full-day pass for US$10, and Sugar King (☎ 322 8778), which costs US$3 a ride. All run from about 10 am to 10 pm; ask your hotel or call for the exact schedule.

Car The following car rental agencies have booths at the airport: Hertz (☎ 234 8336), Dollar (☎ 288 5151), Budget (☎ 234 8232) and Tropical (☎ 288 0373). Thrifty (☎ 234 8356) is nearby on the airport road. Quoted rates for unlimited mileage range from US$40 to US$47 for manual-shift subcompacts, but these rates are liable to climb. Collision damage waivers are available for an additional US$11.

If you don't have a reservation just walk up to each window (they share a single hut) and ask for the best rate – if business is slow there's sometimes room for negotiation.

There are also car rental agents in a few of the larger hotels. Most companies will pick you up anywhere on the island.

Taxi Taxis on Saipan are metered, privately owned and very expensive. It typically costs US$25 to get from the airport to Garapan and Micro Beach, US$40 from the airport to San Roque and US$15 from Garapan to Susupe. Taxis are clearly marked and usually easy to find at the airport and around larger hotels. Bo's Boys (☎ 322 3822) is one of the larger taxi companies.

Bicycle Seashore Dive Shop (☎ 234 5549, fax 233 5901, @ seashore.inc@saipan.com), near the Hyatt in Garapan and across from the American Memorial Park ranger station, rents bikes for US$20 a day and kayaks for US$25.

Tinian

Tinian, a peaceful one-village island just 3 miles (5km) south of Saipan, has a notorious place in history as the take-off site for the aircraft that dropped the atomic bombs on Hiroshima and Nagasaki.

Tinian is the second largest island in the Northern Marianas, about 12 miles (19.5km) long and 5 miles (8km) wide, and

is the least mountainous, with a top elevation of 690 feet (210m). It's an attractive island with ancient *latte* stones, ranch land with grazing cattle, secluded sandy beaches and scenic vistas.

Tinian's fertile soil was used to advantage by the Japanese, who levelled the forests and turned the island into a chequerboard of sugar cane fields. Its level terrain was also ideal for the airfields that were built later. Only a few Chamorros lived on Tinian during the Japanese occupation and they were greatly outnumbered by the nearly 18,000 Japanese, Okinawans

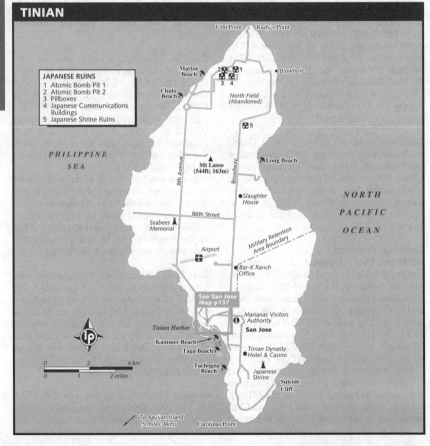

TINIAN

JAPANESE RUINS
1 Atomic Bomb Pit 1
2 Atomic Bomb Pit 2
3 Pillboxes
4 Japanese Communications Buildings
5 Japanese Shrine Ruins

Ushi Point   Rudy's Point

Marine Beach
Blowhole
Chulu Beach
North Field (Abandoned)

PHILIPPINE SEA

8th Avenue

Mt Lasso (544ft; 163m)
Long Beach

Slaughter House

NORTH PACIFIC OCEAN

86th Street
Broadway

Seabees Memorial

Military Retention Area Boundary

Airport

Bar-K Ranch Office

See San Jose Map p137

Marianas Visitors Authority
San Jose

Tinian Harbor
Kammer Beach
Taga Beach
Tachogna Beach

Tinian Dynasty Hotel & Casino

Japanese Shrine

Suicide Cliff

0   2   4 km
0   1   2 miles

To Aguijan Island (5 miles; 8km)   Carolinas Point

and Koreans, most of whom were farm labourers.

Homesick Americans who captured the island in 1944 and quickly developed it into a huge airbase decided that the shape of Tinian was not too different from New York's Manhattan Island. They named their roads Broadway, 42nd St and 8th Avenue, and called one section of the island Harlem and another Central Park. Some of the road names are still used today, though having an 86th St seems a bit out of place on an island that now has little traffic and only a few paved roads!

After the war Tinian reverted to pastoral ways and ranching took hold. The island became known for its beef and dairy products, which were exported to neighbouring islands.

In the mid-1990s Tinian voters, eager to get some of the overseas money pouring into Saipan, approved the development of casinos. In 1998 this blossomed into the US$200 million Tinian Dynasty Hotel, a tower of glitter that is happily (if peculiarly) isolated from the rest of island life, which continues at its same tranquil pace.

Military Presence

Should the USA again build up its presence in the western Pacific, Tinian could become the next US military base in the region. The northern third of the island has been leased to the US military for its sole control and use. The middle third is also leased to the military, though it includes some areas in joint use with the Tinian government (such as the airport and harbour) and other areas such as pastureland that are being leased backed by Tinian residents.

Though there aren't yet any permanent military facilities, Tinian is sometimes used by US forces for training and military exercises. These manoeuvres have been more frequent since the closure of bases in the Philippines, especially by the US navy's special warfare SEALS unit.

Access to the northernmost part of the island is restricted whenever military exercises are taking place.

Information

Tourist Offices The helpful Marianas Visitors Authority (☎ 433 9365, fax 433 0653), on Broadway, is open from 8.30 to 11.30 am and 12.30 to 4.30 pm weekdays.

Money The Bank of Guam is open from 10 am to 3 pm Monday to Thursday and until 6 pm Friday. A 24-hour ATM machine is outside, and the bank will cash travellers cheques in US dollars and give cash advances. Most businesses on Tinian do not accept credit cards. A Bank of Saipan, across the street, will also cash travellers cheques and is open on Saturday.

Post & Communications Tinian's post office is open from 9.30 am to 3 pm weekdays, and from 9 am to noon Saturday. There are pay phones (US$0.25 for local calls) and debit-card phones all over. At Tinian Center you can place international calls (US$0.40 a minute to the US).

Libraries There's a small public library at the Tinian branch of the Northern Marianas College; it's open from 9 am to 5 pm weekdays, with a noon to 1 pm lunch break.

Newspapers *LPS: What's In Tinian*, a very small local paper, is published bimonthly. The mayor's office also publishes a free monthly newsletter, but the best source of local news is the well-trafficked notice board at the post office.

Guam's *Pacific Daily News* and Saipan papers are sold at grocery stores.

Laundry There are small coin-operated laundries next door to the Fleming, Lori Lynn and Tinian Hotels.

Emergency In case of an emergency, call ☎ 911. The police and fire station can be reached on ☎ 433 9222, and the Tinian Health Center on ☎ 433 9233.

San Jose

The quiet village of San Jose, where most of Tinian's few-thousand residents live, was once the site of an ancient village of 13,000

Chamorros. The current population is partly comprised of a group of Chamorros who had been living on Yap since the German era and were resettled in San Jose by the US after WWII.

The town is fronted by a big deepwater harbour that was constructed by US Seabees for unloading the scores of bombs that were dropped on Japan in the final months of the war.

San Jose is a small village and easy to walk around, although streets are not marked.

Taga House San Jose's most notable attraction is Taga House, an impressive collection of *latte* stones said to be the foundations of the home of Taga the Great, legendary king of the ancient Chamorros.

The grassy park contains a dozen or so pitted limestone shafts with capstones, some as large as five feet (1.5m) in diameter and 15 feet (4.5m) in height. One *latte* stone still stands upright in its original position, while the others now lie horizontally. The site is on the US National Register of Historic Places.

There are some small Japanese memorials on both sides of Taga House.

Taga Well A few minutes' walk east of Taga House is the Taga Well, which in ancient times supplied spring water to the island. The water has long since disappeared and these days there's nothing to see other than a small pit surrounded by stones.

Kammer Beach Kammer Beach, also called Jones Beach, is a nice white-sand beach east of the harbour and an easy walk from the centre of town. It has coconut palms, half a dozen pavilions, picnic facilities, restrooms, showers, a water-sports hut (see the Activities section earlier in this chapter for equipment rental details) and a view of Aguijan Island to the south.

During WWII, Americans staged a fake diversionary landing at Kammer Beach just hours before the actual invasion on the north-west shore.

South of San Jose

Taga & Tachogna Beaches Taga Beach Park is ½ mile (800m) south of town on Broadway. From the cliff above the beach there's a striking view of San Jose and some of the most brilliant turquoise waters you can ever expect to see; it's a great sunset spot. Stairs lead down the cliff to a small sandy beach. The water gets deep fairly quickly, which makes for good swimming.

Tachogna Beach Park, immediately beyond, has a broad white-sand beach and is another good swimming area. The water may be a bit choppy at high tide, but at low tide snorkellers can wade out to the shallow coral patch visible just offshore.

Both beaches can be reached by foot from San Jose by following a coastal walkway (known as the jogging trail) that starts past the easternmost pavilion at Kammer Beach. Taking this route, it's only about a 10-minute walk to Taga Beach, and another five minutes from Taga Beach to Tachogna Beach.

Japanese Shrine The best-preserved Japanese shrine on the island is in the hills above Taga Beach. To get there, drive uphill on the road that curves up just past the Dynasty turn-off. Go straight past the stop sign, then curve left with the road. Continue about half a mile (1.1km) along the dirt road, past rows of coconut trees. Just past the triangular dirt road intersection with the road leading downhill, turn left; follow that road until it swerves left and take the first right-hand turn up an overgrown road. If you get lost, just flag down a passing car and ask. The shrine is reached by passing through a *torii* (gate) and up some stone steps that are gradually being overrun by vegetation.

Suicide Cliff To get to Suicide Cliff, follow the road inland from Taga Beach another 4 miles (6.5km), bearing right first at the crossroads and then at the fork. Along the way there are excellent views of the south-west side of the island looking back toward San Jose. The grassy road to

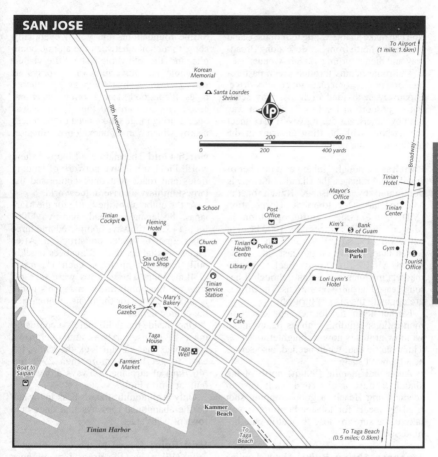

SAN JOSE

To Airport
(1 mile; 1.6km)

Korean
Memorial

Santa Lourdes
Shrine

0   200   400 m
0   200   400 yards

Broadway

Tinian
Hotel

Mayor's
Office

Tinian
Center

School

Post
Office

Kim's

Bank
of Guam

Tinian
Cockpit

Fleming
Hotel

Church

Tinian
Health
Centre

Police

Baseball
Park

Gym

Tourist
Office

Sea Quest
Dive Shop

Library

Lori Lynn's
Hotel

Tinian
Service
Station

Mary's
Bakery

Rosie's
Gazebo

JC
Cafe

Taga
House

Taga
Well

Boat to
Saipan

Farmers'
Market

Kammer
Beach

Tinian Harbor

To
Taga
Beach

To Taga Beach
(0.5 miles; 0.8km)

8th Avenue

Suicide Cliff is usually negotiable in a sedan.

In the hills above the cliffs are the natural and soldier-dug caves that were the last defence position and hide-out for the Japanese military. Though Tinian was secured by the USA after nine days of combat, it took an additional three months to rout out the Japanese from the caves in these cliffs. Most of the 4000 Japanese defenders never accounted for are assumed to have committed suicide inside the caves.

A peace memorial at the site remembers the Japanese civilians who leapt from the cliffs in a smaller version of the suicidal jumps on Saipan. The jump site along the cliff is now barricaded by a fence.

Cow patties (step lightly!) attest to the grazing done in the area, Polynesian rats hop across the road, and on a clear day you can see Rota.

On the way to Suicide Cliff, a new mile-long (1.6km) trail, called the Carolinas Limestone Forest Trail, on the right side of the road is a nice spot to wander and learn the names of trees. If you stray off the path watch out for wasps in the surrounding trees.

North of San Jose

You can make an interesting tour of the island by heading north from San Jose along Broadway and then returning via 8th Avenue.

The route begins through green pastureland and makes for a pleasant country drive. Broadway, a divided highway, may seem out of proportion for tiny Tinian – it was built by Americans during WWII to connect the harbour with bustling airstrips at the north end of the island.

Ranches Although Tinian has a number of small, local ranches, the island's ranching is dominated by the Bar-K Ranch of the Micronesian Development Corporation (MDC), the largest cattle operation in Micronesia. MDC grazes over 1000 head of cattle on 11¾ sq miles (30.5 sq km) of leased land, mostly on the east side of the island. MDC still exports beef to supermarkets in Guam and Saipan, though it has long ceased its dairy operations. The offices are opposite the airport turn-off.

Farther north, the former Japanese communications building with its heavy metal window grates is now a slaughterhouse for Tinian cattle and, when needed, also serves as a typhoon shelter.

About half a mile (800m) north of the slaughterhouse a dirt road leads east to scenic Long Beach, a good camping spot used by locals for lobster hunting; if you take it, be sure to close the cattle gate behind you.

Japanese Shrine Ruins About 4 miles (6.5km) from the airport turn-off a large Shinto torii gate on the left, visible from the road, marks the entrance to the site of a former Japanese shrine.

Just ahead, the road circles a roundabout, which has another old Japanese shrine in its centre called the Hinode Shrine; in 1995 the Americans added markers to those who died in the invasion of Tinian. Four corners are Japanese lanterns. A little past this, Saipan comes into view. Along the rocky north-east coast, waves crash against the cliffs, in places bursting up through spectacular blowholes.

Blowhole Turn right just after the Japanese Shrine roundabout, and you'll eventually come to a choice between the atomic bomb pits and the blowhole. The little-visited blowhole has towering water sprays as waves crash against the wave-weathered holes. It's a good place to bring a beer and relax. The area around the blowhole was once a firing range – take heed of the fences nearby, which warn of unexploded ordnance.

North Field The main road loops around North Field, a massive network of landing fields and roads that once comprised the largest military airbase in the world.

At the outbreak of the battle for the Marianas, the Japanese already had two 4700-foot (1432m) runways completed and three other airstrips under construction. After Tinian was taken, the US Seabees quickly built four new airstrips, each 1½ miles (2.4km) long. These strips were take-off sites for fire-bomb raids on Japan's home islands and later for the planes that carried the atomic bombs.

Once inside the field, there's a confusing maze of roads, airstrips and overgrown crossroads that can all look the same. It's easy to get lost – more than 29 miles (46.7km) of airplane taxiways alone were built at North Field!

Only lazy monitor lizards bask in the sun on the abandoned runways that once held rows of warplanes.

Ushi Point A road to the east, about 8 miles (13km) past the airport turn-off, goes to Ushi Point, the northern tip of Tinian. A cross and memorial stand on the point in remembrance of Tinian islanders who have died at sea.

If you follow the cliff road east it will take you to another memorial marker, known locally as Rudy's Point and dedicated to a fisherman who lost his life near here in 1989. It has a good view of Saipan.

Atomic Bomb Pits Back on the main road circling North Field a dirt road leads to the loading pits for the atomic bombs that were dropped on Japan.

The road to the pits is on the left, about three-quarters of a mile (1.2km) beyond the turn-off to Ushi Point and 4½ miles (7.25km) from the Japanese shrine roundabout. The pit sites are neat and sterile, marked with signs, plaques and plumeria trees.

Japanese Communications Buildings
There are some Japanese WWII installations nearby in the overgrown brush. Go south a few hundred yards from the loading pits until the road splits and turn to the left, then take the first right and the first right again onto a runway. Continue on the runway until you notice a small overgrown road to the right, which goes straight in to the complex.

The reinforced concrete building on the right is the easiest to spot, but hidden, straight ahead, is a larger two-storey former communications building. It was once used in conjunction with an underwater cable system that connected Tinian to Saipan. Low concrete **pillboxes** with gun holes are concealed in the brush to the left as you face the main building.

Invasion Beaches From the Japanese buildings turn right, back onto the runway, and at the end of the road turn left, then take the next right to get to Chulu Beach. A little to the north of Chulu Beach is Marine Beach. Both are attractive white-sand beaches.

Chulu and Marine beaches, which were dubbed White Beach I and II by American forces, are the invasion beaches where more than 15,000 US troops landed in July 1944.

The Chulu Beach area is undergoing one of the largest archaeological excavations ever undertaken in the Mariana Islands. Although the excavations, which were contracted by the US navy, are not yet complete, they have already uncovered three layers of Chamorro civilisation, ranging from 1500 BC to the Latte Period of AD 1000 to AD 1500.

Mt Lasso About 1½ miles (2.4km) south on 8th Avenue, a side road leads east to the 544-foot (163m) Mt Lasso, northern Tin-

Little Boy & Fat Man

In the early evening of 5 August 1945 a uranium bomb code-named 'Little Boy' was loaded aboard the *Enola Gay*, an American B-29 aircraft. The four-tonne bomb had been brought to Tinian from San Francisco aboard the heavy cruiser *Indianapolis*.

The *Enola Gay* and its 12-man crew took off from Tinian at 2.45 am on 6 August and headed for Hiroshima, 1700 miles (2735km) away. The bomb was dropped at 9.15 am Tinian time. It exploded in the air above the city, forming a fireball that quickly mushroomed into a dark-grey cloud three miles (5km) wide and 35,000 feet (1050m) high. More than 75,000 people perished that day from the explosion, beginning the age of atomic warfare. Because of the lingering effects of radiation, the final death toll in Hiroshima has now reached an estimated 200,000.

The second atomic bomb loaded on Tinian was a 4.5-tonne plutonium bomb named 'Fat Man'. It was dropped on Nagasaki on 9 August 1945, immediately killing 75,000 of the city's 240,000 residents. It's estimated that another 75,000 people have since died from the effects of that bombing.

ian's highest point. At the top of the mountain there's a Japanese shrine and a very scenic view of the island.

Seabees Memorial A memorial on the corner of 86th St and 8th Avenue has a plaque and a map of wartime Tinian. The plaque is dedicated to the men of the US Naval Construction Battalion (Seabees) who built the 'world's largest air base' on Tinian. It finishes with the plea, 'May God help us to avoid WWIII'.

Korean Memorial Seven miles (11.3km) south of Chulu Beach on 8th Avenue, turn east onto a grassy path lined with palm trees. Not far from the road is a memorial, built on the back of a carved stone turtle, honouring Koreans who died during WWII. Through the grass, to the left of the turtle, is a brick oven which was a crematorium for Koreans who died before the war.

Honeycombed into the nearby hills are caves where the Japanese hid from invading US forces. One huge cave to the right of the memorial has recently been turned into the Santa Lourdes Shrine, with a statue of the Virgin Mary and a few candles.

Aguijan Island

Aguijan is an uninhabited island less than 5 miles (8km) south of Tinian. During the Spanish and Japanese administrations it was sporadically inhabited but now it is nicknamed 'Goat Island' after its current residents. Goat and coconut crab hunting takes place in season.

Aguijan is part of Tinian's political district and you need to get a permit from Tinian's mayor before visiting the island. From Tinian it takes about 20 minutes to reach Aguijan by boat, but there are no beaches and landings are usually made by jumping ship close to shore and wading in. Thorns can be a deterrent to exploring the interior.

Diving & Snorkelling

Tinian has clear waters, an ocean bottom that slopes rapidly from the shore and a number of good dive sites a short distance from San Jose. One of the most popular is Dump Coke, which was a huge dumping ground for WWII junk. Small Japanese tanks, jeeps, trucks, shell casings and other munitions can be easily spotted there.

Sea Quest Dive Shop (☎ 433 0010), across from the Fleming Hotel, is Tinian's only dive shop. It offers a one-tank beach

Fortunately the fearsome coconut, or robber, crab is nocturnal.

dive for US$45 or a two-tank boat dive for US$90. Introductory beach dives for beginners cost US$75 and hour-long snorkelling tours cost US$35. Diving equipment (not included in tour prices) rents for US$40 a day, and snorkel sets for US$15. Another way to dive Tinian is to arrange a trip with Abracadabra or Stingray on Saipan; both lead cheaper Tinian dives. See the Saipan section earlier in this chapter for details.

The best snorkelling from shore is at Tachogna Beach.

Fuji Marine Sports (☎ 433 0648), based at Tachogna Beach, rents snorkel sets for US$10 a day. A short snorkelling outing by boat costs US$35 and includes all-day gear rental. It also has 'banana boat' rides (US$25 for 30 minutes) and parasailing (US$60 an hour).

Organised Tours

Neither of the two tour companies on Tinian offer English-speaking tours; ask at the tourist office about options.

Special Events

Tinian's fiesta is held during the last weekend in April or the first weekend in May in honour of San Jose, the island's patron saint. Everyone is welcome to join the feasting, dances and cultural events, although finding accommodation at that time can be a challenge.

Tinian holds a fun run in late September and a cliff fishing competition on the third weekend in February. Tuna weighing a good 60 pounds (27kg) have been caught from Tinian cliffs. A Tour de Tinian bike race is held annually in late March.

Places to Stay

Camping Tinian is one of the better islands in Micronesia for camping and no permission is needed to camp on public beaches.

Kammer Beach, at the edge of town, has a nice sandy beach, toilets, outdoor showers, barbecue pits, electricity and picnic tables.

Taga and Tachogna beach parks, about a mile (1.6km) from town, both have picnic tables, barbecue pits and showers. Tachogna is the better bet for camping as it has shady trees and a sandy beach.

For a more remote experience, try the white sands of Chulu Beach on the northwest coast.

Hotels In addition to the Dynasty, Tinian has three small hotels, all in San Jose. Rooms in each have private bathrooms, cable TV, air-con and small refrigerators, but no phones or ceiling fans. A 10% tax is added to room rates below.

Lori Lynn's Hotel (☎ 433 3256, fax 433 0429) is owned by Vicente and Rita Manglona, a friendly local couple who work at the post office. The 14 rooms in this two-storey hotel cost US$35 for singles/doubles including tax. There's a good restaurant on site, and airport transfers can be provided on request. Cash only is accepted.

The older, two-storey *Fleming Hotel* (☎ 433 3232) has 13 good-sized but run-down rooms with balconies, two double beds, a refrigerator and bathtubs. The cost is US$60/80 for singles/doubles. Fleming's (officially named the Meitetsu Fleming Hotel) caters largely to Japanese tourists, which explains the high prices – quality does not measure up. There's a restaurant and store on site. Cash only is accepted.

The renovated *Tinian Hotel* (☎ 433 7000, fax 433 7700), across Broadway from the Tinian Center, is the best deal, with nice rooms from US$33 (tax included). There are laundry facilities, a restaurant and a poker room at the back, which draws locals. Other than Dynasty, it is the only hotel in town that accepts major credit cards and has in-room phones.

The finest – albeit least local – place to stay is of course the 412-room, US$140 million *Tinian Dynasty* (☎ 328-2233, fax 328-1133, ✉ casino@saipan.com), Saipan's new casino-hotel complex. Exquisite soft pink rooms come complete with minibar and safety box. At the time of writing, the price for independent travellers was US$70 plus tax, but if the economy improves this will quickly jump. Queen suites are available.

Places to Eat

All restaurants on Tinian are in San Jose or in the Dynasty.

Rosie's Gazebo has a pleasant outdoor dining area, a bar, good food and an extensive multiethnic menu. A variety of Western-style breakfasts cost US$5. There are beef or chicken dishes for US$7 and fancier 'cook's specials', such as prawn thermidor or pepper steak, for around US$12. It's open 11 am to 4 am daily; happy hour is 11 am to 8 pm daily. Lunch specials are US$5.

JC Cafe has a varied menu that includes tasty chicken, beef, fish, squid and mussel dishes averaging US$8 to US$9. Sandwiches are US$3.50 and plate breakfasts average US$6. At happy hour, from 4 to 8 pm daily, beer costs US$1.50. It's open until 2 am Sunday to Wednesday, and to 3 am Thursday to Saturday.

Lori Lynn's Restaurant, at the hotel of the same name, serves Western and Japanese dishes and is known for its good Chamorro food. Breakfast averages US$5 to US$8, lunch and dinner US$7 to US$12. It's open from 6.30 to 9.30 am, 11.30 am to 1.30 pm and 5.30 to 9.30 pm.

Broadway, the upscale Italian/Pacific restaurant in the Dynasty, has a US$25 Sunday brunch from 10.30 am to 3 pm, with one drink included for paying guests. The nightly buffet costs US$25, lunch is US$20 and breakfast is US$12. The restaurant is open from 6.30 to 10 am, 11.30 am to 2.30 pm and 5.30 to 10.30 pm.

The island has several small grocery stores, including *Kim's*, *Tinian Center* and *Fleming's*, in the hotel of the same name. The *Farmers' Market*, near the harbour, has a sparse selection of seasonal fruit and is open from 7.30 am to 4.30 pm weekdays.

It's best to avoid drinking unboiled tap water. Bottled water is readily available in stores.

Entertainment

When you tire of the 400 slot machines and 80 gaming tables at the *Dynasty*, there's the Dynasty's cover-free disco called *Club De Macau* nightly from 7 pm to 2 am.

Other evening entertainment is limited. *Rosie's Gazebo* has a billiards room. *JC Cafe* has karaoke and will play disco music if anyone wants to dance. For serious local flavour, the *Tinian Cockpit* has cockfights on weekends and holidays.

Shopping
A jar of Tinian hot chilli pepper sauce (US$4.50 at the Farmers' Market) is a worthy investment, dabbed on to local fruit. Be careful – it's VERY hot.

Getting There & Away
Air All flights to Tinian leave from Saipan, a hop that takes just over 10 minutes.

Freedom Air (☎ 433 3288) flies a dozen times daily between Saipan and Tinian, with a one-way fare of US$20.

PIA (☎ 433 3600) has two daily flights each way between Tinian and Saipan, one in the morning and one in the afternoon for US$25 one way.

Tinian's unexpectedly modern airport is 2½ miles (4km) from San Jose. It has airline and car rental counters, restrooms and an ATM, and a snack bar that's open until 6 pm.

Boat The *Tinian Express* (☎ 234 9157), a large passenger vessel owned by the Tinian Dynasty, chugs over from Saipan six times daily around the clock. Reservations are not usually needed, but you should call in advance (on Saipan ☎ 287 9933; on Tinian ☎ 433 3075) to verify departure times. The pricing system is worth taking note of: It is free going to Tinian and US$20 coming back. (Hint: Take the boat over and fly back!)

Yachties wanting to visit Tinian must first go through customs on Saipan. Call Tinian's port authority on ☎ 433 9296 for info on the Tinian harbour.

Getting Around
To/From the Airport The hotels provide free airport transfers.

Car Tinian's main roads are paved, though the undergrowth seeps through on the north of the island. Budget (☎ 433 3104),

Avis (☎ 433 2847) and Islander (☎ 433-3025) have booths at the airport; Budget also hides out in the Dynasty. The cheapest car, usually a manual-transmission Toyota Tercel, rents for about US$39 a day. Make reservations before heading out to Tinian to ensure the best rates and that someone will meet your plane or boat. Credit cards are accepted.

Bicycle Sea Quest Dive Shop (☎ 433 0010) in San Jose rents bicycles out for US$15 a day.

Hitching It's often possible to hitch from the airport to San Jose. San Jose itself is OK for lifts, but outside the village there isn't enough traffic to count on hitching – to get to Suicide Cliff or North Field you really need a vehicle. People on Tinian are hospitable and the island has very little crime but, as elsewhere, the usual safety precautions apply.

Rota

The island of Rota, about halfway between Guam and Saipan, is just beginning to get an overflow of tourists from those larger islands. Nevertheless, the island retains a distinctively slow pace – the main village, Songsong, still gets by without a single shopping centre.

Rota measures about 10 miles (16km) by 3 miles (4.8km) and has a hilly interior. The island has small farms, good spring water, enough deer to have a hunting season and fiery orange sunsets that light the evening skies. Locals call the island Luta.

Rota has also earned the moniker 'The Friendly Island'. Without fail, Rotanese drivers wave to each other as they pass, a tradition so strongly entrenched that non-wavers are immediately recognised as visitors. One Lonely Planet reader wrote in that his efforts to learn stick-shift driving on Rota were continually bedevilled by the need to wave!

Songsong, which means 'village' in Chamorro, is the island's business centre, while the newer homestead development of

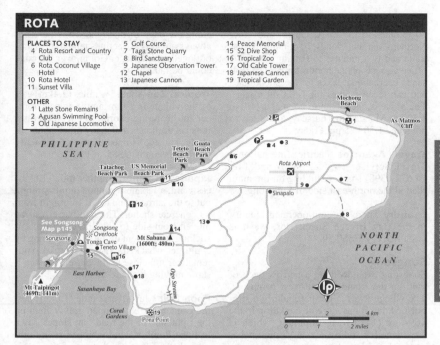

ROTA

PLACES TO STAY
4 Rota Resort and Country
   Club
6 Rota Coconut Village
   Hotel
10 Rota Hotel
11 Sunset Villa

OTHER
1 Latte Stone Remains
2 Agusan Swimming Pool
3 Old Japanese Locomotive

5 Golf Course
7 Taga Stone Quarry
8 Bird Sanctuary
9 Japanese Observation Tower
12 Chapel
13 Japanese Cannon

14 Peace Memorial
15 S2 Dive Shop
16 Tropical Zoo
17 Old Cable Tower
18 Japanese Cannon
19 Tropical Garden

*PHILIPPINE
SEA*

Mochong
Beach

As Matmos
Cliff

Tatachog
Beach Park

US Memorial
Beach Park

Teteto
Beach
Park

Guata
Beach
Park

Rota Airport

Sinapalo

*NORTH
PACIFIC
OCEAN*

See Songsong
Map p145

Songsong
Overlook

Songsong

Tonga Cave
Teneto Village

Mt Sabana
(1600ft; 480m)

East Harbor

Sasanhaya Bay

Mt Taipingot
(469ft; 141m)

Ogo Stream

Coral
Gardens

Pona Point

0   2   4 km
0   1   2 miles

Sinapalo, just south of the airport, has rapidly grown into the island's second village.

Several new hotels, including a country club resort, have recently sprung up with the aim of siphoning tourists off the Guam-Saipan thoroughfare. But the recent Asian economic crisis left businesses high and dry and hotels dropped their prices while the beaches remained gloriously deserted. The friendly new hostel – the only one of its kind in Micronesia – makes Rota accessible to budget travellers.

The scale of construction has brought hundreds of foreign workers onto the island (mostly from the Philippines and other East Asian countries) and, as on Saipan, the Rotanese are grappling with the changing demographics.

But while the island may be in flux, Rota's laid-back character and pristine beaches remain its leading attraction. Where else can you swim right in town and still have the beach all to yourself?

Information

Tourist Offices The Marianas Visitors Authority (☎ 532 0327, fax 532 4000) is up the hill across from the fire station. Hours are 7.30 to 11.30 am and 12.30 to 4.30 pm weekdays.

Money The Bank of Guam, on the main road in Songsong, changes currency, cashes travellers cheques (American Express only) and issues commission-free credit card cash advances. It is open from 10 am to 3 pm Monday to Thursday and until 6 pm Friday. An ATM is outside.

Post & Communications The post office is open from 6 to 11.30 am and 12.30 to 3 pm weekdays and from noon to 1 pm on Saturday.

Rota's telephones operate by both coin or card; the latter are sold at some hotels or at GTE (☎ 532 3499, fax 532 0101), on the north-east side of town a block from the tourist office. A US$10 phone card will buy 30 minutes to the USA, Guam, and other Northern Mariana islands, 10 minutes to Australia and two minutes to Britain. The GTE office also has phone booths for card calls. It sends international faxes for the phone rates and can receive faxes for US$0.50 a page. The office is open 8 am to noon and 1.30 to 4.30 pm Monday to Thursday, and 8 am to noon and 1.30 to 5 pm Friday.

Travel Agencies Pacific International Travel Services (☎ 532 3800) and PIA (☎ 532 0398) share a building on the main road at the north-east side of Songsong.

Laundry There's a coin-operated laundry in the Bay Breeze Snack Bar; wash is US$0.75, dry US$0.50.

Songsong

Songsong extends along a narrow neck of land on the island's south-west peninsula. The village itself is not particularly distinguished, but it has a scenic backdrop in the 469-foot (141m) Mt Taipingot, which is nicknamed Wedding Cake Mountain because of its layered appearance.

Songsong boasts an abundance of *latte* stones, some of which adorn public buildings like the library while others simply landscape front yards. The most notable building in town is the San Francisco de Borja Church, the bell of which dates to the period of German occupation, though the present church was built in the 1940s.

You can get a good view of Songsong by taking the rough dirt road that leads to the hilltop above Tonga Cave. The road, which begins behind Dean's Mobil petrol station at the north end of Songsong, makes a nice hike, though it could also be negotiated in a 4WD.

East of Songsong

The packed coral road that heads east of Songsong edges along Sasanhaya Bay. Along the way there are scenic views across the bay's brilliant turquoise water to Mt Taipingot. The road alternately cuts along the coastal cliffs and dives through tropical jungle canopies. Beware of very steep drops along the edge of this road, which are not always obvious as sections tend to get camouflaged with foliage. Going over the edge could be fatal.

Tropical Zoo About 1½ miles (2.4km) east of the village is a fun family-owned tropical zoo featuring enormous coconut crabs, iguanas, fruit bats and many other small animals. The zoo is open 9 am to 5 pm daily and admission is US$5.

Japanese Cannon Another mile (1.6km) eastward, a Japanese cannon points straight out to the harbour and to Mt Taipingot from its concrete shelter. The gun barrel can be moved from side to side but don't leave it sticking straight out or the next car going by could get whacked. Also, don't park your rental car too close to the barrel, as once it starts moving it's hard to stop.

Pona Point Just over a mile (1.6km) past the cannon there's an open grassy field on the right side of the road that slopes down to Pona Point, a wind-whipped rocky outcrop that offers a good view of the area's rugged coastal cliffs as well as excellent cliff fishing. Although you may be able to drive all the way down to the point, it's only a three-minute walk from the field.

Half a mile (800m) farther down, the main road passes above Ogo (also spelled Okgok) Stream, which features some small **waterfalls**. If you want to visit them you must first get permission from the landowner; inquire in advance at Joe & Sons grocery store in Songsong.

A bit further east is a **tropical garden** (☎ 532 3394), which is a great place to learn to identify tropical fruit trees. For US$10 one of the garden's workers will lead you through the plantation's innumerable groves of breadfruit, coconut, papaya, banana, star-apple and other trees. If you're lucky, he'll probably pluck a bagful of take-home fruit samples. Call ahead to find a good tour time, as the mornings tend to be crowded with large Japanese tour groups.

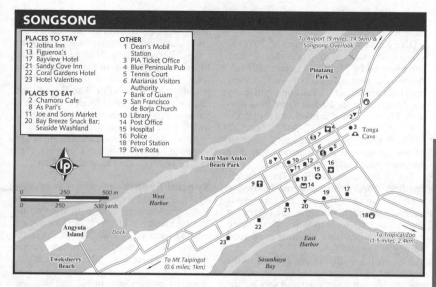

SONGSONG

PLACES TO STAY
12 Jotina Inn
13 Figueroa's
17 Bayview Hotel
21 Sandy Cove Inn
22 Coral Gardens Hotel
23 Hotel Valentino

PLACES TO EAT
2 Chamoru Cafe
8 As Pari's
11 Joe and Sons Market
20 Bay Breeze Snack Bar;
   Seaside Washland

OTHER
1 Dean's Mobil
  Station
3 PIA Ticket Office
4 Blue Peninsula Pub
5 Tennis Court
6 Marianas Visitors
  Authority
7 Bank of Guam
9 San Francisco
  de Borja Church
10 Library
14 Post Office
15 Hospital
16 Police
18 Petrol Station
19 Dive Rota

To Airport (9 miles; 14.5km) &
Songsong Overlook

Pinatang
Park

Tonga
Cave

Unan Man Amko
Beach Park

West
Harbor

Angyuta
Island

Dock

Tweksberry
Beach

To Mt Taipingot
(0.6 miles; 1km)

Sasanhaya
Bay

East
Harbor

To Tropical Zoo
(1.5 miles; 2.4km)

0   250   500 m
0   250   500 yards

NORTHERN MARIANA ISLANDS

Central & Northern Rota

The remains of a two-storey Japanese building that once served as an **observation tower** are on the left side of the road a quarter of a mile (400m) east of the airport. After continuing another half-mile (800m), a road to the right leads to the Taga Stone Quarry.

If you don't turn down to the quarry, the dirt road circles around the airport, past fenced-off farms, pastures and an old Japanese locomotive and continues around to the main paved road.

Taga Stone Quarry The Taga Stone Quarry has nine *latte* shafts and seven capstones still sitting in the trenches where they were being quarried before they were inexplicably abandoned. Mosses, grasses and tiny ferns have grown up around them.

The early Chamorros were able to quarry the *latte* stones without the benefit of metal tools. It's believed they built fires in trenches around the stones and then used basalt stone adzes to cut into the softened limestone.

For anyone interested in Chamorro culture, this is an impressive sight. The road

into the quarry is signposted and easily negotiable in a car. The quarry itself, which is half a mile (800m) from the turn-off, is in a grassy park alongside the road.

According to legend, the ancient Chamorro king Taga the Great jumped from Guam to Rota to establish a kingdom here. He then put the island's inhabitants to work quarrying these *latte* stones, which he used as foundation pillars for royal buildings.

Bird Sanctuary Rota's bird sanctuary lies on the eastern side of the island, down a rough dirt road about 1½ miles (2.4km) from the airport. Watch carefully for the turn-off sign to the right. A cliff-top wooden walkway is a wonderful spot to watch or photograph all manner of seabirds and shorebirds; a bird poster at the sanctuary entrance can help with identification. The best time to go is at sunrise or sunset. Those staying at the Rota Resort and Country Club can join the US$30 guided trip at 7 am to the sanctuary.

Diving

Rota diving stands out for its excellent visibility; on normal days you can see 100 feet (30m) down. Interesting cave and tunnel dives, and now two sunken wrecks, complete the scene.

Dive Rota (☎ 532 3377, fax 532 3022) is a small personalised dive operation owned and operated by Mark and Lynne Michael. A one-tank boat dive costs US$50, a two-tank boat dive costs US$80 and night dives can be arranged for US$60. Dive Rota also rents filled tanks and snorkel sets for US$5.

S2 Dive Shop (☎ 532 3483, fax 532 3484, ✉ s2rota@gtepacifica.net), just east of Songsong, is a new Japanese-run dive company with higher prices.

For shore-side snorkelling, Teteto Beach has large coral formations just below the surface, but you'll have to time your snorkelling with high tide as the coral is in shallow water. Closer to town, the entrance to Sasanhaya Bay has soft corals and a good variety of tropical fish.

The small island at Pinatang Park, at the north end of Songsong, has rather sparse marine life, but swimming and snorkelling between the rock formations can be interesting and the water is clear and calm.

Coral Detonation

The zenith of Rota's diving used to be Coral Gardens, in Sasanhaya Bay. Besides its huge platter corals, the area was home to the wreck of the *Shoun Maru*, a Japanese freighter sunk by an aerial torpedo during WWII, which lay offshore with two other Japanese boats about 90 feet (27m) under water in Sasanhaya Bay. The wreck contained coral-encrusted trucks and assorted paraphernalia such as bathtubs, bicycles and motorcycles.

But the US navy decided that the wrecks were a hazard because they contained unexploded ordnance, and in 1996, to the outrage of divers, blew up the three wrecks and ruined Coral Gardens with it.

The story doesn't end there. In 1998 the US Marshalls office sold two illegal Chinese smuggling boats to Rota for US$2 (US$1 for each boat). In June of that year the navy sank the two boats offshore in Sasanhaya Bay – debatably as compensation for the chagrined divers.

Organised Tours

Many sightseeing tours are in Japanese, so always ask which language will be spoken.

The Rota Coconut Village Hotel (see Places to Stay) has full-day sightseeing tours for US$58 (lunch included) and a half-day tour for US$38. The Rota Resort and Country Club (see Places to Stay) has a variety of tour options ranging from US$15 to US$60; children get discounts.

You can also ask around Songsong to find someone with a pick-up truck who is willing to take you for a spin around the island.

Special Events

The largest and most popular fiesta in the Northern Marianas is held on Rota on the second Sunday in October. The celebration, which honours San Francisco de Borja, the patron saint of Songsong, attracts people from throughout the Marianas. Events include a luau-like feast of Chamorro food, religious processions, music and dancing. The popular fiesta of Sinapalo village falls on the second Saturday in March.

The Rota Road Runners Club sponsors a variety of road races and triathlons year-round; contact the tourist office for dates.

Places to Stay

Camping Many of Rota's public beach parks allow camping. They are easily accessible if you have your own transportation, but be aware that the island is not as crime free as it was in the past.

In addition to public parks, the Sandy Cove Inn (see the following Hotels entry) plans to open up a camping area with A-frames and showers about 2 miles (3.2km) east of Sandy Cove in a prime snorkelling area near Rota's two new wrecks.

Hotels A 10% tax is added to all room rates in Rota.

The new *Sandy Cove Inn* (☎/fax 532 2683), on the south-west end of Songsong right on the bay, is the budget backpacker's dream come true. The inn is operated by Ben and Vicky, charismatic globetrotters originally from the USA. Beds in a hostel room go for US$10 a night; a room with a kitchenette costs US$18.50 and two comfortable single rooms with two and three beds go for US$25. Breakfast is included in the prices. The hostel has a large, clean kitchen, a sitting room, small TV and a pay phone outside. If you ask, Ben just might take you night fishing. Call ahead and they will pick you up from the airport.

The *Coral Gardens Hotel* (☎ *532 3201, fax 532 3204)* commands a gorgeous oceanview vista in Songsong. The rooms are neat and compact with whitewashed walls, cable TV, air-con, refrigerators, oceanfront balconies and either two single beds or one double bed. It's good value at US$45/50 for singles/doubles and has a special car rental deal. A few rooms go for US$33, but these are tiny and lightless and have no ocean view.

Figueroa's (☎ *532 2337)* keeps a handful of tidy rooms above its restaurant. Rooms have air-con, cable TV, showers and minibar; a phone is in the upstairs common sitting room. Rooms go for US$40 singles/doubles.

The *Jotina Inn* (☎ *532 0500, fax 532 0501)* in the centre of Songsong has 12 clean rooms with refrigerator, air-con, phones, refrigerators, cable TV and desks for US$40 singles/doubles. A third person in the room costs US$5.

The *Bayview Hotel* (☎ *532 3414, fax 532 0393)* is a bit older and doesn't have as good a view, but it's still a reasonable option at US$45/50 for singles/doubles. The nine rooms have cable TV, air-con, refrigerators and ceiling fans; various bed combinations are available. There's a small restaurant on site.

Three miles (4.8km) north-east of Songsong, the new *Sunset Villa* (☎ *532 8445, fax 532 8458,* @ *sunsetv@gtepacifica.net)* is right on the water and offers sparkling rooms with TV, phone, refrigerator, air-con, minibar and free airport transfers. Ask for a room with an ocean view balcony. A lifeguard is on the beach during the daytime. Mama'ti Cafe, the hotel restaurant, serves all meals. Fax and copying can be done at the front desk. Singles/doubles are US$45/$65 (including tax). They are an infinitely better value than the overpriced

Rota Hotel (☎ *532 2000, fax 532 3000)*, just up the road toward the airport, where singles, without ocean view or TV, start at US$210 (tax included).

Hotel Valentino (☎ *532 8466, fax 532 0655)*, west of the Coral Gardens Hotel, is very clean but has the eerily quiet, impersonal feel of a new hotel. The rooms are spacious and have kitchens (ask for a well-equipped one), TVs and phones (local calls US$0.50). Airport transfers are US$12. Rooms are from US$49.

A good upper-end choice is the *Rota Coconut Village Hotel* (☎ *532 3448, fax 532 3449)*, which has 10 duplex cottages with an island motif of peaked roofs, rattan furnishings and small Japanese-style soaking tubs that fill tiny bathrooms. There's a swimming pool and restaurant. Singles/doubles cost US$85/95. If you're driving from the airport, go past the turn-off to the country club and watch for a small, unmarked dirt road leading sharply right along the coast at the bottom of the hill. The staff will ferry small groups to the swimming hole or Teteto Beach for US$5 return and to the airport or Songsong for US$12 return.

The new *Rota Resort and Country Club* (☎ *532 1155, fax 532 1156)*, situated magnificently atop an 18-hole golf course with a view to the sea, is the clear luxury choice for Rota. Beautiful two- and four-bedroom suites with a view of the sea or jungle have all the amenities and start at US$250 for two people, breakfast included. Independent travellers who call beforehand may be able to negotiate a lower rate with the management. Each additional person staying in the same suite costs US$40. The resort's features include a nature spa, a children's activity station, several restaurants and a pool with a swim-up bar. It's a good place to bring children.

Places to Eat

Restaurants in Rota tend to be more expensive than you might expect, but the food is hearty and usually quite good. Don't be surprised if you're the only customer – Rota has too many restaurants for its size. Unfortunately there is no farmers' market to sell Rota's abundance of tropical fruits, as most goes overseas, but if you become friendly with the locals they will ply you with fruits from their gardens; otherwise try to get a sample from the tropical garden (see the Pona Point entry earlier in this section).

As Pari's restaurant and bar, on the main road in Songsong, is a perennial favourite. It's comfortable, with well-prepared food, reasonable prices and music that's at a lower decibel than most places. A variety of full breakfasts are available for around US$6. Noodles, spaghetti and fish dishes average US$8, while an extensive selection of meat dishes with rice cost around US$8 to US$10. It's open daily from 6 am to 2 pm and 6 pm to midnight.

For wholesome, fresh food, the restaurant at the *Sandy Cove Inn* is an excellent choice. The fish are caught by Ben, one of the inn's co-proprietors. An order of fried or grilled reef fish, served with a tasty salad and a big bowl of rice, goes for US$10. The place is also deservedly famous for its large pizzas (US$10) with thick homemade crusts, which it cheerfully delivers. The restaurant is open daily for breakfast, lunch and dinner.

Figueroa's, a popular bar and grill next to the post office, is American-owned and flaunts it. There's a Budweiser basketball, a dartboard, graffiti on the walls, chequered tablecloths and piles of peanuts under the tables. Its menu is a smorgasbord of fajitas, seafood, steaks, and burgers; most entrees cost US$12 to US$15. Figueroa's thick-crust, cheesy pizza goes for US$14; unless you're exceptionally hungry, it can feed two. It's open daily until midnight.

Another good if pricey choice is the *Chamoru Cafe*, a modern spot at the north end of Songsong, which makes a tidy breakfast omelette for US$5 and serves up a mix of Filipino, American, and Chamorro food for roughly US$10 to US$20.

The *Bay Breeze Snack Bar*, across from Dive Rota, serves a variety of quick foods at more reasonable prices than you're likely to find elsewhere; a plate of fried chicken or beef with steamed rice goes for US$6,

sandwiches cost US$2 to US$5 and burgers go for US$5 to US$6.

For those who venture afield to Sinapalo, the *Acoustic Cafe*, not far off the highway, is recommended. Food here includes pizza, burgers and omelettes, with Chamorro and Filipino dishes. The prices are a bit lower than in Songsong.

One of the best stocked of the grocery stores in Songsong is *Lucky Store*, around the corner from the Sandy Cove Inn. It serves cheap platefuls of food (US$2 to US$3) in the late morning through to lunchtime. Sinapalo also has several small grocery stores; the best-stocked is *Sinapalo Safeway*.

Rota's drinking water comes from a spring in a natural water cave and may be the best in Micronesia.

Entertainment

The biggest entertainment hit around Rota is the laser karaoke, which consists of video renditions of pop songs with the lyrics written in English across the screen and a live microphone for would-be stars to croon along. *As Pari's*, the *Blue Peninsula* and several other restaurants become late-night karaoke venues; ask the locals for the current hot spot.

Getting There & Away

Air PIA (☎ 532 0398) flies to Rota from Saipan four times daily, with the first flight leaving at 8.15 am and the last at 5.45 pm. The fare is US$65 one way, US$130 return. PIA's two daily flights from Guam – the first departing at 7.45 am and the second at 5.15 pm – cost US$75 one way, US$150 return.

Freedom Air has flights at 9.45 am and 5.15 pm from Saipan to Rota and at 8 am and 3.30 pm from Guam to Rota. The return flights leave Rota 50 minutes later. The fare is US$43 one way and US$86 return. From Saipan the price is US$57 one way, US$94 return.

The small airport is 9 miles (14.5km) north-east of Songsong. It has an ATM, car rental booths outside, phones and a restaurant called Cafe Chadd's.

Boat Yachties should dial the Rota seaport on ☎ 532 8489 (fax 532 9499) in advance of their visit. Though yachts can come directly to Rota rather than going through customs on Saipan first, bear in mind that Rota's harbour facilities are in worse shape than Saipan's and Tinian's.

Getting Around

Rota's one paved road runs between the airport and Songsong, though Songsong itself is slowly getting paved. Otherwise most of the island's road system is packed coral or dirt. Depending on recent rains and how long it's been since the roads have been graded, you may not be able to manage some of Rota's more remote and rutted dirt roads in a sedan without scraping the bottom. Getting to most of the main sights, however, usually isn't a problem. If you want to do a lot of exploring it's best to avoid a low-slung compact car in favour of something that rides a bit higher.

To/From the Airport As there are no taxis or other public transport on Rota, you'll either have to rent a car, make arrangements for your hotel to pick you up or hitch a ride with someone leaving the airport.

Car Rota has four car rental agencies. All but Budget have booths at the airport. All take major credit cards and offer optional collision damage waivers (US$12.50). Coral Rent-A-Car (☎ 532 1996) has an excellent room-and-car package with the Coral Gardens Hotel for US$68. Otherwise the cars start from US$38. Discounts are available for government and military.

Islander Rent-A-Car (☎ 532 0901, fax 532 0902) rents Toyota Tercels for US$46 and other cars for up to US$111. Drivers must be at least 25.

Paseo Drive Car Rental (☎ 532 0406) has cars starting at US$37.50 a day. Budget (☎ 532 3535) is on the road to Songsong about half a mile (800m) from the airport.

Bicycle For those in tip-top shape, bicycling is a wonderful way to see Rota. Bicycles can be rented at Sandy Cove Inn or at the Rota Hotel for US$15 a day.

Hitching It's possible to get lifts around the main parts of the island, such as between the airport and Songsong, though traffic may be too infrequent elsewhere to make hitching practical. The usual safety precautions apply.

Marshall Islands

The Marshall Islands consist entirely of slender coral atolls and islands sprinkled with coconuts, pandanus and breadfruit trees. Few other crops grow in the atolls' salty sand, so the Marshallese long ago turned to the sea for their resources. They became, of necessity, expert fishers and navigators.

Between the two world wars the Japanese used the Marshall Islands as an anchor to lay claim to the central Pacific. After ousting the Japanese, the USA found the Marshalls' isolation ideally suited for testing nuclear weapons. Sixty-seven nuclear bomb tests were performed on Bikini and Enewetok atolls during the post-war years, and though the bomb tests are long over, the Marshallese are still grappling with the lingering effects of radiation and displacement. Bikini Atoll has just opened up to divers, who flock to see the wrecks created by the nuclear testing.

Majuro, the Marshall Islands capital, is quite Westernised and, with a newly opened Outrigger Hotel and revamped tourist office, is pouring energy into improving visitor services. Kwajalein, Continental's other Marshall Islands stop, is leased to the US military for missile testing. It is off-limits to most visitors, who are shuttled off to the tenements on nearby Ebeye. Most of the outer islands, meanwhile, retain the more pristine nature you'd expect to find in the tropical Pacific.

HIGHLIGHTS

- Underwater wrecks – Bikini's newly accessible residue from the nuclear debacle
- Unspoilt island life – the outer Marshalls' rustic experience, with innumerable atolls where the only accommodation available is with families or in a tent
- WWII relics – covering some of the outer atolls end to end

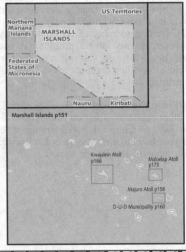

Marshall Islands p151

Kwajalein Atoll p166

Maloelap Atoll p173

Majuro Atoll p158

D-U-D Municipality p160

Facts about the Marshall Islands

HISTORY
Early Settlers
Though the Marshalls were never unified under a single leader, one chief often controlled several atolls. At times the entire Ralik chain came under the reign of a single chief. Chiefs had absolute authority, but their wealth and power depended upon loyalty and tribute payments from commoners.

Land control has always been an extremely important issue for the Marshallese because there is so little land. They married for land, went to war for land and, when all else failed, employed magic to get land.

Because their islands are so widely scattered, the Marshallese developed some of the finest canoe-building and navigational skills in the Pacific.

Pandanus was an important food in the northern islands, breadfruit equally so in the south, while coconut production and fishing were important everywhere.

In 1986 an American archaeologist studying the nuclear-bombed Bikini Atoll discovered bone fragments and the remains of a village. These artefacts have been carbon dated to 1960 BC, making Bikini the site of the earliest human settlement yet discovered in all of Micronesia.

European Contact

The Marshall Islands were off the main trade routes and consequently received few visits from early European explorers.

In 1525 a Spaniard named Alonso de Salazar became the first European to sight one of the islands. Although other Spanish expeditions landed in the Marshalls during the 1500s, Spain took little interest in the islands and did not colonise the area.

The islands were named after the English sea captain, John Marshall, who in 1788 sighted Arno, Majuro, Aur, Maloelap, Wotje

and Ailuk, and docked at Mili. His visit was probably the first made by Europeans in 200 years and the brief exchange between the British and the 'Marshallese' was friendly.

The German-Estonian explorer Otto von Kotzebue, sailing under the Russian tsar, made more thorough expeditions in the early 1800s and drew up the first detailed maps of the islands.

Whalers, Traders & Missionaries

Traders and whalers first showed up in the region in the early 1800s but they began to avoid the Marshalls after contact with the islanders turned violent. The 30-year period from the mid-1820s was a time of brutal attacks on European and American traders. In case after case, ship officers putting into port at various atolls in the Marshalls recorded the death of a captain or crew members. Sometimes the scouting parties that went ashore just completely disappeared and in the early 1850s the entire

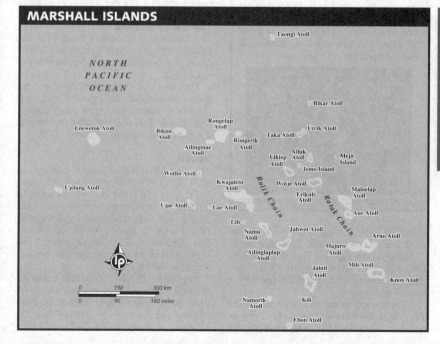

MARSHALL ISLANDS

Stick Charts

The low elevation of the Marshalls and the distances between the atolls make them particularly difficult to sight from the sea. In travels between islands, early inhabitants learned to read the patterns of the waves by watching for swells which would show when land was ahead.

Stick charts were used to teach the secrets of navigation. They were made by tying flat strips of wood together in designs which imitated the wave patterns. Shells were then attached to these sticks to represent the islands.

Three kinds of charts were used. The *mattang* showed wave patterns around a single island or atoll and was used first to teach the basic techniques. The *medo* showed patterns around a small group of atolls and the *rebillit* mapped an entire chain, showing the relationships between the islands and the major ocean swells.

All the information contained on the stick charts was memorised, so the charts were not actually taken on journeys. Nowadays not many Marshallese know how to read them, but due to the charts' popularity as souvenirs many islanders can still make them.

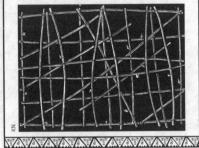

crews of three trading ships were massacred, one each at Namorik, Ebon and Jaluit.

Some of the fighting was prompted by the stealing of island women. Other incidents were essentially reprisals for earlier hostile encounters.

Violence was on the decline when the first Protestant missionaries to the Marshalls arrived on Ebon in 1857. The missionaries were at first welcomed, or at least tolerated, by the chiefs. Schools and churches were opened side by side and conversions came quickly. By the time the chiefs realised their traditional authority was being usurped by Western values and the Christian god, the missionaries had become well entrenched. Within a couple of decades Marshallese graduates of the mission schools were running most of the churches themselves.

German Period

Germany annexed the Marshalls in 1885, but didn't place government officials on the islands until 1906. Instead, island affairs were left to the Jaluit Gesellschaft, a group of powerful German trading companies.

Coconut plantations and copra facilities had been set up as far back as the 1860s, including a coconut-oil factory on Ebon in 1861 and trading stations on Mili, Ebon, Jaluit, Namorik, Majuro and Aur atolls. Though never highly lucrative, these outposts did cull a thin profit for the Germans.

Japanese Period

The Japanese took control from 1914 and colonised the Marshalls extensively, developing and fortifying large bases on many of the islands.

They also took over the copra business, but unlike the Germans the Japanese sold copra directly to traders instead of going through local chiefs. This policy further undermined the traditional authority of island chiefs.

WWII

The first Micronesian islands captured by the USA in WWII were at Kwajalein Atoll in February 1944. The atoll's Roi-Namur Island, the main Japanese air base in the Marshalls, fell first, followed by Kwajalein Island with its almost-completed airstrip. The offensive, code-named Operation Flintlock, marked the first seizure of pre-war Japanese territory.

Majuro Atoll, which had been left undefended, was taken next and quickly developed into a base for aircraft carriers. From Majuro and the air base at Kwajalein, the USA staged attacks on the Caroline Islands.

The USA bypassed four Marshallese atolls still in Japanese hands, but within weeks had captured Enewetok Atoll and about 30 more Marshallese islands before continuing their westward naval assault across the central Pacific.

Americans & Atomic Bombs

After the war, the USA immediately moved in and started atomic bomb experiments on Bikini and Enewetok atolls. Kwajalein Atoll was later established as a missile testing site.

Some of the islanders who breathed radio-active air or lived on contaminated land have since died from radiation-related ailments. Others have lingering health problems. Many suspect that they were deliberately used as test subjects for monitoring radiation's long-term effects on humans.

For specific information on the testing's effects on Bikini Atoll and surrounding atolls, please see the individual sections later in this chapter.

GEOGRAPHY

Of the 1225 islands and islets of the Marshalls, only five are single islands. The rest are grouped into 29 coral atolls, which together comprise more than one-tenth of all atolls in the world.

The atolls run roughly north-south in two nearly parallel chains about 150 miles (240km) apart and 800 miles (1280km) long. The eastern chain is called *Ratak*, which means 'toward dawn', and the western chain is *Ralik*, 'toward sunset'.

Although only 70 sq miles (182 sq km) in land area, the Marshall Islands are scattered across 750,000 sq miles (1,950,000 sq km) of ocean. True atolls, the islands are narrow and low and encircle large central lagoons. The widest island, Wotje, is less than a mile (1.6km) across; the highest elevation, just 34 feet (10.2m), is on the island of Likiep.

The southern islands have more vegetation than those in the north. Virtually all of them have gorgeous white sand beaches.

CLIMATE

In Majuro, the average daily temperature is 81°F (27°C). As the lowest temperatures occur during heavy rains, and most heavy rains fall during the day, night-time temperatures actually average a couple of degrees higher than daytime temperatures.

The northern Marshalls are quite dry, averaging just 20 inches (500mm) of rain each year. Rainfall increases as you head south, with some islands getting up to 160 inches (4060mm) a year. A severe drought caused the Marshallese government to declare a disaster in March 1998. While the drought has eased somewhat, the lack of water remains particularly problematic on Ebeye, where islanders must fetch water from nearby Kwajalein.

On Majuro, the wettest period is September through November, which averages about 14 inches of rain per month, while the driest period is January through March, which sees about eight inches of rain a month.

Full-blown tropical storms or typhoons are rare, but can be devastating when they whip across these low, unprotected islands.

GOVERNMENT & POLITICS

To gain political independence from other Micronesian islands, the Marshallese withdrew from the Congress of Micronesia in 1973. Their constitution became effective on 1 May 1979.

Like other Trust Territory districts, the Marshallese signed a Compact of Free Association with the USA. Almost 90% of the Bikinians voted against it, however, afraid the USA would use conditions of the compact to limit compensation and deny further responsibility for cleaning up Bikini Atoll, which had been devastated by nuclear testing. But the compact eventually passed and took effect in 1986.

The Marshallese government is modelled after a combination of both the British and US systems. The unicameral 33-member parliament, called Nitijela, meets in Majuro in January and August for a total of about 50 days each year. The Nitijela elects one of its members as president of the Marshall Islands. The last president, Amata Kabua, held the office from 1979 till his sudden death in December 1996. He was succeeded by his cousin, Imata Kabua.

MARSHALL ISLANDS

In addition to the elected offices there's a national Council of Iroij, composed of hereditary tribal chiefs, which acts as an advisory board.

The Marshall Islands are divided into 24 municipalities, each of which has its own mayor and is represented by at least one senator in the Nitijela. The major district centres are Majuro, Ebeye, Wotje and Jaluit.

ECONOMY

The Marshallese economy is almost wholly reliant on US funding. Land leases and other payments connected with the USA's US$4 billion missile project on Kwajalein Atoll provide about US$30 million annually to the Marshalls over 30 years. Even more lucrative is the 15-year compact with the USA, which by 2001 will have funnelled about US$1 billion to the Marshalls and comprises over 55% of the Marshall government annual funds.

In recent years the US Congress has also allocated US$240 million to compensate victims of nuclear testing in return for their pledge to drop lawsuits against the US government. Some of the money was paid directly to individual victims, some is being distributed as an annual stipend to the still-displaced Bikinians and other money is set aside as an investment trust. However, supported by new reports that health damage has been more extensive than previously thought, Bikinians are considering launching an appeal to the USA to recover additional damages.

Ironically, during the past decade some Marshallese government officials have flirted with the idea of accepting nuclear waste from Japan, South Korea and Taiwan among others. However, the idea provoked great outcry both from the Marshallese people – who suffer the highest incidence of nuclear diseases worldwide – and neighbouring countries, and in 1998 the Cabinet voted to bar all nuclear waste deposits in the Marshalls.

US cash infusions aside, most Marshallese maintain a mainly subsistence lifestyle, especially on the outer islands.

Small-scale domestic income is derived from copra production, handicraft and aquaculture projects. A garment factory opened in Majuro in 1998 but was shut down one unsuccessful year later. On a brighter note, El Niño-induced weather alterations redirected schools of tuna towards the eastern Marshalls. Taiwan and South Korea hastily signed up for fishing licences for 70 purse seine fishers and annual revenue from licensing foreign fishing vessels, usually US$1.5 million, soared to more than US$4 million in 1998.

POPULATION & PEOPLE

The population of the Marshall Islands is approximately 60,000, with the majority of islanders living on Majuro and Kwajalein atolls. As elsewhere in Micronesia, population growth is a huge problem.

More than 95% of the people living in the Marshalls are Marshallese; they are supplemented by a smattering of Americans and Australians.

ARTS

Marshallese handicrafts are among Micronesia's best; they include stick charts, carved models of outrigger canoes and intricately woven items such as baskets, wall hangings and purses made from pandanus leaves, coconut fronds and cowrie shells.

SOCIETY & CONDUCT

The Marshallese are a soft-spoken people with a rich oral tradition of chants, songs and legends.

Marshallese society has always been a stratified one, and despite increasing Westernisation and the introduction of a monetary economy, social status still derives as much from kinship as it does from economic achievement. Chiefs continue to wield a great deal of authority over land ownership and usage.

Men and young people generally wear Western-style clothing such as T-shirts and pants, while older women often wear loose-fitting floral print muu-muu dresses. On Majuro, school children wear T-shirts of specific colours that identify their schools.

Basketball is the most popular sport on Majuro. Children commonly play street versions of other Western games with rudimentary equipment like a stick and tennis ball substituting for a baseball and bat.

RELIGION

The Protestant 'Boston Mission' that started converting the Marshallese in the mid-1800s effectively wiped out the ancient religion of the islanders.

There are many Protestant sects in the Marshalls, including Congregationalists, Baptists, Seventh-Day Adventists and the Assembly of God. There's also a large Catholic church, a Baha'í centre, a Salvation Army mission and a rapidly growing Mormon presence.

LANGUAGE

Marshallese is the official language, but English is taught in schools and is widely understood. The islanders' gentleness is reflected in their traditional greeting *Yokwe yuk*, which means 'Love to you'. 'Thank you' is *Kommol tata*.

Facts for the Visitor

SUGGESTED ITINERARIES

The charm of the Marshalls is the outer atolls, but if you have only a few days, you'll have to stay on Majuro because Air Marshall Islands (AMI) generally serves outer atolls just once a week. Mili is a good choice, or Wotje or Maloelap for WWII buffs. Divers, of course, should visit Bikini. Ebeye is only for very keen divers.

TOURIST OFFICES

The office of the Marshall Islands Visitors Authority is on Majuro (see Information under Majuro).

VISAS & DOCUMENTS

The immigration office on Majuro (☎ 625 3181), where visa extensions are given, is in the capitol building in D-U-D. For more information see Visas & Travel Permits in the Regional Facts for the Visitor chapter.

MONEY

The Marshall Islands use US dollars (see Exchange Rates under Money in the Regional Facts for the Visitor chapter). Credit cards are increasingly accepted on Majuro and have limited use on Ebeye, where you should expect a surcharge. Tipping is customary in the high-end restaurants but not elsewhere.

POST & COMMUNICATIONS

Majuro uses the US postal system. For postal codes and abbreviations and international telephone codes see the Post & Communications section of the Regional Facts for the Visitor chapter. There are no area codes in the Marshall Islands. Calling Kwajalein Island from other islands in the Marshalls is like making an international call to the USA. To make an international call, dial ☎ 011.

INTERNET RESOURCES

See the Internet Resources section of the Regional Facts for the Visitor chapter for details of Web sites related to the Marshall Islands.

BOOKS

The *Marshall Islands Guidebook* (Micronitor News & Printing Co) gives good cultural information, as well as nice descriptions of individual outer islands. It's available at the tourist office, library, major stores and some hotels on Majuro for US$9, although it might go for less if it hasn't been updated for a while.

MEDIA

Majuro gets cable TV; Ebeye gets US military TV, a unique combination of news, soaps and military propaganda.

Majuro has one AM radio station and one Christian FM station. The local TV station is Channel 11. The Marshalls Broadcasting Company also provides 12 cable TV channels, including HBO, CNN and Fox.

MARSHALL ISLANDS

The weekly US$0.50 *Marshall Islands Journal* has interesting and relevant coverage of the islands and is readily available in stores around town. Guam's *Pacific Daily News* is available at some large stores.

ELECTRICITY
The Marshalls' electricity is 110/120V AC, 60Hz. Plugs are US style with two flat blades.

WEIGHTS & MEASURES
The Marshalls use the imperial measurement system. See the table at the back of this book if you need to convert to metric.

HEALTH
Avoid unboiled tap water.

BUSINESS HOURS
Most businesses and government offices are open Monday to Friday from 9 am to 5 pm.

PUBLIC HOLIDAYS & SPECIAL EVENTS
Public holidays in the Marshalls include:

New Year's Day 1 January
Nuclear Victims Day 1 March
Easter early April
Constitution Day 1 May
Fisherman's Day 1st Friday in July
Labor Day 1st Monday in September
Culture Day last Friday in September
Independence Day 21 October
President's Birthday 17 November
Gospel Day 1st Friday in December
Christmas Day 25 December

Constitution Day is marked by children's sporting events.

Every May 1, Majuro hosts the Outrigger Marshall Islands Cup, held at the Outrigger Hotel. Inter-atoll competition features *korkor* (small canoe) racing. It's a good place to find traditional Marshallese crafts. Dancing and food are also featured.

Majuro has a number of fishing tournaments each year. The largest are held on the weekend before the fourth Thursday in November and on the weekend closest to the 4th of July. Lots of islanders, expats and a growing number of international sportsfishing enthusiasts participate; yellowfin tuna commonly reach 125 pounds (56kg) and the record for Pacific blue marlin is 407 pounds (185kg). For more information ring ☎ 625 7491 or write to the Marshalls Billfish Club, Box 1139, Majuro, Marshall Islands 96960.

ACTIVITIES
The Marshall Islands have excellent diving and snorkelling. Great diving sites can be found on Bikini, Kwajalein and some of the outer islands.

ACCOMMODATION & FOOD
There are no hotels in most of the outer islands but it may be possible to stay with a family or camp, though you should always check with a property's owner before doing so. Only Majuro and, to a lesser extent, Kwajalein have a fair smattering of hotels and restaurants. Travellers going to the outer islands will have to make their own arrangements for food. See the Outer Islands section later in this chapter for details.

DRINKS
Nonalcoholic Drinks
As elsewhere in Micronesia, the ubiquitous drinking coconut is an ideal natural refresher on a hot day.

Alcoholic Drinks
Until very recently, Majuro had its own locally produced brew called Taka – named for one of Marshalls' smallest islands – but the brewery went defunct in 1999 and its future is uncertain. Note that drinking alcohol is not favourably looked on in many of the outer islands.

Getting There & Away

AIR
Airports & Airlines
Majuro and Kwajalein are the only islands with airports served by international flights, with flights from Continental and Aloha

Airlines. AMI also has, in addition to its numerous flights within the Marshalls, a service from Majuro to Tarawa in Kiribati.

AMI (☎ 625 3733, fax 625 3730, @ amisales@ntamar.com) has an office in the Small Island section of D-U-D on Majuro, open weekdays from 8 am to 5.30 pm and from 8 am to 1.30 pm on Saturday. On Ebeye (☎ 329 3036) the office is near Triple J Variety. All tickets must be purchased two days in advance.

Continental has an office on the ground floor of the RRE (Robert Reimers Enterprises) Hotel building in Majuro (☎ 625 3209). This office is open weekdays from 8.30 am to noon and 1 to 4.30 pm.

Continental's Kwajalein office (☎ 355 1013), near Macy's in Kwajalein's central business complex, is open Monday to Friday from 8 am to noon and Tuesday to Saturday from 8 am to 5 pm. The airport office can be reached at ☎ 355 2660. Note that to get to the Kwajalein office you will need a day pass to the island. See Entry to Kwaj later in this chapter.

Departure Tax
Majuro has a US$15 airport departure tax.

Honolulu
Continental has a Honolulu-Majuro flight which costs US$700/1400 one-way/return. Aloha Airlines flies weekly from Honolulu to Majuro for US$800 return and to Kwajalein for US$900 return.

Getting Around

AIR
AMI has numerous flights between Majuro, Kwajalein and the outer islands. See those islands' sections for details.

BOAT
Travel between the islands is usually by privately owned speedboat or diesel inboards, and there are numerous field-trip ships servicing the outer islands. See the individual islands and atolls sections that follow for details.

Majuro Atoll

Most travellers to the Marshalls get only as far as Majuro Atoll, the nation's political and economic centre with a population of 30,000. The name Majuro means 'many eyes' and it has always been one of the more heavily settled Marshallese atolls.

The atoll has 57 small islets curving 63 miles (102km) in an elongated ellipse. The larger islets have been connected by a single 35-mile (56.4km) stretch of paved road, giving most of Majuro the appearance of one long, narrow island. The highest elevation is a mere 20 feet (6m).

Although it is the most populated and most Westernised of the Marshall Islands, Majuro nonetheless retains a simple island flavour. Even in the main municipality of D-U-D you might wake to crowing roosters or see pigs rooting through fallen coconuts. When author Robert Louis Stevenson visited Majuro in 1889 he called the atoll the 'Pearl of the Pacific'. Fragments of Western junk – aluminium cans and wrecked cars – have made Majuro less pristine than it was, but a cleanup effort has done wonders, and the island is abuzz with construction and improvements.

There's a lot that can be learned about life in the Marshalls just from visiting Majuro. Just imagine what it's like to live on a ribbon of land so thin that you can often see the ocean on both sides. Peaceful Laura Village mirrors the rural lifestyle of the outer islands.

Orientation
The airport is about 12 miles (19km) east of the D-U-D municipality. The D-U-D area comprises the three towns of Delap, Uliga and Darrit (Rita), where almost all of Majuro's main services and sights are clustered.

Information
Tourist Offices The new and improved Marshall Islands Visitors Authority (☎ 625 6482, fax 625 6771, @ tourism@ntamar .com) now has an office of its own in the Small Island section of D-U-D. Its helpful

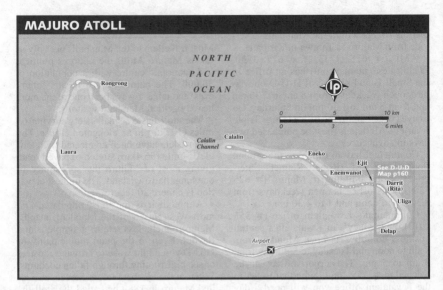

MAJURO ATOLL

NORTH PACIFIC OCEAN

Rongrong

Laura

Calalin Channel

Calalin

Eneko

Ejit

Enemwanot

See D-U-D Map p160

Darrit (Rita)

Uliga

Delap

Airport

0　　5　　10 km
0　　3　　6 miles

staff proffers brochures, a few maps and plenty of information. The office is open weekdays from 9 am to 5 pm.

Money The Bank of Guam is on the 1st floor of the RRE Hotel building, the Bank of the Marshall Islands is next to the main post office and the Bank of Hawaii is beside Gibson's department store. There is an ATM in the RRE grocery store in Uliga.

Post & Communications Majuro's main post office, next door to Robert Reimers Enterprises in Uliga, is open from 8 am to noon and 1 to 4 pm on Tuesday and Thursday, from 8.30 am to noon and 1 to 4 pm other weekdays and from 8 to 11 am on Saturday. Mail sent general delivery to Majuro should be picked up here; it will be held for 30 days.

The Delap substation post office next to Gibson's department store is open from 8.30 am to noon and 1 to 4 pm weekdays.

Continental's reduced flight schedule reportedly caused some mail delivery backlog in 1998; inquire before sending priority mail.

Long-distance calls, faxes and telexes can be made 24 hours a day from the two-storey building behind the National Telecommunications Authority's satellite dish in Delap. Calls to the USA cost US$2 per minute between 7 am and 7 pm and US$1.70 per minute at other times. Calls to Guam cost US$2.50 per minute between 3 am and 9 pm and US$2 at other times. Calls to other countries cost the same at all hours: US$2.50 per minute to Saipan; US$3 per minute to the FSM, Palau, Australia, Nauru, Kiribati and Japan; US$3.50 to New Zealand and Canada; and US$4 to most other destinations. The upper-end hotels also allow guests to call overseas but may add a surcharge.

To call Ebeye from Majuro costs US$0.75 a minute between 7 am and 7 pm and US$0.25 at other times.

All islands other than Majuro and Ebeye are reached only by radio transmission, which costs US$0.50 per minute from Majuro. Calls are made from the NTA building. It's wise to call ahead (☎ 625 3363) to ask when the island you're trying to reach will be on-air, as the outer islands only staff their radios during certain hours.

Pay phones (local calls US$0.25) can be found at Robert Reimers Enterprises,

Gibson's department store, the airport, the hospital and the bowling alley. Dial ☎ 411 for directory assistance.

Email & Internet Access The Tourist Trap store near Gibson's department store has two Internet terminals and charges US$6 per hour plus a US$1 access fee. The store is open weekdays from 9 am to 5 pm and from 9 am to noon on Saturday.

Libraries The public library next door to Alele Museum has a Pacific room with a good selection of books, magazines and journals on Micronesia. It's open Monday to Friday from 10 am to noon and 1 to 5 pm, Saturday from 9 am to 1 pm.

Weather Information For weather information call ☎ 625 3076.

Medical Services Majuro's relatively modern 80-bed hospital (emergency ☎ 625 4144; switchboard ☎ 625 3399) in Delap is adequate for routine medical procedures. The hospital clinic opens daily from 1 to 5 pm and visitors queue with everyone else. There is only one private practice on Majuro, across the street from the tourist office.

Laundry There's a coin laundry on the main road in Delap about a third of a mile (half a kilometre) west of Gibson's department store and others sprinkled around D-U-D.

D-U-D Municipality

Three of Majuro's islands – Delap, Uliga and Darrit (Rita) – are joined into one municipality with the unappealing moniker 'D-U-D'. (Pronounce each letter separately, rather than spitting out the single syllable 'dud'.)

D-U-D is the nation's capital and home to the majority of Majuro's residents. D-U-D also has the greatest concentration of commercial services on the Marshall Islands. There are some problems though – the lagoon around D-U-D is awash with pollution and not suitable for swimming. Poor sanitation conditions are compounded by causeways and bridges that close up the lagoon and block water circulation.

Delap The community of Delap begins as you cross over the Majuro Bridge coming from the airport.

The Marshall Islands government offices are spread around Delap, with the centre of it all being the US$9 million **capitol building** – a singularly modernistic structure of bright reflective glass that looks like no other building this side of Guam. The capitol building has a circular parliamentary hall for the Nitijela, a meeting room for the House of Iroij and a 200-seat spectator gallery.

Next to the dock where the field-trip ship pulls in is the **Tobolar Copra Processing Plant**. A field-trip ship carries supplies to the outer islands and returns loaded with the copra, which is then piled high in the plant warehouse. It's hard to believe that this mountain of gritty brown coconut meat gets transformed into pure transparent oil! If you're interested in looking around, call ☎ 625 3494 or ☎ 625 3116 for a tour.

Uliga Most of Majuro's businesses and services are in Uliga.

The **Alele Museum** and the public library are housed in a two-storey building next to the courthouse. The museum is small but has quality exhibits of early Marshallese culture, including stick charts, model canoes and shell tools. One highlight is the **collection of photographs** of the Marshalls taken at the turn of the century by Joachim deBrum, the son of a Portuguese whaler who lived on Likiep Atoll. There's also a display of hundreds of different seashells collected in the Marshall Islands. The museum is open from 8 to 11 am on Monday, from 11 am to noon and 5 to 7 pm Tuesday to Friday and from 10 am to 1 pm on Saturday. There's no entrance fee, though donations are appreciated.

Darrit (Rita) & Around US forces stationed on Majuro during WWII gave the island of Darrit the nickname 'Rita', after pin-up girl Rita Hayworth, and the name has stuck. (They also named Laura after another Hollywood favourite, Lauren Bacall.)

Die-hard sightseers may want to seek out the **Japanese bunker**, which is Majuro's

MARSHALL ISLANDS

D-U-D MUNICIPALITY

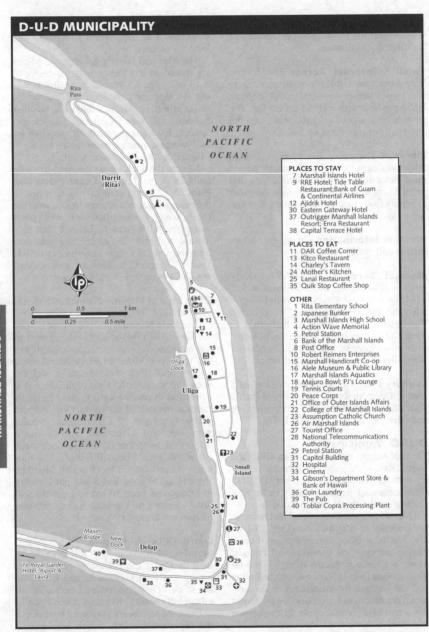

PLACES TO STAY
7 Marshall Islands Hotel
9 RRE Hotel; Tide Table
   Restaurant; Bank of Guam
   & Continental Airlines
12 Ajidrik Hotel
30 Eastern Gateway Hotel
37 Outrigger Marshall Islands
   Resort; Enra Restaurant
38 Capital Terrace Hotel

PLACES TO EAT
11 DAR Coffee Corner
13 Kitco Restaurant
14 Charley's Tavern
24 Mother's Kitchen
25 Lanai Restaurant
35 Quik Stop Coffee Shop

OTHER
1 Rita Elementary School
2 Japanese Bunker
3 Marshall Islands High School
4 Action Wave Memorial
5 Petrol Station
6 Bank of the Marshall Islands
8 Post Office
10 Robert Reimers Enterprises
15 Marshall Handicraft Co-op
16 Alele Museum & Public Library
17 Marshall Islands Aquatics
18 Majuro Bowl; PJ's Lounge
19 Tennis Courts
20 Peace Corps
21 Office of Outer Islands Affairs
22 College of the Marshall Islands
23 Assumption Catholic Church
26 Air Marshall Islands
27 Tourist Office
28 National Telecommunications
   Authority
29 Petrol Station
31 Capitol Building
32 Hospital
33 Cinema
34 Gibson's Department Store &
   Bank of Hawaii
36 Coin Laundry
39 The Pub
40 Toblar Copra Processing Plant

MARSHALL ISLANDS

A chorus of islanders, Pohnpei

Yapese woman in traditional dress

Dancing in Yap

Preparations for a village feast, Yap

Making *sakau*, Pohnpei

Yapese men's house

Preparing a pig for feasting, Pohnpei

only remaining WWII fortification, or the overgrown **Action Wave Memorial** raised after a tidal wave destroyed the area in November 1979. Neither is particularly interesting or easy to find. The bunker, beyond the high school, is reached by tramping through private yards.

People commonly wade across the reef to and from the islands north of Rita – it's such a well-trodden route there's even a footpath over the reef. If you catch low tide the water should be less than a foot deep, and at its lowest you might even be able to cross without getting your feet wet. However you should be careful to watch the tides if you intend to come back the same way. The local newspaper has a tide chart.

The second island past Rita, Ejit, is home to about 250 people from Bikini Atoll. The Bikinians are protective of their privacy and their way of life and maintain an alcohol-free community. Because of a few problems they've had with inquisitive media people tromping through, permission to visit Ejit should be obtained in advance from the Bikini Trust Liaison Office (☎ 625 3177) in Uliga.

A few islands beyond Rita, Enemwanot (also spelled Enamanit) is locally popular for weekend picnics and beer drinking. Its **pleasant beach** and palm-lined shores offer some fine snorkelling. Kirtley Pinho (☎ 625 0155) takes picnickers over for about US$25 return. For a midweek trip, ask for Abacca Maddison at Outrigger, whose husband Yuri sometimes does full-day charters.

Laura

Laura, a quiet green refuge 30 miles (48km) away from the bustle of D-U-D, is the atoll's agricultural centre. This pleasant village is as neat as a pin compared to the D-U-D area and the outing to Laura makes a lovely drive.

The tip of Laura is fringed with a **pretty white sand beach**, Majuro's finest. During the week visitors may well have Laura to themselves. On the weekends it's a popular place for family picnics.

The road to Laura passes the airport, the runway of which is sloped as it also serves

as Majuro's main water catchment area. A dirt path to the left, immediately past the runway, goes straight out to the beach, where there's a **shipwreck** on the shore.

Farther up the road on the right is **Majuro Peace Park**, built by the Japanese, which has a memorial in Marshallese, English and Japanese dedicated to those who died in the East Pacific during WWII. The park's amphitheatre, cement monument and flag-poles all look rather lonely and out of place on this remote beach. There are shady spots for picnicking, though the flies can be a bit thick.

The Japanese erected a **stone memorial marker** for a major typhoon that hit Laura in 1918. To find it, drive to the end of the paved road, continue on the dirt road for about 160 yards (150m) and then stop in front of the pink house; the monument is in the yard on the opposite (inland) side of the road, visible from the road but partially shaded by a bougainvillea bush.

The **beach** is farther along on the same dirt road; bear left at the first intersection and right at the next. The nicest section of the beach is at the end of the road. The landowner charges US$1 for adults and US$0.25 for kids to enter; as they clean up the beach and maintain some picnic facilities it's quite a reasonable fee.

On Sunday, **roadside stands** spring up near Laura, selling coconut frond picnic baskets to people headed to the beach. The baskets are filled with such local treats as drinking coconuts, breadfruit, IQ (coconut pudding), pumpkin, reef fish and barbecued chicken. The price varies, but you can usually get a basket that will fill a few hungry people for about US$20.

Activities

Diving & Snorkelling Majuro is a good place to find rare varieties of tropical fish as well as lots of white-tipped and grey reef sharks. In addition there are a couple of plane wrecks off the airport, and scuttled ships and barges in the waters off Rita.

Diving is possible year-round, though the calmest months are May to October. A popular dive is the Calalin Channel, which has a

MARSHALL ISLANDS

fairly good reef and enough shark activity to be dubbed 'Shark Alley'. The farther from Rita you go, the clearer the water gets. Enemwanot has good snorkelling and Calalin, the last island before the channel, is even better, but beware of currents. Delap Point also is good for reef fish and occasional sharks.

If you want to snorkel without having to find boat transportation, there's a shallow coral reef at Laura Beach, at the west end of Majuro.

Dive Operations Marshalls Dive Adventures (MDA; ☎ 625 5131 ext 215, fax 625 3505, ℮ rreadmin@ntamar.com), run by the RRE Hotel, occupies a waterfront hut at the south side of the hotel. MDA charges US$90 for a two-tank dive in Majuro Atoll. It's US$110 for a two-tank dive in neighbouring Arno Atoll, which is about a 45-minute speedboat ride from Majuro and has a nicer reef with better coral. Dive prices include tanks and weights; add about US$25 more if you need to rent complete gear. MDA also sells and rents snorkelling gear; complete sets cost US$10 a day. A three-day certification class costs US$300. RRE hotel guests get a 10% discount. MasterCard and Visa are accepted.

MDA has also powered Majuro's most notable tourist development – the reopening of diving on Bikini. See the Bikini section later this chapter for more details.

Matthew Holly (☎/fax 625 3669, ℮ aquamar@ntamar.com) of Marshall Islands Aquatics offers two-tank beach dives for US$60, as well as boat and night dives; it's US$100 to go on their boat in Majuro for the day. Snorkel sets rent for US$6.

Tennis & Bowling There are two public tennis courts, with lights for night use, in Uliga.

Also in Uliga is the six-lane Majuro Bowl, the island's first bowling alley, which opens at 10 am (Sunday at 2 pm) and stays open late, locking its doors once the customers finally thin out. The cost is US$2 a game.

Sportsfishing Sportsfishing – mostly trolling for tuna, wahoo and marlin, and bottom fishing for reef fish – is catching on in Majuro. Contact the tourist office for details.

Places to Stay

Majuro has several fine hotels. Those at the lower price range tend to be rather dismal, making Majuro a good place to splurge. There's a hotel tax of US$3 per room per night plus 8%; add this to the prices below unless otherwise noted. Most hotels provide complimentary airport transfers if you call in advance.

Places to Stay – Budget

The **Ajidrik Hotel** (☎ 625 3171, fax 625 3712) in central Uliga has 15 air-con rooms with mini-refrigerators, TV and private bathrooms with showers. Singles/doubles cost US$40/50. It's rather run-down and quite basic, but if US$50 is your limit it's the best option.

The **Capital Terrace Hotel** (☎ 625 3831) in Delap, variously described in Lonely Planet's last edition as 'dingy', 'bug-infested' and 'overpriced', was getting a facelift in spring 1999; call for an update.

Opposite the capitol building is the multi-storey **Eastern Gateway Hotel** (☎ 625 3259, fax 625 3512). One of the Republic of Nauru's myriad investment bloopers, this hotel was erected during a decade of on-and-off construction and was then mothballed just prior to completion. That is to say, the mammoth and dilapidated structure contains no functioning hotel rooms, though there are five unappealing motel rooms (US$40) in a dingy block house flanking the hotel. Six small, run-down concrete bungalows on the lagoon go for US$30. All rooms and bungalows have a mini-refrigerator and private bath.

The nicest by far of the lower-end hotels is the new **Hotel Marshall Islands** (☎ 625 3002, fax 625 3004, ℮ journal@ntamar .com). Though it's directly above the Marshall Islands Club, the noise is effectively blocked by thick walls and floors. The 10 immaculate rooms have a nice natural-wood feel about them; each has a TV, mini-refrigerator and phone (local calls US$0.25). The private bathrooms are clean and modern. Singles/doubles are US$68/83 (tax included); the abysmal quality of other budget hotels makes it worthwhile to spend a little more. Visa and MasterCard are accepted.

If you're looking for a long-term place to stay, Brian & Nancy Vander Velde (☎/fax 625 3811, @ vndvelde@ntamar.com) have a couple of simple studio and one-bedroom apartments that might be available. Known as *Garden Apartments*, they're south of Marshall Islands High School in Rita. Each has air-con, hot water and cooking facilities and costs from US$150 to US$250 a week, depending on demand.

Places to Stay – Top End

The newly refurbished *RRE Hotel (also called Hotel Robert Reimers;* ☎ *625 3250, fax 625 3505,* @ *rreadmin@ntamar.com)* is a comfortable, modern 39-room hotel in central Uliga that's deservedly popular with business travellers. Rooms have a refrigerator, air-con, phones (free local calls), cable TV and rattan furnishings, including a table, chairs and a settee. Purified water is also available. Rooms on the inside corridor are larger, have bathtubs and cost US$75/80 for singles/doubles, while rooms with balconies and views of the lagoon cost US$90/95 for singles/doubles. MasterCard and Visa are accepted.

Another upmarket option that is past its peak but still nice is the *Royal Garden Hotel (*☎ *247 3701, fax 247 3705)*, 2 miles (3km) west of D-U-D across the Majuro bridge. Its 24 large rooms occupy a two-storey complex overlooking a little white sand beach. Rooms have TVs, bathtubs, phones, air-con, carpeting, refrigerators and ocean views. The rates are US$60/70 for singles/doubles (tax included). There's a decent restaurant on the premises.

The Hawai'ian-based Outrigger hotel chain has just opened up the sprawling, 150-room *Outrigger Marshall Islands Resort (*☎ *625 2525, fax 625 2500; in the USA* ☎ *1-800-688 7444)* about a quarter-mile (400m) west of Gibson's department store. The hotel is very comfortable and the staff accommodating. Rooms have all the ex-

pected amenities – bath, TV, phones (local calls US$0.50) and mini-refrigerator, and most have a marvellous lagoon-side beach view. The flat room rate for singles or doubles is US$125; add US$25 for an extra bed. Healthy discounts are given to commercial travellers and government workers. MasterCard and Visa are accepted.

Places to Eat

Food in Majuro is reasonably priced and fresh fish is found in most restaurants. Water is not safe to drink from the tap; you can find bottled water in grocery stores.

Places to Eat – Budget

One of Micronesia's better budget breakfast spots is the *DAR Coffee Corner*, located behind the library in Uliga and a few minutes' walk from the Hotel Marshall Islands and Marshall Islands Club. It is simple, clean, cheap and smoke-free. Two or three fluffy US$0.25 pancakes plus a US$0.60 cup of coffee make a great morning starter. Later in the day quality local food is served buffet-style. It's open from 6 am to 9 pm daily.

Kitco Restaurant, in the centre of D-U-D, is also locally popular for its inexpensive fare, but unlike the DAR it is dark and smoky. Pancakes cost US$1, breakfast combos US$2 to US$3. There's also a full chalkboard of dishes from *ramen* to teriyaki steak for under US$5. It's open daily from 6 am to 9 pm.

Mother's Kitchen, next to Momotaro's store at Small Island, has eight tables in a cosy non-smoking environment. Recommended are the grilled tuna on salad greens and the teriyaki chicken plate, each US$4. There are also sandwiches and vegetarian tofu dishes. At breakfast you can get US$0.75 banana pancakes or various omelettes from US$3 to US$4. It's open from 6 am to 2 pm daily except on Sunday.

The Deli, attached to the RRE store in Uliga, has ordinary burgers and sandwiches for US$2 to US$3, as well as simple, cheap breakfast items. There are picnic tables at the side where you can sit and eat. It's open Monday to Saturday from 6 am to 7.30 pm and Sunday from 7 am to 5.30 pm.

MARSHALL ISLANDS

Savannah's is a new eatery next to Gibson's department store that has attracted a flock of locals and expats. It's a good place for a steak-and-egg or fish-and-rice meal, as the good cooking aroma attests. The restaurant is open Monday to Saturday from 7 am to 10 pm and Sunday from 9 am to 6 pm. It metamorphoses into a popular bar late on weekend evenings.

Charley's Tavern, next to Kitco Restaurant, has the reputation for having the island's best pizza, though its reign is being challenged by the Marshall Islands Club, which also spins out pizza. Both places open in the late afternoon and charge about US$9 for a small pizza.

Of the numerous grocery stores in D-U-D, *Gibson's department store* has the freshest food and best prices. In Uliga, the *RRE Store* has the best variety.

Places to Eat – Top End
Tide Table Restaurant, upstairs at the RRE Hotel, is a popular place with excellent food and fine views of the lagoon. Standard breakfast fare – eggs, pancakes and the like – costs US$3 to US$5 and is served until 11 am. Lunch features burgers and sandwiches with fries and salad for US$4 and a few hot dishes for a bit more. Seafood and steak dinners cost US$10 to US$15, including soup, salad and rice. It's open daily from 7 am to 2 pm and from 5 to 9.30 pm.

The *Lanai Restaurant*, on the lagoon at Small Island next to the AMI office, has a varied Chinese menu. At lunch everything on the menu is US$5, including satay beef, Peking stir fry and chicken curry – all served with rice. At dinner seafood and meat dishes are priced from US$10 to US$13 and vegetarian tofu dishes average US$7. Lunch is from 10 am to 2 pm weekdays and dinner from 5 to 10 pm Monday to Saturday.

Enra Restaurant, downstairs at the Outrigger Hotel, has fine food to accompany a wonderful lagoon view – you can sit inside and gaze through the glass walls, or relax outside on the patio. The menu is an impressive array of steaks, seafood and salads, all reasonably priced for an upmarket establishment. Lunch-time pizzas are from US$7. The restaurant is open daily from 6.30 am to 9.30 pm and for Sunday brunch from 10 am to 2 pm. The Outrigger also offers pricey dinner cruises (US$38 without drinks).

Entertainment
The locally popular *Marshall Islands Club* in Uliga now brews its own golden ale, called Whiteball. It also has a nice ocean view, simple eats and a band most nights.

Other local hang-outs include *PJ's Lounge*, above Majuro Bowl in Uliga, which is open from 4 pm to 2 am and has a live band playing rock, reggae, jazz or soul from 10 pm. There's generally a cover charge. *Charley's Tavern* in the centre of Uliga has live music from 10 pm to 2 am on Friday and is also a popular spot to knock back a beer. *The Pub*, a popular early evening spot beside Ace International in Delap, has both a bar and a disco.

Lanai Restaurant on Small Island changes from restaurant to disco on Thursday, Friday and Saturday and draws a good crowd. Expats patronise the *Tide Table Restaurant* at the RRE Hotel, which has a bar open from 4 pm daily and a good sunset view, as the restaurant faces west across the lagoon. The *Outrigger* also has a bar.

Shopping
The Marshall Handicraft Co-op, behind the museum, is open weekdays from 9 am to noon and 1 to 5 pm, and is a good place to watch women weaving. Busy Hands, on the road near the Assumption Catholic Church, is open more sporadically. Other handicrafts include MIKA Handicrafts between Gibson's department store and Outrigger Marshall Islands Resort, Am Mon Keke behind Gibson's Wallace Theaters in Delap and the Leipajid Club, a small shop across from the Assumption Catholic Church in Uliga. There are also two handicraft booths at the airport, the larger of which carries unique outer island handicrafts.

Locally made coconut oil soap is sold in Majuro stores. You can get colourful commemorative postage stamps at the post office and first day covers at the Alele Museum. The Alele Museum also sells stick charts, T-shirts and cassette tapes of Marshallese chants and stories. The library beside the museum sells books on Micronesia.

Getting There & Away

Air Majuro is a free stopover on Continental's 'Circle Micronesia' island-hopper flight between Honolulu and Guam. (See the regional Getting There & Away chapter for air passes and all airline contact details.)

AMI has only one international destination: Tarawa in Kiribati. The plane flies from Majuro to Tarawa and back on Tuesday and Thursday for a one-way fare of US$197.

The open-air airport has some simple snack bars, a handicraft shop and a couple of car rental booths.

Boat Visiting yachts must check in with Port Authority upon arrival at Majuro. There is a US$50 entry fee.

Getting Around

To/From the Airport Most hotels provide a free minivan service to and from the airport; call ahead so they will be sure to meet you. Otherwise, an unmetered taxi from the airport to D-U-D costs US$2 to US$4. The drive takes about 15 minutes.

Car Visitors can drive in Majuro for 30 days with a valid driving licence from their home country, or pick up a local driver's licence for a small fee.

The speed limit is 25mph (42km/h) in the D-U-D area and 45mph (75km/h) between the airport and Laura, except for school and church zones where the speed limit is 15mph (25km/h) per hour.

Several companies keep booths at the airport, though they're not always staffed. One is DAR (☎ 625 3174, fax 625 3344), which has an office next to the DAR Coffee Corner in Uliga. It charges US$50 to US$60 per day for an air-con sedan, plus US$7 for insurance. DAR may be the only rent-a-car company in Micronesia with hourly rates (US$7.50).

The RRE Hotel (☎ 625 3250, fax 625 3505) rents cars for US$47, insurance included. Other companies with similar rates include the Royal Garden Hotel (☎ 247 3701, fax 247 3705) and Deluxe Car Rental (☎ 625 3665, fax 625 3663). The Outrigger Hotel (☎ 625 2525, ext 7901) has cars from US$65 (a 10% government discount is available). Both RRE and Royal Garden give priority to their hotel guests. There are also any number of signs around town advertising car rental, and a list of car rental agencies at the tourist office as well; if you're on a budget, call around and negotiate for the best price.

Taxi Majuro has a fine, inexpensive shared taxi system. Most taxis are sedans, clearly marked with taxi signs. You stand at the side of the road and wave them down and if they're not full they'll pick you up. It costs just US$0.50 to go anywhere within D-U-D.

Anyone going to Laura can travel on a public minivan from the parking lot of the RRE Hotel ($2). There's no fixed schedule – the minivan leaves whenever it's full. If time is a priority, it might be better to rent a car.

Boat Hotels can arrange boat rentals but you may be able to save money by making arrangements yourself with someone who has a speedboat. Ask around at the docks and bargain. Marshallese are generally very fair and won't cheat you, but if you throw money around they'll take it.

Kwajalein Atoll

Nowhere in Micronesia is the US military presence so pronounced as on Kwajalein Atoll, home of a US$4 billion space tracking and missile defence facility.

Kwajalein is the world's largest coral atoll. Its 97 islands have a total land mass of just 6.5 sq miles (17 sq km) but they surround an immense 1100 sq mile (2860 sq km) lagoon.

The lagoon, sometimes called 'the world's largest catcher's mitt', is the target and splashdown point for US intercontinental

MARSHALL ISLANDS

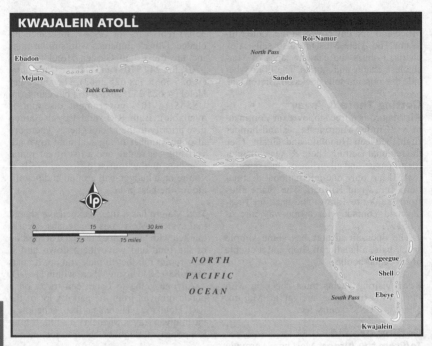

KWAJALEIN ATOLL

Roi-Namur
North Pass
Ebadon
Mejato
Sando
Tabik Channel

NORTH
PACIFIC
OCEAN

Gugeegue
Shell
South Pass Ebeye
Kwajalein

0   15   30 km
0   7.5   15 miles

ballistic missiles (ICBMs) fired from between 260 to 4900 miles (420km to 7900km) away. Many come from the Vandenberg Air Force Base in California, a distance of 4200 miles (6700km).

The missile tests, which occur roughly five to 10 times a year and generally at night, light up the night sky when the dummy warheads enter the earth's atmosphere.

Kwajalein's facility is currently used for space tracking, to test missiles of all ranges, and to test the prototype for the National Missile Defense (the successor to Star Wars).

The Kwajalein missile range (officially called US Army Kwajalein Atoll, or USAKA) includes Kwajalein Island in the southern part of the atoll, Roi-Namur island in the north and some smaller islands between the two. It's a world of radar tracking systems, telemetry, optic sensors, huge antennae and sophisticated computers.

Kwajalein was also the site of heavy fighting during WWII. Under Operation Flintlock, US forces took the atoll in early February 1944 (the army took Kwajalein, the marines took Roi-Namur). The victory helped cut Japanese lines of communication across the Pacific and penetrate the Japanese line of defence.

Orientation

Kwajalein is the arrival point for Continental flights, though the island is off-limits to visitors without a special pass (see the Entry to Kwaj section later in this chapter). Kwajalein is good for changing money and is home to Continental's offices, though all unofficial visitors will stay on Ebeye.

Information

Tourist Offices There are no tourist offices on Kwajalein.

Money There's a bank of the Marshall Islands and a Bank of Guam on Ebeye. The

Bank of Guam is open only on Wednesday and Friday. To avoid the queues, try the clean, efficient Bank of Guam on Kwajalein where credit card advances (MasterCard and Visa) are available.

Post & Communications Ebeye's post office is one minute's walk from the Anrohasa Hotel. There is a 24-hour National Telecom Agency (NTA) toward the south end of Ebeye; it's US$0.75 per minute to call Majuro (US$0.25 from 7 pm to 7 am), and US$2 per minute to call the USA ($1.70 from 7 pm to 7 am). Calling Kwajalein from Ebeye (and vice-versa) is considered an international call between the Marshalls and the USA. It's much cheaper to take the ferry to the dock on Kwajalein and use the Kwajalein phone in the dock area; dial ☎ 5 and then the four-digit number.

Media Ebeye has two television stations. Channel 9 shows more soaps and movies, while Channel 13 alternates between news and sports. Commercials on both consist of US military propaganda and historical snippets. *Stars & Stripes*, the US military newspaper, is sold at the Kwaj dock for US$0.50.

Kwajalein Island

About 2700 US civilian contract workers and their families live on Kwajalein Island, commonly referred to as 'Kwaj'. In many respects, it is US suburbia transplanted.

Recreational facilities include a golf course, two swimming pools, baseball diamonds, tennis courts, a cinema, handball and basketball courts, a bowling alley and a dive club. Attractions of a more local variety include a **pond full of giant turtles** and a new air-conditioned **Marshallese Cultural Center** filled with WWII photos and relics, woven mats, canoes and other artefacts. Virtually everything is free to residents.

WWII has left a palpable presence on Kwajalein. There is a well-preserved **bunker** and a manicured **Japanese cemetery**, site of the mass grave for Japanese soldiers defending Kwajalein.

The island today has several enormous, globe-shaped radar units and a US$425 million Defense Control Center.

Entry to Kwaj Kwajalein Island is off-limits to unofficial visitors except as a transit point to neighbouring Ebeye. To stay overnight on Kwaj, you must have an official 'sponsor' on the island who can arrange for your stay. Veterans who fought on Kwajalein during WWII can ask the American Legion for sponsoring assistance.

However, day passes are not difficult to obtain. Many Marshallese go to Kwaj for the day to do their laundry and haul water back to Ebeye. Visitors to Ebeye can also obtain these day passes, which are issued by the Ebeye police. The day before you want to visit Kwaj, go to the Ebeye police station about 7.30 am and join the throng of waiting Marshallese. When the police station opens at 8 am, the officer will put your name on a list. The next morning, take the ferry to Kwaj. The day passes are available for pick-up in the Kwaj dock waiting room at 8 am. You must turn in your pass by 2 pm.

Visitors to Kwaj can pick up a US$1 taxi ticket at the harbour or at cafe counters; this will pay for a ride anywhere on the island.

Ebeye Island

• **pop 13,000**

Over 1300 Marshallese labourers work on Kwajalein and live on 78-acre (32-hectare) Ebeye Island, 3 miles (4.8km) to the north. They support close to 12,000 more relatives and friends in inadequate, overcrowded tenement conditions.

The contrasts between the two islands are startling. Workers are shuttled by boat between their meagre homes and their affluent work sites. Marshallese are not allowed to shop at Kwajalein's fancy subsidised stores or swim in its 'public' pools. On the other hand, Ebeye's inhabitants seem relatively contented.

In 1935 Ebeye had 13 people in three households. With the development of the Kwajalein missile range in the early 1960s, Kwajalein Island residents were evacuated to Ebeye. Other Kwajalein Atoll islanders soon joined them, as the atoll's 'mid-corridor' islands were also evacuated to free up most of the lagoon for catching missiles launched from California.

The US army constructed apartment units, a saltwater sewage system, a power plant and a freshwater system on Ebeye, but allotted no money for maintenance. The systems soon fell into disrepair.

As if concentrating all the atoll's people on tiny Ebeye wasn't problem enough, the menial jobs that opened up on the base on Kwajalein Island attracted Marshallese from other atolls, particularly those who had relatives on Ebeye. With traditional Marshallese custom dictating that members of each extended family take in relatives in need, the neat little apartments built by the military were on their way to becoming Micronesia's most overcrowded ghetto.

In 1968 Marshallese workers at Kwajalein began receiving the US minimum wage, which was much higher than the average salary elsewhere in the Marshalls. By 1970 Ebeye had 4000 people and by 1978 the population had swelled to 8000 – on an island just 1 mile (1.6km) long and less than 200 yards (183m) wide. One-room shacks and lean-tos of plywood, tin, cinder block and plastic sheeting were jammed side by side, with no room for greenery and trees. The island came to be known as the 'Slum of the Pacific'.

A new sewage system built in 1979 broke down soon after its completion, electrical power was out more often than not, running water was restricted to as little as 15 minutes a day and sanitation conditions were appalling. Pollution levels in the lagoon were hundreds of times higher than those considered safe by World Health Organization standards, yet those same waters were the children's only playground. Typhoid, diabetes, malnutrition and dysentery were all in epidemic proportions. It wasn't until the early 1980s, after islanders had disrupted military tests by staging a series of 'sail-ins' to restricted parts of the atoll, that the US government finally began taking Ebeye's problems seriously. The lease agreement

granting the USA continued use of Kwajalein Atoll was renegotiated, with the rent increasing from a couple of hundred thousand dollars to US$9 million a year.

About half of that money was allotted to development and the Kwajalein Atoll Development Authority (KADA) was established to coordinate projects; it has made some headway in turning things around.

As part of KADA's projects, Ebeye's dusty potholed roads have been paved, sidewalks built and the sewage system rebuilt, and things are generally improving. However, poor infrastructure remains one of Ebeye's greatest handicaps. Ebeye's desalinisation plant has not worked for years, which forces residents to go to Kwajalein and haul water back, via the ferry, to Ebeye. Electricity too is spotty.

A causeway stretches 6 miles (9.6km) northward from Ebeye to neighbouring islands, joining half a dozen of them in an effort to relieve Ebeye's overcrowding.

Gugeegue, the island at the far end of the causeway, is being developed as an outlet for overflow housing. Already it has a branch of the College of the Marshall Islands. At 59 acres (24 hectares), Gugeegue is the largest of these islands and is expected to eventually house up to 3000 people; several hundred live there now.

Needless to say, Ebeye is not a big tourist spot, but it is a real eye-opener. The people are very friendly, especially the children.

Roi-Namur & Sando Islands

Fifty miles (80km) north of Ebeye, Roi-Namur houses radar and other tracking equipment. Like Kwajalein, it's a restricted military facility and another 'little America' with modern amenities available to Americans only.

Sando is the home of Marshallese workers commuting to Roi-Namur, much like Ebeye is to Kwajalein. The Japanese had communications facilities on Sando and large bomb shelters still stand, though they were damaged by heavy bombing during WWII. Live shells are still occasionally found on Roi-Namur and Sando.

Sando is so close to the missile touch-down site that the USA built a modern bomb shelter for the 400 residents. But the islanders, who once dutifully practiced drills, no longer bother to go to the shelter when US missiles are shot their way.

Mejato Island

Mejato, in the north-west part of the atoll, is home to 350 Rongelapese, many of whom were exposed to radiation in US nuclear testing.

After years of US failure to respond to the islanders' concerns about radioactive contamination on Rongelap, Greenpeace helped the Rongelapese relocate to Mejato in 1985. During their first few years on Mejato the Rongelapese suffered food shortages due to the difficulty in bringing supplies from Ebeye, 70 miles (110km) to the south. One of the obstacles was the waters around Mejato, which are too shallow for most cargo boats to land.

Greenpeace came to the rescue again in 1988, providing the islanders with US$50,000 to build a 40-foot (12m) catamaran to transport food and supplies.

Diving

Kwajalein Atoll has more than 30 WWII-era Japanese ships at the bottom of the lagoon. Until recently they were the exclusive playground of US divers stationed on Kwajalein Island, but Ebeye now has an established dive operation, Kwajalein Atoll Dive Resort (☎/fax 329 3297), which has opened up the area to civilian divers. Dive master Steven Gavegan, who moved here from the Caribbean, has a small office in the KADA building beside the telecommunications office. The dive sites include coral pinnacles, a dozen ships at the south end of the atoll and an aeroplane graveyard off Roi-Namur, but the real highlight is the wreck of the *Prinz Eugen*, a German pocket battleship, off the coast of Carlson just west of Kwajalein Atoll. The *Prinz Eugen* served as an escort to the *Bismarck* during its legendary battle against the British *Hood* during WWII. After the war it was commandeered by the USA for use in its nuclear tests on Bikini Atoll. The old ship settled to its current depth in 1957.

A two-tank dive with Kwajalein Atoll Dive Resort costs US$95 and includes tanks and weights; other gear can be rented for US$45. Visa and MasterCard are accepted (4% surcharge).

There is also a scuba club on Kwajalein Island accessible to guests there.

Places to Stay

Official visitors to Kwaj can stay in the *Kwaj Lodge*, which has rooms for US$20 to US$75.

All three of Ebeye's hotels are impressively overpriced and rooms in some of the hotels can be verging on the decrepit. Add US$2 local tax plus 8% to the rates below. Book several weeks in advance if you want to stay in one of Anrohasa's cheaper rooms or in one of the other hotels.

The nicest place to stay is the two-storey *Anrohasa Hotel* (☎ 329 3161, fax 329 3248), a family-owned hotel belonging to Fountain and Ann Inok. The 26 rooms have air-con, refrigerators, phones and TVs. There are six small rooms in an older wing for US$65. The newer, spiffier rooms cost US$85, US$95 with limited cooking facilities, and suites are US$150. Visa and MasterCard are accepted (4% surcharge). A hefty deposit of US$100 is required for a one-night stay (more for multiple nights).

The best budget option is the *DSC Hotel* (☎ 329 3194), which has seven decent rooms with double bed, TV and refrigerator for US$52.

The Place Hotel (☎ 329 3210, fax 329 3292), huddled amidst Ebeye's tenements not far from the Anrohasa Hotel, has eight cheerless box-like, rooms with air-con and a TV if you insist. There's no hot water, cold water only on request and no room service. Rooms are US$57 (tax included).

Places to Eat

Bob's Island Restaurant, a block from the Anrohasa Hotel, has a little balcony with a sea view, good prices and the best food on Ebeye. Try the French toast or the pancakes for breakfast ($2.50). Bob's is open for all meals except Sunday dinner.

The **Anrohasa Hotel Restaurant** has a varied menu with US-style food as well as Chinese and Japanese dishes. Eggs are a reliable breakfast choice, and fish or beef for lunch or dinner. It's open for three meals a day, prices are moderate and there's a bar across the hall.

Triple J Variety Store near the Ebeye dock has the regular line of groceries as well as a few takeaway sandwiches. Ice-cream cones are US$0.50.

If you make it to Kwaj, try the **Three Palms** snack bar beside the Bank of Guam. It has classic American fare – burgers, fries, pizza and Baskin-Robbins ice-cream – as well as some pastries.

If desperation arises (and it will), try the **snack bar** at the Kwaj dock, which serves fresh pastries in the morning, as well as a good selection of sandwiches ($2.50 or less) and imported apples, oranges and bananas.

Getting There & Away

Air Continental stops on Kwajalein Island as part of the island-hopper flight. There is also an Aloha Airlines weekly flight from Honolulu. See the Getting There & Away section earlier in this chapter for details.

Although Kwajalein Island is a closed military base, it is the transit point if you're entering Ebeye by air. Once you're on Kwajalein, you'll be instructed to go to the dock and take a ferry (free) or a water taxi ($4 one-way) to Ebeye. Citizens of countries other than the USA and the Marshall Islands will receive an escort to the dock; US citizens and Marshallese can catch taxis at the airport. The boat, a US army catamaran, is free and takes 25 minutes; ask for a ferry schedule at the DSC dock before you leave.

When you're flying out of Kwajalein, it's wise to check in as early as possible as Continental's reduced flight schedule means that flights are often full. When you show your ticket at the Kwajalein dock you will be allowed to proceed to the airport; if you have an open ticket, obtain a print-out of your flight times to show at the dock.

AMI flies direct between Majuro and Kwajalein daily except Friday and Sunday for US$125 one way.

Boat Field-trip ships stop at Ebeye about once a month. For more information, see Getting There & Away under Outer Islands later in this chapter.

Getting Around

From Ebeye's dock you can get a minivan taxi to anywhere on the island for US$0.50, though it takes only 20 minutes to walk from one end of the island to the other.

It's possible to rent boats on Ebeye to visit islands around the atoll; ask around and bargain. Before setting off to any of the other islands you need to get permission from the landowner on Ebeye first, but this shouldn't be hard to do. Stay clear of military installations around the lagoon, as you could be arrested for trespassing.

Outer Islands

Something of Marshallese traditional island life still remains in the quiet village communities away from Majuro and Kwajalein. The pace on the outer islands is relaxed and very s-l-o-w.

Usually a few people on each island speak English and nearly everyone is friendly. Because of the language barrier some people may appear shy while others will strike up a conversation just to practise their English.

If you're visiting somebody special you might even rate a real Marshallese welcome. On these occasions a group of women singing in harmony and bearing baskets piled with food will surround the visitors. The women give the guests flower headbands and leis and then everybody stands around exchanging compliments.

One Peace Corps volunteer, describing a visit by her brother, told how some of the older village women welcomed him by rubbing baked breadfruit on his stomach and chanting about how good-looking he was.

For better or worse, this isn't something the average traveller will encounter!

Although some outer islanders still use the *korkor*, a dug-out fishing canoe made from a breadfruit log, 'boom-booms', or motorboats, are steadily gaining in popularity. Both kinds of boats are used for frequent *jambos* (trips or picnics) to uninhabited atoll islands.

Accommodation

The Marshallese living beyond Majuro and Kwajalein are used to weekly flights dropping off the occasional visitor now and again. Some atolls have formal arrangements for visitors; on others, you should be able to find a family to stay with or a place to camp as the Marshallese are quite hospitable. Needless to say, you need to get permission before setting up a tent, as all land belongs to someone.

If you have time before your arrival to the Marshalls, you could try writing in advance. Just direct the letter to, for example: Mayor of Wotje, Wotje Atoll, Marshall Islands 96960. However, you're not likely to get a response, and it's best to radio ahead to the mayor of the atoll you wish to visit once you arrive on Majuro (see Post & Communications earlier in this chapter).

The tourist office on Majuro, the only tourist office in the Marshalls, keeps up to date on current accommodation options on the outer islands. The AMI office in Majuro is another potential resource.

Don't expect this to be a freebie. Many islanders are quite fond of money so you should be prepared to pay; it's wise to agree on cost before jumping on a plane.

Trade items are sometimes more useful than cash, especially if they are things not readily available from the field-trip ships. Coffee, printed T-shirts, D-size batteries and cassette tapes of Western music are popular items. Cigarettes too are also a very big hit.

Most outer islands do not have electricity, running water or flush toilets. Some houses are of concrete and others are made of thatch with coral rock floors. Instead of beds, pandanus mats are piled on the floor.

The Marshallese take excellent care of guests and will share what they have.

Food & Drink

Restaurants don't exist outside the major atolls. You can make do with local store provisions, eat with the family you stay with or bring food with you from Majuro which you can then either eat or trade for local fresh foods.

Usually there are a couple of small stores with a very limited inventory of rice, flour, tea, canned meats and other staples. Island meals generally consist of a combination of those items and local foods like breadfruit, pandanus, pumpkin, taro and fish.

Most of the outer islands are dry. Although alcohol is often illegally made and consumed, visitors who drink are not usually appreciated.

All water should be boiled, even if it's from catchments – and without fail if it's not.

MILI ATOLL

Mili is a good choice for travellers who want to visit one of the outer atolls, as it has friendly people and beautiful beaches and, as it's not far from Majuro, is relatively cheap to reach.

After Kwajalein, Mili has the most land area of the Marshallese atolls – just over 6 sq miles (15.6 sq km). The population is about 850.

Famed US aviator Amelia Earhart, who disappeared in this part of the Pacific during an attempted round-the-world flight in 1937, was reportedly seen in Mili under Japanese custody long after her disappearance – though this theory is merely one of many about her mysterious disappearance. (See the boxed text in the US territories chapter for the latest speculation.)

Toward WWII's end, some 17,000 Japanese soldiers were isolated on Mili. As a result of a US blockade, near-starvation conditions existed and the execution of Mili islanders who failed to turn their food over to the Japanese were so commonplace that the people of Mili sued the Japanese government for war crimes and were compensated.

As a major WWII Japanese base, Mili has many abandoned weapons, Japanese and US war planes and bombed-out buildings still scattered around.

The plane lands on Mili Island, the atoll's main island. It's a pleasant quarter-mile (400m) walk to the village from the airstrip. Along the way you'll see **large bomb craters** now covered with vines and coconut trees. Mili has a mosquito problem as these bomb craters make perfect spawning grounds. Bring mosquito repellent or coils or both with you. (Mosquito coils and coffee also make nice gifts for people on Mili.)

The whole lagoon side of Mili Island is trimmed with **sandy white beaches**, while shell collecting is good on the ocean side. At low tide you can easily walk along the reef to the neighbouring islands, some of which have only a single house upon them. Mili's pristine waters are great for diving.

Places to Stay & Eat

Majuro-based Marshalls Dive Adventures maintains several *thatched cottages* on Wau Island as part of the Wau Island Giant Clam Farm. Each has a private bathroom, one queen-size and one single bed, running water and solar power. For US$750 and with a six-person minimum, divers can spend a week on the island, which includes airfare from Majuro, dives, food and accommodation. Fishing packages can also be arranged and, depending on availability, shorter stays may be possible (a three-day stay costs divers US$460).

Getting There & Away

AMI flies between Majuro and Mili on Tuesday for US$56 one way.

The RRE ship *Lona* sometimes makes the 10-hour trip to Mili; the tourist office on Majuro will also be able to tell you about other ship options.

MALOELAP ATOLL

Taroa (Tarawa) Island, in Maloelap Atoll, was the main Japanese airbase in the eastern Marshalls during WWII and most visitors these days come to see **war relics**.

There are numerous twisted wrecks of Zeros and Betty bombers, pillboxes, guns and the remains of an airfield, a narrow-gauge railroad and a radio station. The southern tip of the island has coastal defence guns, including a 127 mm anti-aircraft gun and a Howitzer on wheels.

You can stumble across some of the stuff on your own, but a lot of it is hidden under thick jungle foliage and difficult to find. A few islanders are willing to trek with visitors and show them the sites, so if you're interested just ask around.

Off Taroa's lagoon beach the **Japanese freighter** *Toroshima Maru* lies half submerged where it was sunk by US bombers. Periscopes and the mast can still be seen, but it's pretty well stripped, except for some live depth charges. If you swim out around it, watch for the grouper (a type of sea bass) that is said to be as large as a human. The lagoon also has its share of sharks, so watch out for them too! After the war ended, Taroa was not settled again by Marshallese until the 1970s. Now it's the centre of atoll activity because of its airport, stores and copra cooperative.

Maloelap Atoll, with a population of 800 people, has four other inhabited islands. Airok is 16 miles (26km) south of Taroa; Ollet, Jang and Kaben are respectively 6, 18 and 32 miles (9.6, 29 and 51.5 km) to the north-west. Not many Japanese were stationed on the other islands so they don't have the same amount of war junk as Taroa does.

Maloelap has two chiefs. One is head of Taroa, Ollet, Jang and Kaben islands, as well as the northern atolls of Wotje, Utrik and Ailuk, while the other presides over Maloelap's Airok Island and parts of Aur Atoll.

Taroa's Location

Legend has it that Taroa Island used to be in the centre of Maloelap's lagoon in a spot where it was easy for all canoes to sail to. But the legendary figure L'etao, who demanded food from each of the atoll islands, got irritated with the stingy offerings given by the Taroa islanders and kicked Taroa to where it is now.

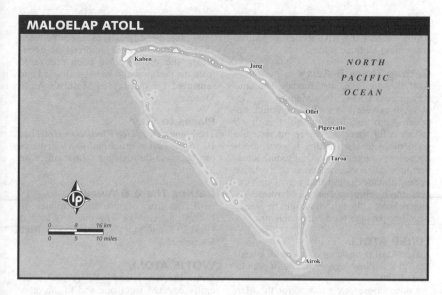

MALOELAP ATOLL

Kaben

Jang

NORTH
PACIFIC
OCEAN

Ollet

Pigeeyatto

Taroa

Airok

0   8   16 km
0   5   10 miles

Just a few miles (about 4km) from both Taroa and Ollet is uninhabited Pigeeyatto, which is sometimes called 'Papaya Island' because of its fresh fruit. It has ruins of a wartime radio transmitter station where cables ran to Taroa's radio receiving station.

Places to Stay
Maloelap is used to visitors and sometimes *simple houses* can be arranged for stays through the mayor's office. You might also be able to stay at the *schoolhouse* on Taroa if school's not in session.

Getting There & Away
AMI flies from Majuro to Kaben on Tuesday for US$69 one way, and from Majuro to Taroa on Thursday for US$77 one way.

Getting Around
Inter-island commuting is via either privately owned speedboats or diesel inboard motorboats that are owned by the island government. An inboard boat ride to Kaben from Taroa costs about US$20 and takes around 4½ hours, depending on the roughness of the water in the lagoon. From Taroa to Airok it takes about one hour by speed-

boat or just over two hours by diesel inboard, and costs about US$20 one way.

ARNO ATOLL
Arno is the closest atoll to Majuro, just 9 miles (14.5 km) away. It has 133 islands, two airstrips and nearly 1700 people.

The Longar area in Arno is famed for its **'love school'** where young women were once taught how to perfect their sexual techniques.

The waters off Longar Point are known for superb deep-sea fishing, and yellowfin tuna, marlin, mahi-mahi and sailfish abound.

About 10,000 pounds of tuna and reef fish caught near Arno are sold on Majuro each month, thanks in part to a Japanese-funded fishing project on Arno Island, which paid for fishing boats, a cold storage facility and an upgrade of the dock.

Places to Stay
Arno offers visitors several small places to stay. RRE's *Arno Black Pearl Farm Island* has two cottages on the far northern tip of Arno. Francis Reimer's *Arno House* is on Arno Island, the closest to Majuro Atoll. Francis Reimer's *Enedrik Island House* is

MARSHALL ISLANDS

on Enedrik Island, in the eastern part of the Atoll. Contact the RRE Hotel in Majuro concerning all three places.

Getting There & Away

AMI flies to Tinak on Monday. The one-way price is US$41 from Majuro.

Small private boats often commute between Arno and Majuro, but there's no schedule for these. If you're interested, a good place to start asking is your guest-house – it's largely a word of mouth situation in which someone knows of a relative or acquaintance going that way. Don't expect it to be cheaper than the Maritime Authority boat, although you might be able to negotiate passage for a reasonable price.

LIKIEP ATOLL

Likiep Atoll is made up of about 60 islands around a shallow lagoon and has a population of 500.

Likiep houses are unusual for the Marshalls in that they're built in a sort of Western style with porches and railings. Because of this, Likiep has been dubbed by some islanders 'The Williamsburg of the Pacific', although the comparison does stretch the imagination.

In 1877, during the German era, Jose deBrum, a Portuguese harpooner who arrived aboard a US whaling ship, and Adolf Capelle, a German trader from a Honolulu-based company, bought Likiep Atoll from the high chief who owned it. They both married Marshallese women and settled in, began by planting coconut and fruit trees and started profitable copra and shipbuilding companies.

Descendants of deBrum and Capelle still own Likiep and operate it as a copra plantation. The sale of the island is still a source of contention 120 years later as current traditional leaders question its validity, claiming the document of sale was written in a foreign language that the high chief wasn't able to read.

Jose deBrum's son Joachim designed ships and homes and the mansion he built for his family still stands on Likiep. Joachim was also a photographer with a keen historian's perspective. More than 2300 glass plate negatives, taken between 1885 and 1930, and hundreds of documents and diaries have been recovered from the mansion and were catalogued and reprinted for display in Majuro's Alele Museum.

Places to Stay

The brand new *Likiep Plantation Hotel* has 10 rooms and a restaurant. Arrangements can be made through the tourist office on Majuro.

Getting There & Away

AMI flies from Majuro and Kwajalein to Likiep on Saturday. The one-way cost is US$120 from Majuro, and US$77 from Kwajalein.

WOTJE ATOLL

Wotje, the main island in Wotje Atoll, is literally covered from one end to the other with remnants of WWII. Huge Japanese-built structures loom out of the jungle, some bombed to pieces but others still habitable.

Large portions of the island were once paved in concrete, and machinery, fuel tanks and all sorts of unidentifiable war junk stick out everywhere. Right in the centre of the village is a large Japanese gun that can still be moved on its pivot. The lagoon is also full of wreckage, including a few submerged ships which would probably make interesting diving.

The lagoon beaches of Wotje Island are quite beautiful and relatively clean. The nearby small islands are even better as they're mostly deserted and at low tide you can walk right over to them.

Wotje, known as the 'Marshallese garden centre', is a sub-district centre with about 650 people. It's said that its abundant produce is due to topsoil the Japanese shipped over from Japan.

Places to Stay

There's a *council house* on Wotje where visitors may be able to stay, and sometimes families are willing to put people up as well.

Mayor Tony Philips may be able to help you find a place to stay.

Another possibility is to contact Charles Domnick through DAR Car Rentals (☎ 625 3174) in Majuro. His family has a *two-bedroom house* with an ice box, kitchen and living room on Wotje that is sometimes available for rent.

Getting There & Away
AMI has flights from Kwajalein and Majuro to Wotje on Saturday. The cost is US$93 one way from both islands.

MEJIT ISLAND
Mejit is a single coral island, about ¾ sq mile (2 sq km) in area, with a population of about 450 people. It's a beautiful island, with lush taro patches in the centre and an abundance of coconut, breadfruit and pandanus trees.

As Mejit lacks a protective lagoon, fishing and the unloading of field-trip ships can be quite perilous. This is especially true in November and December, months which also have pleasantly cooling winds. From May to July it's very humid and the mosquitoes are out in full force.

Mejit has a small **freshwater lake**, a rarity in the Marshalls, which even attracts a few wayward migrating ducks in the winter. If you can ignore the algae the lake is a nice place to swim.

California Beach, a beautiful beach on the north-west side of the island, is the best beach for swimming. Snorkelling is good north of the beach.

Mejit has lots of seasonal tuna, as well as lobster and octopus and, unlike other islands, no poisonous fish. Fishing is still very traditional on Mejit. The men go out fishing every morning, except Sunday, in traditional korkor. They are hesitant to take foreigners out fishing and consider it plain bad luck to have a woman on board.

The island is known for its quality pandanus-leaf mats.

Mejit has one of the best outer island schools and quite a few islanders speak fluent English. The people of Mejit are friendly and used to visitors as Peace Corps training sessions are sometimes held here.

Places to Stay
There's a government *council house* where you might be able to stay, but you should offer to pay something for the privilege.

Getting There & Away
AMI flies from Majuro to Mejit on Thursday. The cost is US$117 one way.

The field-trip ship usually takes about eight days from Majuro, though it can take twice that long on the return as it loads up with copra along the way.

JALUIT ATOLL
Traditionally Jaluit was the home of the high chief of the southern Ralik islands. Today it's a sub-district centre with a population of 1700 people and the only outer island with a public high school.

Jaluit's main island, Jabwor, was the headquarters of Jaluit Gesellschaft, a powerful group of German copra traders. It later became the German capital and Marshallese from other islands moved in, attracted by the schools, churches and higher standard of living. Now about 800 people live on Jabwor.

In 1890, during his trans-Pacific cruise aboard the *Janet Nicoll*, Robert Louis Stevenson visited Jaluit and was greeted with fine European wine.

When the Japanese took over they fortified the islands and started a fishing industry. The ruins of Japanese buildings and bunkers still remain, and some people have even converted them to bungalows. The USA captured the atoll during WWII but then mostly ignored it. In the 1950s Catholic and Protestant missions were set up and Jabwor began to prosper again.

In 1958 Typhoon Ophelia swept waves and wind over Jaluit, flooding the islands with water several feet deep, washing away most of the homes and coconut trees and killing 16 people. Jaluit is not a good place to be during typhoons; one in 1904 swept away at least 60 people.

You can see the **wreck** of the *Alfred* still on the reef at Jabwor Pass, where it sank in 1899.

Jaluit Atoll, with its **wrecks of airplanes and ships**, has some of the best diving in the Marshalls.

Places to Stay & Eat
On Jabwor Island, there's an *RRE affiliated shop* selling doughnuts and noodles, and the *Jaweij Hotel* run by Marshall Electric Company where visitors can stay. There are four units with double occupancy, two bathrooms, air-con and a washer and dryer. For reservations call ☎ 625 3829 in Majuro or @ meccorp @ntamar.com.

Betto's Store also has two small cabins; contact Antari Jason (☎ 625 3450) on Majuro for reservations.

Both places charge US$50 per night per person.

Getting There & Away
AMI flies from Majuro to Jaluit on Friday. The cost is US$86 one way.

The RRE store sends a resupply boat about once a month; inquire at the store.

KILI ISLAND
In 1948 the US government resettled the displaced Bikinian people on 200-acre (81-hectare) Kili, a single isolated island which was uninhabited before they arrived.

The Bikinians soon learned that the canoes they had brought with them to Kili were useless as the island has no easy access to the sea; there is no lagoon, no port – not even a nice beach. The surf is so rough that nearly half of the year it's inaccessible by boat. Once a society of famed navigators, the Bikinians' are now losing their seafaring skills with the passing away of their older men.

Kili is now home to about 900 of the 2050 Bikinians (nearly as many live in Majuro). Despite the fact that a Bikinian trust fund distributes a US$2000 annual stipend to each islander, most people still live in the ramshackle shacks that the US built for them in 1948, albeit now furnished with TVs and VCRs.

The biggest annual event on Kili is still Bikini Day, held in March on the anniversary of the day in 1946 that the Bikinians became 'nuclear nomads'. There are sporting events and feasts, but much of the day is taken up by wistful speeches

from the elders about returning to their homeland.

Getting There & Away
AMI flies from Majuro to Kili on Monday, Wednesday and Friday. The cost is US$93 one way.

The RRE sends a boat to Kili about once a month.

AUR ATOLL
Aur Atoll has a population of 450 people who are equally divided between Tobal and Aur islands. The atoll is 75 miles (121km) north of Majuro and just a few miles (about 4km) south of Maloelap. The other islands in the atoll are officially uninhabited, though they're used for copra production and families sometimes live on these islands for stretches of a month or two.

Aur is a scenic atoll with a beautiful lagoon and excellent snorkelling. Not only is there a good variety of tropical fish and corals, but it's not uncommon to see turtles and small sharks.

Aur is a fairly traditional atoll and a good place to see both men and women making handicrafts. The people of Aur specialise in making model canoes and large wall hangings.

Getting There & Away
AMI flies from Majuro to Aur on Thursday. The one-way fare is US$56.

AILINGLAPLAP ATOLL
Ailinglaplap is the Marshall Islands' third-largest atoll, with a land area of 5¾ sq miles (14.7 sq km). It is home to over 1700 people, surpassed in population only by Majuro and Kwajalein. Ailinglaplap is also one of the Marshall Islands' biggest copra producers.

Woja, one of the main islands, is about 7 miles (11km) long and has approximately 600 people. There are few 'sights' as such, but Woja is a lovely, lush island with white sand beaches – though many of its trees took a brutal beating from Typhoon Paka in December 1997. The **large protected lagoon** offers good snorkelling, swimming

Bikini Relocation

The Bikinians were first moved to Rongerik Atoll, a place of ill omen in Marshallese legend. There they got sick from eating poisonous fish from the lagoon and nearly starved because of inadequate food supplies. Two years later they were moved to Kwajalein Atoll and then later to Kili Island.

In the 1970s the Bikinians were told it was safe to move back home and a resettlement program began. Though two entire islands had been blown away and the others were treeless and debris-covered, the people remained on Bikini and tried to get their lives back in order.

In 1978 US tests showed that by eating food grown in the caesium-contaminated soil the Bikinians had collected huge levels of radioactivity in their bodies, so they were moved back to Kili again. It was later reported that the return program was a US blunder: The islanders were supposed to have been put on Eneu Island, the other main island in Bikini Atoll, not on Bikini Island, which is eight times more radioactive.

and fishing. The island has a good school with some US-educated teachers; many people speak English and are friendly to visitors. There's an abundance of local food, particularly in the summer, and a couple of stores, though no restaurants or hotels. A few pick-up trucks act as taxis.

Getting There & Away

AMI flies to three islands in the atoll: to Airok on Monday (from both Kwajalein and Majuro), to Jeh on Wednesday and to Woja on Friday. The one-way fare from Majuro is US$82 to Jeh ($72 from Kwajalein) and US$98 to Woja ($66 from Kwajalein) and from Kwajalein to Airok it's US$74.

Small private boats can take you across the expansive lagoon from one island to another for about US$50 one way, and sometimes there are government boats around which can do the same at nominal cost.

BIKINI ATOLL

For the Marshallese, Bikini is a name that will live on in infamy. Home to the earliest known habitation in Micronesia, Bikini was selected by President Truman, without the knowledge of a single Micronesian, as the site for the first peacetime explosion of the atomic bomb.

Early in 1946 the US military governor of the Marshalls met with the fervently religious Bikini islanders, following church services, to inform them that their islands were needed for 'a greater good'. After deliberations, Bikini's Chief Juda responded that if the USA wanted to use Bikini for the 'benefit of all mankind' his people would go elsewhere. Still awed by the US firepower that had recently defeated the Japanese Imperial Navy, the Bikinians felt in no position to balk. The US was also well aware that challenging authority was contrary to the very fibre of Marshallese custom.

Bikini's 161 residents were relocated on the assurance they could move back once the tests were over. A few months later the USA exploded a nuclear device 500 feet (150m) over Bikini's lagoon, the first of 23 nuclear tests that would leave the islands uninhabitable, the Bikinians displaced and their society irreparably disrupted.

The final cleanup of Bikini will require replacing all the current topsoil with imported soil. The cost of that procedure alone is about US$200 million, nearly double the amount of money allocated to the entire cleanup project.

Bikini now is home to a mixture of scientists, construction workers and divers. Scientists from the Lawrence Livermore Laboratory in California are using Bikini as a study in ways to clean up radiation. So far they've successfully used potassium fertiliser to block the uptake of caesium in plants, but there are still long-term problems with eating anything grown on the island. The US Department of Energy also has a few dozen construction workers involved in cleaning up the main atoll islands, Eneu and Bikini. Eneu, which they use as a base, is currently considered safe.

MARSHALL ISLANDS

The Marshallese are currently receiving over US$500 million for the atoll cleanup through the compact and affiliated programs. However, the government is contemplating an appeal to the US government for a higher amount; their potential case is buoyed by newly declassified top-secret US research, which indicates that the adverse effects of the nuclear tests stretched well beyond the four named atolls – Bikini, Enewetok, Rongelap and Utrik – and puts the health damage much higher.

Diving

Thanks to its ominous nuclear history, Bikini is one of Micronesia's premier dive spots. The Majuro-based Marshalls Dive Adventures, which began diving Bikini in 1996, was first to the market. One highlight is the **USS Saratoga**, the world's only diveable aircraft carrier, which still visibly holds planes and racks of bombs. Another memorable dive is the **Nagato**, the Japanese battleship from the deck of which Admiral Yamamoto ordered his warplanes to attack Pearl Harbor. Bikini is a great spot for diving with sharks – grey reef sharks abound, and spotting a silvertip on the wrecks is not uncommon. The Bikini Atoll Web site (www.bikiniatoll.com) is an excellent resource.

Places to Stay

Marshalls Dive Adventures (MDA) in Majuro operates a small eight-unit *Bikini Atoll Dive Resort* on Bikini. Rooms are simple but have air-con and 24-hour generator electricity. There's hot and cold water and a recreation room with a TV/VCR, pool table and table tennis. The minimum stay is one week – the interval between AMI flights – so MDA arranges its payment on a package basis. The price for one week is US$2750, which includes 12 dives, lodging and meals on Bikini and one night's accommodation at the RRE hotel in Majuro. AMI airfare between Majuro and Bikini is not included. The hotel's maximum capacity is 13 people for one week.

MDA can also arrange sportsfishing packages; the fly-fishing in particular is

quite good. A one week trolling package, similar to the diving package, costs US$3750. A fly-fishing package costs US$2750. If you want to take a dive package but substitute a day's trolling or fly-fishing, arrange with MDA in advance.

Getting There & Away

AMI flies on Wednesday to Bikini from Majuro via Kwajalein. The one-way fare from Majuro is US$215, from Kwajalein US$108.

ENEWETOK ATOLL

Enewetok islanders were evacuated to Ujelang Atoll before atomic bomb tests began in 1948. Over a 10-year period 43 atomic bombs were detonated from Enewetok.

In 1980, after a US$120 million clean-up program, the islanders were allowed to return to Enewetok Island, in the southern part of the atoll.

Ten miles (16km) north of Enewetok is Runit Island, where contaminated items from the atoll were stashed under a huge 18-inch-thick concrete dome nicknamed Cactus Crater. The radiated debris and soil will supposedly be safe in 50,000 years. The concrete may last 300!

A 9.8-megaton hydrogen bomb exploded in 1958 on Enewetok was the focus of an extensive geological study conducted in the 1980s which showed the bomb had blasted a mile-wide, 200-foot-deep (1.6km, 60m) crater in the lagoon and fractured the rock to a depth of 1400 feet (420m) beneath the crater's surface. The geological impact of such massive bending and breaking of the earth's crust remains unknown.

Getting There & Away

AMI flies from Majuro to Enewetok via Kwajalein on Tuesday. The one-way fare is US$264 from Majuro, US$154 from Kwajalein.

RONGELAP ATOLL

The immensely powerful hydrogen bomb 'Bravo' that exploded on Bikini on 1 March 1954 sent clouds of deadly radioactivity toward inhabited Rongelap Atoll,

100 miles (160km) to the east. The fallout came down as powdered ash six hours after the blast.

Signs of radiation sickness including nausea, hair loss and severe burns occurred within hours, yet it wasn't until three days after the blast that the US military evacuated the 82 inhabitants of Rongelap to Kwajalein for decontamination. The Rongelapese were returned to their atoll in 1957.

The Rongelapese have continuing health problems that include high rates of mental retardation, leukemia, stillbirths and miscarriages. Almost 75% of the people who were under the age of 10 on the day of the blast have had surgery for thyroid tumours.

Despite an aerial survey showing that some of the islands of Rongelap were as 'hot' as islands in Bikini, and despite a ban placed on eating shellfish because of accumulated radiation, the USA insisted that Rongelap was safe and refused to help resettle the islanders.

In 1985 the Greenpeace ship *Rainbow Warrior* moved the Rongelapese to a new home on Mejato Island in Kwajalein Atoll, 110 miles (177km) to the south. (The boat was later sunk in New Zealand by French agents who hoped to stop the *Rainbow Warrior*'s activities aimed at ending nuclear testing in the South Pacific.)

In 1994 a US Congressional Committee re-examined the Bravo test and discredited the previously held US position that the Rongelapese were irradiated only because of an unexpected last-minute change in wind direction. Testimony by atomic energy officials revealed that the day before the bomb test US meteorologists reported that the winds had shifted in the direction of Rongelap and a warning had been issued that contamination of the islands would occur if the test were to proceed.

The following year the USA established a US$45 million trust fund for the Rongelapese. Rehabilitation of the island began soon after; thus far, base camp facilities and infrastructure, including a new lagoon-side dock, are under construction as a precursor to resettlement.

Getting There & Away
AMI now flies to Rongelap on Saturday from Majuro and Kwajalein; the one-way price from Majuro is US$200, from Kwajalein US$93.

UTRIK ATOLL
Although their plight is not as well known, the islanders of Utrik Atoll also received fallout from the Bravo test on Bikini and have similar radiation-related medical problems.

Getting There & Away
AMI flies from Majuro to Utrik on Tuesday for US$153 one way.

OTHER ATOLLS
Many Marshallese claim that Wotho, with a population of 120, is the **most beautiful atoll in the world**. It has a pretty lagoon full of giant clams that are harvested by the islanders. Wotho is a traditional place and it helps if visitors speak a little Marshallese, though the mayor knows some English.

Although **flying fish** are caught throughout the Marshalls, they are especially associated with Ailuk Atoll, figuring in Ailuk's music, dance and legends. The fish are caught at night using lights and scoop nets, and Ailuk is known for its delicious flying fish cuisine. The atoll has a population of about 500 people. Many of the finer woven baskets sold in Majuro are made in Ailuk.

Namorik is a lovely diamond-shaped atoll with about 800 people and a plan to build a little two-storey hotel in the centre of the village. Robert Louis Stevenson visited briefly on his 1890 Pacific swing.

Bikar, Taka and Taongi atolls and Jemo island are uninhabited by people, but are home to birds, coconut crabs and sea turtles.

Researchers from the East-West Center in Honolulu and the South Pacific Regional Environment Programme inspected atolls in the Marshalls a while back and recommended designating Taongi and Bikar as National Preservation Areas. The team called Taongi (also known as Bokaak) 'possibly the only example of a completely

MARSHALL ISLANDS

natural, unaltered, semiarid atoll ecosystem remaining in the world today'. Taongi has an abundance of shearwaters, a kind of seabird which burrows into the sand to nest. Bikar has an especially large population of green sea turtles.

Getting There & Away

Air The government-owned AMI (☎ 625 3733 in Majuro), with a fleet of two 19-passenger Dorniers, operates services to about two dozen islands, touching down at every inhabited atoll. Some flights hop across a couple of islands at a time, so it can be possible to visit a few different islands without returning to Majuro each time. See the individual atoll sections for details.

The flight schedule changes periodically, so if you're intent on using AMI ask the Majuro office for a schedule.

Boat The Marshalls have four field-trip ships – *Micro Chief*, MV *Jojoltae*, *YFU76* and MV *Juk Ae* – which service the outer islands about once a month, dropping off supplies and picking up copra.

Seven privately owned field-trip ships, some run by RRE, also service the outer islands about once a month. These include: *Charlies Angel*, MV *Libubu*, *Ocean Glory*, *Boujlab II*, *Lona*, MV *Kawewa* and *Angilina*. These ships also service the outer islands once a month.

These ships ply a number of different routes, typically spending two or three days at each stop. The longest run is the western field trip which goes to Kwajalein, Lae, Ujae, Wotho, Enewetok and Ujelang, a round-trip distance of 1510 miles (2435km) that takes about three weeks. The eastern route takes in nine islands in Arno Atoll and six in Mili Atoll, covering 175 miles (282km) in two to three weeks. The southern route takes two weeks and goes to Jaluit, Kili, Ebon and Namorik, a trip of 680 miles (1097km). The remaining atolls

are covered in the northern and central routes. There's no air-con in the cabins.

Scheduling and fare information is available from the Transportation Office (☎ 625 3469, fax 625 3486), at Uliga Dock in Majuro. The boats leave from the new dock near the copra processing plant.

Yachts must obtain a permit from the Ministry of Internal Affairs in Majuro before continuing to the outer islands. They should also radio ahead from Majuro and check in with the mayor of each atoll upon arrival in the lagoon.

The only atolls with suitable docks for yachts are Jaluit, Likiep and Bikini. Arno, Mili, Jaluit, Ailinlaplap, Namu, Aur, Maloelap, Likiep, Wotho, Rongelap and Bikini all have safe lagoon-entry passages. The tourist office in Majuro has nautical charts you can can ask to look at.

Some of the outer atolls do not charge entrance fees; others charge between US$25 and US$100.

Getting Around

Some islands have pick-up trucks or motor scooters, but most of the time people just walk.

Outer islands usually have at least one motorboat and trips to other islands within the atoll can generally be arranged; US$25 might be a reasonable price for an hour's trip.

Sometimes the uninhabited atoll islands are used for copra production or to raise livestock. The more remote islands often have the best beaches and occasionally have thatched shelters for overnight stays.

For a price, it should be fairly easy to get someone to take you fishing, lobstering, coconut-crab hunting and the like. Ask the mayor if there's a local fishing ordinance or a fee.

Marshall Islands Aquatics (☎/fax 625 3669, ✉ aquamar@ntamar.com) offers outer island packages for US$200 a day; these include walking tours to WWII sites in Mili and Jaluit atolls.

Kiribati

The tiny Republic of Kiribati (population 86816) takes up a good spread on the globe. Although comprising only 810.5 sq km in land area, its 33 coral atolls span 3.5 million sq km of ocean and have an east-west distance approximating New York to Los Angeles.

The passing centuries have had little impact on Kiribati (pronounced Kiri-**bahs**), particularly on its outer islands, where people continue to gather coconuts, giant prawns, octopuses and other fish as they have for centuries. Even on the main island, Tarawa, most people live in traditional thatched huts – though cars, extensive litter and even the Internet give notice of mounting Western influence.

Twenty years after gaining independence from the British, Kiribati is still struggling to cope with the logistical challenges of governing such a diverse, geographically far-flung area. Christmas Island – a magnet for US sportsfishers and Kiribati's largest tourist draw – is two weeks by ship from Tarawa, though only three hours by plane from Honolulu.

The I-Kiribati are a joyful people, revelling in life and in their rich natural resources. Small, wide-eyed children will chirp a bold 'hello' or *'mauri'* to passing strangers, while the elders relax in thatched *maneaba* (village meeting houses; see the boxed text 'The Maneaba'). Traditional singing and dancing remain an integral part of everyday life.

Facts about Kiribati

HISTORY
Early Settlers
The first settlers, most likely from the Caroline and Marshall islands, settled the Gilbert Islands and Ocean Island more than 3000 years ago. The Phoenix Islands and Line Islands never supported permanent settlements, though archaeological evi-

dence suggests occasional pre-European landings.

The early Gilbertese settled in distinct *kainga* (villages), within which extended families lived together. Except on Butaritari and Makin, the two northernmost islands in the Gilbert chain where centralised chiefs

---

HIGHLIGHTS

- Traditional dancing – colourful, vibrant and easy to arrange – just get yourself invited to a *maneaba*
- North Tarawa – relax with a fresh coconut in a house on stilts over the aqua lagoon
- South Tarawa – the enormous WWII guns from the 1943 Battle of Tarawa
- Outer Islands – life at a relaxed pace, with locals salting clams or weaving thatch
- Christmas Island – bonefishers and birdwatchers unite!

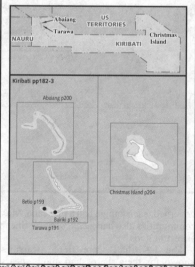

Kiribati pp182-3

Abaiang p200

Christmas Island p204

Betio p193

Bairiki p192

Tarawa p191

KIRIBATI

181

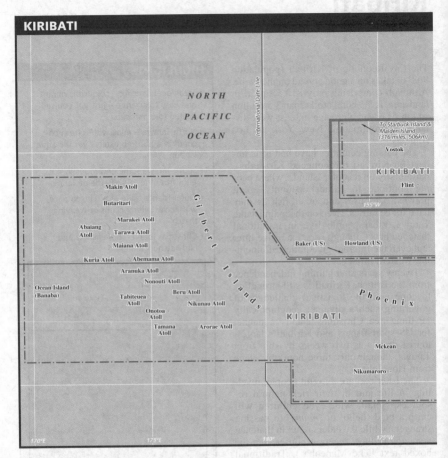

KIRIBATI

NORTH
PACIFIC
OCEAN

International Date line

To Starbuck Island &
Malden Island
(316 miles, 506km)

Vostok

KIRIBATI

Flint

155°W

Makin Atoll

Butaritari

Marakei Atoll

Abaiang
Atoll
Tarawa Atoll

Maiana Atoll

Gilbert Islands

Kuria Atoll
Abemama Atoll

Baker (US)
Howland (US)

Aranuka Atoll

Nonouti Atoll

Ocean Island
(Banaba)

Beru Atoll

Tabiteuea
Atoll
Nikunau Atoll

Onotoa
Atoll

Phoenix

Tamana
Atoll
Arorae Atoll

KIRIBATI

Mckean

Nikumaroro

170°E
175°E
180°
175°W

governed, each kainga had a maneaba. Most communities also had a *bangota*, a shrine to ancestral gods.

The I-Kiribati were fierce warriors, known for their sharp shark-tooth spears, but inter-tribal skirmishes, while not unknown, were not serious until the Europeans introduced modern weaponry.

European Contact
Because of the remoteness of Kiribati's Gilbert Islands and relative lack of natural resources, Europeans drifted in more slowly than they did to other Micronesian islands.

In 1606, Spanish explorer Pedro Fernandez de Quirós was the first European to land on the Gilbert Islands. The next European did not arrive until 1766 when Commodore John Byron put ashore on Nikunau, an island in the southern Gilberts.

Twenty-two years later, Captain Thomas Gilbert, for whom the Gilbert Islands were named, spotted several more islands as he sailed to China.

European visits increased in the 1830s and 1840s, as European whalers pursued sperm whales around the southern Gilberts. Missionaries and traders also made their

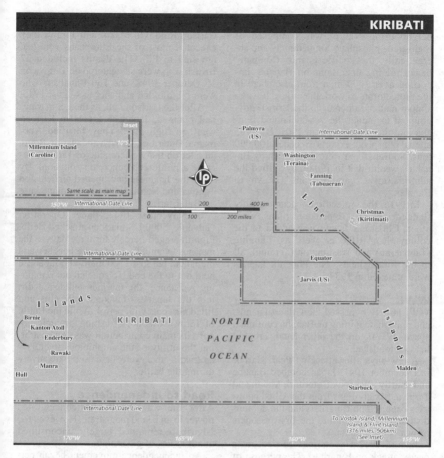

way to the Gilberts. The latter made use of Butaritari's trading port, where they swapped manufactured goods for coconut oil and turtle shells. Blackbirders moved in during the late 19th century, taking islanders to work on plantations in Fiji, Australia and Hawai'i.

British Rule

Kiribati was never subject to successive rule by the Spanish, German, Japanese, and US. Instead, the islands fell largely under British dominion. Towards the end of the 19th century the British assumed informal governance of the Gilbert Islands and the Ellice Islands (present-day Tuvalu; see the boxed text 'The Making of Tuvalu' later in this chapter). This power structure was formalised on 27 May 1892, when British captain EHM Davis of the HMS *Royalist* raised the British flag at Abemama and declared the Gilbert & Ellice Islands a British protectorate. Three years later, Tarawa was designated the protectorate's administrative capital, largely because of its excellent anchorage and relatively wide lagoon passage.

In 1900, geologist Albert Ellis of the Pacific Islands Company discovered that

KIRIBATI

Banaba (also known as Ocean Island), like neighbouring Nauru, was composed of high-grade phosphate. Immediately and energetically, the Pacific Islands Company began mining operations on Banaba, importing over 1000 men from elsewhere in the protectorate to work the mines. It was a simple matter to persuade the British government to induct the yet-unclaimed Banaba into the protectorate in 1901. By 1905 annual phosphate exports exceeded 100,000 tons. So transfixed were the British by Banaba's wealth that in 1908 they shifted the administrative capital from Tarawa to Banaba.

In 1916, the protectorate became a fully fledged colony. Expansion plans were afoot: Christmas Island was added to the colony in 1919, as well as Fanning (Tabuaeran) and Washington (Teraina), all in the Line Islands. The Phoenix Islands were annexed in 1937.

WWII

WWI largely bypassed the Gilbert Islands, and phosphate mining on Banaba continued apace. WWII, on the other hand, brought heavy bloodshed.

A few days after attacking Pearl Harbor in December 1941, Japan bombed Banaba and shortly after took Butaritari, Makin and Tarawa. Six civilians from the Allied countries captured on Butaritari had the dubious distinction of becoming the first prisoners of war sent to Japan.

In mid-1942 US marines carried out a decoy attack on Butaritari. The purpose of this attack – called the Carlson Raid – was to distract the Japanese from the planned US strike in the Solomon Islands. The marines swooped in, forcing the Japanese to flee, and then back-pedalled out the next few days. Furious and humiliated, the Japanese bombed Butaritari a few days later and killed 47 Gilbertese – just punishment, in the Japanese view, for alleged Gilbertese betrayals.

The Japanese acquired a hideous human rights record during their occupation of the Gilbert Islands and Ocean Island. Upon retaking Butaritari, they beheaded nine un-

fortunate US marines left behind from the Carlson Raid. On Makin and Tarawa they executed most of the Europeans who had not fled to Fiji. The deaths included 22 British who were slaughtered on Tarawa on 15 October 1942, and 160 Banabans who were blindfolded and shot in August 1945.

After the Carlson raid, as the US marines had planned, Japanese forces in Kiribati went on high alert. They fortified Abemama, Butaritari, Banaba and Nauru. Betio, an islet on the western side of Tarawa, became a reinforced concrete stronghold. By 1943 the Japanese had opened airfields on Tarawa and Nauru and had a seaplane base on Butaritari.

In November 1943, under Operation Galvanic, 5000 US marines attacked Betio. Fighting raged fiercely for three days as the marines eventually gained the beaches and the island but lost 1500 men. The Japanese held out to the end. To squelch out remaining resistance, the marines bulldozed dirt into the Japanese bunkers' rifle slits and filled air vents with petrol. While the Battle of Tarawa was not of lasting strategic import, its main contribution was demonstrating the utility of the amphibious tractors – amtraks – that were first used extensively during the battle.

Road to Independence

After the war the British concentrated power in an island magistrate. However, the I-Kiribati remained largely unconsulted about issues of governing.

An independence movement began percolating in the mid-1950s, when governmental training and leadership programs for the Gilbertese were expanded. The winds of change gathered strength in the 1960s, when the Solomon Islands and Fiji, also British colonies, were also agitating for independence.

In 1963 an executive council was established, comprising eight members (four official, four unofficial) appointed by the resident commissioner, along with an advisory council. Both bodies were supposed to advise the resident commissioner; in effect, it was practice for real power. In 1967 the

The Making of Tuvalu

The Gilbert & Ellice Islands union was largely an artificial construct of British rule. During the mid-1960s, as Tarawa's independence movement grew, the Ellice Islanders began agitating strongly for their own independence. They feared that the more populous Gilbertese would have greater political clout – this became apparent in the 1967 House of Assembly, when the Gilberts were allotted 18 seats and the Ellice Islands just five. The Gilbertese, meanwhile, resented the Ellice Islanders' disproportionate hold on civil service positions.

In a 1974 referendum, the Ellice Islanders voted overwhelmingly for separation from the Gilberts. Official separation came in October 1975, though they were administered together under Tarawa until 1 January 1976. Over this period, Ellice Islanders departed Tarawa en masse for their homeland, though a few hundred Ellice Islanders remain today on Tarawa.

On 1 October 1978 the Ellice Islands became the independent nation of Tuvalu.

advisory council became the elected House of Representatives, with 18 representatives from the Gilbert Islands and five from the Ellice Islands. Still later, in 1974, the House of Assembly was born.

Finally, a year after the secession of the Ellice Islands (present-day Tuvalu), on 12 July 1979, the Republic of Kiribati – consisting of the Gilbert Islands, the Phoenix Islands, the Line Islands and Banaba (whose own secessionist movement had been squelched) – became an independent nation, ending 87 years of British rule.

Modern Kiribati

British rule left Kiribati less developed than other Micronesian countries. The new nation's most pressing problem was money: At the same time as Kiribati achieved independence, it lost its main source of revenue, as Banaba's rich phosphate reserves had finally been drained. Overcrowding on South Tarawa, rapid urbanisation and the govern-

ing of such widely spread atolls have presented further challenges.

GEOGRAPHY

Land is the exception rather than the rule in Kiribati. Land area totals just 810.5 sq km, whereas Kiribati's oceans stretch 3870km east to west and 2050km north to south.

Kiribati is composed of three main island groups: The 16 atolls of the Gilbert Islands chain and the eight atolls each of the Line and Phoenix chains. There is also Banaba, which lies 400km west of the Gilberts. Almost all the islands but Banaba are flat coral atolls with central lagoons, flecked with coconut palms, pandanus and breadfruit trees.

The Phoenix Islands lie south of the equator, whereas the Line and Gilbert Islands are split by the equator.

CLIMATE

Kiribati lies in the dry belt of the equatorial oceanic climate zone. Butaritari in the north consistently has the highest rainfall (318cm in 1998), followed by Tarawa.

Easterly trade winds blow most of the year, bringing high humidity. Most atolls maintain a fairly even temperature year-round. Tarawa's monthly average hovers around 25° to 26°C, and there is no real rainy season. Because of Kiribati's proximity to the equator, it is out of the classic typhoon path.

The El Niño-induced drought that afflicted all Micronesia in 1998 prompted the Kiribati government to declare a state of emergency in March 1999, but immediately thereafter the rains began.

Rising sea levels associated with higher sea temperatures have caused mild erosion on some of the atolls.

GOVERNMENT & POLITICS

Kiribati is a member of the Commonwealth and operates on a Westminster-style parliamentary system. Thirty-nine members of the 41-member *Maneaba ni Maungatbu* (House of Parliament) are popularly elected every four years. The Maneaba nominates three or four candidates for president, after which a popular election is held. Upon taking office, the president *(Beretitenti)* selects a cabinet. The attorney general, nominated by the president, and the Rabi Island Council-nominated representative for Banaba are then appointed to join the Maneaba. The Maneaba currently convenes in a traditional community meeting house in Bairiki, but there are plans to soon relocate to Ambo.

Teburoro Tito, who was re-elected in 1998 to a second four-year term, is Kiribati's current president.

The island councils control local government, and are advised by the *unimane*, the traditional village elder men.

ECONOMY

In the years leading up to independence, phosphate mining on Banaba accounted for 45% of Kiribati's GDP and 85% of its exports. With the phosphate exhausted by 1979, the economy endured a difficult shift and acquired an unfavourable trade balance and a large budget deficit.

However, their land full of coconut trees and their seas rich with fish, most I-Kiribati still maintain a largely subsistence lifestyle. On the outer islands, some derive a marginal income from cutting copra (dried coconut flesh). Copra is now the principal export item, fetching A$4 million annually. Most of the copra goes to Bangladesh, where it is made into soaps and other cosmetic products. Pet fish, incidentally, are the nation's second-leading export item, accounting for A$700,000 in 1997! Seaweed cultivation is also catching on, especially in the outer islands.

Tourism contributes minimal revenue to Kiribati. Christmas Island is the tourist hub, and with 1564 visitors in 1998 it received almost half as many as did Tarawa over the years 1990 to 1997.

Kiribati's principal asset is the 3.5 million sq km Exclusive Economic Zone (EEZ), which generates revenue from foreign fishing licences (A$42,464,000 in 1998). Attempts to strengthen its own fishing industry by creating Te Mautari Ltd, a government-sponsored fishing company, flopped miserably due to a lack of efficient

fishing vessels. However, a new port facility, due for completion by 2001, should expedite ship loading.

About 1500 I-Kiribati seamen work on foreign (mostly German) vessels. The money they send home is a major source of income for their families.

Kiribati relies heavily on Australia, Japan and Fiji for imports and gets a fair amount of aid from Australia.

POPULATION & PEOPLE

One-third of Kiribati's people live on South Tarawa. With an average of 4.5 children born to each woman, problems associated with population pressure are becoming more severe and an internal resettlement program has been instituted to shift people from overcrowded Betio to the Line Islands.

ARTS

Typical I-Kiribati crafts include wooden baskets, mats and conical fishermen's hats made from pandanus, carved outrigger canoes, woven bags and purses, and necklaces of fibres and shells. Most are made on the outer islands and shipped in to Tarawa.

Kiribati's colourful, rhythmic chants and dances are one of the highlights of Micronesia. Dancing remains an important part of local culture, and the largest hotels in each district centre – the Captain Cook Hotel on Christmas Island and the Otintaai Hotel on Tarawa – both have regularly scheduled dance performances.

SOCIETY & CONDUCT

Society in Kiribati remains very traditional, despite the advent of Western clothing, foods and religion. Life centres around the maneaba (see boxed text 'The Maneaba'), and almost all houses are still constructed in the traditional style.

Visiting women should show respect by wearing long, loose shirts. It's a good idea not to wear shorts anyway as the mosquitoes can be fierce. Many local men wear colourful *lava lava*.

If you are invited to attend a maneaba meeting or a party, you will be expected to

The Maneaba

The *maneaba*, or traditional meeting house, is found throughout Kiribati. The word maneaba derives from *manea* (to accommodate) and *te aba* (people and land). Traditional maneaba have thatched roofs and locally woven mats cover the floors (though a few new maneaba in South Tarawa have tin roofs and concrete floors). Typically the largest building in the village, the maneaba is built on respect and social hierarchy. By design, the pointed roof drops below the average height of an adult, so that you must duck upon entering to show respect.

The *unimane*, or elder men, sit cross-legged in the centre of the maneaba and conduct the meeting. If a party is held in the maneaba, the unimane are always served first. So respected is the sanctity of the building that if a man commits rape and is pursued by the woman's family seeking vigilante justice, his best option is to run to the nearest maneaba where he will be protected.

People sleep in the maneaba only in times of celebration, such as the Independence Day festivities.

---

participate in full by giving a speech and/or singing a song. Prepare your best patriotic melodies and reminiscences.

RELIGION

Before the arrival of Europeans, there was belief in *anti* (spirits) and *tabunea* (sorcery). Nareau the Wise was believed to be the god of creation. However, Christianity now has a stronghold.

The Roman Catholic Church, headquartered in the village of Teaoraereke on Tarawa, is the religion of about half of Kiribati. The next largest denomination is the Kiribati Protestant Church (a Congregational church), though on some outer islands Protestants outnumber Catholics. The I-Kiribati are a religious people, and mingling with the locals at a Sunday church ceremony is an excellent way to meet people.

There are a few Baha'í on Tarawa, and Seventh-Day Adventists, Mormons, Muslims and Church of God followers also have places of worship.

LANGUAGE

English is the official language, but Gilbertese, an Austronesian language, predominates in conversation. Even on South Tarawa many locals know only a smattering of English words, and on the outer islands it is even more limited.

Some of the more far-flung outer islands, such as Butaritari and Makin in the northern Gilberts, have a few variations on standard Gilbertese but in general the words are the same, albeit pronounced with a slightly different accent.

'Hello' is *'mauri'*; thank you is *'ko rabwa'*. The letters 'ti' at the end of a word signal pronunciation 's' – thus, Kiribati is pronounced 'Kiri-bahs'.

The name Kiribati is a transliteration of 'Gilberts', which in turn is named after the British captain who spotted the islands in 1788. Locals still sometimes refer to the Gilbert chain as Tungaru, the original local name.

Facts for the Visitor

SUGGESTED ITINERARIES

If you have one week it's best to tour the war relics on South Tarawa, the main island, and then head for Abaiang (the only outer island readily accessible by boat) or to rustic North Tarawa. Those with more time and flexibility might consider Butaritari. From Honolulu, Christmas Island is a one-week trip.

PLANNING
Maps

Nice topographic maps of Kiribati's islands are available from the Department of Lands & Survey (DL&S; ☎ 21 283), on the second floor of the building behind the library. Buying a map is a classic bureaucratic exercise: You look at the map at DL&S, and they send you to the next building (the

KIRIBATI

Department of Home Affairs) to pay and then you bring your receipt back to DL&S and they give you the map. The maps are quite large and even rolled up, they will be bulky to carry home. They're also pricey at A$7.50 to A$8.50, as some islands are so long and narrow that they require three maps.

TOURIST OFFICES

See Information in the Tarawa and Christmas Island sections for local tourist offices.

Kiribati is represented abroad by the Tourism Council of the South Pacific (TCSP). Visit the Web site at www.tcsp.com.

VISAS & DOCUMENTS

Citizens of Britain, Canada and New Zealand can enter Kiribati visa-free for a 28-day maximum stay. Citizens of other countries, including the USA and Australia, require a visa. See the Regional Facts for the Visitor chapter for detailed information.

When they're around, the immigration officials occupy the large breadfruit container beside the Foreign Affairs building in Bairiki, down the street opposite the market. The office is open from 8 am to 4.15 pm weekdays, with a 12.30 to 1.30 pm break for lunch.

MONEY

The accepted currency in Kiribati is Australian dollars, though you'll see occasional A$2 Kiribati commemorative coins.

The main branch of the Bank of Kiribati is in Bairiki, on Tarawa; it has branches in Betio and Bikenibeu and on Christmas Island.

POST & COMMUNICATIONS

Kiribati has no postal code. Letters/postcards to Australia cost A$0.60/30 and to the USA A$0.75/40.

Kiribati's international telephone code is ☎ 686; there are no area codes. Only South Tarawa and Christmas Island have more than one telephone. North Tarawa (☎ 027 100), Maiana (☎ 027 101), Abaiang (☎ 027 102) and Marakei (☎ 027 103) each have

one telephone. The remaining outer islands have ham radios that are turned on at scheduled times. To book your call, dial ☎ 21 411.

INTERNET RESOURCES

Kiribati's government Web site (www.tskl.net.ki/kiribati) has links to some useful tourist information. Try also the TCSP site (www.tcsp.com).

BOOKS

For a good history, particularly of the Gilbert & Ellice Islands' failed marriage, try *Cinderellas of the Empire: Towards a History of Kiribati and Tuvalu*, by Barrie Macdonald (1982).

Atoll Politics – The Republic of Kiribati (Macmillan Brown Centre for Pacific Studies, 1993), edited by Howard Van Trease, is a collection of informative essays by leading I-Kiribati politicians and scholars.

MEDIA

Radio Kiribati Broadcasting, on FM 98, has occasional 15-minute Australian news broadcasts. Bring a portable short wave radio to receive more in-depth news. There is no television station in Kiribati. A weekly local news leaflet, *Uekera*, publishes some items in English.

TIME

Tarawa's time is GMT + 12; Christmas Island is GMT + 14.

PUBLIC HOLIDAYS & SPECIAL EVENTS

As well as New Year's Day, Easter, Christmas and Boxing Day, Kiribati celebrates the following holidays:

World Health Day May 9
Independence Day July 12 (also July 11)
Youth Day August 1
Human Rights/Peace Day December 12

Independence Day, which commemorates the 1979 break from British rule, is marked by a sports bonanza: track and field events, canoe races, wrestling and local dancing and singing competitions. The main road in Bairiki closes for the day.

As is the case elsewhere in Micronesia, Easter is a very important holiday; festivities extend into Easter Monday, when women's groups fill the churches with traditional dancing and singing.

ACTIVITIES
Diving, snorkelling and swimming are key activities for visitors to Kiribati (see island sections below for details). Christmas Island also offers great bird watching, and is a popular destination for sportsfishers.

But sports of all kind are extremely popular in Kiribati, as people use their idyllic natural setting to its best recreational advantage. Along the road, you'll pass people playing pick-up soccer and volleyball, which you can generally join.

ACCOMMODATION
Most of the outer islands have simple resthouses run by the local island council. The tourist office can help you arrange your stay, or contact the island council yourself by radio in advance. Bear in mind that even the best resthouses are primitive, with no hot water and with electricity generators that operate for a few hours in the evening if at all. The food, however, will be a hearty blend of local fish and coconut dishes (but be sure to boil or filter the local water). Most island council guesthouses cost A$30 a night, with three meals included; mosquito nets are provided along with sheets, a mattress and a pillow. The guesthouses vary widely in quality year to year, so it's best to ask at the tourist office before deciding on accommodation.

SPECTATOR SPORTS
A soccer tournament on New Year's Day draws teams from the outer islands, who ride for a day or more in a boat to reach the event, which is held in Tarawa. Tarawa usually wins the tournament, and local sports analysts opine that while the outer islands teams are generally more fit, Tarawa has superior ball handling skills.

SHOPPING
Wood carving and weaving predominate in I-Kiribati handicrafts (see Arts under Facts about Kiribati earlier this chapter) as well as necklaces made of fibres and shells. Most of these are made on the outer islands. There aren't too many palm-sized items so spare a bit of room in your bags.

If you collect stamps you may also want to visit the Philatelic Bureau in Betio, South Tarawa.

Getting There & Away

AIR
Airports & Airlines
Tarawa is the main entry point into Kiribati. Air Nauru flies Nauru-Tarawa-Fiji-Tarawa-Nauru twice each week. Similarly, Air Marshall Islands flies to Kiribati twice weekly, connecting Majuro and Tarawa. Air Kiribati also flies weekly between Honolulu and Christmas Island. See Getting There & Away under Tarawa, Outer Gilbert Islands and Christmas Island for further details.

The Bonriki International Airport, located in the north-east of South Tarawa, is a basic, mostly open-air terminal with one ancient coin-operated pay phone, hard-to-find toilets and a VIP lounge that is usually locked. There is no snack bar. As at the FSM airports, expect a warm and curious reception from the sea of locals waiting for the plane.

SEA
Kiribati Shipping Services has ships going periodically to Fiji, Tuvalu, Suva and Christmas Island, and WKK Shipping Line and Fern Store boats also travel intermittently through the islands. See Getting There & Away under Tarawa, Outer Gilbert Islands and Christmas Island.

Visiting yachts can anchor in Betio's harbour at Tarawa. Whether you're sailing to Tarawa or the outer islands of Kiribati, you must first go through customs at Tarawa or Christmas Island. Before leaving Kiribati yachts must return to Tarawa (or Christmas Island) for exit clearance and to pay the departure tax.

KIRIBATI

Departure Tax

Tarawa and Christmas Island each have a A\$10 departure tax.

ORGANISED TOURS

Most tourists to Christmas Island go on package sportsfishing or diving tours; see the Christmas Island section for details. Valor Tours (☎1-800-842 4504, 415-332 7850, fax 415-332 6971) in the USA, which specialises in WWII history, can help arrange a trip to Tarawa.

Getting Around

AIR

Air Kiribati flies to most outer Gilberts at least once a week. Its planes are occasionally grounded for lack of fuel or encounter some other trouble, so it's wise to allow a bit of extra time if you're planning a visit to one of the outer islands. There are no flights to the Phoenix or Line islands (except the Aloha plane from Honolulu to Christmas Island).

BOAT

Most of the outer Gilberts are serviced by supply ships from Tarawa every month or two, and ships go very occasionally from Tarawa to Christmas, Fanning and Washington. There is an almost daily boat to Abaiang, the closest of the outer islands.

LAND

Tarawa has an efficient minibus service, while Christmas Island's fledgling service has a one-bus fleet. On both islands car rentals are available; on the outer islands you may be able to rent a bicycle or a motor scooter or get a boat ride, but there likely won't be many trucks.

Driving is on the left side of the road.

Tarawa

Tarawa, shaped like two sides of a triangle, is a long, narrow coral atoll with a total land area of 32.5 sq km.

Tarawa is Kiribati's administrative seat. Divided into North Tarawa (population 4361) and South Tarawa (population 28,968), the south is the locus of all government activity and services, while the rural north approximates an outer island experience.

South Tarawa is home to more than one-third of Kiribati's population, most of whom cluster in open-air huts on the islet of Betio at Tarawa's westernmost tip. Betio was also the site of the US marines' bloody 1943 victory over the Japanese. Huge guns still preside over its beaches and rusting tanks rest just offshore, while trash is a reminder of present-day lifestyle. Bairiki, in South Tarawa between the airport and Betio, is home to most of the government buildings. The airport is about an hour's drive east of Betio.

A system of causeways, traversed by one main road, links all of South Tarawa and runs to Buota in North Tarawa. From Buota you must take a small canoe at high tide to reach the northern islets.

Information

Tourist Offices The tourist office (☎ 26 157, fax 26 233, @ commerce@tski.net.ki) is tucked away from the main road, on a small dirt road behind the large shipping storage facilities in Betio. The sign for the Ministry of Commerce, Industry & Tourism is on the left. The helpful, friendly staff will proffer a surprising number of useful (if dusty) brochures. The office is open from 8 am to 4.30 pm weekdays, though there is often an extended lunch break.

Money The overseas transaction counter at the large Bank of Kiribati in Bairiki changes cash and travellers cheques. It also does MasterCard and Visa cash advances (\$15 per transaction) and accepts wire transfers. Banking hours are from 9.30 am to 3 pm weekdays, but be aware that the every other Friday is payday. The bank also has branches in Betio and Bikenibeu.

Credit cards are accepted only by the Otintaai Hotel, Tobaroai Travel and the banks.

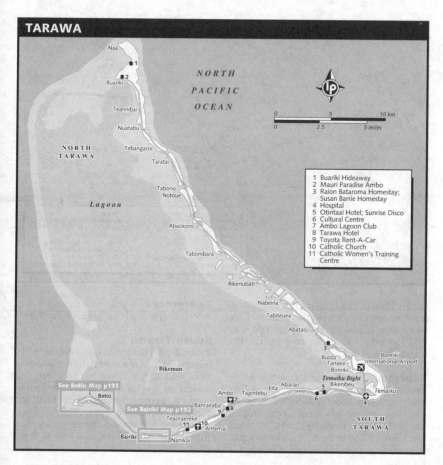

TARAWA

Naa
1 Buariki
2 Buariki
Tearinibai

NORTH
PACIFIC
OCEAN

Nuatabu

NORTH
TARAWA

Tebangaroi
Taratai

Taborio
Notoue

Lagoon

Abaokoro

Tabonibara

1 Buariki Hideaway
2 Mauri Paradise Ambo
3 Raion Bataroma Homestay;
   Susan Barrie Homestay
4 Hospital
5 Otintaai Hotel; Sunrise Disco
6 Cultural Centre
7 Ambo Lagoon Club
8 Tarawa Hotel
9 Toyota Rent-A-Car
10 Catholic Church
11 Catholic Women's Training
   Centre

Bikenubati

Nabeina

Tabiteuea

Abatao

Buota
Tanaea
Bonriki
Bonriki
International Airport

Bikeman

See Betio Map p193
Betio

Ambo
Banraeaba
Teaoraereke
Nanikai
Bairiki
Antemai

Eita
Tagintebu
Abarao

Temaiku Bight
Bikenibeu

Temaiku

See Bairiki Map p192

SOUTH
TARAWA

Post & Communications The central post office in Bairiki is open from 9 am to 3 pm weekdays, and has branches in Betio and Bikenibeu. The Philatelic Bureau is in Betio, on the right not far past the roundabout (see Shopping later this chapter for details).

International telephone calls can be made from the main Telecom Services Kiribati Limited (TSKL) office in Bairiki (it also has branches in Betio and Bikenibeu). The per-minute cost to Australia, New Zealand and Nauru is A$3, and to most of the rest of the world it's A$6. It's A$0.90 a minute to

call the outer islands and there's a three-minute minimum for most calls (see Facts for the Visitor earlier in this chapter for outer island telephone numbers). The office also has new coin and card-operated phones. For 24-hour directory assistance dial ☎ 103 and for the international operator dial ☎ 910.

Sending faxes costs A$0.07 a minute to Australia, New Zealand and Nauru and A$0.09 a minute elsewhere. Faxes sent to fax 21 416 can be received for A$1.50 per page. The office is open from 8 am to 5.15 pm weekdays.

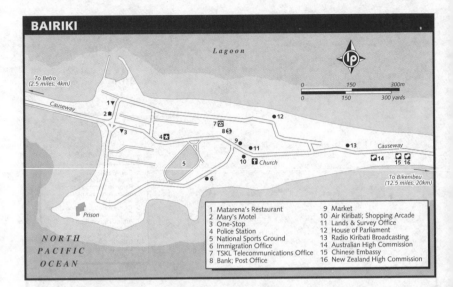

BAIRIKI

1 Matarena's Restaurant	9 Market
2 Mary's Motel	10 Air Kiribati; Shopping Arcade
3 One-Stop	11 Lands & Survey Office
4 Police Station	12 House of Parliament
5 National Sports Ground	13 Radio Kiribati Broadcasting
6 Immigration Office	14 Australian High Commission
7 TSKL Telecommunications Office	15 Chinese Embassy
8 Bank; Post Office	16 New Zealand High Commission

The Bairiki TSKL office has one public Internet terminal behind the counter. One week after it was introduced the rate was A$30 an hour – an experimental price that hopefully will drop.

Bookshops The University of the South Pacific Bookshop is the best place to find books on Kiribati, but it doesn't have much else. The bookshop is usually open from 9 am to 5.45 pm weekdays, with a lunch break from 12.30 to 2 pm. If it's locked, ask the nearby administrative office to open it for you.

Libraries Kiribati National Library stocks several shelves of books on the old South Pacific, but unfortunately most on Kiribati have been lost. The University of the South Pacific also has a one-room library with Pacific literature shelves and with longer hours.

Medical Services The island's sea-green hospital (☎ 28 100) is a 10-minute ride from the Otintaai Hotel towards the airport. It has limited air-con and drugs are often out of date.

Emergency For police emergencies dial ☎ 992; for medical emergencies dial ☎ 994.

South Tarawa

Bikenibeu The new cultural centre, a 20-minute walk in the direction of the airport from the Otintaai Hotel, has an interesting collection of local artefacts, including weaving, a coconut and pearl fish hook and torso armour made from coconut fibre. Admission is free and the centre is open from 8 am to 12.30 pm and 1.30 to 4 pm weekdays.

Betio At the western end of South Tarawa, Betio is connected to the rest of the island by a causeway. Completed in 1987, the causeway has contributed to lagoon-side coastal erosion by choking up the formerly free-flowing water. The road makes a loop in Betio, so don't get confused if all the minibuses go in one direction.

On 20 November 1943 20,000 US marines stormed Betio's beaches, and after several days of fierce fighting proclaimed victory. Casualties on both sides were severe: 1113 US marines were killed and 2290 wounded; the Japanese lost close to

4500 men. Betio retains an impressive array of WWII relics, including eight-inch guns, bunkers and a machine-gun command post.

Wear solid footwear (ie, not sandals) if you're going on a war tour, as the relics lie among piles of broken glass and trash. See Organised Tours below for details on an excellent war tour of Betio.

Towards the end of the causeway are numerous large **eight-inch guns** easily visible from the road. The lagoon-side of the causeway was once a minefield, but is now cleared. Coming from Bairiki, turn right at the end of the causeway onto a small dirt road, and you'll see an **anti-aircraft gun** in good condition on the right-hand side behind the fence.

Just beyond the causeway in Betio is a large sports field on the right. This is actually an overgrown runway built by the Americans after they took the island; it extends to the western tip of Betio.

Further west, the **cemetery**, on the left side of the road, is laced with a smattering

of **bunkers**, some quite large. There's also a moving **memorial** to 22 British soldiers killed by the Japanese on 15 October 1942. Its plaque reads, 'Standing unarmed to their posts, they matched brutality with gallantry, and met death with fortitude'. Beside the epitaph are the names of the dead, who included wireless operators, civilians and one church reverend. They were shot in probable retaliation after the US raid on Butaritari.

At **Temakin Point**, the western tip of Betio, there's an **eight-inch gun**, which is easily visible from the road. You can climb up to it if you have a local to assist you. Unfortunately, this area is rather popular as a local toilet.

As you proceed along the road, you'll be unable to miss the rubbish tip, which has a gun emplacement. A **Japanese Memorial Garden**, in front of the tip, was built in the mid-1970s. It has a number of monuments inscribed in Japanese and English. One

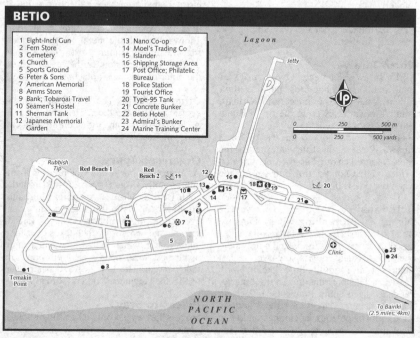

BETIO

1 Eight-Inch Gun
2 Fern Store
3 Cemetery
4 Church
5 Sports Ground
6 Peter & Sons
7 American Memorial
8 Amms Store
9 Bank; Tobaroai Travel
10 Seamen's Hostel
11 Sherman Tank
12 Japanese Memorial Garden
13 Nano Co-op
14 Moel's Trading Co
15 Islander
16 Shipping Storage Area
17 Post Office; Philatelic Bureau
18 Police Station
19 Tourist Office
20 Type-95 Tank
21 Concrete Bunker
22 Betio Hotel
23 Admiral's Bunker
24 Marine Training Center

Lagoon
Jetty
Rubbish Tip
Red Beach 1
Red Beach 2
NORTH PACIFIC OCEAN
Temakin Point
Clinic
To Bairiki (2.5 miles; 4km)

0   250   500 m
0   250   500 yards

poetic epitaph reads 'Where have you gone, my dear/ In this Lagoon? Standing on sand/ With my soles burning/ I feel your soul coming.' There is a Shinto shrine and a Korean shrine here as well as an anti-aircraft gun.

Red Beach One and **Red Beach Two** are just beyond the tip. They have more orange-coloured sand than most beaches and are where some marine contingents landed.

The **American Memorial** in front of the Betio town council, was built in 1987. It is a time capsule that's scheduled to be opened on 29 November 2043, 100 years after the Battle of Tarawa.

Turn left at Peter & Sons store and proceed towards the sea wall at the beach. A **Sherman tank** is visible at low tide, as is a Type-95 light **Japanese tank** that was in front of the command bunker but pushed into the lagoon.

The yellow structure by the Marine Training Centre is the old **command bunker**.

Throughout Betio's back roads small guns and bunkers dot the way among the pigs and children.

North Tarawa

North Tarawa, connected by a series of small roads and canoe crossings, is an excellent place to experience rural Kiribati. South Tarawa buses go to the tip of Buota and the road is decent.

Getting from Buota to the rest of North Tarawa is easy; you can wade across the aqua-coloured channel at low tide, or catch a ride (A$0.30) on the tiny outrigger canoe when the tide is higher.

Activities

Diving & Snorkelling Mauri Paradise (☎ 21 646, fax 21 416, ✆ mp@tskl.net.ki), based in Ambo, runs the island's only dive operation. Usually divers stay overnight at Mauri Paradise's idyllic little hotel in North Tarawa, a 1½ hour ride on a 29-foot outrigger canoe from South Tarawa (see Places to Stay for details). The diving there is quite good, with napoleons, anemones and even giant prawns. For hotel guests, a two-tank dive costs A$88, a night dive costs A$68, scuba rental A$22 and snorkelling equipment A$10. As a day trip from South Tarawa, a two-tank dive costs A$140, including lunch and transportation – prices fall to A$120 if there are two or more people – and diving equipment is rented for A$5. Mauri Paradise also charters its boat for bottom fishing (A$290) and trolling (A$350).

Some of the outer islands have good diving and snorkelling, but you must bring your own gear. Expat John Thurston (☎/fax 28 661) charters his 36-foot cruising trimaran *Martha*, which rests just outside the Otintaai Hotel, for $400 per day. This is a good option for visiting the outer islands or North Tarawa. John will bring along a couple of snorkelling masks too. The 20-passenger boat sleeps six comfortably.

Swimming Swimmers should stay well clear of South Tarawa's lagoon. It has become heavily polluted as the causeways have created a garbage collecting point. If you must swim try the channel on the way to Betio. Another decent spot is in North Tarawa, beneath the metal bridge connecting Tanaea to Buota. North Tarawa has other swimming spots further afield, as do the outer islands; ask your hosts or guide.

Other Activities The Hash House Harriers runs on Wednesdays. The cost to run is A$1. The Australian High Commission can give you details.

Organised Tours

A fascinating tour of the war relics is available at Molly's Tours (☎/fax 26 409) in Betio. John Brown, Molly's Australian husband, drives around Betio reliving the battle, and even shows a 15-minute Battle of Tarawa video at the end. Molly then takes over for a cultural tour, which includes an explanation about how local houses are built and how toddy is cut. The tour is A$30 per person (A$15 for Volunteer Workers Abroad).

Places to Stay

Hotels Tarawa has only a handful of hotels, none of which could be mistaken for luxury

KIRIBATI

accommodation. A tax of 10% will be added to the rates listed here, and no hotels besides the Otintaai Hotel accept credit cards.

Most foreign business travellers stay at the government-owned *Otintaai Hotel* (☎ *28 084, fax 28 045)*. Its 40 rooms, undoubtedly overpriced and not particularly spectacular, at A$70 to A$80 for singles, smell musty if it rains. But each room does have air-con, private bath, refrigerator, phone (local calls A$0.25) and, most notably, reliable hot water. Bring earplugs to block out the Friday and Saturday night disco. The hotel is about a 20-minute drive from Bairiki and 45 minutes from Betio.

Mary's Motel (☎ *21 164)*, in Bairiki at the start of the causeway to Betio, has two nice new rooms, each with two single beds, air-con, a clean shower (hot water not guaranteed), a little outdoor sitting area, a refrigerator and the beginnings of a minibar. Four similar rooms were under construction at the time of writing. Four older rooms in a concrete building, each with refrigerator, air-con and private bath, are so rundown that some showers lack a showerhead. Singles/doubles in the newer part cost A$77/85, in the older part A$55/66. Mary charges A$1 for a local call.

Seamen's Hostel (☎ *26 566)*, behind Nano's store in Betio, is just A$20 per night – but it's very basic, with a dirty shower and toilet area. It's really for seamen and can be a bit rough – the fact that they give a $5 refund if the room is not damaged when you leave says a great deal.

Tarawa Hotel (☎ *21 445)* is a single-storey, concrete-block building a few minutes' walk from the Ambo Lagoon Club. Six basic but decent rooms have ceiling fans (no air-con) and share two toilet and shower areas. The kitchen facilities – a refrigerator and icebox, stove and some pans – make the A$25/35 rate for singles/doubles quite a good deal.

Betio Motel (☎ *26 361, fax 26 048)*, not far from the causeway relics, has ten small, plain rooms with air-con and private baths for A$45/65 (tax included). The place is friendly if not immaculate and the bar has satellite television (when the dish is working). Airport transfers are available upon request.

Mauri Paradise Ambo (☎ *21 646, fax 21 416; in Japan fax 81-466 45 0745,* ☻ *mp@tskl.net.ki)* is the lone 'hotel' on North Tarawa, with two bungalow-style places accommodating four people total. The price is A$80 per person per night and includes tasty meals, starting with pancakes with coconut syrup for breakfast. The 1½-hour ride in a 39-foot outrigger costs A$122 return. Basic shower facilities are available, and there's a generator and lanterns for evening light. See also the Diving & Snorkelling section earlier in this chapter.

Homestays North Tarawa has many excellent homestays that allow you to sample local culture and local food – for cheaper prices than the hotels.

Some of North Tarawa's homestays are in Abatao, just a short canoe trip from the end of the South Tarawa bus line. More remote homestays are over an hour away by boat, so it's best to decide how close you need to be to the 'civilisation' of South Tarawa. You can generally arrange meals at a minimal addition to the prices listed below.

As North Tarawa has only one telephone at the moment, it's best to contact the tourist office to arrange a homestay.

Raion Bataroma in Abatao, has a couple of gorgeous bungalows on stilts over the lagoon, just across the canoe passage from where the road ends at Buota. Instead of air-con there's a fresh sea breeze. The price is A$25/30 for singles/doubles.

Susan Barrie, who can be contacted through Tobaroai Travel Agency (☎ *36 567, fax 26 000)*, has a resthouse in the same vicinity for A$35 per person. A breakfast of pancakes with coconut syrup and a dinner of fish with local vegetables are included.

Further away, at the far end of North Tarawa between Buariki village and Naa, is the *Buariki Hideaway* (☎ *26 695, 30 222, fax 26 250,* ☻ *buariki@tskl.net.ki)*, a group of brand-new, well-kept bungalows managed by Swiss-German Mike Strub. Prices are by bungalow not by person. It's A$20

KIRIBATI

per day for any of the three one-bedroom bungalows and A$40 for the large two-bedroom bungalow; add A$50 to A$60 for meals, though the bungalows have cooking facilities. Snorkelling, fishing and boat and bike hire can be arranged for reasonable rates. There is generator electricity and running water. Transportation is just A$20 round-trip for the one- to two-hour ride in a covered canoe.

Places to Eat

Most of Tarawa's food comes from Australia at approximately monthly intervals. You'll know if a ship has come in because suddenly half-bare shelves will swell proudly with goods. Small stores stock plenty of tinned goods and sodas, and you can often find the excellent local bread, which is a touch sweeter than regular bread. *Amms* and *One-Stop*, both with branches in Bairiki, are Tarawa's largest stores.

The main *market*, selling local fruit and featuring women fanning fish, is open from 8 am to 5 pm Monday to Saturday. Here you'll find drinking coconuts for A$0.50.

The small *shopping arcade* opposite the market has two cheap and fairly clean local eateries on opposite sides of the walkway. A hearty plateful of chicken or fish with rice won't cost more than A$3.

Otintaai Hotel guests can walk east 40m and take the dirt road off to the right to reach a *shop* next to the Music Store. It has supplies including bread and undersells the hotel on VB (Victoria Bitter) by A$0.30.

Kiribati's water, pumped from a water lens or a reservoir, is not safe to drink without filtering or boiling.

If you're in Betio around mealtime, check behind Amms store for the *small restaurant* that serves up a variety of fish, chicken, and pork dishes (depending on availability) for A$3.50 to A$4. Amms is open from 10 am to 2 pm and 5 to 8 pm weekdays, from noon to 2 pm and 5.30 to 7.30 pm weekends.

Good food at a reasonable price is served at the outdoor tables at *Mary's Motel* in Bairiki. Try the Tarawa chick tropical, which comes feathered in breadcrumbs and with cheese, bacon and pineapple mixed in (A$9.50). Grilled fish comes with a small salad and rice or chips (A$5.50) – a nice choice. Breakfasts are around A$4, and beer is A$1.70. The service can be a bit slow, and many diners claim that the food is better when Mary is around. It's open from 7 am to 10 pm daily.

Matarena's Restaurant, next door to Mary's, does an excellent job with fish. Try the crispy fish in chilli sauce (A$7.50), which is four tender chunks of fried fish with rice or chips and a couple of fried fruit pieces, or go for a plateful of fish chop suey. The restaurant is open from 6.30 am to 9.30 pm daily.

The *Otintaai Hotel* has a good restaurant with worthwhile specials. Friday is 'Cheap Cheap Night', when all entrees cost A$5.50 and come with chips or rice; if you're absolutely starving the smallish platefuls might not be enough but otherwise it's a good night to come. On other days the food is good but pricey, starting at A$10 an entree (check the back of the menu for budget options). Barbecues are held on Tuesday and Thursday nights, when fish costs A$6 and A$9 respectively. The restaurant is open from 7 to 9 am, noon to 2 pm and 7 to 9 pm daily.

Entertainment

Any number of wild local bars clustered in Betio keep things swinging – try the *Islander*, beside the roundabout in Betio, or the *Royal Saloon*, which has a popular raffle Friday nights. If you're out to make a night of it, be aware that minibuses stop running at 8.30 pm Monday to Thursday and 10 pm Friday and Saturday. The *Otintaai Hotel* bar attracts a hefty expat following before dinner, while the *Sunrise* disco on the hotel grounds, open Friday and Saturday nights, lures droves of local youth.

Local dance competitions are held annually during the 12 July Independence Day celebrations, and are a marvellous spectator event. If you ask your hotel to arrange a local dance performance, it's essential to have a large group as the dancers like an energetic, clapping audience. The Otintaai

Cutting Toddy

Kiribati's famed local brew is called *kaokioki*, or sour toddy, which is much like the *kaleva*, fermented coconut juice from Tokelau. Essentially kaokioki is sap tapped from coconut trees that has been fermented for a few days. (The syrupy 'sweet toddy' skips the fermentation stage.) 'Cutting toddy', as the extraction procedure is called, is done by Kiribati men and demands technique and skill.

First, the man shimmies up a coconut palm and tightly laces a rope (made from local materials) around the branch. Using the hanging end of the rope, he ties on a container so that the sap, collected twice daily, drips into the container. Most men 'cut their toddy' – take down the bottle – twice a day, mid-morning and again mid-afternoon. (So sacrosanct is toddy quality that local men who are not toddy experts cut theirs late at night while no-one else is around to observe how little toddy they may have obtained. Particularly on the outer islands, men sing merry adulations of their girlfriends or wives as they cut toddy.

Sour toddy is ubiquitous but you won't find it in restaurants or bars. Instead, ask a local to point you to the nearest toddy purveyor. A word of caution: Often the toddy is diluted with tap water, which is not likely to be boiled, so think twice before trying.

Most toddy-tied branches are unable to produce coconuts.

Hotel has dancers on Thursday nights to accompany its barbecue.

The *Ambo Lagoon Club*, a popular expat hangout with a pool table and copious VB, has a weekly movie on Thursday and occasional barbecues. Visitors must purchase an A$5.20 temporary membership. The Club is open until 10 pm Sunday to Thursday and until 2 am Friday and Saturday; happy hour is from 5 to 7 pm daily.

Shopping

An excellent selection of handicrafts is stocked by the Catholic Women's Training Centre in Teaoraereke, about a 10 minutes

drive from Bairiki towards the airport. The choice items are the traditional swords with shark-tooth spikes and giant prawn tentacles extending from a coconut-wood shaft (from A$18). The outrigger canoe models (from A$12) are also tempting. Bottles of hand-pressed coconut oil are A$4.50.

Anyone interested in I-Kiribati music should bring a blank cassette to the Radio Kiribati Broadcasting office in Bairiki. The staff will make up a tape for A$9.40 if you say what album or group you want.

Stamp collectors will find everything from Kiribati lobsters to Japanese seaplanes at the Kiribati Philatelic Bureau (☎ 26 515, fax 26 193) in Betio. They also sell a few nice stamp postcards (A$0.60). Mauri Paradise in Ambo also stocks good A$0.50 postcards of classic Kiribati scenes.

Getting There & Away

Air Air Nauru flies Nauru-Tarawa-Fiji-Tarawa-Nauru on Tuesdays and Thursdays. To Tarawa from Nauru the excursion fare is A$325. The efficient Tobaroai Travel Agency (☎ 26 567, fax 26 000), above the bank in Betio, handles Air Nauru bookings. The office is open from 8 am to 4.30 pm weekdays. Visa and MasterCard are accepted but carry a A$20 surcharge.

Air Marshall Islands (☎ 21 577, fax 21 579) has an office behind the bank in Bairiki. It flies between Majuro and Tarawa on Tuesday and Thursday and fares cost A$279/558 one-way/return. The service, however, is not hugely reliable.

Boat Kiribati Shipping Services (☎ 26 195, fax 26 204) sends ships to Fiji, Tuvalu and Suva every two months or so. One-way fares are A$192.50 for Fiji, A$103.40 for Tuvalu and A$116.80 for Christmas Island. The fare doubles for cabin accommodation. Food is included.

Ship arrivals and departures are generally announced on the public radio – sometimes even in English – so keep your ears open or ask a local to keep you posted.

Visiting yachts can anchor in Betio's harbour for A$0.50 per gross tonnage per day;

pulling alongside the wharf costs A$0.20 extra per gross tonnage per day.

Getting Around

To/From the Airport The airport is in Bonriki, about a 50-minute drive east from Betio. The Otintaai Hotel sends a van to the airport to meet arriving international flights. Other hotels generally provide free airport transport if you call first. If you take the bus, the fare from the airport to Betio is A$1.50; by taxi it is about A$25.

Bus Tarawa's bus system is excellent. Minivans sporting a cardboard 'BUS' sign and blaring American pop music whizz by between 6 am and 8 or 9 pm (10 pm on weekends). A conductor will collect the fare when you get off.

The buses eliminate the need to rent a car, as you'll rarely go three minutes during working hours without spotting one. There are no actual stops; just flag down the bus from the roadside. When you want to get off yell 'stop' or, if you're feeling particularly local, yell '*kai*'. The minibuses tend to stage races among themselves, so they can be slightly hazardous.

Car Toyota Rent-A-Car, at Tarawa Motors in Bairiki (☎ 21 090, fax 21 451), has cars for hire at A$50 a day. The Otintaai Hotel (☎ 28 084, fax 28 045) can also arrange cars for the same price. Otherwise ask around.

Overseas driving licences are valid for two weeks from arrival in Kiribati. If you need a licence for a longer period, bring your current licence and A$5 to the Tarawa Urban Council in Teaoraereke, about a 10-minute drive from Bairiki on the way to the airport.

Driving is on the left side of the road. Watch for periodic speed bumps, people ambling along the roadside and minibuses screeching to a halt.

Taxi Some private taxis are available; try TJ taxi service (☎ 21 292). Taxis are hired mainly by locals wishing to see their relatives off in style.

Boat Boats occasionally connect North and South Tarawa, but the only way to find out who's going is to ask around.

Outer Gilbert Islands

Visiting the outer Gilbert islands is an excellent way to experience traditional I-Kiribati life, where it's rare to find more than a few trucks and some motorbikes. The trash that has marred the beauty of South Tarawa is nowhere to be found on the outer islands, as packaged Western products are a rarity. People live off fish from the sea and coconuts from the land, and occasionally earn revenue by selling salted clams to Tarawa or copra abroad.

All of the outer islands have a resthouse operated by the island council. See Accommodation under Facts for the Visitor earlier in this chapter for details.

Getting There & Away

Air Air Kiribati (☎ 21 550, 21 227, fax 21 188), which has an office in the shopping arcade across from the Bairiki market in Tarawa, flies to most of the outer Gilberts at least once a week. Be aware that Air Kiribati occasionally contends with problems (eg, fuel shortages) that can ground its three aircraft for weeks at a time, so be sure you have plenty of flexibility. The following are standard one-way air fares (students get a 25% discount and children under 11 years fly half-price) from Tarawa:

destination	flights weekly	fare (A$)
Abaiang	3	29
Abemama	3	45
Aranuka	1	49
Arorae	1	116
Beru	1	116
Butaritari	3	61
Kuria	1	48
Maiana	3	28
Makin	1	68
Marakei	3	35
Nikunau	1	124

destination	flights weekly	fare (A$)
Nonouti	2	76
Onotoa	1	116
Tabiteuea North	3	94
Tabiteuea South	1	104
Tamana	1	136

Boat A ferry leaves the harbour in Betio almost daily for Abaiang. Ask at the tourist office.

Most of the other outer Gilberts are serviced by supply ships from Tarawa once every month or two. One option is travelling with Kiribati Shipping Services (☎ 26 195, fax 26 204), which sends ships on a weekly basis along different routes through the Gilbert Islands.

WKK Shipping Line (☎ 26 352, fax 26 007) sends ships to the outer islands roughly 25 times a year depending on supply needs. Fern Store (☎ 26 596) in Betio also sends boats to the outer islands.

Abaiang, Maiana, Nenos, Tabiteuea South, Onotoa and Abemama are the only outer Gilbert Islands with lagoons that can handle large boats. Ask at the Ministry of Information, Communications & Transport (☎ 26 003).

ABAIANG

Four hours by boat or 15 minutes by plane from Tarawa, Abaiang (population 4361) – the name means 'north land' – is the most easily accessed of the outer islands, but it still offers a typically remote experience. Small children shout a timid 'mauri' to an *I-Matang* (white person) and women can be seen weaving thatch or salt clams to send to Tarawa. The dirt road running the length of the island is empty except for an occasional motor scooter or push bike, or the church truck spilling over with excited children.

The airstrip is about 3km south of the island council base at the village of Taburao. Though the boat docks north of Taburao, you can get dropped off in a small skiff on the southern tip of the island, at the village of Tabontebike, where the island council's rest house is located.

The rest house, called *Hotel Nikuao*, is among the outer islands' most pleasant accommodation. Four spacious thatched cottages surround a large central dining area (request the cottage with the private shower), where you can enjoy the delicious fish, and a spongy cake made from *babai* and coconut cream. You can swim at the beach at high tide.

Ask around in the village about renting a bicycle for the day (A$5). If you're in good shape, you can cycle up past the government station to Koinawa – the village with the **Catholic church**. Though badly in need of renovation, the church still has rainbow coloured window frames. Ask a local to escort you up the rickety wooden steps so you can join the Virgin Mary for the view. From Tabontebike to Koinawa it's about 15km.

BUTARITARI

Averaging over 300cm in annual rainfall, Butaritari (13.5 sq kms) is Kiribati's greenest island. Breadfruit, coconut, pandanus and other fruit-bearing trees flourish on its rich soils.

Butaritari (population 4905) was one of Robert Louis Stevenson's stops during his Pacific journey aboard the *Equator*. When Stevenson arrived in July 1889, he found the whole island drunk in the wake of the 4 July celebrations hosted by the resident American traders. Seeing a man deprived of an earlobe in a barroom brawl persuaded Stevenson to lobby for temperance.

Butaritari has a sobering WWII history, as the lopsided wreckage of a **Japanese seaplane** near Butaritari village attests. Together with its northern neighbour Makin – whose northernmost reaches are known as the home of 'Naa's tongue', the traditional jumping-off point for I-Kiribati spirits en route to the underworld – Butaritari was the first Gilbert Island to be occupied by the Japanese during WWII. In December 1941, the Japanese landed close to 300 troops in Ukiangang village in the south and then advanced north, settling in Butaritari village.

In August 1942, more than 200 US marines beat back the Japanese in a battle near the present-day airfield. The US, which was only employing a diversionary

KIRIBATI

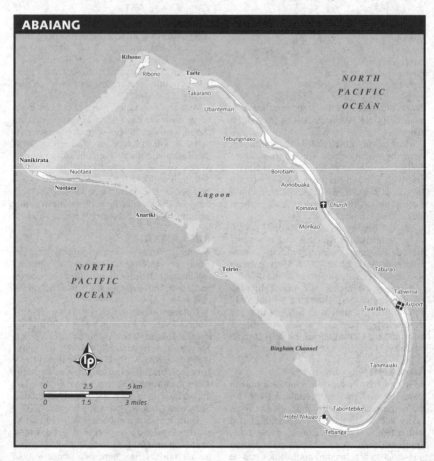

ABAIANG

Ribono
Ribono
Taete
Takarano
NORTH
PACIFIC
OCEAN
Ubanteman
Tebunginako
Nanikirata
Nuotaea
Borotiam
Aonobuaka
Nuotaea
Lagoon
Koinawa   🕆 Church
Anariki
Morikao
Teirio
Taburao
Tabwiroa
NORTH
PACIFIC
OCEAN
Tuarabu   ✈ Airport
Bingham Channel
Tanimaiaki
0   2.5   5 km
0   1.5   3 miles
Tabontebike
Hotel Nikuao
Tebanga

tactic, pulled out a day later, and angry Japanese air raids on the village of Keuea killed 41 locals. The Japanese set local men to work building the wharf, bunkers and roads.

There is strong speculation that the Gilbertese men would have been killed by the Japanese but for the intervention of a Japanese trader sympathetic to the locals. Such plans were in any case disrupted by a second US counter-invasion on 20 November 1943. The US won the island after three days of heavy fighting that left 818 US and 550 Japanese dead. To this day, a celebra-

tion takes place on 20 November, called the Remembrance of Underground Cave Openings, at Ukiangang village. It commemorates the emergence of village elders from their hideaway caves.

In addition to the usual island *resthouse*, there's the new *Pearl Shell Resthouse*, a private guesthouse operated by a local family, about a 10-minute walk from the government complex. Snorkelling, swimming and generator electricity are available. Contact Linda Uan and John Anderson at NTNK video resource unit (☎/fax 21 629, ✉ kirivid@hotmail.com).

BANABA (OCEAN ISLAND)

Just under 6.5 sq km in area, Banaba (population 344) is Kiribati's only uplifted limestone island. Its highest point rises 78m above sea level, dwarfing Kiribati's other high points by a factor of 26.

In 1804 the European vessel *Ocean* gave her name to the island, but the I-Kiribati retain the island's original name, Banaba.

Like its nearest neighbour Nauru, Banaba's fate took a turn when Albert Ellis of Britain's Pacific Island Company, analysing rock in an Australian lab in 1900, realised that Banaba was rich in phosphate reserves. Ellis hastily boarded a ship and arrived at Ocean Island on 3 May 1900. By the afternoon, he had coerced the Banabans into giving the Pacific Islands Company (later renamed the British Phosphate Company) exclusive rights to mine the island for 999 years.

Phosphate mining began that same year. The following year Banaba was brought into the British protectorate and in 1908 it replaced Tarawa as the protectorate's administrative capital – a distinction it retained until after WWII, when Tarawa reassumed administrative control.

The Japanese arrived in 1942 and found the phosphate works sabotaged in expectation of their arrival. Their fury led to numerous atrocities, and in 1943 most Banabans and Gilbertese were relocated to the Carolines and Tarawa. In August 1945 a kill-the-natives order was issued against the 160 Banabans remaining on the island. The Japanese rounded up the locals, forced them to kneel blindfolded at a cliff top then stabbed or shot them over the cliff. One man, Kabunare, crawled out of a cave months later and relayed the horror to the Australians.

Inspired by neighbouring Nauru's example, the Banabans sought self-government after WWII, but Britain stalled. During the mid-1960s, Banabans also angled for a higher percentage of phosphate revenues. They received mining royalties of 15% in 1965, and 50% by the 1970s.

In 1972 the Banabans also demanded rehabilitation money for the mined-out lands, as well as an additional A$38.5 million in owed taxes and royalties. The British offered close to A$500,000, and the judge at a British high court ordered the British to pay A$11,000.

The British volunteered to pay an additional A$10 million, but Banaba would only accept this if it won self-government, separation from the Gilberts and free association with Fiji. But the British delayed and Banaba's phosphate ran out in 1979, the year Kiribati achieved its independence. Banabans took the A$10 million two years later but independence, strongly opposed by the Tarawa government, remains an impossibility.

Banaba today has four villages and is a graveyard of rusting equipment, with old staff-housing that has fallen into disrepair. A **Sir Albert Ellis memorial** near the sea marks the site of Ellis' first camp in 1900. Many of Banaba's young people leave for Tarawa or Rabi Island.

To stay on Banaba, you should obtain a government permit from the Home Affairs office on Tarawa. Guests will most likely be put up at the former British Phosphate Company resthouse, called the *Banaba House*, near the harbour. Four trucks and a few motorbikes make the rounds on the island.

ABEMAMA

Alone among the outer islands, Abemama (27.37 sq km) still has a 'royal family' who retain their title, if not their power. The king's old house is not preserved.

Abemama (population 4022) has a high copra output, rich fish resources and a good water lens. There's a causeway bridge linking the atoll's two islands.

The introduction of a few trucks to supplement the scooters made an interesting kink in one cultural tradition. When riding by a maneaba meeting on a scooter or bike, the rider customarily dismounts and pushes the vehicle past out of respect. However, one would be hard-pressed to push a truck past, so allowances have been made for modern technology.

Along with Butaritari and Tarawa, centrally located Abemama was under consideration in the late 19th century for the capital of the Gilbert Islands, but it lost out to Tarawa because its lagoon passage was considered slightly dangerous.

Abemama's once-numerous private guesthouses have closed, and only the *island council resthouse* remains.

MARAKEI

Visitors to Marakei (population 3645), a 14-sq-km atoll north of Abaiang, will encounter a rather astonishing custom. All first-time visitors must travel counter-clockwise around the ring-shaped island. Aided by a guide, you will visit four or five small, distinctive **shrines** to the spirits of the ancestors. At these shrines, you must lay a stick of tobacco so that the ancestors will bless your stay.

You will discover one of two things during this tour. Either the guide, professing to be an agent of the ancestors, will seize your tobacco within a minute of your depositing it; or the hollow in which you place your tobacco will actually have no back, and as soon as you deposit the tobacco it will be snatched from the opposite side by an over-eager ancestor who, assuming the form of a small child, will scurry back into the coconut trees and deliver the booty to its elders.

Most outer islands have a similar tradition, but it is most firmly entrenched on Marakei. One might note in passing that some 'ancestors' presumably existed before the European traders' 17th century introduction of tobacco.

OTHER ISLANDS

Each of the Gilbert Islands has a distinctive character. **Tabiteuea**, divided into north (population 4286) and south (pop 1788), is the third-largest island in Kiribati at 29.5 sq km. It is the home of Kiribati's current president, Teburoro Tito. Tabiteuea quite literally means 'Forbidden to Kings' – no king system has ever been permitted here.

Onotoa (population 2598) is known locally for its wrestlers, as are **Tamana** (population 1862) and **Arorae** (population 1983).

Phoenix Islands

Most of the eight Phoenix Islands, all south of the equator, were added to the Gilbert & Ellice Islands colony in 1937. The Treaty of Friendship, approved by the US Congress in 1982, gave Kiribati sovereignty over Kanton, Hull and Enderbury although the US reserved the right to build military facilities there.

Remote and uninhabited – except for Kanton (population 33) – these islands are low atolls with enclosed lagoons. **Wildlife sanctuaries** have been established on some.

Getting to the Phoenix Islands is difficult. **Kanton**, which has a pier for small boats and a wharf for larger boats, is sometimes visited by supply ships en route to the Line Islands.

Line Islands

The eight Line Islands, the westernmost group in Kiribati, straddle the equator. Only the northern Line Islands – Washington, Fanning and Christmas island – are inhabited, whereas the five islands south of the equator are not. As with the Phoenix Islands, the lack of freshwater in the southern Line Islands prevents human habitation. Under Tarawa's government, the Line Islands are administered separately from Christmas Island.

The population of the northern Line Islands is growing rapidly, spurred by the Kiribati government's 1988 program to resettle people from overcrowded South Tarawa. The Line Islands have about 60% of Kiribati's total land area but only 7% of the population. The resumption of air service between Honolulu and Christmas Island has allowed the latter to attract tourists, while Washington and Fanning are being left behind.

Although their climates are different, the three northern Line Islands all supported copra plantations during the 19th century. Christmas Island is prone to droughts, while Washington is quite wet and Fanning's climate is in between.

Millennium

The International Date Line used to split Kiribati down the middle – until January 1 1995, that is, when Kiribati shifted its part of the date line eastward. The stated purpose of the move was to unite all of Kiribati's dispersed atolls on the same side of the dateline. Previously the date line had split the country, so that when it was Friday in Christmas Island it was already Saturday in Tarawa, a situation that posed obvious administrative complications. As the International Date Line has no binding legal status, this move met no opposition from the Royal Greenwich Observatory in England.

With this swift move, tiny Kiribati found itself on the cutting edge of Millennium Fever. Kiribati was now the first country to see the year 2000 sunrise (if you don't count Antarctica, where the sun rose in August). Caroline Island, an uninhabited southern Line Island newly renamed Millennium, was the first to see the sun rise, at 5.43 am local time, and the first to celebrate the midnight New Year in the round-the-world millennium television extravaganza.

There are resthouses on Fanning and Washington but no air service; the only way to get there is by ship. In Tarawa contact Kiribati Shipping Services (☎ 26 195, fax 26 204), WKK Shipping (☎ 26 352, fax 26 007) and Fern Store (☎ 26 596). All send annual or semi-annual boats to the northern Line Islands.

To the south, Caroline Island, recently rechristened Millennium Island, is the easternmost of the group. Thanks to Kiribati's jiggering of the international dateline (see boxed text 'Millennium'), 'Millennium Island' became the first land area in the world – barring Antarctica – to see the sunrise of the year 2000.

FANNING (TABUAERAN)
Ring-shaped Fanning (population 600) has six small villages and a land area of 34 sq km. Fanning's local name, Tabuaeran, derives from a Polynesian word meaning 'sacred footprint'. When the island was found in 1798 by Captain Edmund Fanning, of the whaler *Betsy*, there were no inhabitants, though traces remain of ancient Polynesian occupation.

A few miles north of the harbour is an overgrown runway, the site of a 1902 cable station that formed part of the first trans-Pacific cable that ran from Australia to Fiji to Fanning and through to Canada. In 1916, a German cruiser flying a French flag cut the cable though it was later restored.

A **six-inch gun** sits between the airport and the cable station, put in place by US troops early in WWII.

The island council runs a small *resthouse* on the south side of the harbour entrance. Also ask about the three thatched *bungalows* run by Tabia Baraniko, facing the lagoon and ventilated by the trade winds. Like the resthouse, Tabia charges A$20 to A$25 a night with meals included.

Fanning's wide, deep channels and good natural harbour makes it a good cruise-ship destination, and it's only 1½ days by boat from Christmas Island; use the channel at English Harbour. Docking costs A$1 per passenger. Yachties should contact port authority at Christmas Island or Tarawa.

WASHINGTON (TERAINA)
North-west of Fanning by 187km, oblong-shaped Washington (population 610) was named in 1798 by Captain Fanning after the first US president. Uniquely, Washington has a **freshwater lake** enclosed by peat bogs, so that it looks a bit like an Everglades with coconut trees. A small *resthouse* on the island's west side fronts a sandy beach, from where you can enjoy the sunsets.

Washington lacks the good anchorage of Fanning.

CHRISTMAS ISLAND (KIRITIMATI)
Pincer-shaped Christmas Island (population 3571), transliterated as Kiritimati in Gilbertese, is a paradisiacal playground for visiting sportsfishers, bird-watchers and divers. At 338.9 sq km, Christmas has 48%

KIRIBATI

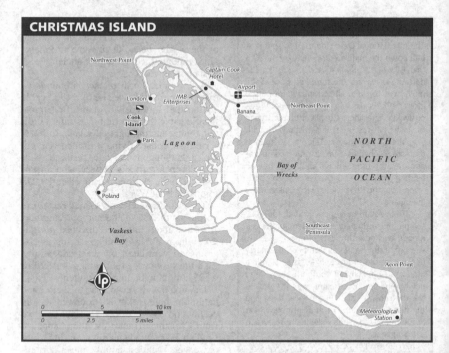

CHRISTMAS ISLAND

Northwest Point

Captain Cook Hotel

Airport

London

JMB Enterprises

Northeast Point

Cook Island

Banana

Paris

Lagoon

NORTH

PACIFIC

Bay of Wrecks

OCEAN

Poland

Vaskess Bay

Southeast Peninsula

Aeon Point

0   5   10 km
0   2.5   5 miles

Meteorological Station

---

of Kiribati's total land area. In terms of land size it's the largest coral atoll in the world, and it is home to 18 bird species and a dazzling variety of fish. The whole island is a wildlife sanctuary.

Captain Cook, who anchored near Cook Island (see Around Christmas Island later) on Christmas Eve in 1777, named the island. In his diary Cook reported a barren, desolate island with only a handful of coconut trees. Coconut plantations were later established, and the island's topography is now a patchwork of coconut palms and desolate flats.

From 1957 to 1959 the British Operation Grapple used the island as a nuclear-testing area. The Americans arrived in 1961, after pulling out of Bikini Atoll, but stayed only one year. Unlike on Bikini, the Christmas Island tests were performed high up from balloons, so that the trade winds swept away all nuclear debris.

The 1997 resumption of weekly Aloha Airlines charter flights from Honolulu has made Christmas easily accessible, and American sportsfishers have heeded the call of the bonefish. However, tourists are not the only newcomers. Most of the I-Kiribati now on Christmas migrated there within the last 30 years. The population almost tripled from 1979 to 1999, and new arrivals continue to arrive from Tarawa and the outer Gilbert Islands.

Thanks to Kiribati's 11th-hour rejigging of the International Date Line, Christmas Island was the fifth place in the world (not including Antarctica) to hail the dawn of the new millennium. Of more lasting import, the Japanese are building facilities for the Hope X landing craft, due to be completed in 2002.

Information

Most government services are in London, at the tip of Christmas Island's northern pincer.

The Ministry of Commerce, Industry & Tourism (☎ 81 198, fax 81 316) runs what could be called a tourist office in London, open from 8 am to 4.15 pm weekdays.

The Fish & Wildlife Service (☎ 81 217, fax 81 278) has an office in the building marked Ministry of Line & Phoenix Development in London. You can obtain permits and information here.

The Bank of Kiribati changes travellers cheques and does Visa and MasterCard cash advances (US$15 commission). Much better rates are available at JMB Enterprises near the Captain Cook Hotel. Some establishments, such as the Mini Hotel, will accept US dollars.

London also has a post office and a telecommunications building for international calls and faxes. Faxes can be received for A$1.50 a page at fax 81 201.

Fees & Restrictions There's an A$35 fishing and diving permit required on Christmas Island. Applications are distributed at the airport upon arrival.

Visitors to any of the four reserve areas, including Cook Island, must obtain a A$10 permit from the Fish & Wildlife Services, which the Captain Cook Hotel can arrange. In real terms, a visit to Cook Island can become costly, as fees for the guide and the boat to visit the restricted areas can run to A$50 or A$100. Negotiate the price ahead of time.

Around Christmas Island
The small town of **London**, home to one-third of Christmas Island's population, has a few small offshore kelp farms near the harbour.

Across the channel, a 20-minute ride south of London by boat, is **Cook Island**, a mecca for nesting birds. To venture onto Cook Island you'll need a permit (see Information earlier) and a guide, otherwise you can get a feel for the thicket of birds by swinging near on a boat.

South of Cook Island, across another channel, is **Paris**, which was named in honour of French priest Father Rougier, who once bought part of Christmas Island. The area is a former coconut plantation.

Heading overland clockwise around the island from London, you come to a run-down **NASDA satellite tracking station** built in 1977 by the Japanese. Further along is the Captain Cook Hotel, built atop the remains of barracks that the British used during their 1959 to 1962 nuclear tests.

Fifteen minutes' drive further is the runway. During the British operations, a three-field runway was constructed; the 7000-foot main runway remains the site of the current airfield.

Continuing south, the long, flat road runs beside the undivable **Bay of Wrecks**, named for the handful of 19th-century square-riggers unwittingly blown into Christmas Island.

At the south-eastern tip of the island, about a two-hour drive from the Captain Cook Hotel, is the **Korean wreck**, which has some nice picnic tables and a beach. Nearby is a meteorological station used in the balloon tests of the 1950s and 60s.

Christmas Island's interior consists largely of desolate flats adorned only by saltbrush, a locus for sportsfishers in pursuit of bonefish. It is very easy to get lost among the rough tracks that skirt the flats. Do not venture in without a guide.

Activities
Fishing Fly fishing is the most popular activity on Christmas Island, the endless flats of which hold enormous bonefish. For package tour information, see the Getting There & Away section later in this chapter.

For off-shore fishing, you'll find tuna, wahoo, billfish and trevally all lurking off the coast of Poland (which is south of Paris). Dive Kiribati (☎/fax 81 139 on Christmas Island, ✉ divekiribati@juno.com, Box 1583, Kaneohe, Hawaii 96744) in London runs a mostly 'catch & release' operation. Half/full-day tours cost US$200/300, including all gear.

Diving & Snorkelling Diving on Christmas Island is outstanding for its variety and sheer numbers of fish. Almost all dives are done in the two coral-rich channels flanking Cook Island, where the reef drops off sharply. The fish are large and divers come away with tales of manta rays, black-tipped and white-tipped sharks, dolphins, stingrays and huge turtles – all sighted between London and Paris! None of the seven square-riggers at the bottom of the temptingly named Bay of Wrecks, on the island's east side, are divable.

Knowledgeable California transplant Kim Andersen, who at the time of writing had been on Christmas seven years, heads up Dive Kiribati (see above for contact details), the island's only dive shop. He and his staff captain the *Spirit of Christmas*, a 380-foot outrigger canoe that holds six to eight divers. Walk-in dives cost US$75/100/120 for a one/two/three-tank dive, tanks and weight belt included; gear technically rents for US$20 more than this but Kim may throw it in for free. Kim is a certified dive chamber operator and has a small dive decompression chamber. See also Organised Tours below for diving options.

Kim rents snorkel gear and knows excellent channel snorkelling spots. For a separate boat it's US$35 per person (with a three-person minimum).

Bird-watching Christmas Island's myriad sea bird colonies include tropicbirds, black noddies, white and grey terns, shearwaters, petrels and boobies. Many cluster on Cook Island, and even offshore the sound of birds is deafening. The savannah-like grassland covering much of Christmas makes an ideal resting place for sooty terns and their predator, the frigate bird. Feral cats have been eradicated.

Organised Tours
Most sportsfishers go through Frontiers in the USA (☎ 1-800-245 1950, 724-935 1577, fax 935 5388, ✆ info@frontierstrvl.com), which has fishing trips with meals and accommodation at the Captain Cook Hotel for US$1785 per person per week, double occupancy. A fishing and diving combo runs to US$1820 per person and a nonfishing nondiving costs US$970 per person (add $127 to all rates for a single person). Not included are the air fare, alcoholic beverages, surcharge for an air-con room or extra guide charges. Diving packages cost US$1600.

Royal Journeys (☎ 1-888-483 5495, 425-483 5495, fax 402 0300) also arranges sportsfishing tours with accommodation and meals at the Captain Cook Hotel. A one-week package, including charter air fare from Honolulu, costs US$2535.

Christmas Island Outfitters (☎ 1-800-694 4162, 804-823 1937, fax 717-281 7121) has fly-fishing tours for US$1995 during summer months, or US$2295 from October to May. The price includes Mini Hotel Kiritimati accommodation and the charter air fare from Honolulu.

Check the refund policy of each company before committing yourself.

Places to Stay
Christmas Island's two hotels tend to fill up in January and February, so travellers should arrange accommodation well in advance. Add a 10% tax to the hotel rates listed below.

Almost all sportsfishers stay at the *Captain Cook Hotel* (☎ 81 230, fax 81 425), about halfway between the airport and London. The hotel, built on the foundations of British military barracks, has 24 clean rooms and six duplex bungalows. Each room has a mini-refrigerator and a jug of drinking water is delivered daily; you can also request a telephone. The hotel is geared towards moneyed Americans, but it's certainly no Hilton – the rooms are pleasant but a bit worn. Singles/doubles in regular rooms cost A$89/119 (minus A$14 for non-air-con rooms); for the bungalows it's A$95/105. Pay for accommodation in cash (Australian dollars).

Beware – if you look rich, the hotel may pull out a very different rate sheet in US dollars at astronomical prices. This hotel gives priority to package visitors.

The *Mini Hotel Kiritimati* (☎ 81 371, fax 81 336) has four basic, dorm-like rooms, each with two single beds and a shared toilet and shower. There's no air-con but there are ceiling fans. The place is clean and the management friendly. A bar shares the building so it could get noisy weekend nights. A kitchen is available for guest use.

Singles/doubles are US$40/50 and the prices are 20% lower from May to October.

Father Bermond (☎ 81 365, 81 251), a French priest who has lived on Christmas for 37 years, runs the *Fare Tony Hostel*, a very basic one-room affair on the grounds of the Catholic church in London. Your payment is a donation to the Catholic church; A$10 to A$20 per night should be a fair price. There is a toilet and shower facility nearby, but there's no kitchen equipment. He will be delighted if you speak French.

The Mitsubishi Corporation is also planning a new hotel for 2002. Contact Mitsubishi (☎ 03-3210 3363, fax 3210 9983) in Japan for the latest developments.

Places to Eat
The tap water on Christmas Island is brackish and unsafe to drink.

Snack items and drinks are available on the second floor at *JMB Enterprises* near the Captain Cook Hotel. The home-made tuna jerky (A$5) makes a fabulous hors d'oeuvre or take-home treat. The store is open from about 8 am to 6 pm daily and the owners live on the premises. The *Mini Store* at the Captain Cook Hotel has a similar selection of goods, plus overpriced fruit. In London try the retail store *Dojin*, next to the Fish Restaurant. Supplies (particularly beer) tend to dwindle before the monthly resupply.

The *Captain Cook Hotel* has a restaurant that serves food from a fixed menu. The fresh fish, a dinner mainstay, is reliably good. Breakfast costs A$10, lunch A$13 and dinner A$20. There are barbecues twice a week and local entertainment is held after dinner some nights. You may be charged more for the lovely Saturday night *luau*, complete with fresh local lobster and after-dinner local dancing. The restaurant is open daily for all meals.

The *Mini Hotel Kiritimati* has a restaurant that's open upon advance request. Meals can be cooked for guests for US$30 per day.

The *Fish Restaurant* in the centre of London is Christmas Island's only nonhotel restaurant. It's a classic local establishment, in a closet-like, rather dingy room. Fair-sized fish and rice plates go for A$2, though you might find the pork and chicken fresher – it's wise to ask. Make any special requests in advance. The restaurant is open from 7 am to 10 pm Monday to Saturday and from 11 am Sunday.

Shopping
The Captain Cook Mini-Store has a few ancient A$0.50 postcards. Father Bermond at the Catholic church near London has a much nicer selection. JMB Enterprises has nice Christmas Island T-shirts and sometimes sells shark-tooth swords.

Many of Christmas Island's finest handicrafts come out only when cruise ships visit. Determined handicraft seekers can contact Kim Andersen at Dive Kiribati, who knows where the island's reclusive handicraft-makers hide away.

Getting There & Away
Air Air Kiribati (in the USA ☎ 1-888-800 8144, 808-839 6680, fax 839 6681) has chartered an Aloha Airlines 737 jet for a weekly service to Christmas Island. The flights are on Tuesday morning Honolulu time (though you arrive Wednesday, due to the date line crossing). An economy-class return fare is US$750. You can pay with a credit card in advance or buy the ticket in cash at the airport.

Visas can be obtained at the airport in Hawai'i immediately before departure; see Visas & Documents in the Regional Facts for the Visitor chapter.

Boat Christmas' shallow channel is not good for large boats. WKK Shipping Line (in Betio ☎ 26 352, fax 26 007) sends boats to Christmas Island from Tarawa four to five times annually; a spot on deck costs A$149 one way, double for a cabin. Fern Store (☎ 26 596) in Betio also sends boats to Christmas from Tarawa.

Getting Around
A van from the Captain Cook Hotel meets all arriving flights. Mini Hotel guests

KIRIBATI

should arrange in advance for an airport transfer (US$20 return).

One minibus drives between London and Banana – most reliably during working hours. The price is A$1. Hitchhiking is easy – if you see a car.

JMB Enterprises (☎ 81 501, fax 81 505) rents vehicles to nonfishers for US$60 per day or US$350 per week. For fishers the price is US$95 per day or US$120 per day with a driver and guide. Rates at Dojin store

(☎ 81 110, fax 81 321) in London are more reasonable at A$50 per day for a pick-up with a house structure in back, plus A$15 for insurance. The Mini Hotel Kiritimati (☎ 81 371) also has pick-up trucks starting at US$60 per day. Petrol is about A$0.70 a litre.

JMB Enterprises sometimes rents bikes for US$5 per day. Try also at Dojin.

Boat hire can be arranged through the Mini Hotel Kiritimati. Rental costs US$600 per week, but call them for the daily rate.

Nauru

Just 18km in circumference, potato-shaped Nauru discovered early this century that guano brings Western powers a-courting – in droves. High-grade phosphate on Nauru was found accidentally in 1900, which ignited over half a century of scuffling among Germany, Australia, New Zealand and Britain, all of whom wanted a cut of the riches. When Nauru gained its long-sought independence in 1968, the government-owned Nauru Phosphate Corporation (NPC) took the helm at the mines and Nauru became one of the richest per capita nations in the world. Annual phosphate exports soared to two million tons, much of it going to Australia or New Zealand for fertiliser. Today, the phosphate industry remains the basis of Nauru's economy, but the long-term outlook is grim: Nauru's phosphate resources are expected to be exhausted within 20 years, leaving the island's interior a treeless moonscape of coral pinnacles and its once-wealthy population clinging to the coast. Regardless, this sunny island nation makes for an interesting one-day visit – to view the towering phosphate works, WWII relics, and most of all the unique island itself.

HIGHLIGHTS

- Coral moonscape – the fascinating, bizarre, bleached moonscape that will remain long after the phosphate has gone
- Phosphate works – the mammoth machinery that once made Nauru's people among the richest in the world

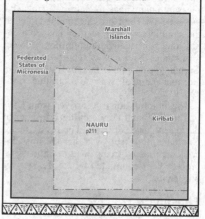

Facts about Nauru

HISTORY
Early Settlers
Very little is known about Nauru's early history as there are no written records, but Nauruans are believed to be of Polynesian and Micronesian descent, a hybrid of Gilbertese, Carolinians and Marshallese. Traditional Nauruan society was made up of 12 tribes; some bore the names of Nauru's marine life, such as Eamwit (eel) and Deboe (a small black reef fish). Two tribes, the Iwi and the Iruti, died out in the first half of the 20th century. The Eamwit tribe, from which Nauru's last queen came, were the island's most powerful.

Nauru's tribes were matrilineal, with children belonging to the tribe of their mother. Each tribe developed its own songs, legends and crafts.

Nauruans have always had a strong belief in private ownership. Even the reef and the sea beyond it were owned, though this belief came to lose currency in the 20th century.

European Contact
In 1798, British captain John Fearn, sailing between New Zealand and China aboard the *Hunter*, spotted Nauru and, in a burst of originality, named it 'Pleasant Island' because of the 'pleasant appearance and manner of its inhabitants'. Starting in the 1830s, European whaling boats passed through and used the island to stock up on supplies.

Some Europeans remained and intermarried with Nauruans.

Within half a century of the European influx, traditional society began to disintegrate. Using European guns, the 12 Nauruan tribes collapsed into a civil war in 1878. After 10 years of battle, Nauru's population was reduced by 40%, to 900 people.

In 1886 Nauru was given to Germany under the auspices of the Berlin Anglo-German Convention. German administrators, who changed the island's name from Pleasant Island back to Nauru, began arriving in 1888. Their presence helped quench the smouldering war, as they banned alcohol and confiscated ammunition. Eleven years later Nauru was incorporated into Germany's Marshall Islands Protectorate. German control was to continue until WWI.

The first missionaries arrived from Kiribati in 1887 and they continued to pour in during the next 30 years. The result, many Nauruans now feel, was that the missionaries suppressed many local traditions – a process later completed by the frenzy over phosphate.

Phosphate

Nauru's phosphate was created tens of thousands of years ago by guano deposited by birds, some species of which may now be extinct. Periodic geological submergence of the island washed away the phosphate's impurities and left 85% pure phosphate lime. The phosphate resembles light brown soil or rock and is found in cavities between pinnacles of coral.

Phosphate prospectors who combed the Western Pacific during the 19th century and found small deposits on islands such as Peleliu and Angaur in Palau and Howland and Baker in the unincorporated US territories discounted Nauru as a phosphate site. Nauru's German administrators gave Jaluit Gesellschaft, the large German trading conglomerate, the right to probe Nauru's guano deposits but it turned up nothing. The Germans were stunned in 1900 when Albert Ellis of the Pacific Islands Company found

Dream Doorstop

Albert Ellis, a geologist with the Pacific Islands Company, wrote later of his discovery, 'My attention was arrested by a large block of rock used for keeping open the door of the laboratory. In some ways it resembled a rare kind of phosphate rock ... I was told it was a lump of "petrified wood" found on Pleasant Island (Nauru) some three years previously, and that one or more geologists had agreed as to its nature. This seemed decisive enough, but somehow when working in the laboratory, the piece of rock repeatedly attracted my attention and some three months afterwards the thought occurred "Why not test it?" A chip was knocked off, ground up and tested for phosphate with such a decided reaction that a complete analysis was made, and the humble doorstop proved to be phosphate of the highest quality.'

high-grade calcium phosphate on Nauru and its neighbour, Banaba (Ocean Island; now in Kiribati).

Tranquil Nauru was suddenly transformed into a businessmen's battleground. The Pacific Islands Company, shortly to be renamed the Pacific Phosphate Company, obtained the right to mine phosphate on Nauru in 1901. But when the German administrators awoke to the riches beneath them, they stalled for several years while negotiating their way into PIC shares and per-ton royalties.

Mining operations commenced in 1906, but it was not an auspicious beginning: Loaded with almost 2000 tons of phosphate, the ill-fated SS *Fido*, Nauru's first phosphate ship, foundered off the coast of New South Wales, Australia, in 1907. It was Nauru's only phosphate shipment ever to sink.

By the end of 1907 over 11,500 tons of phosphate – all mined by pick, shovel and sweat – had been loaded onto ships to Australia. In 1908 the overhead cableways were installed to transport the mined phosphate to the phosphate train, which in turn delivered it to the crushers and dryers.

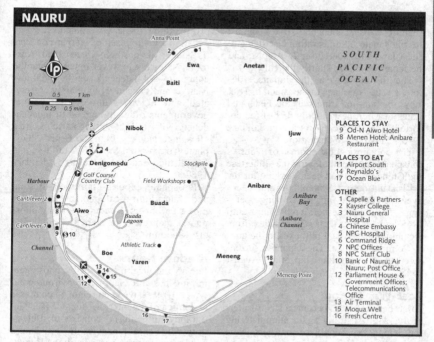

NAURU

SOUTH
PACIFIC
OCEAN

PLACES TO STAY
9 Od-N Aiwo Hotel
18 Menen Hotel; Anibare
  Restaurant

PLACES TO EAT
11 Airport South
14 Reynaldo's
17 Ocean Blue

OTHER
1 Capelle & Partners
2 Kayser College
3 Nauru General
  Hospital
4 Chinese Embassy
5 NPC Hospital
6 Command Ridge
7 NPC Offices
8 NPC Staff Club
10 Bank of Nauru; Air
   Nauru; Post Office
12 Parliament House &
   Government Offices;
   Telecommunications
   Office
13 Air Terminal
15 Moqua Well
16 Fresh Centre

WWI

When hostilities broke out in 1914, Nauru's German administrators declared a state of martial law and deported their British ex-colleagues to Banaba, where the British colonisers maintained a healthy phosphate operation. But when the HMAS *Melbourne* sailed into Nauru in November 1914 it was the 23 Germans' turn to be deported. They were sent to Australia and the German shares of the British Phosphate Commission were auctioned off in London for £600,000. The British exiles returned and the mining resumed, using Chinese and Pacific island labour.

At the war's end, Australia, New Zealand and Great Britain, after some bickering, agreed to joint trusteeship of Nauru under the League of Nations. An Australian commissioner was appointed to run the island, while Britain and New Zealand retained voices on the board of administrators. The three countries jointly established the British Phosphate Commission (BPC); Australia and Great Britain were given rights to 42% of the phosphate and New Zealand 16 percent. To accommodate soaring post-war demand, Nauru's first cantilever was built in 1930 off the west coast. Fed by a wide conveyor belt, the cantilever's huge swinging arms were able to load the phosphate much quicker than before, and phosphate exports subsequently rose by a third.

WWII

On 6 December 1940 the Germans sank four ships off the coast of Nauru. Three weeks later they were back and heavily shelled the phosphate works. Though the cantilever survived the attack, the adjacent fuel storage tanks were hit and burst into flames. The heat of the burning oil caused the steel bin that fed the cantilever to collapse.

In August 1942 the island again came under attack, this time from the Japanese.

Nine Japanese planes bombed Nauru and offshore cruisers launched strikes against the phosphate administration's settlement. The island surrendered on 24 August, and the Japanese landed shortly thereafter.

The following year, the Japanese deported 1200 Nauruans to the island of Truk (now the state of Chuuk in the Federated States of Micronesia). Only 737 of the deportees were alive to return in January 1946; many died of starvation.

The Japanese took control of Nauru's phosphate works, employing the Gilbertese and Chinese who had been working for the British, but daily US bombing raids effectively scuttled the Japanese mining operations. The Japanese held onto Nauru until 1945; evidence of their stay remains, from the ubiquitous coastal pillboxes to the guns at Command Ridge. The Japanese surrendered to an Australian ship on 21 August 1945.

Post-War Period

After the war, Nauru became a UN trust territory, with Australia again administering the island on behalf of partners New Zealand and Great Britain. Nauru's local population had been decimated, particularly by the deportations to Truk – according to an Australian census, Nauruans accounted for only 591 of the 5200 people on Nauru after the war.

The phosphate works underwent major repairs and the cantilever became operational again in 1949. Phosphate exports rose again, so that in the period 1950 to 1964 Nauru accounted for 60% of Australia's total phosphate. More Gilbertese and Ellice Islanders came to work the mines, and a second cantilever was built in 1960.

Independence

As it groped toward independence in the mid-20th century, Nauru entertained a series of local governing structures: a Council of Chiefs was formed in 1927; it was replaced in 1951 by the Nauru Local Government Council. Though neither had real power, the symbolism of self-government resonated with the people.

Foreseeing the end of the phosphate supply, the three partner governments drew up a plan in 1964 to resettle Nauruans on Curtis Island, off northern Queensland, Australia. Nauruans, however, opted to steer the course toward independence. In 1965, legislative and executive councils were created, and in 1967 Nauru and the partner governments officially agreed to independence. NPC bought the rights to Nauru's phosphate industry from the British Phosphate Commission for US$21 million, and formal independence came on 31 January 1968.

Phosphate exports continued to soar, and Nauru built a calcination plant to remove carbon and cadmium from phosphate marketed to Japan, India and elsewhere in Asia.

Modern Nauru

For all the wealth brought by phosphate, mining has left Nauru an environmental wreck. Trees have been removed en masse and much of the interior – topside (see Geography following) – consists of lifeless, grey-white coral pinnacles. In 1989 Nauru filed a suit against Australia in the Hague-based International Court of Justice for the damages caused by mining while the island was under Australian jurisdiction. In 1993 the suit was settled out of court for A$109 million; part of the agreement binds Australia to assist Nauru with rehabilitation and development. Ironically, Nauru itself has followed the same path toward environmental destruction, and mining operations are expected to continue until the phosphate runs out in 10 to 20 years.

GEOGRAPHY

Forty-two kilometres south of the equator, Nauru is a stunning sight from the air – an isolated blot on the blue seascape, with an interior of blazing white rock ('topside' or 'phosphate land'), a narrow coastal fringe ('coconut land') and an encircling coral reef. Nauru's total land area is 21.3 square kilometres; its highest point, along Command Ridge, rises 65 metres above sea level. Most of the population hugs the coast, where the coconut trees offer shade.

There is a small lagoon, Buada Lagoon, tucked in the centre of Nauru that once teemed with milkfish, but a fish called *taripia* killed them all. Now stone walls mark out plots where families have established milkfish farms.

Nauru's closest neighbour is Kiribati's Banaba, 307km to the east, which also has been a centre for phosphate mining.

GEOLOGY

Nauru's interior is a parched sea of jagged, white, coral pinnacles, some towering up to 15m high. Before it was mined, the phosphate was deposited between blocks of corals. When the phosphate was extracted, the coral pinnacles were exposed. Removal of the pinnacles may provide an opportunity for secondary mining: There is still up to 10% more phosphate lurking in the troughs between the pinnacles, but the mining machinery cannot scoop deep enough to get it.

With the end of phosphate fast approaching, Nauru is also considering the viability of marketing crushed coral, which can be used as aggregate for the construction of roads, buildings and airstrips. If Nauru ever wants to rehabilitate its mined-out land, the coral pinnacles will have to be removed anyway.

A Sad Legacy

The phosphate mining industry has wreaked havoc on Nauru's climate. Deforestation – the precursor to surface mining – has exposed bare white coral rock, which reflects the sun's rays back upwards and, in turn, chases away the clouds and rain. This is called the 'oven effect'. If you take a close look at the phosphate pinnacles, you can distinguish between the new pinnacles (white) and the ones that were mined a while back (grey).

Most indigenous birds, including the rapidly disappearing frigate birds (Nauru's national symbol) and beloved noddies, are dying out as a result of the deforestation.

CLIMATE

Nauru's climate is tropical – hot and humid but tempered by sea breezes. North-east trade winds blow from March to October, and westerly winds may bring more rain from November to February. Nauru's average rainfall is 206cm; its average shade temperature is 24.4°C.

GOVERNMENT & POLITICS

Nauru joined the British Commonwealth on 1 May, 1999. The country applies a Westminster-style parliamentary system to one of the world's smallest parliaments. Eighteen MPs are elected from eight regions; representation is roughly apportioned by population. The parliament, elected every three years, then elects a president who remains a member of parliament. The president in turn taps four or five MPs as his cabinet ministers.

Voting is mandatory for all Nauruans over 20, and the next election is scheduled for February 2000. As dissatisfaction grows over the government's poor investment record and retrenchments (see the Economy section following), so too does political turmoil. In April 1999 the government of five-term president, Bernard Dowiyogo, was forced to step down because of a no-confidence vote, and a new president was appointed in his place. In 1997 the situation was so bad that Nauru churned through four presidents in as many months.

Nauru recently had a female MP, Ruby Dediya, but she was voted out of office in 1997.

The government used to own everything but is slowly 'privatising' or 'corporatising' its holdings. It relinquished ownership of Air Nauru in 1998 but still owns the NPC. Roughly 1600 Nauruans work for the government and 1400 work for the phosphate industry.

ECONOMY

Phosphate has been Nauru's sole export and source of revenue since the turn of the century. As annual phosphate exports reached two million tons in the heyday of the late 20th century the island became rich. Many of the rich were landowners, who received a cut of the profits from leasing their land to the mining companies.

But in the early 1990s, a slumping demand for phosphate from Australia and New Zealand, coupled with ageing equipment and the recognition that phosphate supplies would soon be exhausted, caused Nauru's exports to fall gradually to their current annual level of 500,000 tons. At more than A$60 a ton, phosphate remains a tremendously lucrative industry. However, even the most optimistic estimates predict that Nauru's phosphate supplies will be exhausted in 20 years.

In preparation for the post-phosphate world, the government of Nauru invested a hefty proportion of mining proceeds. Those investments have been a case study in financial mismanagement. From ill-timed real estate investments in Melbourne and Honolulu to several million squandered on a London musical, the government has earned the ire of private citizens. Its banks are so critically low on cash that the government has sometimes lagged in wage payments to its workers.

In March 1999 the government began a program of retrenchment, laying off over 400 workers as part of a cost-cutting operation. Retrenchment will further complicate the already murky political terrain: The government leases all of its land from private landowners, who may well be among the very people the government retrenched!

To add to Nauru's woes, a task force from the Organization for Economic Cooperation and Development recently named Nauru as one of four Pacific island countries that were laundering Russian Mafia funds.

In recent years the government has been scrambling to diversify Nauru's economy. A major new fish market is being built on Nauru's west side. A further boost in the fishing arena may come from Japan, which plans to fund a new harbour on Anibare Bay north of the Menen Hotel. This would provide harbour access from the calmer of Nauru's two channels. Revenue from international fishing licences sold to Japan, the

USA, Taiwan and the Philippines brings in A$2.8 million annually. The licences offer up the right to fish in Nauru's waters, which extend in a roughly 320km radius around the island.

Another glimmer of hope came in spring 1999, when the Asian Development Bank pledged a multi-million dollar loan to Nauru. Tourism as yet is nonexistent.

POPULATION & PEOPLE

Nauru's population was estimated in 1999 to be 11,300, up from 9920 in 1992. This indicates a 2% growth rate, which is alarming for an island so small. Over 70% are Nauruans, with the balance comprised of other Pacific islanders, Asians (predominantly Chinese and Filipinos) and a few Europeans. The Gilbertese and the Ellice Islanders comprise the majority of unskilled workers for the phosphate industry, while the Chinese, originally brought to work on the mines, tend to be carpenters or restaurateurs. Most Nauruans are of Polynesian or Micronesian descent; Polynesian characteristics predominate.

The Boe district by the north end of the airport is the most populous of Nauru's 14 districts.

Nauru has had more exposure to Western products than most Pacific island nations, and health problems such as diabetes are correspondingly severe. Most Nauruans live in houses that are quite modern by Micronesian standards.

SOCIETY & CONDUCT

As elsewhere in Micronesia, celebrations such as birthdays are important. The night before a birthday, friends and family sing and give gifts to the celebrant at midnight. On the actual birthday, the person typically hosts a party and, if the birthday is a milestone such as 21 or 50, gives gifts such as T-shirts or cups inscribed with the date of birth.

Land ownership has traditionally been very important to Nauruans and can be the source of intra-family feuds, particularly given the current high birth rate.

Nauruans are fanatical about Australian Rules football. The Nauruan season follows the Australian schedule as closely as possible, starting in April and ending in September. There are seven teams on Nauru that compete among themselves and on occasion internationally. The oval in Ewa district on the north end of the island hosts the games every Saturday afternoon, while children have games there Saturday mornings.

Another Nauruan forte is weightlifting – not illogical because Nauruans tend to be on the hefty side. Watch for signs around the island, particularly at the government complex, for the next competition. Weightlifting events are held at Centennial Hall opposite the Congregational Church.

Last but not least, prepare to encounter Nauruan time: Everything operates well behind schedule – and nobody minds.

RELIGION
Most Nauruans are Christians, with a fairly even split between Catholics and Protestants.

LANGUAGE
Nauru's language, like its people, is a unique blend of Polynesian and Micronesian. Some German words have filtered in from Protectorate days and English numbers are used for counting. Though official government transactions are recorded in English, most telephone discussions among government officials are conducted in Nauruan, and most Nauruans are bilingual.

Facts for the Visitor

ORIENTATION
One day is plenty to see the main points of interest on Nauru – the phosphate works, the dramatic interior coral pinnacles and Command Ridge.

A paved 18km road circles the island's coast. The main road into the interior branches off near the NPC buildings. Smaller roads of crushed coral, used for mining, criss-cross Nauru's interior. Some of the roads may be impassable since the

machines surface-mine them as they pull out. The airport lies on the south-west corner of the island, directly across the runway from the government offices. A paved road makes a 3km circle around the runway, which cannot be crossed. Most of Nauru's services, such as the post office and bank, cluster just north of the runway; the NPC offices are just north beyond that.

TOURIST OFFICES
There is an Office of Culture & Tourism on the second floor of the government complex.

VISAS & DOCUMENTS
For visa information see Visas & Travel Permits in the Regional Facts for the Visitor chapter. The Nauru immigration office (☎ 444 3165) is in the government complex. If you have arranged a meeting, allot at least an extra half-hour for the proper official to show up.

MONEY
Nauru's official currency is the Australian dollar (exchange rates are given under Money in the Regional Facts for the Visitor chapter). Only Air Nauru and the hotels accept credit cards. The cash-strapped Bank of Nauru has difficulty changing money and travellers cheques, so bring sufficient Australian dollars into the country.

POST & COMMUNICATIONS
There is no postal code. The international telephone code is ☎ 674 and there are no telephone area codes. For 24-hour directory assistance, dial ☎ 444 3197. For international calls, dial ☎ 00.

Internet & Email Access
The excellent Air Nauru Web site (www.airnauru.com.au) notwithstanding, currently there is no place to access the Internet in Nauru. However, a Nauru server (www.cenpa.net.nr) has just been created.

INTERNET RESOURCES
See Internet Resources in the Facts for the Visitor chapter for information on Nauru-related Web sites.

MEDIA

The *Bulletin*, a government-issued news leaflet, comes out every two weeks and is very difficult to find. Nauru has a government-owned TV station, NTV, which plays mostly live CNN and some movies. Nauru's other channel is the brand-new Sports Pacific Network (SPN), which was popularised during the 1998 Micronesian games in Palau. The sole radio station is the government-owned 1323 AM. And don't forget about the 'coconut wireless', the gossip chain that transmits all news, great and small, with lightning speed across this small island.

LAUNDRY

The hotels can do your laundry for you for a surcharge; otherwise take your laundry to one of the innumerable shacks with a sign Wash & Iron; they'll do your laundry in one day for up to A$0.50 an item.

DANGERS & ANNOYANCES

Swimming can be dangerous on Nauru due to the strong currents around the island.

Dogs, too, can be a hazard. See Running under Activities later in this chapter.

PUBLIC HOLIDAYS & SPECIAL EVENTS

Nauru celebrates the following public holidays:

New Year's Day 1 January
Independence Day 31 January
Easter Sunday, Monday and Tuesday in late April
Constitution Day 17 May
Angam Day 26 October
Christmas Day 25 December

On Independence Day there is an early-morning fishing competition, with prizes for the largest catch or the widest variety of fish caught. Angam ('Homecoming') Day commemorates the day in 1932 when the birth of a baby girl boosted Nauru's population to 1500. This was regarded as an important landmark in the battle for survival of the Nauruan race, which had just been decimated by an influenza epidemic. A sec-ond Angam Day, on 31 March 1949, was celebrated when the 1500 mark was achieved once more after WWII's devastation. Angam Day celebrations are marked by family feasts and gatherings, which often include the traditional Nauruan card game *eporeitid*.

The Nauru Arts Festival, held 8 August at Centennial Hall, features dance, poetry, crafts, painting and carving.

ACTIVITIES

Diving & Snorkelling

There are currently no dive shops on Nauru; diving would be quite dodgy anyway due to the reef's sharp drop-off. In any case, the fish aren't as exciting as elsewhere in Micronesia. Snorkellers might be able to tag along with a sportsfishing boat (see below). A very limited selection of scuba and snorkel gear is available at Capelle & Partner; don't count on a complete set.

Swimming

Swim only with great caution in Nauru; strong currents can create sudden surges and sweep you away from the shore. That said, there are three primary swimming areas – the Gabab Harbour, the Anibare Channel north of the Menen Hotel, and another channel off Boe district north of the airport. Beware of currents, and don't swim beyond waist deep.

If you go swimming in the harbour you may be offered a fish from a returning fisherman – it's Nauruan custom. Keep tabs on the wind and the current in the harbour because there's a sewage outlet not far away.

You'll see occasional reef-walkers behind the Menen Hotel collecting octopuses, periwinkles and reef fish; if you venture out to join them, be sure to wear shoes or thongs (flip-flops) because the rocks are sharp and there are stinging jellyfish.

Tennis

The Menen Hotel has two tennis courts, one of which is in reasonable shape, but you'll have to ferret out your own gear as they have no rackets or balls. Two community

Noddy Hunting

Grilled noddy is a particular Nauruan delicacy, and hunting black noddy birds is a popular pastime in the Topside area. There's a bit of an art to the hunting expedition. Hunters don camouflage clothing and head out to Topside after dark. In earlier times they would make noddy-like whistles; now, in the era of modern technology, they take stereo systems with pre-recorded noddy songs. Hearing their own songs attracts the birds, and the hunters are able to snag them using a net at the end of a long bamboo stick.

After they are caught, the noddies are shaken so that they cough up any food they have ingested; then their neck is bitten or wrung. After being taken home and feathered, the birds are barbecued. If you are in Nauru long enough and make friends with the locals, you may be invited to go noddy hunting – though it is banned during mating season in October and November.

tennis courts with night lighting are located near the NPC buildings. It's difficult to get a court, however, as they are monopolised by the nearby school in the afternoons and by locals in the evenings.

Golf

Nauru has one nine-hole golf course on the west side; there's an annual charge for members but none for foreigners. Technically a member is supposed to invite you, but if you walk into the clubhouse you'll make friends anyway and be invited. There is no golf equipment for rent, so you'll need to arrange to borrow someone's gear.

Running

Nauru is in many ways a jogger's dream – a flat circle road by the seaside with an occasional stiff sea breeze. Locals don't see many runners and will gawk or wave hello. The dogs, however, are worrisome; they can spring out of nowhere and can be vicious. When walking around the island, too, it's best to wear long pants in case of dog attack.

Sportsfishing

Nauru's waters are good for catching marlin, yellowfin tuna, skipjack, wahoos, and more; contact the Oppenheimer family at Capelle & Partner (☎ 555 6333, fax 555 6477). The boat can be chartered for A$90 an hour, which isn't too steep if you fish with a couple of buddies. For longer outings they'll bring along some food and drink and snorkel equipment. Sometimes the Oppenheimers let rooms at Capelle & Partner to people who are chartering the boat.

Getting There & Away

AIR
Airports & Airlines

Nauru has a clean, modern airport with restrooms, phones and a snack bar with hot sandwiches – though for a more wholesome meal try Reynaldo's next door (see Places to Eat later in this chapter). There are also a currency exchange booth, a post office and a VIP lounge, none of which reliably opens for flights.

Air Nauru is the only airline serving Nauru and has earned a reputation for reliability. It has one jet, a Boeing 737-400, that flies on separate routes to Fiji and Tarawa (twice a week); Brisbane and Melbourne (once a week); Pohnpei, Guam and Manila (once a week). Economy fares from Melbourne are A$875; from Brisbane A$817; from Guam A$673; from Guam A$622. Excursion fares are generally quite reasonable; A$325 to Tarawa, for example, and A$470 to Fiji.

There are, curiously, separate but adjacent Air Nauru offices in town. The spiffier one (☎ 444 3141) is on the second floor of the post office building; the other (☎ 444 3218) is at the back of the civic centre, across from the supermarket. The main office, the spiffy one, is open weekdays from 9 am to 5 pm; the smaller office is open Monday to Saturday from 8:30 am to noon and Monday to Friday from 1:30 to 4:30 pm. There is also an airport counter (☎ 444

3218) open for flights. The main office accepts American Express cards.

SEA
At time of writing Nauru did not have a harbour, but a small new harbour, for which there may be fees and regulations, is planned in Anibare. Contact the harbourmaster (☎ 555 4189) for details.

Getting Around

TO/FROM THE AIRPORT
Both hotels send vans to meet arriving planes. Hotel vans taking passengers to departing flights leave the hotel two hours before departure time.

CAR
Unfortunately none of the car rental agencies has hourly rates. The Menen Hotel has two cars for rent at A$50 a day. Kinza Clodumar (☎ 444 3856), one of Nauru's string of former presidents, runs PPH Budget Car Rentals, which has 4WDs for A$35 to A$45 a day. Jeremiah's (☎ 555 4385) has cars for A$75 to A$85 a day, and Kogo's Car Rentals may have a good deal – ask around.

Petrol costs 75 cents a litre. As it is sometimes rationed, there can be long lines at petrol stations; try to arrange to pay for the petrol rather than refill the tank.

Many Nauruans get around by scooter; ask around at your hotel and you may find someone willing to rent you one.

TAXI
The only two taxis on Nauru roost at the Menen Hotel, which owns them. They are metered; a trip around the island costs about A$16.

HITCHING
Hitching is not common because most people have transportation of their own – cars or motor scooters. Nonetheless people are friendly and may pick you up if you're walking in the hot sun; a plaintive wave never hurts.

ORGANISED TOURS
The Od-N Aiwo Hotel offers its van for tours for A$10; the Menen Hotel sends guests around in its taxis and may, if you insist, come up with a more formal tour. Nauruans are not used to giving tours, and it's up to you to take the initiative by asking questions and telling the driver where you want to go.

The tourist office also keeps a notebook entitled *Nauru: Educational Visits Guide*, which lists a range of tours (mostly free) of the island. These range from an airfield tour to a fisheries tour; contact the tourist bureau for information well in advance. A group is generally preferred.

For a tour of the phosphate mines, contact the NPC offices (☎ 555 4209) directly; they should be willing to briefly take you around.

Around Nauru

ORIENTATION
Maps
The Lands Department near the NPC headquarters sells a nice poster-size map of Nauru for A$20. The Menen Hotel puts a colourful sketch-map into its welcome packet for guests, and the Od-N Aiwo Hotel has a map available upon request.

INFORMATION
Tourist Offices
Julie Olsson, the Director of Culture & Tourism (☎ 444 3292, fax 444 3791) in the Ministry of Internal Affairs, has a small office on the second floor of the government complex. She has the keys to the NPC museum and the Arts & Crafts Centre and can help arrange tours. She can be quite difficult to reach, however. Be persistent. The office is open weekdays from 9 am to 5 pm, with a lunch break from 1 to 2 pm.

MONEY
The hotels exchange money at roughly 10% lower than the international rate; if you arrive late on a flight or during a holiday, you'll be fleeced. It's best to have Australian currency with you anyway as the Bank of Nauru faces a chronic cash

shortage and will change only US$200 maximum in traveller's cheques. Service is languid at best; someone may promise to help you and then vanish into a back room. Banking hours are Monday to Thursday from 9 am to 3 pm and Friday from 9 am to 4.30 pm. Credit cards are accepted by the Air Nauru office and the two hotels.

POST & COMMUNICATIONS

The post office in Aiwo district is open weekdays from 9 am to 4.30 pm. A letter to the US costs 90 cents (10 cents less to Australia). Nauru's philatelic bureau is here and has some nice stamps. The post office also has two international phones and a fax machine.

International telephone calls can be made 24 hours a day from the five phones inside the rather dismal telecommunications office, which lies directly across the runway from the airport and has a satellite dish outside. The per-minute rate to Australia, New Zealand, Kiribati and Palau is A$2; to the USA, FSM, Guam and the Northern Mariana Islands it's A$4.50; and to Britain it's A$5.50. There is a three-minute minimum charge; you avoid this if you call internationally from the hotels.

The post office also has two international phones, though they charge a A$0.50 per minute commission in addition to the regular rate. Faxes can be sent from here (for the

Ragow Pinnacle

The largest coral pinnacle on Anibare Beach has a secret. If you find the pinnacle, which is across the road from the church, go around to its rear side. Where there is an indentation press your face to the rock and look up, and you'll see a cylindrical hole. According to legend, ancient giant Nauruans used this hole to test the coconut palm trunks that they used for weapons. They would jam the palms against the rock to make sure they did not break, thus creating the hole. For that reason the pinnacle is named *ragow* pinnacle – ragow being the Nauruan word for weapon.

price of an international call) and received, for A$2 a page, to fax 444 3201.

LIBRARIES

The NPC library opens spotty hours. The University of the South Pacific (USP) library is open weekdays until 6 pm.

MEDICAL SERVICES

Nauru has two hospitals – the Nauru Phosphate Corporation Hospital (☎ 555 4155) and the Nauru General Hospital (☎ 555 4302). The NPC hospital is the better choice, particularly when it comes to after-hours care as the nurses live just up the hill.

EMERGENCY

The police emergency number is ☎ 110. For an ambulance dial ☎ 118 or 117, for fire ☎ 119.

THINGS TO SEE
Command Ridge

Command Ridge, where the Japanese kept watch in the 1940s, is the highest point on Nauru and still holds WWII guns, though some were taken by Nauru's commonwealth administrators after the war and a few others are in the NPC museum.

To get to Command Ridge, take the road inland from Aiwo toward Buada lagoon. Go down to Buada, turn left at the first dirt road and turn left at the end of this road, crossing the railway tracks. Follow that road as far as you can; it's not well maintained, so if you're in a rental car you might not want to risk it. Continue on foot, turning left at the three large water tanks near where the road ends. Just past the tanks, in the bushes off to the right of the path, is the first small rusted gun.

WWII Relics

Not much further along, also off to the right, is a **bunker** with a metal pipe still sticking out. The pipe was used for communications purposes. You can enter this bunker if you have a flashlight or lantern and if you look closely you'll see some Japanese writing. Near the bunker, though heavily obscured, is a **13mm gun mounting**.

Further along off to the right is a large ro-tating **six-barrel gun**, and about 150m be-yond the first big gun, among some rubbish, is a second one. These guns could fire 90-pound shells. Some of the muzzles were damaged by the Australians.

A **square well** is off to the left along the trail to the big guns, well hidden in the bushes.

Besides Command Ridge, a web of smaller **shelters** and **cliff-top gun nests** cir-cle the island, particularly on the west side. It's best to ask the tourist bureau to help find you a guide.

Japanese bunkers, visible from the road, are spaced fairly evenly along the coastline.

Government Complex

The government complex across the run-way from the airport on the west side is worth a visit. Watch for a sign announcing 'Parliament in Session' – that's your cue to join the viewers in the parliament. The de-bates tend to get quite contentious as Nauru's leadership writhes under the eco-nomic squeeze.

Above the airport are eight British-built single-shot, six-inch **naval guns** from the early 20th century. More guns are on the cliffs inland from Kayser College, but you can't see them from below.

Phosphate Works

The two giant **cantilevers**, one by the Od-N Aiwo Hotel and the other near the NPC of-fices, are an impressive sight; their power-ful arms help speed up ship-loading, which otherwise would be tricky given Nauru's prohibitive reefs. Cantilever 1 is no longer functioning.

To view the phosphate works in Nauru's interior, head up the road branching inland near the first cantilever. Take a right at the major intersection (a left will take you to Buada Lagoon), and follow the road until you reach the **Stockpile** of topsoil and wait-ing phosphate. This is a good place to take a look at Nauru's coral pinnacle moon-scape. If you look toward the south-west, you may notice that the landscape looks vaguely striped; this denotes the area where

phosphate was mined in the early days, with pick and shovel rather than modern ma-chinery.

Just below the stockpile is a **crushing plant**, where the phosphate is reduced to pellet-size pieces and shuttled to the train waiting nearby. The trains run back to the cantilevers; the total track distance is about 5km.

Back in town near the NPC offices is a **drying plant**, where the phosphate is heated and tossed to remove the moisture. This is done because buyers want phosphate with no more than 3% moisture. If you venture into this plant, bring a handkerchief – it can be mighty dusty! Like other parts of the phosphate works, the drying plant is only half used; the cutbacks since the golden days of phosphate means that only three of the six machines need to be used.

A **calcination plant** nearby was built shortly after Nauru's 1968 independence, when Nauru was trying to expand its phos-phate clientele beyond Australia and New Zealand. Impurities were melted out of the phosphate, which had to be 99% pure, by roasting it at 1000°C.

The NPC head office served as the Japanese wartime headquarters and was damaged only slightly during WWII shelling.

Nauru Phosphate Corporation Museum

The NPC museum in Aiwo district is one of Micronesia's best. The ambitious one-room museum features colonial-era cannons, a large Japanese cannon, and a plethora of other artefacts from WWII and the 20th cen-tury – old bottles, bullets, shell cases, Japan-ese pottery, and innumerable black-and-white photos (including one of Albert Ellis' porten-tous doorstop). The only drawback is that the museum is not normally open: Contact the Director of Culture & Tourism (see Informa-tion earlier in this chapter) for the key.

Arts & Crafts Centre

Heaped with a variety of crafts, the Arts & Crafts Centre is as much a swan song to a dying tradition as a cultural display.

Baskets, stone tools, fishing nets, an old pandanus grater, and *ingurig* (grass skirts made from hibiscus) are among the fine collection. Only a handful of Nauruans still know how to make these treasures. Contact the Director of Culture & Tourism (see Information earlier in this chapter) for the key.

PLACES TO STAY

Camping is not an option as all land on Nauru is privately owned. Nauru's two hotels both have plenty of space and send vans to the airport, so no reservations are necessary unless you need a document to present to immigration upon arrival (see Visas & Travel Permits in the Regional Facts for the Visitor chapter).

The government-owned **Menen Hotel** (☎ *444 3300, fax 444 3595*), on the coast 4km east of the airport, is the best-value hotel in all of Micronesia. Standard rooms are immaculate, with wooden desk, two single beds, good air-con and ceiling fan, glass shower recess, porch, phone and TV (no cable), and coffee and tea-making facilities. There's also a swimming pool but it's not likely to be full. Even if you're a budget traveller, it's worth the mini-splurge to stay here and soak up the comforts. Standard rooms are A$85/120 for singles/doubles, ocean view rooms are A$115/140 and suites are A$230. Couples should call in advance to specify a room with a double bed, as most rooms have two single beds. Children under 12 are free; extra beds are A$25. All major credit cards are accepted. The only drawback is that 'town' is halfway around the island and public transportation is nonexistent.

The concrete-block **Od-N Aiwo Hotel** (☎/*fax 444 3591, fax 555 4555*) has 30 clean but plain rooms, with refrigerator, air-con, and a double bed or two twins. The ocean view from the rooms is blocked by the rusting cantilever. A suite, similar to the other rooms except larger and with TV, can accommodate five people. The prices are much lower than Menen's and the hotel is right in town. Singles are A$45, doubles A$60, triples A$70, and the suite is A$120. American Express and Diners Club are accepted for a 5% surcharge. A mini-store, a

small but adequate restaurant and a 24-hour mini-shop are on the premises, but no alcohol is available.

PLACES TO EAT

There are no indigenous Nauruan restaurants as Nauruans have ceded all culinary matters to the Chinese – which, considering the quality of the food, is not a bad choice. Small Chinese eateries sprout up every 200m or so along the more populous roadway strips; these serve quick, hearty meat-and-rice plates for around A$2.50. *Eren ankiwi* – sashimi in coconut juice – is an island speciality you'll find at most of these small Chinese shops. Keep a careful eye on the current health situation – it would be best to stick with the few licensed restaurants if there's a typhoid outbreak. The Chinese also have a variety of tea shops, where Chinese can be seen sipping tea and consuming *mimpos* – Chinese dough – from the early morning hours.

Both hotels have adequate restaurants, though the Menen Hotel's **Anibare Restaurant** is predictably pricier and more heavily attended. The Menen Hotel hosts an outdoor barbecue on Wednesday and Friday nights (A$15).

Ocean Blue, which contrary to its name occupies a lavender building, is about half a kilometre from the runway in the Menen Hotel direction. It is very clean and has scrumptious Chinese food. The vast menu includes soups, pork, beef, seafood and noodle dishes. An excellent choice is the fish slices in black bean sauce (the medium size portion makes a hefty plateful at A$8); supplement this with steamed rice on the side (A$2 small, A$4 large) to soak up the sauce. The restaurant is open daily from 9 am to 10 pm.

Right beside the airport, **Reynaldo's** is a good place to find dinner if you've checked in early for your flight. The menu is the same as at the other restaurants – duck, pork, noodles, chicken and copious seafood – and the prices, starting at A$5, are reasonable. As at Ocean Blue, dishes are offered by size; opt for medium, which is plenty to fill you up. Reynaldo's is open daily from 8 am to 2 pm and 5 to 10 pm.

Airport South, directly across the runway from the airport, is a clean if slightly worn Chinese eatery. The prices are a bit higher than at Ocean Blue, with entrees generally A$10 and up. If you want to go cheap, stick to fried rice, a big plateful of which costs A$3 to A$7.50.

Self-Catering

By far the largest selection of groceries is at *Capelle & Partner*, on the north side of the island. There is an abundance of imported Australian packaged cookies and cereals, but little bread and some none-too-savoury fruit and vegetables. Keep an eye on the date labels. It's open Monday to Saturday from 9 am to 9 pm; the liquor shop through the rainbow streamers is open Monday to Saturday from 10 am to 6 pm.

The Nauruan version of fast food is served up at a small booth next door to Capelle & Partner, with fish and chips for A$5, chips for A$2.50, chicken nuggets for A$2, doughnuts, and so on – though half the menu items may not be available at a given time. It's best to go in the late morning as most of the food is cooked between 9 and 10 am, and by 4 pm the 'fresh hot' chips have gone rather limp. The fast-food joint opens from 9 am to 6 pm Monday to Saturday.

Nauru's home-grown fruits, unfortunately, are not commercially available; if you must have vitamins try *Fresh Centre*, next to Jet Video on the way to the Menen Hotel, which has expensive but wholesome fruits and vegetables imported from Australia. The store is open from 8.30 am (11.30 am on Sunday) to 10 pm daily.

Avoid drinking Nauru's water, most of which is desalinised and carried around in tanks that don't seem too sanitary. Unfortunately, however, bottled water is expensive and somewhat difficult to come by – 1.5L bottles are sold for A$6 at the Menen Hotel. Use the boiler in your room or drink juice.

ENTERTAINMENT

Keep abreast of payday, which is every second Thursday for NPC workers and every second Friday for government workers. The two are alternated, so payday comes essentially every week.

The *Menen Hotel* has two bars. The Reef Bar downstairs by the lobby has a limited selection of mixed drinks and of course cans of Victoria Bitter (VB) for A$3 – but be smart and go upstairs to the casino, where VB sells for A$2. If you don't like the smoky games room, bring your beer downstairs and sit outside in the calm by the ocean. The casino opens until 2 am most nights, later than the Reef Bar.

The spacious and pleasant *NPC Staff Club*, on the second floor of the building behind the tennis courts, is a good spot to meet locals. Ignore the 'Members Only' sign and proceed upstairs. VB is A$2 and a brandy and cola is A$1.30. The club has a pool table and is open until 10 pm weeknights and until midnight on weekends. There's a popular, rather wild monthly disco, usually on the last Friday of each month.

Another drinking hole is at Nauru's *Country Club*, where golf types collect at the few tables and consume A$2 VBs.

The only things Nauruans show up on time for is *bingo night*, every Wednesday and Friday at 8 pm, when they clog the Aiue Boulevard and play bingo on picnic tables and in the streets. By 9 pm everything is over and the street deserted.

In the heyday of phosphate Nauru used to have drive-in cinemas, but those are all boarded up now; all that remains is a small theatre, *Lazer Island* on the west coast, which has nightly video screenings except Sunday.

SHOPPING

Nauru has few handicrafts for sale. Basket-weaving and other traditional arts have faded in the face of the country's single-minded pursuit of phosphate production. Now only a handful of ageing Nauruans have the knowledge or skills to make handicrafts. But phosphate has spawned its own beautiful souvenirs. Phosphate rock, carved to resemble the island of Nauru and embedded in glossy native *tomano* wood (also in the shape of Nauru), is available at the NPC's engineering office near the second cantilever. These souvenirs come as paperweights (A$20) or as plaques (A$50). You can get the paperweight or plaque inscribed for no additional charge, but depending how busy they are it may be a day or two before it's ready. You can also bring your own small clock and they'll embed it in the phosphate and tomano (A$40). You can also order coffee tables in the same style – tomano embedded with phosphate rock. These are gorgeous but are too big to fit in your luggage and would have to be shipped home.

Elizabeth Garden, a store just before the bridge, has a few assorted foreign-made trinkets – 'Nauru' ashtrays, mugs and the like. Check the top shelf to see whether locally made outrigger canoes are in stock.

Nauru also has a nice philatelic bureau. You can buy stamps at the post office or write for an order form to Nauru Philatelic Bureau, Post Office Building, Republic of Nauru, Central Pacific.

Federated States of Micronesia

FED STATES OF MICRONESIA

The Federated States of Micronesia (FSM) consists of the four states of Kosrae, Pohnpei, Chuuk and Yap. All are part of the Caroline Islands and share similar colonial histories under Spain, Germany, Japan and the USA, yet each of the four geographically distant states has its own distinctive cultures, traditions and identities. Kosrae is known for its preponderance of true believers, Pohnpei, the capital, boasts lush landforms and ancient ruins, Chuuk is renowned for its diving, and Yap for its traditional culture.

Given the diversity of cultures, lifestyles and natural attractions within the FSM, a trip island-hopping through the region will bring novel experiences and sights at every stop.

Facts about the Federated States of Micronesia

HISTORY

Some FSM islands are believed to have been settled around AD 200.

Medieval Pohnpei was ruled by the Saudeleurs, a tyrannical royal dynasty which reigned from Nan Madol, an elaborate city of stone fortresses and temples. By 1400 stratified Kosrae was unified under one paramount chief, or *tokosra*, who ruled from the island of Lelu. While the commoners lived on the main island, then called Ualang, the royalty and their retainers lived inside more than 100 basalt-walled compounds on Lelu and nearby islets. With its canal system and coral streets, the fortressed island of Lelu would have rivalled its medieval counterparts in Europe.

The first Europeans arrived in Yap and Ulithi Atoll around 1526. The Spanish, arriving later, claimed sovereignty over the Caroline Islands until 1899, when it sold its holdings to Germany.

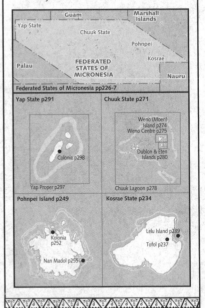

The infamous 1910–11 Sokehs Rebellion was sparked when a Pohnpeian working on a labour gang on Sokehs Island was given a beating by a German overseer. The Pohnpeians killed the overseer, and the revolt was on. The Germans promised revenge, though it took more than four months for ships with reinforcements to arrive from Melanesia. The Germans then blockaded Kolonia and sent Melanesian troops charging up Sokehs Ridge. The uprising was suppressed and 17 rebel leaders were executed and thrown into a mass grave. Not wanting to see the incident repeated, the Germans exiled 426 Sokehs residents to Palau and then brought in people from other Micronesian islands to settle on Sokehs.

In 1914 the Japanese navy took control of the islands and their population dwarfed that of the locals. Chuuk's huge, sheltered lagoon became the Japanese Imperial Fleet's most important central Pacific base, so impenetrable that it was called the 'Gibraltar of the Pacific'.

On 17 February 1944, the US navy airbombed the Japanese fleet docked in the lagoon and sank some 60 ships, which lie on the bottom today.

After the war, when the USA took over and the Trust Territory was set up, Kosrae was included in the Pohnpei district, but in 1977 Kosrae broke away from Pohnpei and later became a separate state.

In July 1978 the Trust Territory districts of Pohnpei, Kosrae, Chuuk, Yap, the Marshall Islands and Palau voted on a common constitution. The Marshalls and Palau rejected it and went on to establish separate countries. What was left became, by default, the Federated States of Micronesia.

In October 1982 the FSM signed a 15-year Compact of Free Association with the USA, which guaranteed annual funding to the islands in exchange for granting the USA exclusive military access to the region. The compact was officially implemented in November 1986. In 1991 the FSM was admitted to the United Nations.

While the compact pretty much gives the US military carte blanche in the FSM, the end of the Cold War kept military development essentially at nil.

GEOGRAPHY

The FSM has 607 islands sprinkled across more than one million square miles (2.6

million sq km) of the Pacific and extends 1800 miles (2899km) from east to west. About 65 islands are inhabited.

The total land area is 271 sq miles (705 sq km). Pohnpei has nearly half the land area, with the rest almost equally divided between the other three states.

CLIMATE

The average annual temperature in the region is 81°F (27°C). See Climate under individual states for more information.

GOVERNMENT & POLITICS

The FSM has three levels of government: national, state and municipal.

The national government is divided into executive, legislative and judicial branches. The FSM Congress is unicameral, with 14 senators. Each state elects one senator-at-large and the other 10 are elected on the basis of population apportionment (five from Chuuk, three from Pohnpei, one each from Kosrae and Yap). The president and vice president, who cannot be from the same state, are elected by Congress from among its members. The last elections were held in May 1999. The national capital is in Palikir on Pohnpei.

Each state has its own governor elected by popular vote for a four-year term, an elected state legislature and a state court. Election outcomes generally hinge on *peneinei* (family) and *keinek* (clanship).

On a municipal level, the traditional village leaders play an active role in government in some of the states, particularly Yap. They often select candidates for political office, and whether the village leaders approve or disapprove legislation usually determines how people vote. It's common for the mayor of a municipality to be a local chief.

In Kosrae mayors have fully supplanted the traditional system of village chiefs.

ECONOMY

The FSM economy is still hugely reliant on US money. By the time its 15-year compact with the USA expires, the FSM will have received a total of US$1.3 billion in direct compact monies, as well as tens of millions of dollars in additional grants and in aid programs.

The compact funding began top-heavy with a five-year capital infusion that was intended to expand the islands' infrastructure and serve as seed money to stimulate small businesses. However, even now there's still not much to show besides a few new airstrips, more paved roads and a couple of electrification projects. As the compact winds down, there is significant anxiety about renegotiation because unlike the Marshall Islands, which have Kwajalein, the FSM holds no compelling incentive for the USA to invest more. Some states, such as Kosrae, have downscaled working hours and given people early retirement packages in 11th-hour efforts to economise.

As in other Micronesian countries, the government is the dominant employer, and the import-export balance is disastrous, with imports totalling US$84 million annually while exports total just over US$10 million.

The waters around the FSM are some of the world's most productive tuna-fishing grounds. A catch worth more than US$250 million is taken annually, mainly by fleets of Chinese and Taiwanese purse seiners. The US$15 to US$20 million collected by the FSM each year as fishing fees from these foreign boats is its largest source of income following US aid. The FSM would like to get local fishing operations going but is hampered both by poor equipment and by the difficulty of adjusting to efficient commercial fishing techniques.

Efforts are being made to build up tourism in the FSM, but the economic crisis which hit Asia in the 1990s dealt the fledgling industry a painful blow, practically wiping out Japanese visitation. In 1998 Pohnpei drew the greatest number of foreign visitors (6575), followed by Chuuk (5467), Yap (4782) and Kosrae (2686).

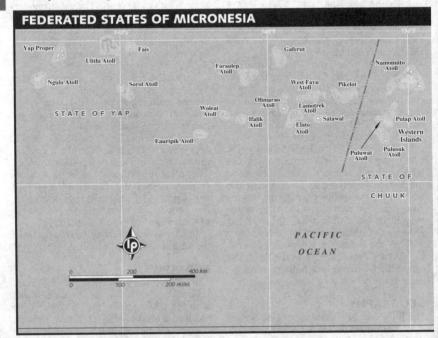

FEDERATED STATES OF MICRONESIA

Kosrae

Most people in Kosrae still rely on subsistence farming and fishing for their livelihood. For government workers, cutbacks in the local budget have resulted in scaled back working hours (see Business Hours under Facts for the Visitor).

Some produce is exported to Majuro, Pohnpei and Guam, the main crops being bananas, limes, tangerines and taro. The FSM Aquaculture Center in Lelu grows giant clams for export to restaurants in Pohnpei and Chuuk. Fruit bats caught in Utwe are exported to Saipan.

The Chinese fishing company, Ting Hong, which was active in Kosraean waters until 1997, has moved to the Marshall Islands, and another fishing company, Pacific Fishing Ventures, has moved in to replace it. As much as Kosrae would like to fish its own waters commercially, the small island still lacks the infrastructure to do so, and so fails to make best use of its own resources.

Pohnpei

As the FSM government is centred in Pohnpei, the majority of workers in the monetary system are on the government payroll. These include a number of American lawyers, most of whom act as advisers to FSM officials.

Agriculture is important on Pohnpei and subsistence farming is still widespread. The island is home to PATS (Ponape Agriculture & Trade School), Micronesia's only agricultural trade school.

Pohnpei also has a sprinkling of pepper plantations. Pepper grows on climbing vines which in the wild sometimes reach to the top of full-grown trees. When cultivated, the vines are usually trained up posts 6 to 8 feet high for easy picking. Pohnpei pepper, which is shipped overseas to gourmet food shops, is a leading export crop, along with copra.

Other exports include trochus shell buttons and coconut oils, soaps and shampoos.

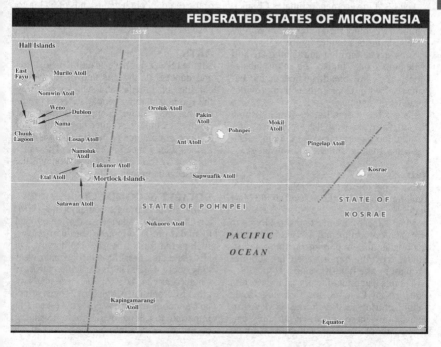

FEDERATED STATES OF MICRONESIA

Among more creative ways of gaining revenue, Pohnpei has recently begun selling its Internet domain name (.fm) to FM radio stations, a venture which pulled in US$150,000 in 1998.

Chuuk

As elsewhere in the FSM, Chuuk is largely dependent on US compact monies. This money is intended for government operational expenses and social and economic development, but much of it has been squandered on a bloated government bureaucracy of about 3000 employees. Chuuk is commonly the target of criticism by other FSM states who feel that it is misappropriating the FSM funding and failing to pay legitimate bills. As a result of Chuuk's growing budget problems there's not always enough fuel to run government boats and the school year has been shortened. The situation became so bad that even the tourist office closed for a few years.

The FSM government estimates Chuuk's unemployment rate as 20%, but the vast numbers of young men loitering on Weno's streets suggests a higher figure.

Subsistence farming and fishing are still widespread on Chuuk. The main subsistence crops are breadfruit, coconuts, bananas and taro. Copra production provides some local income.

Chuuk has a small state-owned fishing fleet that provides fresh fish for the local market, but the biggest players are foreign fishing boats, mainly Chinese and Taiwanese.

Yap

Yap's economy is largely reliant upon US funding, though it's the best-off of the FSM states.

Most Yapese continue to make a living in subsistence farming and fishing. Copra production is still important on the outer islands, with the copra traded for supplies brought by the field-trip ship.

There's a garment factory on the western outskirts of Colonia, the first large-scale manufacturing facility in the FSM. A primarily Taiwanese venture, it currently employs about several hundred Chinese workers who are on Yap mostly on two-year contracts, working in sweltering conditions and living in barracks. Most of the garments are shipped to the USA, which gives the FSM duty-free access.

The US fishing company Mid Pacific recently signed an agreement to bring nine fishing boats into Yap. Fish processing also contributes significantly to Yap's economy. As elsewhere in Micronesia, the boats, which lack sanitation facilities, are a serious source of contamination.

Tourism plays an increasing role in Yap's economy.

POPULATION & PEOPLE

Chuuk has 57,300 people, Pohnpei 36,900, Kosrae 7700 and Yap 11,900. As the US compact permits FSM citizens 'habitual residence' in the USA, 7000 FSM citizens have decamped to Guam, 3000 to the Northern Mariana Islands (CNMI) and about 5000 to the US mainland. The people of the remote Pohnpeian islands of Nukuoro and Kapingamarangi are the only Polynesians in Micronesia.

ARTS

All the FSM states have beautiful handicrafts and dances. Pohnpei is known for woodcarvings of dolphins and sharks created by the Kapingamarangi people. In terms of traditional architecture, Pohnpei has traditional ceremonial buildings called *nahs*, while Yap has *pebai* (community meeting houses) and *faluw* (men's meeting houses). The most noteworthy form of indigenous money is the Yapese stone money, called *rai* or *fae*.

SOCIETY & CONDUCT

Clans remain strong throughout the FSM. On Chuuk, other islanders are often obliged to make presentations to the clan leader, such as the fruits from the first harvest. On all islands it's best if visiting women wear long, loose skirts. This is particularly true on Chuuk and Yap. The Yapese, more than any other Micronesian peoples, have been reluctant to adopt Western ways – it's especially important to ask permission before walking on private land or into buildings on Yap.

RELIGION

On Kosrae, about 85% of people are Congregationalists. Pohnpei and Chuuk residents are fairly evenly divided between Protestant and Catholic faiths, while on Yap Catholicism predominates. On all islands you'll find a small following of Mormons, Jehovah's Witnesses, Baha'i and other religions.

LANGUAGE

The 113,000 residents of the FSM have eight major indigenous languages between them; no two states have the same native

Constitution of the Federated States of Micronesia – Preamble

WE, the people of Micronesia, exercising our inherent sovereignty, do hereby establish the Constitution of the Federated States of Micronesia.

With this Constitution, we affirm our common wish to live together in peace and harmony, to preserve the heritage of the past, and to protect the promise of the future.

To make one nation of many islands, we respect the diversity of our cultures. Our differences enrich us. The seas bring us together, they do not separate us. Our islands sustain us, our island nation enlarges us and makes us stronger.

Our ancestors, who made their homes on these islands, displaced no other people. We, who remain, wish no other home than this. Having known war, we hope for peace. Having been divided, we wish unity. Having been ruled, we seek freedom.

Micronesia began in the days when man explored seas in rafts and canoes. The Micronesian nation is born in an age when men voyage among stars; our world itself is an island. We extend to all nations what we seek from each: peace, friendship, cooperation and love in our common humanity. With this Constitution we, who have been the wards of other nations, become the proud guardian of our own islands, now and forever.

tongue. They communicate with each other in English, the language of their most recent colonial administrator.

Kosraean Basics

English is the official language of the government and is widely spoken in Kosrae, though Kosraean, the native language, is more commonly used in everyday conversation.

It's said that early whalers used the expression 'ah shit' so often that the islanders picked up on it and identified the whalers as *ahset*. This is still the common word for 'foreigner' today.

Hello.	*Lotu wo.*
Goodbye.	*Kut fwa osun.*
Good morning.	*Tu wo.*
Good afternoon.	*Lwen wov.*
Good evening.	*Ekwe wo.*
Good night.	*Fong wo.*
How are you?	*Kom fuhkah?*
I'm well.	*Nga ku na.*
Please.	*Nunakmuna.*
Thank you (very much).	*Kulo (ma lunhlhp).*
Yes.	*Aok.*
No.	*Moohi.*

Pohnpeian Basics

Pohnpeian is the main indigenous language. Other Micronesian languages spoken on Pohnpei are Mokilese, Pingelapese, Ngatikese and Nukuoro-Kapingamarangi, as well as Mortlockese, a Chuukese dialect. English is widely spoken, and is the language of instruction in schools. Pohnpei was known as Ponape until 1984, and the name still appears on occasion.

Hello/goodbye.	*Kaselehie.*
How are you?	*Ia iromw?*
I'm well (thanks).	*I kehlail (kalangan).*
Please.	*Menlam.*
Thank you.	*Kalahngan.*
Yes.	*Eng.*
No.	*Soo.*
Foreigner.	*Mehnwhi.*

Chuukese Basics

The native language is Chuukese, but there are also several minority dialects, the most widely spoken being Mortlockese. English is widely understood.

Many native words and place names have more than one spelling. This is due not only to inconsistencies among those who transcribed the native language into the Roman alphabet, but also because most people living in Chuuk Lagoon pronounce 'l' as 'n'.

Itang, a specialised and highly metaphorical language taught only to chiefs and people of high rank, has been in use since the 14th century. It is used to pass down secret knowledge and to call on supernatural powers.

Hello.	*Ran annim.*
(lagoon Chuukese) or	*Ran allim.*
(outer islanders).	
Goodbye.	*Kone nom.*
How are you?	*Ifa usum?*
I'm well (thanks).	*Ngang mei pochokum (kilisou).*
Please.	*Kose mwochen.*
Thank you (very much).	*Kiniso* or *Kilisou (chapur).*
Yes.	*Wuu.*
No.	*Apw.*

Yapese Basics

The local languages are Yapese, Ulithian, Woleaian and Satawalese. The last three are the languages of outer islanders.

Hello.	*Mogethin.*
Goodbye.	*Kefel.*
How are you?	*Ke us rogom buoch?*
I'm well.	*Kab fe'l rogog, kam magar.*
Please.	*Wenig ngom.*
Thank you.	*Kam magar.*
Yes.	*Arrogo'n.*
No.	*Danga'.*
Excuse me	*Siro.*

Facts for the Visitor

SUGGESTED ITINERARIES

As all islands except Pohnpei are accessed by only two international flights a week,

it's best to plan a trip with the individual islands in mind, rather than the entire FSM. If you have only one week, Yap, with its traditional culture and excellent diving, is a worthwhile choice; it is a free stopover on the way to Palau on Continental Airlines.

On the other side of Guam, Chuuk, Pohnpei and Kosrae are sequential stops on Continental's island-hopper. Spending three days on each provides a varied sample of FSM life.

TOURIST OFFICES

Each state within the FSM has a tourist office in the district centre.

VISAS & DOCUMENTS

Passports are not required of US citizens, but it's a good idea to have one anyway. Each of the states has its own immigration process so you automatically get a new entry permit, good for up to 30 days, each time you fly into a new district centre. Entry permits can be extended through the immigration offices for a total stay of up to 90 days, or up to 365 days for US citizens.

See Immigration in the individual states' sections later in this chapter for details about immigration offices.

EMBASSIES & CONSULATES

For addresses of FSM embassies and consulates abroad and foreign embassies in FSM see Embassies & Consulates in the Regional Facts for the Visitor chapter.

MONEY

The US dollar is the currency throughout the FSM. Pohnpei and Chuuk each have one ATM. Credit cards are accepted at most top-end hotels and many dive shops.

POST & COMMUNICATIONS

The FSM uses the US postal system – letters should be addressed 'via USA'. Postal codes are: Kosrae 96944, Pohnpei 94941, Chuuk 96942 and Yap 94943.

Each state has a 24-hour telecommunications centre where you can place international calls, send and receive faxes and check your email and surf the Internet (minimum one hour). Calls between FSM states cost US$1 per minute from 6 am to 6 pm weekdays and US$0.50 a minute at other times.

International calls have a three-minute minimum charge; however, you can avoid the charge by purchasing an FSM phonecard to use in the telecommunications centres. The per-minute rate is US$2.50 to the USA or Guam (US$2 on Sunday); US$3 to the Marshall Islands, Palau, Saipan, Nauru, Kiribati or Australia; US$4 to Canada, the UK or Germany; US$5 to most everywhere else. International rates are discounted 25% from 6 pm to midnight and 50% from midnight to 6 am.

The FSM's international telephone code is ☎ 691.

INTERNET RESOURCES
Check for information at the FSM's government Web site (www.fsmgov.org).

BOOKS
Lonely Planet's Pisces series includes *Diving & Snorkeling Chuuk Lagoon, Pohnpei & Kosrae*, and *Diving & Snorkeling Guam & Yap*.

Stephen D Thomas' *The Last Navigator* tells of the author's stay on Satawal studying under the famous traditional navigator Mau Pialug. Oliver Sacks' *Island of the Colour Blind* discusses the hereditary colour blindness which arose on Pingelap after the population bottleneck caused by a cyclone that killed 90% of the island's population.

MEDIA
Kosrae and Yap have no TV services. Yap has a government-owned TV station which broadcasts US programs. All states have their own radio stations.

ELECTRICITY
The electricity supply is 110/120V AC, 60Hz. Plugs are US-style with two flat blades.

WEIGHTS & MEASURES
The FSM uses the imperial system. See the conversion table at the back of this book.

DANGERS & ANNOYANCES
While other islands are placid tropical backwaters, Chuuk has idle flotillas of young men lining the streets who harass Western women. See Dangers & Annoyances under Chuuk (Truk) later in this chapter.

BUSINESS HOURS
Business hours are from around 8 am to 4.30 pm on weekdays. Banking hours are typically from 10 am to 3 pm Monday to Thursday and 10 am to 5 pm on Friday. On Kosrae, government cutbacks have reduced the working week to Monday to Thursday.

PUBLIC HOLIDAYS & SPECIAL EVENTS
The four-yearly Micronesian Games will be held in Pohnpei in 2002. They feature track events and classic Micronesian-style events, such as outrigger canoe races. See the boxed text 'Micronesian Games 2002'.

Yap's big traditional celebrations are *mitmit*, all-out feasts accompanied by giftgiving, singing and dancing. One village gives a mitmit for another village to reciprocate for one they received in previous years. The completion of a major village project such as a new community house is also a time for major festivities in Yap.

National Holidays
National public holidays are as follows:

New Year's Day 1 January
Easter Sunday March/April
Good Friday Before Easter
Cultural Day 31 March
FSM Constitution Day 10 May
United Nations Day 24 October
FSM Independence Day 3 November
Christmas Day 25 December

Kosrae State Holidays
Kosrae celebrates the following days:

Kosrae Constitution Day 11 January
Kosrae Liberation Day 8 September
Thanksgiving Last Thursday in November

Kosrae Liberation Day Commemorates the day the Americans liberated Kosrae from the Japanese at the end of WWII, and is marked by spirited sports competitions and canoe races between village teams. A sincere effort is made to include everyone in the festivities and there's usually an *ahset* (foreigners') team that visitors are welcome to join.

Pohnpei State Holidays

Pohnpei celebrates the following holidays:

Sokehs Rebellion Day 24 February
Good Friday March/April
Pohnpei Liberation Day 11 September
Pohnpeian Constitution Day 8 November

Each municipality in Pohnpei has its own constitution and thus its own Constitution Day holiday. They are: 27 February in Kitti, 1 May in Madolenihmw, 26 May in Uh, 2 August in Sokehs, 25 August in Nett and 20 September in Kolonia.

Chuuk State Holidays

Chuuk has the following public holidays:

Chuuk State Constitution Day 1 October

Yap State Holidays

Yap celebrates the following public holidays:

Yap Day 1st week of March
Yap State Constitution Day 24 December

Yap Day includes ceremonial dancing and sporting events.

ACCOMMODATION

Camping is not customary as all land is privately owned, but there are exceptions (see the respective states' sections for details). Each island has a good range of accommodation. Traditional-style hotels, one each on Yap, Kosrae and Pohnpei, allow visitors to stay in pleasant open-air thatched roof cottages. All top-end hotels accept MasterCard and Visa, though budget hotels may not.

FOOD

Fish (usually tuna) and rice are staples; also common is breadfruit, taro and bananas.

Western foods like hamburgers, sandwiches, fried chicken and steak are often found, as is fresh sashimi, teriyaki and ramen.

Pohnpeians are big on yams and yams can be big on them. It can take 12 men just to carry one yam, as they can grow up to 10 feet in length and weigh as much as 1500 pounds! Yams take on almost mystical qualities and there's a lot of prestige attached to growing the biggest yam in the village. You've heard of the Inuit having dozens of words for 'snow' – well, the Pohnpeians have more than 100 words for yam. Oddly (or is it?), yams are rare on restaurant menus. In the home, though, breadfruit and yams are commonly covered with breadfruit leaves and cooked by means of *uhmw* – flame-heated stones.

DRINKS

Kosrae ostensibly requires drinking permits and Chuuk is officially dry (but isn't). Local drinks include *tuba* (coconut wine) on Yap and *sakau* (the intoxicating drink known in Polynesia as kava) on Pohnpei. Within Micronesia, sakau is unique to Pohnpei, although the Kosraeans enjoyed it before the missionaries came along. See the boxed text 'Sakau' in the Pohnpei section.

Getting There & Away

AIR

Chuuk, Pohnpei and Kosrae are open stopovers on Continental's island-hopper ticket between Guam and Honolulu, and can be part of a Circle Micronesia or Visit Micronesia itinerary. See the Getting There & Away chapter for details.

Yap lies between Guam and Palau on Continental's flight route. In other words, to get to Yap from other FSM islands you must stop in Guam.

Continental is the only international carrier for Kosrae, Chuuk and Yap. Pohnpei is also served twice a week by Air Nauru, which flies to Nauru (with connections to

Australia, Tarawa and Fiji) in one direction, and to Guam and Manila in the other. For regional airlines contact details see the Getting Around chapter. For airline office locations see Getting There & Away under the respective FSM states later in this chapter.

Departure Tax
Departure taxes are: US$10 from Kosrae, US$10 from Pohnpei, and US$15 from Chuuk. Yap has no departure tax.

SEA
Yachties will find regulations detailed under specific FSM state sections. Note that you must obtain clearance at an official port of entry for each state that you visit. Getting clearance for Kosrae does not allow you free movement within Pohnpei or Chuuk.

You can apply for a vessel entry permit before entering the FSM from the Division of Immigration and Labor (☎ 320 2605, fax 320 7250, ✆ imhq@mail.fm), Pohnpei.

Ports of entry are Lelu and Okat harbours in Kosrae, Kolonia in Pohnpei, Weno anchorage in Chuuk and Tomil Harbor and Ulithi anchorage in Yap.

ORGANISED TOURS
A number of US-based dive operators come to the FSM, particularly Chuuk and Yap. See under Organised Tours in the Getting There & Away chapter.

Getting Around

Yap and Pohnpei both have local carriers that fly to the outer islands.

Chuuk and Pohnpei have excellent shared taxi systems. Kosrae and Yap have small private taxis.

All islands have rental car agencies; prices typically start around US$45 per day with unlimited mileage.

Hitching is simple on Kosrae, difficult on Pohnpei where the taxis will pick you up, definitely discouraged on Chuuk and culturally inadvisable on Yap. See Getting

Around under the individual FSM state sections for more information.

Field-trip ships connect the islands every few months; their schedules are unreliable.

Kosrae

Kosrae is a casual, unpretentious backwater, where people consistently return a smile. It is one of the least spoiled and least developed areas in Micronesia, an unhurried place that retains a certain air of innocence.

A high volcanic island with peaks draped in lush tropical greenery and sometimes shrouded in clouds, Kosrae is rich in natural beauty. It has an interior of uncharted rainforests, a pristine fringing reef and a coast that is a mix of sandy beaches and mangrove swamps. Flowering hibiscus, bananas and coconuts are abundant and the island is known for its citrus fruit, especially oranges, tangerines and limes.

The ruins of Kosrae's ancient stone city, Lelu, while not as well known as Pohnpei's Nan Madol ruins, are nearly as impressive and more easily accessible.

The introduction of jet service to Kosrae in the late 1980s has had a surprisingly limited impact. Having more than a few dozen visitors on the island at any one time is still unusual and, in a friendly way, people take note when someone new is in town. Though the number of faiths is slowly diversifying, religion perseveres as strong as ever, and church is the *only* thing to do on Sunday.

Kosrae, pronounced 'ko-**shrye**' (last syllable rhymes with 'rye'), was formerly called Kusaie. It is divided into four districts, called municipalities, which are named after the main village in each: Lelu, Malem, Utwe and Tafunsak. Kosrae's administrative centre is in Tofol, 2 miles (3.3km) south of the causeway to Lelu Island.

Historically Kosrae's population was dispersed around the coast in about 70 villages and many of the names of now-uninhabited villages are still used to designate sites.

The airport is on an artificial island off the north-west side of Kosrae. From the airport the main road runs clockwise around

FED STATES OF MICRONESIA

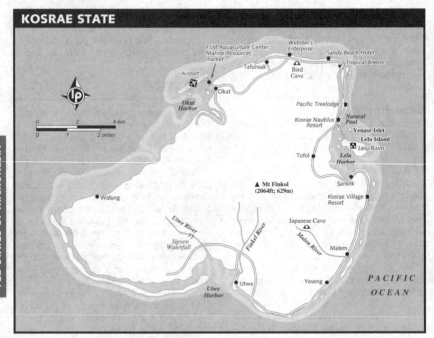

KOSRAE STATE

FSM Aquaculture Center;
Marine Resources;
market

Webster's
Enterprise

Sandy Beach Hotel

Tropical Breeze

Tafunsak

Bird
Cave

Airport

Okat

Okat
Harbor

0   2   4 km

0   1   2 miles

Pacific Treelodge

Kosrae Nautilus
Resort

Natural
Pool

Yenasr Islet

Lelu Island

Lelu Ruins

Tofol

Lelu
Harbor

▲ Mt Finkol
(2064ft; 629m)

Sansrik

Kosrae Village
Resort

Walung

Utwe River

Sipyen
Waterfall

Finkol River

Japanese Cave

Malem River

Malem

Utwe

Yeseng

Utwe
Harbor

PACIFIC
OCEAN

the coast, ending several miles after Utwe. The road between the airport and Tofol is paved, and there are plans to eventually pave the section between Tofol and Utwe – though the current compacted coral road is quite passable.

Walung, a major village on the west coast that maintains traditional ways, can only be reached by boat.

History
Early Settlers Kosrae once had the most stratified society in Micronesia. By the year 1400 it was unified under one paramount chief, or *tokosra*, who ruled from the island of Lelu. Essentially a handful of high chiefs owned the land, low chiefs managed it and the mass of commoners worked it. It was a feudalistic system with each group passing a percentage of their produce up the ladder.

While the commoners lived on the main island, which was then called Ualang, the royalty and their retainers lived inside more than 100 basalt-walled compounds on Lelu and the nearby islets of Pisin, Yenyen and Yenasr. With its canal system and coral streets, the fortressed island of Lelu would have rivalled its medieval counterparts in Europe.

There are indications that Kosrae was once an important power in the region. Pohnpeian legend says that around the 14th century Kosraean warriors sailed to Pohnpei and overthrew the tyrannical Saudeleur dynasty that ruled that island. Chuukese legends also suggest cultural influences from Kosrae around the same time.

European Contact Kosrae was sighted by Europeans at least as early as 1801. It became known to sailors as Strong's Island, named in 1804 by the captain of the Nantucket whaler *Nancy* after the governor of Massachusetts.

It wasn't until 1824, however, that a Western ship finally pulled into harbour. It was just one of many stops in the Pacific for the sailors of the French ship *Coquille*, captained by Louis Duperrey, but for the Kosraeans it was their first contact with westerners.

Duperrey and his crew stayed on Kosrae for 10 days and provided the outside world with an excellent account of the island. They estimated the population to be about 5000, with about 1500 living on Lelu, the ruling centre. The Kosraeans, a peace-loving people who had no weapons, were awed by the foreigners who gave them iron hatchets, a pig and other presents.

In 1827 the Russian ship *Senyavin*, captained by Fedor Lutke, docked at Kosrae and also received a hospitable welcome. Lutke noted that although the Kosraeans had dugout canoes as long as 30 feet, they had no need to go outside their own island and had no boats equipped for the open ocean.

Whalers and traders started calling at Kosrae in the early 1830s, attracted by deep-water harbours and reports of plentiful supplies of food, water, wood and women.

Not all early confrontations were peaceful, however. In 1835 Kosraeans torched the Hawai'ian ship *Waverly* and massacred the entire crew, apparently as retribution on the sailors who had boldly bedded island women without first getting permission from Kosraean men. The Boston trading ship *Honduras* was similarly attacked the same year, with only two of its crew managing to escape.

In the early 1840s relations again became harmonious under the reign of chief Awane Lapalik I, who was known as 'Good King George' by visiting westerners. From then until the decline of whaling in the Pacific in the mid-1860s whale ships visited Kosrae by the dozens each year.

Missionaries By 1852, when the first missionaries arrived from Hawai'i, the contagious diseases introduced by foreign sailors had already begun taking a disastrous toll on the islanders. The Kosraean people were in serious danger of being completely obliterated.

Ironically this made the missionaries' goal of total conversion considerably easier, not only by lessening organised resistance but by lowering the number of souls which needed saving. Around 1880, when the population hit an all-time low of about 300, virtually every remaining Kosraean was converted to Christianity.

The conversion was thorough. Traditional songs, dances, myths and other oral histories were discouraged or banned and ultimately forgotten. Tattooing went out of fashion, alcohol was forbidden and the ceremonial use of *seka*, a narcotic drink like Pohnpei's sakau, was no longer allowed.

Under church influences, Kosrae's traditional matrilineal society developed into a Western-style patrilineal system.

Traders Traders started arriving in full force in the 1870s. One of Kosrae's most famous visitors during this time was the American 'Bully' Hayes, a notorious swindler and trader who roamed the Pacific after years of involvement in the China opium trade. He was a frequent visitor to Kosrae, where he traded in beche-de-mer, copra and coconut oil.

In March 1874 Hayes' 218-ton brigantine *Leonora* sank in Utwe Harbor during a sudden storm, becoming Kosrae's most famous shipwreck. Hayes was murdered at sea three years later in a brawl with his ship's cook, Dutch Pete.

Some believe that at the time of his death Hayes was on his way back to Kosrae to recover the treasure he had rescued from the sinking *Leonora* and reputedly buried somewhere on the island. These rumours have inspired many a treasure hunt on Kosrae.

Japanese Period The Japanese, who arrived in 1914, exploited Kosrae's natural resources and took over three of the island's four coastal villages, forcing the Kosraeans to move inland.

Developments in agriculture, forestry, fishing and copra helped support the Japanese war effort during WWII, as well as provide for the 7000 Japanese living on the island. Kosrae was never invaded by Allied forces during the war.

Post WWII After the war, when the USA took over and the Trust Territory was set up, Kosrae was included in the Pohnpei district. For three decades thereafter Kosrae played only a secondary role as development was centred on Pohnpei, 350 miles (563km) to the north-west.

In 1977 Kosrae became a separate district within the Trust Territory and later a separate FSM state. Although Kosrae gets more funding this way than it would as an appendage of Pohnpei State, a desire for a bigger slice of the pie was not the only motive: Kosraeans and Pohnpeians had never before considered themselves one political unit until lumped together at the whim of the US administration.

Geography

Kosrae is the easternmost island of both the Federated States of Micronesia and the Caroline Island chain. It is the only state in the FSM with no outer islands. The island is roughly triangular, covering an area of 42 sq miles (109 sq km). It's one-third the size of Pohnpei, an island it resembles in shape and topography.

Kosrae has a rugged interior of mountain ridges and river valleys. A full 70% of the island is mountainous and another 15% is given over to mangrove swamps. Mt Finkol, the highest point, rises to 2064 feet (629m).

Lelu, Utwe and Okat are the main deepwater harbours and all villages are along the coast.

Climate

Temperatures on Kosrae average 80°F (27°C) year round. Rainfall averages 185 to 250 inches (4699 to 6350mm) per year and is heaviest in summer months (June-August), with more falling on the west coast than on the east. Trade winds come mainly from the north-east and are weakest from May to November. Kosrae is fortunate to lie outside the main typhoon tracks and even strong storms are relatively rare.

Population & People

Kosrae is home to 7700 people, accounting for just 6.8% of the FSM's total population. Approximately 2600 people live in the Lelu and Tofol areas, 1500 in greater Malem, 1150 in the Utwe area, 2200 in Tafunsak and 300 elsewhere.

Society & Conduct

In Kosrae when you talk about the culture you talk about religion – the most essential part of modern Kosraean society. About 85% of all Kosraeans are Congregationalists, though the numbers and types of faiths are slowly expanding.

The religious beliefs and practices of the late 19th century that so totally overtook the islanders have changed little over the years, though today the ministers are Kosraean.

On Sunday it's polite to refrain from working, scuba diving, fishing and drinking.

Health

Water is not safe to drink from the tap in Kosrae as it comes down from the mountains untreated and can be contaminated by

---

Sunday Best

Attending church at 10 am on Sunday is a wonderful way to experience Kosraean culture – besides, there's nothing else going on! The Congregationalist Church in Lelu attracts the largest following, and your hotel can easily arrange a ride to church since everybody's going anyway.

The congregation, dressed in its formal Sunday best, begins drifting in about 45 minutes before the service starts, to sit quietly and listen to the organ music. Women sit on one side of the room, men on the other, and the choir (men and women together) occupies the centre front.

Services are held in Kosraean but most likely the pastor will notice a new face in the audience and ask you to stand and be welcomed. The service includes prayers, a sermon, hymns, glorious choral singing and psalm readings.

wild pigs and rats that live in the interior. Although it's not terribly common, leptospirosis can be transmitted from these animals to humans via fresh water.

Most islanders drink catchment water and, although few people bother, it's not a bad idea to treat or boil catchment water as not all catchment systems are equally sanitary. Most hotels and restaurants serve catchment water.

Drinks

Visitors officially need a drinking permit to purchase alcoholic beverages in Kosrae, though enforcement waxes and wanes. Both Kosrae Nautilus Resort and Kosrae Village Resort have restaurants that serve alcohol and can issue diners the permit for US$3. Valid for 30 days, the permit can also be picked up at the police station in Tofol. Webster's Enterprises in Tafunsak sells beer and spirits, as does Joanna's store in Sansrik between Tofol and Kosrae Village Resort. Spirits but no beer are sold in small shops on Lelu Island and in Malem. It's simplest just to ask your taxi driver to take you liquor-shopping. Alcohol is not sold or served on Sunday.

Information

Tourist Offices The tourist office in Tofol (☎ 370 2228, fax 370 2066, ✉ kosrae@mail.fm), in a traditional-style Kosraean building with a high thatched roof, has basic brochures, can arrange guided tours and sells a few handicraft items. It's open from 8 am to 4 pm Monday to Thursday.

A very useful guide to Kosrae, *Kosrae, a Travel Planner,* can be obtained from the tourist office or at any FSM embassy or consulate.

Money Kosrae's two banks, the Bank of FSM and the Bank of Hawaii, are both in Tofol and are open weekdays from 9.30 am to 2.30 pm (the Bank of Hawaii closes a half-hour later on Friday). Both can exchange American Express travellers cheques for a small commission. The Bank of Hawaii can also do credit card advances and

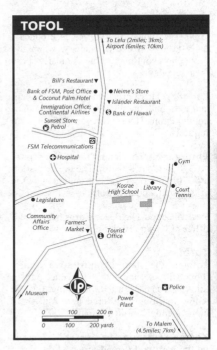

TOFOL

To Lelu (2miles; 3km);
Airport (6miles; 10km)

Bill's Restaurant ▼
Bank of FSM, Post Office ● ● Neime's Store
& Coconut Palm Hotel
Immigration Office; ▼ Islander Restaurant
Continental Airlines ● 🏦 Bank of Hawaii
Sunset Store; ⛽ Petrol
FSM Telecommunications ☎
✚ Hospital
Gym
Kosrae Library
High School Court
● Legislature Tennis
Community Farmers'
Affairs Market
Office 🛈 Tourist
Office
LP
● Museum ✚ Police
Power
Plant
0   100   200 m
0   100   200 yards
To Malem
(4.5miles; 7km)

exchange Australian currency. Credit cards are accepted by most hotels, Continental Airlines and the telecommunications office, but expect most other transactions to be in cash.

Post & Communications The post office is open weekdays from 8 am to 3.30 pm.

Local and long-distance telephone calls can be made from the FSM telecommunications centre in Tofol. Local calls are free. For directory assistance dial ☎ 411.

Immigration The Immigration office, above the Continental office in Tofol, is open weekdays from 8 am to 5 pm.

Libraries You can read the *Pacific Daily News* and browse magazines and books about Micronesia at the library, which is at Kosrae High School. It's open from 8 am to 4 pm weekdays and 9.30 to 11.30 am Saturday.

Media Kosrae's only radio station is at 1500 AM; Voice of America is broadcast daily at 10 am except Sunday, when the radio plays continuous church music. There is no television.

Laundry There are laundrettes in Malem and Lelu but none in Tofol, though the Coconut Palm Hotel can do laundry on request.

Emergency The island's small hospital (☎ 370 3012) is in Tofol. The police station (☎ 370 3333 or ☎ 911 for emergencies) is at the south end of Tofol.

Peace Corps The Peace Corps has a small office at Kosrae High School.

Tofol

Tofol is the state administrative centre, though it's so small that it seems odd to think of it as the centre of anything. It's just a few buildings scattered here and there along a couple of dusty roads.

Kosrae Museum The Kosrae Museum is up the narrow dirt road just past the farmers' market. It's about a 10-minute walk though you can also drive, and the top of the hill affords a nice view of Tofol and Lelu Island. Though it has only one room, the museum is certainly worth a look. It has charts and drawings detailing different parts of Lelu's history and photos of the archaeological work done at the ruins. Other compelling artefacts include ancient basalt food pounders, adzes (tools for dressing timber) made from giant clam shells, a model traditional house, an outrigger canoe made from a breadfruit tree trunk and the ship log from the *Leonora* which foundered in 1874 off Kosrae's coast.

The museum is open from 8 am to 4 pm Monday to Thursday. While there's no admission fee, a donation is appreciated.

Lelu Island

Lelu (also spelled Leluh) is a separate island connected to the rest of Kosrae by a causeway.

The early Kosraeans artificially extended the low part of Lelu by piling stones and packing coral upon the surrounding reef. They then used the new land to build a massive walled city for Kosraean royalty.

Lelu Hill, the island's high point, has a scattering of caves and tunnels used by the Japanese during WWII. There's a good view of the harbour from the top of the hill, which once held a Japanese observation tower and gun emplacements. A trail goes up the hill, but as it crosses private land, it's best to find a local guide; just ask around and someone will be glad to show you.

Lelu Ruins The construction of Lelu dates back at least as far as AD 1400, and probably as early as AD 1250. In its heyday this royal city and feudal capital covered the entire lowland area of Lelu Island, and though the outskirts of the massive complex have been torn down the remaining ruins still cover a third of the island.

A ride around Lelu's perimeter road reveals only a sleepy waterfront village and a smattering of homes and businesses, with not a single stone wall in sight. However, Lelu is deceptive as the ruins are just behind these homes, beyond their backyards, and are almost completely hidden by thick tropical vegetation.

Once inside the complex, Lelu's walls rise up around you and your perspective changes completely. Suddenly you're in an ancient, hidden city, the kind of isolated setting you might imagine trekking hours through dense jungle to find.

Still extant are the dwelling compounds of some of the high chiefs, two royal burial mounds, a few sacred compounds and numerous large walls of huge hexagonal basalt logs that have been stacked log-cabin style. Pounding stones used for food preparation or making seka are identifiable by their smooth, indented surfaces.

To enter the ruins, take the driveway that runs between a store and Lelu Elementary school. Follow the path past the houses and continue walking straight back along the right side of the pigsty; within a minute you'll be within the ruins. Continue straight

LELU ISLAND

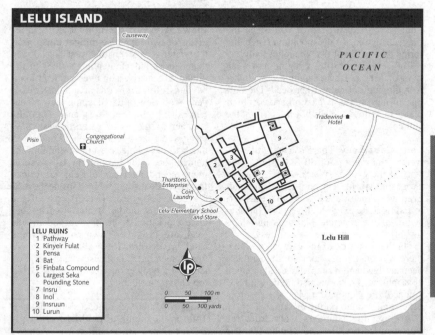

Causeway

PACIFIC
OCEAN

Pisin

Congregational
Church

Tradewind
Hotel

Thurstons
Enterprise
Coin
Laundry

Lelu Elementary School
and Store

Lelu Hill

LELU RUINS
1 Pathway
2 Kinyeir Fulat
3 Pensa
4 Bat
5 Finbata Compound
6 Largest Seka
  Pounding Stone
7 Insru
8 Inol
9 Insruun
10 Lurun

0   50   100 m
0   50   100 yards

FED STATES OF MICRONESIA

ahead through the complex and just before crossing the canal take the stone footpath on the left to get to **Kinyeir Fulat**, one of the most impressive sections of the ruins. Kinyeir Fulat, which has stacked prismatic basalt walls reaching 20 feet (6m) high, is believed to have served as both dwelling compound and meeting house.

The compounds opposite Kinyeir Fulat are called **Pensa**. The walls at Pensa are mostly of medium-sized round basalt stones, with some brain coral added in (a later-day architectural feature). The high chief's feast house was used for food preparation and occupied the south-east compound and the adjacent areas of Pensa. It still contains about 20 pounding stones.

Bat is the large dwelling compound across the canal from Pensa. Its high basalt walls are thought to be among the newest in town, dating from around AD 1600.

The **Finbata Compound**, to the south of Bat, contains the remains of a feast house,

while **Lurun**, a high-walled dwelling compound, offers another example of impressive stacked prismatic architecture. **Insruun**, at the north end of the complex, is thought to have originally been a dwelling compound that was later converted into other uses.

Insru and **Inol** contain mounded tombs which served as temporary resting places for deceased royalty. It was a sacred area, closed to commoners except for a group of wailing female mourners who, from the time the king was laid in the crypt, kept a continuous watch over his tomb and decaying body. After the king's flesh decomposed, the bones were ceremoniously carried to Yenasr Islet and dropped into a deep, natural hole in the reef.

In 1910 a German excavation found a male skeleton in one of the tombs. It was presumed he was the last king to be buried on Lelu and that in the whirlwind of Christian conversion his bones, and with them Kosraean traditions, were quickly abandoned.

Sleeping Lady If you look south across Lelu Harbor toward Tofol you'll see the rugged ridgeline of the mountain range that forms the profile of the 'Sleeping Lady'.

To view the profile, imagine a woman lying on her back facing south-east, with her hair flowing out behind her head. The outline of her breasts is easy to spot. A good place to enjoy a clear view is from the church.

Lelu Causeway There's a natural saltwater **swimming pool** off to the left at the start of the causeway to Lelu Island. This expansive, deeply cut pool is full of water even when the tide is low and the flats surrounding it are exposed. It's a good place to swim, and a concrete platform and stairs just off the road provide easy access.

On the west side of the causeway, where there was once a tiny airstrip, the land has been dredged and reshaped to create a small boat marina. This area also holds the FSM Aquaculture Center, the Marine Resources office and a small public market.

At low tide islanders walk from the causeway across the reef (about 500m) to Yenasr Islet (see Snorkelling & Swimming under Activities later in this section), but visitors shouldn't attempt the walk without reef walkers or canvas shoes as the coral can be sharp.

The area between Lelu causeway and the north-east point of Kosrae is good for shell collecting when the tide is low. On full moon nights some islanders go out 'moon-shelling' along the reef.

Sleeping Lady

According to legend, the gods were angry with a woman so they laid her in the sea in a sleeping position and turned her into the island of Kosrae. The woman was menstruating at the time, so the story goes, which accounts for the rich red soil found in the jungle at the point of her inner thighs. Kosraean men used to trek into the interior to gather the red soil from this sacred place and use it to make a paint for their canoes.

South of Tofol

Views & WWII Remains The rusted remains of two **Japanese midget tanks** sit at the water's edge on the west side of the thatched-roofed elementary school in the village of Sansrik, a bit over a mile (1.6km) beyond Tofol. From this area there's also a very good view of the Sleeping Lady mountain ridge to the south-west and of Lelu Island across the bay to the north-west.

Viewed from Sansrik, Lelu Island looks much like a whale, the hill resembling the humped body, the flat part the tail. According to legend, the island of Lelu was formed from a whale that got trapped inside the reef.

About 350 yards (320m) east of the school, partly hidden behind a small concrete block house on the right side of the road, are 115 overgrown **concrete steps** heading skyward. It's a climb to nowhere these days, but a Japanese weather station and lookout tower once commanded the hill top above the stairs.

Malem Malem, 5 miles (8km) south of Tofol at the mouth of the Malem River, is Kosrae's third largest village.

Behind the municipal building in Malem there's a small **stone monument** put up by the Kosraean-Japanese Friendship Society to honour the island's 700 WWII dead.

The first road to the right past the municipal building goes by the Malem Congregational Church and up to a small dam that marks the beginning of a short, overgrown trail leading to the old **Japanese command post**. Nothing remains of the commander's house, but you can see the cave that served as his bunker by walking up the right side of the river for a few minutes. Look carefully for a cave opening on the right.

If you want to see the cave, you can contact Hamilson Phillip (☎ 370 4405) who owns part of the land. He charges US$18 for a guided tour of the caves, though the price drops to US$12 with three or more people. There have been unverified reports that Mr Phillip can be overly flirtatious, so joining a group tour might make the cave tour more enjoyable for solo women travellers.

Yeseng, the next village, has several concrete **WWII bunkers** scattered along the beach behind people's homes.

Utwe The village of Utwe (also called Utwa) is 5 miles (8km) past Malem, at the mouth of the Finkol River.

This is a pleasant village to stroll around. People can often be seen sitting outside their homes cooking over an open fire while naked children play nearby. For a quick bite, there's a little bakery in the centre of the village with coffee and doughnuts.

If you want to hike there's a pretty walk from Utwe up the Finkol River. After about 45 minutes or so walking across rocks and through mud, you'll come to some nice pools. You can do this first section on your own; ask anyone in Utwe how to get started.

With a guide you could continue walking upriver all the way to the top of Mt Finkol. It's a strenuous all-day walk which will reward you with a splendid view that includes all three of the island's harbours (see Hiking under Activities later).

Utwe-Walung Marine Park (☎ 370 2321, fax 370 2322, ✉ marinepark@mail.fm), a conservation area extending between Utwe and Walung, is being developed in Utwe. Plans call for a boardwalk extending the length of the mangrove channel from Utwe to Walung, but for now the office in Utwe is more active in organising activities, such as culture shows, guided walks and camping, and can rent out outrigger canoes.

Inland Road Some 4½ miles (7km) beyond Malem, at the eastern outskirts of Utwe, there's a wide dirt road leading inland opposite a utility pole marked with an 'X', which is just before the Mormon church. This is the start of a new road along the southern part of the island that's intended to eventually complete the circle-island route. It currently ends after about 6 miles (10km). Driving along this road gives an easy passage into the island's jungle interior.

If you're searching for sights, you might want to visit the **Sipyen Waterfall**, which is 3½ miles (5.6km) up the inland road. After

the road climbs through a cut in the mountains it descends steeply. Park off to the right side of the road at the bottom of the descent, where the guardrail stops. You can hear the falls from the road. It's a five-minute walk up the river, though there's not a real trail and you must walk along the stream bed rocks, some of which are mossy. The waterfall, about 25 feet high and 4 to 5 feet wide, is pleasant enough but by no means spectacular, and the shallow pool beneath the falls is not deep enough for swimming.

Tafunsak

The municipality of Tafunsak stretches along the entire west flank of Kosrae. It includes the remote Walung village, Okat Harbor, the airport, Tafunsak village and several smaller villages on the northern side of the island.

Airport to Lelu The drive between the airport and Lelu is the prettiest on the island, offering views of both the mountains and the coast, as well as close-up looks at Kosrae's luxuriant greenery.

The bridge that connects the airport with the main island crosses a **reef channel** of striking turquoise waters, which are popular with snorkellers. Just beyond the bridge there's a **mangrove swamp** where you might spot a grey Pacific reef heron (nok-lap) scenically perched on one of the swamp's bleached white logs.

Approaching Lelu there are picturesque white sand **beaches** lined with coconut palms. Along the shallow reefs fronting the beach you can sometimes watch fishers casting nets in the reef pools.

Bird Cave A large swampy cave at the west side of the rock quarry in the Wiya area is home to a sizable colony of swiftlets (kalkaf) who cling to the cave walls by their claws and build nests from dried saliva and moss. When flying they look like small bats.

Islanders collect the bird droppings in the cave bottom to use as a rich fertiliser. Like lots of other places in Kosrae, this big swampy cave is thought to be haunted. In this case the belief is spurred on by rumours of Kosraean bodies left in the back of the cave by the Japanese.

Although the tourist office promotes the cave as an attraction, if you're not keenly interested in caves and swiftlets this is a good site to be viewed from a distance. The cave can readily be seen from the road and the swiftlets can often be spotted circling just outside the entrance. If you must go closer, tread gently. Swiftlets are vulnerable to disruption by humans and may abandon a cave that is visited too often. At any rate, the cave itself is not particularly attractive up close and smells of decaying matter.

Tafunsak Gorge There's a steep gorge with 70-foot (21m) walls in Tafunsak village which could be an interesting place to explore on a sunny day. As the gorge is extremely narrow, just eight to 10 feet wide in places, it has the potential to flash flood so it can be dangerous during a downpour.

To get there, take the path running southeast from Stop n Shop at the crossroads in Tafunsak village. It's a 45-minute walk up the gorge, following an old steel water pipe. Be careful crossing the pipe as it can be slippery under foot. A few minutes up the trail there's a shallow pool where neighbourhood kids swim, the first of a number of waterfalls and pools along the way.

Circle-Island Road The section of a new road that will eventually circle the island leads south off the main road at the east side of the bridge to the airport. The road construction, abandoned since the early 1990s, is expected to resume under the current government – but then again, the same thing was said five years ago. Currently the road runs about 3 miles (4.8km), passing above mangrove swamps and through jungles thick with bananas, tapioca and wild ginger. **Stone ruins** of residential compounds and canoe platforms uncovered during road construction can be seen a short way down on the left side of the road.

Walung The new circle road will eventually connect Walung on the west coast with the rest of the island. Home to just a few hundred people, Walung is the island's most traditional village and not everyone there is happy about ending their isolation. For now it's a quiet place with few visitors.

Walung is lined with lovely sandy **beaches** that stretch intermittently for a couple of miles. Just inland, craggy green peaks poke their heads up above the mist, creating a scenic backdrop.

Walung has a church and elementary school as well as the foundations of an old mission. The village is cut by tidal channels that are spanned by log footbridges.

One way to get to Walung is an arduous all-day hike following the southern coast, for which a guide is essential. It is far preferable to journey by boat; the tourist office can make arrangements. The tourist office or the Utwe-Walung Marine Park can also arrange an outrigger canoe equipped with an outboard motor to take you on a fascinating trip through the mangrove channel from Utwe to Walung. You'll pass by some of the largest and oldest mangrove trees to be found in all Micronesia and see herons and scurrying monitor lizards. The trip takes about 45 minutes and costs US$35 return (it's a flat trip rate, so the more people the cheaper the trip). The boat ride within the channel can only be made at high tide, though it's also possible to make a quicker, less scenic, journey outside the reef. You can get tide information from the Marine Resources office (☎ 370 3031) in Lelu.

The other way to get to Walung is by private speedboat from Okat dock. The ride takes about 15 minutes, but it's not nearly as interesting. There's no scheduled service, but you can usually find someone willing to take you over for a reasonable fee by inquiring at the Okat Marina kiosk.

It's worthwhile to spend more than the short stay allowed by the tides on Walung. The tourist office can arrange a homestay. Inquire about the 'mansion', a large house that was built by an American and which sometimes has rooms. It has a great location, right up against breakers on one side, the lagoon on the other.

Activities

Diving Kosrae has unspoiled coral reefs close to shore and both walk-in and boat diving. The confluence of two currents makes for prolific and varied marine life. Underwater visibility can easily reach 100 feet (30m), and in summer as much as 200 feet (60m)!

There's a US PBY **search plane** in about 60 feet (18m) of water at the mouth of Lelu Harbor. Also in Lelu Harbor are two Japanese boats, including a 300-foot (91m) freighter, which were skip-bombed and blown apart, and the remains of a whaling ship. All these dives are best done during a spell of clear weather, as rain can substantially cut harbour visibility.

The Blue Hole in Lelu is also good for diving, and harbours coral heads, lionfish, stingrays and lots of big fish, including barracuda.

In the south, a nice dive spot is Hiroshi's Point, which is a drift dive over beautiful soft corals.

Bully Hayes' ship, the *Leonora*, remained untouched in Utwe Harbor for more than 90 years. After a diving team from the Scripps Oceanographic Institute in California and a private group from Kwajalein stripped artefacts from the wreck the site was officially designated off-limits to sport divers. Now the wreck is protected under law and can only be visited with advance notice and with the accompaniment of a guide authorised by the Historic Preservation Office – but despite the ship's infamous history there's not much to see besides a few planks.

There's good diving between Utwe Harbor and Walung, where large groupers, barracuda and hump-headed parrotfish can sometimes be spotted. At several places you can just step into the water at high tide, swim out 50 to 100 feet (15m to 30m) and start diving.

Kosrae is not the place to see sharks, except for the small docile whitetips found between Walung and Okat.

Dive Shops There are several good dive operations on the island. The fees given for both include tanks and weights; other gear can be rented.

Kosrae Village Resort (☎ 370 3483, fax 370 5838, @ kosraevillage@mail.fm) has a five-star PADI dive operation. Single divers and handicapped divers are well accommodated. Two-tank dives cost US$80, including lunch, tanks and weight belt. Other gear can be rented for under US$30. A five-day open-water certification course is available for US$395, and a referral course for US$295. KVR has a good repair shop with plenty of extras.

The Australian-run Kosrae Nautilus Divers (☎ 370 3567, fax 370 3568, @ nautilus@mail.fm), at Kosrae Nautilus Resort, also caters to English speakers. The resort has a 27-foot boat that can carry up to 10 divers. A two-tank boat dive costs US$90, including tanks, weights and lunch. An escorted shore dive to the Blue Hole costs US$45. Other equipment is available for rent.

Phoenix Marine Sports (☎ 370 3100, fax 370 3509, @ jun@mail.fm), 350 yards (320m) south of the CAT Camp, is a branch of the Japanese dive operation based in Pohnpei. Although it caters predominantly to Japanese divers on package tours, it takes English-speaking divers as well. You'll have more flexibility if you go out independently with Phoenix rather than join a group, as Japanese package-tour divers prefer to plan their diving destinations in advance and stick to the schedule. Rates are US$100 for a two-tank dive (including lunch) for two or more people.

Dive Caroline (☎ 370 3239) is a small operation based at Sandy Beach Hotel.

Snorkelling & Swimming The best spots for snorkelling and swimming change with the seasons and the trade winds. Conditions are usually good between Malem and Utwe in the winter, though there are treacherous currents and rogue waves around Malem itself. The areas near Tafunsak, around the bridge to the airport and off Kosrae's northeast point, are usually good in the summer, but can be rough from December to February. Among these, the north-east side of the airport runway is a favourite snorkelling spot, with 15- to 20-foot (4 to 6m) walls, lobsters, giant clams, stingrays and good visibility. Be cautious of currents in the channel.

The natural swimming hole formed in the reef alongside Lelu causeway is good for swimming, although because it tends to silt up it's not suitable for snorkelling. However, farther out on the reef, near Yenasr Islet, there's another natural pool, the Blue Hole, that's larger and deeper and harbours lots of marine life and coral. This is where the early Kosraeans deposited the bones of their kings. Snorkelling is good here – if you dare!

Snorkellers who go out with the dive companies are often taken to Walung, which has coral gardens. Utwe-Walung Marine Park (☎ 370 2321) can arrange snorkelling trips through the mangrove channel.

Kosrae Nautilus Divers rents snorkel sets for US$11 and has reef walkers for US$4. Phoenix Marine Sports rents snorkel sets for US$10, Dive Caroline for US$20 and Kosrae Village Resort (KVR) for US$10. KVR sends snorkellers out with the dive boat for half the diving price.

Kayaking & Canoeing The Mutunnena Channel, which wends past Kosrae Village Resort on the east side of the island, and the Utwa/Walung Mangrove Channel along the island's south-west fringe, are laced with thick mangroves, and a canoe or kayak trip through them is magical. The east side channel, which actually winds beneath the wooden walkway that leads to Kosrae Village Resort, is too narrow for an outrigger canoe but is perfect for kayaking. Kosrae Village Resort offers a five- to six-hour guided kayaking tour for US$39, including lunch.

Kosrae Nautilus Divers rents kayaks for US$15 a day and arranges canoe rentals for US$20 (US$15 each for two or more people). Utwa/Walung Marine Park (☎ 370 2321) organises nice four- to six-hour canoe trips through its mangrove channel. The

Snaking Through the Mangroves

Legend has it that long ago a beautiful girl who was the daughter of a mother-snake was swimming in Okat Harbor. Her astonishing beauty caught the attention of the king of Kosrae, who had his servants spirit the girl away to his palace in Lelu. When her daughter did not return, the agitated mother-snake set off to find her. Frantically she slithered all around the island until, exhausted, she arrived at Lelu Harbor.

The kidnapped girl was told by a servant who had seen the snake that her mother was nearby. Joyously they reunited and the girl hid her mother in the roof of the king's palace. But another servant espied the snake in the rafters and informed the king, who immediately deduced that it was the girl's mother. So while all the women were at the river washing clothes, the sly king set the building on fire. The young girl rushed back but it was too late – her mother had already perished in the flames. Distraught, the girl flung herself on the fire and died with her mother.

The mangrove channels on Lelu are said to be carved by the frantic mother snake in search of her child.

cost is US$35 per person including lunch and hotel pick-up. A US$5 fee is charged to private canoeists or kayakers passing through the Utwa/Walung Marine Park.

Hiking Kosrae has a number of wonderful hikes, though some require guides as they go through private land and the trails are difficult to find. For a short hike in Tofol the easy stroll up to the museum offers a nice view of the surrounding area and of Lelu. For something more substantial, the hike up the Tafunsak Gorge (see Tafunsak earlier) makes for a pleasant little afternoon outing. The Japanese caves (see Malem under South of Tofol earlier in this section) is another, more novel option.

The most rewarding and challenging hike on the island is the hike from Utwe to the top of Mt Finkol. The whole trip takes eight to 10 hours and hikers should be in good shape as it's a strenuous climb. Much of the trail follows the Finkol River. Expect to get wet as the route jumps across river rocks and sloshes through mud. At the top you'll be rewarded with an incredible view that includes all three of the island's harbours.

The Mt Finkol hike requires a guide. Hanson Nena (☎ 370 3036, 370 5230 after hours) of Utwe does a great job and charges US$50 for a group of one to four people, or US$15 each for five people or more. He prefers to arrange tours on weekends, but if given advance notice he can shuffle his work schedule to accommodate weekday hikers. Otherwise, ask at the tourist office or your hotel for an alternate guide.

Another arduous hike is up Mt Oma, beyond the Japanese caves near Malem. A guide is necessary for the six-hour trip.

Another good hike is to the Menke ruins on the south side of the island. The ruins were the sacred spot of Ninlaku, the goddess of nature and breadfruit. Contact Tadao Wakuk (☎ 370 5080) who gives an excellent, painstaking tour. The Marine Park (☎ 370 2321) can also arrange a hike for US$25.

Other Activities Kosrae has a big gym behind the high school in Tofol that doubles as a meeting hall for special events. There's also an adjacent athletic field, a track and a tennis court, all open to the public. More adventurous types can accompany Hamilson Phillip (☎ 370 4405) on a half-day wild pig-hunting tour (US$20). There have been unverified reports that Mr Phillip can be overly flirtatious, so joining a group tour might make the 'wild pig-hunting' more enjoyable for solo women travellers.

Organised Tours
Kosrae is small enough to tailor tours to individual needs: Explain what you want to see and your hotel or the tourist office should be able to arrange a guide for a reasonable fee.

Places to Stay
Camping Camping, once a foreign concept, is increasingly common in Kosrae. People have even camped in the centre of Tofol on a grassy spot near the Coconut Palm Hotel! But there are much better spots than Tofol. If you want to camp, it's best to approach the mayor of the village where you want to camp; he can find locals willing to let you camp on their land. The tourist office and the Marine Park should also have some suggestions.

Hotels For a place with relatively few tourists, Kosrae supports a handful of pleasant hotels.

A tax of 5% is included in the rates listed below. All hotels accept Visa and Master-Card except Pacific Treelodge, which accepts Visa only (for a 4.5% surcharge), and Sandy Beach, which accepts Visa and American Express.

The only hotel in Tofol is the *Coconut Palm Hotel (☎ 370 3181, fax 370 3084)*, above the post office in Tofol. The hotel has three simple rooms that are clean and commodious with comfortable beds, a sofa, desk, refrigerator and air-con. Eight more rooms are scheduled for renovation. A long-time favourite with businesspeople, the hotel is good value at US$37/42 for singles/doubles.

Sandy Beach Hotel (☎ 370 3239, fax 370 2109), on the beach between Tafunsak and Lelu, has adequate rooms in two-storey duplex and fourplex buildings. Rooms have two double beds, air-con, refrigerator and an oceanfront porch. All have private bathrooms, most with tubs. The buildings' thatch facade lends a nice element to the beachfront location. Rates are US$55/70; a smaller freestanding cottage nearby goes for US$35/50.

Tradewind Hotel (☎ 370 3991, fax 370 3988), on Lelu Island, is in the process of replacing its five wooden cottages with concrete ones. Current rates are US$35/50. Room and car packages are available as it belongs to the same family that owns TE car rentals.

Pacific Treelodge (☎ 370 2102, fax 370 3060) has modern rooms in duplex cottages that are nicely spread around a mangrove pond. Rooms have a queen and twin bed, private bathroom, air-con, phone and refrigerator, and cost US$55/75. It's opposite the beach, half a mile (800m) north of Kosrae Nautilus Resort. It might be a good idea to inquire whether the restaurant has reopened before committing.

One pleasant upmarket option is the Australian-run *Kosrae Nautilus Resort* (☎ 370 3567, fax 370 3568, ✉ nautilus@mail.fm). The rooms are very comfortable, clean and modern, each with two double beds, a mini-refrigerator, bathroom with tub, air-con and a VCR. The hotel, located a few minutes' walk from the Lelu causeway and the natural swimming hole, has a restaurant, dive shop and Kosrae's only swimming pool. Rooms cost US$90/109. Discounts are given to government workers and groups of 10 or more.

A few miles south of Tofol, *Kosrae Village Resort* (☎ 370 3483, fax 370 5839, ✉ kosraevillage@mail.fm) offers nine thatched bungalows that are pleasantly secluded amidst the tropical forest between the mangrove channel and the ocean. Each bungalow has been carefully constructed with native materials and has a queen and a single bed with mosquito netting, mini-refrigerator, coffee-maker and ceiling fans. The bungalows are handicapped-accessible, part of the Californian owners' emphasis on personal touches. The resort, complete with an excellent restaurant and dive shop, makes for a peaceful getaway. Rooms cost US$70/95.

Places to Eat

Bill's Restaurant in Tofol has good food and is a popular local spot. Beef teriyaki and chicken in peanut sauce are priced from US$5 to US$6 at lunch and dinner. Bill's also has good sashimi with rice for US$3.25, moderately priced sandwiches and *ramen* (noodle soup), and breakfasts for US$2 to US$5. Coffee with free refills is just US$0.50. It's open from 6 to 9.30 am, 10.30 am to 1.30 pm, and 5.30 to 9.30 pm. On Sunday only dinner is served.

The *Islander Restaurant* in Tofol is a popular spot for breakfast, with a pleasant local atmosphere and reasonable prices. Pancakes cost US$1.50, eggs, toast and ham costs US$4, and various fish and meat dishes are about a dollar more. With a day's advance notice it can serve local food – mangrove crab, soft taro, drinking coconuts and more. It's open weekdays from 6 am to 2.30 pm. On prior request they'll open for dinner as well.

The *Pacific Treelodge Restaurant*, at the end of a long boardwalk behind its namesake hotel, was closed for renovations in spring 1999.

The *Sandy Beach Hotel* has a small waterfront restaurant with good, reasonably priced food but snail-pace service. Pass the time by bringing your own Budweiser for an evening cocktail. Try any of the fish options (US$4.50 to US$6). A stack of breakfast pancakes is US$2.50 and coffee is US$0.50. The restaurant purports to be open daily for all meals but hours are unreliable, so call ahead to the hotel, particularly if you plan to dine on Sunday.

The restaurant at the *Kosrae Nautilus Resort* has a pleasant air-con dining room that's smoke-free. Breakfast is priced from US$3 to US$6. At lunch, burgers with fries cost up to US$5. Dinners include spaghetti with garlic bread, grilled tuna or chicken teriyaki for US$6 to US$10.50. Side-orders of local foods are available. Try the breadfruit chips, but save room for the house dessert. Beer, spirits, wine and champagne are available, and margaritas, made with Kosraean limes, are a pricey US$6. The restaurant is open daily from 7 to 9 am, 11.30 am to 2 pm and 6 to 9 pm.

The thatched-roof, open-air restaurant at *Kosrae Village Resort* serves some of the island's best food at reasonable prices. Dinner is from an ever-changing menu that overflows with fresh tuna options. The big, healthy mangrove crabs (priced according to weight) are a worthwhile treat. Drinking coconuts are US$1, as is the excellent fresh lime juice. The seafood salads, made with tuna and mangrove crab, have a reputation as the island's best. The restaurant opens daily from 8 am to 10 pm but closes on Sunday at 9 pm.

Tropical Breeze, on the coastal road just east of the CAT Camp, is a small store with a bakery that makes tasty banana bread, turnovers and other treats. It's open daily from 6.30 am to 9 pm and 10 am to 2 pm Sunday.

If you will be in Kosrae over a Sunday, be aware that all grocery stores close; stock up on bottled water and munchies before-hand. *Webster's Enterprises* in Tafunsak and *Thurston's Enterprise* in Lelu are Kosrae's largest grocery and general stores. There are no grocery stores in Tofol, but you can pick up bottled water and a few snack items at *Neime's Store*, which opens from 7.30 am to 7.30 pm Monday to Satur-day; plate lunches, available in the late mornings, cost US$1.50.

Fresh fish, live lobster and mangrove crabs are sold at the little dock at *Okat Harbor*, just before crossing the causeway to the airport. Sashimi-lovers should also stop at the *FSM Aquaculture Center* on the causeway to Lelu, which sells mango-size giant clams priced by weight. The *Causeway Market* next door has a supply of local fruits, including drinking coconuts. Jars of Kosraean peppers are sold here for under US$2.

There's a *farmers' market* opposite the tourist office in Tofol that's generally open on weekday mornings. In addition to locally grown bananas, citrus and the occasional watermelon, you might also be able to buy local foods such as boiled breadfruit, boiled taro or baked bananas. A real treat would be *fafa*, a sweet poi (a Hawai'ian dish) made from pounded taro with a coating of co-conut milk and sugar, a Kosraean delicacy made on special occasions.

Entertainment

Entertainment in the conventional sense is limited on Kosrae. There are no discos, staged cultural shows or movie theatres. Kosrae Nautilus Resort accommodation has TVs and a small library of free videos for guests.

Shopping

Typical Kosraean crafts include wooden taro pounders, carved wooden canoes, woven bags and purses and wall hangings of fibres and shells.

The Community Development Office, in the unmarked building with the brown door on the left-hand side behind the old court-house, is an excellent place to find sou-venirs. Tucked away in boxes at the back is a plethora of beautiful handicrafts, includ-ing coconut spears and taro pounders, out-rigger canoes, head wreaths made of shells, and much more – all for reasonable prices.

A few handicrafts are also available at the Causeway Market en route to Lelu.

Postcards and T-shirts are sold at the tourist office, Kosrae Village Resort and Kosrae Nautilus Resort. There's a hut next to the tourist office where you can watch and photograph Kosraean craft-makers at work.

Getting There & Away

Air All of Continental's island-hopper flights between Guam and Honolulu stop in Kosrae as a free stopover.

Flights between Pohnpei and Kosrae cost US$135 one way, and between Kosrae and Majuro (Marshall Islands) US$310. Return tickets cost double.

Airports & Airlines Kosrae has an open-air airport terminal with several snack stands (treats include drinking coconuts), rest-rooms and an abundance of choice handi-crafts. There's a debit-card phone in the lobby, or just ask to use the phone at one of the snack stands.

The Continental Airlines office (☎ 370 3024, fax 370 3112) in Tofol is open week-days from 9 am to 4 pm and 9 am to 11 am Saturday. The airport office (☎ 370 2024) is open weekdays from noon to 4 pm and 11 am to 4 pm Saturday.

Boat SeAir Transportation sometimes takes passengers on its cargo runs between Pohnpei and Kosrae, but the schedule is very irregular. See Getting There & Away in the Pohnpei section for more details.

Yachts should notify the Department of Public Works (☎ 270 3011) or the dock (☎ 370 2154) of their intended arrival date. Lelu Harbor is an official port of entry;

bring the yacht in to dock so it can be boarded for immigration procedures and inspection. The Department of Public Works charges an entry fee of US$0.15 per gross tonnage, a dockage fee of US$0.9 per gross tonnage, and an anchorage fee of US$0.7 per gross tonnage; these are per-day fees. If there is no registered tonnage then the fee will be assessed by measurement. Lelu Harbor currently has no mooring buoys but at time of writing had vague plans to establish some in late 1999. Okat Harbor, though also a port of entry, is for commercial shipping.

Getting Around
To/From the Airport The airport is about a 20-minute drive from Tofol or Lelu. The hotels provide free airport transportation for their guests. They don't usually send a van to meet all arriving flights. If you haven't made advance arrangements, give a call from the airport and the hotel will send someone out to fetch you.

Otherwise, getting a ride into Lelu or Tofol should be no problem, as most people head that way and will gladly give a ride.

Car DJ Car Rental (☎ 370 2308) has cars for US$39 and US$49, the cheapest in town. TE's (Thurston's Enterprise) Car Rental (☎ 370 3991) in Lelu has cars for US$45. Webster George Car Rental (☎ 370 3116) in Tafunsak also rents cars for US$45.

Outside of built-up areas, the speed limit is 35 mph (56km/h), but most people drive a bit slower than that. Driving is on the right-hand side of the road. There are eventual plans to pave the roads with asphalt but for now they are paved with compressed coral.

Petrol costs about US$1.70 a gallon.

Taxi Thurston Taxi (☎ 370 3991), Kosrae's sole taxi service, has a four-car fleet. During working hours the service is fairly prompt. After-hours and Sunday it becomes rather spotty, so prepare to do some hitching. Prices are very reasonable – it's US$1 from Tofol to Kosrae Village Resort and US$3 to Malem. In general, it's much

cheaper to rely on taxis and hitching than to rent a car.

Hitching It's quite easy to get rides around Kosrae. In fact, people will often go out of their way to drop you off. If waving doesn't work, it's only because people think you're simply being friendly; the thumb should do the trick.

Bicycle Kosrae Village Resort (☎ 370 3483) currently rents bicycles but may discontinue; call to check.

Pohnpei

Pohnpei's lush vegetation, jungle hillsides and flowering hibiscus fits the typical South Sea island image, albeit a wet one, as abundant rainfall feeds a multitude of streams, rivers and tumbling waterfalls. The damp rainforest interior, which is uninhabited and difficult to reach, has soft, spongy ground and moss-covered trees.

Pohnpei's boldest landmark is the scenic Sokehs Rock, a steep cliff face often compared to Honolulu's Diamond Head. The ancient stone city of Nan Madol, abandoned on nearly 100 artificial islets off the south-east coast, is Micronesia's best known archaeological site and makes a fantastic boat trip.

The main town of Kolonia (not to be confused with Colonia in Yap), though sizable by island standards, still retains an unhurried small-town character. Outside the Kolonia area Pohnpei is unspoiled and undeveloped, with just a smattering of small villages. The small islands in Pohnpei's lagoon offer a range of excellent day trips, and diving is also varied and rewarding. Kolonia is the capital of Pohnpei State, while Palikir, 5 miles (8km) outside Kolonia, is the capital of the FSM.

History
Early Settlers Although Pohnpei was inhabited at least as early as AD 200, virtually nothing is known of Pohnpeians prior to the Saudeleurs. The Saudeleurs were a tyrannical royal dynasty which ruled from Nan

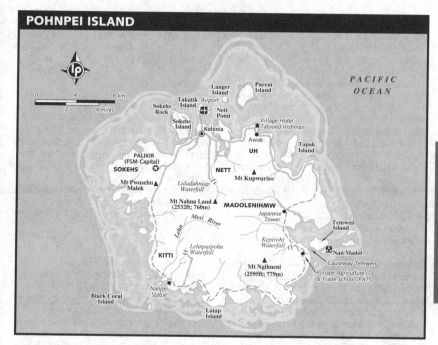

POHNPEI ISLAND

PACIFIC OCEAN

Langer Island
Parem Island
Takatik Island *Airport*
Sokehs Rock
Nett Point
Sokehs Island
Village Hotel; Tatooed Irishman
Kolonia
Awak
UH
Tapak Island
PALIKIR (FSM Capital)
SOKEHS
NETT
Mt Pwusehn Malek
Liduduhniap Waterfall
Mt Kupwuriso
Mt Nahna Laud (2532ft; 760m)
MADOLENIHMW
Japanese Tower
Mesi River
Lehn
Temwen Island
Kepirohi Waterfall
Nan Madol
Lehnpaipohn Waterfall
KITTI
Causeway Temwen
Ponape Agriculture & Trade School (PATS)
Mt Ngihneni (2595ft; 779m)
Black Coral Island
Nanpei Statue
Laiap Island

Madol, an elaborate city of stone fortresses and temples. The dynasty apparently reached its peak in the 13th century.

After the fall of the Saudeleurs Pohnpei was divided into districts, each with two separate families of nobles. The senior man of the highest ranking family was the *nahnmwarki*. The head of the other royal line was the *nahnken*, or secondary leader. The victorious Isokelekel, who had led the invaders (see the boxed text 'The Saudeleurs' Demise'), became nahnmwarki of the region called Madolenihmw, the highest ranked district on Pohnpei and the one which included Nan Madol.

Sometime before the arrival of westerners in the 1820s Pohnpei was divided into the five districts of Madolenihmw, Uh, Kitti, Sokehs and Nett. These districts are the same municipalities in existence today, with the addition of the town of Kolonia, which previously was part of Nett. Each municipality still has its own nahnmwarki

and nahnken, and the system of ranked titles remains largely intact. The current nahnmwarki of Madolenihmw, Ilden Shelten, traces his lineage back to Isokelekel.

European Contact In 1528 a Spaniard, Alvaro de Saavedra, became the first known European to sight Pohnpei, but it wasn't until 1595 that the island was actually claimed for Spain by Pedro Fernandez de Quirós. Even then, like most of the Carolines, Pohnpei was virtually ignored by the Spanish who were concentrating their efforts in the Marianas.

In 1828 Fyodor Lutke, of the Russian sloop *Senyavin*, christened the island of Pohnpei and the atolls of Ant and Pakin 'the Senyavin Islands' and for a while the name stuck.

Whalers, Traders & Missionaries
Whalers, traders and Protestant missionaries began arriving in Pohnpei around the

mid-1800s. During each of the peak whaling years of 1855 and 1856 more than 50 whale ships dropped anchor in the island's lagoon. During this period Pohnpei was known as Ascension Island.

As in other Micronesian islands, the diseases spread by visiting westerners took their toll. The worst was the smallpox epidemic of 1854, introduced by the crew of the US whaling ship *Delta*, which killed between 2000 and 3000 Pohnpeians. The indigenous population dropped from an estimated 10,000 in the early 19th century to less than 5000 by the end of the century.

In 1870 the naval cruiser USS *Jamestown* pulled into Pohnpei and forced island chiefs to sign a treaty which, among other things, allowed foreigners to buy Pohnpeian land. Kolonia was then named Jamestown.

Spanish Period The Spanish began to occupy Pohnpei in 1886, following the papal arbitration that gave Spain authority over the Caroline Islands. The Spanish didn't receive a hospitable welcome in Pohnpei, however. Just three months after his arrival, the island's first Spanish governor was killed in a rebellion by Pohnpeians who were protesting the use of forced native labour to build a Spanish fort in Kolonia.

The Saudeleurs' Demise

The most common story of the demise of the Saudeleurs tells of conquests from Kosrae. The Thunder God, who had been severely punished for having an affair with the wife of a Saudeleur on Pohnpei, set out for Kosrae in his canoe. The canoe sank, but the Thunder God was able to continue on when a floating taro flower changed into a needlefish and guided the god to the island. On Kosrae he made a woman of his own clan pregnant, and the child, Isokelekel, was raised on stories about the cruel Saudeleurs back on Pohnpei. After reaching adulthood Isokelekel gathered an army of 333 men and went to Nan Madol. He conquered the Saudeleurs and established a new system of royalty.

Spain's occupation of Pohnpei continued to be plagued by uprisings, a few of which concerned the Catholic missions that the Spanish were trying to introduce into communities that were by now staunchly Protestant.

German Period The Germans arrived in 1899 after buying the Carolines from the Spanish. Their interest was in copra and other commercial products and they were rather heavy-handed in going about their development projects, relying upon forced labour for much of the work.

The Sokehs Rebellion of the early 20th century led to major reprisals by the Germans (see History under Facts about the FSM for more information).

Japanese Period The Japanese took over in 1914. As elsewhere in Micronesia, Pohnpei became a site of intense commercial and agricultural development. The Japanese cultivated trochus shells and set up a sugar plantation in order to make alcohol.

At the beginning of WWII there were nearly 14,000 Japanese, Okinawans and Koreans living on Pohnpei and only about 5000 Pohnpeians.

Although Japanese military fortifications on Pohnpei were hit by US aerial bombings throughout 1944 and Kolonia was virtually levelled, Pohnpei was not invaded.

Geography

Pohnpei island is high, volcanic and roughly circular, its coast edged with coves and jutting peninsulas. The interior has rugged mountain ridges and deep valleys. Averaging 13 miles (21km) in diameter and with a land mass of 129 sq miles (334 sq km), it's the largest island in the FSM and the third largest island in Micronesia.

The centre of Pohnpei island is Mt Nahna Laud but the highest peak is the 2595-feet (791m) Ngihneni. The coastline is mainly tidal flats and mangrove swamps. In between the island and its surrounding circular reef is a 70-sq-mile (181-sq-km) lagoon containing dozens of small islands, many with lovely white sand beaches.

Pohnpei State also includes eight outlying atolls, each covering less than 1 sq mile (2.6 sq km) of land. To the south-east, almost like stepping stones down to Kosrae, are the atolls of Mokil and Pingelap, 80 and 140 miles (129 and 225km) from Pohnpei island. To the south-west are Sapwuafik (formerly Ngatik) Atoll, 90 miles (145km) away; Nukuoro Atoll, 250 miles (402km) away; and Kapingamarangi Atoll, 445 miles (716km) away. Oroluk Atoll is 180 miles (290km) to the north-west and Pakin and Ant atolls are a few miles west of Pohnpei island.

Climate
The town of Kolonia has an average annual rainfall of 192 inches (4877mm) and Pohnpei's interior often gets a whopping 400 inches (10,160mm), making it one of the rainiest places on earth. The lowest rainfall occurs between January and March, while the wettest months are April and May. A typical Pohnpei day is cloudy with intermittent showers and the sun breaking through now and then.

Temperatures average 81°F (27°C) and for most of the year there are north-easterly trade winds. However, from July to November the winds die down, the humidity inches up and the nights can be especially oppressive.

Pohnpei lies within typhoon spawning grounds, although outside the major tracks.

Population & People
About 95% of Pohnpei's inhabitants live on Pohnpei island. Of those, 20% are Kapingamarangis, Mortlockese, Pingelapese, Mokilese and, in smaller numbers, Kosraeans, Palauans, Filipinos, Americans, Japanese and Australians.

Society & Conduct
Traditionally Pohnpeian society has been a stratified one, with a person's status derived from membership in a particular clan. Each clan had its own chief, its own territory and a 12-tiered ranking system. Although Pohnpeian society is more Westernised today,

many Pohnpeians retain a title related to the clan system.

Funeral feasts are important social events that can last three days, and everyone brings gifts of food and sakau. Dog is a traditional feast food, but the casual visitor is unlikely to come across it.

Information
Tourist Offices The tourist office (☎ 320 2421, fax 320 6019), on Main St in Kolonia, is open weekdays from 8 am to noon and 1 to 5 pm. It has a few brochures on Pohnpei. The equally helpful nonprofit Pohnpei Visitors Bureau (☎ 320 4851, fax 320 4868, ✉ pohnpeivb@mail.fm), in the old Agricultural Station in the botanical gardens just south of town, is open weekdays from 8 am to 5 pm.

Money The Bank of Guam and the Bank of Hawaii are together with a couple of

Sakau
'After four cups of sakau, one leg struggles south while the other is marching due north.' So wrote Englishman FW Christian, who did archaeological research at Nan Madol in the 1890s, in his book *The Caroline Islands*.

Sakau is made from *Piper methysticum*, the roots of a pepper shrub. A seemingly mild but potent narcotic, sakau tends to have a sedative effect: First your tongue and lips go numb and then feel quite mellow and, while your thinking seems clear, your body doesn't always respond quite as you think it should.

In ancient times, the drinking of sakau had religious significance and generally was restricted to times when the *nahnmwarki* (district chief) was present. There were strict rules governing how it was passed from hand to hand, with the highest chief served first.

In the traditional method, the pepper roots are pounded on a stone and the pulp squeezed by hand through hibiscus bark. The juices are then mixed with a little water and poured into a coconut shell, which is passed around communally. Nowadays many shops do.

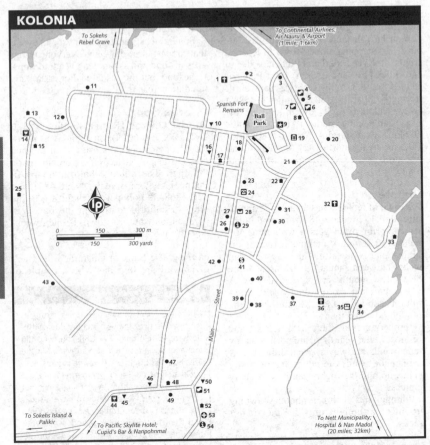

KOLONIA

To Sokehs
Rebel Grave

To Continental Airlines;
Air Nauru & Airport
(1 mile, 1.6km)

Spanish Fort
Remains

Ball
Park

FED STATES OF MICRONESIA

To Sokehs Island &
Palikir

To Pacific Skylite Hotel;
Cupid's Bar & Nanpohnmal

To Nett Municipality;
Hospital & Nan Madol
(20 miles; 32km)

Main Street

travel agencies in a small complex just off Kolonia's Main St. The Bank of Hawaii is open from 9 am to 3 pm Monday to Thursday and 9 am to 5 pm Friday, while the Bank of Guam closes at 4 pm on Friday. A 24-hour ATM is outside. The Bank of FSM is beneath the Australian embassy along the waterfront road.

Post & Communications Pohnpei's main post office, on Main St, is open weekdays from 8 am to 4 pm. The only other post office is in the new FSM capitol complex in Palikir.

Local and long-distance telephone calls can be made and telex, faxes and telegrams can be sent from the FSM telecommunications centre on Main St. Faxes can be received free of charge (at fax 320 2745) and sent for the price of a phone call. Local calls are free from the counter phone. Local calls are free from most hotels.

The FSM telecommunications centre has two fast computers with Internet access for US$4 per hour.

Travel Agencies Village Travel (☎ 320 2777, fax 320 3797), opposite the post office

KOLONIA

PLACES TO STAY	OTHER		
8 Sea Breeze Hotel	1 Catholic Church	30	GP Car Rental; Tennis Courts
13 South Park Hotel; South Park Restaurant	2 German Bell Tower	31	Kolonia Town Hall
15 Cliff Rainbow Hotel	3 Iet Ehu Tours	32	Protestant Church
17 Joy Hotel; Joy Hotel Restaurant	4 Japanese Embassy	34	Ace Hardware
21 Nara Gardens	5 Ponape Coconut Products	35	Pohnpei Cinema
22 Yvonne's Hotel	6 Chinese Embassy	36	Kosrae-Kolonia Congregational Church
25 Pohnpei Hotel	7 Australian Embassy; Bank of FSM; H&E Rentals	37	College of Micronesia
33 Nantehlik Hotel; PCR Restaurant	9 Police Station	38	Pohnpei Supreme Court
48 Hotel Nicho	11 Coin Laundry	39	Office for Island Affairs
52 Penny Hotel; Penny Rent-A-Car	12 German Cemetery	40	State Legislature
	14 Across the Street	41	Bank of Hawaii; Bank of Guam; Travel Agencies
PLACES TO EAT	18 SeAir Transportation	42	Immigration Office
10 Cafe Ole; Ambros Store	19 Pohnpei Lidorkini Museum	43	Kapingamarangi Village
16 Joy Restaurant	20 Public Market	44	Jungle Bar
45 China Star Restaurant	23 Budget Rent-A-Car	47	Coin Laundry
46 Palm Terrace Store	24 FSM Telecommunications	49	Library
50 Yaeko's; Sei Restaurant	26 J&T Store	51	US Embassy
	27 Pohnpei Pharmacy	53	Pohnpei Family Health Clinic
	28 Post Office	54	Agricultural Station; Pohnpei Visitors Bureau
	29 Tourist Office		

FED STATES OF MICRONESIA

on Main St, is helpful and competent. It's open weekdays from 8.30 am to 5 pm and 8.30 am to noon Saturday.

Immigration The immigration office at the south end of town is open from 8 am to 5 pm weekdays.

Libraries The public library, due for expansion soon, is open weekdays 8 am to 5 pm.

Media The government-owned radio station is at 1449 AM. 101 FM is a Christian station and 105 FM plays general music.

Cable TV including live CNN is available at most hotels; the local station is Channel 6.

The *Island Tribune* is the local newspaper. Earlier issues of Guam's *Pacific Daily News* can be picked up at larger Kolonia stores. The Australian embassy on the waterfront road has Australian newspapers that visitors can drop by to read.

Film & Photography Phoenix of Micronesia, next door to Phoenix Marine Sports, does quality 24-hour film processing, with a 24-exposure roll of prints costing US$8. They also sell print and slide film.

Laundry There's a coin laundry with plenty of machines one minute's walk north of the Palm Terrace Store, and another a three-minute walk from the South Park and Cliff Rainbow Hotels: walk down the hill, turn left, and you'll see machines at the back of Fisherman's Store on the left-hand side of the road.

Medical Services The hospital is a mile south-east of Kolonia, on the main road heading down the east coast. Fees are usually only a couple of dollars for simple treatments, but it's a rudimentary and somewhat dirty facility and people who can afford it usually fly to Guam or Honolulu for major medical services.

For a non-emergency, a better option is the clean Pohnpei Family Health Clinic (☎ 320 5777, fax 320 2229, ✉ khni@mail.fm), a few hundred metres from the US embassy and up a short dirt road. Hawai'ian-trained Dr. Bryan Isaac sees walk-in patients for US$15 a visit. It's open weekdays from 9 am to noon and 1.30 to 5 pm and 9 am to noon Saturday. The Pohnpei Pharmacy on Main St in Kolonia sells prescription and over-the-counter drugs, as does the Genesis Pharmacy by the hospital.

Emergency For police emergencies, dial ☎ 320 2221; for medical emergencies, dial ☎ 320 2213.

Pohnpei Island

Kolonia Though it's the largest town in the FSM and experiences occasional 'rush hour' traffic, Kolonia (population 3258) still feels much like an old frontier town. The rural character is most evident on the town's back streets: Dogs laze on the side of the roads and it seems that every other yard, no matter how small, contains a pen of squealing pigs.

Main St is the town centre. About midway down the street, beside the tourist office, there's a small **Japanese tank** painted in camouflage splotches. A few blocks south, the state legislature buildings sit on the highest hill in Kolonia.

Along the waterfront road on the east side of town you'll find old warehouse-style businesses, a public market, a few retail stores and the island's largest **Protestant church**, built in the early 1930s. The most colourful church in town is the new Kosrae-Kolonia **Congregational Church**, near the college, which has a unique design and is the place of worship for the island's 500 Kosraeans.

The one-room **Pohnpei Lidorkini Museum** has a handful of photographic and showcase displays, including one with shell adzes, coral pounders, pottery shards and beads found at Nan Madol (see later). Another display features a sakau-pounding stone housed in a small ceremonial nahs. There are also weavings, traditional fibre clothing and a few WWII items such as rusted helmets from the Japanese occupation. Located on the dirt road loop off the baseball field, the museum is open weekdays from 10 am to 5 pm. Admission is free.

Pohnpei's original Catholic mission was founded at the north end of town in the late 19th century by Capuchin missionaries. Additions during the German administration include a **bell tower** built in 1907. Today that tall grey tower is the only structure surviving the WWII bombing raids that took down the rest of the mission.

Also in this area are the moss-covered remains of Spanish **stone walls**, which were built around 1887 and once enclosed Fort Alphonse and large sections of the Spanish colony. One notable section of the old wall is at the side of the ball park, while another starts across the street and runs along the road leading down to the waterfront.

The cemeteries where the casualties from the Sokehs Rebellion were laid to rest are both in the north-west part of Kolonia. The **German cemetery**, behind the church that's down the hill from the South Park Hotel, holds the remains of sailors from the German cruiser *Emden* who died fighting the Sokehs rebels. It also has the grave of Victor Berg, the German governor who died suddenly in 1907 after excavating a grave in Nan Madol (see boxed text 'Mysteries of Nan Madol'). Unfortunately, the cemetery is overgrown and enclosed by a fence, so it's hard to make out the gravestones.

The **mass grave site** for the executed Pohnpeian rebels is in a residential area to the north-east of the German cemetery. Look for the small unmarked cement enclosure at the left edge of the road shortly before it dead ends.

Nan Madol Nan Madol was an important political, social and religious centre built during the Saudeleur dynasty, a place for ritual activity and the homes of royalty and their servants. It is comprised of 92 artificial islets which were built on the tidal flats and reef off the south-east side of Pohnpei, near Temwen Island. The islets extend nearly a mile in length and a half-mile in width.

Basalt pillars, which had formed naturally into hexagonal columns, some of them 25 feet in length and 50 tons (45,350kg) in weight, were quarried on Pohnpei island and hauled to the site by raft.

The columns were stacked horizontally around the edges of the islets to serve as retaining walls, which were then filled with coral rubble and rock. In this manner the

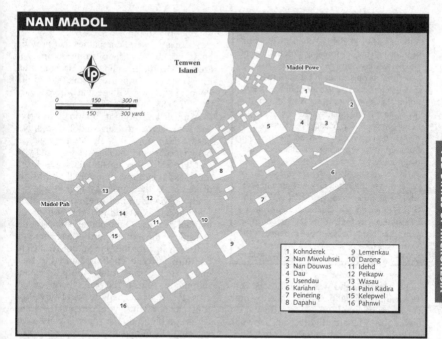

NAN MADOL

Temwen Island

Madol Powe

0   150   300 m
0   150   300 yards

Madol Pah

1	Kohnderek	9	Lemenkau
2	Nan Mwoluhsei	10	Darong
3	Nan Douwas	11	Idehd
4	Dau	12	Peikapw
5	Usendau	13	Wasau
6	Kariahn	14	Pahn Kadira
7	Peinering	15	Kelepwel
8	Dapahu	16	Pahnwi

islets were eventually raised and the twisting canals shaped into what is sometimes referred to as the 'Venice of Micronesia'. On the level surfaces were built temples, burial vaults, meeting houses, bathing areas and pools for turtles, fish and eels.

The eastern half, Madol Powe (upper town), was the section for priests and rituals. The western half, Madol Pah (lower town), was the administration section.

The construction of Nan Madol began in force between AD 1100 and AD 1200 and continued for another 200 to 300 years. It was uninhabited when the first westerners came ashore in the 1820s, but it was a recent abandonment. In 1852 missionaries recorded that elderly Pohnpeians could still remember when Nan Madol was densely populated.

The best time to visit is at high tide, when small boats can easily navigate the twisting mangrove-lined channels which wind through the complex.

Although many of the ruins have collapsed, it just adds to the dramatic impact, especially as you round a sharp corner in the canal and suddenly find yourself in the shadow of the massive Nan Douwas.

Nan Douwas is the largest structure still standing and the most impressive sight. The outer walls of the compound stand 25 feet high. The inner compound contains four crypts which were burial places for the Saudeleur dynasty and later the nahnmwarki. The largest crypt is rectangular and lies in the centre of two sets of enclosing walls, covered by basalt stones about 18 feet long and weighing a ton each. There is a small trail around the main island.

Kariahn islet also has high walls surrounding a tomb.

The administrative centre of Nan Madol was probably **Pahn Kadira**, which also featured the temple of the Thunder God. A large, low platform is all that remains of the temple.

Mysteries of Nan Madol

Although Nan Madol is Pohnpei's foremost sightseeing spot for foreigners, not all Pohnpeians feel comfortable there and the local belief that people shouldn't disturb the ruins may be more than mere superstition. In 1907, Pohnpei's German governor died of a mysterious ailment immediately after excavating a burial tomb on Nan Madol. The German administration claimed it was heat exhaustion but a lot of older Pohnpeians still doubt that diagnosis.

Nan Madol holds its mysteries well. Some believe that the legendary lost continent of Mu, or Lemuria, may lie off its waters and that Nan Madol was built as a mirror image of a sunken city that, at the time of construction, could still be seen lying beneath the water's surface.

The islet of **Idehd** was the religious centre. An annual ritual performed here by high priests culminated with the offering of cooked turtle innards fed to Nan Sanwohl, the 'holy eel' that was kept in the compound pool. The ritual was part of a two-week religious ceremony which included canoe-building competitions, feasting, singing, dancing and sakau drinking.

Darong, an important ritual area, has a natural reef pool in its centre which may have been used for raising clams. Near one wall is a large stone once used for pounding sakau.

Other major islets are **Usendau**, an area where priests lived; **Nan Mwoluhsei** ('Where the Voyage Stopped'), the ocean entrance to Nan Madol; **Pahnwi**, a multipurpose islet that included burial tombs; **Kelepwel**, a residential islet for servants and visitors; **Wasau**, an area where food was prepared; **Kohnderek**, a site for funeral services; **Dapahu**, an islet where canoes were made; **Dau**, a place where warriors lived; **Peikapw**, an islet which had two pools for turtles; **Lemenkau**, the medical centre; and **Peinering**, a coconut processing centre.

Getting to Nan Madol Visiting Nan Madol via boat through the canals is a scenic, traditional and practical way to see the majority of the islets.

There are several companies that provide boat tours of Nan Madol from Kolonia for around US$40, including Joy Hotel and Iet Ehu Tours (see Organised Tours later in the Pohnpei section), Village and Micro Tours (☎ 320 2888, fax 320 5528).

A much less inviting option is to drive and wade across to Nan Madol. The drawbacks: the road will badly scrape your car belly (see Around the Island later) and you won't be able to see most of the islets. From the Madolenihmw municipal building, drive across the causeway to Temwen Island. Continue on that road approximately 1½ miles (2.4km) and turn right on an unmarked dirt road (a telephone pole is on the left side of the road). Shortly thereafter you will see a sign for the Nan Madol Trail Center; turn left and continue until the road ends. A pleasant rock footpath leads through the ruins to the reef, where you can cross the water and explore Nan Douwas on foot. At low tide you can easily wade across; at high tide the water is waist-deep so bring a bathing suit.

If you walk over, expect to pay the nahnmwarki of Madolenihmw US$3. You don't need to hunt him down – he'll generally find you. If you take a boat tour, the permit fee is usually included in the tour price.

You can also arrange to have kayaks or canoes taken to Nan Madol and paddle through.

Kapingamarangi Village This village, on the west side of town in an area called Porakiet, is home to the Polynesians who moved to Pohnpei from Kapingamarangi and Nukuoro atolls following typhoon and famine disasters earlier in the century. They live a more open and outdoor lifestyle than other Kolonia residents. Their breezy thatched homes with partially open-air sides are built on raised platforms a couple of feet off the ground.

The Kapingamarangi men make woodcarvings and the women weave. In recent years this enclave has sprouted a few outstanding craft shops. Try the Carving Spot

Utwe village, Kosrae

Wooden walkway, Carp Island, Palau

Children playing on Chuuk

Washing day, Weno, Chuuk

MICHAEL AW

Girls on Yap making local handicrafts

ASTRID WITTE & CASEY MAHANEY

Children dwarfed by stone money, Yap

SIMON ROWE

Stone money *(rai)* can weigh up to five tons

Handicraft Shop and the Kapingamarangi Gift Shop.

Agricultural Station & Botanical Gardens An agricultural station, started by the Germans and expanded by the Japanese, is in the southern part of town. While not a formal botanical garden, there are some nice old trees on the grounds, including a breadfruit grove near the road, tall royal palms flanking the driveway, traveller's palms and a big fern-draped monkeypod tree. Many of the trees originally came from Borneo or Sumatra. One of the tourist offices is now on site, making the place even more worthy of a look.

The **three-storey building** on the grounds once had a Japanese weather station on top. It was one of the few structures left standing in Kolonia after WWII but the building is now abandoned and condemned.

Sokehs Island To get to Sokehs Island, take the road to the right at the fork past the Palm Terrace Store. Once you cross the causeway onto the island the road divides, following the coast in both directions. Both ways finish in a dead end, as the island road doesn't connect around the northern tip.

It's possible to walk around Sokehs Island, but it takes half a day. The northern part, where there's no drivable road, is made up of large rough rocks, so sturdy shoes are essential. This is the road the Germans ordered to be built with forced labour in 1910, prompting the labourers to resist in what became the Sokehs Rebellion.

After the rebellion, all Pohnpeians living on Sokehs Island were exiled and the land resettled by people from the Mortlocks in Chuuk and from Pingelap, Mokil and Sapwuafik atolls. Their descendants still live on Sokehs Island today.

Sokehs Ridge The 900-foot Sokehs Ridge is loaded with **anti-aircraft guns**, **naval guns**, **pillboxes** and **tunnels** and there's an excellent **view** of Kolonia and the surrounding reef from the top. Naturalists should be able to spot **nesting tropicbirds** and **fruit bats**. The walk up to the ridge takes about 45 minutes and is not difficult. The trail starts on a 4WD road behind the municipal office, the yellow building just to the right after coming over the causeway. If you come by car, you can park at the municipal office. The trail doesn't cross private property and you can do this walk on your own.

Sokehs Rock The steep 498-feet (152m) Sokehs Rock can be climbed by those who like a challenge. After crossing the causeway, take the road to the right, which ends 1¾ miles (2.8km) down. The trail begins shortly before the end of the road, near the Danpei United Church of Christ. The climb up takes 45 minutes to an hour and a local guide is advisable – this can be arranged at the municipal office.

The trail can be fairly intense as it climbs the rock's sheer basalt face. It can be very slippery when wet, and may not be in the greatest condition. Along the steepest part of the trail there's a wrapped cable you can use to pull yourself along. The reward is the good view of Kolonia and the reef you get from the top.

Palikir The 135-acre (54-hectare) **FSM capitol complex** in Palikir Valley, built on the site of a Japanese WWII airfield, is 5 miles (8km) south-west of Kolonia.

The complex incorporates traditional Micronesian architectural designs. The building roofs are peaked, like those of ancestral Kosraean homes. Supporting pillars cast of black concrete resemble the basalt columns of Nan Madol. The ends of the beams on the 1st storey are in the shape of Yapese rai, whereas those on the 2nd storey look something like the bow of a Chuukese outrigger canoe.

The US$13 million complex, built in 1989, has four legislative and judicial buildings grouped together, including an attractive Congressional chamber with a pyramidal roof topped by a huge skylight. A second cluster contains five buildings used for the executive branch, which administers day-to-day operations. Beyond the entrance are the four buildings comprising the brand-new campus of the College of the FSM.

The paved road to Palikir heads uphill to the left just before the causeway to Sokehs Island. This is also the start of the circle-island road. This section of the road is in excellent condition, though it has no shoulders and you'll need to watch out for children who walk along the road oblivious to cars. The entrance to Palikir is 3½ miles (5.6km) down.

Pwusehn Malek Legend says this high volcanic cone formation in Palikir was created during the defeat of Pohnpei's Saudeleur dynasty. The ruler of Palikir changed himself into a giant rooster to fly to Nan Madol and along the way he left a huge pile of droppings.

Pohnpeians call the hill Pwusehn Malek. The English translation so stumped Pohnpei's tourist office that their brochure simply lists it as 'Mount' followed by a long blank space. The popular translation is 'Chickenshit Mountain'.

A trail up Pwusehn Malek starts by the telephone pole on the right-hand side of the road, a little over 1½ miles (2.4km) south of the FSM capitol complex. It's about a 10-minute walk on a grassy and overgrown trail up to the first ridge. It's an easy trail, though when wet it can be muddy and slippery.

Nett Municipality A popular swimming spot on the Nanpil River, the **Liduduhniap Waterfall** is a 15-minute drive from Kolonia. To get there, take Kolonia's waterfront road heading south and half a mile past Yamaguchi Store turn right onto the paved road that starts just before the tyre shop. After 2¾ miles (4.4km) up this riverside road there's a small power plant; continue for just over half a mile to where the road forks, turn left at the fork and stop at the kiosk 350 yards (300m) in.

The trail to the waterfall begins at the small village directly opposite the kiosk. One of the villagers will collect US$1 from you as you enter. It's but a five-minute walk to the falls along a pleasant hibiscus-lined path. The falls, which drop about 50 feet (15m), have nice, wide pools both above and below them. The one at the base of the falls is about 35 feet (11m) across. It's a

moderate scurry down to the base of that pool, but it only takes two minutes.

About halfway between the tyre shop and the waterfall, on the east side of the road, there's a beautiful **ceremonial house** *(nahs)* owned by the local nahnken that's well worth a look.

The nahs, which has been restored to showpiece condition, is made of native materials in the traditional manner. Split reeds and thatch make up the roof and walls, hand-twisted coconut sennit rope ties the beams, and all the wood pillars are set on stones so as not to touch the ground.

A black granite plaque on the grounds, presented by the Oomoto Foundation of Japan, waxes poetic:

Into the dim reaches
Beyond cloud haze
I make my way
Toward Ponape.

Another popular place for swimming and picnics is **Nett Point**, though the area does have a noticeable number of rats. As in most places, it's safe if there are families around, but you might want to avoid the area if there are only drinkers hanging out.

To get there, turn left onto the dirt road immediately after crossing Dausokele Bridge, a half mile past the hospital. The road leads 2 miles (3.2km) down to an old dock that offers good views of the lagoon islands and a distant glimpse of the thatched cottages of the Village Hotel to the east. From the pier there are steps leading down into clear waters, good for swimming, though be cautious of boat traffic in the channel.

The drive itself is nice too, passing both modern and thatched homes, and providing excellent views of Sokehs Rock across the bay.

Around the Island A 54-mile (87km) road circles Pohnpei. Close to two-thirds of it is paved; the remaining third, on the southern part of the island between the Village Hotel and Nan Madol, is a very rutted dirt road and the pothole-laced driving will cause great pain to a rental-car belly. The dirt road west of Nan Madol is in slightly better condition than the portion east of it. Plans call for the remainder of the road to be paved, but with the compact funds in a tenuous state it's dubious.

For now, it takes about 1½ hours to go the 22 miles (36km) from Kolonia to the Ponape Agriculture & Trade School (PATS) and the Madolenihmw municipal building, and about four hours to circle the entire island.

East Pohnpei The circle-island road, taken clockwise, leads south out of Kolonia, through small villages in Nett, Uh and Madolenihmw municipalities.

You'll see a nice cross-section of village life on this drive. The men walk along carrying machetes, and sometimes a stalk of bananas or a basket of yams as well, naked children play at the roadside and women gather in the streams to do laundry. If you drive at night you'll see cars collected outside sakau bars.

A mile (1.6km) out of Kolonia the road crosses the **Dausokele Bridge**, which spans a wide river. The turn-off to the Village Hotel is 3½ miles (5.8km) beyond the bridge, on the left.

A half-mile past the Village Hotel you'll cross a bridge and enter Awak village in Uh Municipality. The **church** on the right, with a picturesque mountain backdrop, is worth a look.

Six miles past Awak Village there's a nice **hillside view** looking down onto lagoon islands that resemble Palau's Rock Islands.

Six miles farther, in the village of **Namishi**, an old Japanese lookout tower covered with vines is visible on the right side of the road.

This side of the island is Pohnpei's wetter, windward side and there's an abundance of tropical flora, including plumeria, bougainvillea, beach hibiscus, African tulip trees, breadfruit, pandanus, mangoes and bamboo.

You'll probably have seen **Kepirohi Waterfall** before you get there, as this is the impressive waterfall pictured in tourist brochures. The broad 70-foot (21m) falls cascade over a basalt rockface into a pool that's good for a refreshing midday dip.

The waterfall is at the far end of the village of Sapwehrek. One-third of a mile past Sapwehrek Elementary School you'll cross a river followed by a small church on the right side of the road. Park at the church and walk back about 50 feet (15m) to the trail, which begins on the north side of the church property. It takes about 15 minutes to walk up to the falls. The property owner charges visitors US$3.

Just a few hundred yards past the church there's a road junction. If you're planning to visit the **Ponape Agriculture & Trade School** (better known as PATS) or are on your way to Nan Madol, then go straight ahead on the sole paved road at this intersection rather than taking the sharp left or veering right. (If you want to continue around the island, take the road to the right.)

PATS is a private Jesuit-run high school that offers four-year courses in agriculture, construction and mechanics to boys from all over Micronesia. The school is surrounded by about 200 acres (80 hectares) of land, some of which has been developed as an experimental farm.

Students give free tours of the school by appointment. Call a day or two in advance (☎ 320 2991) to schedule a time. The tours last about an hour and are generally offered between 1 and 3.30 pm.

To get to the Madolenihmw municipal building, or to go over to Temwen Island, drive straight through the PATS complex. Across from the municipal office is Ponape Coconut Products, a small business started by PATS but now independent, which makes the coconut-oil soaps and shampoos sold in gift shops around Kolonia.

South-West Pohnpei Continuing counterclockwise on the circle road, you'll pass through a eucalyptus grove and then up and down a series of hills, the steepest of which offers a beautiful **ocean view**.

This rear side of Pohnpei remains largely in a natural state, with only a few clusters of houses here and there, many made of thatch and mangrove wood. This side is also drier, with less jungle and more open vistas into the interior. On the south coast of Pohnpei is the now-closed Enipein Marine Park.

A bronze **statue** of Henry Nanpei (1860–1928), an influential Pohnpeian nationalist involved in the struggle against the Spanish colonists, is one of the few conventional 'sights' in the area.

The dirt road to the statue leads off to the left 12½ miles (20km) from the turn-off to PATS and a quarter mile (400m) before reaching the cement bridge that crosses Lehn Mesi River, the widest on Pohnpei's south side. The statue is almost half a mile down the side road, off to the right in a small grassy clearing. Nanpei was buried a little farther down the road, in a **church cemetery**. Also in this area is the Lehnpaipohn Waterfall (see later in this section).

As the cross-island road continues it edges along mangrove swamps, winds inland and back to the coast, crosses dozens of streams and goes through a run of small villages.

The picturesque Pwudoi Sanctuary, with its long boardwalk meandering above a mangrove swamp, has closed indefinitely.

The distinctive conical mountain called Pwusehn Malek marks the beginning of the Palikir area and Sokehs Municipality. The FSM capitol complex is just ahead and the road continues back to Kolonia.

Lehnpaipohn Waterfall is a pleasant 30-foot fall which drops into a wide, deep pool that's ideal for swimming. To get to the trailhead coming from Kolonia, continue 10 miles south of Palikir, at which point you'll cross the wide bridge that spans the Lehn Mesi River. Exactly a mile farther turn inland at the school bus stop, pass the Pohn Alamwahu Church and continue on the dirt road for another 1½ miles (2.4km). After going over a rise look for a stand of bamboo; the unmarked trail starts on the left side of the road opposite the bamboo. Road conditions vary with the rain, but you can usually reach the trailhead by car.

The trail is well defined, beginning down carved clay steps, and takes about 15 minutes in all. It's a neat walk through a jungle

of ferns and tropical trees. There's a stream crossing about 10 minutes down, but unless the water is high you can usually make it across the rocks without getting your feet wet. The trail ends at a hillside ledge above the falls. If you walk about 15 yards to the south-east there's a short but steep trail that scurries down the hillside to the edge of the pool. Watch your footing and take your time.

Islands in Pohnpei Lagoon

The number of islands in Pohnpei's lagoon depends on the tide and how you make the count. Not including the artificial islets of Nan Madol, there are about 24 basalt islands, 30 coral islets on the barrier reef and some islands of alluvial sands.

Langer Island The basalt island of Langer figures in colonial history. German traders had copra operations there and the Japanese built a seaplane base on the island that survived US bombings in 1944. After WWII the seaplane ramp was used as Pohnpei's only runway, with all air travel by Grumman SA-16 amphibians until 1970, when the current airport was built on Takatik.

Today Langer Island, equipped with covered picnic tables, is a popular place for weekend family picnics and has clear waters with good swimming and snorkelling.

Black Coral Island Black Coral Island, a small island on Pohnpei's south-western barrier reef, is owned by a friendly Pohnpeian family and makes a fine place for either a day outing or an overnight getaway.

There's nice coral around the island and splendid marine life on the ocean side. Be careful of strong tidal currents in the channel. In addition to swimming and snorkelling, the island can be a fun place for shell searching or just lying on the beach.

Outer Atolls

Ant Atoll Ant, a beautiful atoll with a palm-fringed lagoon, lies a few miles southwest of Pohnpei island. It has pristine white sand beaches and aqua waters with abundant coral and fish, and is one of Pohnpei's most popular dive destinations.

Ant has a large sea bird colony, including brown noddies, great crested terns, sooty terns and great frigate birds.

The atoll is part of Kitti Municipality and belongs to descendants of Pohnpeian nationalist Henry Nanpei.

The largest of the atoll islands, Nikalap Aru, once had a little thatched-cottage resort under development, but a typhoon nipped the project in the bud and the island remains uninhabited.

Pakin Atoll Pakin is a small atoll about 25 miles off Pohnpei island's north-west coast. Its half-dozen islands are inhabited by a single family. It has good beaches and, like Ant, is a popular dive spot.

Oroluk Atoll Oroluk has a tiny population of only a dozen people, but a sizable population of hawksbill and Pacific green turtles. Although its 19 islands total less than a quarter of a square mile of land it has a large lagoon.

Mokil Atoll Mokil (also called Mwoakilloa) was once commonly visited by Marshallese and Gilbertese and later became a popular stop with whalers.

Mokil Atoll's three islets total about half a square mile. About 450 people live on Kahlap, the largest and only inhabited islet. The other two, Urak and Mwandohn, are farmed.

Mokil is a tidy little place, with friendly people, a pretty lagoon and a 1000-foot (304m) airstrip served by Caroline Islands Air.

Pingelap Atoll Pingelap has three islands but all of the atoll's 182 people live on Pingelap Island, which is unfortunately thick with flies and mosquitoes. Sukoru and Deke islands are visited to gather coconuts and crabs.

Early foreigners did not find a ready welcome in Pingelap until about the 1850s when the first whaling ships arrived. In the 1870s, Congregationalist missionaries trained two Pingelapese teachers on Pohnpei and sent them back to their home islands. In just two years they had not only converted practically the entire population, but had adults and children alike all wearing Western clothing.

Pingelap is known for *kahlek*, a kind of night fishing which uses burning torches to attract flying fish into hand-held nets. Kahlek means 'dancing' and refers to the way the men holding the torches have to sway to keep their balance when they're standing up. This type of fishing is done from January to April.

Like Mokil, Pingelap has a 1000-foot airstrip serviced by Caroline Islands Air.

Sapwuafik (Ngatik) Atoll With the drawing up of its municipal constitution in 1986, Ngatik Atoll renamed itself Sapwuafik Atoll, correcting an inaccuracy it had been carrying for 150 years as a result of careless European cartographers. The name Ngatik now, as in pre-European times, refers solely to the largest and only populated island in the atoll.

Sapwuafik, with 327 people, is well known for its outrigger sailing canoes, made from breadfruit logs and assembled using wooden pegs and coconut fibre twine. Unlike on other Pohnpeian atolls, where islanders have switched to speedboats or have attached small outboard motors to their canoes, Sapwuafik's traditional canoes are powered solely by the wind using sails lashed to bamboo poles.

The FSM government is currently building an airstrip on Sapwuafik, but as it has languished in the 'building' stage for a while there is no knowing when it will be completed.

Nukuoro & Kapingamarangi Atolls The 400 or so people of Nukuoro and Kapingamarangi atolls are physically, linguistically and culturally Polynesian. Both atolls are beautiful, with good beaches.

Nukuoro has 42 tiny islets formed in a near-perfect circle around a lagoon 4 miles (6.4km) in diameter. The total land area is just 380 acres (150 hectares). Most of the

Bloody Hart

A visit to Ngatik by the British ship *Lambton* in 1837 left an indelible mark on the island. Charles 'Bloody' Hart, the Australian captain of the ship, was after fine pieces of tortoise shell he had seen on an earlier excursion. However, the shells had religious significance to the Ngatikese and they refused to trade. In fact, during the first visit trading negotiations were halted by a group of armed islanders who attacked the crew and forced them to run for their lives back to the ship.

Hart was a swindler, accustomed to getting his own way, and although his crew had escaped unharmed they sought revenge. The Ngatikese, armed only with clubs and slings, had little defence against the muskets of the *Lambton's* crew, and the sailors massacred all the island men.

As a result, the 600 people of Sapwuafik Atoll are largely descended from a mix of Ngatikese women and British, American, Pohnpeian and Gilbertese men, many of them crew members of the *Lambton*.

---

population live on the largest island, a third of which is covered by taro. Subsistence comes largely from taro farming and fishing.

Nukuoro is a real haven, with welcoming Polynesian hospitality, and would be a fine place to spend some time just lazing around on beaches, picking up seashells and playing with island children.

Kapingamarangi Atoll is just one degree, or 65 miles, north of the equator. Its 33 islets total just over half a sq mile, with a lagoon 7 miles (11.6km) across at its widest point. The population is about 625. There are no arrangements for visitors to stay on Kapingamarangi, and overall the island is not terribly welcoming to outsiders.

Both Nukuoro and Kapingamarangi are hit from time to time by severe droughts, resulting in food shortages on the islands.

Activities

Diving & Snorkelling Pohnpei has pretty coral reefs, manta rays and lots of fish. If the sea is rough, divers may have to stay in-side the barrier reef, which lies from 1 to 5 miles (1.6 to 8km) offshore, and be content to explore the lagoon waters. However, visibility is much better outside the reef. Night diving is available and it's also possible to dive Nan Madol.

While snorkelling is not good on Pohnpei island itself, there are a number of small nearby islands accessible by short boat rides that have clear waters and good coral and marine life.

Ant and Pakin atolls are favourite diving spots. Ant has sheer coral drop-offs, schools of barracuda and lots of reef-shark action; it's good for snorkelling too. Pakin has virgin reefs with gorgonian fans and other coral as well as abundant marine life. The one-way boat ride takes one hour to Ant and two hours to Pakin. Spring, summer and autumn months are the best times for diving. From the winter months of December to February the waters between Pohnpei and Pakin are rough. If you go outside the reef it's a good safety precaution to make sure your boat has two engines.

Dive Shops Phoenix Marine Sports (☎ 320 5678, fax 320 2364) is a Japanese dive operation with the latest equipment, comfortable boats, friendly staff and a good reputation. Two-tank boat dives cost US$65 inside Pohnpei reef, US$75 outside (rates apply to groups of four or more people – they increase for smaller groups.) For Ant or Pakin, add US$10. Weight belts and tanks are included in the rate; other equipment can be rented. Snorkelling tours that include a visit to Nan Madol and Kepirohi Waterfall cost US$55, lunch included. Visa and MasterCard are accepted.

The Village (☎ 320 2797, fax 320 3797, ✉ thevillage@mail.fm) also runs a nice dive operation. The rates vary with the number of people, so contact them for a specific price quote. Village rents scuba gear to those who use its service for US$20. It also accepts MasterCard, Visa and American Express cards.

Iet Ehu (☎ 320 2958, fax 320 2958) is a local operation that's short on equipment but otherwise friendly. Two-tank boat dives within Pohnpei reef cost US$65, to Ant and Pakin US$85 (prices assume a minimum of three people in the boat). They also offer a one-tank manta ray dive that's combined with a tour of Nan Madol for US$65. Iet Ehu does not rent scuba equipment (and few places have scuba equipment except for their own divers), so if you don't have your own gear try elsewhere. Visa, MasterCard and American Express are accepted.

Pohnpei Aqua World (☎ 320 5941, fax 320 4221) has two-tank dives for US$85 and night dives for US$60. Scuba equipment and snorkel sets are available by rental. Visa and MasterCard are accepted.

Joy Ocean Service (☎ 320 2447, fax 320 2478), behind Joy Hotel, is a small operation run by dive-master Yukio Suzuki. Very little English is spoken and it's rather expensive – US$100 for a two-tank boat dive around Pohnpei (including lunch).

For other dive shops, see Organised Tours in the Getting There & Away chapter.

Kayaking Pohnpei's lagoons, with their mangroves and the ruins of Nan Madol, make nice, relaxed kayaking locations. The Village rents single kayaks for US$25 and double kayaks for US$35. The Pohnpei Paddle Club (☎ 320 7706) can arrange kayak lessons and rentals.

Hiking The two main hikes in the greater Kolonia area are on Sokehs Island, one an easy hike up the ridge and the other a difficult one up the rock face. Both offer great views (see Sokehs Island earlier in this chapter).

You can also make hardy hikes into Pohnpei's jungle interior though you'll need a guide; ask the tourist office for assistance.

Langer Island also has a short but decent walking trail.

Tennis There are two busy tennis courts at the south side of Kolonia Town Hall, a building originally constructed during the Japanese era and marked only in Japanese script. If you want to play, there's usually somebody from the local tennis club around who can explain the proper protocol.

Fishing Pohnpei waters have a good variety of fish, including yellowfin tuna, mahimahi, marlin, barracuda and numerous reef fish. Trolling, bottom fishing and spearfishing trips can be arranged through most tour companies or dive shops. For a listing of companies, see Organised Tours following.

Organised Tours

Iet Ehu Tours (☎ 320 2958), a flexible local tour operation, offers the widest range of sightseeing tours, from overnight trekking outings in the jungle (US$80) to trips to Sokehs Rock (US$30). The Nan Madol trip (US$40) includes snorkelling and a dip under Kepirohi Waterfall; try and ask for freshly speared fish for lunch. Iet Ehu also goes to Mt. Nahna Laud (US$60) and to various waterfalls (US$50). Note that the above prices apply to groups of three or more. Singles or couples will be charged triple the price. Iet Ehu can also take you to any of Pohnpei's nearshore islands, including Langer and Black Coral.

Micro Tours (☎ 320 2888, fax 320 5528), based in the Micro Office Supply Building near the public market, has a variety of tours including boat trips to Nan Madol (US$38 per person), Ant Atoll (US$50), and Black Coral Island (US$38).

The Village Hotel (☎ 320 2797) can arrange a variety of tours; call for prices. Also try Pohnpei Aqua World (☎ 320 5942, fax 320 2391, ✆ pwohmariabeach@ mail.fm) and Joy Hotel (☎ 320 2477). Many of the tour operators can be flexible and will bend to accommodate your wishes.

Places to Stay

Camping Camping is not a custom on Pohnpei island and because of crime issues it's not advisable. Camping can be arranged, however, on the uninhabited islands of Ant and Pakin atolls for a modest fee, though you'll also have to pay for the boat ride. The tourist office or the dive companies can usually help make arrangements.

Micronesian Games 2002

The 5th Micronesian Games will be held in Pohnpei in 2002. The Games are held every four years, when states from around Micronesia send athletes to participate in over 60 events. These include outrigger canoe racing, spearfishing, weightlifting, table tennis, soccer and rugby. The most popular spectator event is the Micro All-Around Competition which consists of climbing coconut trees, coconut husking and grating, and swimming and diving.

The last Micronesian Games, held in Palau in 1998, were a tremendous success. Broadcasting was aided by the kickoff of Nauru's Sports Pacific Network television.

It's a good idea to have a local guide stay out with you for safety's sake.

Hotels Pohnpei has a 6% hotel tax which should be added to the rates below unless otherwise specified. Almost all of the hotels accept MasterCard and Visa and a few (including the Village Hotel) accept American Express. Most hotels will provide free airport transfers if you call ahead.

Kolonia Yvonne's Hotel (☎ 320 5130, fax 320 4953) has pleasant rooms on the ground floor of a four-storey apartment building, each with air-con, TV, refrigerator and private bathroom. It's a few minutes walk from the centre of town and reasonable value at US$50/56 for singles/doubles (tax included). You can also get a room/car package for US$80; check with GP Car Rental at the airport.

One of Micronesia's nicest new budget spots is *Nara Gardens* (☎/fax 320 2774, @ bnn@mail.fm), which has three immaculate apartments for overnight guests (and three for long-term stays). Each apartment has twin beds, TV and kitchenette. It costs US$50 a night for singles/doubles; it's US$30 to add a bed. The friendly management lives just across the street. It's advisable to make advance reservations given the limited space. Credit cards are not accepted.

Other apartment options are the two apartments, one two-bedroom and one three-bedroom, above the *Nihco Store* (☎ 320 4659, fax 320 6504, @ nihco@ mail.fm) near the US embassy. Both are fully furnished with TV, air-con and kitchen facilities. They cost US$50 a night, but they're often rented out to long-term guests.

Also reasonably priced is the *Sea Breeze Hotel* (☎ 320 2065, fax 320 2067) on the harbour road near the Australian embassy. Good-sized rooms have a single and a double bed, bathroom, refrigerator and TV. Rooms with an ocean view cost US$50/60; others cost US$10 less. In addition to tax, the hotel charges a 5% service fee.

Hotel Pohnpei (☎ 320 2330, fax 320 5983), a few minutes walk beyond the South Park and Cliff Rainbow Hotels, has rustic thatch and wood cottages. It was closed for renovations in Spring 1999 without a definite reopening date; call for details.

The 18-room *South Park Hotel* (☎ 320 2255, fax 320 2600, @ southparkhotel@ mail.fm) has a fine hillside location on the west side of Kolonia. The new wing has pleasant rooms, refrigerator and a sliding glass door opening to a veranda with an unspoiled view of Sokehs Rock. Rooms cost US$75/85. The old wing also has fine ocean views but has a more cottage-like atmosphere. These rooms are basic but also have TV, air-con and bathroom and are good value at US$40/45.

The *Cliff Rainbow Hotel* (☎ 320 2415, fax 320 5416, @ cliffrainbow@mail.fm), across the road from the South Park Hotel, has 32 rooms with air-con, refrigerators and TVs. Rates range from US$40 to US$85/US$48 to US$95. The cheaper rooms are in an older section, which is quite ordinary but clean and adequate.

The clean 18-room *Pacific Skylite Hotel* (☎ 320 3672, fax 320 3708, @ pacskylite@ mail.fm), about 200m beyond the Jungle Bar, has nice rooms, some with a lagoon view, with a king, queen and single bed, or two single beds. Rooms come with refrigerator, TV and tub, and cost US$66/77 (tax included) for singles/doubles. Children under 5 stay free; extra persons cost US$15.

There is a pool and a restaurant. A room and car package is available for US$85/100.

Joy Hotel (☎ *320 2447, fax 320 2478,* ✉ *joy_ponape@mail.fm)* is a pleasant, central hotel with nicely furnished rooms, each with refrigerator, air-con, fan, cable TV and a small balcony. Rooms with one double bed cost US$69/74 and rooms with two double beds cost US$90 for doubles (tax included).

Penny Hotel (☎ *320 5770, fax 320 2040,* ✉ *penny@mail.fm)* is adjacent to the US embassy, about a 10-minute walk from the town centre. The rooms are comfortable, with air-con, refrigerators, cable TV, bathtubs and either a king bed or two twins. All rooms have large balconies, but ask for one of the quieter rear-facing ones, which have pleasant garden views. Rooms cost US$71.50/82.50 (tax included). Call ahead for airport transfers.

Airport Area The ***Pwohmaria Beach Resort*** (☎ *320 5941, fax 320 2391,* ✉ *pwohmariabeach@mail.fm)* consists of a run of beachside cottages squeezed between the commercial dock and the backside of the airport. Considering that Pohnpei has several late night flights, the runway proximity could certainly disrupt sleep. The cottages themselves are quite clean and have a rustic appeal with wood interiors, wicker furniture, and refrigerators; ceiling fans and a stiff sea breeze keep them cool. Singles/doubles cost US$65/72. This near-deserted hotel is suffering severely from Asian no-shows.

Outside Kolonia The popular ***Village Hotel*** (☎ *320 2797, fax 320 3797,* ✉ *thevillage@mail.fm)*, widely considered *the* place to stay in Pohnpei, has 20 native-style thatched cottages perched on a hillside in a natural setting 5 miles (8km) south of Kolonia. Rooms have two queen waterbeds, wicker furniture, private baths and fans. Rates are US$80 to US$95/US$90 to US$105 for singles/doubles. Additional guests are US$10 and children under 12 stay for half-price. Airport transfers cost US$8 return.

The ***PCR-Nantehlik Hotel*** (☎ *320 4981, fax 320 4983)*, on the river opposite Nett Point, was under renovation at the time of writing. Its thatched roofs and pleasant lagoon setting will make it worth a look.

If you're looking for a long-term rental, one of the easier places to book is ***C-Star Apartelle*** (☎ *320 3398, fax 320 3399,* ✉ *cstar@mail.fm)*, on the road to Nanpohmnal, a couple of miles south of Kolonia. This modern apartment complex has 25 units, with cooking facilities, living room, air-con and cable TV. Rates begin at US$700 a month. Units can also be rented by the day for US$60/70.

Outer Islands Caroline Islands Air (☎ 320 8406) can arrange for homestays in Mokil or Pingelap, but contact them well in advance of your visit. Otherwise, contact the mayor of the island you intend to visit. With a little persistence, you can usually track him down by calling the Congress (☎ 320 2324) or the Office for Island Affairs (☎ 320 2710, fax 320 2505) for help.

Bear in mind that homestay accommodation on the outer islands is extremely rustic. There is no electricity, water consists of rainwater collected in vats and Western comforts are lacking. However, it's an excellent way to learn about Pohnpei's traditional lifestyles.

On Langer Island there are seven bright-green, simple *cottages* on stilts where visitors can stay for US$7, mattress and sheets included. There is no electricity or air-con but the huts are cross-ventilated by the coastal winds. The 15-minute boat ride over can be arranged for US$2 return. Bring your own food; you can use their kerosene stove. For more information contact Jerry Barbosa (☎ 320 2769). These are undoubtedly the better choice on Langer, but if they are taken, try Higinio Weirlangt (☎ 320 2159), who operates one *cottage* and a ***Pohnpeian nahs*** – essentially a shelter where people can bed down. The cottage, which gets quite toasty without air-con, costs US$15. The nahs costs US$7.50 per person, mattresses and sheets included.

Black Coral Island has seven simple but adequate *huts* that cost US$13.50 per person, with mattresses, pillows and sheets. You should bring your own food and supplement it with the only meal offered, a fresh fish plate for US$5 (request in advance).

On Nukuoro Island there is a guesthouse on the pier available for overnight or longer stays and the local senator has a traditional wooden house on stilts that is sometimes available. To make advance arrangements call ☎ 320 2750 in Kolonia and ask for the Nukuoro senator, or radio Nukuoro Atoll via the FSM telecommunications office.

Places to Eat

Pohnpei has excellent fresh tuna. Sashimi is often the cheapest dish on the menu; grilled or fried fish dishes are not much more. Most restaurants offer a combination of Japanese and Western food.

Tap water is not safe for drinking unless it has been treated or boiled. Distilled water is available in grocery stores.

Kolonia *Cafe Ole*, a simple cafe at the side of Ambros Store, makes good milkshakes and has reasonably priced breakfast fare. There are also good toasted sandwiches, burgers with fries for US$3 to US$5 and plate lunches from US$5. Try the sashimi platter (US$5.25). It's open from 6.30 am to 7 pm daily.

Joy Restaurant at the north side of Kolonia is a perennial favourite with excellent Japanese food. Fresh fish is the speciality, though they also have beef and chicken dishes. The popular 'Joy Lunch' of fried tuna, rice, sashimi, soup and salad costs just US$5.50. You can also get a fried fish burger to go (US$1.50). It's open for lunch from 11 am to 3 pm daily except Saturday.

Joy Hotel Restaurant, not to be confused with the nearby Joy Restaurant, is off the lobby of the Joy Hotel and serves a variety of Japanese and Western foods. A dinner of tuna includes a big piece of fish, soup, salad and French fries for US$7. Chicken teriyaki plates cost US$7.25. At lunch they have sandwiches for US$3.50 to US$4, and *oyako donburi* (sweetened chicken and egg

atop rice) and other dishes for not much more. At breakfast, French toast, pancakes or egg dishes cost around US$1.50 to US$3. It's open for breakfast, lunch and dinner daily.

Yaeko's in front of the Sei Restaurant has four dishes on the menu, including an omelette and tasty fried chicken. All dishes cost US$5. Helpings are huge.

PCR Restaurant has varied and delicious offerings. Its famous Napolitan spaghetti comes loaded with fish, octopus and green peppers and arrives on a sizzling platter with tasty garlic bread for US$6.50. It's a popular place, with a great waterfront setting and consistently excellent food. It's open from 10 am to 2 pm and 5 to 9 pm daily.

Sei Restaurant, at the southern end of Kolonia, is tucked in a very pleasant wood building and is a great place to go if you're starving. Sei's speciality is a fabulous all-you-can-eat Japanese buffet for lunch and dinner. The offerings include shrimp rice, sashimi, fried tuna, noodle and vegetable dishes. The lunch/dinner buffet costs US$7/9. Sei is open weekdays only from 9 am to 2 pm, and from 6 to 9 pm daily.

The *China Star Restaurant* near the library aspires for the elegant look, with padded, high-backed black metal chairs. It has a good, if a bit pricey, selection of Chinese dishes. Especially popular are the Sichuan chicken (US$7) and the seafood combo (US$12.50). It's open from 11.30 am to 1.30 pm and 5 to 9.30 pm. On weekends it's open for dinner only.

The popular *South Park Restaurant* at the South Park Hotel has a nice view of Sokehs Rock through louvred windows. The varied menu includes oyako donburi and various fish, chicken and pork dishes for US$7 to US$10 at dinner. At lunch there are some good-value specials; opt for the fish set (US$5.50). Western-style breakfasts also cost around US$5. It's open from 7 am to 2 pm Monday to Saturday and 5 to 9 pm daily.

There's a public market along the waterfront road by the Chinese embassy, where you can buy produce and drinking coconuts. Small stands selling fruit, snacks, and sandwiches have sprouted along the roads in and around Kolonia.

The modern *Palm Terrace Store*, the island's best and largest grocery store, is open from 8 am to 8 pm on weekdays, 8 am to 7 pm Saturday and 10 am to 5 pm Sunday. It has a good bakery section, a deli with fresh roasted or batter-fried chicken and a wine and spirits section. The *Ambrose Store* beside Cafe Ole is also well-stocked and has a nice bakery section, including US$1 bags of fresh doughnuts.

Outside Kolonia The open-air thatched restaurant at the *Village Hotel* has an unbeatable hillside setting, with a distant view of Sokehs Rock across the lagoon. This is a good place to stop for breakfast if you're on your way around the island. If you have a sweet tooth, try the platter of Pohnpei hot cakes topped with thick fruity syrup (US$3.50). At lunch there are sandwiches and omelettes for US$4 to US$5. Dinners include seafood and meat specials ranging from US$14 to US$20; the quasedillas and sashimi appetisers are good warm-ups. On Sunday there are some nice brunch items as well as US$2.50 glasses of champagne.

Entertainment

Bars Drinking scenes in Pohnpei can sometimes get a bit rough, with fist fights breaking out and the like, particularly in venues where there's dancing. The bars listed in this entry are among the tamer spots. Alcohol and cigarettes are taxed at 25%.

Across the Street, a bar opposite Cliff Rainbow Hotel, is in a large open-air thatched-roof spot with a great hill-top view of Sokehs Rock. It's open daily from noon to midnight weekdays. The US$1 beers at happy hour (5 to 7 pm) are the island's best bargain. Otherwise beer costs US$1.50 and mixed drinks start at US$4.50.

Rumors, an open-air bar at the side of the marina, has a pleasant harbourside locale that attracts a nice mix of islanders and younger expats. There's a happy hour from 4 to 6 pm on weekdays with US$1.50 beers and US$1.75 mixed drinks.

The new *Jungle Bar* is a relaxed, covered outdoor setting beyond the Penny Hotel. At happy hour (5 to 7 pm weekdays and noon to 6 pm on weekends), beer drops from US$1.75 to US$1.50 and tequila is US$2. The place is a bit hard to find – peer through the jungle opposite the Nissan sign.

The *Tattooed Irishman*, the bar at the Village Hotel's open-air restaurant, has a more genteel atmosphere. For a breathtaking view, order up a tropical drink and head for the thatched gazebo.

Cupid's Bar, high on a hill past the Pacific Skylight Hotel, is worthwhile for its stunning overlook onto Kolonia; opt for the outdoor hillside seats in good weather.

Sakau Bars Every neighbourhood has a sakau bar, though most are small, casual and inconspicuous. Most commonly they are a simple thatched-roof, open-air structure in someone's backyard. If you see a sign hung on a shack saying *mie sakau pwongiet* it means sakau is being served there that night.

Though sakau bars are thick outside Kolonia, within Kolonia people tend simply to stop by and fill their flasks. The bars are also a bit hard to find – ask the locals (who always know), or bring your flask to the Jungle Bar (which has a sakau bar nearby) and they'll fill it for US$3.

Unlike alcohol drinkers who tend to be boisterous and temperamental, sakau drinkers are quiet and relaxed. Sakau partakers generally sit in a circle sharing stories, passing the sakau bowl and gradually falling into quiet contemplation.

Cultural Shows Pohnpei's cultural centres offer shows of traditional dances, songs and demonstrations of coconut husking and crafts. Shows usually include ritual sakau making, with samples handed around to the audience, weaving of grass skirts and baskets, and native food making. The cultural centre that most frequently gives shows is the one in Nett Municipality and the other in Uh Municipality by the Village Hotel.

The cultural show in Nett usually includes a wonderful array of traditional

Pohnpeian foods roasted in an earthen oven. You'll witness *uhmw* – the local method of cooking breadfruit.

Performances can be arranged either by calling the cultural centre at Nett directly (☎ 320 3622) at least 24 hours in advance, or by contacting the Pohnpei Visitors Bureau (☎ 320 4851). The price is US$50 for one to four people, or US$10 for five and more persons. Iet Ehu tours can also arrange for groups to see local dance performances in Nett or Kitti; the price is US$35 a head and can drop to US$20 with larger groups.

Shopping

Pohnpei has Micronesia's highest quality woodcarvings, virtually all made by Kapingamarangi islanders who live in Kolonia. Most common are dolphins, sharks with real shark teeth, turtles and outrigger canoe models with woven sails, all carved of mangrove or ironwood. Other items made by the Kapingamarangi people are amulets of manta rays and dolphins finely carved from the nut of the ivory palm, a hard seed that resembles real ivory.

Other local handicrafts that make good souvenirs include fans, woven fibre pocketbooks, baskets, trochus shell buttons and brightly coloured appliquéd skirts.

Packages of gourmet Pohnpei pepper make nice lightweight presents. A 3oz pack of black or white peppercorns costs about US$3.50, while 5oz attractively bottled and packaged in a woven basket costs around US$12.

Pohnpei soap, massage oil, suntan lotion and shampoo that are made from coconut oil are sold separately in stores for local use or gift-packaged in woven boxes at the handicraft shops. Or, for slightly lower prices, check the tiny stock at the Ponape Coconut Products office, just north of the public market, which is open weekdays from 8 am to 4.30 pm.

Joy Restaurant is a particularly good place to find handicrafts. The Village Hotel's T-shirts are also nice.

The best method of all is to purchase items directly from craftspeople at the workshops in Kolonia's Kapingamarangi Village; try the Carving Spot Handicraft Shop or the Kapingamarangi Gift Shop.

Getting There & Away

Air Continental flies to Pohnpei on its island-hopper route, with flights coming from both directions twice a week. The regular one-way fare is US$255 between Chuuk and Pohnpei and US$430 between Guam and Pohnpei, though FSM residents pay only US$160/255 on those routes.

The regular one-way fare from Kosrae to Pohnpei is US$145, and from Majuro it's US$400.

For travellers island-hopping between Guam and Honolulu, Pohnpei is a free stopover. Otherwise, Honolulu to Pohnpei costs US$750 one way, or US$1238 return.

Air Nauru flies into Pohnpei twice a week and continues to Guam and Manila. The one-way Pohnpei-Guam fare is US$195; the one-way Pohnpei-Manila fare is A$550; A$590 excursion. The one-way Pohnpei-Nauru fare is A$425, or A$470 return. There's also a Pohnpei-Fiji ticket for US$495 one way, US$550 for a 30-day excursion. Tickets are best booked through Village Travel, which accepts American Express but not Visa or MasterCard.

Airports & Airlines Pohnpei's airport is on Takatik Island, connected to Kolonia by a mile-long causeway. The terminal has a snack bar, a small but good souvenir shop, car rental booths and restrooms.

The Continental Airlines office (☎ 320 2424) is at the airport. It's open from 9 am to 3.30 pm, but they're not always at the counter. If no-one is out front knock on the door behind the counter. Air Nauru (☎ 320 5963) also operates from its airport counter; an agent works spotty hours there during the day.

Boat Kolonia Harbor is the official port of entry in Pohnpei. Yachts dock at the marina near Rumors bar.

SeAir Transportation (☎ 320 2865, fax 320 2866) on Main St in Kolonia is a private company that operates the MS *Caroline*

Islands, a boat similar to the government field-trip ship. It runs on an irregular basis between Pohnpei and Kosrae, and sometimes also goes to Chuuk and Yap, depending upon its cargo schedules. Fares are calculated according to distance. The one-way fare to Kosrae costs US$10, to Chuuk US$12 and to Yap US$20. Cabin fares cost US$51 to Kosrae, US$62 to Chuuk and US$192 to Yap. There's meal service on board (US$12 per day), but you'll probably want to bring your own food. The *Caroline Islands* may soon be replaced by the Japanese-built *Caroline Voyager*.

For information on the field-trip ship to Pohnpei's outer islands see Getting Around later in this chapter.

Yachties heading to Pohnpei should notify the Port Authority (☎ 320 2793) at least 24 hours in advance so that Environmental Protection Agency officers can inspect the ship before it docks. Visitors permits will be issued upon arrival. The Port Authority charges visiting yachts a US$25 entry fee and US$20 for navigational aids. Staying at the dock costs US$35 a day.

Getting Around

To/From the Airport Most hotels will provide free airport transfers on request. Taxis generally don't run out to the airport, as it's off their main route. If you don't have somebody coming to pick you up, try to catch a ride from someone heading into town – otherwise it's a two-mile (3.2km) walk.

Air The only airstrips on Pohnpei's outer atolls are on Mokil and Pingelap, although one is under way on Sapwuafik. Division among islanders on Nukuoro has stalemated plans for building an airstrip there.

Caroline Islands Air (CIA; ☎ 320 8406) flies to Mokil and Pingelap on Monday and Friday, provided there are enough passengers. CIA's one-way fare from Pohnpei island is US$50 to Mokil, US$65 to Pingelap. Return fares are double.

Flights leave Pohnpei from the two-storey cement building on the western side of the main airport terminal.

Car Of the car rental companies with offices at the airport, the more reliable is GP Car Rental (☎ 320 5648), which has sedans for US$40 per day; add US$5 for a collision damage waiver.

Budget Rent-A-Car (☎ 320 8705/8760) has an office by the FSM telecommunications building in town and rents sedans for US$49 and vans for US$80; collision insurance is US$16. Budget accepts major credit cards and usually meets arriving flights.

H & E (☎/fax 320 2413), just behind the Australian embassy, has sedans, vans, and a pick-up for US$50; no insurance is available. Visa and MasterCard are accepted.

PCR Car Rental (☎ 320 5252), behind PCR Restaurant, may revive when its Nissan shipment arrives. Penny Rent-A-Car (☎ 320 5770), with the Penny Hotel, has Nissan sedans for US$55. Pacific Skylite Hotel (☎ 320 3672) has cars for US$45. If you plan to do much dirt road driving it's a good idea to call around and try to get a jeep or other high-riding vehicle; in low-riding sedans, lost oil pans are not uncommon and the rental companies will hit you up for the repair costs.

Petrol costs US$1.90 a gallon on Pohnpei.

Taxi Pohnpei has a system of radio-dispatched shared taxis. The taxis are marked. Some are sedans, others are minivans. You can call to have a taxi pick you up, or flag them down. Either way, the fare is US$1 anywhere within greater Kolonia, including Palikir, as long as you don't go off the paved road. To go onto dirt roads there's an extra US$1 charge.

It costs US$2 to go from Kolonia to the Village Hotel and at least US$12 to the Madolenihmw municipal office. These fares are per person; taxis will stop and pick up other passengers along the way. Two of the biggest of Pohnpei's taxi companies are Waido (☎ 320 5744) and Lucky 7 (☎ 320 5859). Taxis operate from 6.30 am to midnight daily.

Hitching Hitching has mixed results. If you've got your thumb out it will often be one of the taxis that stops to pick you up – and they expect payment. On the other hand, when you're just walking along the road, people who have had some passing contact with you, such as a customs officer, will often stop and offer you a ride. The usual safety precautions apply.

Boat The government field-trip ship, *Micro Glory*, used to go once a month to the outer islands, but at the time of writing lack of government funding had the ship dry-docked on Pohnpei for much of the year. It runs more reliably before election-time, when the politicians are out to rouse support. The ship holds 125 passengers and has six two-person cabins. Fares are calculated on a per-mile basis.

The eastern islands trip goes to Mokil and Pingelap, returning in about five days. The return fare is US$12 on deck, US$62 for a cabin. The southern islands trip goes to Sapwuafik, Oroluk, Nukuoro and Kapingamarangi and takes a week to 10 days. The return fare costs US$30 on deck, US$155 for a cabin. You can take along your own food or pay US$4 for breakfast, US$5 for lunch and US$6 for dinner.

The field-trip ship leaves from the commercial dock on Takatik Island. For more information, contact the Office for Island Affairs (☎ 320 2710, fax 320 2505). If you go in person, it's the first building on the left (marked Office of Public & Governmental Relations) as you go up the hill toward the legislature building in Kolonia.

To get to Black Coral Island, contact Micro Tours or Iet Ehu Tours, which can drop visitors there; otherwise make arrangements through Dakio Paul (☎ 320 4869) to be picked up behind the Seinwar Elementary School in Kitti, which is less than a mile south of the Pwudoi Sanctuary. The 15-minute boat trip costs US$35 for one to four people, and US$7.50 each for more than four. For those on day trips, there's a US$5 landing fee.

Chuuk (Truk)

Chuuk is colourful, lively and rough around the edges. Houses are commonly painted in several bright contrasting colours. On hot days village women sit bare-breasted in streams doing laundry and young children run around naked. Speedboats zip back and forth across the lagoon and from Weno you can watch the sun set behind the Faichuk Islands, often with a brilliant light show.

Chuuk's biggest draw card is its sunken wrecks, which draw enthusiastic divers from all over the world. A whole Japanese fleet rests on the lagoon floor – a moment in time captured in an underwater museum. Most of the wrecks lie off the islands of Dublon, Eten, Fefan and Uman, and together they represent the largest naval loss in history.

The waters of Chuuk Lagoon are clear and calm and you don't have to be an experienced diver to take a look at its underwater attractions. Some shipwrecks are only a few feet under the water's surface and can readily be snorkelled.

With the passing of its state constitution in 1989, Truk officially renamed itself Chuuk (pronounced 'chuke'). Most islanders have managed the change, but many US dive tour companies still insist on 'Truk', as do WWII veterans and some other Micronesian residents.

History
Early Settlers Legend says that sometime around the 14th century the great leader Sowukachaw came by canoe to Chuuk with his son Sowooniiras. Where they really came from is anybody's guess but most people put their money on Kosrae since in Chuuk (as in Pohnpei) there are many legends relating to Kosrae.

From Truk to Chuuk

To outsiders the name change from Truk to Chuuk may be confusing, but the Chuukese have always called the islands in the main lagoon 'Chuuk' when speaking in their native language. The word 'Truk', a Germanic corruption of the name, was used only when speaking in English. *Chuuk* means 'mountain'. The outer islands are *fanabi* – *fanu* is 'island', *bi* is 'sand'.

CHUUK STATE

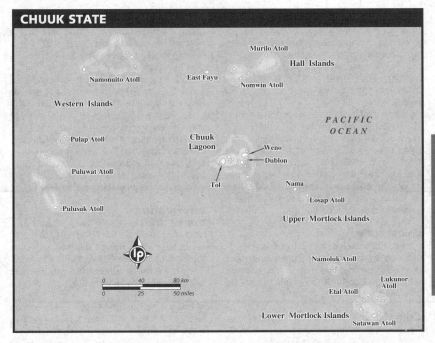

Murilo Atoll

Hall Islands

Namonuito Atoll

East Fayu

Nomwin Atoll

Western Islands

PACIFIC
OCEAN

Pulap Atoll

Chuuk
Lagoon

Weno

Dublon

Puluwat Atoll

Tol

Nama

Pulusuk Atoll

Losap Atoll

Upper Mortlock Islands

Namoluk Atoll

Lukunor
Atoll

Etal Atoll

Lower Mortlock Islands

Satawan Atoll

0   40   80 km
0   25   50 miles

The arrival of these leaders represented something analogous to the end of medievalism. They are credited with introducing new varieties of breadfruit as well as methods to preserve it. That's important because at the time breadfruit was the staple food crop. The arrival of Sowukachaw also represented the beginning of clan history and some sort of social ranking system. When the Chuukese trace their ancestry they go back as far as that time, but never any further.

European Contact The first Europeans to sight Chuuk Lagoon were with the Spanish ship *San Lucas*, captained by Alonso de Arellano, in 1565. The Chuukese responded with hundreds of canoes filled with armed warriors. The Spaniards stayed only long enough to fire a few cannon shots and make their way across the lagoon and out another passage.

When Manuel Dublon, captaining the *San Antonio*, came to Chuuk in 1814 to collect beche-de-mer he became the first European to enter the lagoon in 250 years.

The Germans took possession of Chuuk from the Spanish in 1899 and developed a copra trade, with their headquarters on Dublon Island.

Japanese & WWII The Japanese navy began building bases on Dublon immediately after occupying the islands in 1914.

During the war Chuuk Lagoon became the Japanese Imperial Fleet's most important central Pacific base. The fortification of the islands was thought to be so impenetrable that the lagoon earned the nickname 'Gibraltar of the Pacific'. As the huge sheltered lagoon had only a few passageways it could be easily defended against naval invasion, making for a perfect, calm anchorage. Unfortunately for the Japanese, these same conditions also made it easy to trap their fleet.

On 17 February 1944 the US navy launched an air-bomb attack, code-named

'Operation Hailstone', against the Japanese Fourth Fleet, which was docked in the lagoon. Like sitting ducks, the Japanese ships were bombed nonstop for two days and by the finish some 60 ships had sunk to the bottom. The islands of Chuuk Lagoon, however, were never invaded by Allied forces.

When the US military moved in after the war, Dublon was crowded with the 30,000 Japanese soldiers who had survived the air raids but had no means of leaving the island. Since it was easiest to keep them on Dublon until they could be repatriated to Japan, the USA established its headquarters on Weno, which has been the administrative centre ever since.

Geography

Chuuk State includes 192 outer islands in addition to the 15 main islands and more than 80 islets that make up Chuuk Lagoon. All in all, about 40 of the state's islands are inhabited.

Climate

The average annual temperature is a fairly constant 81°F (27°C). Annual rainfall averages 143 inches in Chuuk Lagoon. Humidity is high year round and can get particularly uncomfortable between July and November when the north-easterly trade winds die down. The most agreeable time of the year is the dry season from January to March.

Although Chuuk lies outside the main typhoon belt, it has been hit by a number of severe storms in recent years.

Population & People

Chuuk is the one of Micronesia's most populous island groups, with 57,300 people. Approximately one-third live on the island of Weno.

Society & Conduct

In Chuuk each island has a predominant clan, the members of which are generally the descendants of the first people to settle that island. While the head clan no longer owns all the island's land, the members still enjoy limited privileges. For instance, other people on the island are often obliged to present the clan with some token of respect, such as the fruits from the first harvest.

Today the chief of the predominant clan has only nominal power over those outside his own clan, though he is still occasionally called on to mediate disputes between other clans on the island.

Many Chuukese women wear *nikautang*, a dress with puffed sleeves, a dropped waist with lace trim and a gathered skirt that hangs below the knee. Also popular are brightly coloured appliqued skirts called *uros*.

Information

Tourist Offices The Chuuk Visitors Bureau (☎ 330 4133, fax 330 4194, ✆ cvb@ mail.fm), tucked behind the post office on Weno, is open weekdays from 8 am to 5 pm. They have few brochures but can be quite helpful with enough prodding.

Money The Bank of Guam has a branch next to Shigeto's Store, which is open weekdays from 9 am to 3 pm, and from 9 am to 1 pm on Saturday. The bank can exchange currency, including Australian dollars, and can cash US dollar travellers cheques. There's a 24-hour ATM outside the bank that attracts curious onlookers. The Bank of FSM is open from 9.30 am to 2.30 pm Monday to Thursday, and until 3 pm on Friday. On payday Friday expect long queues at the counters.

Social Highs & Lows

Anyone who observes the Chuukese closely, in the store or in the tourist office, will note that many duck when entering a room. This is a reflection of the traditional social hierarchy: young men bow to old men, women bow to men, and young women bow to old women. Technically one's head is supposed to be low enough so that it will not block the sight of the higher-status person, but the custom is not usually carried to this extreme in practice.

Credit cards are increasingly accepted on Weno, though there may be a commission for using them.

Post & Communications Chuuk's only post office is in Weno centre. It's open weekdays from 8 am to 4 pm, and from 9 to 11 am on Saturday.

Telephone calls can be made and faxes, telex and telegrams can be sent from the FSM telecommunications centre, east of the airport. Local calls and incoming faxes (fax 330 2777) are free.

The FSM telecommunications centre has one computer available 24 hours for Internet use; the price is US$4 per hour. The tourist office also has Internet access that visitors can, at a pinch, request to use – offer to pay a bit to defray cost.

Immigration The FSM Immigration Office (☎ 330 2335) is on the main road in Weno.

Media The one Chuukese newspaper, *Chuuk Sunrise*, comes out biweekly (or less). Days-old editions of Guam's *Pacific Daily News* are sold at larger grocery stores. Weno has one radio station, 1590 AM, which has a Civic Action Team (CAT) show on Friday evenings. Chuuk's cable TV includes live CNN.

Weather Information You can get a 24-hour recorded weather forecast by calling ☎ 330 4349.

Laundry There are a number of coin laundries in town. One, convenient for the northernmost hotels, is near the Island Mart on the north side of town. Another is in the unmarked blue building on the north side of Susumi's store.

Medical Services The hospital (☎ 330 2216) is in Weno centre, up from the government offices.

Emergency For police emergencies, dial ☎ 330 2223; for medical emergencies, dial ☎ 330 2444.

Dangers & Annoyances Despite its dive charms, Chuuk is not among Micronesia's safer islands. A high unemployment rate, combined with general languor and plenty of black market alcohol, means that young men idle on the streets all day – and making catcalls is one of their tamer diversions.

Male and female travellers alike should under no circumstances venture out after dark, even in a car. Recently a carload of doctors driving at night between Blue Lagoon Resort and Weno's town centre had their car stoned, and one man's glasses shattered into his eye. Travellers should not accept lifts in vehicles or boats from strangers, and hitching is definitely discouraged.

Foreign women walking alone will be subject to constant verbal harassment. It's much better to take taxis or go around in a group (walking with a man would be helpful).

Weno (Moen) Island

Weno, formerly Moen, is the capital and commercial centre of Chuuk. At just over 7 sq miles (18 sq km), it is the second largest island in the lagoon. Tropical forests make up much of the interior, with the highest point, the 1214-foot (370m) Mt Tonoken, nearly in the centre.

Villages circle the outer edges of Weno. The district centre, government offices and airport are on the north-west side of the island. A coastal road extends most of the way around Weno, broken by a narrow gap of mangrove swamp between the tiny villages of Nukunap and Winipis on the east side of the island.

Many outer islanders come to Weno in search of job opportunities, of which there are few for those without political connections, and thus they end up living in poverty conditions. As one of the most densely populated islands in Micronesia, Weno has its share of pollution problems, including sewage that runs into the lagoon and streets littered with trash.

Mt Tonaachaw When the legendary Sowukachaw arrived on Chuuk he brought

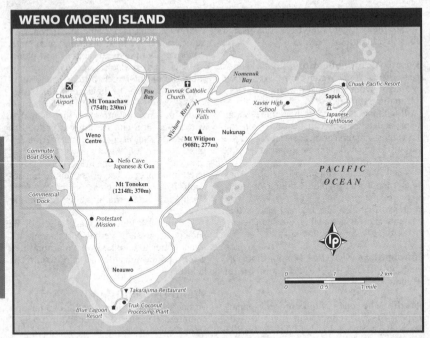

WENO (MOEN) ISLAND

See Weno Centre Map p275

Chuuk Airport

Mt Tonaachaw
(754ft; 230m)

Pou Bay

Tunnuk Catholic Church

Nomenuk Bay

Wichon River

Wichon Falls

Xavier High School

Sapuk

Chuuk Pacific Resort

Japanese Lighthouse

Weno Centre

Mt Witipon
(908ft; 277m)

Nukunap

Commuter Boat Dock

Nefo Cave
Japanese & Gun

Mt Tonoken
(1214ft; 370m)

Commercial Dock

PACIFIC OCEAN

Protestant Mission

Neauwo

Takarajima Restaurant

Blue Lagoon Resort

Truk Coconut Processing Plant

0   1   2 km
0   0.5   1 mile

a lump of basalt rock with him, stuck it on the summit of Mt Tonaachaw and built a meeting house on the mountain top from where he ruled all of Chuuk Lagoon.

The steep-sided 754-foot (230m) mountain, with its lone tree on the knobby top, is the backdrop for the airport and harbour. Although there's a trail to the top, Chuukese are wary of climbing this mountain because Neawacha, the ghost of an old woman who lives there, is believed to have the power of curses.

The US Air Force Civic Action Team (CAT) has a barracks on the side of the mountain above Weno centre, at an elevation of 250 feet (76m). The CAT crew is made up of a dozen people who spend eight-month stints on the island doing public works projects such as road and school construction.

The narrow dirt road to the CAT camp begins just east of Island Mart and ends a half mile up at the barracks, where there's a

lagoon view that's particularly nice at sunset. You can see the Faichuk Islands straight ahead past the runway and the flat island of Param to the left.

A trail that goes to the top of Mt Tonaachaw begins at the left side of the main CAT building. Follow the trail past the small house above the CAT camp and continue on up. The path starts out well defined and then becomes less so, but it's not hard to follow. The walk can be slippery when wet but otherwise, if you avoid the midday sun, it's not too strenuous. It takes about 30 minutes to get to the top where there's a Japanese bunker and good panoramic views.

Ethnographic Center A small one-room museum at the tourist office, known as the Ethnographic Center, has **love sticks** (see boxed text 'Love Sticks'), **outrigger canoe models** and a few other interesting traditional items, such as a coconut grater and a

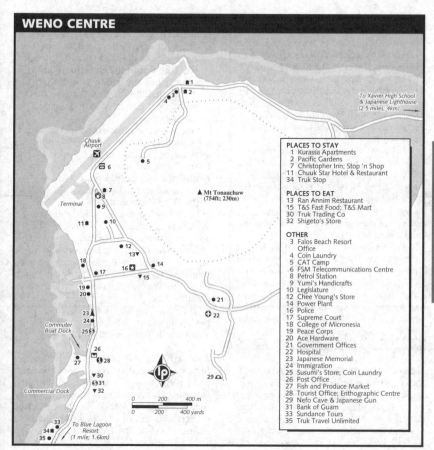

WENO CENTRE

To Xavier High School
& Japanese Lighthouse
(2.5 miles; 4km)

Chuuk
Airport

▲ Mt Tonaachaw
(754ft; 230m)

Terminal

Commuter
Boat Dock

Commercial Dock

33 To Blue Lagoon
34   Resort
35   (1 mile; 1.6km)

0   200   400 m
0   200   400 yards

PLACES TO STAY
1 Kurassa Apartments
2 Pacific Gardens
7 Christopher Inn; Stop 'n Shop
11 Chuuk Star Hotel & Restaurant
34 Truk Stop

PLACES TO EAT
13 Ran Annim Restaurant
15 T&S Fast Food; T&S Mart
30 Truk Trading Co
32 Shigeto's Store

OTHER
3 Falos Beach Resort
   Office
4 Coin Laundry
5 CAT Camp
6 FSM Telecommunications Centre
8 Petrol Station
9 Yumi's Handicrafts
10 Legislature
12 Chee Young's Store
14 Power Plant
16 Police
17 Supreme Court
18 College of Micronesia
19 Peace Corps
20 Ace Hardware
21 Government Offices
22 Hospital
23 Japanese Memorial
24 Immigration
25 Susumi's Store; Coin Laundry
26 Post Office
27 Fish and Produce Market
28 Tourist Office; Enthographic Centre
29 Nefo Cave & Japanese Gun
31 Bank of Guam
33 Sundance Tours
35 Truk Travel Unlimited

ulong, a special food bowl that was used to present the season's first harvest to the high chief.

There are also artefacts from the lagoon shipwrecks, including the compass, a ship lantern and a coral-encrusted machine gun from the bridge of the *Fujikawa Maru*, and a propeller blade. A **display of photos** taken during the two-day US bombing assault on the Japanese fleet shows all the ships in the lagoon during the attack, the layout of Weno's South Field with its seaplane ramps and the then densely developed island of Dublon.

It's open weekdays from 8 am to 4.45 pm and admission is US$1. There is no air-con so don't linger too long.

Coastal Views Looking toward the beach next to the Peace Corps building, you'll see what looks like a big black marble. It's actually a **Japanese memorial** to war dead with the script character for peace, *wa*, carved into the pedestal.

This is also a vantage for viewing some of the nearshore **shipwrecks** and rusting hulls that have been abandoned in the lagoon.

Love Sticks

In the days of thatched houses, love sticks were used by courting males to get a date for the evening. These slender sticks of mangrove wood were each intricately notched and carved in a design unique to its owner.

A young man would at some stage show his love stick to the object of his desire, so she could then recognise the carving at the appropriate time.

If all went well the suitor would wait until the young woman had retired for night and then push the love stick in through the side of the thatched house and entangle it in her long hair. She would be woken by his gentle tugging, feel the carving to determine who was outside and, if tempted, would sneak out into the night for a secret rendezvous.

It seems like a mating ritual with a built-in potential for disaster, with incidents such as poking the young woman in the eye or tangling the stick in her mother's hair instead as likely scenarios, but perhaps there was more to it than is usually told. When thatched houses went out of fashion, so did love sticks. Replicas make popular souvenirs.

Nefo Cave & Japanese Gun A large cave above the town holds a Japanese naval gun and offers a good view of Weno centre. To get there, head east from downtown Weno, take the paved road to the right after the hospital and follow the road up the hill to where it dead-ends at a big water tank. The second house from the end, incidentally, is the governor's official residence, though not all governors opt to live there.

Directly across the street from the driveway of the last house there's a path leading up the hill. It's a two-minute walk to the cave. Go straight through the cave, which is 75 feet long (23m), to get to the gun.

If you step out a few feet beyond the gun, you can also get a good view of Mt Tonaachaw to the right.

South Field South Field, at the southern tip of Weno, was once a large Japanese seaplane base. The three-mile drive from Weno centre to South Field offers pretty views of both the lagoon islands and Weno's west coast, with intermittent patches of taro, mangroves, bananas and breadfruit trees.

The **Truk Coconut Processing Plant** is in the corrugated tin building to the left just before the gate to the Blue Lagoon Resort. If you want to see how soap is made from copra, go inside.

One of the old **Japanese seaplane ramps**, now used to unload copra, is behind the soap factory, as is a beached ferro-concrete boat, the result of a failed government-funded small industries project.

At the southernmost point of South Field is the Blue Lagoon Resort, which has the only easily accessible **sandy beach** on Weno and a splendid lagoon view. There's another **seaplane ramp** here, as well as grass-covered Japanese **bunkers** and a few other war artefacts on the hotel grounds. There's also a traditional **outrigger canoe** from the Western Islands, made from a breadfruit tree.

The road heading east from South Field gets rougher as it goes along, with only about a mile of it passable in a sedan.

East of the Airport From the airport heading east, the road edges along the coast and passes through small villages. After the Bethesda church comes up on the right, the road goes across Pou Bay. The attractive **church** with red trim on the hill to the right is the Tunnuk Catholic Church.

Wichon Falls Wichon Falls are not very big, but the walk up the river is pleasant and will get you a little closer to village life. On sunny mornings, the stream is busy with women doing laundry and after school lets out, kids play in the water holes.

To reach the falls go 1¼ miles (2km) past Tunnuk Catholic Church to the innermost part of Nomenuk Bay, where the Wichon River empties into the lagoon. Just before a very small bridge, you'll see a rough dirt road to the right which leads into Wichon village.

Walk one-third of a mile up this road, turn on the first drive to the left, go behind the house and begin walking up the river. There's a crossing over rocks in the stream not far from the house, and from there the falls are just a couple of minutes up. As you are crossing private property, you should ask permission to continue if you see anyone along the way.

Petroglyphs in the shape of triangles, parallel lines and other geometric shapes have been carved into the smooth rock both above and near the base of the falls. Most are quite weathered, but can be made out with a determined eye.

The Wichon area figures in many Chuukese legends. One story tells of a ghost who scooped up part of nearby Mt Witipon (908 feet, 277m), creating the Wichon Valley, and then flew to the Mortlocks where he dropped the land in the sea to form Losap Atoll.

Xavier High School

The Jesuit-run Xavier High School opened in 1953 as the first four-year high school in Micronesia and maintains a reputation as the region's best.

Originally the site of a German chapel, the land was taken by the Japanese in 1940 and a fortress-like wartime communications centre was constructed. The main building, with 2-foot-thick (600mm) reinforced concrete walls and vault-like steel doors and windows, survived two direct hits by US bombers, amazingly requiring only a patch job on the roof. The building now houses the school's classrooms.

Visitors are welcome to climb the roof for a panoramic view of Chuuk Lagoon and to walk around the grounds, provided they don't disturb classes. Cars should be parked under the big mango tree at the far right of the main building.

Go quietly through the centre doorway of the main building, past the study hall and up the stairs on the left. At the top of the stairs go through the door on the left marked Faculty, then turn right to get outside, where there are stairs up to the roof. You can see many of the lagoon islands from the rooftop. There's a gorgeous **view** of the Faichuks and in the opposite direction you can see the old Japanese lighthouse on the hill in Sapuk.

A **display cabinet** at the top of the stairs on the 2nd floor holds objects from sunken ships, including dishes, sake bottles and a porthole. The landing below has a collection of Chuukese seashells.

Be careful if driving there, as the driveway leading up to the school, along which a network of Japanese tunnels are burrowed, can be quite treacherous in the rainy season.

Japanese Lighthouse Even better than the view from Xavier is the one from the Japanese lighthouse in Sapuk. The lighthouse, which was built in the early 1930s, sits atop Newech Hill at an elevation of 348 feet (117m), but it's on private property. The best way to visit is to contact the property owner, Rively Walter (☎ 330 2222), who can arrange to pick visitors up at their hotel and take them to the top for US$10 per person. The whole thing takes less than two hours, although you can extend it with a trip to Xavier High School. If you're going alone, you'll need to pay US$5; park your car where the road briefly plateaus at a house, and walk the rest of the way up. As at Xavier, the road can be very muddy, rocky and treacherous even with a 4WD car.

Islands in Chuuk Lagoon

Outside Weno the most easily accessible populated islands in Chuuk Lagoon are Dublon, Eten and Fefan. Uman and Param are not particularly receptive to visitors and the Tol islanders have a reputation for being a bit rough and rowdy. Many of these islanders commute by boat to jobs on Weno while others have subsistence farms or earn money through fishing or copra. Fananang Island, also called Blue Lagoon Island and owned by Blue Lagoon Resort, is an option for peaceful camping. See Camping under Places to Stay later.

It's a more traditional Chuukese lifestyle on the islands in the outer lagoon. On some islands people still live under thatched roofs and cook outdoors over open fires. Roads are scarce and vehicles are few.

There's no established accommodation for visitors on any of the following lagoon islands, except for Falos and the camping area at Blue Lagoon Island.

Dublon Dublon is also called Tonoas, which was the island's original name until 1814 when Manuel Dublon landed there and humbly renamed it.

Dublon is a peaceful island today, with a population of only about 3000, but there are many remnants of its colonial past that reveal its former importance under occupying powers. Both the Germans and Japanese made Dublon their administrative centres; the Japanese military headquarters there included submarine, seaplane and coastal defence bases. Intense US bombings left nearly all of them in ruins.

After the war Dublon became sleepy and overgrown. Although it has received development funding, which brought electricity to the island, Dublon still provides a good glimpse of rural Chuukese life.

There are docks at Sapou, in the northeast corner of the island and in the south. Most of the WWII relics are on the west side of the island. A rut-filled road runs

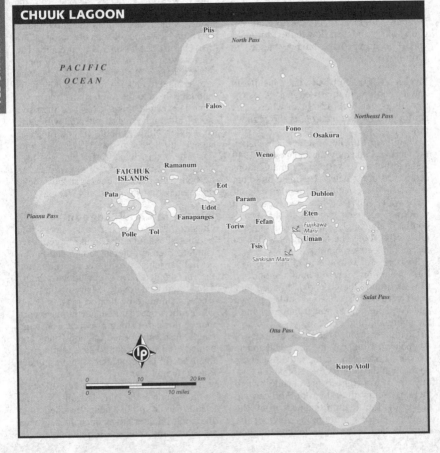

CHUUK LAGOON

around the island and there are private pick-up trucks, but no taxis. Visitors to the memorials on the island should be aware that locals commonly pop up making shaky demands for money to see the memorials. One reader's solution was to bring no money whatsoever to the island and show the locals his empty wallet.

Sapou Overgrown vegetation in Sapou village partly conceals the remains of what was once a city. The wooden buildings are long gone, but the cement footings they were built upon are still there. Broad cement sidewalks, once covered with tin awnings to shelter the Japanese against sun and rain, are now shaded by breadfruit trees. The remains of the **Japanese naval hospital** can be explored on the hill above the youth centre for US$2.

Sapou's colourful **village church**, which is dark grey trimmed with bright primary colours, sports a sign in Old English lettering reading *kinamue*, which means 'peace' in Chuukese.

South Dublon If you drive anticlockwise from Sapou to the south side of Dublon, you'll see a large Japanese dome-like **concrete bunker** on the right side of the road. An iron pipe protruding from the top served as an air vent.

Ahead, where the road splits in two, you can take the right fork, which takes you to a **fortified Japanese building** with heavy metal doors and windows.

A little farther on is the junior high school, built on the concrete airfields of the old **Japanese seaplane base**. There's a seaplane ramp leading down into the water.

Back on the main road, on the left, are the remains of a collapsed **Japanese oil storage tank**, now used by a local family as a garage. Ahead, up a grade to the left, an aluminium geodesic dome covers a large freshwater **reservoir**. The concrete water tank was built by the Japanese, who secretly placed a steel tank in the centre to serve as a hidden fuel reserve.

Turn right at the next road to get to Dublon's **deepwater dock** and multi-million

dollar fisheries complex and freezer, which was built with Japanese aid and now serves as a dock for Chinese fishing boats.

East-Central Dublon Continuing on the main road, you'll see more burned-out **oil storage tanks** on the right. At the crossroads, turn left and you'll pass a small **Japanese memorial**. Just past the municipal building turn left, then keep an eye out to the left for the entrance to a massive **cement tunnel** built under the mountain. The tunnel looks big enough to run a subway through and did in fact hold a fleet of military vehicles. It ran under the Japanese governor's residence and still has a rusted electric generator inside. You'll probably be charged US$1.

Farther down on the left, a sign in Japanese announces a **naval cemetery**. Steep stairs lead up to the site, but this is private property so you should ask permission if you want to climb up, and the owner may charge US$1.

Down the road on the left look closely to see the narrow overgrown entrance to the **general's cave**, one of five openings to an interconnecting network of tunnels. The road finishes in a dead end a little farther on at a Protestant church.

Go back the way you came and take the road diagonally opposite the municipal building. After passing a school on the left, you'll come to the ruins of the **Japanese civil hospital** at the crossroads. What remains of the hospital is basically just the arched concrete entrance hall, now covered in graffiti. Straight ahead are the stairs to a former Shinto shrine.

Eten Island From a distance Eten looks like a huge aircraft carrier which, in effect, it was. The Japanese used Chuukese labour to tear down the mountaintops and carry away half the island in order to recreate Eten as an airfield.

If you dock on Eten's north-west side, directly opposite the fisheries complex on Dublon, then it's a 10-minute walk inland to a complex of concrete and steel **bombed-out buildings**.

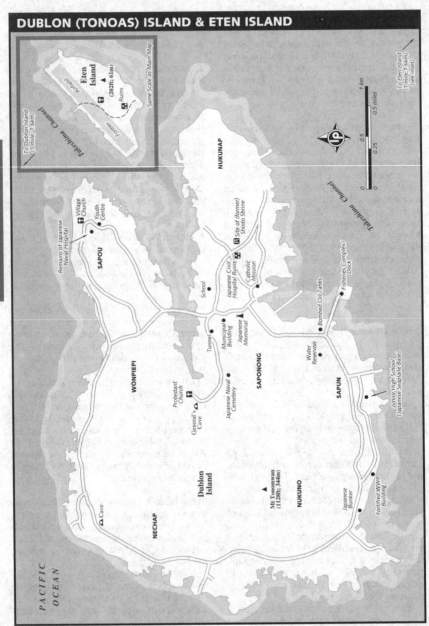

DUBLON (TONOAS) ISLAND & ETEN ISLAND

Eten Island

Airfield

(202ft; 61m)

Former

Ruins

Takeshima Channel

Same Scale as Main Map

To Dublon Island
(1 mile; 1.6km)

To Eten Island
(1 mile; 1.6km)
(see inset)

1 km

0.5 miles

0.5

0.25

0

0

NUKUNAP

Takeshima Channel

Remains of Japanese Naval Hospital

Village Church

Youth Centre

SAPOU

School

Site of (former) Shinto Shrine

Japanese Civil Hospital Ruins

Catholic Mission

Fisheries Complex/Dock

WONPIEPI

Tunnel

Municipal Building

Japanese Memorial

SAPONONG

Bombed Oil Tanks

Water Reservoir

Protestant Church

General's Cave

Japanese Naval Cemetery

SAPUN

Junior/High School (Japanese Seaplane Base)

Cave

Dublon Island

Mt Tonomwan (1128ft; 344m)

NUKUNO

NECHAP

Japanese Bunker

Fortified WWII Building

PACIFIC OCEAN

FED STATES OF MICRONESIA

From the dock you pass a couple of houses, then walk up to the right through the village and follow the path to the right of the **Catholic church**. It's a well-defined trail, much of it on the pavement still left from the old airstrip.

The path leads directly to a massive two-storey concrete structure, which islanders say was hit by 15 to 20 bombs. The roof and 2nd floor are partly caved in, with twisted steel reinforcement rods hanging down, but one room is amazingly still intact.

Beyond are three more two-storey **Japanese buildings** with 2-foot-thick (60cm) concrete walls and vault-like steel windows and doors. There's a **demolished tower** and a **big gun** on top of the hill, as well as **wrecked planes** in the water around the island.

Fefan Island Fefan is known for its abundance of fresh produce and for its high-quality basketry woven of banana and hibiscus fibres. Mangrove swamps line much of the shoreline, while the forested interior reaches an elevation of 984 feet (300m). Pieces of pottery found in archaeological digs on Fefan date back more than 1500 years.

Mesa Wharf is on the east side of Fefan and you can take in the whole village of **Mesa**, such as it is, in a 10-minute stroll. The **village church** is a few minutes walk to the right of the wharf.

On Fefan, kids come up and touch you to see if you're real. They smile, ask your name, follow you around for a minute or two and then go back to whatever they were doing.

Most WWII relics are inland on the hills and difficult to reach. The hike up to some **anti-aircraft guns** which are spread out on top of a hill directly up from Mesa Wharf would take about 30 minutes, but there's no real trail.

A couple of pick-up trucks drive the rough circle-island road, charging US$2 or more per person, but as it's about 1½ hours around the island and the trucks run sporadically don't count on catching one.

Faichuk Islands The Faichuk Islands, in the western part of Chuuk Lagoon, include Tol, Polle, Pata, Udot, Eot, Ramanum and Fanapanges.

Tol, the largest and most populated of the Faichuks, is about a one-hour boat ride from Weno. Tol's Mt Tumuital, which rises 1453 feet (443m), is the tallest mountain in Chuuk. The island's high jungle forest is the sole habitat of the Truk greater white-eye, a rare bird with one of the most restricted ranges of any in Micronesia.

The Japanese once had vehicles on Tol but the roads took a beating during the war bombing and today there are no cars.

In the 1970s, when Chuuk's political future was being debated, most Faichuk Islanders wanted Chuuk to opt for commonwealth status with the USA, similar to that of the Northern Marianas. When the majority of Chuukese voted instead to become a state in the FSM, the Faichuks started statehood attempts of their own.

In the late 1970s the FSM Congress actually approved the Faichuks as a new FSM state after 98% of Faichuk voters chose by referendum to break away from the rest of Chuuk. The movement failed with a veto by the FSM president, who was incidentally from Chuuk, but the secessionist movement revived somewhat in the late 1990s.

With one-third of Chuuk's population, the Faichuk Islanders feel they're entitled to one-third of the state budget, but they only get a trickle of that. They want electricity and paved roads, and perhaps most importantly, they want a reliable water system, as during severe droughts they sometimes run out of water completely and have to rely on drinking coconut milk.

Picnic Islands There are numerous small uninhabited coral islets scattered around the lagoon, which the Chuukese use as fishing grounds and picnic or drinking spots. Many of them have white sand beaches and small stands of coconut palms.

The waters are generally clear and snorkelling can be excellent, though in some spots dynamiting has damaged the coral, and near the shore you'll often see as many empty beer cans as fish.

Deserted or not, all the islands are owned and you're supposed to get permission to visit from the owners. However, your guide will generally arrange that.

Falos Island Falos is a tidy little island circled with soft white sand beaches and thickly shaded with coconut palms. For the casual visitor to Chuuk this is the easiest of the Picnic Islands to visit, as it's been set up for both day trips and overnight stays.

Coral close to the shore makes for good snorkelling, and the deeper waters just a short way out have larger fish and even an occasional shark or two. From the beach you can see Weno, Dublon, Fefan and the Faichuks.

If you visit on weekdays you may well have the beach to yourself, while on weekends it's usually a bit livelier with locals from Weno coming over to picnic. A caretaker family lives on the island, with other 'staff' boating over when there are overnight visitors.

Outer Islands

Outside Chuuk Lagoon are the far-flung Mortlocks, Hall Islands and Western Islands. Together they comprise 11 atolls and three single islands. All are flat coral formations, some just wisps of sand barely rising above the surface of the ocean.

In their isolation, the outer islands maintain a more traditional lifestyle than can be found in Chuuk Lagoon. They have footpaths but virtually no cars or roads. A day's work might include fishing, cultivating the taro patch, preparing copra or making sleeping mats and coconut fibre ropes.

The Mortlocks The Mortlocks stretch about 180 miles in a south-easterly direction from Chuuk Lagoon.

The Upper Mortlocks include the single island of Nama, and Losap Atoll with its main islands of Losap and Piis. The Mid-Mortlocks include Etal and Namoluk atolls, as well as Kuttu and Moch, the northernmost islands in Satawan Atoll. The Lower Mortlocks incorporate Lukunor Atoll with its islands of Lukunor and Oneop as well as the southernmost Satawan Atoll islands of Satawan and Ta.

The Mortlockese are a gentle, easy-going people and are more Westernised in their dress than other outer islanders. They also tend to be a more religious bunch overall, perhaps because it was in the Mortlocks that Christian missionaries established Chuuk's first church in 1875, long before they reached Chuuk Lagoon. Many religious prohibitions, such as those against building fires on Sunday, have only recently been abandoned.

The Mortlockese still make traditional masks of hibiscus wood. Once worn by men during battle and to ward off evil spirits, they are now carved for Chuuk's tourist trade.

For visitors, one of the handiest Mortlock destinations is **Satawan Atoll**. It is the largest of all Chuuk's outer island groups, though its four populated islands and 45 islets cover a total area of only 1200 acres (485 hectares).

The main island, Satawan, is a sub-district centre with about 500 people. The island is fringed with white sand beaches and dotted with coconut palms and breadfruit trees. It has two churches (one Catholic, one Protestant), a regional high school and a couple of small stores. There's a single pick-up truck that's used to haul cargo from boats to the village. The electric generator has closed indefinitely, but some people have small, private generators. You can find half a dozen rusting **Japanese tanks** in the village centre and a fairly intact **Japanese Zero** in a banana patch.

Ta Island is separated from Satawan Island by about 200 yards (180m) of shallow reef that can readily be walked across at low tide. Home to about 300 people, Ta is just a couple of hundred yards wide, though it extends for 5 miles (8km). It's a lovely, unspoiled place with empty beaches, perfect for relaxing. Unlike many of Chuuk's other islands, the Satawanese welcome outsiders. A nice way to meet people is simply to walk the wide road that goes down the middle of the island built by the CAT team.

The swimming and snorkelling is great off Satawan and Ta islands, with an abundance of turtles, fish and coral, and sometimes **dolphins** as well. The lagoon waters are usually placid and have excellent visibility. You can walk along the fringe reef for miles at low tide and find all sorts of seashells.

The Hall Islands The Halls, north of Chuuk Lagoon, include the single island of East Fayu, Murilo Atoll with its islands of Murilo and Ruo, and Nomwin Atoll with its islands of Nomwin and Fananu. Fananu Island, one of the most attractive of all the Halls, had an airstrip under construction at the time of writing.

These islands are, in a sense, a satellite community of Chuuk Lagoon. They were once allied with Weno and with islands on the Chuuk Lagoon reef, with whom they share a common dialect.

The Western Islands The Western Islands, Chuuk's most remote and traditional islands, share close ties with the outer islands of Yap. Though political distinctions divvy them up into two separate states, outer islanders in the central Carolines have more in common with each other than they do with the high islands of Yap or Chuuk Lagoon to which they belong.

On these islands the men still wear bright loincloths and the women wear only woven fibre or grass skirts. Houses are made of thatch, subsistence comes from the sea and men continue to sail single-hulled outrigger canoes carved from breadfruit logs, relying on centuries-old navigational methods.

Young women from the Western Islands who attend the University of Guam have been known to enter classrooms crawling on their knees if any of their male relatives are in the room. This would be expected of them in their home islands but university tutors, not too keen on the custom, eventually get them to make some concessions to Western culture (see the boxed text 'Bowing').

The Western Islands include Namonuito, Pulap, Pulusuk and Puluwat atolls. As a group, the latter three are also called Pattiw.

Namonuito is a triangular atoll so large that all the islands are widely separated and it's a very long boat ride between them. The main island, **Ulul** (also called Onoun), is at the western side of the lagoon. Ulul is a rather traditional place with as much Japanese influence as American. The wreck of a wartime **Japanese plane** lies just off the runway. There's no established accommodation on Ulul, although elderly Japanese sometimes return here to visit old friends, with the chief arranging a hut for them to stay in.

The people of **Pulap Atoll**, which has two small and lightly populated islands, Pulap and Tamatam, are said to be Chuuk's best navigators. They also hold on to other traditions and if you're lucky enough to arrive on a special occasion you can expect to see young women performing custom dances and village men performing stick dances, with dancers wearing beaded necklaces and colourful ceremonial dress.

Pulusuk Atoll has just one island, Houk, but it's fairly large for the Westerns, covering a little over 1 sq mile (2.6 sq km). The island has Chuuk's only freshwater pond. There's an airstrip under construction.

Puluwat's five islands almost surround its small lagoon, leaving just one passageway and an excellent anchorage with a safe refuge from storms. The Japanese had an airstrip and lighthouse on one of the now uninhabited islets.

Outer islanders used to have a reputation for being tough fighters, and the people of Puluwat were probably once the most feared people in all the central Carolines. However, around the late 19th century they took to religion and became as gentle as lambs.

Activities
Diving Chuuk Lagoon is a wreck diver's dream. On its bottom rest about 60 Japanese ships, including oil tankers, submarines, cruisers, tugboats and cargo ships, as well as scores of US and Japanese planes.

The ships lie just as they sank in 1944 – some upright, some intact, some in pieces strewn across the lagoon floor. Each is a separate time capsule. The holds are full of guns and trucks and fighter planes, the dining areas are littered with dishes, silverware and sake bottles and the skeletal remains of the perished crews lie 'buried' at sea.

The wrecks have become artificial reefs for hundreds of species of vividly coloured corals, sponges and anemones that have attached themselves to the metal. These shelters also attract large schools of fish. The water is warm, about 85°F (29°C), and visibility is generally 50 to 100 feet (15 to 30m).

The largest wreck in the lagoon is the *Heian Maru*, a 535-foot (163m) passenger and cargo ship lying on its port side at 40 to 110 feet (12 to 33m). Divers can see the ship's name and telegraph mount on the bow, as well as large propellers, periscopes and a torpedo.

The *Fujikawa Maru*, an aircraft ferry that landed upright in 40 to 90 feet (12 to 27m) of water, is one of the most popular dives. Until recently the stern mast stuck up out of the water, but damage caused by local fishers using dynamite near the wreck caused the mast to collapse. The main deck is 60 feet (18m) below the surface, while the hold, which contains four Zero fighters, is at 90 feet (27m).

Underwater photographers like the *Sankisan Maru* for its excellent soft coral formations. This half-destroyed munitions freighter is upright at 50 to 100 feet (15 to 30m) and still has a cargo of trucks, machine guns and ammunition.

While it's the wrecks that make Chuuk special, the walls on the outside of the lagoon reef also make good diving. Visibility outside the lagoon can be up to 200 feet (60m).

Although strictly illegal, some islanders tear the shipwrecks apart looking for stores of explosives, which they then use to dynamite the reefs for an easy catch of fish. Unfortunately there's a ready market for fish caught this way.

Dive Shops To keep souvenir hunters at bay, the wrecks in Chuuk Lagoon have been declared an underwater historical park and can't be visited without a guide.

The Blue Lagoon Dive Shop (☎ 330 2796, fax 330 4307, ❢ bldiveshop@ mail.fm) at Blue Lagoon Resort, in the south of Weno Island, was Chuuk's first dive operation. It was started in 1973 by Kimiuo Aisek and is now managed by his son Gradvin. Blue Lagoon is by far the larger of Chuuk's two dive operations. The rack rate for a one-tank dive is US$60, a two-tank dive is US$90, and a night dive US$65. The wholesale rate available to package tourists is US$40, US$70 and US$45. These prices do not include equipment or lunch.

The smaller Sundance Tours & Dive Shop (☎ 330 4234, fax 330 4451, ❢ sundance@mail.fm) is beside the Truk Stop hotel. A two-tank dive costs US$70, a third dive US$40 and a night dive US$65. Travellers cheques and cash only are accepted.

Dive Boats Two popular live-aboard dive boats are based in Chuuk Lagoon. The SS *Thorfinn* has a seven-day diving package with up to five dives a day. The cost, including meals, alcoholic beverages, ship services and accommodation, is US$2195 (or US$345 for the off-weekly daily rate). If you want to go along as a non diver, subtract US$600 from the price. A more extended option is a 14-day diving tour of islands between Chuuk and Yap, which comes to US$3495 plus an US$800 boarding fee (paid to the islands for their cultural shows). This expedition emphasises cultural exploration along with the diving. The *Thorfinn*, a converted whaler, holds 22 passengers in 11 air-con rooms, with private showers and toilets. Although the ship is not new, it's quite comfortable and even has a hot tub on deck, and the food is good. Reservations can be made direct through Seaward Holidays (☎ 330 3040, fax 330 4253, ❢ seaward@mail.fm).

The *Truk Aggressor II* (☎ 330 2198, fax 329 2629), the reincarnated *Palau Aggressor*, has weekly trips that include 5½ days of diving. The seven private, carpeted staterooms each have a queen and single bunk and individual air-con controls as well as a private bath and toilet. There's also an E-6 slide processing lab on board.

The cost is US$2295 which includes everything except the air fare and alcoholic beverages. Reservations can be made through Live/Dive Pacific (☎ 1-800-344 5662, 808-329 8182, fax 808-329 2628, ℮ livedive@compuserve.com), at 74-5588 Pawai Place, Building F, Kailua-Kona, HI 96740, and other dive tour operators.

Snorkelling Boat trips for snorkellers usually include a visit to the *Dainihino Maru*, a small coral-encrusted transport ship that lies on its starboard side in 40 feet (27m) of water off Uman. It has a bow gun just 3 feet (900mm) underwater and its deck is about 8 feet (2.4m) down. Other wrecks visited for snorkelling are a Zero fighter in shallow waters off Eten and the *Susuki Maru*, a sub-chaser off the coast of Dublon, with its deck about 10 feet (3m) underwater.

Blue Lagoon Dive Shop charges US$55 for its snorkelling tour (US$35 wholesale). If three or more snorkellers are going out they'll usually take a separate boat and snorkel around the shallow airplane wrecks or the reef, but otherwise snorkellers go out with divers.

Sundance Tours & Dive Shop (see Organised Tours later) in Weno can arrange a snorkelling trip and picnic on an island in Chuuk's lagoon for US$50.

Both dive shops rent snorkel sets for US$10 a day including fins. Chuuk Pacific Resort (see Hotels under Places to Stay later) in north-east Weno provides complimentary snorkel sets to guests.

Organised Tours

Truk Land & Sea Tours (☎ 330 2438), in the lobby of the Blue Lagoon Resort, offers 2½-hour land tours of Weno for US$20 per person, four-hour lagoon boat tours for US$60 to US$65 per person and shopping tours for US$5.

Sundance Tours & Dive Shop (☎ 330 4234), next to the Truk Stop hotel, can arrange a variety of sightseeing tours. A land tour of Weno, including Nefo Cave, Xavier High School and the Japanese lighthouse, costs US$20; a boat tour costs US$50.

In addition, the tourist office can arrange local tour guides for about US$20. If they're not busy, they may provide a free tour themselves.

In general, land tours of Chuuk don't tend to be very inspiring, and most of what they cover you could easily see yourself.

Places to Stay

Camping Camping should not be done on Weno, the foremost reason being safety. Blue Lagoon Dive Shop organises an overnight excursion to Blue Lagoon's shelters on Fananang Island (Blue Lagoon Island), a 20-minute boat ride from Weno. Along with 15 coconut trees, the island has a small hut that sleeps six and plenty of tent space. A small generator is turned on when needed. It's a nice getaway but can be a bit pricey – check with Blue Lagoon Dive Shop (see Snorkelling under Activities earlier).

Hotels All hotels except Blue Lagoon Resort and the Chuuk Pacific Resort are in town or in residential neighbourhoods. Most provide free airport transfers. Many of the larger hotels charge extra for late checkout (generally US$30), which you will be stuck paying if your flight is in the late afternoon or evening. Smaller hotels tend to negotiate, as does the Chuuk Star Hotel. Chuuk has a 10% room tax which should be added to the following prices unless otherwise noted.

Kurassa Apartments (☎ 330 4415, fax 330 4355), ¾ mile (1.2km) east of the airport, is the best budget option in town. Its nine one-bedroom and studio apartments are pleasant and safe and go for the fair price of US$48 (US$600 a month without maid service), tax included. There's also a room-and-car package for US$80 a day. All rooms have air-con in the bedroom, a ceiling fan in the living room, kitchen facilities, TV and VCR The major drawback is frequent electricity outages. There is no restaurant (but there is a store downstairs), although the Pacific Gardens has a restaurant.

Pacific Gardens (☎ 330 4639, fax 330 2334) is a 10-room local hotel opposite Kurassa Apartments. The units have a small separate area with a table, sink and refrigerator but no cooking facilities, and a small bedroom with a double and single bed, a TV if you ask and air-con – it's OK but nothing special. Singles/doubles cost US$55/65. There's a simple restaurant and bar downstairs.

Christopher Inn (☎ 330 2652, fax 330 2207), in central Weno above the Stop n Shop, is a very local hotel with 19 basic, run-down singles/doubles that are over-priced at US$47/57 (including tax). The rooms have air-con, TV, refrigerators and bathrooms, but the cleaning service is less than impressive. Locals loitering in the lobby and at the store below make the place feel unsafe.

The *Chuuk Star Hotel* (☎ 330 2040, @ chuukstar@mail.fm) is a clean, mid-range hotel just south of the airport. The rooms have cable TV, balconies with water views and bathrooms with tubs. Singles or doubles cost US$70.50 (including tax). There's a fine restaurant on site.

Truk Stop hotel (☎ 330 4232, fax 330 2286, @ trukstop@mail.fm) is a popular 23-room hotel about a mile (1.6km) south of the airport. Rooms are spacious, comfortable and clean with two double beds, cable TV, air-con, refrigerator and private bathroom. There are fine lagoon views from the balconies of the oceanfront units (US$99), while the standard units (US$90) are without a view. Fax, copy, and email services are all available for a fee. Visa, MasterCard, and American Express are accepted, though it's cheaper to pay in cash.

Blue Lagoon Resort (☎ 330 2727, fax 330 2439, @ bldiveshop@mail.fm), at the island's southernmost point, is the only hotel on Weno with a beachside setting. An upmarket, pleasantly landscaped hotel for divers, it has 52 comfortable, well-furnished rooms in several two-storey wood buildings, each with a balcony facing the lagoon. Rooms have air-con, refrigerators and two beds. Given the safety situation on Chuuk, this may be the best place for divers – you certainly don't have to drive to get to the dive shop. There's a restaurant, two bars and a gift shop. Rooms cost US$100/117;

add US$3 for TVs. There are also two suites. Diving packages are available. Airport transfers are US$5 each way. All major credit cards are accepted.

The Korean-run *Chuuk Pacific Resort* (☎ 330 2723, fax 330 2736, @ gocpr@ mail.fm) is Chuuk's newest hotel, on a gorgeous, isolated coastal stretch north-east of Weno. Each room has a twin and single bed, a fridge and a gorgeous lagoon-view porch. The handheld showers are not as inviting as you might expect of a new resort hotel. The clientele, when anyone is there, is almost exclusively Korean. Prices are US$77/99 for singles/doubles (including tax). Airport transfers are free. There is a restaurant on site serving American and Asian food. MasterCard and Visa are accepted.

Outside Weno On Falos Island, *Falos Beach Resort* (☎/fax 330 2606) has 10 simple concrete, tin-roofed cottages with linoleum floors, electric lights and futons on wooden bases. Ask for cottage No 1, 5, 6 or 7, as each one is free-standing with screened, louvred windows on all four walls to catch the breeze. Toilets and showers are outside and shared. Price is the main drawback: US$45/55 for singles/doubles, plus 10% room tax and the boat fare. The kind family who lives on the island may offer you drinking coconuts in the morning, but plan on bringing your own food to cook.

Arrangements to visit Falos Island should be made in advance at the office in Weno (☎ 330 2606), next door to Island Mart on the main road near the runway's north end.

On Ta Island, Binte and Reiko Simina have four simple cottages, known as *Simina's Sunset Bungalows*, located on a white sand beach. The cottages are simple but adequate, with comfortable mattresses, clean sheets and towels, mosquito netting and generator-powered electricity. All in all, it makes a good getaway if you're looking for a quiet place on a remote tropical island. The cost is US$30/40 for singles/doubles. Activities, including traditional net or spearfishing outings and motorboat tours, can be arranged at reasonable costs, as can meals (about US$10 a day). Call Binte (Weno, ☎ 330 4469) to make arrangements.

If you want to stay on Satawan Island, Representative Harper (Weno, ☎ 330 2666) has a four-bedroom *house* and sometimes rents out a room to visitors. If that is occupied, he or his office in Weno may suggest alternative arrangements.

There are no guesthouses on any of the outer islands, but the governor's office on Weno can sometimes make arrangements with island magistrates to find accommodation for visitors. Bring food or tobacco as gifts.

Places to Eat

Most restaurants offer a combination of American and Japanese cuisine, while the stalls along the main street provide an opportunity to sample a few traditional Chuukese dishes.

The unmarked *Ran Annim Restaurant*, in the same shack as the bakery near the power plant, is an inexpensive favourite of Peace Corps volunteers. It's a simple hole-in-the-wall but a friendly place. Six fat half-slices of French toast go for US$1.50, large burgers for US$1.50, fabulous fried fish plates for US$4, cinnamon rolls for a mere dime (US$0.10) and coffee for US$0.40. It's open weekdays from 6 am to 4 pm and closes at 2 pm on weekends.

T&S Fast-Food, next to T&S Mart, is a cafeteria-style snack bar serving breakfast and lunch from a *bain marie*. It's cheap enough, though at any given time some of the items may be unavailable. Meat-heavy lunch specials are US$4 and breakfast plates are US$3. It's open from 6.30 am to 3 pm daily.

The *Chuuk Star Hotel* has good food at reasonable prices; a plate of tuna steaks in braised onion sauce costs US$6. Curiously, almost no fish is on the lunch menu but the dinner menu is full of it.

Slightly pricier is the *Truk Stop restaurant* at the Truk Stop hotel, which occupies a pleasant setting looking out at the lagoon. At breakfast you can get a serving of banana pancakes for US$5 or bacon and egg plates for US$4.50, and fresh drinking coconuts.

At lunch there are sandwiches or burgers with fries from US$4.50; dinner meals are pricier, averaging US$9 to US$15. Truk Stop serves the island's only pizza. Breakfast is served from 6 to 11 am, lunch from 11 am to 2 pm and dinner from 6 to 10 pm.

Takarajima Restaurant, just a few minutes' walk from Blue Lagoon Resort, has the best Japanese food on Weno. The oyako donburi comes with miso soup and is one of the better deals at US$6.50, while tempura dishes cost US$15 and mangrove crab and lobster cost from US$10 to US$35. It's open from 11 am to 2 pm weekdays and from 5 to 10 pm daily. Saltwater aquariums spread around the restaurant add a nice touch.

Blue Lagoon Resort has good if pricey food, a pleasant atmosphere and a terrific lagoon-side setting. The popular local breakfast with fish is US$6. Dinner ranges from chicken yakita for US$7 to black pepper steak at US$18. There are good views from the dining room of the islands of Faichuks, Fefan and Dublon. The restaurant is open daily from 6.30 am to 2 pm and from 6.30 pm to 10 pm. The lounge bar, which is open from 1.30 to 5 pm daily (later if there's an incoming flight), also has lunch

Preserved Breadfruit

One customary Chuukese food speciality, *oppot*, is made by filling a pit with alternating layers of ripe cut breadfruit and banana leaves, then covering the top with rocks and leaving it for months, or even years. Uninitiated noses might think it rotten, but preserved breadfruit is highly valued and has traditionally served as an important staple, feeding islanders through long canoe journeys or during months when fresh breadfruit was not in season.

food and doles out sandwiches to returning divers.

The *fruit stalls* at the fish and produce market opposite the post office sell drinking coconuts for US$0.50 to US$1. Other items include pounded taro wrapped in green taro leaves, boiled breadfruit, preserved breadfruit, sea cucumber in vinegar and fresh produce such as bananas, mangoes and cucumbers, most of which comes from Fefan. You can also pick up a fragrant *mwaramwar* (head wreath) for US$1. Booths behind the fruit stalls sell inexpensive fried reef fish and barbecued chicken for take-away.

Truk Trading Co, *Shigeto's Store* and *T&S Mart* are Chuuk's largest grocery stores and have the freshest food. T&S has the best selection of produce; Truk Trading Co has the widest selection and Shigeto's carries US culinary delights. Truk Trading Co has a simple snack bar with inexpensive sandwiches and fried chicken by the piece.

Stay clear of Chuuk's tap water. You can buy fruit juice and bottled water in grocery stores.

Entertainment

Though Weno is officially dry, you'd never know it. Beer sells for US$3 a can at the *Blue Lagoon Resort* and at a number of restaurants, but you can get bottles of Budweiser at local stores – watch out for the giveaway sign 'Cold Beer Here'.

Don't go out to local bars in Chuuk. The raucous bars can become bottle-hurling scenes in a flash, and payday weekend poses a particular hazard. Stick to the tamer hotel bars at the Truk Stop hotel, the Chuuk Star Hotel and Blue Lagoon Resort.

Chuuk has no movie theatre, but there's many a video shop.

Shopping

Popular souvenirs include love sticks, hibiscus fibre fans, woodcarvings, wooden masks, baskets, seashells and shell jewellery.

Yumi's Handicrafts, opposite the airport, and Sundance Tours, next to Truk Stop hotel, have the widest selections of quality handicrafts. There's a gift shop at the Blue Lagoon Resort that also sells some handicrafts and T-shirts. The dive shop sells copies of LP's *Diving & Snorkeling Chuuk Lagoon, Pohnpei & Kosrae* by Tim Rock.

Body oils and bath soaps made from coconut oil at the Truk Coconut Processing Plant are sold in shops around town.

Combs, jewellery and other items made from the shells of endangered sea turtles are sold all around Chuuk, but cannot be imported into most Western countries, including the USA and Australia.

Getting There & Away

Air Continental is the only airline that flies to Chuuk, connecting Weno with Pohnpei and Guam on the island-hopper routes. The one-way fare is US$192 between Guam and Chuuk, while the return fare is US$300. From Pohnpei to Chuuk it's US$160 one way and US$225 return.

Airports & Airlines Chuuk's open-air airport terminal has a tourist information booth that usually opens briefly at flight times, car rental booths that are seldom staffed, a simple snack bar and toilets.

Continental Airlines' only office (☎ 330 2424) is at the check-in counter in the airport. It's open every day but at different hours depending on flight times. It's best to try between 9 am and 3.30 pm Monday to Saturday.

Chuukese Magic

Believers say Chuukese magic is powerful and they take it very seriously. It surfaces in many forms – as a curse, a love potion, a way to remove evil spirits or a form of protection. Satawan Atoll is said to have the strongest magic.

Perfumed love potions, called *omung*, may contain such exotica as centipede teeth and stingray tail mixed with coconut oil. If a beautiful woman falls in love with a plain-looking man, people will joke and say he used omung. Magic aside, Chuukese say that nowadays money is a more effective way to win someone's heart.

Rock archway over the aquamarine waters of Palau

MICHAEL AW

The ancient ruins of Nan Madol

NED FRIARY

WWII tank on Saipan

MICHAEL AW

Prinz Eugen, propeller in water, Kwajalein Atoll

NED FRIARY

WWII gun on Mañagaha Island, Saipan

Truk Travel Unlimited (☎ 330 2701, fax 330 2798), next to its affiliate Truk Stop Hotel, is quite helpful and can make reservations on most airlines. It's open weekdays from 8 am to 5 pm and accepts major credit cards.

Boat Visiting cruise ships should request an application for entry from the Chuuk Immigration and Labour Department (☎ 330 2335) and submit it to the FSM Immigration and Labor Division in Palikir, Pohnpei (☎ 320 4844).

There is currently no harbour fee on Weno, though you might want to contact Chuuk's harbourmaster (☎ 330 2592) in advance of your visit. Of all of Chuuk's islands, Weno and Puluwat have the best anchorage and channels.

Getting Around

To/From the Airport Weno's airport is smack in the centre of town. Taxis wait out front, but most hotels provide airport transfer if given advance notice.

Car Truk Stop Car Rentals (☎ 330 4232), at the Truk Stop hotel, rents cars for US$45/55 to guests/nonguests. Kurassa Apartments (☎ 330 4415) has an old sedan for US$45, as well as a larger, pricier car. Taxis are more economical.

Petrol costs US$1.70 a gallon.

Taxi Practically every other car is a 'taxi' on Chuuk, as you'll see by the ubiquitous cardboard signs perched on car windscreens. Many of these are unlicensed: If you're alone and concerned about safety, it's better to either get in a car with other people or call for a legitimate taxi. You can try calling Mo's (☎ 330 2668), but pick-up service is impressively sluggish. There are fewer taxis outside downtown Weno. It should cost US$0.50 to go anywhere around the downtown area or as far as the Blue Lagoon Resort, and US$1 to Xavier High School. Most taxis stop running around 8 pm.

Boat Commuter boats leave the main lagoon islands for Weno on weekday mornings and return from Weno in the early afternoons, as do many private speedboats. They're obviously convenient for islanders commuting to Weno, but the schedules are backwards for anyone planning a day trip from Weno.

Boats from Fefan tie up at the Weno dock, on the side opposite the post office, where the Fefan women market their vegetables. Boats from Dublon and Tol are usually moored on the other side of the dock. The cost is US$1 to US$2 each way, depending on the island. For speedboats you may hop on for the price of petrol money. Be aware, however, that taking rides with strangers can be dangerous in Chuuk.

The tourist office can also arrange boat rentals, but don't expect any bargains.

Blue Lagoon Dive Shop (☎ 330 2796, fax 330 4307, ✉ bldiveshop@mail.fm) sometimes takes divers to Dublon but more often they go to Blue Lagoon Island for camping.

A full-day tour to Falos Island costs US$29.50 per person, minimum two people. An overnight tour (which does not include hotel costs) is US$45 per night. Both tours include lunch. Boat rides can be arranged for US$10 per person if you're staying overnight, or US$30 per person return for up to four people if you're just going over for the day (two-person minimum). The ride takes about 30 minutes one way when the lagoon waters are calm.

Since the local airline shut down, boat is the only way to reach Chuuk's outer islands. Two field-trip ships, the *Micro Trader* and the *Micro Dawn*, together aim to make a total of about 40 to 50 trips a year. Most trips are approximately one week long. Separate trips are scheduled to the Lower and Mid-Mortlocks, the Upper Mortlocks, the Halls and Namonuito, and to Pattiw.

The ships commonly leave late and occasionally skip a sailing completely due to fuel shortages or other contingencies, so take a sceptical approach to the schedule which, with some persistence, you can obtain from the Transportation Office (☎ 330 2592, Chuuk State Government, Chuuk). On the other hand, the ships sometimes make extra trips for medical evacuation or other emergency purposes. Each ship carries about 150 people and generally spends at least a few hours unloading supplies at each island stopover.

It costs US$0.03 per mile on deck or US$0.10 per mile plus US$2 per night for a cabin. There are only seven two-bunk cabins, however, and they are often reserved for government officials. Chuukese aren't known for their tidiness, so expect deck passage to be in disarray. From Weno it's 170 miles (274km) to Satawan, 160 miles (257km) to Pulusuk and 80 miles (129km) to Murilo.

You can buy breakfast for US$3.50, lunch for US$4.50 and dinner for US$5.50 on board but it's probably better to bring your own food and water.

The field-trip ships are a good way to spend a few days on an outer island. It can drop you off with the supplies on one of the islands nearer to Weno and then continue to its final destination before returning to pick you up along the way. If you go this route, be sure to speak with the mayor's or governor's office of the island you want to visit. You can track down contact information from the tourist office or the Transportation Department. They will radio to the island and arrange for your trip.

The Nama Island government sends a boat to the Upper Mortlocks every other week, on payday Friday or Saturday. A return fare to Nama Island, Losaap or Piis, each less than six hours from Chuuk Lagoon, costs US$20.

For the Mid- and Lower Mortlocks, one option is the *Truk Queen 7* (☎ 330 4151), which makes a trip every month and charges passengers US$0.09 a mile.

To reach the Lower Mortlocks, the best option is private boat. Contact Chee Young's Family Store (☎ 330 2015). Chee Young's boat heads to the Lower Mortlocks roughly every two weeks and charges visitors US$10 for the trip.

Other private boats head out to the islands. If you call *Truk Queen 7* or Chee Young, and ask (with some persistence), they should be able to direct you to the next boat.

Yap

Yap, the land of giant stone money or rai, is the FSM's most traditional district.

You know you're in a unique place as soon as you catch your first glimpse of Yap at the airport. Most people dress in Western clothes but a fair number of men and boys wear bright-coloured loincloths and the woman greeting the passengers wears only a woven hibiscus skirt. Everyone, including the very official-looking customs officers, has a cheek bulging with betel nut. Apparently the dirt floors of the old airport were so deeply stained with betel nut juice that the designers of Yap's new airport terminal opted to paint the cement floors betel-nut red!

Out in the villages, which are connected by centuries-old stone footpaths, faluw (men's houses) are still built in the elaborate, traditional style of wood, thatch, rope and bamboo. The caste system survives and village chiefs still hold as much political clout as elected public officials.

The Yapese are a shy yet proud people. They are offended by the occasional tourist who brazenly points a camera at them as if they were subjects in an anthropological museum yet, at the same time, they're receptive to travellers who respect their customs and culture. For the traveller who treads gently, it's still a rare place to visit.

History

Early Settlers Pottery and other archaeological finds on Map Island date the earliest known Yapese settlement at around AD 200.

A Land Called Wa'ab

According to one story, when early European explorers first arrived, a group of islanders paddled out to meet them. The explorers pointed and asked the name of the island but the islanders, with their backs to the shore, misunderstood the question. Holding up their paddles they replied, 'yap', the word for paddle. Ever since, the islands known to its people as Wa'ab have been known to those outside its shores as Yap.

The Yapese once reigned over a scattered island empire, extending as far north as the Mariana Islands and encompassing Chuuk to the east. In ancient times lengthy ocean-going voyages were not uncommon.

The Yapese empire was built upon the powers of magic rather than conquest. The high chiefs of Yap Proper employed sorcerers who were believed to have powers to induce such calamities as famine, sickness and typhoons. Fearful of this sorcery, the outer islanders offered the high chiefs annual tributes in the hope of remaining in good favour.

European Contact The first contact with Europeans was in 1526 when the Portuguese explorer Dioga da Rocha landed on Ulithi. The islanders were 'without malice, fear or cautiousness' and da Rocha and his crew remained on the island for four months. Over the next 300 years the rest of Yap's islands were gradually 'discovered' and added to the charts.

Early attempts to settle Yap were half-hearted at best. In 1731 a Spanish Jesuit mission was established on Ulithi but when a supply ship returned a year later they found that all 13 people of the colony had been killed by the islanders.

Apparently Europeans got the hint and for the next 100 years their visits to Yap were few and far between. Strangely, however, Dumont d'Urville, the only European known to have visited the main Yap islands in the early 1800s, found a people who spoke enough Spanish to request cigars and brandy. It's largely thought that the islanders' knowledge of Spanish was the result of their own inter-island commerce with places as distant as the Marianas.

In the 1830s two Spanish ships came to gather beche-de-mer on Yap but at some point during the operation the crews were attacked and brutally murdered. In 1843 the English captain Andrew Cheyne made a similar attempt to secure a cargo of beche-de-mer. Yapese chiefs seemed cooperative at first, but a brush with would-be assassins and contact with an enslaved survivor of the Spanish massacre convinced Cheyne to drop the venture before suffering a similar fate. It wasn't until the 1860s that regular trade with the West was gradually established. The Germans opened the first permanent trading station in 1869.

FED STATES OF MICRONESIA

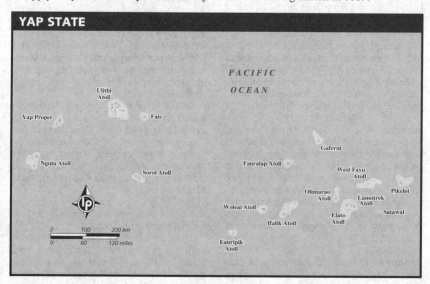

YAP STATE

PACIFIC OCEAN

Ulithi Atoll

Fais

Yap Proper

Gaferut

Ngulu Atoll

Fauralap Atoll

West Fayu Atoll

Sorol Atoll

Olimarao Atoll

Pikelot

Lamotrek Atoll

Woleai Atoll

Elato Atoll

Satawal

Ifalik Atoll

Eauripik Atoll

0   100   200 km
0   60   120 miles

Yapese Stone Money

Legend has it that the ancient navigator Anagumang set sail in search of the ideal stone to be used as Yapese currency. On Palau's Rock Islands he found a hard crystalline limestone that the Yapese then quarried into huge flat discs. Holes were carved in the centre so logs could be slipped through and the stones were then lugged down to barges and towed by canoe 250 miles (402km) to Yap.

With their weighty cargo, entire expeditions were sometimes lost in storms at sea. The most valuable stones were not necessarily the largest, but those that were transported at the highest cost of human lives. These stones commonly bore the names of the lost mariners.

Stone money, which the Yapese call *rai*, can range up to 12 feet (3.6m) in diameter and weigh as much as five tons. The Japanese civilian government counted 13,281 coins in 1929.

Most rai is kept in 'banks' lined up along village pathways. The money is not moved, even when ownership changes. Rai remains in use today for some traditional exchanges, although the US dollar settles most transactions.

Although Spain had long laid claim to Yap, it wasn't until the Germans attempted to annex the islands in 1885 that the Spanish established a permanent garrison. Formal colonial occupation of Yap was to continue in one form or another for the next 100 years.

In 1899, in the aftermath of the Spanish-American War, Spain sold Yap to Germany, whose interest in the islands was primarily commercial. Concerned about the shortage of labourers to work their plantations and mines, the Germans developed health and sanitation services in the hope of stemming the rapid depopulation. The Germans were the first to use forced Yapese labour, both on Yap and in the phosphate mines on Angaur in Palau.

Japanese Period The Japanese took control of Yap in 1914 when the outbreak of WWI forced the Germans to quickly withdraw from the islands.

Concern over Yap's transpacific cable station, on a line between the USA and Shanghai, led the USA to demand access to Yap as a precondition to recognising Japan's League of Nations mandate over Micronesia. Japan and the USA eventually came to an agreement and signed a treaty in 1921.

The Japanese then began to emigrate to Yap and set up stores, farms and sea-based industries. Their numbers were not as great as in other parts of Micronesia but they nonetheless came to vastly outnumber the dwindling Yapese population.

As WWII approached the Yapese were forced to build airfields and military fortifications for the Japanese. As punishment for noncooperation the Japanese would smash pieces of Yap's highly valued rai, sometimes using the broken pieces as road fill.

During WWII, US forces decided not to invade Yap Proper although they bombed the island during air raids. Ulithi Atoll was captured and developed into a major Allied support base in 1944.

Geography

Yap Proper consists of the four tightly clustered islands of Yap, Tomil-Gagil, Map (pronounced 'marp', and also spelt Maap) and Rumung. All but Rumung are connected by bridges. The islands are 515 miles south-west of Guam.

Unlike other high islands in Micronesia which are volcanic in origin (see Geology in the Facts about the Region chapter), Yap Proper was formed by land upheavals of the Asian continental shelf. Consequently the interior regions are not mountainous, but have gentle rolling hills. The highest point, Mt Matade on Yap Island, is 571 feet (174m). Yap Proper has 38¾ sq miles (100 sq km) of land, which accounts for 84% of the state's total land mass.

There are also a handful of small islands within Yap Proper's fringing coral reef. Three of these – Pekel, Bi and Tarang (O'Keefe's) – sit in the channel between

Tomil-Gagil and Yap islands and total about 10 acres (4 hectares) combined. Garim (Bird Island), off the south-east tip of Yap Island, is an uplifted 300-foot-long (91m) chunk of coral undercut by the sea.

Strung out some 600 miles (966km) to the east of Yap Proper are 134 outer islands, with a combined land area of 7¼ sq miles (18.8 sq km). Most are mere strands of coral and sand rising precariously above the water. A major typhoon could easily sweep these islands clean of coconut trees or wash them into the sea.

Trade winds blow onto the northern and eastern sides of the islands, leaving the southern and western shores with good sandy beaches.

Climate

Yap has an average year-round temperature of 81°F (27°C) with an approximate 10°F variance between noon and night. The average annual rainfall is 121 inches (3073mm).

The north-east trade winds prevail on Yap from November to May when the rainfall is lighter and the humidity lower. From June to October the breezes falter, the humidity climbs, rainfall rises and the evenings are less comfortable.

Fully developed typhoons are uncommon near Yap, as most of them pass to the north; however, they're not unknown.

Government & Politics

In addition to an elected state legislature, Yap's constitution establishes two councils of traditional leaders. The Council of Pilung is made up of chiefs from Yap Proper and the Council of Tamol consists of chiefs from the outer islands.

The chiefs wield a lot of power and pretty much decide who runs and who wins in general elections. Although the Yapese can vote for whomever they like for political office, people still generally follow the advice and leadership of their chiefs. The councils have the right to veto any legislation that affects traditional customs.

If the governor is from Yap Proper, then the lieutenant governor must be from the outer islands, and vice versa.

Population & People

The physical characteristics of the Yapese are western Pacific in origin, with traits that indicate Philippine, Palauan and Indonesian influences.

During the colonial era there was little intermarriage with Europeans or Japanese, which makes the Yapese unique among Micronesians. Attempts by the Japanese to assimilate the Micronesian peoples by offering privileges to the offspring of mixed Japanese-Micronesian parents had no impact on the Yapese. They continued to marry traditionally in accordance with their caste system and foreigners remained excluded.

For reasons that are still unclear, the Yapese population dropped by half under the Japanese administration. The entire population in 1945 was only 2582. With the birth rate among the world's lowest, there was serious concern that the Yapese as a people were on the verge of extinction.

The US reacted by sending medical teams and a slew of anthropologists. Fortunately the latter needn't have made such haste, for the population slowly edged back upwards.

The current population is 11,900, with about 65% living on Yap Proper.

Society & Conduct

The Yapese, more than any other Micronesian peoples, have been reluctant to adopt Western ways. Despite four colonial administrations, their culture remains largely undiluted by outside influences and they still retain their own customs and traditions.

Caste A complex caste system was developed over time as a consequence of warfare between Yapese villages. The victors demanded land ownership rights and the patronage of the defeated village. The defeated people retained rights to use the land in their village but were compelled to perform menial tasks for their new landlords, such as road construction and burial of the dead. In this manner the victorious villages climbed to the top of the caste system while the defeated ones sank to the bottom.

To this day, the village in which one is born determines one's name and caste. Members of a village belong to the same caste, although their rank within that caste varies. Every plot of land in the village has a name and a rank, with the highest ranked plot belonging to the village chief.

Depending on how you differentiate them, there are either seven or nine castes in Yapese society today. Each village has its own chief with the paramount chiefs of Yap coming from the three highest caste villages (Gachpar, Teb and Ngolog).

It's not really obvious where a village stands in the caste hierarchy just by looking at it. Caste has a more profound effect on people's status than upon their standard of living.

Women's Roles Traditionally women have had subservient roles in Yapese society. They did the cooking and tended the fields, harvesting from one plot for male family members and from another for the females. The food then had to be prepared in separate pots over separate fires. Not only could men and women not eat together but neither could members of different castes share the same food.

Although these restrictions are not so strictly adhered to today, this could perhaps have some bearing on why there are so few restaurants on Yap.

Traditional Community Houses A faluw is a large thatched structure with a sharply pitched roof, supported by heavy wooden pillars and resting atop a stone platform. Traditionally the faluw served as a school for young boys, as quarters for bachelors and as a meeting place for the village leaders.

Pebai are community meeting houses. They often look much like men's houses, only they're larger and have open sides. Pebai are mostly built inland whereas faluw are usually by the water.

Once common throughout Yap, women's houses or *dapal* are now only found on the outer islands. When a girl reached puberty she was ushered off to a dapal for initiation and all women in the village went there to wait out their menstrual periods, using the time to weave, bathe and relax.

Traditional Dress The cotton loincloth worn by men and boys is called a *thu* and most commonly is one of three colours: red, blue or white. Young boys wear just one thu, either red or blue. Upon reaching 18-years, young men on Yap Proper switch to two layers of different coloured cloth, and in their mid-20s they add a third layer. Older men affix strands of hibiscus fibre on top of their thu. Men on the outer islands generally wear just one layer of cloth.

Women have two kinds of traditional dress – grass skirts and *lava-lava*. The latter is a wide strip of cloth woven from hibiscus and banana fibres or from cotton thread. The cotton ones are becoming more common, as they take only about a third of the time to make. Lava-lava are wrapped around the lower body, extending from the waist to the knee.

Traditionally, neither men nor women wore clothing on their upper bodies, though today T-shirts are sometimes worn, to the chagrin of more traditional chiefs. Western-style clothing has largely overtaken Colonia (not to be confused with Kolonia in Pohnpei), but both Western and traditional dress are seen all around Yap.

Orientation
Maps The Land Management office (☎ 350 2164, fax 350 2414), up the hill from the post office and beside the telecommunications office, sells USGS maps of Yap for US$7.50.

Information
Tourist Offices The Yap Visitors Bureau (☎ 350 2298, fax 350 7015, ✉ yvb@mail.fm), on the north side of the bridge in Colonia centre, is open weekdays from 7.30 to 11.30 am and 12.30 to 4.30 pm.

Money The Bank of Hawaii and the Bank of FSM are near each other in Colonia centre. Both are open from 9.30 am to 3 pm Monday to Thursday and until 5 pm on

Dos and Don'ts

Exploring Yap requires a grasp of Yapese etiquette. Once you step off the road anywhere in Yap (except for some parts of Colonia), you're on private property. Even some of the stone pathways through villages are private and walking along them is somewhat similar to cutting across someone's backyard. The Yapese themselves try to avoid entering a village other than their own once the sun has set. Once inside a village there are more rules of etiquette; some villages for example, have areas that women are not allowed to enter.

The official line is that you need to get permission and sometimes a guide to visit most beaches, *pebai* (community meeting house) or villages. Unofficially, the word is that because you're a foreigner and don't know the rules, the Yapese will understand as long as you're considerate and don't overstep the bounds.

The catch-22 is that if you have a guide with you, there are certain things you won't be able to see or do, because the guide knows precisely where he is and isn't allowed to take you.

In reality it's not difficult to go off on your own, asking people along the way for directions and permission when appropriate. Smiles go a long way in Yap. In a village you should greet everyone you see so it doesn't look as if you're sneaking around. Be prepared to back off when it's obvious you're intruding, and always ask permission before snapping someone's picture. Yapese don't like to be stared at or have things pointed at them, so video cameras are especially distasteful.

To the Yapese, not asking permission is an insult, but they're a very generous people and if you do ask, they'll probably let you go nearly anywhere and see almost anything you want.

Friday. The Bank of Hawaii is the place to change foreign currency or obtain cash advances on credit cards. Both banks change US-dollar travellers cheques. Many businesses on Yap now accept credit cards. There is no ATM machine.

Post & Communications Yap Proper's only post office, on the northern side of Chamorro Bay, is open weekdays from 8.30 am to 3 pm. Mail goes off-island only twice weekly, on Wednesday and Sunday.

Long-distance phone calls can be made and telexes can be sent from the FSM telecommunications building in Colonia. Faxes can be sent for the cost of a phone call, plus a dollar. You can receive faxes at the office (at fax 350 4115). There are no coin phones on Yap, but there are a handful of debit-card phones at stores in Colonia and at the telecommunications building. You can also buy phonecards in both places.

The telecommunications office has one PC with Internet access that costs US$4 an hour. It's best to go between working hours (7.30 am to 4.30 pm), when computer-literate employees are most likely to be around. Most hotels are connected to the Internet and may allow you to use their connection for a small fee.

Immigration The immigration office (☎ 350 2126, ✉ yil@mail.fm), on the 2nd floor of the Bank of FSM building, is open from 8.30 am to 4.30 pm weekdays.

Libraries Colonia's little public library, which is south of the Marina Restaurant, is open weekdays from 9 am to 4 pm.

Media Yap has a government-owned AM radio station and a Christian FM station, and a government-owned TV station, WAAB, which shows recorded programs from the US mainland. YCA sells Guam's *Pacific Daily News*, albeit several days old.

Laundry The coin laundry behind the YCA charges US$0.50 to wash, US$0.75 to dry.

Emergency There's a public hospital (☎ 350 3446) at the north side of Colonia, on the main road leading to Tomil-Gagil Island. For police emergencies, dial ☎ 350 3333 or ☎ 911.

Yap Proper
The major islands of Yap, Map and Tomil-Gagil are all tightly clustered and connected by bridges, and contain 65% of Yap's

population. Yap Island is the westernmost and largest island, with half of Yap Proper's land area and two-thirds of its people. Rumung is separated from the rest of Yap Proper by Yinbinaew Passage and can only be reached by boat. Rumung is not receptive to visitors – outsiders need an invitation to go there. Yap Proper has 10 municipalities with more than 100 small villages.

The landscape of the main islands is mainly rolling hills with a green cover of grass interspersed with sparse pandanus and palm trees. In the south-west the lowlands have thick growth and a marsh-like jungle floor. Yap Proper has some sandy beaches, but much of the coast is lined with mangrove swamps.

The most interesting sights by far are not WWII relics or scenic views, but glimpses into Yapese culture.

The sparsely populated villages outside the capital of Colonia are quiet, peaceful and tidy. On weekdays, when the children are at school and adults are off fishing or at work either in Colonia or in their taro patches, the villages can look semi-deserted.

Bechiyal, a traditional village on a sandy beach at the tip of Map Island, has opened itself to visitors as a living cultural centre. It offers the kind of experience you'd hope to find by journeying to a distant outer island, yet is only a US$10 taxi ride away from Colonia. You can sleep overnight in a faluw, eat breadfruit and freshly speared fish, drink homemade tuba and learn from the villagers about Yapese culture. See Bechiyal Cultural Center later in this section for details.

Colonia Colonia (population 1188), on Yap Island in Yap Proper, is the state capital, the business and administrative centre and the only part of Yap that is the least bit modern. Even so the town, known as Donguch in Yapese, would be considered a village almost anywhere else.

Colonia wraps around Chamorro Bay, offering sea views most everywhere. The bay, incidentally, got its name during the German era when the area was settled with

Chamorro labourers who were brought in from Saipan to build the transpacific cable station. These days the south side of Chamorro Bay is home to a sizable Palauan community.

For all practical purposes Colonia's town centre is the YCA complex, a cooperative that was started by an expat Quaker in the 1950s. The old, quaintly jumbled YCA department store embodied Yapese small-town character for nearly four decades before being torn down and replaced by a more modern building. While the charming sidewalk bamboo benches and thatched awnings are gone, the complex is still a meeting place of sorts and it's common to find Yapese men in thu standing around chatting.

There's quite a bit to see in the Colonia area and the best of it can be explored on foot: the stone footpath across town, the trail up Medeqdeq Hill, and a walk to the stone money bank and faluw in the nearby village of Balabat. These all make pleasurable strolls and you don't need special permission to do them on your own.

The **government administration building** was constructed on the site of the old Spanish fort, of which only remnants of a wall and the foundations remain. Among the offices here are those of the governor and of outer island affairs.

The **state legislature building** is on the site of a former Japanese Shinto shrine. The main vestiges of the shrine are the cement *torii* (pillared gate) in the middle of the parking lot and a pair of stone lanterns flanking the steps leading to the front entrance.

The 482-foot (147m) **Medeqdeq Hill** is topped with a light beacon and has a panoramic **view** of Colonia, the harbour and Yap's east coast. The top of the hill is about a mile up from Colonia on the road past **St Mary's Catholic Church**, which incidentally dates back to Yap's first Spanish Capuchin missionaries.

Although the walk starts out on pavement, the last half is along a rough dirt road that's not passable without a 4WD vehicle. Beware of a low-growing groundcover with

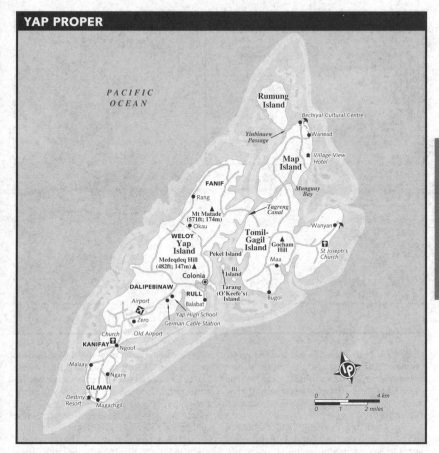

YAP PROPER

PACIFIC
OCEAN

Rumung
Island

Bechiyal Cultural Centre

Yinbinaew
Passage

Wanead

Map
Island

Village View
Hotel

FANIF

Rang

Munguuy
Bay

Mt Matade
(571ft; 174m) ▲

Okau

Tagreng
Canal

WELOY
Yap
Island

Tomil-
Gagil
Island

Gocham
Hill

Wanyan

Pekel Island

Medeqdeq Hill
(482ft; 147m) ▲

Bi
Island

St Joseph's
Church

Maa

Colonia

DALIPEBINAW

RULL

Tarang
(O'Keefe's)
Island

Bugol

Airport

Balabat

Zero

Yap High School

German Cable Station

Church

Old Airport

KANIFAY

Ngoof

Malaay

Ngariy

GILMAN

Destiny
Resort

Magachgil

0   2   4 km
0   1   2 miles

FED STATES OF MICRONESIA

fuzzy purple flowers and small razor-sharp thorns that draw blood at the slightest touch. The hike up and back takes about an hour from the church.

There's a lovely traditional **stone footpath** that starts opposite the waterfront just south of the Ocean View Hotel. The path is peaceful and shady, and lined with flowering hibiscus and green ti plants much of the way. When the path splits, take the left fork and you'll come out to the paved road just above the Catholic school.

To continue on a second footpath that will bring you down to the north side of Chamorro Bay, turn right and go up the road for about 20 feet (6m). The second path begins near a pigsty. This path is not as well-lined with stones as the first, but it does offer some glimpses of taro patches and **village houses**.

The whole walk only takes about 15 minutes and is a very pleasant way to get across town.

The **Ethnic Art Institute of Micronesia** attempts to preserve traditional art forms by providing a place for local artists to create and sell their art. To revive and expand the arts, village elders have been invited to

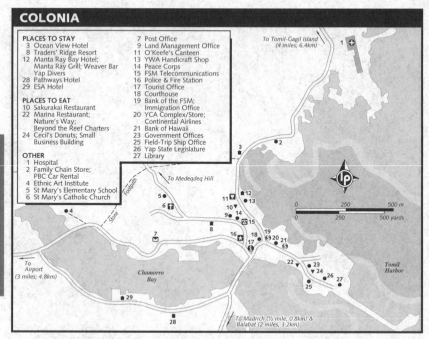

COLONIA

PLACES TO STAY
3 Ocean View Hotel
8 Traders' Ridge Resort
12 Manta Ray Bay Hotel;
   Manta Ray Grill; Weaver Bar
   Yap Divers
28 Pathways Hotel
29 ESA Hotel

PLACES TO EAT
10 Sakurakai Restaurant
22 Marina Restaurant;
   Nature's Way;
   Beyond the Reef Charters
24 Cecil's Donuts; Small
   Business Building

OTHER
1 Hospital
2 Family Chain Store;
   PBC Car Rental
4 Ethnic Art Institute
5 St Mary's Elementary School
6 St Mary's Catholic Church

7 Post Office
9 Land Management Office
11 O'Keefe's Canteen
13 YWA Handicraft Shop
14 Peace Corps
15 FSM Telecommunications
16 Police & Fire Station
17 Tourist Office
18 Courthouse
19 Bank of the FSM;
   Immigration Office
20 YCA Complex/Store;
   Continental Airlines
21 Bank of Hawaii
23 Government Offices
25 Field-Trip Ship Office
26 Yap State Legislature
27 Library

To Tomil-Gagil Island
(4 miles; 6.4km)

To Medeqdeq Hill

To Airport
(3 miles; 4.8km)

Chamorro Bay

Tomil Harbor

To Madrich (½ mile; 0.8km) &
Balabat (2 miles; 3.2km)

teach their craftsmanship and techniques to younger artists. Part of the program involves research to determine the exact form of original idols, discover what natural pigments were used before Western contact and so forth.

The artists live on-site in thatched homes and work in an open-air carving shelter. The institute has an exhibition in the tourist office and is open weekdays from 9 to 11 am and 1 to 3.30 pm.

Balabat The mile-long walk to the village of Balabat in Rull Municipality is a good way to see a traditional faluw and stone-money bank without having to drive around the island.

The road starts at the petrol station near the bridge in south Colonia. A few minutes along you'll pass Madrich, a point of land sticking out into the bay which is home to a settlement of outer islanders. Madrich, once the site of a Spanish trading station, was named after Madrid.

The walk continues along the waterfront until it reaches Rull municipal office, where the road is lined with an impressive collection of **rai**. Just before you reach the municipal office you'll come to Sav-Way Mart, where foreign tourists are expected to stop and pay US$2.50 to enter Rull.

At the municipal office the pavement ends and the road curves to the right. Two-tenths of a mile (300m) past the municipal office look on the left for a dirt road about as wide as the main road. It's just a couple of minutes down that road to more **rai** and a **seaside faluw** in a setting of coconut palms.

The main road ends at two raised **stone platforms** used for community gatherings. Traditional **dances** sometimes take place on the pathway between the platforms. The village of Balabat is neatly landscaped with betel nut trees, taro patches, hibiscus and lilies. You can usually spot bright red cardinal honeyeaters in the trees along this walk.

Around Yap Island In 1905 the **German cable station** on Yap completed a link to Shanghai through Guam and the Philippines via an undersea cable system. Shelling from a British warship in August 1914 destroyed the station's 200-foot steel radio tower, breaking Germany's communications link to its Pacific territories and marking the start of WWI activity in Micronesia.

To see the graffiti-decorated concrete remains of the station, one of the few remnants of German occupation in Yap, head west out of Colonia on the road to the airport. Pass the pond that serves as the town's water reservoir on the right, then turn left onto the unmarked dirt road that leads up to Yap High School. The station remains are clearly visible opposite the school parking lot. The whole distance from the westside bridge in Colonia is 1¾ miles (2.8km).

To see the remains of some **Japanese Zeros**, continue past the entrance to the new airport for exactly one mile and then turn left onto an unmarked dirt road. Continue on that road for half a mile, at which point you'll reach the old telecommunications station followed by the weather station.

The two planes that are best preserved and easiest to see are about 100 yards (90m) north of the weather station. To get to them, take the dirt road that runs back between the telecommunications and weather stations. You can visit them for free. However, if you want to photograph them, you're supposed to first see Martin at the weather station and pay US$2.50.

The Zeros were destroyed on the ground by US aerial bombings during WWII. The planes are missing engines and other parts that were taken away by Japanese collectors, but the wings are still largely intact and they're interesting to see. The area around the planes is a good place to find low-growing, insectivorous pitcher plants.

There's a well-preserved **Japanese anti-aircraft gun** under a big mahogany tree on the weather station lawn about 20 feet (6m) from the road, just beyond the little chain-link enclosure. After you pass the gun, keep looking on the left to find a Yapese-style **tree house** complete with a thatched roof.

The road continues on to an abandoned 5000-foot (1.5km) **airstrip** built by the Japanese. The old thatched-roof terminal still stands, but it's difficult to spot the remains of the 727 that landed short of the runway in 1980, lost a wheel and skidded off into the bush at the eastern end of the airstrip.

You can turn right onto the runway to get back to the main road that goes to Gilman municipality.

Southern Tip of Yap South of the old airport is the village of **Ngoof**, marked by St Ignatius of Loyola church and the adjacent cemetery. A mile beyond on the left is Nathan Store (no sign), where you can buy a cool drink while checking out the store's old **Spanish cannon**, which is sandwiched between two pieces of rai. The friendly proprietor is a school teacher who enjoys chatting and sharing insights.

After another 1½ miles the road reaches the coast at **Gilman**, the southernmost end of the island. It's a neat community with much of the shoreline bordered by coconut palms and Yapese mahogany trees. There are some attractive **traditional houses** in this area, landscaped with rai, hibiscus hedges and chenille plants with velvety red tails.

The road going up the west side skirts the mangrove-studded coast, in places narrowing to just one lane elevated a few feet above the swamps. Tiny lipstick-red **fiddler crabs** are easy to spot running around in the black mud between the sharp spikes of the mangrove shoots, and with a little luck you might also see **mangrove crabs** and **monitor lizards**. The lizards, which can reach a length of several feet, were introduced onto Yap and Ulithi by the Japanese both to control the rat population and to serve as a food source.

The road ends at Malaay village, where an extensive moss-covered **Japanese stone wall**, part of WWII defence fortifications, runs along the side of the road. At Malaay, turn east on the side road that's strung with power lines to get back on the main Gilman-airport road. Just 200 yards (180m) along this side road look to the left to see a grassy **rai path**.

Okau Village The village of Okau in Weloy municipality has one of Yap's best **meeting houses** and **stone money banks** at the end of a very pleasant stone footpath.

To get there from Colonia you take the road west, as if heading toward the airport, but instead of turning left with the main paved road take the right fork onto the wide dirt road, which is three-quarters of a mile (1.2km) from the westside bridge on Chamorro Bay.

When the road forks again, bear right, continuing on the wider road. The stone pathway, which is just over 3 miles (4.8km) from the airport road, starts on the right opposite a stone platform and just before two small houses and a bridge.

One section of the path meanders alongside taro patches and interesting mud flats, while another part is lined with hibiscus and lush variegated plants. Moss grows in the cracks between the stones. It's very quiet and peaceful, almost like walking through a Japanese Zen garden.

The large pebai about 10 minutes down the pathway is built on a raised stone platform. The supports are made of mahogany, the inside floor planks of betel nut and the roof is nipa palm lashed onto bamboo.

Yap's most valuable rai is generally thickest in the middle and thinner at the edges, with circular gouge markings across the face. You can see an example of this type of rai in front of the pebai to the left.

Across a little footbridge opposite the pebai entrance is a *wunbey*, or **meeting platform**. There in the open air the elder men of the village have their meetings, sitting against stone backrests. Traditionally a low stone table is placed in the centre to hold food and betel nut, which young men sitting around on the edges serve to the elders.

Fanif Municipality From Okau the road continues through Fanif Municipality around the northern end of Yap Island. En route it skirts extensive mangrove swamps, crosses little bridges and goes through a few sleepy villages.

Nearly 2 miles (3.3km) from Okau you'll enter the village of **Rang**. The chief's house is the first house on the left, surrounded by rai – if he's on the front porch be sure to give a wave and if you're interested in using the beach, stop and ask for his permission. Rang Beach is a long brown-sand beach. Swimming might be good at high tide, but at low tide it's all sea grass and sand flats.

The dirt road continues another 12 miles (19km), washboard-like in places but usually passable in a standard car, before coming out to Yap's main paved road. At this intersection, turn right to get to Colonia, left to go to Tomil-Gagil.

Tomil-Gagil Island Tomil-Gagil was once connected to Yap Island at the upper end of Tomil Harbor by mangrove flats. During the German occupation the shallow Tagreng Canal was dug between the islands to allow boat passage to Map and Rumung from Colonia.

Most visitors to Tomil-Gagil are on their way to the beach in Wanyan or to Bechiyal on Map Island. For the most part the interior is dry, with open rolling meadows and dusty red earth, while the coast is lusher, with coconut palms, mangroves and bananas.

Shortly after crossing the Tagreng Canal you'll go by the Seventh-Day Adventist school. When the road forks a mile farther, veer left, continuing on the main road. The road north to Bechiyal will come in after ¼ mile (400m), but to get to Wanyan continue straight ahead. The Wanyan road runs through the **Micronesian Maritime & Fisheries Academy**. The top of an inland hill may seem like an oddly landlocked location for a maritime academy, but it owes its location to the otherwise suitable facilities that were left at this site by the former US Coast Guard Loran Station.

Gocham Hill, south of the road near the academy, is a sacred place that is considered the centre of Yapese wisdom and the spot where Yap is said to have been formed.

Wanyan To get to the coastal village of Wanyan, bear left at the fork three-quarters of a mile after the academy, on the road that parallels the power lines.

Yap's largest rai is on Rumung Island, but since its islanders have decided they're not ready for foreign visitors, you'll have to settle for the second largest rai, which is in the centre of Wanyan village.

Upon entering Wanyan, you'll pass St Joseph's Catholic Church, which has an interesting **mural** painted above its door showing Yapese men presenting gifts of rai, lava-lava, food and storyboards.

Just a little farther on, you'll pass a meeting house and will then see two **huge rai** standing along the ocean side of the road. The piece on the left is Yap's second largest.

One of Yap's most accessible beaches is **Wanyan Beach** (also called Seabreeze Beach), at the end of the road. This brown-sand beach is backed by lots of loaded coconut trees – if you're driving, be careful where you park! There are thatched picnic shelters, restrooms and showers. Pay the US$2 beach use fee at the unmarked tin-sided store that's on the ocean side of the road 350 yards (320m) before the beach. You can borrow a volleyball net there if you're so inclined. They've also got a couple of kayaks for rent and there is a bar called *Coco-Shade*, which is open from 5 to 9 pm Wednesday to Sunday.

Swimming is best at high tide, as otherwise the water is shallow and there's lots of sea grass near the shore. About halfway out to the reef there are several **circular drop-offs** with good fish and coral. If you look straight out from the beach you can identify these snorkelling holes by the water colour, which changes from dark blue to aqua. The closest is directly out from the beach at 11 o'clock and takes about 10 minutes to swim out to.

Bechiyal Cultural Center Bechiyal is a special place. This friendly seaside village at the northern tip of Map has not only decided to accommodate overnight guests, but has set itself up as a low-key cultural centre, providing visitors with an opportunity to more closely observe traditional Yapese village life.

Bechiyal is on a lovely beach, one of Yap Proper's best, though you'll usually need to wade out for about 10 minutes to reach water deep enough for swimming. Between the coastline and reef are two large V-shaped **stone fish traps** of ancient origins. When the tide goes out the bigger fish get stuck in the narrow end of the traps, making it a cinch for villagers to go out and spear fish for their next meal.

Visitors are welcome to use the **beach** in front of the faluw, though the beaches just beyond the village are even nicer, and as they're more secluded women can sunbathe without having to worry about offending anyone. There's a freshwater shower in the village. For US$10 to US$15, **snorkellers** can be taken out by boat to the channel, where the manta rays feed, and even do a scenic loop around the forbidden island of Rumung on the way back. However, advance planning is required.

Bechiyal's **pebai** is the largest on Yap, while its **faluw**, on a high stone platform above the beach, is one of the oldest on the island. The faluw is crafted in the centuries-old manner with openings that hinge in and out, and thatch that catches cool ocean breezes. Inside there are dried turtle skulls as well as a carved wooden figure that represents the *mispil*, which in times past was a woman captured from a neighbouring village and used as the mistress for the faluw.

The entrance fee to Bechiyal is US$2.50 for adults, US$1.75 for children aged from 10 to 17, and under 10 years are free. If you ask, one of the villagers will probably give you a guided tour. There's no extra charge for still photography, but previous negative experiences with video cameras makes their use frowned upon and there's a fee to use one. Souveniring shells is strictly forbidden.

Your guide can pick you a drinking coconut from a nearby tree and serve it up with a fresh-cut papaya-stem straw. Meals are available for US$3 to US$4 each, but should be arranged a day in advance. Dinner might well be a hardy Yapese meal of fish or crab, breadfruit, taro and fried banana, all from the village. Bechiyal's tuba has such a good reputation that Rumung islanders regularly come ashore to buy it, and those who spend the night at Bechiyal (see Places to Stay later) commonly pass the evening sipping away.

There's a handicraft hut in Bechiyal that sells locally made woven bags, baskets, pandanus place mats, betel nut bags and toy bamboo rafts. Ask to see the little museum display stored here, which includes shell money called *yar*, a pig's tooth necklace, shell adzes and other artefacts.

Getting to Bechiyal The nicest way to get to Bechiyal is on a delightful mile-long footpath that begins at the end of the Map road. To get started, drive or take a taxi (US$10) to the end of the road (or, if you're overnighting, take the public school bus). When you reach a fork with the sea in view, stay left. You can park at the end of the road and then walk across the log footbridge. The path passes through **Wanead** and **Tooruw**, two traditional villages of thatched houses spread along the coast, then leads through a jungle setting with lots of bird calls, dragonflies and scurrying lizards. There's also several examples of **rai** along the way.

About 15 minutes along the route you'll reach another road. Turn right onto it for the simplest route into the village or continue on the old path straight ahead for the most scenic route. Either way, you're only about ten minutes from Bechiyal.

If you have a real time-crunch you could instead drive directly to Bechiyal on the other road, which starts off the main paved road at Maap Elementary School. However, this road could be a bit tougher on your car.

Outer Islands

The outer islands are made up of 11 atolls and four single islands. Of these 15 outer island groups, 11 are populated.

Yap's outer islanders are some of the most isolated people on earth. Little is known of their origins, although it's believed that their islands were settled quite independently of Yap Proper. Yap's east-

ernmost islanders and Chuuk's westernmost islanders have more physical, cultural and linguistic similarities with each other than they do with either of their district centres.

Most outer islanders live the same way they have for centuries, wearing thu and lava-lava and living in thatched huts. Some of the elderly men still have elaborate body tattoos, though the practice has been all but abandoned by younger generations.

For the most part the outer islanders maintain a subsistence livelihood of fishing and farming. To earn a little money, many of the islanders produce copra which they load onto the field-trip ship when it stops by.

Uninhabited islands are visited in outrigger canoes to gather turtles, turtle eggs and coconuts. On Lamotrek Atoll, for instance, turtle meat is the staple food between April and August.

Some of the smaller atolls have so little land that every spare bit is used for growing crops. During severe dry spells some islanders are forced to rely solely on drinking coconuts when they run out of catchment water.

Ulithian is the native language on Ulithi, Fais and Sorol atolls. Satawal Islanders speak Satawalese, which is closely related to the language of Chuuk's western islanders. The native language on Yap's other outer islands is Woleaian.

Permission to Visit There's concern that Yap's more isolated outer islands may be very vulnerable, should the 20th century (not to mention the 21st century) suddenly appear upon their shores clad in board shorts or a bikini and grasping a video camera. It's largely because of this that visitors are screened.

In a government survey some years back, 99% of outer islanders said they thought visitors should be accompanied by a Yapese guide (but 96% would like to share Yap's traditional culture with outsiders), the Governor's Office and the Council of Tamol (composed of chiefs from the outer islands) established a formal set of guidelines for visiting the outer islands. The guidelines aren't meant to discourage 'appropriate' visitors, but rather to make the process smoother for everyone and to assure the respect of traditional ways.

You should make a request to the Yap Visitors Bureau at least a month before the date you're hoping to visit. The office will then take the request to the chief of the island you want to visit. Upon the chief's approval, the office will issue a pass authorising the visit and stating the length of stay. You can then purchase a ticket from either the field-trip ship or PMA (Pacific Missionary Aviation). Upon landing the pass needs to be presented to the island chief, along with a visitor fee of US$20. A gift of cigarettes or canned food is appropriate for your host family.

Ulithi Atoll Ulithi Atoll, 100 miles northeast of Yap, has the most land and the most people of any of the outer islands. Its huge lagoon, which covers 209 sq miles (541 sq km), is the world's fourth largest. All in all, there are 49 islands with a total land mass of just 1¾ sq miles (4.6 sq km).

Ulithi's inhabited islands – Falalop, Mogmog, Asor and Fassarai – have a total population of just over 1000. All have nice sandy beaches. The only airstrip is on Falalop and the terminal building has Yap's only outer island post office.

Ulithi is the most developed of the outer islands. It has the only outer islands high school, public electricity and even a little laundrette built with Australian aid. Concrete houses are more common than thatched houses. Partly because the US military left so much corrugated metal, there are more tin roofs on Ulithi than on any of the other islands.

Ulithi played an important role in WWII. The Japanese came in numbers that must have seemed enormous to the Ulithians – that is until the USA moved in with temporary population densities that rivalled those of major cities.

The Japanese had established a seaplane and naval base as well as a radio and weather station on Ulithi. When the Americans closed in, the Japanese evacuated to

Yap Proper taking most of the able-bodied Ulithians along with them.

In September 1944 the Americans landed on Ulithi unopposed. They quickly constructed an airstrip on Falalop Island and a hospital, and a recreation centre on Mogmog Island that eventually entertained as many as 20,000 soldiers a day.

Strategically located, Ulithi served as a major anchorage and supply and repair base for the final six months of the war. Its extensive lagoon held 617 Allied naval vessels prior to the Okinawa invasion.

Somehow folks on Ulithi survived these encounters with uninvited visitors from the 'civilised' world. These days if you want to visit the atoll you have to seek permission.

Flights between Yap and Guam often fly over Ulithi Atoll. It's an impressive sight from the air, with islands spread so far apart that they scarcely seem related.

Woleai Atoll For many reasons Woleai makes a nice choice for an outer island visit – it has an appealingly simple lifestyle and friendly people and is serviced by both field-trip ship and plane. If you were to take the field-trip ship from Colonia you could stay about a week and then catch the same boat back on its return leg.

Of the outer atolls, Woleai ranks a close second to Ulithi both in land size and population. About 850 people live on five of Woleai's 22 islets and the atoll has a junior high school. Several of the islands are clustered close together, some separated only by narrow mangrove channels and others joined at low tide by sand bars. Woleai has beautiful sandy beaches, and canoes are favoured over motorboats.

Woleai holds onto its traditional ways more firmly than Ulithi does. At a recent community meeting it was decided to strictly enforce rules against wearing T-shirts, pants, baseball caps and other Western clothing. While foreign visitors are exempt, it aids your acceptance if you endeavour to wear traditional clothing – lava-lava for women, thu for men. There aren't shops on Woleai that sell these items, but you can generally find someone willing to trade canned foods or other items for them.

During WWII the Japanese fortified Woleai, and shells of wrecked ships and planes, old tanks, bunkers, field guns and monuments are all around the islands. Even the airfield used by PMA is a former Japanese fighter airstrip.

The runway and main village are on Falalop Island, the atoll's largest. In the village, at the southern end of the runway, there are taro patches behind the school where you can find the remains of **Japanese planes**, including an intact **Zero**. From Falalop you can wade across to Paliau Island, where there's a sandy beach with a **bunker** and **WWII guns**. If you want to explore other war sights, it's usually possible to arrange for someone to take you by boat elsewhere around the atoll. You could even go snorkelling and explore a **US bomber** that sits on the lagoon floor.

The governor's representative sometimes lets visitors sleep the first night in his office near the runway. If you want to camp, this can generally be arranged at a rocky beach on the ocean side of Falalop. If you prefer to stay with a family you may be assigned one of the small huts on the edge of extended family compounds.

Fais Island Fais is a single island of raised limestone with just over 1 sq mile (2.6 sq km) of land. It has a partial fringing reef, sandy beaches, cliffs and sea caves. With an elevation of 60 feet (18m), Fais is the highest of Yap's outer islands and was once known for its agricultural production.

Both the Germans and the Japanese had phosphate mines on Fais that scarred the island. You can find the remains of a **Japanese dock** hit by US bombers during WWII, parts of a **steel observation tower** and the base of a shore **defence gun**. Fais has one village, a population of 300 and a 3000-foot (914m) crushed coral airstrip. The women are known for their skilled weaving of lava-lava, many of which are created during their stays in the village dapal.

Satawal Island Satawal, Yap's easternmost inhabited island, is home to some of the world's most skilled traditional navigators, who still sail vast expanses of ocean in outrigger canoes without charts or compass, relying on their knowledge of star positions, ocean swells and other natural phenomena. It was Satawal master star-path navigator Mau Piailug who was chosen to navigate the double-hulled sailing canoe *Hokulea* on its historic journey between Hawai'i and Tahiti in 1976. Using traditional navigational skills preserved in Satawal but long forgotten elsewhere in the Pacific, the trip retraced the ancient routes of the early Polynesian seafarers who settled Hawai'i.

Satawal is a single raised island of ½ sq mile (1.3 sq km) of land with no lagoon. It has a fringing reef and is a difficult island to land on: The *Micro Spirit* (see Getting There & Away later in this section) cannot anchor close to shore and even its lighters cannot reach the island when the tide is low.

Satawal is rather densely populated, with about 560 residents. Most live in the main village, which fronts a large sandy beach. After Typhoon Owen hit in November 1990 only nine of the island's 90 houses were left standing.

Another disaster struck in 1994, when the Greek ship *Oceanus* bashed the fish-rich reef. The islanders sued in a court on Yap and were awarded US$2 million.

Lamotrek Atoll Lamotrek Atoll is shaped a bit like a deflated triangle, with an island at each of the three points. At the south-east end of the atoll is Lamotrek Island, the largest and only populated island. The interior is swampy, while the lagoon side of the island has a lovely beach that's thickly lined with coconut palms. It takes only about 10 minutes to walk from one side of Lamotrek Island to the other and the total land area for the entire atoll is a mere 245 acres (100 hectares).

The population is about 300, and despite the surrounding reef and an abundance of land crabs and fruit, severe droughts occasionally cause famine conditions on the island. The Japanese occupied Lamotrek and the remains of **WWII planes** can still be found.

Ifalik Atoll Ifalik Atoll has long, white sandy beaches, lots of coconut palms and a lagoon in a near-perfect circle. The two inhabited islands were one island until a typhoon hit and broke a narrow channel through the middle. With a land area of just over ½ sq mile (1.3 sq km), Ifalik is home to 650 people. The atoll is very traditional. There's a taboo area in the main village where no-one may enter and the chief reportedly won't allow motorboats into the lagoon.

Faraulap Atoll Faraulap Atoll has a small lagoon and five islets totalling just 100 acres (40 hectares), with most of the 220 residents living on Faraulep and Pig. A large sand spit has built up on the south side of Faraulep islet and the field-trip ship cannot enter the lagoon.

Eauripik Atoll Eauripik Atoll has 120 people living on a mere 60 acres (25 hectares) of land, giving it the highest population density of any of Yap's outer islands. Every speck of the island is used either for homesites or food crops. Copra is not made as all coconuts are eaten. Houses are built on raised stone platforms and the church is one of only two on the outer islands still of traditional-style construction.

Elato Atoll Elato Atoll has seven islets, comprising 130 acres (50 hectares) of land, in a lovely lagoon setting with a curving sandy beach. From its shores you can see Lamotrek, 13 miles (21km) to the east. There is a relatively large area set aside for copra production, though food is sometimes scarce. Elato has about 120 people.

Sorol & Ngulu Atolls These two atolls have small land areas and only about 40 people combined – three for Sorol, 38 for Ngulu. Ngulu has a very large lagoon of 148 sq miles (383 sq km), with nesting areas for sea turtles and excellent commercial fishing.

Gaferut, West Fayu, Pikelot & Olimarao These atolls have no permanent inhabitants and are nesting grounds for turtles and birds.

Activities

Diving & Snorkelling Yap has good diving, including virgin reefs with excellent coral, vertical walls, sea caves, channel drifts, schools of grey sharks and barracuda, sea turtles and a couple of shipwrecks.

The reef off Gilman at the southern tip of Yap Proper slopes gently with extensive branching corals, huge lettuce corals and spectacular coral heads.

Yap's most novel attraction, however, is its manta rays. In winter months (December-February) divers go to Manta Ridge in Miil Channel, where a school of manta rays cruise about. These gentle creatures, which can have a wingspan of 12 feet (3.6m), swim through the channel as divers cling to a ledge about 30 feet (9m) below the surface. The manta rays often come close enough to brush divers with their wingtips. The rays, which are cleaned by parasitic wrasses in the channel, are an awesome sight, especially when they open their wide mouths.

In summer the manta rays move to Gofnuw Channel, at the north-east end of Tomil-Gagil, an interesting dive that often has sleeping sharks as well.

Dive Shops The rates at each of Yap's three dive shops include tanks, weights and lunch. BCDs (buoyancy control devices), regulators and other equipment can be rented for an additional cost. If you sign up in advance for a dive package lasting more than two days find out if you'll be going to different sites, as there's a tendency to go back to the Gofnuw Channel every second day.

Yap Divers (☎ 350 2300, fax 350 4567) at the Manta Ray Bay Hotel is Yap's largest dive shop. This five-star PADI operation offers two-tank dives for US$95. Snorkellers can go out on the boat for US$45, but as trips are generally geared to divers ask in advance about destinations and water conditions. A choppy water surface that won't affect divers can make for less than ideal snorkelling. If you go to Miil Channel it can be interesting watching the rays from above, even though it's a distant view, and you'll be close enough to the reef to swim over and do a little reef snorkelling as well.

Beyond the Reef Charters (☎ 350 3483, fax 350 3733, ✉ beyondthereef@mail.fm) in the Marina Restaurant is a friendly alternative dive company that offers one-tank boat dives for US$60 and two-tank boat dives for US$90. They also have a half-day snorkelling tour, with the destination depending on the tides and customer preference, for US$35 per person, lunch included.

Nature's Way (☎/fax 350 3407, ✉ naturesway@mail.fm) is a little Yapese-owned operation with an amiable Japanese dive instructor, Sue Yasui, who speaks English. Nature's Way charges US$60/90/125 for one/two/three-tank boat dives, and has a snorkelling tour for US$45. All dives include lunch.

Yap ORC (☎ 350 3956, fax 350 4640) is a new but out-of-the-way diving operation based at the Village View Hotel, which is geared toward Japanese tourists. A two-tank dive including lunch costs US$95, snorkel rental costs US$10, and dive equipment rental is US$20, though business is so slow that prices are negotiable.

Both Nature's Way and Beyond the Reef offer a one-day introductory scuba course and dive for US$120, and all three major operations offer night dives for US$50. Beyond the Reef has a five-day open water certification course for US$295.

All shops rent snorkel gear for US$5 to US$10 a set.

Swimming   There aren't many good beaches on Yap and even fewer open to use by non-villagers. The most accessible beaches are Wanyan Beach in Tomil-Gagil and the beach at Bechiyal Cultural Center.

Out of respect for local mores, women may wear a swimsuit in the water as long as it's not too skimpy, but should cover up on the beach.

Fishing   Yap waters have marlin, yellowfin tuna, barracuda and trevally. Beyond the Reef Charters (☎ 350 3483, fax 350 3733) offers trolling, casting and bottom fishing from its 22-foot boat; half-day/full day charters cost US$95/130, equipment and lunch included. Nature's Way has rates that range from US$35 for bottom fishing to US$120 for a full-day charter. Yap Anglers at Manta Ray Bay Hotel (see Places to Stay later) specialises in looking for giant trevally; its rates vary.

Organised Tours

Guided sightseeing tours can be arranged through the hotels.

Nature's Way (☎ 350 2542) provides half-day tours that include a sampling of local fruit for US$45, and full-day tours for US$65. They also offer a mangrove boat tour of the Tagreng Canal for US$35. The Pathways Hotel (☎ 350 3310) runs a series called Monarch Tours, which run from US$20 for an unguided kayak tour to US$60 for a guided land tour of Guam. Snorkel tours cost US$35 a person, and full-moon kayak tours are planned. The Ocean View Hotel also has a half-day tour for US$35, though the per person price drops as more people join, and ESA Hotel runs tours for US$45 to US$75 with a two-person minimum.

If you want to piece together your own little tour, you could also rent a taxi for the day and use the driver as your guide. Taxis can be chartered for US$15 an hour or US$50 and up a day.

Places to Stay

Although Yap has fewer than 100 visitor rooms in all, they represent a surprisingly wide variety in both cost and type. Accommodation ranges from a US$20 guesthouse in a traditional village at the northern end of Yap to US$175 for a room at Traders' Ridge Resort. In Colonia itself there are five small hotels, one quintessentially Yapese.

Yap has a 10% hotel tax; add it to the hotel rates below unless otherwise indicated.

Camping   Camping can be complicated on Yap as every speck of land is privately owned, so you'll need to obtain permission from the landowner. The tourist office should be able to help if you aren't successful on your own. Laurence at the Pathways Hotel (see Places to Stay later) may also be able to arrange camping.

For the most part islanders think camping is a bit odd and may insist you pitch your tent in their backyard where they can keep an eye on you. They'll need to explain it all to the neighbours and will most probably breathe a sigh of relief once you've gone.

The one notable exception is Bechiyal Cultural Center on Map Island, where arrangements have been made to accommodate campers. It costs US$5 per person to pitch a tent and the location, near the men's house, is unbeatable.

Homestays The tourist office keeps a list of Yapese families who are interested in taking travellers into their homes. It is preferred that you write to the tourist office a month in advance to tell them when you're coming, how long you'd like a homestay and a little about yourself. However, it's also possible just to come by the office when you arrive, as homestays can sometimes be arranged on the spot. Either way, the tourist office can arrange for you to visit a home or two, allowing you and the families to check each other out. You should plan to stay in a hotel for one night first until arrangements are complete. Rates are negotiable between you and the family, and the tourist office doesn't charge for its service. Expect to pay about US$20 per person; this generally includes meals.

These are not established guesthouses, by any means, so this is a good opportunity to experience authentic Yapese home life while saving a bit on travel expenses. Expect accommodation to be very modest, but warm and homely.

While it's best to go through the tourist office, you might also try Cyprian Mugunbey (☎ 350 3344, fax 350 7074, ✉ cmugunbey@mail.fm), whose place on glorious Wanyan Beach has a cosy two-person open-air bungalow on stilts for US$25/35 single/double; includes one meal.

He also rents single kayaks (US$3/10 per hour/day), and double kayaks (US$5/15).

Bechiyal Cottage & Men's House
Bechiyal has a wood-and-bamboo *cottage* for overnight guests. It's a simple place on stilts, with a loft and glass-louvred windows all around. Guests are provided with futons on the floor, pillows, sheets, mosquito nets and lanterns. The cost is US$20 per person, or the same price for a homestay, plus traditional-style meals for US$3 to US$4.

Visitors can also stay overnight at the *faluw*, where a couple of village boys occasionally sleep. Despite the place's name, the locals will generally make exceptions for foreign visitors and allow women to stay as well. It costs US$10 for mat space on the floor.

Reservations for overnight stays can be made through Chief John Tamag (☎ 350 2939), Bechiyal Cultural Center, Box 37, Colonia, Yap, FM 96943.

Hotels in Colonia The *ESA Hotel* (☎ 350 2139, fax 350 2310, ✉ esayap@mail.fm), run by a Palauan family, is an older motel-style place that overlooks Chamorro Bay. There are 16 plain but clean rooms with two comfortable twin beds, air-con, private bathrooms, refrigerators, phones and TVs. The rate is US$96.50/104.50 for singles/doubles (including tax); rooms in the older wing go for US$38.50/49.50 (including tax). The hotel has a nice family atmosphere with a guest lounge on the 2nd floor.

The *Ocean View Hotel* (☎ 350 2279, fax 350 2339), at the north-east side of Colonia, is a clean 17-room hotel with a decidedly budget feel. The adequate rooms have two twin-beds, air-con, fans, and a small Japanese-style bathtub. Singles or doubles cost US$44 (including tax), and the airport transfer cost is US$2 per person one way and US$0.75 per bag. Credit cards are not yet accepted.

The *Pathways Hotel* (☎ 350 3310, fax 350 2066, ✉ pathways@mail.fm) has hillside cottages that nicely balance modern comforts with traditional Yapese aesthetics. Each cottage was built using native materials. There are pleasant sitting verandas, many with a clear view of Chamorro Bay. Rooms have two single beds, fans, air-con, bathroom and refrigerator. The friendly, knowledgeable management help make Pathways one of Micronesia's best hotels. The rate is US$115/125 for singles/doubles, which includes continental breakfast and airport transfers.

Catering largely to divers, the three-storey **Manta Ray Bay Hotel** (☎ 350 2300, fax 350 4567, @ billacker@mail.fm) has 23 large, comfortable rooms with rattan furnishings and modern conveniences. All have air-con, a room safe, VCR, telephone (unusual in Yap) and minibar, and there are waterbeds in the ground floor rooms. Rates are US$132/167 for street-side rooms and US$152/187 for rooms with verandas facing the water. For high rollers there's a luxury suite with a king-size bed and a spiral staircase leading to a private jacuzzi for US$222/265. Airport transfers are free and all major credit cards are accepted. The hotel has its own dock and dive shop, a restaurant on the third floor and a bar downstairs.

A new upmarket hotel overlooking the bay is **Traders' Ridge Resort** (☎ 350 6000, fax 350 4279, @ tradersridge@mail.fm), built on the former site of the German cable station. The resort has landscaped grounds, a bar, restaurant and swimming pool. Veranda rooms cost US$185, patio rooms are $165, and a grand suite costs $275.

Hotels Outside Colonia The **Village View Hotel** (☎ 350 3956, fax 350 4640) is at the northern end of Map Island, about 2 miles (3.2km) south-east of Bechiyal. Run by a former tourism officer, it has five Western-style duplex units. The rooms have air-con, two twin beds and a bathroom. It's on a nice and quiet but sometimes windy beach and could make an interesting getaway, though it's a pretty long haul into town if you want to dine out, and it could get rather lonely as there aren't many guests. The rate is US$55/65 for singles/doubles and you

could probably negotiate breakfast into the price. A bar and restaurant are under slow construction. The ORC dive shop is on-site.

Destiny Resort (☎ 350 4188, fax 350 4187) is a tiny 'resort' in the quiet village of Anoth in Gilman, at the southern tip of Yap Island. The cottages are nice but deserted, a random casualty of the fact that some of Micronesia's rustic resorts take off but others struggle. The two A-frame bungalows are studio-like and roomy, with a kitchenette, fans, bathroom with tub, two twin-beds and a futon. The rate is US$75 for singles or doubles. Bring mosquito repellent for the beach.

At time of writing a 14-room hotel, with 10 air-con rooms and four thatched bungalows, was scheduled to open on Ulithi. Contact the tourist office for more information.

None of the other outer islands has established accommodation for visitors. Overnight visitors will probably end up with a host family. Where you stay and what it will cost will be the chief's decision, and won't necessarily be cheaper than staying on Yap Proper. Plan to bring enough food and supplies for the duration of your stay. Coffee, bread, canned meats or other food items unobtainable on the islands make welcome gifts.

Places to Eat

Cecil's Donuts, in the Small Business Building across the street from the Marina Restaurant, is the cheapest and quickest breakfast spot in town. Yummy doughnuts start at US$0.35 and coffee is US$0.75. The shop is open weekdays from 7.30 am to 5.30 pm and weekends from 7.30 am to 1 pm.

Sakurakai Restaurant, next-door to O'Keefe's Canteen, has decent but unexciting Filipino and American food; prices hover around US$6. It's open daily from 6 am to 9 pm.

A great place to dine is the **Marina Restaurant**, a casual, open-air eatery on the waterfront beside the marina. At breakfast a waffle or French toast with an egg and bacon is US$4, and throughout the day you can get a fresh fish sandwich for US$2.50.

A hearty fish or chicken dinner with taro, breadfruit, rice, fruit and a drink costs US$6 to US$7 at lunch and US$10 at dinner. The restaurant is open weekdays from 7 am to 10 pm, 4.30 to 9 pm Saturday, and 10 am to 4 pm and 5 to 9 pm Sunday.

The *Pathway Hotel's* little open-air courtyard makes a nice setting for any meal. The food is excellent – popular seafood dishes cost US$8, and beef dishes cost around US$8.50. During happy hour (4.30 to 7.30 pm) alcoholic drinks drop US$1. Tuesday and Saturday are buffet nights – it's US$25 for a fabulous all-you-can-eat spread. Tuba is served on buffet nights, which is a rare treat (it's not widely available because it spoils quickly). It's necessary to make a reservation on buffet night.

The *Manta Ray Bistro,* on the third floor of the Manta Ray Bay Hotel, has a bayside, breezy view through large windows. The food is standard American fare, which is quite good, if a bit pricey. At breakfast you can get fruit, banana bread and coffee for US$3.50. At lunch, a cheeseburger or fish sandwich with French fries cost US$8.50. The cheese pizza is the best (and nearly the only) pizza on Yap. Otherwise à la carte main dishes include vegetarian pasta, chicken coconut curry and pepper steak in the US$10 to US$22 range. The restaurant is open daily from 6 am to 9 pm.

There are no restaurants outside Colonia, though the outlying villages often have small roadside stores.

YCA is Yap's biggest grocery/general store and is open from 8 am to 5.30 pm weekdays, 8.30 am to 2.30 pm Saturday and 8.30 am to 1 pm Sunday. You can buy alcoholic beverages at YCA and in the Liquor Shoppe in the YCA complex. The nearby video shop sells soft-serve ice cream for US$0.50. Not far beyond the Ocean View Hotel is another food store, the *Family Chain Store*, which stocks a good supply of bread from the bakery down the street.

The Farmers' Market has closed, but *Gardeners Enterprise*, on the south-west corner of the lagoon, has some local produce and occasional coconut drinks. It's open weekdays from 9 am to 5 pm, 9 am to 2 pm Saturday.

Colonia's water is not safe to drink from the tap. If you arrive on a Sunday, be sure to grab some bottled water before the stores close.

Entertainment

There's not much to do in the evening around Colonia in terms of standard entertainment. Yap has no movie theatre. Payday is Wednesday night and so Wednesday and Friday night are the liveliest.

Colonia has four places with open-air bars and water views. Yap's cheapest drinks (US$1.80 for a beer) are at the *Marina Restaurant* during the 4.30 to 7 pm happy hour; on Friday there are live bands and the place stays open until 2 am. The most atmospheric spot is the little thatched gazebo

---

Betel Nut

Everyone, but everyone, in Yap chews *buw*, as betel nut is called. Betel nut is split open while green, sprinkled with dry coral lime, wrapped in pepper leaves and then chewed. The effect is a mild high that lasts for about 10 minutes. Sometimes tobacco, or tobacco soaked in vodka, is added. Betel nut turns the saliva (stimulated by the lime) bright red and stains the teeth red and eventually black.

According to old timers, even ghosts chew betel nut. If, for example, an outrigger canoe were to stop for no obvious reason in the middle of a lagoon, the sailor would prepare a special betel nut mixture, wrap it in extra leaves and tie it up tightly with many knots. He would then throw it overboard and sail away easily, while the ghost who'd been holding his canoe was kept busy untying the knots.

at the **Pathways Hotel**, where a Foster's costs US$2 until 7.30 pm, US$3 after that. The Weaver Bar in the **Manta Ray Bay Hotel** is a bit pricey but has the widest selection, including wines.

Colonia's newest bar is **O'Keefe's Canteen**, built on the historic site of an 1874 canteen owned by an American entrepreneur who hauled Yapese rai back from Palau (see boxed text 'His Majesty O'Keefe'). The popular Canteen has both indoor and outdoor seating and is open from 4 to 11 pm nightly, with happy hour from 4 to 8 pm. On Wednesday, Friday and Saturday there's local entertainment. On Friday night there's also a barbecue on the upper patio; arrive about 6 pm before the food runs out.

The legal drinking age is 21 and island residents need to obtain a liquor permit at the police station. At most places, including the bars listed here, foreign visitors can buy alcohol without the permit, though clerks in some smaller stores refuse to sell you beer without one.

Cultural Shows Maa village on Tomil-Gagil Island opens up to tours on request, with traditional dancing by costumed boys and girls, a village stroll along a stone footpath and a sampling of local fruits. The tour is good fun, offers an opportunity to see a traditional men's house and provides a rare chance to take photos of Yapese (no fee) without worrying about giving offence. It lasts about two hours and costs US$45. The Pathways Hotel and other hotels should be able to arrange the tour for you.

Shopping

Yap has some fine native handicrafts. Lava-lava skirts hand-woven from cotton or hibiscus and banana-tree fibres can make attractive wall hangings; they sell for US$20 to US$60. Other crafts are handbags or betel nut pouches woven of pandanus leaves, wood carvings of outrigger canoes and toy bamboo rafts.

You can buy crafts directly from the artists at the Ethnic Art Institute of Micronesia (see its entry earlier in this section).

His Majesty O'Keefe

The most colourful character of Yap's 19th-century history was David 'His Majesty' O'Keefe, a shipwrecked Irish-American who washed ashore in 1871. Near death, he was nursed back to health by the Yapese and spent the next 30 years of his life on the islands.

Where the Germans had failed in getting the Yapese to produce copra in quantity, O'Keefe saw a golden opportunity. He noted that the colourful cloth and trinkets that traders used to entice other Pacific islanders raised little curiosity among the Yapese, who stubbornly preferred traditional hibiscus clothing and grass skirts.

Realising that the enormous stone money the Yapese quarried in distant Palau offered more leverage as a medium of exchange, O'Keefe decided to get into the stone money trade. He went off to Hong Kong to buy a Chinese junk, then returned to Yap and began making runs down to Palau to pick up newly quarried stone money. Yapese chiefs paid for the stone money with copra and O'Keefe soon came to dominate the copra trade in Yap.

O'Keefe's Irish temper and penchant for feuding with colonial administrators made him legendary among the Yapese. In 1901 he disappeared at sea. His former home on Tarang Island in Tomil Harbor is now in the Register of National Historic Places, though only a couple of bricks and a stairway remain.

The Pathways Hotel has a little gift shop with a variety of items from lava-lava to pencil sketches.

Another option is the new Yap Art Studio and Gallery (☎ 350 4180, 🖂 rglenn@ mail.fm), where Yapese artists and illustrators work and produce. Lava-lava cost from US$50 to US$120. It also sells paintings, baskets and jewellery.

The YWA (Yap Women's Association) Handicraft Shop has a wide selection and good prices, and the nearby ILP Handy Craft (☎ 350 3880) has lots of T-shirts with Yapese designs and some fine Ulithi-made pandanus purses. Both are in the YCA complex.

Tropical Touch in the YCA complex is a newish store and sells handicrafts (baskets and lava-lava) for higher than normal prices.

YCA has T-shirts and tank-tops for US$10 and up.

O'Keefe's Canteen sells copies of *His Majesty O'Keefe*, a lively read about the bar's unwitting ancestor.

Getting There & Away

Air Continental, the only airline which services Yap, flies on Sunday and Wednesday. The flight originates in Guam, touches down on Yap on the way to Palau, and lands again on Yap on the return to Guam.

The one-way fare between Guam and Yap is US$263, while the return fare is US$330; both are unrestricted and have no advance-purchase. The one-way fare between Palau and Yap is US$160; return US$335. Micronesia residents can obtain a substantial discount on the one-way fares. Yap is a free stopover on flights between Guam and Palau.

Most foreign visitors will find it cheaper to have Yap added onto their original ticket to Micronesia rather than buy a separate ticket to Yap from Palau or Guam.

The Continental office (☎ 350 2127) in the YCA complex has chequered hours, as the staff also handles airport flights. The office is open from 8 to 11 am and 12.30 to 3 pm Monday, Tuesday, Thursday and Friday. It is closed Wednesday, Saturday, and Sunday. The airport office (☎ 350 2788) is staffed on Wednesday and Sunday only.

Boat Yap does not have a clear harbour or dockage fee in place for visiting yachts, though this is because they haven't hosted very many. The islands with the best facilities for visiting yachts are Ulithi, Woleai, Ifalik, Elato, Lamotrek, Sorol and Ngulu.

Yachts will have to obtain special permission from the Council of Tamol (☎ 350 2343, fax 350 4271) to visit the outer islands and, as always, they must come into the main island (Yap Proper) for immigration and other formalities. Contact FSM Immigration in Pohnpei (☎ 320 5844, fax 320 5488) prior to your visit.

Getting Around

To/From the Airport The airport is 3 miles (4.8km) from Colonia. Hotels provide airport transfers for their guests and most meet each flight. There are no car rental booths at the airport; if you want to rent a car you can ask the ESA Hotel representative; ESA generally has cars and meets arriving flights. There are usually no taxis at the airport, but you can call for one – or just grab a ride back to Colonia with the flood of locals.

At the western end of the terminal there's a reasonably priced gift shop and a new cafe-bar where all the locals relax while waiting for flights. Entry to the private Traders Club lounge, a sanctuary of comfortable sofas and magazines, far removed from the hubbub of the airport, costs US$5; complimentary coffee is available. The airport also has a debit-card phone.

Air A great way to start a journey to the outer islands is by chatting with islanders at the dock or airport counter. Yapese are curious about visitors and it's easy to strike up a conversation once people realise you're headed for their island. Not only will this help you gain insights into the place you're about to visit, but knowing someone generally smooths the way once you arrive.

Pacific Missionary Aviation (PMA; ☎ 350 2360, fax 350 2539) flies a nine-passenger plane to Ulithi, Fais and Woleai. Its office is at the west side of the main airport terminal.

Scheduled flights are from Yap to Ulithi on Monday and Friday, from Yap to Fais and from Ulithi to Fais on Friday, and from Yap to Woleai on alternate Wednesdays. When there are enough passengers PMA sometimes schedules flights on the off-days as well, and flights are also made from Woleai to Ulithi or Fais on demand.

The one-way fare is US$60 between Yap and Ulithi, US$25 between Ulithi and Fais, US$75 between Yap and Fais, US$150 between Yap and Woleai, US$110 between Woleai and Fais and US$130 between Woleai and Ulithi.

Bus School buses run between Colonia and outlying villages transporting students and commuting workers, generally heading toward Colonia in the early morning and going back to the villages in the late afternoon. Visitors can use them on a space-available basis for US$0.50. If you're going to Bechiyal, buses usually leave Colonia around 3 pm carrying students and at 5 pm for workers. The buses return from Bechiyal (leaving from the log bridge at Wanead) at about 7 pm. In Colonia, most buses park at the north side of the Bank of FSM.

Car The island's main paved road begins at the airport, curves through Colonia, and continues through Tomil-Gagil to the northeast end of Map, finishing at a hill called Duweli'l. There are also a few paved roads around Colonia, but most other roads on the island are packed dirt. By Micronesian standards Yap's dirt roads are in very condition.

ESA Hotel (☎ 350 2139) and PBC Car Rental (☎ 350 2266) at the Family Chain Store rent sedans for US$45 a day; PBC rents one old double-cabin pick-up for US$25 a day. There are no car rental booths at the airport. If you don't want to chase down a car by yourself, the front desk at your hotel can generally make arrangements. Islander Rentals (☎ 350 2566, fax 350 2555, @ 7d@mail.fm), across from the Manta Ray Bay Hotel, has some sedans from US$38 a day. There's a 10% tax on car rentals.

Petrol costs approximately US$1.55 a gallon.

Taxi Yap's taxis are radio dispatched, not hailed down by the side of the road. They don't have meters, but rides around the Colonia area are usually US$0.50 to US$0.75 (per taxi, not per person).

The taxi fare from Colonia is US$2 to the airport, US$5 to Okau, and US$10 to Gilman Municipality or Wanyan or the beginning of the Bechiyal footpath.

The main taxi companies are:

Wanyo Taxi (☎ 350 2120)
Mid-Land Taxi (☎ 350 2405)
Savway Taxi (☎ 350 2120)

Hitching There isn't enough traffic outside of Colonia to be able to really depend on hitching, though if you're walking along the road you might get offered a ride. Sticking out a thumb is not a custom here.

Boat The field-trip ship *Micro Spirit*, (capacity 125) runs between Yap Proper and all the populated outer islands. The full trip generally takes about 14 days, though it's not uncommon to be a day or two behind schedule. The ship averages about 10 trips a year. Although the departure days vary, the boat generally starts a trip by leaving Colonia around 6 pm and arriving at 5 am the next morning in Ulithi.

Deck fares vary with the distance: from Yap Proper to Ulithi or Fais the fare is US$6, to Woleai or Ifalik it's US$15 and to Satawal, the most distant island, it's US$18. Children aged four to 12 pay half fare, while younger children travel free. One option for those not wanting to do the whole trip by boat is to fly to an outer island with PMA, and then arrange pick-up by the *Micro Spirit*.

There are also cabins. However, they're made available to travelling government officials first and can only be booked by visitors after it's been assessed that they're not needed by higher authorities. The most crowded time is summer, when students take the boat back and forth to the outer islands. Visitors can book only 2 to 3 days in advance. Cabin rates are calculated at US$0.16 per mile and cost US$17 to Ulithi, US$60 to Woleai and US$87 to Satawal. There's an additional berthing charge of US$3 per night.

Meals can be purchased for US$3 at breakfast, US$4 at lunch and US$4.50 at dinner but the food's pretty basic so you may want to bring your own.

The boat generally docks at each island for four to 12 hours, depending upon how much cargo needs to be loaded and unloaded. If you get a general permit from the governor's office in advance it's possible to disembark and visit the islands while the boat is in port and get back on when it's ready to leave. However, if you want to stay on the island for a few days until the boat returns you'll need to get advance permission from the island chief (see the Permission to Visit entry earlier).

Arrange permits in Colonia from the unmarked Office of Outer Islands Affairs, the small blue-and-white metal shed at the north-west corner of the government offices complex. Book the boat through the Office of Sea Transportation (☎ 350 2403, fax 350 2267), past the Marina Restaurant and Small Business Center on the east side of Colonia. They'll make you take the ticket to the Office of Finance to pay for it.

Palau

The Republic of Palau showcases Micronesia's richest flora and fauna, both on land and under water. Exotic birds fly around the island, crocodiles slip through the mangrove swamps and orchids sprout profusely in people's yards.

Palau's waters hold an incredible spectrum of coral, fish and other marine life, including giant clams that weigh a quarter ton and many rare sea creatures.

The shores of the scenic Rock Islands have some of Micronesia's finest snorkelling and diving, and beyond them lie the sleepy southern islands of Peleliu and Angaur.

The native name for the islands is Belau, although the new nation, born in 1994 after 50 years of colonial-style US rule, calls itself the Republic of Palau. Koror has the bulk of the nation's 17,225 people, and by Micronesian standards it's a busy town.

The 1996 collapse of the famous K-B Bridge that linked Koror to Babeldaob, Palau's largest island, dealt a major blow to the young country's pride. The Asian economic crisis deepened the hurt by reducing tourism from that region. However, Palau has proved remarkably buoyant: The pontoon bridge erected to replace the K-B bridge will soon itself be replaced by a permanent bridge; the Hawai'i-based Outrigger chain has just opened a gorgeous first-class hotel in downtown Koror, and construction is scheduled to begin soon on a new road to circle Babeldaob.

HIGHLIGHTS

- The Rock Islands – a maze of divinely green, mushroom-shaped islands
- Babeldaob – the powerful waterfalls and traditional *bai* of Micronesia's second-largest island
- Peleliu – a WWII-ravaged island, now a tranquil retreat with good dive sites
- Palau dining – mangrove crab, lobster or exquisite sushi in one of Palau's many outstanding restaurants

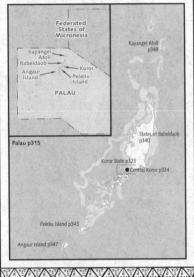

Facts about Palau

HISTORY
Early Settlers

It is generally believed that Palau's first inhabitants came from eastern Indonesia. Carbon dating of ancient habitation sites has established that the Rock Islands were settled by at least 1000 BC.

Traditionally, the women of Palau tended the taro swamps and the men fished the reef and harvested breadfruit and betel nut. With a fairly vast land area offering an abundance of vegetation, Palauans were not compelled to journey far beyond their shores. They spent their leisure time working on projects such as the construction of *bai* (men's meeting houses), with each village home to its own skilled artisans who did the tasks of woodworking and thatching.

PALAU

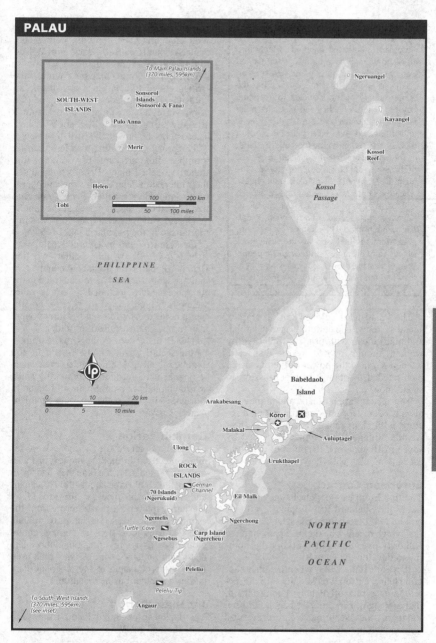

PALAU

PALAU

To Main Palau Islands
(370 miles, 595km)

SOUTH-WEST
ISLANDS

Sonsorol
Islands
(Sonsorol & Fana)

Pulo Anna

Merir

Helen

Tobi

0   100   200 km
0   50   100 miles

Ngeruangel

Kayangel

Kossol
Reef

Kossol
Passage

PHILIPPINE
SEA

Babeldaob
Island

Arakabesang

Koror

Malakal

Auluptagel

Ulong

Urukthapel

ROCK
ISLANDS

German
Channel

Eil Malk

70 Islands
(Ngerukuid)

Ngemelis

Turtle Cove

Ngesebus

Ngerchong

Carp Island
(Ngercheu)

NORTH

PACIFIC

OCEAN

Peleliu

Peleliu Tip

To South-West Islands
(370 miles, 595km)
(see inset)

Angaur

0   10   20 km
0   5   10 miles

The Creation Myth

According to Palauan legend, in ancient times an island woman gave birth to a son named Uab, who grew so quickly and had such an insatiable appetite that it soon became the primary chore of the islanders to keep the boy fed. The more they fed him, the more food he demanded and the larger he grew, until one day he was taller than the coconut trees and had eaten all the food on the island.

The villagers reluctantly decided they must destroy the giant boy in order to survive. One night they set fire to the men's meeting house where he slept. Uab's bloated body exploded and parts of it were flung in all directions. Kayangel was created from his head, Babeldaob from his body, Peleliu from his legs, Angaur from his feet and all the little Rock Islands from his fingers and toes. The people then settled the new islands believing that as they had fed Uab, he would now feed them.

The Palauans developed fairly complex social systems. The culture was matriarchal and matrilineal, with property inherited by women, though owned by the clan. The women retained the power of the purse and men needed to obtain their permission to spend money.

The accumulation of land and money has always been very important in Palauan society, with clans ranked according to their wealth. Villages were typically settled by seven to 10 clans and the chief of the highest ranking clan was the village leader.

European Contact

The first European to sight Palau was most likely the Spaniard Ruy Lopez de Villalobos in 1543. He named the islands Arrecifos, which means 'the reefs'. Spain claimed authority over Palau in 1686 but did nothing to develop the islands.

It wasn't until 1783, when English captain Henry Wilson wrecked his ship the *Antelope* on a reef off Palau's Ulong Island, that any significant contact began between Palauans and Westerners. The crew was treated well by Chief Ibedul of Koror, who helped them rebuild their ship from the wreckage and then sent his young son, Prince Lebuu (Lee Boo), back with Wilson to England for schooling.

Gifts from the Palauans, which the British called the 'Pelew Curiosities', included a bracelet made from a dugong (sea cow) vertebrate, a dagger made from a stingray stinger and turtle shell dishes. These items are now in the British Museum.

The prince died of smallpox less than six months after arriving in London; the tragedy touched many Britons and piqued their interest in Palau. There was even a romantic melodrama called *Prince Lee Boo* that played on London stages at the time.

The story of Wilson and his crew was immortalised in the popular book *An Account of the Pelew Islands* by George Keate, published in 1788, which further whetted Britain's appetite for trade between the two nations. Unfortunately, favoured trade items for the Palauans included guns and other weapons, which served to increase hostilities among local tribes and at times were also turned against European traders.

The British were Palau's main trading partners until Spain finally moved in and expelled them in 1885. Spanish missionaries managed to introduce Christianity and a written alphabet before Spain sold Palau to Germany in the wake of the Spanish-American War.

German Period

Unlike the Spanish, the Germans were far more interested in making money in Palau than saving souls. By the time they had taken control in 1899 only about 4000 Palauans had survived the diseases introduced by Western explorers, a drastic drop from the estimated pre-contact population of 40,000. The Germans took steps to contain contagious diseases by providing inoculations and instituting sanitary controls. They then used Palauan forced labour to start coconut plantations and other business ventures.

Japanese Period

The Japanese occupied Palau from 1914 until the end of WWII. It was during this

Palauan Money

The early Palauans developed an intricate system of money that was used as a mode of exchange and as gift offerings at traditional events. Beads, called *udoud*, were the most common type of Palauan money. The beads were made of clay or glass and were usually yellow or orange.

Common round beads were used for daily transactions, while beads that were oval, faceted or cylindrical were more prestigious and valuable. The beads were not made in Palau and although no-one today knows exactly where they came from it is thought they may have originated in Indonesia or Malaysia.

One legend, however, says they came from a mysterious Yapese island called Kablik. Kablik was said to be so magical that stones thrown from the island towards the sea never touched the water, but returned instead to the thrower.

The beads still have value but are in limited use today, exchanged mainly at times of birth, marriage and death. Strings of udoud are worn as necklaces (called *iek*) by high-ranking women on special occasions, and it's common to see Palauan women wearing a single bead on a black cord as an heirloom necklace.

Another type of traditional Palauan money is *toluk*, made by steaming hawksbill turtle shell and pressing it into a wooden tray-shaped mould. The shell is hardened into the shape of an oval plate; the larger and lighter-coloured the toluk, the more value it has.

time that Palauan culture went through its most radical transformation, as the Japanese established a colonial administration. Free public schools were opened, teaching islanders in a subservient dialect of the Japanese language, and village chiefs lost power to Japanese bureaucrats.

Japan expanded the commercial ventures started by the Germans and developed many more. Thousands of Japanese, Korean and Okinawan labourers were brought in to work in phosphate mines, rice fields, pineapple plantations and other businesses that thrived under Japanese administration.

Traditional inheritance patterns were shattered as Palauans lost their land, either through sale or confiscation.

After 1922 all of Japan's Pacific possessions were administered from Koror, which the Japanese developed into a bustling modern city complete with paved roads, electricity and piped-in water. Out of its 30,000 residents, only about 20% were Palauan.

In the late 1930s, Japan closed Palau to the outside world and began concentrating its efforts on developing military fortifications throughout the islands.

WWII

During the final stages of WWII, as the Allied offensive moved westward across the Pacific, Japanese installations in Palau became a target for attacks. US aerial bombings of Malakal Island and Airai state in March and July 1944 destroyed numerous Japanese ships and planes, and set fuel tanks and military facilities ablaze. However, the real battles in Palau took place in September of that year on the southern islands of Peleliu and Angaur.

Before the USA's invasion, most Palauans were rounded up by the Japanese and sent to central Babeldaob. The reason for the forced relocation is not entirely clear. Some islanders insist that the Japanese had plans to kill the Palauans and even had ditches dug to use as mass graves. Nonetheless, historians tend to credit the Japanese for getting the islanders out of harm's way and undoubtedly the action did save the lives of many Palauans who otherwise would have been caught up in major assault zones.

Despite the fierce fighting that took place on Peleliu and Angaur, the more heavily populated Koror and Babeldaob were never invaded and the 25,000 Japanese soldiers stationed on those islands remained there until the war's end.

Independence & the Compact of Free Association

When the USA began to administer Palau after the war, it had hoped to spin off Palau

PALAU

with the rest of Micronesia into a single political entity.

Palauans, however, voted in July 1978 against becoming part of the Federated States of Micronesia, forming instead a separate political entity. In July 1980 Palauans adopted their own constitution. Koror was named the provisional capital, though Palau's constitution stipulates that the capital eventually be moved to Melekeok state in Babeldaob.

A nuclear-free provision Palauans wrote into their constitution proved unacceptable to the US government, which saw Palau as part of a 'defensive arc' – a fall-back, together with Guam and Tinian, in case the USA lost its bases in the Philippines.

Disregarding the anti-nuclear constitutional provision, the USA drafted a Compact of Free Association that not only allowed it to bring nuclear weapons into Palau, but gave the USA the right of eminent domain over virtually all Palauan territory. In exchange, the USA offered Palau millions of dollars in aid.

After eight heated referenda, each of which failed to override the constitution's anti-nuclear provision, the pro-compact government finally amended the constitution itself, allowing the compact to be ratified with a simple majority vote. In November 1993, under the amended constitution, Palauans voted with a 68% majority in favour of the compact. Most held, thus far correctly, that the Cold War's end makes the USA unlikely to build military installations on Palau.

In its final version the compact limits US military access to one-third of Palauan territory. In return, Palauans got a hefty US$450 million financial package for the first 15 years of the 50-year compact.

On 1 October 1994 Palau officially became an independent nation, ending 47 years as a trust territory. In December of the same year it was admitted to the United Nations as its 185th member.

Modern Palau

Palau's struggle to emerge as a new nation had a troubled beginning. President Hauro Remeliik, Palau's first president, was assassinated in June 1985. Three years later his successor, Lazarus Salii, was found shot in an apparent suicide. The situation has since stabilised, however, and at time of writing the next elections were scheduled for 2000.

Implementation of the compact and the new Western style of government triggered a power struggle between elected officials and Palau's traditional authorities. These issues are slowly being litigated, case by case and state by state. The transition has also opened the door to corruption, as chiefs angle to become paid elected officials. Palau's youth, however, is largely embracing the new Western forms of power.

Palauans are hawkishly watching their neighbours in the Federated States of Micronesia and Marshall Islands, which squandered much of their compact funding early on and must renegotiate their compacts over the next few years.

Palau has other preoccupations as well. In 1996, Palau's 700-foot (213m) reinforced concrete bridge, called the K-B Bridge, collapsed due to a mechanical flaw shortly after the bridge had undergone repair work. Palau sued several international companies involved in the repair, and the case was settled for US$17 million.

Palauans endured several months of painfully slow commuting by ferry between Babeldaob and Koror, but a temporary floating bridge was soon put in place. The Japanese have offered US$30 million in aid to build a new permanent bridge. It is hoped that a new bridge will be up sometime in 2000.

Transportation infrastructure is a hot topic in Palau. On the down side, Palau's national airline, Paradise Air, suffered a fatal crash in 1998 and service has been discontinued for the foreseeable future. On a cheerier note, construction of a US$149 million, 53-mile (85.5km) road circling Babeldaob Island is expected to begin soon and should be completed by 2001.

Palauans have also voiced concern in recent years about environmental issues, particularly regarding overtourism, overfishing, erosion, litter and pollution. This has resulted in the creation of preservation areas, both in and around the Rock Islands and Babeldaob.

GEOGRAPHY

As part of the western Caroline Islands, Palau is the westernmost part of Micronesia, lying 470 miles (756km) east of the Philippines.

The tightly clustered Palau archipelago consists of the high islands of Babeldaob, Koror, Peleliu and Angaur; the low coral atolls of Kayangel and Ngeruangel; and the limestone Rock Islands, of which there are more than 200. The islands run roughly from north to south, covering about 125 miles (201km). Except for Kayangel and uninhabited Ngeruangel in the north and Angaur in the south, all islands in the Palau group are inside a single barrier reef.

The nation's boundaries also encompass six other small, isolated islands: the Sonsorol Islands (Sonsorol and Fana), Pulo Anna, Merir, Tobi and Helen. Known as the South-West Islands, they extend 370 miles (595km) south-west from the main Palau Islands, reaching almost as far as Indonesia.

The thickly vegetated Babeldaob, the largest island in Micronesia after Guam, is 27 miles (43.5km) long and has a land area of 153 sq miles (398 sq km). The other Palauan islands together total just 37 sq miles (96 sq km).

CLIMATE

In Koror the average daily high is 87°F (30°C) and the average daily low is 75°F (24°C). Humidity averages 80% and the annual rainfall is 147 inches (373cm).

February and March are the driest months, averaging about eight inches (200mm) of rainfall each, and June to August is the wettest period, averaging about 15 inches (38cm) each month. June sees numerous thunderstorms, which have been known to drop as much as an inch of rain in 15 minutes. Although Palau lies outside the main typhoon tracks – most storms originate here and travel to Guam or the Philippines – it does occasionally get hit.

GOVERNMENT & POLITICS

The Republic of Palau has a democratic form of government headed by an elected president.

Palau's national congress, a 30-seat bicameral legislature, is called Olbiil Era Kelulau, which means 'meeting place of whispers'. The House of Delegates has 16 members, one from each state. The Senate, whose representation is based on district populations, has 14 members. Each branch of Congress, as well as the president, is elected for a four-year term.

There's also a council of chiefs, composed of one traditional chief from each state, which advises the president on legislation affecting Palauan customs.

Palau has a political framework similar to both the US federal and state governments – except that its population is not 250 million but a mere 17,225. Some of Palau's 16 states have fewer than 100 people, yet each has a governor, a legislature and a state (or governor's) office. It would be hard to find another nation where so few are governed by so many.

ECONOMY

Despite its political independence, Palau's economy remains heavily dependent upon US aid.

Palau's 15 year compact with the USA entitles it to a total of US$450 million in funding until 2008. In an effort to develop infrastructure and entrepreneurship, the funding is most substantial in the early years of the compact and narrows towards the end.

Palau's per capita GDP of US$5000 is one of Micronesia's highest, but government employment remains the largest economic sector. Tourism, an important industry in Palau, took a hit with the Asian financial crisis: After a near-doubling of visitor arrivals in the mid-1990s, visitation plunged 13% from 1997 to 1998. Nonetheless, Palau's natural wonders and commitment to development virtually ensures that the economy will rebound once the crisis passes.

Palau, like some of its Micronesian neighbours, is flirting with the introduction

PALAU

of garment factories to speed economic development. A minimum wage law passed in early 1999 set US$2.50 per hour as the minimum wage for local workers (but no minimum was set for foreign workers). Although this is undoubtedly garment-factory friendly legislation, it remains to be seen if the factories will follow.

POPULATION & PEOPLE

Palau's population is approximately 17,225. An estimated 4500 foreign workers, the majority of whom are Filipino, also live in Palau.

Most Palauans have large extended families. If you spend much time with a Palauan, you'll likely meet a never-ending stream of cousins, uncles and aunts.

ARTS

Traditional Palauan arts are more commonly found outside built-up Koror. Intricately carved storyboards make wonderful souvenirs. Traditional dancing is no longer as strong in Palau as of yore.

SOCIETY & CONDUCT

Though Palauans are among Micronesia's most Westernised people, they also retain many traditional ways. Family and kinship ties are strong, age-old competition continues between clans and chiefs still command an important role in the social hierarchy. Shoes are removed when entering a private home.

Betel nut has a hefty Palauan following. Betel-nut chewers can be recognised by their red teeth and their tendency to spit a lot – the betel nut induces salivation and the juices are not swallowed. Beware of car doors flying open as the driver spits a stream of betel-nut juice onto the street.

RELIGION

Most Palauans are Christian, and both the Catholic and Protestant churches are well established. Other religions include Seventh-Day Adventist, Jehovah's Witness and Baha'í.

Modekngei is a revived form of indigenous religion. Some Palauans still hold some form of traditional belief, based on nature spirits, clan-ancestral worship and village deities. Some Palauan homes leave a light on through the night to ward off unwanted spirits.

LANGUAGE

Palauan is spoken at home and in casual situations, while English is more common in business and government. Both are official languages and most Palauans are bilingual from an early age.

The South-West Islanders speak Sonsorolese and Tobian languages, which are more closely related to Yapese or Chuukese dialects than to Palauan.

In Palauan, 'hello' is *alii* and 'thanks' is *sulang*.

Many Palauan words begin with 'ng' – which is a nasal sound, pronounced like the ending of the word 'bring'. The 'ch' spelling is pronounced 'uh'.

Islanders borrow the Hawai'ian term *haole* to refer to Caucasian foreigners.

Facts for the Visitor

SUGGESTED ITINERARIES

If you have just a few days in Palau, it's best to stay on Koror and see the Rock Islands. If you have weeks, you should do the same thing! For variety, consider exploring Babeldaob's *bai* (traditional men's houses) and waterfalls, camping on the Rock Islands or spending a few days on Peleliu.

TOURIST OFFICES
Local Tourist Offices

The Palau Visitors Authority (PVA) is the tourist information office for the country. PVA's central office is in Koror (see the Koror State section later in this chapter) and it also has a branch at the airport.

Tourist Offices Abroad

Overseas offices of the Palau Visitors Authority include:

Germany (☎ 089-16 62 11, fax 13 23 12) c/o
ZFL Public Relations GmbH, Schulstrasse 34,
D-80634 Munich, HR Munich B 101063
Japan (☎ 03-3354 5500, fax 3354 5200) 5th
floor, 201 Pare Cristal, 1-1 Katamachi,
Shinjuku-ku, Tokyo 160-001
Taiwan (☎ 02-2561 1580, fax 2511 4687) 2/F –
B, No 100, Nanking East Road, Sec 2, Taipei
USA (☎ 808-591 6599, fax 591 2933) c/o The
Limtiaco Company, 1210 Auahi St, Suite 208,
Honolulu, Hawai'i 96814

VISAS & DOCUMENTS
Tourists can stay without a visa in Palau for
a period of 30 days, which can be extended
for up to 60 days. See the Regional Facts for
the Visitor chapter for further information.

The Palau Immigration Office (☎ 488
2498) is on the second floor of the Supreme
Court, near the library in Koror. It's open
from 7.30 to 11.30 am and 12.30 to 4.30 pm
weekdays.

MONEY
The US dollar is the currency used in Palau
(see the Regional Facts for the Visitor chapter for exchange rates). You'll find the Bank
of Guam and the Bank of Hawaii represented here. Credit cards are accepted at
most hotels, car rental agencies, dive shops
and larger restaurants.

POST & COMMUNICATIONS
Palau's only post office is in central Koror.
Palau uses the US postal system but has its
own stamps. Palau's postal code is 96940;
its international telephone code is ☎ 680
(there are no area codes).

INTERNET RESOURCES
The Palau Visitors Authority has a useful
Web site at www.paulaunet.com, which has
links to other sites.

BOOKS
Diving & Snorkeling Palau (from Lonely
Planet's Pisces series) gives an excellent
overview of Palau's best dive spots.

MEDIA
Guam's *Pacific Daily News* comes to Palau
a day after publication, and the local papers,

Tia Belau and *Palau Horizon*, come out
biweekly.

Koror has one private TV station and 13
cable channels, including round-the-clock
live CNN.

The government radio station, TA88, is
on the air at 1584 AM from 6.30 am to midnight. It broadcasts Voice of America and
other overseas newscasts several times a
day. Of the five FM stations, two are
Christian.

PHOTOGRAPHY
The best place in Palau to have slide film
developed is at the photo lab at Palau Pacific Resort, on Arakabesang Island, just off
Koror.

LAUNDRY
Laundrettes are quite common in Koror,
and most budget motels have laundry
facilities.

DANGERS & ANNOYANCES
There is a midnight-to-dawn curfew in
Koror which was instituted after the assas-
sination of the president in 1985 and is still
in place to control errant elements and
late-night rowdiness.

PUBLIC HOLIDAYS & SPECIAL EVENTS
As well as Easter, New Year and Christmas, Palau celebrates the following public
holidays:

Youth Day 15 March
Senior Citizens Day 5 May
President's Day 1 June
Constitution Day 9 July
Labor Day 1st Monday in September
Independence Day 1 October
Thanksgiving 4th Thursday in November

Youth Day features concerts and sporting
events, while Senior Citizens Day features
a parade with floats, handicraft exhibits
and a dance competition. The Belau Arts
Festival, held on Constitution Day, includes craft exhibits, dances and cooking
contests. Some states also celebrate state

PALAU

constitution, while Peleliu and Angaur have a WWII Memorial Day coinciding with the day US forces landed on each island.

ACCOMMODATION & FOOD

Palau's Rock Islands are excellent camping spots, and camping is possible at other islands outside Koror. Homestays are possible on Babeldaob and Kayangel (see those sections, later). Koror's top-end hotels are excellent. Fresh fish – tuna, crab, lobster and sushi – are served at Palau's excellent restaurants. There are no restaurants outside Koror and Babeldaob's Airai State.

Getting There & Away

AIR
Airports & Airlines

Palau's international, though basic, airport terminal is north-east of Koror, on the southern end of Babeldaob Island. It has a PVA office, car rental booths (not always operating), several gift shops, a lounge and a few snack bars. These services open daily for flights. See the Koror State section for information on Airline offices in Palau.

Asia

Continental flies from Manila to Koror on Wednesdays and Saturdays. Its one-way/return fare is US$360/710, but the price drops by US$125 for three-day advance purchase fare.

Japan Airlines runs twice-weekly charter flights from Japan but is considering a commercial service.

Within Micronesia

Continental has daily flights to and from Guam. The one-way/return Guam-Koror fare is US$357/755. You should be able to stop over in Yap – if the agent says you can't, try elsewhere.

The only other commercial airline servicing Koror is Far Eastern Air Transport.

Flights arrive from Taipei on Tuesday and Saturday. The 3½-hour trip costs US$350/690 one way/return.

Departure Tax

There's a departure tax of US$20 for all non-Palauans exiting the country.

SEA

Visiting yachts should notify the immigration office and harbour master (☎ 488 5789) before arrival. Yachts moor at Malakal port and at M-Dock. Harbour fees are given under Boat in the Koror State section later in this chapter.

Getting Around

CAR

Most car rental agencies are in Koror State (see Getting Around in the Koror State section). It's possible to rent a vehicle on the other islands, though you will need to do this either privately or through your accommodation.

Generally, cars have steering wheels on the right-hand side. Watch out for potholes and unmarked speedbumps. If you're driving deep into Babeldaob, rent a high-riding vehicle that can handle the bumps. The maximum speed limit is 25 mph (40km/h) and passing is not allowed, though neither law is observed.

HITCHING

Hitching is not common in Palau. Outside central Koror, however, if you start walking you might get offered a ride. The usual safety precautions apply, particularly for women.

BOAT

Many Palauans commute between islands in privately-owned boats. You can often hitch a ride on one of these by contributing to fuel costs. Some state-owned boats also make journeys between their home island and Koror. See Getting Around under the island sections later in this chapter for details.

PALAU

Koror State

Koror, the economic centre and capital of Palau, is home to almost two-thirds of the republic's population. Many of Koror's 12,300 people have been drawn from outlying villages by employment opportunities.

In prewar days the population of Koror was three times its present size and the town was jammed with military facilities, geisha houses, Shinto shrines, kimono tailors and public baths.

Today's Koror is more nondescript and less crowded, though if you look closely you'll often find the past and present juxtaposed. One interesting example is the Koror governor's office, which is fronted by an ancient platform with stone backrests in each corner where traditional leaders once sat in meeting.

The greater Koror area is best used as a base for trips to Babeldaob, the Rock Islands, Peleliu, Angaur and other islands.

Orientation

Koror state consists of the inhabited islands of Koror, Malakal and Arakabesang, all of which are connected by causeways. The island of Koror is also connected to neighbouring Babeldaob via a floating bridge, the makeshift successor to the K-B Bridge.

Traffic tends to choke up in downtown Koror, particularly during rush hour, as there is only one road into it from Babeldaob. Koror's sprawl makes it time-consuming to get around on foot, particularly since there are no pavements.

The airport is in Airai state, at the southern end of Babeldaob, a 25-minute drive from central Koror.

Information

Tourist Offices The friendly, knowledgeable Palau Visitors Authority (☎ 488 2793, fax 488 1453, ✆ pva@palaunet.com), on the western side of town, keeps a good collection of English-language brochures on

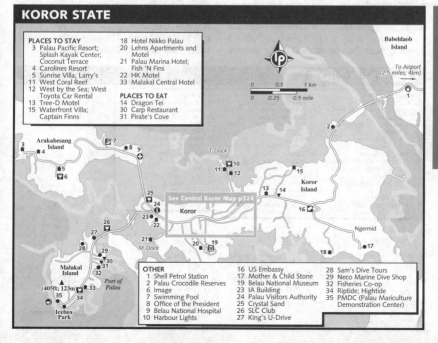

tours, dives and hotels. *Wow! Palau* is a colourful monthly pamphlet telling what's new on the tourist scene. You can also request a tide calendar (free). The Koror office is open from 8 am to 5 pm weekdays. The airport booth opens for arriving flights.

Money Both the Bank of Hawaii and the Bank of Guam are on Koror's main road and both have 24-hour ATMs outside. The Bank of Guam is open from 9.30 am to 2.30 pm Monday to Thursday, to 5 pm on Friday. The Bank of Hawaii is open from 8.30 am to 3 pm Monday to Thursday, and to 5 pm on Friday.

Post & Communications Palau issues attractive postage stamps of tropical fish, flowers and shells as well as commemorative stamps of historic events. These are available from Palau's single post office, in central Koror, which is open from 8 am to 4 pm weekdays.

International phone calls can be made 24 hours from the spiffy new Palau National Communications Corporation (PNCC) building near the airport. Rates per-minute

to other Micronesian islands and the USA are US$3 from 7 am to 6 pm weekdays, US$2 from 11 pm to 4 am and US$2.50 at other times. Calls to most other destinations are about US$4 a minute, though they drop to US$2 a minute between 11 pm and 4 am. There's a three-minute minimum charge.

International calls can more conveniently be made at the PNCC office in central Koror, which is open from 8 am to 5 pm weekdays. This office handles faxes, which can be sent for the same price as a phone call and received (fax 488 1725) free. The PNCC main office also offers this service.

For directory assistance, dial ☎ 411. To reach an international operator, dial ☎ 0.

Email & Internet Access The Rock Islands Computer Institute, on the second floor of the large IA building across the main road from the PVA tourist office, has eight computer terminals with Internet access. The high price (US$10 per half-hour) reflects the cost of the Palaunet server (US$15 per hour). The terminals are open from 8 am to 5 pm weekdays.

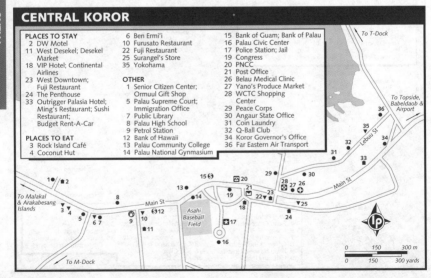

CENTRAL KOROR

PLACES TO STAY
2 DW Motel
11 West Desekel; Desekel Market
18 VIP Hotel; Continental Airlines
23 West Downtown; Fuji Restaurant
24 The Penthouse
33 Outrigger Palasia Hotel; Ming's Restaurant; Sushi Restaurant; Budget Rent-A-Car

PLACES TO EAT
3 Rock Island Café
4 Coconut Hut

6 Ben Ermi'i
10 Furusato Restaurant
22 Fuji Restaurant
25 Surangel's Store
35 Yokohama

OTHER
1 Senior Citizen Center; Ormuul Gift Shop
5 Palau Supreme Court; Immigration Office
7 Public Library
8 Palau High School
9 Petrol Station
12 Bank of Hawaii
13 Palau Community College
14 Palau National Gynmasium

15 Bank of Guam; Bank of Palau
16 Palau Civic Center
17 Police Station; Jail
19 Congress
20 PNCC
21 Post Office
26 Belau Medical Clinic
27 Yano's Produce Market
28 WCTC Shopping Center
29 Peace Corps
30 Angaur State Office
31 Coin Laundry
32 Q-Ball Club
34 Koror Governor's Office
36 Far Eastern Air Transport

To T-Dock
To Topside, Babeldaob & Airport
Main St
Lebuu St
To Malakal & Arakabesang Islands
To Malakal & Arakabesang Islands
Main St
Asahi Baseball Field
To M-Dock

0   150   300 m
0   150   300 yards

Libraries The Palau Public Library (☎ 488 2973) has now reopened after being closed for renovations in early 1999. The Palau Community College library is well-stocked with Pacific books and keeps some reasonably up-to-date magazines and newspapers.

Weather Information A 24-hour forecast can be obtained from the Palau Weather Service on ☎ 488 1103.

Maps Maps of Kayangel, Ngeruangel, Peleliu and the Rock Islands (1:25,000 scale), and some nautical charts, can be purchased for US$12 each from Blue Line (☎ 488 2679), a business centre just south of the SLC Club on the road to Malakal. The Palau Visitors Authority also gives out a large, helpful map of downtown Koror.

Medical Services Belau Medical Clinic (☎ 488 2688), in central Koror, is recommended for nonemergency attention. It's open from 8.30 am to 3 pm on Monday, Tuesday, Thursday and Friday, and a gynaecologist consults from 6 to 9 pm the same evenings. The clinic opens from 8.30 am to 1 pm Wednesdays and Saturdays. A first-time visit costs US$17, plus additional tests or medicines. Appointments are preferred, but foreign visitors without appointments will likely be seen within an hour or two.

The Belau National Hospital (☎ 488 2558) on Arakabesang Island, just over the causeway from Koror, gives emergency treatment and has a decompression chamber.

Emergency The police emergency number is ☎ 911; the nonemergency number is ☎ 488 1422. For an ambulance or the fire department dial ☎ 488 1411.

Koror Island

Belau National Museum To get to the small two-storey Belau National Museum, follow the signs from Koror's main street. The sights begin at the door, which is intricately carved in the manner of a storyboard. Other displays include bead and turtle shell money, as well as local artefacts and crafts. The museum building once served as a Japanese weather station – the current weather station has moved next door. The museum is open from 8 am to 4 pm weekdays, from 10 am to 4 pm Saturday. Admission is US$3 for adults, US$2 for students and free for locals.

Next door is a **research library** with a good collection of books on the region, which museum staff will open on request.

On the museum grounds is a beautiful **wood-and-thatch bai** carved and painted with depictions of Palauan legends, including that of Uab, whose body created the Palau islands. Although this is a re-creation of an older bai that burned down in 1979, it's built in a traditional manner, constructed of rough planks with notched jointing and set above the ground on stone stacks – a splendid example of traditional architecture.

There is also a **lily pond**, a few **anti-aircraft guns** and other Japanese-era artefacts, a small **war memorial** to Palauans who died during WWII and a bronze **bust of Haruo Remeliik**, Palau's first president.

Etpison Museum A private art museum, housing artefacts from early Palauan cultures, opened in mid-1999. It is located on Koror's main road. It is open Monday to Saturday 9 am to 9 pm and closed on Sunday.

Palau International Coral Reef Center The US$10 million centre, located on M-Dock and funded by the Japanese government, is expected to be completed in early 2001 (contact the PVA office for up-to-date information). The complex will include an aquarium with indoor and outdoor displays, and information on coral reef preservation.

Eastern Koror For a superb **view of the Rock Islands** head towards the airport from Koror. When you get out of central Koror take the paved road to the right that winds down to the Hotel Nikko. The view from the hotel is worth catching at any time of day, but it's particularly nice at sunrise.

PALAU

Follow the stairs up past the swimming pool to the top of the hill to see two **anti-aircraft guns** and get a sweeping view.

Near the beginning of the hotel driveway there's a rebuilt Japanese **Shinto shrine** that dates to prewar times.

Continuing on the road half a mile (800m) past the hotel is Ngermid, which despite its rather modern appearance is one of Koror's most traditional villages, having been home to the same families for generations. The only 'sight' per se is the **Mother & Child Stone**, which is said to be the Lot-like remains of a mother and child who were turned to stone after the mother took a forbidden peek inside the village men's house. Look for the small sign on the left side of the road and follow the footpath. Within a minute or so you'll reach a corrugated-iron house where you are expected to pay the landowner US$2 to see the sight.

The **Palau Crocodile Preserves**, on a causeway island between Koror and Babeldaob, has pens with three dozen native crocs, plus a few Angaur monkeys. Admission is US$3 for adults and US$2 for children, plus an extra charge for using still or video cameras. It's open from 8 am to 4 pm Monday to Saturday.

Malakal Island

Malakal Island, across a causeway west of Koror, has the Fisheries Co-op, the deepwater commercial port, small-boat docks and other marine businesses.

At the southern tip of the island is **Icebox Park**, so named because it was the site of an ice-making plant during the Japanese era. It's now a grassy public park and although there's no sandy beach there is access to the clear waters for swimming and snorkelling.

Palau Mariculture Demonstration Center The PMDC (☎ 488 3322), at the end of the road on Malakal Island, is a research marine laboratory engaged in conservation and commercial projects. It has received international recognition for its success in cultivating the threatened giant *tridacna* clam.

Giant Clams

Micronesia's endangered giant tridacna clams (*tridacna gigas*) regularly grow more than four feet (1.2m) in length and can weigh more than 500 pounds, making them the world's largest bivalve mollusc. Their fleshy mantles have intriguingly mottled designs of browns, greens and iridescent blues. Some live more than 100 years.

Palauans have long eaten the meat of the clams, sold the huge shells to tourists and ground the smaller shells into lime powder to chew with betel nut.

The main threat to the clams, however, comes from outside poachers, mainly from Taiwan, who are wiping out the tridacna on coral reefs around the Pacific, overharvesting to a point where few are left for breeding. The poachers often take only the profitable adductor muscle of the clam, which is prized as a delicacy and aphrodisiac, while the rest of the clam is left to rot.

The PMDC raises millions of seed clams to be planted in reefs around Palau and other islands in Micronesia – especially in places that can be guarded against illegal harvesting – and trains islanders in sea farming technology. The young clams have edible meat and these farm-raised 'baby giant clams' have found their way onto menus around Micronesia, commonly as sashimi.

You can wander around the PMDC complex and peer into long shallow tanks of giant clams. Further back in the complex are deep round tanks containing various species of sea turtles. There's a visitor centre selling a few souvenirs, including shells, posters, postcards and T-shirts. PMDC is open to visitors from 8 to 11.30 am and 1 to 4 pm on weekdays, and has a US$2 admission fee. Fish posters cost US$10 and are sold in the adjacent Division of Marine Resources office.

Malakal Hill You can get an excellent view of the nearby Rock Islands by going halfway up Malakal Hill, where the road ends at a water tank. After leaving Icebox Park, take the steep, narrow dirt road to the left, just past the green sewage plant. It only takes about 10 minutes to walk up.

It's possible to continue to the top of the 405-foot (123m) hill for even better views. It's about a 15-minute hard climb from the water tank, though there really isn't much of a path and you may need a guide.

Arakabesang Island

Once a Japanese military base, Arakabesang Island is now a 'suburb' of Koror. On the south side of the island there's a village that has been settled by people from Palau's South-West Islands, complete with traditional outrigger canoes.

After crossing over the causeway northwest of Koror, the first road to the right past the PNCC satellite station leads to the Office of the President and other national government offices. If you're interested in WWII sites, make note of the concrete pillars flanking the entrance to this road, because the next road to the right with similar pillars is the turn-off to one of the Japanese-era **seaplane ramps**. Simply follow the road to the water. There's another seaplane ramp on the beach at Palau Pacific Resort on the west side of the island.

Activities

Snorkelling The beach fronting the Palau Pacific Resort has some of Koror's best snorkelling. The water is calm, shallow and clear. Snorkellers will find colourful tropical fish, platter and mushroom corals and giant tridacna clams with iridescent mantles. Breakfast in the open-air restaurant followed by a morning of snorkelling from the beach isn't a bad way to kick off the day. The resort officially charges nonguests a US$25-per-day fee to use the beach.

For children, a nice swimming and snorkelling spot is the Long Island Clam Project, on a small peninsula en route to Malakal. There is a barbecue grill and covered picnic area here.

Snorkelling is also good off Icebox Park and the Palau Mariculture Demonstration Center (PMDC) grounds on Malakal Island.

From Icebox Park, the best snorkelling is to the right towards PMDC where there are fairly calm waters and a beginners' reef for those comfortable with overhead depths. Expect to find clownfish hiding in anemone shelters as well as crown of thorns starfish. In front of PMDC giant clams are lined up in underwater cages just offshore. Watch out for the spiny urchins that cling to the sides of the wall, and also for motorboats that sometimes cut the corners sharper than they should.

But no-one really comes to Palau to snorkel in Koror. The real action is in and around the Rock Islands.

Information on diving in Palau, and on dive shops based in Koror, is in the Rock Islands section. Dive shops that rent snorkelling gear include Palau Diving Center, Sam's Dive Tours and Splash. Each place charges around US$5 a day for mask and snorkel, and another US$2.50 or US$5 for fins or booties.

Most or the upmarket hotels have swimming pools.

Tennis There are three public tennis courts at Airai Elementary School, en route to the airport. The Palau Pacific Resort also has courts for guest use.

Gymnasium Palau has a new basketball gymnasium in central Koror, built for the 1998 Micronesian Games.

Running The local Hash House Harriers run every other Saturday (on payday weekends). Runners meet at the post office at 3.45 pm. Inquire at expat hangouts such as Rock Island Cafe or at Sam's Dive Tours.

A new track, built for the Micronesian Games, is in Koror centre.

Kayaking The Rock Islands are ideal for ocean kayaking and the sport has recently taken off in Koror. Planet Blue Guided Kayak Tours (☎ 488 1062, fax 488 5305, ℮ samstour@palaunet.com), a subsidiary of Sam's Dive Tours, runs excellent kayak trips with half day/full day/overnight options for US$55/85/130, including lunch and drinks. Planet Blue can transport the kayaks by speedboat to your site to spare you the paddlework.

Splash Kayak Center (☎ 488 2600, fax 488 1606, Ⓔ splash@palaunet.com), operating out of the Palau Pacific Resort, has a full-day kayak tour, including lunch and drinks, for US$85.

Eric Carlson of Adventure Kayaking of Palau (☎ 488 1694) and Palau Kayak Tours (☎ 488 5885, Ⓔ kayakmary@palaunet.com) also run recommendable tours.

If you enjoy seclusion, ask your guides to take you to Ngeremeduu Bay on Babeldaob Island, where kayaking is good on rivers feeding into the bay. The bay is Micronesia's largest estuary and offers the chance to see birds, mangroves and an occasional crocodile.

Canoeing The fledgling Canoe Association of Palau holds periodic practices and events that visitors can join. Contact Joe Aitaro at the Palau Visitors Authority for the latest. Canoe excursions generally leave from the Palau Pacific Resort.

Sportsfishing International Anglers (☎ 488 5305, fax 488 5003), a new branch of Sam's Dive Tours, uses a 41-foot (12m) flybridge sportsfisher, the *Virgo IV*, and the 26-foot (8m) *Seacat* for offshore trolling. Half-day tours run from US$350 to US$550, and full-day tours are US$600 to US$900.

Prices at Fish 'N Fins (☎ 488 2637, fax 488 5418, Ⓔ fishnfin@palaunet.com) are better – a half day of fishing costs US$300 and a full day US$475, both options including lunch. Island Nation (☎ 488 5322, Ⓔ islandnation@palaunet.com) offers half-day trolling or night fishing for US$300 and full-day bottom fishing for US$400, including lunch.

You must have a licence to fish, which costs US$10. The company you use should obtain one for you.

Places to Stay

All of the top-end hotels, except the new Outrigger Palasia, are outside the town centre. Most of the low and middle range places are in Koror, either in the centre or on the outskirts of town. The budget options, as a rule, are not terribly appealing. Unless otherwise noted, they have private baths.

Koror hotels can get booked out from around Christmas to mid-January and during the Japanese Obon holidays, from late July through August. Add a 10% room tax to all prices listed below.

If you're in Palau to dive, it's worth researching possible package deals, which can cut the overall rate substantially (see the Getting There & Away section at the beginning of this book).

Places to Stay – Budget

The *Tree-D Motel* (☎ 488 3856, fax 488 4584), in the Topside area, is a friendly family-run hostelry and the best budget option in Koror. The rooms are small and simple but clean and come equipped with a refrigerator, ceiling fan and air-con. Guests can use the office phone. Free airport transfers are provided with advance notice. The rate is US$45 for a double-bed room, US$55 for a room with two single beds; there's a 10% discount for a week's stay. A coffee shop downstairs serves breakfast. Visa cards only are accepted.

Lehns Apartments and Motel (☎/fax 488 1486, Ⓔ lehns.motel@palaunet.com) is tucked away from the traffic of Koror's main road, but still central. If you're driving from the airport, take a left turn just past the post office; when the road curves left, go right. The budget rooms are small and basic, with hall bathrooms and shower, but the friendly management keeps them clean and air-conditioned. They go for US$38.50 (including tax). Larger rooms are US$66.50 and each includes cooking facilities, cable TV and a private bath. Airport transfers are available, and there are laundry facilities on the premises. All major credit cards, except American Express, are accepted.

The *DW Motel* (☎ 488 2641, fax 488 1725) has 17 tired but adequate rooms with refrigerators, air-con and private bathrooms. There's a television and free coffee and tea in the guest lounge, as well as a laundrette on site. Complimentary transport is provided to and from the airport. Once you clear customs ask for Wilfred Williams, the manager's son, who meets nearly every flight. Rates are US$35/45 for singles/doubles and all major credit cards are accepted.

The neon-green **HK Motel** (☎ 488 2764) is an unpretentious eight-room budget motel. Its rooms are fairly bare, with only a shower, refrigerator and twin beds. Call ahead for airport transfers (US$5 each way). Laundry facilities are available. Rooms cost US$40 (including tax) and one closet-like room goes for US$30. Credit cards are not accepted.

The centrally located **New Koror Hotel** (☎ 488 1159, fax 488 1725) has 25 very basic, unappealing, carpeted rooms, with refrigerators, air-con and private bathrooms – shop around for a room with a fresher smell. Rates are US$33/38.50 for singles/doubles (including tax) and there's a 3% tax on use of credit cards.

Places to Stay – Mid-Range

The West Plaza Hotel group has a number of separate locations, though booking is done centrally (☎ 488 2133, fax 488 2136, @ west.plaza@palaunet.com). All rooms have telephones with free local calls, TVs, air-con and mini-fridges, and all West hotels provide complimentary airport transfers. West has good dive packages with Fish 'N Fins: a four/seven-day package is US$420/820.

West by the Sea (☎ 488 2133) is a 36-room seaside hotel near T-Dock. Rooms facing the lagoon are reasonable value at US$90, with kitchenettes that include microwaves. The rooms are plain but comfortable enough, and there's a good Chinese restaurant and the West Toyota Car Rental on site.

West Coral Reef (☎/fax 488 5332), down the street from West by the Sea, is among the newest of the Wests and it's also the emptiest. The great-ocean-view promotion neglects to mention that the view takes in a rather uninspiring parking lot and there is no restaurant on site. Rooms are US$90 for deluxe, US$120 for a suite.

More conveniently located is **West Desekel** (☎ 488 2521, fax 488 6043), which consists of 30 nice, relatively spacious rooms above the Desekel Market grocery store. The hotel is one of the newest in the chain so the rooms feel a bit fresher. Each room has a microwave and twin beds. The rate is US$70 for singles or doubles and there are a couple of larger suites with kitchenettes for US$80.

The 22-room **West Downtown** (☎ 488 1671, fax 488 5521) in central Koror has adequate rooms at moderate prices. It is US$55 for a standard room, US$65 for a larger room with a partial kitchenette.

The best deal in town is at the tawny new **Waterfront Villa** (☎ 488 2904, fax 488 4904, @ waterfront.villa@palaunet.com), though it's slightly out of the way. Coming into Koror from Babeldaob, take the first right after Dragon-Tei restaurant and turn right again at the stop sign. About a quarter-mile (400m) farther on take a left into the first paved road and follow this road to its end. Comfortable, immaculate rooms with two large, comfy beds, phones and marble-floored bathrooms with tubs are US$60/75 in low/high season. Suites with one king-size bed and a kitchen area are US$75/95. Airport transfers are free, and if you reserve ahead they'll include breakfast in the price. The hotel can also provide cheap transportation to Koror. Diving packages are available with Neco Marine, Sam's Dive Tours and Palau Diving Center. Ask about monthly rentals.

The 77-room **Airai View Hotel** (☎ 587 3530, fax 587 3533), on Babeldaob near the airport, is a newly renovated hotel with an old-fashioned character. It has rich mahogany floors, a grand lobby decorated with the island's largest storyboard, a balcony restaurant and piano bar. The standard rooms (US$80) are plain yet elegant, each with two double beds, air-con, wooden furniture, a TV and refrigerator. The deluxe rooms (US$100) have huge balconies looking across the jungle towards the ocean. There's a large pool and a restaurant downstairs. The hotel targets Taiwanese tourists but welcomes independent travellers.

The **VIP Hotel** (☎ *488 1502, fax 488 1429)*, is a pleasant 22-room hotel upstairs from Continental's Koror office. The rooms are spotlessly clean and the atmosphere quite personable. Free coffee and tea are available on each floor and there's a small reading lounge. Rooms are large, each with a single and a double bed, table and chairs, phone, balcony, air-con, ceiling fan, TV and refrigerator. Singles/doubles cost US$65/85 and there's a surcharge for using credit cards. Airport transfers are free.

The three-storey **Palau Marina Hotel** (☎ *488 1786, fax 488 1070,* @ *marina@ palaunet.com)* is on the water at M-Dock. The 28 rooms are standard but adequate, with balconies, cable TV, desks, refrigerators and phones. It's geared for divers, who can practically step out of their rooms and into the dive boat. Rates are US$80/120 for singles and doubles in low/high season, and major credit cards are accepted. Airport transfers are US$10 return.

The Penthouse (☎ *488 1941, fax 488 1442)* is a quiet, centrally located 14-room hotel off the main road behind the Palau Hotel. The rooms are comfortable with modern amenities including TVs with cable, VCRs, minibars, bathtubs, air-con, refrigerators and phones. A room with two single beds costs US$90/93.50 for singles/ doubles (tax included); larger deluxe rooms with balconies are US$104.50. All major credit cards are accepted and airport transfers are US$12 return.

Places to Stay – Top End

The new nine-storey, 165-room **Outrigger Palasia Hotel** (☎ *488 8888, fax 488 8800; in the USA* ☎ *1-800-688 7444; in Australia* ☎ *1-800-124 171,* @ *outrigger@palaunet .com)* in central Koror is a terrific choice, the lack of beach aside. It has all the resort amenities and more – a business centre, swimming pool, health spa and fitness centre, not to mention excellent restaurants, duty-free shops and Budget Rent-A-Car downstairs. All rooms have air-con, phones (local calls US$0.50), cable and pay TV, a shower/tub combo and refrigerators. There are nonsmoking floors and the building is

wheelchair accessible. Airport transfers are US$10 one way. Rates start at US$200/270 during low/high season and business, government and military personnel can get considerable discounts.

For those who enjoy a rustic feel, the **Carolines Resort** (☎ *488 3754, fax 488 3756,* @ *carolines@palaunet.com)*, built on a hill on the way to Palau Pacific Resort (see later), offers seven pleasant, clean and comfortable bungalows, each with air-con, cable TV, a VCR, private bath, coffeemaker and minibar. The best views are from cabins 4 to 7 and cabins 6 and 7 are slightly bigger. A tennis court and private beach are nearby and available for guest use. The price is US$150 per night, and a full breakfast, which can be delivered to your room, costs US$4 to US$7. Currently, only Visa is accepted.

Sunrise Villa (☎ *488 4590, fax 488 4593,* @ *sunrise@ite.net)*, on Arakabesang Island, has 21 posh, comfortable rooms and a friendly staff. All rooms are carpeted, have fine views over the lagoon, TVs, refrigerators and phones. Huge double rooms with two queen-size beds cost US$160. The single rooms, which are smaller but also a good size, are on the top floor and have the best views; request a king-size bed and bathtub room. Singles go for US$130. The two-bedroom, kitchen-equipped executive suite is US$210. The presidential suite, at US$295, may be the nicest room on Palau, with corner windows offering 180° views, a jacuzzi, VCR and a second bedroom. Corporate and military discounts are available and airport transfers are free. The hotel has an excellent restaurant and a pool, and a cosy bar overlooking the bay.

The **Hotel Nikko Palau** (☎ *488 2486, fax 488 2878,* @ *nikko@palaunet.com)*, once Palau's premier hotel, was eclipsed when the beachside Palau Pacific Resort opened a decade ago. But the Nikko still boasts a gorgeous hillside setting overlooking Palau's northernmost Rock Islands. The 51 rooms are conventional and a bit worn, but adequate, with air-con, two double beds, a refrigerator and phone but no TV. Standard rooms cost US$150. Some rooms are quite a hike uphill from the reception area. The hotel has a small swimming pool, bar and restaurant.

Palau Pacific Resort (☎ *488 2600, fax 488 1606,* ✆ *ppr@palaunet.com),* a 20-minute drive from Koror on Arakabesang Island, is one of Micronesia's finest resort hotels and Palau's only beach-side hotel, a protected strand that's the best in Koror. The 160 rooms have rattan furniture, block prints, tile floors, ceiling fans, air-con, private *lanai* (verandas) and either a queen-size bed or twin beds. Room rates range from US$250/220 for a garden view in high/low season to US$290/250 for an ocean view, while suites are more pricey. Add a 5% service charge to the bill. Airport transfers are US$7.50 each way. There's a beachside swimming pool, tennis courts, a fitness centre and a dive shop. Local events such as dance competitions and the presidential inaugural ball also take place here. Reservations can also be made through Pan Pacific Hotels and Resorts (in North America ☎ 1-800-327 8585; in Australia ☎ 1-800 252 900; in Japan ☎ 0120-001 800; in London ☎ 020-7491 3812).

Places to Eat

Palau offers excellent food, at both budget and full price. Seafood, especially fish, crabs and shellfish, abounds. Crocodile, giant clam, pigeon and fruit bat are some of the more unusual local delicacies, though these are unlikely to appear on many restaurant menus. Most places in Koror serve both Japanese and Western-style dishes.

Don't drink the tap water in Koror, though ice and water are OK in most restaurants.

Places to Eat – Budget

Palauans affectionately refer to *Ben Ermii*, a burgers-on-wheels van parked opposite the high school, as the McDonald's of Palau. Burgers start at US$2.75, milkshakes are US$3, and a side order of fries is US$1. There's no fish, and vegetarians must opt for the egg and cheese sandwich (US$2.50). Ben Ermii opens at 10 am weekdays; it closes at 10 pm Monday and Tuesday, 2 am

Wednesday to Friday. Saturday it's open from 7 am to 2 am and Ben Ermii's spends Sunday at Airai's baseball field. The long hours make it a very handy snack spot.

The clean, deli-style *Coconut Hut* (☎ *488 2124),* adjacent to the Rock Island Cafe, has tables but is more popular for takeaway. Call ahead for a burger or a sandwich (US$2.75 to US$3.50) and head for a picnic spot. Generous scoops of ice cream (US$1.25) are also served. The Coconut Hut is open from 7 am to 7 pm but is closed Saturday.

Furusato Restaurant, next to the Bank of Hawaii, is another popular place with good-value meals. At breakfast you can get a boiled egg, toast and coffee for US$3.50 or a full breakfast for a few dollars more. For lunch and dinner, curry rice, noodle and oyako donburi are US$5, while various beef, pork and fish dishes average US$6 to US$8. The kitchen is open from 6 am to 10.30 pm daily.

Yokohama, on Lebuu Street, is a popular local restaurant serving generous portions at honest prices. Sandwiches cost around US$2, sashimi or ramen US$3 and lunch or dinner dishes, including teriyaki chicken, grilled fish and beef curry, are US$5 to US$6. It's open from 5.30 am to 9 pm Monday to Saturday, from 5.30 am to 2 pm Sunday.

The *Carp Restaurant*, beside the waterfront on Malakal Island, is a little Japanese-run place with inexpensive home-style food. Dishes include sashimi for US$5, fried fish for US$5.50 and fish and vegetable tempura for US$6. It's open from 11 am to 2 pm and from 3 to 9 pm.

Self-Catering *Yano's Produce Market*, a small country-style store beside the WCTC Shopping Center, is a great place to buy local produce and freshly cooked Palauan food. You could easily concoct a meal from the fried fish, teriyaki squid, turtle with coconut milk, and fried bananas, which are either pre-wrapped or sold by the piece from steaming platters. It's open from 6 am to 9 pm weekdays and from 6 am to 8 pm Saturday.

PALAU

The *WCTC Shopping Center* has a large modern supermarket with reasonable grocery prices and fresh produce. There's an ATM in the lobby leading to the store. The nearby *Surangel's Store* has a slightly narrower selection.

Places to Eat – Mid-Range

The *Rock Island Cafe*, centrally located in downtown Koror, is an expat favourite for excellent pizza, seafood and steaks, and for its relaxed atmosphere. A small pepperoni pizza costs US$5, while a medium, which feeds two, is US$9.50. You can get pasta and Mexican food for US$5 to US$7 and a big portion of fresh sashimi or a good burger with fries for US$5. It's open from 6.30 am to 10 pm daily except Saturday, when it opens from 6 pm to 10 pm.

The new *Captain Finn's* at Waterfront Villa, which is angling to be an expat hangout, is a pleasant spot for a meal or a drink and overlooks the water. The service is a little slow and the prices a tad high, but the food is good enough. Burgers with fat fries start at US$6, lunch salads topped with fish are US$8. Captain Finn's is open until midnight Thursday to Saturday, and until 10 pm other days.

Larry's at the Sunrise Villa, half a mile (800m) before the gate to Palau Pacific Resort, is a pleasant hotel restaurant with a fine hillside lagoon view and good food at surprisingly reasonable prices. A full breakfast is US$6. At lunch, grilled chicken or fried fish with rice or fries costs US$6.75, and dinner ranges from spaghetti with meatballs for US$8 to T-bone steak for US$17. Lunch and dinner specials are about US$14. Breakfast is served from 6.30 to 11 am, lunch from 10.30 am to 5 pm and dinner from 5 to 10.30 pm.

Pirate's Cove, near the Fisheries Co-op on Malakal Island, has a water view and well-prepared food. Dishes range from spaghetti in fish sauce for US$6.75 to teriyaki steak with rice and salad for US$12 to T-bone steak for US$18. There's both indoor and balcony dining and it's open from 8 am to 2 pm and 4 to 11 pm daily except Sunday, although the bar may open later.

Places to Eat – Top End

The *Arirang Restaurant* (☎ 488 2799) is a Korean barbecue-style restaurant in Koror centre. The menu features various meats cooked on a small grill at your table (US$15) – the short ribs are especially popular. Lunch is the best deal, with specials for about US$5. Lunch is from 11 am to 2 pm and dinner from 5 to 10 pm. It's closed for lunch on Sunday. Call ahead and they'll fix up a bento lunch (US$10).

The popular *Fuji Restaurant*, in the same complex as West Downtown Hotel, is a good upmarket place for seafood and Japanese dishes. Sweet and sour fish or a pork cutlet cost US$8 while there's a set dinner with sashimi, land crab and various side dishes for US$25. It's open from 10.30 am to 1 pm from 5.30 to 9 pm; dinner only is served on Sundays.

There is a wide consensus that the Japanese-run *Dragon Tei* (☎ 488 2271) in Topside serves the best food in Palau. It's Okinawa with a touch of Palauan; specialties include coconut crab (US$11 a pound – 450gm) and a tasty Napoleon fish sauteed in white wine. Dishes are served à la carte, and most are priced between US$6 and US$8. There's a teppanyaki grill used to make huge okonomiyaki, which they dub 'Japanese pizza'. The interior has a pleasant decor, including tatami mats, and the service is excellent. It's open from 5 to 10.30 pm nightly.

The open-air *Coconut Terrace* restaurant at Palau Pacific Resort has average food at higher-than-average prices. The restaurant has a breakfast buffet from 7 to 10 am for US$14, and lunch is served from 11 am to 5 pm, with burgers or sandwiches with fries at US$7.50. At both lunch and dinner there are dishes such as nasi goreng or Thai prawn curry for US$15.

Ming's Restaurant, on the second floor of the Outrigger Palasia, is a pleasant, airy restaurant with gorgeous crystal-dripping chandeliers and with tasty Chinese cuisine prepared by a Shanghai chef. Many of the entrees, from popular sweet-and-sour options to an array of seafood, are US$9.50 to US$32. Lunch is served from 11.30 am to 2 pm and dinner from 5.30 to 10 pm.

PALAU

The Outrigger's small *Sushi Restaurant* has great food and is a comfortable place to eat alone. There are breakfast, lunch and dinner specials at US$12, US$15 and US$23, but the best deal is a US$10 'special set', which comes with miso soup, rice and fruit and a delicious meat or fish entree.

Palau's only dinner cruise, the Sunset Sail or Ngibtal cruise (☎ 488 6141), is popular among affluent locals. The boat leaves M-Dock at 4.45 pm daily and returns 2½ hours later. The US$52 cost includes a steak or fish dinner, two free drinks and live entertainment.

Entertainment
Palau's legal drinking age is 21. All bars close by midnight, when Koror's curfew takes effect. The local brew, Red Rooster, is good and wheaty, and both dark and light are on tap in many bars.

Riptide, an open-air bar on a man-made beach on Malakal Island, is a favourite expat hangout. During the 4 to 7 pm happy hour, Budweiser drops from US$3 to US$2. This is also a popular spot to grab a fish sandwich for lunch. Riptide's sister bar, *Hightide*, is just across the way. Both bars are open from 10 am to midnight daily and serve Red Rooster.

The beach bar at *Palau Pacific Resort* is a fine upmarket place for a sunset drink. Another peaceful evening spot on Arakabesang is the outdoor covered bar above the pool at *Sunrise Villa*.

For a more local scene try the *SLC Club* on the road to Malakal. The slightly tamer *Harbour Lights* is another popular local spot, though a few foreigners are occasionally spotted. Crowds start pouring in around 11 pm. Pool and billiard players will find 10 tables at the *Q-Ball Club* on Lebuu St, for US$6 per table per hour. It's open from 5 pm to midnight Tuesday to Saturday.

Palauans are into karaoke; try *Image*, down the same road as Sunrise Villa, which is open until midnight nightly.

Koror's only disco, *Crystal Sand*, is a popular late-evening spot that attracts both expats and locals.

Storyboards
Palau's unique art form is the storyboard, a smaller version of the carved legends that have traditionally decorated the beams and gables of men's meeting houses. The carving style was suggested in 1935 by Japanese anthropologist Hisakatsu Hijikata, who viewed the smaller boards as a way to keep both the art form and legends from dying out. Today, many of the storyboard scenes depicted have an element of erotica.

The 3½-hour *cocktail cruise* offered by Ngibtal Cruises (☎ 488 4911) costs just US$5, plus drinks. It leaves from M-Dock at 7.30 pm, but may be cancelled if not enough people join so call ahead.

Palau Pacific Resort (☎ 488 2600) has *Palauan Night* every Tuesday, featuring a dinner buffet of Palauan foods (US$25) and a dance performance by local children. Reservations are necessary.

Palau still has no movie theatre but free movies are shown Tuesday through Saturday at 7.30 pm by the *Seabees (☎ 587 1311)*, the US navy division that helps with public-works projects. To get here, take the side road to the airport, but rather than turning into the terminal continue north about half a mile (800m) to the Seabees Camp, which is on the right.

Shopping
Palauan storyboards make excellent, albeit not inexpensive, souvenirs. A good place to find quality storyboards is at the shop in the entrance of the Koror jail.

At the Senior Citizen Center near the DW Motel local craftspeople sit in an open-air shelter painted to resemble a traditional bai and weave hats, baskets and purses out of pandanus and coconut palm. The centre's Ormuul Gift Shop is open from 8 am to 5 pm weekdays and has an excellent craft selection.

The gift shop at the museum sells storyboards, books about Palau, T-shirts, woven baskets and purses, commemorative stamps and posters.

PALAU

Ben Franklin, in the WCTC Shopping Center, sells some rather simple storyboards for US$50 to US$125. It also carries other handicrafts, as well as T-shirts and cassette tapes of Palauan music.

Tropicana, a shop near Ben Franklin, sells storyboards from US$69 and has a good selection of earrings, money, baskets and other handicrafts.

Keep in mind that sea turtles are endangered and the turtle shell jewellery sold in Palau cannot be brought into Guam, the USA, Canada, Australia, the UK or any other country that abides by the Convention on International Trade in Endangered Species.

Getting There & Away

Air Continental Airlines and Far Eastern Air Transport are the only commercial airlines servicing Palau. The Continental ticket office (☎ 488 2448) is behind the post office and is open from 8 am to 4.30 pm weekdays, and from 8 am to noon on Saturday. Far Eastern Air Transport (☎ 488 3931) has an office on Lebuu Street in central Koror.

Japan Airlines, which has a charter service from Japan, is affiliated with Hotel Nikko, located outside of central Koror.

See the Getting There & Away section earlier in this chapter for flight information.

Boat Because Koror is the nation's commercial centre, Palauans commonly commute by private speedboat between Koror and villages on other Palauan islands. You might be able to hitch a ride by offering to help pay for petrol.

Visiting yachts must notify the immigration office and harbour master (☎ 488 5789) before arrival. The following fees are applicable for yachts coming to Koror: baggage fee (gross registered tonnage x US$0.03 x number of days in the dock); entry fee (gross registered tonnage x US$0.03); and line handling fee (US$75 per call). For details call Belau Transfer (☎ 488 2629).

Getting Around

To/From the Airport Most hotels provide airport transport if you call ahead. Neco Tours (☎ 488 1755) offers a shuttle bus service between the airport and any hotel for US$7.50 per person. There are taxis and car rental booths at the airport.

Taxi Taxis are plentiful and can be flagged down. Koror's taxis are private (ie, you don't have to share them with other passengers) and have no meters. Short trips around town are usually US$2 and the fare between central Koror and Palau Pacific Resort is US$5. City Cab (☎ 488 1394) quoted us US$25 from the airport to town, while Koror Taxi (☎ 488 1519) quoted US$15. Always check the fare first and beware of overcharging. Taxis can be chartered for US$20 an hour.

Car The following car-rental agencies have booths at the airport as well as offices in Koror:

West Toyota Car Rental (☎ 488 5599)
I-A Rent-A-Car (☎ 488 1113)
King's U-Drive (☎ 488 2964, fax 488 3273)
Budget Rent-A-Car (☎ 488 6233)

Good deals are offered by King's U-Drive and West Toyota, both of which offer cars in low-season from US$30 a day (though this may rise with a better economy). Budget is more expensive, with prices starting at US$35 in the low season, discounted from the usual US$49.50. Reserve ahead, as the cheaper cars go quickly.

Insurance varies among the car companies – US$7 or more is likely.

Rock Islands

The Rock Islands are the crown jewels of Micronesia.

More than 200 of these rounded knobs of limestone, totally covered with green jungle growth, dot the waters for a 20-mile (32km) stretch south-west of Koror. The bases of the islands have been undercut by water erosion and by grazing fish and the tiny chitons that scrape at the rock. Because of their unique shape, the islands are often likened to emerald mushrooms rising from a turquoise-blue sea.

The waters surrounding the islands contain some of the most abundant and varied marine life to be found anywhere. The islands are also home to crocodiles and fruit bats and are rich with bird life, including kingfishers, reef herons, black noddies, white-tailed tropicbirds, black-napped terns and introduced cockatoos and parrots.

Most of the islands have been undercut all the way round and have no place for boat landings, but some have beaches where soft white sands have washed up and stayed. Most of the under-cut islands are off-limits to visitors, but most with beaches are accessible; ask your guide for details. Ancient rock paintings can be found on Ulong Island, and half-quarried Yapese stone money can be seen in a limestone cave near Airai Channel. Other islands have caves with dripping stalactites, rock arches and underground channels.

Visitors must pay a US$15 Rock Island use tax to Koror state, which goes towards conservation. Most dive operations do not include the tax in their fee. Once purchased, the permit is valid for 30 days and you should carry it on all trips to the Rock Islands lest you be stopped by a ranger. If you switch dive operations, be sure to bring your permit or you'll be required to purchase a new one.

Jellyfish Crisis

Jellyfish Lake holds two kinds of jellyfish – *mastigias* (orange jellyfish) and *aurelia* (white jellyfish). In late 1998, the orange jellyfish population suddenly and dramatically declined. Although there were still orange jellyfish buds at the bottom of the lake, they were dying before they could grow. Most environmental observers attribute this to El Niño and its sidekick, La Niña, phenomena which noticeably increased the lake's water temperature and salinity. In spring 1999 many tour operators had temporarily (and voluntarily) cut their tours to Jellyfish Lake to allow the jellyfish to recover.

Marine Lakes

The Rock Islands hold about 80 marine salt lakes, former sinkholes that are now filled with saltwater and have a limited exchange with the sea. Variations in algae give them different colours and some have soft corals, fish, sponges or jellyfish.

The heavily forested island of **Eil Malk** contains **Spooky Lake**, which has stratified layers of plankton, hydrogen sulphide and gases, and **Jellyfish Lake**, filled with jellyfish that have lost the ability to sting. Eil Malk also has a hot water lake that reaches 100°F (37.4°C) as well as Palau's largest salt lake, **Metukercheuas Uet**, which is 1½ miles (2.4km) long and 200 feet (60m) deep.

Each lake has a unique ecosystem, providing habitat for specialised creatures that have evolved in their waters over the millennia. Travellers rarely get to see the lakes but they're a treasure to the marine biologists who study them.

70 Islands

Ngerukuid, also known as 70 Islands, is an extremely scenic part of the Rock Islands that's popular with aerial photographers. It is a nesting site for hawksbill turtles and sea birds and has been set aside as a wildlife preserve. Visits by divers, tourists and fishers are prohibited.

Carp & Neco Islands

For one-day outings, dive shops can drop you off on a Rock Island beach in the morning and pick you up after their last dive, usually for the cost of the snorkelling tour.

Palau Diving Center and Neco Marine Dive Shop usually take you to their own islands, Carp Island and Neco Island respectively. Carp Island is a good choice for lazing around, plus it's a long south-bound trip through the scenic Rock Islands. For snorkelling, Neco is better, though you'll see only about half as many Rock Islands en route.

Carp Island Ngercheu Island, more commonly called Carp Island, is primarily a divers' basecamp for the Palau Diving Center.

A motorboat leaves M-Dock in Koror around 8 am, zips through the Rock Islands and arrives on Carp an hour later. The boat ride costs US$35 return, US$40 with lunch.

Carp Island is very peaceful, with a white sand beach lined with coconut palms, and hammocks tied to shady ironwood trees. At high tide the Rock Islands across from Carp appear to be floating on the sea. As the water recedes they become encircled by beaches and linked by sand bars, and all around Carp Island beautifully rippled shoals of sand appear.

If the tide is right and the staff isn't busy, someone might give you a boat ride to a reef where there's good coral. Otherwise, snorkelling is not very good around Carp Island itself, as the water is shallow and about all you'll see is sea grass, goatfish and sea cucumbers. (If you want to go snorkelling with the divers instead of staying on the island, it costs an additional US$45!)

Neco Island Neco Marine Dive Shop charges US$50, including lunch, for an outing to the beach at Neco Island. The divers usually have lunch on the island, so you can choose between spending the day there or snorkelling for the full US$85 fee.

Diving & Snorkelling

Palau is one of the world's truly spectacular dive spots. If coral reefs, blue holes, WWII wrecks and hidden caves and tunnels aren't enough, consider the more than 60 vertical drop-offs.

Palau is the meeting place of three major ocean currents that have abundant food supplies to support an enormous variety of marine life. The waters surrounding the Rock Islands are literally teeming with over 1500 varieties of reef and pelagic fish. There are four times the number of coral species in Palau than in the Caribbean, including immense tabletop corals, interlocking thickets of staghorn coral and soft corals of all types and colours.

Divers can see manta rays, sea turtles, moray eels, giant tridacna clams, grey reef sharks and sometimes even a sea snake, rare dugong or chambered nautilus. The sea temperature averages about 82°F (27°C) and visibility extends to well over 100 feet (30m) along drop-offs.

The **Ngemelis Wall**, also called Big Drop-off, is widely considered the world's best wall dive. From knee-deep water, the wall drops vertically nearly 1000 feet (305m). Divers can free float past a brilliant rainbow of sponges and soft corals, whose intense blues, reds and pure whites form a backdrop for quivering 9-foot (3m) orange and yellow sea fans and giant black coral trees. The wall is also good sport for snorkellers, who can see coral, turtles and anemones.

Blue Corner, Palau's most popular dive, is known for its sheer abundance of underwater life. Expect to be totally bedazzled by the incredible variety of fish, including barracudas and schooling sharks, as well as hard and soft corals. Strong tidal currents nourish this chain of life, but also render it a dive for the more experienced.

Both the **German Channel** and **Turtle Cove**, near Peleliu, offer dives that novices can feel comfortable with. Manta rays are frequently spotted in the German Channel, as are mackerels. **Devil Fish City** is also a good place for snorkellers, as is the Turtle Cove beach area.

Eil Malk's **Jellyfish Lake** is a different kind of dive experience. You'll need to hike up over a hill about 10 minutes through the jungle to reach this mangrove-bordered lake, where a floating dock and eco-friendly toilets have been set up. Mark your entry point into the lake to avoid losing your way back out, and be careful of slippery rocks around the shoreline where the water is

The leatherback turtle, which can be over two metres long, is the largest of the sea turtles.

KN

The rare dugong can sometimes be seen in the waters around the Rock Islands.

murky and green. Farther out the water clears and millions of harmless transparent jellyfish, their sting either nonexistent or mild, swim en masse to follow the path of the sun. Snorkelling in this pulsating mass is an unearthly, eerie sensation.

Crocodiles are generally nocturnal creatures, but should you hear a low 'harrumph' you just might want to head in the opposite direction – unless you plan to test the theory that the crocodiles in Jellyfish Lake are more afraid of people than vice versa.

A few Japanese shipwrecks from the WWII Operation Desecrate lie about a 20-minute boat ride from Koror.

Dive Shops Most dive trips leave Koror around 9 am and return around 4 pm, breaking for a lunch on a Rock Island.

Be aware of the company's bad-weather cancellation policy. If you're going to Jellyfish Lake, note also that some of the larger tour operators charge extra for a stopover there. Most of the larger dive shops accept credit cards but smaller ones, such as Dive Palau, may not.

Splash (☎ 488 2600, fax 488 1601), a well-regarded PADI (Professional Association of Dive Instructors) five-star dive centre at the Palau Pacific Resort, has night dives for US$70, while two-tank boat dives with lunch cost US$105. Full-day snorkelling trips are US$55, plus US$15 for gear rental. Trips to Jellyfish Lake are US$15 extra. For novices there are one/two-tank beach dives for US$130/155. Prices drop for groups of five or more. A five-day certification course costs US$605; the more elaborate Discover Scuba course, which includes two Rock Islands beach dives, is US$130. A full four-day certification course costs US$455.

Neco Marine Dive Shop (☎ 488 1755, fax 488 3014, ✉ necomarine@palaunet .com), at a Malakal Island marina, is one of Palau's largest operations and has a good reputation. One/two/three-tank dives cost US$65/98/133, and night dives are US$65 (lunch is included where applicable). Dives to see the chambered nautilus or to Peleliu are available for US$20 and US$15 extra, respectively. Snorkelling tours, boat charters, PADI courses and introductory courses can be arranged. Hotel pick-up is free and diving gear and underwater cameras can be rented. There's a shop selling local books and dive supplies, and E-6 film processing, personalised videos and camera repair work are offered.

Fish 'N Fins (☎ 488 2637, fax 488 5418, ✉ fishnfin@palaunet.com), one of Palau's oldest dive shops run by an enthusiastic Israeli couple, keeps a tidy shop on M-Dock in Koror. A two-tank dive costs US$95. Snorkellers pay US$60 to go out with divers plus another US$20 for Peleliu trips.

PALAU

Fish 'N Fins has a good four/seven-day accommodation and diving package for US$470/820 with the West Plaza hotels. Three-day certification and introductory dive courses are available. Fish 'N Fins also owns the *Ocean Hunter* live-aboard.

The five-star PADI, American-run Sam's Dive Tours (☎ 488 1062, fax 488 5003, ✉ samstour@palaunet.com), has grown over the last several years into a hugely popular operation. Sam's tours are limited to eight divers. One/two-tank dives cost US$65/99, including lunch, and Sam's can also arrange snorkelling, sportsfishing and land tours as well as camping expeditions.

The Palau Diving Center (☎ 488 2978, fax 488 3155) is a Japanese operation beside the Carp Restaurant on Malakal Island. One/two-tank dives cost US$70/115, with lunch, drinks and hotel pick-up included. It is an extra US$10 for Jellyfish Lake. Palau Diving Center owns Carp Island Resort; see earlier.

A smaller operation favoured by Peace Corps volunteers and other small groups or individuals is Dive Palau (☎ 488 3548, ✉ keithpda@palaunet.com), headed by long-time Missouri transplant Keith Santillano. Two-tank dives are US$90, three-tank dives US$120, night dives US$55 and snorkelling trips US$55 (tanks, weights and lunch are included, but not on night dives). Introductory one-tank dives cost US$60 and a full day with an introductory two-tank dive is US$130, including equipment, lunch and drinks.

Live-aboard Dive Boats Three live-aboard dive boats ply Palauan waters. In addition to the fees listed below, you will likely be charged the US$15 Rock Island 'use tax'.

The *Palau Aggressor II* (✉ paggressor@ palaunet.com) is a 106-foot (32m) diesel-powered boat. Week-long Sunday to Saturday cruises include 5½ days of diving. Each of the eight carpeted air-con cabins has a queen-size and a single bed, toilet, sink, shower and individual temperature controls. The boat has a photo centre with an E-6 processing lab. The cost is US$2295, based on double occupancy, and includes meals and unlimited diving. There's a US$200 discount for nondivers and for divers who book back-to-back with the company's boat in Chuuk. Reservations can be made through Live/Dive Pacific (in the USA ☎ 1-800-344 5662, 808-329 8182, fax 808-329 2628). On Palau, information can be obtained from Neco Marine Dive Shop (☎ 488 1755).

The 138-foot (42m) *Sun Dancer II* has ten double cabins, each with a private bathroom and air-con. The boat has an entertainment lounge and a photo lab equipped to process E-6 slide film. The cost for the Sunday to Sunday cruise, based on double occupancy, is US$2195, or US$2395 in a deluxe stateroom. Included are meals, alcoholic beverages, all dives and accommodation on the boat; not included is a US$25 diving permit fee and US$50 port charges. There's a US$400 discount for trips made from late July to mid-October. Reservations can be made through Peter Hughes Diving (in the USA ☎ 1-800-932 6237, 305-669 9391, fax 305-669 9475, ✉ dancer@peterhughes.com).

A smaller vessel is the *Ocean Hunter* (☎ 488 2637, fax 488 5418, ✉ ocean.hunter @palaunet.com) operated by Fish 'N Fins in Koror. This 60-foot (18m), six-passenger boat has trips from seven to 14 days that start at US$2295 per person per week. The fee includes unlimited diving, accommodation in one of three air-con cabins and food. Booking six months ahead is recommended, though last-minute discounts can occur if someone drops out.

Places to Stay
Camping The Rock Islands offer Micronesia's best camping, with tremendous star gazing. Some islands have shelters and picnic tables (and some have enormous piles of Budweiser cans!) though none have fresh water. Bring protection from biting sand gnats and avoid the islands with rat infestations. There are no camping fees, only the cost of transport.

You can make arrangements for one of the dive shops to drop you off on a deserted island and pick you up later at an arranged time. Fish 'N Fins, for example, charges US$40 for this service, though they'll usually drop you for free if you coordinate with diving or snorkelling trips (ie, they'll pick you up from your Rock Island so you can join the dive group, at the same rate as if you came aboard in Koror). They weave through the Rock Islands for most diving tours anyway, and on the return they can drop you back at your island.

For information on a chaperoned camping/diving outing, try Sam's Tours and its subsidiary, Planet Blue Kayaking.

Guesthouses *Carp Island Resort*, booked through Palau Diving Center (☎ 488 2978, fax 488 3155, @ carpcorp@palaunet.com), has a variety of overpriced accommodation options geared towards Japanese divers. Four rooms in duplex cottages, each with two single beds, a shared indoor toilet and a porch overlooking the beach, go for US$85/75 in high/low season. For a bed in plain dorm-style rooms at nondorm prices it's US$65/55 in high/low season. Generator electricity comes on at night and showers for the divehouse are outdoors. There's an informal restaurant with meals (US$7.50 for breakfast or lunch, US$20 for dinner). You can bring your own food and use the kitchen facilities at no charge. You can also camp on the beach near the resort and use the outdoor public shower for US$10 per night – the best deal by far on this island.

The *Ngerchong Boat-el* (☎ 488 2691), on Ngerchong Island, is geared towards groups, with a large building that can accommodate up to 10 people and a smaller self-contained unit for up to four people. The latter is US$40 a night, while the larger place is about US$70. Boat transportation is the whopper – about US$200 return. Meals are available from US$4 to US$8.

Getting There & Away
Most visitors see the Rock Islands via dive shop boat trips (see Diving & Snorkelling earlier in this section). There are also other tour companies that arrange boat tours through the Rock Islands.

The Japanese-operated Rock Island Tour Co (☎ 488 1573), at the northern end of Malakal Island, has a semi-submersible boat that takes passengers on a cruise around the Rock Islands. There are underwater glass windows that allow passengers to view coral and tropical fish. The cost of US$100 includes the boat ride, lunch, snorkelling and hotel transfers. Tours last from 9 am to 4 pm.

Try also Palau Island Adventures (☎ 488 1843).

Babeldaob

Babeldaob, or Babelthaup, is the second-largest island in Micronesia, three-quarters the size of Guam. It has 10 states but a total population of under 4000, with many of the younger people making an exodus to Koror in search of jobs.

Melekeok, a state with just 261 people, has been constitutionally designated Palau's future capital. Grandiose plans have been drawn up, though their implementation is in doubt.

More probable and immediate is the construction of a paved, US$149 million, 53 mile (85.3km) road around the island, which, among other momentous impacts, will make the island much more accessible to tourists. To mitigate the environmental impact of the road, two conservation areas totalling 5 sq km were established in parts of Ngiwal and Melekeok states.

Although Babeldaob is a high volcanic island, the highest of its gently rolling hills, Mt Ngerchelchuus, reaches only 713 feet (217m). Babeldaob's **Lake Ngardok**, about 3000 feet (914m) long and 12 feet (3.6m) deep, is one of Micronesia's few freshwater lakes and is the region's largest natural lake. Parts of the island's dense jungle interior remain virtually unexplored.

The east coast has beautiful stretches of **sandy beach**, particularly from Ngiwal to Ngaraard, while the west coast has a largely mangrove-studded shoreline. Many villages are connected by ancient stone footpaths.

STATES OF BABELDAOB

Babeldaob State Offices

The following are the phone numbers for each Babeldaob state (governor's) office. All are in Koror, except for those of the southern states of Aimeliik and Airai, which are located on Babeldaob.

Aimeliik State	☎ 544 2967
Airai State	☎ 587 3511
Melekeok State	☎ 488 2728
Ngaraard State	☎ 488 1320
Ngarchelong State	☎ 488 2871
Ngardmau State	☎ 488 1401
Ngatpang State	☎ 488 1882
Ngchesar State	☎ 488 2636
Ngeremlengui State	☎ 488 2190
Ngiwal State	☎ 488 3254

to these terraced hillsides. Badrulchau is the only known exception.

Airai State

At the southern end of Babeldaob, Airai, with a population of just under 1500, has Palau's international airport. The state's relatively good roads and its proximity to Koror make it a good area to explore. The most visited attractions are two bai – one is old, the other more recent.

Airai and Koror are connected by the temporary pontoon bridge that succeeded the collapsed K-B Bridge.

To visit the **bai**, continue straight on the main road, rather than turning towards the airport. The bombed-out shell of a **Japanese administration building** is 1¼ miles (2km) farther, on the left just after the pavement ends. Behind the main ruins you can see another old wartime building which is now used as an auto repair shop. A **Japanese tank** and a few **guns** rust in union with a heap of car parts outside.

Continue on the main road for about 200 yards (180m) to a security gate; just past that the road splits. Take the road to the left to the new bai, which is on the right 4½ miles (7.2km) from the bridge. This bai is made mostly of concrete though it incorporates traditional features.

Ngarchelong state, at the northernmost point of Babeldaob, has an open field with rows of large **basalt monoliths** known as Badrulchau. The origin of the monoliths is unknown, but according to one legend the gods put them there to support a bai that held thousands of people. There are 37 stones in all, some weighing up to five tons.

Many of Babeldaob's hillsides were once elaborately terraced into steps and pyramids – archaeological research suggests construction probably began around AD 100 and was abandoned around 1600. Quite mysteriously, few villages seem to have been located close

Just beyond this turn left at the T-junction and after a few hundred yards the road will end at **Palau's oldest bai**, which dates back a century. It is 70 feet (21m) long and 20 feet (6m) wide with a steeply pitched roof reaching a height of 40 feet (12m). It was constructed without nails using native materials of wood and thatch on a stone platform.

Chances are good that as you start walking up the path the keeper of the bai will appear. Expect to pay about US$2, or US$10 if you want to photograph the bai (US$50 for video cameras).

While the most interesting is certainly the older bai, which is the last original structure of its type in Palau, both have legendary scenes and symbolic designs painted inside and out.

Also in Airai is **Metuker ra Bisech**, a quarry for Yapese stone money. This spot has been revamped, with a stairway and handrail and covered rest station. It's about 20 minutes by boat from Koror.

Ngaraard State

Ngaraard has villages on both its east and west coasts, with a road connecting them. Some of Babeldaob's prettiest **beaches** are on Ngaraard's east coast, as is the island's only established guesthouse. Though Ngaraard has only 421 people, that's enough to make it the third most populated state in Babeldaob (after Airai and Ngerchelong).

Ngaraard residents are used to seeing foreigners. Peace Corps volunteers train in this state and Bethania High School, a Christian girls school which takes students from throughout Micronesia, has some American teachers.

Organised Tours

Guided tours of Babeldaob can be arranged from Koror but they tend to be expensive, averaging about US$65 per person for a half day and US$100 for an extensive full day tour. There's usually a two person minimum. Island Nation (☎ 488 5322, @ islandnation@palaunet.com) offers tours for one to four people for US$250, including boat charter. Additional persons are US$50 each. Overnight camping trips for four people are US$475, including meals.

Palau Island Adventures (☎ 488 4511, fax 488 1843, @ pia@palaunet.com) has safari tours to Babeldaob visiting different waterfalls. The price is US$65 to US$100 per person, with minimum of three people.

Ngaraard Traditional Resort (☎ 488 1788) offers its overnight guests guided tours in northern Babeldaob. A tour that includes the stone monoliths of Badrulchau costs US$55, US$25 for children. The boat tour to Ngardmau, followed by an hour-long hike to Palau's largest waterfall, costs the same price.

Places to Stay

Camping can be a problem on Babeldaob as it's not a local custom. You'll need to first obtain permission from the village chief.

Homestays are a new option in Ngarchelong (☎ 488 2871), Ngardmau (☎ 488 1401, 488 2683) and Ngchesar (☎ 488 2636) states. Contact the governors' offices in Koror to arrange homestays. The cost is about US$25 to US$35 per person per night and this generally includes one meal though more, of course, can be arranged.

Ngaraard Traditional Resort *(☎ 488 1788, fax 488 1725, @ jdean@palaunet .com)* has three cottages in a natural beach setting in Ulimang village in Ngaraard. The local-style cottages have thatched roofs and rough-hewn beams, each with two bedrooms with double beds and mosquito nets, an ice cooler and kerosene stove but no cooking facilities. The showers and toilets are outdoors and electricity is supplied from 6 pm to midnight daily. The cost is US$45/55 for singles/doubles and US$15 to US$20 for each additional person (children under 10 can stay for US$10). Meals are US$6.50 for breakfast, US$8.50 for lunch and US$18.50 for dinner. Fax or email ahead, as reaching them by phone can be tricky.

Three new Babeldaob ***guesthouses*** are operated by Lazarus Kodep (☎ 654 1001, 488 2728, fax 654 1003), Melekeok's governor. These lovely spacious guesthouses, side by side on the road, are constructed in beautiful dark wood. There is electricity 24 hours,

PALAU

a hot-water shower and excellent kitchen facilities – refrigerator, freezer, microwave, oven and rice cooker. There's a giant clam farm nearby and local meals are available. The price is US$40 a night (plus tax) and transportation can be arranged for US$25.

The *Airai View Hotel*, on the road between Koror and the airport, is listed under Places to Stay in the Koror section.

Getting There & Away
Private speedboats, fishing boats and state motorboats going to Babeldaob generally leave from Koror's T-Dock or the Fisheries Co-op. Check at the governor's office of the state you're planning to visit or simply go to the docks and ask if anyone's heading in that direction. You can generally join a boat by sharing fuel costs. Some boats return to Koror the same day, some stay overnight.

Ngaraard Traditional Resort can arrange a private speedboat from Koror to Ngaraard for US$50 per adult (US$20 per child) one way or US$100 per boat return (one hour each way).

You may be able to arrange a ride with locals bringing their produce to Yano's market in Koror in return for a contribution towards fuel (US$5 or US$10). Ask at the market or governors' offices.

Getting Around
You can get from Koror to the bai in Airai in a sedan, but beyond that you'll need a 4WD vehicle. It is possible to drive as far as Melekeok on the east coast and Ngeremlengui on the west coast along rough dirt roads (although rental companies may restrict vehicle use in these areas).

Babeldaob has only a few vehicle roads, which generally follow the paths of the once-extensive road system constructed during the Japanese era. Some states have just a mile or two (a few kilometres) of roads which go through a main village and then stop. Because each state works on its own road projects, roads in one state don't always connect up with roads in the next. The planned circle road should improve things.

Wherever you stay, ask around and you may be able to rent a truck.

Peleliu

Peleliu was the site of one of the bloodiest battles of WWII. The island is small, only 5 sq miles (13 sq km), yet in two months of fighting on Peleliu during 1944 over 15,000 men were killed – not much less than Palau's current population.

Battle for Peleliu

The battle for Peleliu was conceived by US military tacticians who were worried that Japanese attacks from bases in Peleliu and Angaur might prevent a successful retaking of the Philippines. By mid-1944, however, US air bombings had reduced Peleliu to a negligible threat and it could easily have been bypassed, as were many other islands held by the Japanese. Instead Peleliu was captured at a terrible, unanticipated cost, with more than 8000 US casualties.

At the time of the US invasion, some 10,000 Japanese soldiers were holed up in the caves that honeycombed Peleliu's jagged limestone ridges. Their goal was not to win, but to stall defeat. Far away from the beaches and the reach of naval bombardment, the Japanese tenaciously defended these caves to their deaths. In the bloody assaults that followed, the caves became mass coffins as American troops used flamethrowers, grenades and explosives to seal them shut.

Rather than the expected quick victory, it took 2½ months for the Americans to rout out the last of the Japanese forces. In the end only 400 prisoners were taken alive and the majority of those were Korean labourers.

In the late 1950s, a Japanese straggler who had been hiding in the jungle was discovered by an elderly woman as he entered her garden. Crouching low to see who had been stealing her tapioca, the woman froze and then screamed, thinking she was seeing a ghost. The man's uniform was torn into shreds, his hair matted and teeth streaked black. Police from Koror hunted down the straggler, bound him with rope and paraded him around for everyone to see. In that inglorious manner, the last WWII soldier left Peleliu.

In pre-war days settlements were scattered around Peleliu. During the final days of Japanese control of the island, however, the islanders were forced to evacuate Peleliu and move to Babeldaob. Upon returning to the battle-scarred island after the war, everyone resettled on the northern tip of Peleliu, where they remain today. The island's current population is about 575.

Several areas in Peleliu have been renamed for their military usage. Koska, at the southern end of Klouklubed, is not really a separate village, but is the area where the coast guard (kos ka) personnel once stayed. Ngerkeyukl, the former village north of Orange Beach, is now called Sina, which is the Palauan word for China, so named because of the nationalist Chinese that came to that area to buy jeeps and other WWII surplus.

During the fighting Peleliu's forests were bombed and burned to the ground. Today the island is alive with the whistles and songs of tropical birds that thrive on the secondary jungle growth of vines and leafy foliage that covers the island's battle scars. If it weren't for the occasional pillbox, rusting tank or memorial, there'd be

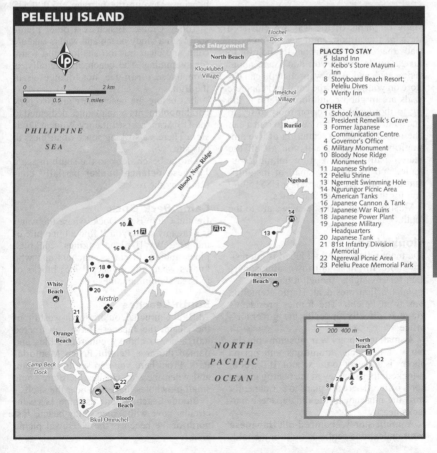

PELELIU ISLAND

Elochel Dock

See Enlargement

North Beach

Klouklubed Village

Imelchol Village

0   1   2 km
0   0.5   1 miles

PHILIPPINE SEA

Ruriid

Bloody Nose Ridge

Ngebad

PLACES TO STAY
5   Island Inn
7   Keibo's Store Mayumi Inn
8   Storyboard Beach Resort; Peleliu Dives
9   Wenty Inn

OTHER
1   School; Museum
2   President Remeliik's Grave
3   Former Japanese Communication Centre
4   Governor's Office
6   Military Monument
10 Bloody Nose Ridge Monuments
11 Japanese Shrine
12 Peleliu Shrine
13 Ngermelt Swimming Hole
14 Ngurungor Picnic Area
15 American Tanks
16 Japanese Cannon & Tank
17 Japanese War Ruins
18 Japanese Power Plant
19 Japanese Military Headquarters
20 Japanese Tank
21 81st Infantry Division Memorial
22 Ngerewal Picnic Area
23 Peleliu Peace Memorial Park

PALAU

White Beach

Airstrip

Orange Beach

Camp Beck Dock

Honeymoon Beach

NORTH PACIFIC OCEAN

Bloody Beach

Bkul Omruchel

0   200   400 m

North Beach

no immediate sense of this island's war history.

Peleliu is also known in some circles for its high-quality marijuana. Fertile soil is brought in from Babeldaob for pot planting in 50-gallon oil drums. Police raids, sponsored by US agents, occasionally swoop in and confiscate the harvest, much to the ire of locals who consider it an attack on their economy.

Peleliu has much more to offer than just war relics. It's a fine place to kick back and take life easy for a while. The old name for Peleliu was Odesangel, meaning the 'beginning of everything'.

Orientation

Many remnants of the war are clustered north of the airport amid a criss-cross of roads that can be confusing. It's helpful to have a guide, but if you don't care about seeing each and every war relic you can explore on your own, as the coral and concrete roads are in good condition. Peleliu is too big to thoroughly cover on foot, so try to find a bicycle if you don't want to rent a car. The island still has a scattering of live ammunition, so take care if you go off the beaten path. Refrain from taking 'souvenirs', no matter how small or insignificant they may seem. There is a US$15,000 fine for the removal of war relics.

Most of Peleliu's best beaches are to the south.

Klouklubed

The main village of Klouklubed is interesting more for its small-town atmosphere than for any sights, though it has a few.

Palau's first president, Haruo Remeliik, was from Peleliu. The former president's **grave** is directly opposite the governor's office.

A small temporary **war museum** containing war artefacts, munitions and period photos is adjacent to the school. If the door is locked, there's a key at the nearby governor's office. There are plans to permanently shift the museum to the old Japanese barracks nearby.

A multi-storey, bombed-out **Japanese communications centre** is right in the mid-dle of the village, tangled with vegetation and encircled by homes. Kids play inside the building and its roof is now a forest floor.

There's a small **US military monument** opposite Keibo's Store. Heading towards the dock you can spot a **cave** and **pillbox** on the right, opposite a sandy beach.

Orange Beach

The first US invasion forces to land on Peleliu came ashore at Orange Beach on 15 September 1944. From concrete pillboxes the Japanese machine-gunned the oncoming waves of Americans as they hit the beaches. Despite the barrage, 15,000 US soldiers made it ashore that first day.

Today Orange Beach is a quiet picnic spot with a sandy beach and waters that are calm and clear but too shallow and warm for swimming. The beach, incidentally, is pronounced o-**ran**-gee, not 'orange' as in the fruit.

Just before the beach there are two grey **coral monuments** with plaques dedicated to the US Army's 81st Infantry Wildcat Division. There's a striking sense of stillness at this site.

On the beach, look to the south to see a Japanese **defence bunker** partially concealed by the rocks.

Camp Beck Dock

Behind Camp Beck Dock, where the water is a creamy aqua, you'll find a huge pile of mangled WWII plane engines, cockpits, pipes, tubing, fuselages, anchors and who knows what, all compacted into blocks of twisted aluminium and steel.

South Beaches

At Bkul Omruchel, on the south-west tip of the island, the Japanese have constructed half a dozen chunky concrete tables and named the area **Peleliu Peace Memorial Park**. From here you can see to the south, and when the surf crashes there are some small blowholes that erupt near the shore.

Bloody Beach, despite its name, is a calm circular cove with a nice sandy beach. Just north of the beach is the Ngerewal picnic area.

North-east of the airport is **Honeymoon Beach**, a long stretch of beach with good seasonal surf.

At the eastern tip of the island is the **Ngurungor picnic area**, which has some mangroves and tiny rock island formations just offshore.

Heading back from Ngurungor, off a grassy road to the right, there's a refreshing little **swimming hole** of half-salt, half-fresh water that bobs up and down with the tides. A metal ladder hangs down the side of the tiny pit, but local kids just jump in from the top.

Diving & Snorkelling

The **Peleliu Wall**, south-west of Peleliu, is one of the world's finest dives, an abrupt 900-foot (300m) drop that starts in about 10 feet (3m) of water. It's a veritable treasure-trove of sharks, hawksbill sea turtles, black coral trees, mammoth gorgonian fans and an amazing variety of fish.

Many of Palau's best dive spots are in fact closer to Peleliu than Koror, but most people start from Koror with the dive shops there.

Both White Beach and Bloody Beach have coral and good snorkelling; Honeymoon Beach also has good snorkelling.

Peleliu Divers (☎/fax 345 1058, @ pdivers@palaunet.com), a small operation beside the Storyboard Beach Resort, knows the best dive spots and charges US$85 for a two-tank dive. It also has land tours for US$20, kayak tours for US$40 and Jellyfish Lake tours for US$70.

Organised Tours

An excellent tour of the island is given by Tangie, a very friendly character and Peleliu's resident historian of sorts. He shares lots of background info as he tours the sights. The tour costs US$77 for one to four people, US$15 per person for five or more. Tangie can generally be reached at the Mayumi Inn. Peleliu Divers (☎/fax 345 1058) also does tours.

Places to Stay & Eat

Camping Camping is easy and acceptable on Peleliu. Some of the beach picnic sites have open-air shelters, tables, barbecue pits and outhouses, but you'll need to take drinking water with you. You'll also need a close-knit screened tent or insect repellent.

While no permission is required to camp, you should first check in at the helpful governor's office. You can arrange in town for a car to drop you off at your camping site and to pick you up later.

Ngurungor picnic area is a good choice for camping. It's close to the swimming hole and it usually has a refreshing breeze.

Orange Beach is another possibility for camping, though the west coast doesn't catch many breezes, and it can be hot and muggy.

Honeymoon Beach, which has covered picnic tables, is also a nice spot, but beware the hard-biting sand gnats that can make for a sleepless night.

Guesthouses No credit cards are accepted on Peleliu, so bring sufficient cash and travellers cheques. There's a 10% hotel tax generally applied to the room rates below. Also, bear in mind that there is no electricity between 6 am and 6 pm.

The *Wenty Inn* (☎ 345 2967), run by Emery Wenty, is a guesthouse with five rooms, each with a double bed. The cost is US$15 per person and meals cost US$7 for breakfast and US$10 for lunch and dinner. There's a nice beach when the tide is in.

Reiko Kubarii (☎ 345 1106) has rooms for US$15 near the governor's office. It was closed for renovation at the time of writing, but is expected to reopen in 2000.

At *Mayumi Inn*, Mayumi Keibo rents three plain rooms behind Keibo's Store. They have air-con and a shared outdoor bathroom. The rate is US$22 per person (including tax), and meals are available for US$7 to US$12.

Down the street towards the dock, *Island Inn* (☎ 345 1090, fax 345 1036), above a small store and under Keibo's ownership, is massively overpriced at US$50/55 singles/doubles for its seven bland rooms, each with a private bath. It's a five-minute walk down to Keibo for meals. Unless you're firmly opposed to shared baths, there is no

PALAU

reason to stay at the Island Inn if you can stay at Mayumi's. The rooms have air-con and twin beds.

Storyboard Beach Resort (☎ *345 1019, fax 345 1058,* @ *pdivers@palaunet.com*), under the same family ownership as adjacent Peleliu Divers, consists of six simple but clean A-frame concrete cottages on the beach in the village just south of Keibo's Store. The cottages have hot showers, lanai and ceiling fans. Some cottages have queen-size beds, others twin beds. Breakfast can be prepared for US$6 and dinner for US$12. But save up for the room rate – a steep US$85 per cottage (plus US$25 for a third guest).

Peleliu has several small ***food stores***, selling mostly canned and packaged goods, but no restaurants.

Getting There & Away

The state boat *Peleliu Islander*, with a 30 passenger capacity, runs between Elochel Dock in Klouklubed and the Fisheries Co-op on Koror. It generally leaves Koror at noon on Mondays and Fridays and returns from Peleliu at 10 am on Thursdays and Sundays. Reservations are not necessary, but you should call the governor's office in advance (☎ 345 1071) to verify departure times. The two-hour ride costs US$6 each way.

Private speedboats sometimes operate between Klouklubed and Koror, so you might be able to get a ride by asking around at the Fisheries Co-op. The governor's offices on Peleliu and Koror will also know who's leaving and when.

Some dive companies take their midday break on Peleliu and can provide guests with a land tour for an additional fee.

Getting Around

Car If you ask around you might be able to rent a pick-up truck or van for about US$40 a day, although it's rather hit-or-miss. Also check at Mayumi's Inn, which rents an old van for US$49.50.

Bicycle Wenty Inn rents bicycles for US$10 a day. It would take a couple of days to see most of Peleliu's sights by bike.

Angaur

For the independent traveller looking to get off the beaten track, low-keyed Angaur, with a population just under 200, has a certain timeless South Seas charm.

Lying 7 miles (11.2 km) south-west of Peleliu, Angaur is outside the protective reef that surrounds most of Palau's islands. Open ocean pounds the north coast where the sea explodes skyward through small blowholes. The south end of the island is much calmer and fringed with sandy beaches.

Orientation

The coastal road circling the island is mostly level and in good condition. Angaur is just 2.5 miles (4km) long, making it easy to get around on foot.

If you're on a day trip, however, you'll probably want to rent a vehicle or be content with walking around just a part of the island. Although it's possible to walk the entire coastal road in a day, the heat and humidity don't make it tempting – at least not at midday. Outside Angaur's one village, tall trees and tropical growth close in, allowing for shady strolls.

Diving

There's good diving around Angaur between January and July, but the rest of the year the water's too rough. Diving arrangements must be made in advance in Koror, as

---

Angaur Monkeys

Angaur has thousands of crab-eating macaques, descendants of a couple of monkeys brought to the island by Germans in the early 1900s to monitor air quality in Angaur's phosphate mines.

Accidentally released, the monkeys took well to Angaur's jungle, despite attempts to eradicate them. As the macaques occasionally raid crops, many islanders consider them a pest.

While their export to other Palauan islands is officially prohibited, they are prized as pets and you may occasionally spot one in Koror.

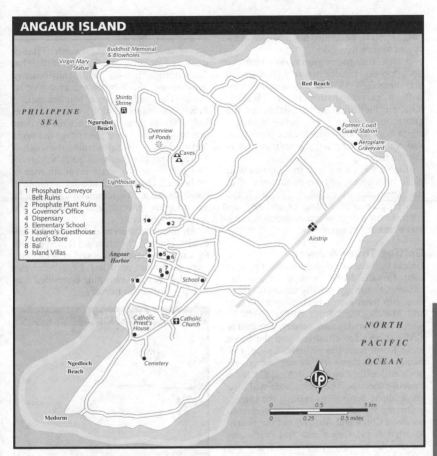

ANGAUR ISLAND

Buddhist Memorial
& Blowholes

Virgin Mary
Statue

Red Beach

Shinto
Shrine

*PHILIPPINE
SEA*

Nguruhei
Beach

Overview
of Ponds

Former Coast
Guard Station

Aeroplane
Graveyard

Caves

Lighthouse

1 Phosphate Conveyor
  Belt Ruins
2 Phosphate Plant Ruins
3 Governor's Office
4 Dispensary
5 Elementary School
6 Kasiano's Guesthouse
7 Leon's Store
8 Bai
9 Island Villas

Airstrip

Angaur
Harbor

School

Catholic
Priest's
House

Catholic
Church

*NORTH
PACIFIC
OCEAN*

Ngedloch
Beach

Cemetery

Medorm

0   0.5   1 km
0   0.25   0.5 miles

PALAU

there are no facilities on Angaur. Most dive companies do not go regularly to Angaur.

Places to Stay & Eat

Camping Camping can be complicated. There are no developed facilities, and as most of Angaur's coastal areas are privately owned you'll need to seek permission from the landowner. Make arrangements at the governor's office in Koror (☎ 488 5282) before you leave.

Guesthouses *Island Villas* consists of two guesthouses managed by Leon Guilbert.

The best one is a spacious, modern house on the beach with a kitchen, ocean-view deck, two bedrooms and a couple of other rooms capable of accommodating larger groups. If the beach house is full, a second guesthouse, on the south side of Leon's store in the village centre, also has a few rooms. The cost at either house is US$20 per person (or US$30 for a double, US$60 for the house). Meals are US$8 for breakfast, US$10 for lunch and US$15 for dinner, and sometimes there are special local delicacies, such as land crabs in coconut milk, for a few dollars more. Reservations are made through the governor's office in Angaur (☎ 277 2967). Leon also has a couple of bicycles to rent for US$5.

A new four-room *guesthouse* near the dock has downstairs rooms with a shared bathroom for US$35 and an upstairs room with a private bathroom for US$45. Kitchen facilities are available as the guesthouse doesn't yet serve meals – check with Kasiano, the owner. Electricity and water are supplied intermittently during the day.

Angaur has a couple of small *stores* with basic provisions, but no restaurants. Call the governor's office on ☎ 277 2967, the only phone number in Angaur, and they can summon the owner of either guesthouse for you to make arrangements.

Getting There & Away
Unless the seas are unduly rough, the state boat *Yamato Maru*, with a 20- to 25-passenger capacity, usually makes the three hour trip from Koror to Angaur on Friday and Monday, and from Angaur back to Koror on Thursday and Sunday. The cost is US$5 (US$3 for children) and the boats leave Koror from the Fisheries Co-op. Departure times can vary, so call the governor's office in Koror (☎ 488 5282) for a current schedule. The office staff will also know about cargo ships making the trip.

Private speedboats sometimes commute between Koror and Angaur, but not nearly as often as between Koror and Peleliu, as the channel between Angaur and Koror can get very rough.

Getting Around
If you don't want to explore Angaur on foot, Island Villas can arrange car rentals for US$35 to US$40 a day and sometimes mopeds (US$15 to US$20) and bicycles (US$5 to US$10). The latter work well because the island is flat.

Island Villas can also arrange guided land tours for US$50 to US$60 for up to four people, plus US$10 for each additional person. Snorkelling and fishing tours by boat can also be arranged for US$50 an hour.

Kayangel

Kayangel, 15 miles (24km) north of Babeldaob, is a picture-postcard coral atoll. It has four islands fringed with sun-bleached beaches and a well-protected aqua-blue lagoon. The main island, Ngcheangel, is barely 1½ miles (2.4km) long and takes only a few minutes to walk across, yet there are two chiefs – one governing the north and a stronger chief governing the south.

Kayangel has just one quiet village of 137 people, which has a predominance of tin houses. There are 41 houses, a couple of small stores, a little ice-making plant and a few mopeds, one car and a phone in the governor's office.

An important recent development is the establishment of Ngeruangel Reserve, a 35-sq-km area where fishing and general entry were prohibited until late 1999. After this Kayangel began welcoming controlled fishing in and visits to the area.

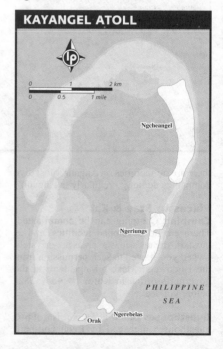

KAYANGEL ATOLL

Ngcheangel

Ngeriungs

PHILIPPINE SEA

Orak Ngerebelas

Kayangel is fairly traditional and welcomes culturally sensitive visitors. Dress is particularly important – women should wear a T-shirt and shorts over their bathing suit when swimming and no-one should wear shorts in the village.

Woven handbags (US$35) and baskets from Kayangel are in demand as they're made of a high quality pandanus leaf.

Tourists need permits to visit Kayangel. These are relatively easy to obtain from the governor's office in Koror. A one-month to one-year permit for scuba diving costs US$20, for sportsfishing US$15, photography US$20 and sightseeing and snorkelling US$8.

Diving & Sportsfishing
Some dive companies occasionally bring divers to Kayangel on request. While diving here may not be on par with the Rock Islands, it does have virgin reefs and offers the opportunity to get well off the beaten path. You can check with the governor's office or the tourist office for companies that bring tourists to Ngeruangel Reserve.

Places to Stay
There are no hotels on Kayangel, but you can contact the Kayangel governor's office (in Kayangel ☎ 876 2967; in Koror ☎ 488 2766) about camping or staying with a family. You should be able to arrange a place for around US$20 to US$50, meals included.

Take rice, coffee, betel nut, baked goods or other provisions as gifts.

Getting There & Away
The state speedboat leaves Kayangel for Koror every second Friday and returns to Kayangel from Koror's T-Dock the following Sunday. It costs US$20 each way and the trip takes just two hours.

Another option is Kayangel's fishing boat, which travels to Koror about every five or six days. The schedule is irregular but the governor's office will know when the boat leaves. Private boats sometimes make the trip – again the governor's office will know. Both fishing and private boats take seven to eight hours and charge US$7.

Private speedboats, if you can find them, take about three hours.

South-West Islands

The South-West Islands are comprised of half a dozen small islands scattered 370 miles (595km) beyond Koror and 100 miles (161km) north of Indonesia. Each of the islands covers less than 1 sq mile (2.6 sq km) of land. The six islands are Sonsorol and Fana (collectively known as the Sonsorol Islands), Pulo Anna, Merir, Tobi and Helen.

South-West Islanders are culturally related to people from the central Caroline Islands, and have more in common with Yapese and Chuukese outer islanders than with people from the main islands of Palau. Their native languages are Sonsorolese and Tobian, which are similar to Yapese. They have a very traditional island lifestyle, with thatched houses, carved canoes and a fishing-based livelihood.

Unlike today the South-West Islands were once heavily populated, as most were used for phosphate mining during the period of Japanese occupation. At last count Tobi had 25 people, Sonsorol had between 20 and 64 (people tend to migrate with visiting ships), Pulo Anna 18 and Merir five. While the island of Fana has remained uninhabited since WWII, the Sonsorolese visit it to fish and capture coconut crabs, turtles and birds.

Uninhabited Helen Island has nesting lesser-crested terns and green sea turtles. South-West Islanders have long sailed to Helen Reef to hunt the turtles and harvest giant clams, as do occasional government supply ships and illegal Indonesian poachers. Merir Island also has nesting green sea turtles.

Other than the occasional researcher, there are virtually no foreign visitors to the islands, but the people are friendly and most speak some English. All of the islands have a radio, so communication is possible with Koror.

While there are no guesthouses in the South-West Islands, it is possible to camp.

PALAU

However, it's best to avoid Merir Island, which has a terrible mosquito infestation. You'll need to bring all your own food and supplies.

According to the governor's office, land is being cleared for an airport on Sonsorol to facilitate supply planes.

Getting There & Away

Sonsorol's state boat visits Sonsorol every second month and visitors can make the 20- to 23-hour ride from Koror free of charge. The Tobi state boat also goes to Tobi and Helen every two months, or more frequently if there's a need. The return fare is US$19.50. The Tobi boat sometimes goes to other islands and you may be able to coordinate transport so that one boat takes you out and another picks you up, if you don't want to stay for two months. Research vessels and a Palauan fishing patrol boat also make their way to the islands occasionally. For information on the boats and accommodation, contact the Sonsorol governor's office (☎ 488 1237) and the Tobi governor's office (☎ 488 2218) in Koror.

US Territories

Since the 19th century the USA has laid claim to nine small landmasses in the Pacific, between Kiribati and Hawai'i: Palmyra Atoll, Johnston Atoll, Navassa Island, Baker Island, Howland Island, Jarvis Atoll, Kingman Reef, Midway Atoll and Wake Atoll. All but Midway and Wake were claimed under the 1956 *Guano Islands Act*, in the heyday of the phosphate hunt – though Palmyra and Kingman turned out to have no guano. Most are narrow coral reefs, with finger-shaped islands surrounding a central lagoon.

Sovereignty issues abound in these unincorporated US territories. Some, like Palmyra and Kingman, are privately owned but are interlocked with US naval history. Jarvis Atoll is claimed by the Marshall Islands, and Kiribati has recently asked the USA to give it Howland, Baker and Jarvis so that it can extend its sea domain (and expand its fishing licence revenue). A movement in the mid-1990s attempted to incorporate Baker, Jarvis, Johnston, Kingman, Howland, Midway and Palmyra into the state of Hawai'i – while a separate bill proposed the induction of Howland and Baker into American Samoa – but these bills, never a high Congressional priority, stalled and faded.

With the exception of Palmyra, none of these islands is open to visitors; many are wildlife refuges and none has the facilities to support large numbers of visitors. For information on national wildlife refuges, contact the Fish and Wildlife Service in Honolulu at ☎ 808-541 1201, fax 808-541 1216.

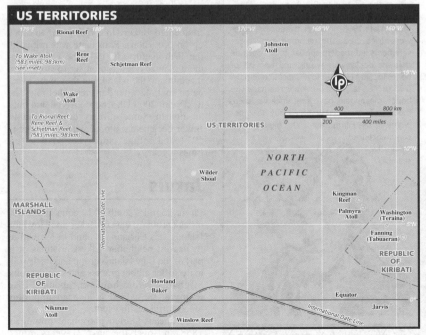

Howland

Treeless and barren, uninhabited Howland is home to birds, turtles and other tiny animals that can subsist in its harsh environment; there is no fresh water and only scrub vegetation. The island, 1500 miles (2400km) south-east of Hawai'i, was mined until 1878. The Fish and Wildlife Service now keeps Howland as a national wildlife refuge.

Howland is most famous as the intended refuelling stop for US aviator Amelia Earhart during her round-the-equator trip in 1937. An airstrip was built there in anticipation of her landing, but Earhart and her navigator, Fred Noonan, never made it. It appears that they could not locate the island and instead came down elsewhere in the Pacific. Her fate remains unknown, but theories abound – the most dramatic being that she was captured by the Japanese during WWII and taken to Mili Atoll in the Marshall Islands. The most recent hypothesis is that the bones found on the island of Nikumaroro, about 1000 miles north of Suva, Fiji, in Kiribati's Gilbert chain, are those of Earhart and her navigator.

Baker

Like its near neighbour Howland, which is 36 miles to the north, Baker belongs to the Phoenix Group. At its highest point it reaches 27 feet.

The island has a fringing coral reef and is a breeding area for pelagic birds and a stop for migrating shore birds; it also has marine turtles and bottlenose dolphins.

During the mid-19th century, whalers frequented Baker (like Howland) to stock up on provisions. Phosphate was mined in the 19th century. In 1935 the US government planted a few 'colonists' to strengthen its claims to the island, but they were evacuated in 1942 after Japanese shelling. The next year, 2000 US troops arrived and built an airstrip. Some military debris remains. Baker became a national wildlife refuge in 1974 and refuge employees visit a few times a year.

Jarvis

Jarvis, 25 miles south of the equator and 700 miles (1100km) east of Baker and Howland Islands, has Christmas Island in Kiribati as its nearest neighbour. Like Christmas, it is part of the Line Islands group and its dry climate stifles all but grasses and small shrubs. Migratory birds, however, abound. Like Palmyra, the island is also an important green-turtle nesting spot.

Europeans started phosphate mining in 1858 and over the next 21 years mined

Was Earhart Found?

When British soldiers discovered two sets of bones and shoes on the remote island of Nikumaroro, Kiribati, in 1941, they immediately sent them to Tarawa, Kiribati's capital, where the examining British physician pronounced them the bones of two European men. In late 1998, however, the doctor's notes were discovered. The recorded bone measurements led modern specialists to conclude that the doctor was wrong and one set of bones in fact belonged to a Caucasian female, 5'7" or 5'8" tall – just like Amelia Earhart. The bones, meanwhile, have long since vanished, though it is suspected that they may be somewhere in the Fiji museum. The museum has commenced an exhaustive search.

300,000 tons. The next inhabitants were colonists, sent by the US government in the 1936 to firm up the US territorial claim. They were evacuated in 1942 and the island remains uninhabited. In 1974 the island, which covers 2.2 sq miles, became a national wildlife refuge. The Fish and Wildlife Service visits every few years.

Palmyra Atoll

Located 350 miles (560km) north of Jarvis, palm-lined Palmyra consists of 52 islets surrounding three lagoons. Americans aboard the ship *Palmyra* first discovered the atoll in 1902, but it was not until 60 years later that Hawai'i claimed it under the *Guano Islands Act*. When the USA annexed Hawai'i in 1898 the annexation act specifically excluded Palmyra – because it turned out to have no guano and had thus been unlawfully claimed.

In 1922, the Fullard-Leo family of Hawai'i bought Palmyra for US$15,000 and has owned it ever since, though the navy built an airstrip and some buildings there during WWII. Since the mid-1990s, however, the family has indicated a desire to sell it. The first major bidder, a New York corporation, was on the verge of purchasing it for US$30 million, but its plans to use Palmyra as a nuclear-waste dump sparked an outcry across the Pacific. The most recent and likely purchaser has emerged as the Nature Conservancy, a major US conservation group that would turn Palmyra over to the US Fish and Wildlife Service.

There is a couple who live on the island, which has large WWII-era rainfall catchments and is relatively fertile. The boat pier and wide harbour make the island an attractive stop for visiting yachts, but you must ask permission beforehand. Contact Palmyra Development Company (☎ 808-942 7701, fax 808-947 5429) and pay US$5 per boat per day plus US$1 per person per day. The Fullard-Leo family permits catch-and-release fishing, snorkelling and diving.

Kingman Reef

Treeless, triangular Kingman, with a maximum elevation of 1m, is little more than a 5000 sq foot coral head surrounded by a massive reef. Like Palmyra 35 miles to the south, Kingman Reef is owned by the Fullard-Leo family. Kingman was discovered in 1798 by a US whaler, but named for Captain WE Kingman of the US vessel *Shooting Star* who came by in 1853. It was claimed under the *Guano Islands Act* under the name 'Danger' because of its proximity to a spot called 'Danger Rock' – though it was later discovered to contain no phosphate.

In 1934 US president FD Roosevelt put Kingman under the control of the US navy, where it remains to this day.

Johnston Atoll

Johnston Atoll, 700 miles (1100km) northwest of Palmyra, consists of two natural coral islands, Sand and Johnston, and two man-made islets, North and East (Akau and Hikina). The reef that encloses the islands is about 21 miles in circumference. Viewed from the air, Johnston Island has a most unusual shape, its shoreline extending out in hard straight lines. This is because soil was scooped up from the lagoon during WWII and used to lengthen the runway.

Johnston's other geographic distinction is its isolation. It's 717 nautical miles south-west of its nearest neighbour, Hawai'i, which makes it a useful refuelling stop for Continental Airlines flights bound for Micronesia. The first recorded sighting of Johnston Island was in 1796, when Captain Johnston of HMS *Cornwallis* came ashore. The atoll was simultaneously claimed by the US and Hawai'i in 1858. Hawai'i arrived three months after the USA and Hawai'ian navigator Samuel Allen of the *Kalama* ripped down the US flag and put up the Hawai'ian flag. When Hawai'i became a state in 1898, Johnston Island was separately annexed by the USA. The island's limited phosphate deposits were mined until the early 20th century. In 1926, Johnston was designated a national bird refuge. Its peace, however, was interrupted in 1934, when the island came under navy control. It was used as a submarine refuelling base as well as an airbase. The air force took the islands in 1948 and the islets North and East were created over the next 15 years.

Since 1990, Johnston Island has served as a disposal site for weapons – it is one of nine US sites devoted to this purpose. Over 1200 US military and contract workers live on Johnston and are busy destroying 6% of the world's weapons arsenal – including mines, missiles, mortars, rockets, bombs and VX nerve gas – which is stored on

Johnston. According to the most recent report, 77% of Johnston's weaponry has been destroyed including all the volatile sarin nerve gas.

Continental passengers cannot disembark without US military permission. Yachts are not permitted within 3 miles of Johnston Island.

Wake Atoll

Wake Atoll, 1250 miles (2000km) west of Johnston Atoll, consists of three small islands (Peale, Wake and Wilkes) with a total land area of 2.5 sq miles. Wake is named for a British captain who landed there in 1796. The USA officially claimed it about a century later when a US ship heading to the Philippines during the Spanish-American war planted the US flag on the island in 1898.

Though originally intended as a cable station, Wake served as a refuelling base for trans-Pacific flights during the 1930s. A 48-room hotel supported the base and its 9800-foot airstrip. After WWII the US navy administered Wake, but left in 1962. The US Army Space and Strategic Defense Command (SSDC) controls Wake and keeps 300 people there, though the Marshall Islands has laid claim to the atoll as well, saying that it's part of the Ratak Chain. The Americans are talking of making Wake into a national wildlife refuge, though for now it's off limits.

Some Wildlife Refuge!

Johnston Island is the Dr Jekyll-and-Mr Hyde of the Pacific. While infamous as a chemical weapons cleanup site, it is simultaneously a national wildlife refuge. Thousands of birds, including boobies, shearwaters and terns, use it as a migratory or nesting stop. All told, Johnston has over 300 species of fish, 20 species of native and migratory birds and 32 species of coral, as well as green sea turtles, dolphins and humpback whales. If the military finishes its operations in 2001 as planned, Johnston will be turned over in full to the Fish and Wildlife Service. Then – at long last – Johnston may slowly return to nature.

Glossary

ahset – foreigner (Kosrae)
atoll – a ring of coral reefs or islands surrounding a lagoon

bai – a traditional men's meeting house in Palau
babai – a large plant resembling taro, commonly eaten in Kiribati
banzai attack – a mass attack by troops without concern for casualties, as practised by the Japanese during WWII
beche-de-mer – trepang or large sea cucumber
betel nut – the fruit of the areca palm tree, which is commonly split open, sprinkled with dry coral lime, wrapped in a pepper leaf, and chewed as a digestive stimulant and mild narcotic
breadfruit – a tree of the Pacific Islands, the trunk of which is used for lumber and canoe building. The fruit is cooked and eaten and has a texture like bread.

cantilever – on Nauru, a projected beam that acts as an arm to facilitate ship loading
Chamorro – the indigenous people of the Mariana Islands
copra – dried coconut kernel, used for making coconut oil

dapal – a women's meeting house in Yap
dugong – a herbivorous mammal, similar to the manatee of Florida; it can be found in the shallow tropical waters around Palau

faluw – a Yapese meeting house for men

I-Kiribati – a Kiribati native
I-Matang – the Kiribati word for foreigner
iroij – traditional Marshallese chief

jambos – Marshallese picnics or trips

kainga – on Kiribati, an extended family
kahlek – night fishing in Pohnpei, in which burning torches are used to attract flying fish into hand-held nets

kaokioki – a beer-like fermented coconut drink in Kiribati, also known as sour toddy
kelaguen – minced chicken, fish, shrimp or Spam mixed with lemon, onions, peppers and shredded coconut
korkor – a Marshallese dugout fishing canoe made from a breadfruit log

lagoon – a body of water that is bound by an encircling reef
lanai – a Hawai'ian word commonly used in Micronesia to refer to a veranda
latte stones – the stone foundation pillars used to support ancient Chamorro buildings in the Marianas. The shafts and capstones were carved from limestone quarries.
lava-lava – a wide piece of cloth of woven hibiscus and banana fibres, worn as a skirt by women throughout Yap and in Chuuk's outer islands
lumpia – a fried food, similar to an egg roll, which is usually dipped in garlic sauce or vinegar

maneaba – a traditional community meeting house on Kiribati
mangrove – a tropical tree that grows in tidal mud flats and extends looping prop roots along the shoreline
men's house – see *faluw*
mimpo – Chinese dough
muu-muu – a long, loose-fitting dress introduced by missionaries
mwaramwars – head wreaths of flowers and fragrant leaves worn throughout the FSM

nahnmwarki – a district chief in Pohnpei
nahs – a traditional ceremonial house on Pohnpei
nahnken – a chief in Pohnpei of lesser rank than the *nahnmwarki*
nipa palm – a palm tree common to the tropics; its foliage is used for thatching and basketry
noddy – a tropical tern, or aquatic bird, with black and white or dark plumage

omung – a perfumed love potion used in Chuuk

oyako donburi – a Japanese dish of sweetened chicken and egg served over rice

PADI – Professional Association of Dive Instructors, the world's largest diving association

pandanus – a plant common to the tropics; its sword-shaped leaves are used to make mats and baskets

pebai – a Yapese community meeting house

phosphate – a primary ingredient in fertiliser

purse seine – a large net generally used between two boats that is drawn around a school of fish, especially tuna. Boats that use this method are called purse seiners.

rai – Yapese stone money

ramen – instant noodles

sakau – a mildly narcotic Pohnpeian drink made from the roots of a pepper shrub

sake – Japanese rice wine

Saudeleurs – a tyrannical dynasty that ruled Pohnpei around the 13th century

seka – a narcotic, ceremonial drink (similar to *sakau*) of Kosrae

tangan-tangan – a shrub that was mass-planted in the Marianas to prevent erosion

taro – a plant with green heart-shaped leaves, cultivated for both its leaf and edible rootstock; the latter is commonly boiled and eaten like a potato

thu – a loincloth worn by Yapese males and by outer island Chuukese

tinaktak katni – beef strips in coconut milk (Saipan)

trade winds – the near-constant winds that dominate most of the tropics and in Micronesia blow mainly from the north-east

Tridacna clam – the giant clam, *Tridacna gigas*. The largest known bivalve mollusc, it is collected and farmed in Palau for its edible flesh, and is poached throughout the Pacific for its valuable adductor muscle, which is considered a delicacy.

trochus – a shellfish commercially harvested for its shell and flesh

tuba – an alcoholic drink made from coconut sap, commonly drunk on Yap

uhmw – on Pohnpei, a method of local cooking on several small, fire-heated rocks; banana and breadfruit are often cooked this way.

unimane – respected old men or village elders on Kiribati

LONELY PLANET

Guides by Region

L onely Planet is known worldwide for publishing practical, reliable and no-nonsense travel information in our guides and on our web site. The Lonely Planet list covers just about every accessible part of the world. Currently there are fifteen series: travel guides, Shoestrings, Condensed, Phrasebooks, Read This First, Healthy Travel, Walking guides, Cycling guides, Pisces Diving & Snorkeling guides, City Maps, Travel Atlases, Out to Eat, World Food, Journeys travel literature and Pictorials.

AFRICA Africa on a shoestring • Africa – the South • Arabic (Egyptian) phrasebook • Arabic (Moroccan) phrasebook • Cairo • Cape Town • Cape Town city map • Central Africa • East Africa • Egypt • Egypt travel atlas • Ethiopian (Amharic) phrasebook • The Gambia & Senegal • Healthy Travel Africa • Kenya • Kenya travel atlas • Malawi, Mozambique & Zambia • Morocco • North Africa • Read This First Africa • South Africa, Lesotho & Swaziland • South Africa, Lesotho & Swaziland travel atlas • Swahili phrasebook • Tanzania, Zanzibar & Pemba • Trekking in East Africa • Tunisia • West Africa • Zimbabwe, Botswana & Namibia • Zimbabwe, Botswana & Nambia Travel Atlas • World Food Morocco
Travel Literature: The Rainbird: A Central African Journey • Songs to an African Sunset: A Zimbabwean Story • Mali Blues: Traveling to an African Beat

AUSTRALIA & THE PACIFIC Auckland • Australia • Australian phrasebook • Bushwalking in Australia • Bushwalking in Papua New Guinea • Fiji • Fijian phrasebook • Healthy Travel Australia, NZ and the Pacific • Islands of Australia's Great Barrier Reef • Melbourne • Melbourne city map • Micronesia • New Caledonia • New South Wales & the ACT • New Zealand • Northern Territory • Outback Australia • Out To Eat – Melbourne • Out to Eat – Sydney • Papua New Guinea • Pidgin phrasebook • Queensland • Rarotonga & the Cook Islands • Samoa • Solomon Islands • South Australia • South Pacific • South Pacific Languages phrasebook • Sydney • Sydney city map • Sydney Condensed • Tahiti & French Polynesia • Tasmania • Tonga • Tramping in New Zealand • Vanuatu • Victoria • Western Australia
Travel Literature: Islands in the Clouds • Kiwi Tracks: A New Zealand Journey • Sean & David's Long Drive

CENTRAL AMERICA & THE CARIBBEAN Bahamas, Turks & Caicos • Bermuda • Central America on a shoestring • Costa Rica • Cuba • Dominican Republic & Haiti • Eastern Caribbean • Guatemala, Belize & Yucatán: La Ruta Maya • Jamaica • Mexico • Mexico City • Panama • Puerto Rico • Read This First Central & South America • World Food Mexico
Travel Literature: Green Dreams: Travels in Central America

EUROPE Amsterdam • Amsterdam city map • Andalucía • Austria • Baltic States phrasebook • Barcelona • Berlin • Berlin city map • Britain • British phrasebook • Brussels, Bruges & Antwerp • Budapest city map • Canary Islands • Central Europe • Central Europe phrasebook • Corfu & Ionians • Corsica • Crete • Crete Condensed • Croatia • Cyprus • Czech & Slovak Republics • Denmark • Dublin • Eastern Europe • Eastern Europe phrasebook • Edinburgh • Estonia, Latvia & Lithuania • Europe on a shoestring • Finland • Florence • France • French phrasebook • Germany • German phrasebook • Greece • Greek Islands • Greek phrasebook • Hungary • Iceland, Greenland & the Faroe Islands • Istanbul City Map • Ireland • Italian phrasebook • Italy • Krakow •Lisbon • London • London city map • London Condensed • Mediterranean Europe • Mediterranean Europe phrasebook • Munich • Norway • Paris • Paris city map • Paris Condensed • Poland • Portugal • Portugese phrasebook • Portugal travel atlas • Prague • Prague city map • Provence & the Côte d'Azur • Read This First Europe • Romania & Moldova • Rome • Russia, Ukraine & Belarus • Russian phrasebook • Scandinavian & Baltic Europe • Scandinavian Europe phrasebook • Scotland • Slovenia • Spain • Spanish phrasebook • St Petersburg • Switzerland • Trekking in Spain • Ukrainian phrasebook • Venice • Vienna • Walking in Britain • Walking in Ireland • Walking in Italy • Walking in Spain • Walking in Switzerland • Western Europe • Western Europe phrasebook • World Food Italy • World Food Spain
Travel Literature: The Olive Grove: Travels in Greece

INDIAN SUBCONTINENT Bangladesh • Bengali phrasebook • Bhutan • Delhi • Goa • Hindi & Urdu phrasebook • India • India & Bangladesh travel atlas • Indian Himalaya • Karakoram Highway • Kerala • Mumbai (Bombay) • Nepal • Nepali phrasebook • Pakistan • Rajasthan • Read This First: Asia & India • South India • Sri Lanka • Sri Lanka phrasebook • Trekking in the Indian Himalaya • Trekking in the Karakoram & Hindukush • Trekking in the Nepal Himalaya
Travel Literature: In Rajasthan • Shopping for Buddhas • The Age Of Kali

Mail Order

Lonely Planet products are distributed worldwide. They are also available by mail order from Lonely Planet, so if you have difficulty finding a title please write to us. North and South American residents should write to 150 Linden St, Oakland CA 94607, USA; European and African residents should write to 10a Spring Place, London, NW5 3BH; and residents of other countries to PO Box 617, Hawthorn, Victoria 3122, Australia.

ISLANDS OF THE INDIAN OCEAN Madagascar & Comoros • Maldives • Mauritius, Réunion & Seychelles

MIDDLE EAST & CENTRAL ASIA Bahrain, Kuwait & Qatar • Central Asia • Central Asia phrasebook • Dubai • Hebrew phrasebook • Iran • Israel & the Palestinian Territories • Israel & the Palestinian Territories travel atlas • Istanbul • Istanbul to Cairo on a shoestring • Jerusalem • Jerusalem City Map • Jordan • Jordan, Syria & Lebanon travel atlas • Lebanon • Middle East • Oman & the United Arab Emirates • Syria • Turkey • Turkey travel atlas • Turkish phrasebook • Yemen
Travel Literature: The Gates of Damascus • Kingdom of the Film Stars: Journey into Jordan • Black on Black: Iran Revisited

NORTH AMERICA Alaska • Backpacking in Alaska • Baja California • California & Nevada • California Condensed • Canada • Chicago • Chicago city map • Deep South • Florida • Hawaii • Honolulu • Las Vegas • Los Angeles • Miami • New England • New Orleans • New York City • New York city map • New York Condensed • New York, New Jersey & Pennsylvania • Oahu • Pacific Northwest USA • Puerto Rico • Rocky Mountain • San Francisco • San Francisco city map • Seattle • Southwest USA • Texas • USA • USA phrasebook • Vancouver • Washington, DC & the Capital Region • Washington DC city map
Travel Literature: Drive Thru America

NORTH-EAST ASIA Beijing • Cantonese phrasebook • China • Hong Kong • Hong Kong city map • Hong Kong, Macau & Guangzhou • Japan • Japanese phrasebook • Japanese audio pack • Korea • Korean phrasebook • Kyoto • Mandarin phrasebook • Mongolia • Mongolian phrasebook • North-East Asia on a shoestring • Seoul • South-West China • Taiwan • Tibet • Tibetan phrasebook • Tokyo
Travel Literature: Lost Japan • In Xanadu

SOUTH AMERICA Argentina, Uruguay & Paraguay • Bolivia • Brazil • Brazilian phrasebook • Buenos Aires • Chile & Easter Island • Chile & Easter Island travel atlas • Colombia • Ecuador & the Galapagos Islands • Healthy Travel Central & South America • Latin American Spanish phrasebook • Peru • Quechua phrasebook • Rio de Janeiro • Rio de Janeiro city map • South America on a shoestring • Trekking in the Patagonian Andes • Venezuela
Travel Literature: Full Circle: A South American Journey

SOUTH-EAST ASIA Bali & Lombok • Bangkok • Bangkok city map • Burmese phrasebook • Cambodia • Hanoi • Healthy Travel Asia & India • Hill Tribes phrasebook • Ho Chi Minh City • Indonesia • Indonesia's Eastern Islands • Indonesian phrasebook • Indonesian audio pack • Jakarta • Java • Laos • Lao phrasebook • Laos travel atlas • Malay phrasebook • Malaysia, Singapore & Brunei • Myanmar (Burma) • Philippines • Pilipino (Tagalog) phrasebook • Read This First Asia & India • Singapore • South-East Asia on a shoestring • South-East Asia phrasebook • Thailand • Thailand's Islands & Beaches • Thailand travel atlas • Thai phrasebook • Thai audio pack • Vietnam • Vietnamese phrasebook • Vietnam travel atlas • World Food Thailand • World Food Vietnam

ALSO AVAILABLE: Antarctica • The Arctic • Brief Encounters: Stories of Love, Sex & Travel • Chasing Rickshaws • Lonely Planet Unpacked • Not the Only Planet: Travel Stories from Science Fiction • Sacred India • Travel with Children • Traveller's Tales

LONELY PLANET

You already know that Lonely Planet produces more than this one guidebook, but you might not be aware of the other products we have on this region. Here is a selection of titles which you may want to check out as well:

South Pacific
ISBN 0 86442 717 4
US$24.95 • UK£15.99 • 190FF

South Pacific Phrasebook
ISBN 0 86442 595 3
US$6.95 • UK£4.99 • 50FF

Diving & Snorkeling Palau
ISBN 1 86450 019 0
US$16.99 • UK£10.99 • 149FF

Healthy Travel Australia, NZ & the Pacific
ISBN 1 86450 052 2
US$5.95 • UK£3.99 • 39FF

Diving & Snorkeling Guam & Yap
ISBN 0 86442 744 1
US$15.95 • UK£9.99 • 120FF

Diving & Snorkeling Chuuk Lagoon, Pohnpei & Kosrae
ISBN 1 86450 029 8
US$17.95 • UK£11.99 • 140FF

Available wherever books are sold.

Index

Abbreviations

Text

A

Abaiang (Ki) 199, **200**
Abemama (Ki) 201-2
accommodation 64-5,
  see also individual countries
Adelup Point (Gu) 100
Aguijan Island (NM) 140
Ailinglaplap Atoll (MI) 176-7
Ailuk Atoll (MI) 179
air travel 67-72,
  see also individual countries
  air passes 67-70
  airlines 91
  to/from Asia 71-2
  to/from Australia 72
  to/from the Pacific 72
  to/from USA 70-1
  within Micronesia 75-6
Airai Channel (Pa) 335
Airai State (Pa) 340-1
airlines 70, 75-6
Airok Island (MI) 172
airports 75
alcohol 66, 156, 237
Angaur (Pa) 346-9, **347**
Ant Atoll (FSM) 260-1
Apra Harbor (Gu) 101
Arakabesang Island (Pa) 327
archaeological sites 139, 340
architecture 35-6
Arno Atoll (MI) 173-4
Arorae (Ki) 202
arts 35-6
Atomic Bomb Pits (NM) 138-9
Aur Atoll (MI) 176

B

Babeldaob (Pa) 339-49, **340**
Babelthaup, *see* Babeldaob
bai, *see* meeting houses

Bold indicates maps.

Bairiki (Ki) 188, 190-2, **192**
Baker Island (US) 352
Balabat (FSM) 298
Banaba (Ki) 201
Banzai Cliff (NM) 123
Bar-K Ranch (NM) 138
beaches
  Asan Beach (Gu) 100
  Bloody Beach (Pa) 344
  California Beach (MI) 175
  Family Beach (Gu) 101
  Honeymoon Beach (Pa) 345
  Ipan Beach (Gu) 105
  Jeffries (Talofofo) Beach
    (NM) 125
  Kammer Beach (NM) 136
  Ladder Beach (NM) 125
  Laulau Beach (NM) 125
  Marshall Islands (unnamed) 161
  Micro Beach (NM) 121
  Obyan Beach (NM) 125-6
  Orange Beach (Pa) 344
  Pau Pau Beach (NM) 122-3
  Profile Beach (NM) 125
  Ritidian Point (Gu) 98-9
  Shark's Hole (Gu) 99
  Tachogna Beach (NM) 136
  Taga Beach (NM) 136
  Tanguisson Beach (Gu) 99
  Tarague Beach (Gu) 99
  Uruno Beach (Gu) 99
  Wanyan Beach (FSM) 301
  White Beach (Pa) 345
  Wing Beach (NM) 123
Bechiyal Cultural Center (FSM)
  301-2
betel nut 29, 309
Betio (Ki) 192-4, **193**
bicycle travel 77
Bikenibeu (Ki) 192
Bikini Atoll (MI) 177-8
Bird Island (NM) 124
bird sanctuary (NM) 145

birds, *see* fauna
Black Coral Island (FSM) 260
Blowhole (NM) 138
Blue Corner (Pa) 336
Blue Hole (FSM) 243
boat travel 72
books 49-51
breadfruit 29, 287
bus travel 76
business hours 62,
  see also individual countries
Butaritari (Ki) 199-200

C

Calalin Island (MI) 162
Camp Beck Dock (Pa) 344
camping 89-90
canoeing
  Federated States of
    Micronesia 244, 263
  Palau 327-8
canoes 36, 37-8, 81, 274
Capitol Hill (NM) 124-5
car travel 76-7
Caroline Island,
  see Millennium Island
Carp Island (Pa) 335-6
caves 241
  Bird Cave (FSM) 241-2
  Gadao's Cave (Gu) 104-5
  Guam (unnamed) 95, 98, 99
  Nefo Cave (FSM) 276
  Tonga Cave (NM) 144
  Yokoi Caves (Gu) 105
Cetti Bay (Gu) 102
Chalan Kanoa (NM) 125
Chamorro people 35, 84
Chamorro Village (Gu) 90, 96,
  104
children 61
Christmas Island (Ki) 203-8, **204**
  travel to/from 207
  travel within 207-8

Bold indicates maps.

Boxed Text

MAP LEGEND

CITY ROUTES

Freeway	Freeway
Highway	Primary Road
Road	Secondary Road
Street	Street
Lane	Lane
	On/Off Ramp

= = = =	Unsealed Road
→	One Way Street
	Pedestrian Street
⊏⊐⊏⊐⊏⊐	Stepped Street
)= = =	Tunnel
	Footbridge

REGIONAL ROUTES

	Tollway, Freeway
	Primary Road
	Secondary Road
	Minor Road

BOUNDARIES

▬·▬·▬·	International
▬··▬··▬	State
▬ ▬ ▬	Disputed
▬▲▬▲▬	Fortified Wall

HYDROGRAPHY

River, Creek	
Canal	
Lake	

Lagoon	
Spring; Rapids	
Waterfalls	

TRANSPORT ROUTES & STATIONS

—●—	Train
+ + + +	Underground Train
—Ⓜ—	Metro
— — —	Tramway
⊬—⊬—⊬—⊬	Cable Car, Chairlift

- - - -◻	Ferry
— — — —	Walking Trail
· · · · · · · ·	Walking Tour
	Path
	Pier or Jetty

AREA FEATURES

Building	
❀ Park, Gardens	

Market	
Sports Ground	

↗ Beach	
Cemetery	

Campus	
Reef	

POPULATION SYMBOLS

✪ CAPITAL	National Capital
◉ CAPITAL	State Capital

⊙ CITY	City
● Town	Town

● Village	Village
	Urban Area

MAP SYMBOLS

■	Place to Stay	▼	Place to Eat	●	Point of Interest
✚ ✖	Airfield, Airport	▣	Fort	▣	Parking	↙	Shipwreck
⊖	Bank	➋	Golf Course	⊙	Petrol Station	⊠	Shopping Centre
▣	Camping Ground	✛	Hospital	☻	Picnic Area	▣	Swimming Pool
⌂	Cave	☨	Lighthouse	✚	Police Station	▣	Telephone
▬ ▣	Church	☀	Lookout	▣	Post Office	■	Tomb
▣	Cinema	▲	Monument	▣	Pub or Bar	❶	Tourist Information
◧ ◎	Diving, Snorkelling	▲	Mountain	▣	Ruins	▭	Transport (general)
▣	Embassy	▥	Museum	▥	Shinto Shrine	▣	Zoo

Note: not all symbols displayed above appear in this book

LONELY PLANET OFFICES

Australia
PO Box 617, Hawthorn, Victoria 3122
☎ 03 9819 1877 fax 03 9819 6459
email: talk2us@lonelyplanet.com.au

USA
150 Linden St, Oakland, CA 94607
☎ 510 893 8555 TOLL FREE: 800 275 8555
fax 510 893 8572
email: info@lonelyplanet.com

UK
10a Spring Place, London NW5 3BH
☎ 020 7428 4800 fax 020 7428 4828
email: go@lonelyplanet.co.uk

France
1 rue du Dahomey, 75011 Paris
☎ 01 55 25 33 00 fax 01 55 25 33 01
email: bip@lonelyplanet.fr
www.lonelyplanet.fr

World Wide Web: www.lonelyplanet.com *or* AOL keyword: lp
Lonely Planet Images: lpi@lonelyplanet.com.au